# RESEARCH HANDBOOK ON BEHAVIORAL LAW AND ECONOMICS

# RESEARCH HANDBOOKS IN LAW AND ECONOMICS

**Series Editors:** Richard A. Posner, *Judge, United States Court of Appeals for the Seventh Circuit and Senior Lecturer, University of Chicago Law School, USA* and Francesco Parisi, *Oppenheimer Wolff and Donnelly Professor of Law, University of Minnesota, USA and Professor of Economics, University of Bologna, Italy*

Edited by highly distinguished scholars, the landmark reference works in this series offer advanced treatments of specific topics that reflect the state-of-the-art of research in law and economics, while also expanding the law and economics debate. Each volume's accessible yet sophisticated contributions from top international researchers make it an indispensable resource for students and scholars alike.

Titles in this series include:

Research Handbook on Public Choice and Public Law
*Edited by Daniel A. Farber and Anne Joseph O'Connell*

Research Handbook on the Economics of Property Law
*Edited by Kenneth Ayotte and Henry E. Smith*

Research Handbook on the Economics of Family Law
*Edited by Lloyd R. Cohen and Joshua D. Wright*

Research Handbook on the Economics of Antitrust Law
*Edited by Einer R. Elhauge*

Research Handbook on the Economics of Corporate Law
*Edited by Brett McDonnell and Claire A. Hill*

Research Handbook on the Economics of European Union Law
*Edited by Thomas Eger and Hans-Bernd Schäfer*

Research Handbook on the Economics of Criminal Law
*Edited by Alon Harel and Keith N. Hylton*

Research Handbook on the Economics of Labor and Employment Law
*Edited by Michael L. Wachter and Cynthia L. Estlund*

Research Handbook on Austrian Law and Economics
*Edited by Todd J. Zywicki and Peter J. Boettke*

Research Handbook on Behavioral Law and Economics
*Edited by Joshua C. Teitelbaum and Kathryn Zeiler*

# Research Handbook on Behavioral Law and Economics

*Edited by*

Joshua C. Teitelbaum

*Georgetown University Law Center, USA*

Kathryn Zeiler

*Boston University School of Law, USA*

RESEARCH HANDBOOKS IN LAW AND ECONOMICS

Edward Elgar
PUBLISHING

Cheltenham, UK • Northampton, MA, USA

Published by
Edward Elgar Publishing Limited
The Lypiatts
15 Lansdown Road
Cheltenham
Glos GL50 2JA
UK

Edward Elgar Publishing, Inc.
William Pratt House
9 Dewey Court
Northampton
Massachusetts 01060
USA


A catalogue record for this book
is available from the British Library


Library of Congress Control Number: 2017953231


This book is available electronically in the **Elgar**online
Law subject collection
DOI 10.4337/9781849805681


Printed on elemental chlorine free (ECF)
recycled paper containing 30% Post-Consumer Waste


ISBN 978 1 84980 567 4 (cased)
ISBN 978 1 84980 568 1 (eBook)

Typeset by Servis Filmsetting Ltd, Stockport, Cheshire
Printed and bound in the USA

# Contents

PART V  HAPPINESS AND TRUST

PART VI  EXPERIMENTS AND NEUROECONOMICS

PART VII  CAUTIONS AND WAYS FORWARD

# Contributors

**Sumit Agarwal**, William G. Droms Term Professor of Finance, Georgetown University, USA

**Ali al-Nowaihi**, University of Leicester, School of Business, Economics Division, UK

**Brent W. Ambrose**, Smeal Professor of Real Estate, The Pennsylvania State University, USA

**Jonathan Baron**, Professor of Psychology, University of Pennsylvania, USA

**Marieke Bos**, Deputy Director, Swedish House of Finance, Stockholm School of Economics, Sweden; Visiting Scholar, Federal Reserve Bank of Philadelphia, USA

**Susan Payne Carter**, Assistant Professor and Research Analyst, United States Military Academy, West Point, USA

**Gary Charness**, Professor of Economics, University of California, Santa Barbara, USA

**Terrence Chorvat**, Professor of Law, George Mason University School of Law, USA

**Gregory DeAngelo**, Assistant Professor of Economics, West Virginia University, USA

**Sanjit Dhami**, University of Leicester, School of Business, Economics Division, UK

**Benjamin Ho**, Associate Professor of Economics, Vassar College, USA

**Peter H. Huang**, Professor and DeMuth Chair of Business Law, University of Colorado Law School, USA and Visiting Scholar, Loyola Los Angeles Law School, USA

**David Huffman**, Professor of Economics, University of Pittsburgh, USA

**Owen D. Jones**, New York Alumni Chancellor's Professor of Law and Professor of Biological Sciences, Vanderbilt University; Director, MacArthur Foundation Research Network on Law and Neuroscience, USA

**Claudia M. Landeo**, Associate Professor of Economics, University of Alberta, Canada

**Barbara Luppi**, Assistant Professor of Economics, University of Modena and Reggio Emilia, Italy

**Kevin McCabe**, Professor of Economics, Law, and Neuroscience, George Mason University, USA

**Gregory Mitchell**, Joseph Weintraub – Bank of America Distinguished Professor of Law, University of Virginia Law School, USA

**Francesco Parisi**, Oppenheimer Wolff & Donnelly Professor of Law, University of Minnesota School of Law, US; Distinguished Professor of Economics, University of Bologna, Italy

**Paige Marta Skiba**, Professor of Law, Vanderbilt University Law School, USA

**Alex Stein**, Professor of Law, Brooklyn Law School, USA

**Joshua C. Teitelbaum**, Associate Dean of Research and Academic Programs and Professor of Law, Georgetown University Law Center, USA

**Tess Wilkinson-Ryan**, Professor of Law and Psychology, University of Pennsylvania Law School, USA

**Erte Xiao**, Associate Professor of Economics, Monash University, Australia

**Kathryn Zeiler**, Nancy Barton Scholar and Professor of Law, Boston University School of Law, USA

# Introduction
## *Joshua C. Teitelbaum and Kathryn Zeiler*

## 1. THE ROLE OF BEHAVIORAL ECONOMICS IN LAW

The subfield of behavioral economics, while still quite young, has made important contributions to our understanding of human behavior. Through a cycle of theory development and empirical investigation, work in behavioral economics taps into lessons from psychology with the goal of improving economics' predictive power. While the focus diverges from that of neoclassical economics, the best work in both subfields has much in common. The most useful insights are produced by faithfully applying the scientific method—the development of explanations of behavior through repeated cycles of data collection and hypothesis testing. Gains in knowledge are incremental, and skepticism is encouraged until assumptions built into theory are able to hold up against data collected in multiple environments. In addition, both subfields strive to integrate relevant concepts—e.g., psychological concepts in the case of behavioral economics—into models that produce well-defined, testable, and falsifiable predictions.

While some have characterized the mission of behavioral economics as an attempt to abandon rational choice theory and replace it with more realistic assumptions that reflect human fallibility, many behavioral economics models that find strong support in existing data assume a set of rational but non-standard preferences (Zeiler, forthcoming). In fact, a great many works in behavioral economics contain multiple theories able to explain large swaths of existing data, some of which assume individuals make systematic, predictable mistakes, while others assume the error-free expression of non-standard, rational preferences. The empiricist's role is to discover ways to separate the theories by developing or observing environments in which the theories lead to divergent predictions. In some literatures models that assume mistake-making are in the lead, and in others models assuming non-standard preferences seem to best explain existing data.

This variation in behavioral economics models and the nature of the scientific method have important implications for legal scholars who import economic theory into legal contexts. First, importers will want to avoid drawing strong descriptive and normative claims from any one empirical study or economic theory. Sophisticated importation recognizes that very few (if any) literatures have converged on a single model to explain observed choices and that they are in constant flux. Second, and for these reasons, keeping up to date on the state of relevant literatures is vital for effective importation of economics into law. Readers of legal scholarship are best armed when they have a complete picture of the state of the science being applied. Third, importers should have a clear sense of the nature of the models they apply. More specifically, they should avoid mistaking models that assume non-standard preferences as theories of error, and vice versa. The chapters included in this volume are intended, in part, to help legal scholars effectively draw on the important findings from the field of behavioral economics.

## 2.   HANDBOOK CONTRIBUTIONS

The purpose of this volume is to assist both researchers and those who apply the research to legal issues in keeping up with the latest developments in the literature. The volume is by no means comprehensive. No such volume could be given the huge numbers of contributions made to the vast literatures each year. The collection of chapters, written by leaders in the field, is designed to provide insights about the foundations of the field, to catch us up on recent developments in the fields of antitrust, consumer finance, crime and punishment, torts, happiness and trust research, experiments, and neuroeconomics, and to demonstrate methods for effective original research. The volume also includes words of caution related to abstraction relevant for both researchers and appliers, and offers some ideas about steps that researchers and the research consumer communities can take to push the field of behavioral law and economics forward.

### 2.1   Foundations

The two opening chapters of the volume set the stage by examining the foundations of behavioral law and economics.

In "Conceptual Foundations: A Bird's-eye View," Jonathan Baron and Tess Wilkinson-Ryan outline the field's conceptual foundations. They concentrate on the behavioral concepts imported into the field from psychology and experimental economics, and survey the normative models, descriptive theories, and prescriptive approaches featured in behavioral law and economics research. They endeavor to point out common themes in the research in an effort to tie together various bunches of findings and counter the criticism that the field lacks the cohesion of standard law and economics.

In "Behavioral Probability," Alex Stein challenges the acceptance by behavioral law and economics of mathematical (Bayesian) probability as the benchmark for rationality in the study of decision-making under uncertainty. Instead, Stein defends as rational the use of common-sense reasoning that generally aligns with causative (Baconian) probability. After making the case against mathematical probability and in favor of causative probability, he revisits and critiques the foundational experiments, carried out by Daniel Kahneman, Amos Tversky, and others, that behavioral law and economics scholars embrace as evidence of people's probabilistic irrationality and on which they rely to make the case for legal and regulatory interventions designed to correct people's probabilistic mistakes.

### 2.2   Antitrust and Consumer Finance

The next three chapters touch on the areas of antitrust and consumer finance.

In "Exclusionary Vertical Restraints and Antitrust: Experimental Law and Economics Contributions," Claudia Landeo reviews theoretical and experimental literatures related to the long-debated question of whether vertical restraints—arrangements between firms up and down the supply chain designed to restrict the conditions under which the firms are allowed to transact with each other and with third parties—add value or mitigate the benefits we get from robust competition in markets. If regulators see these vertical arrangements as threats to consumer surplus when they actually make consumers better off, regulation might reduce social welfare in an effort to increase it. As Landeo explains, understanding the impacts of these arrangements is vitally important to our efforts to best regulate them, if they are in fact in need of regulation at all.

The chapter begins with theory. Economists have developed various theories to aid in our understanding of the impacts of vertical arrangements. The theoretical literature teaches us that we should expect different outcomes depending on the assumptions employed in the models. Some theories suggest that under certain conditions vertical integration can increase consumer surplus by allowing firms along the supply chain to "exploit technological complementarities, reduce transaction costs . . ., gain control over production processes and preclude opportunistic behavior, overcome informational imperfections, and internalize externalities." On the other hand, leverage theory predicts that firms will use exclusionary arrangements to increase their market power in other markets or to take advantage of their monopoly positions. These theories are key to understanding potential motivations behind exclusionary arrangements because motivations drive our regulatory intuitions.

Despite a robust theoretical literature, Landeo points out that regulators tend not to make use of the insights from this literature. She attributes this to the lack of empirical verification of the theoretical models. Empirical verification using field data is difficult given the incentives for parities to vertical arrangements to keep them private. Landeo claims that new experimental tests of the theories help to fill this void. After helpfully describing the main features of sound experimental studies, Landeo describes a number of experimental studies designed to test theoretical predictions of behavior and outcomes in the presence of contractual vertical restraints. Landeo argues that this evidence helps us to sort out which theories are best at informing us about the motivations behind such restraints and should compel regulators to lean toward the set of theories best supported by the experimental literature. Experiments can also be useful in guiding regulators towards the environments that are most likely to be negatively impacted by vertical restraints (e.g., production processes with relatively large fixed costs, relatively small technological advantages of potential entrants, and relatively large economies of scale).

So what does behavioral economics have to do with it? One of the main contributions of the experimental literature in this arena is the discovery, through experiments, of previously non-modeled factors that seem to influence behavior in settings that incorporate as many assumptions of the standard theoretical models as possible. These factors include decision errors possibly resulting from cognitive limitations, preferences over fairness and reciprocity that might vary by levels of social proximity, and beliefs over the intentions of other actors to cause monetary harm. Although the tested theories do not include assumptions related to these factors, some experimental results suggest that adding them will increase the models' predictive value. Once hints of these factors appear, models can be revised and then retested using experiment design techniques to determine the roles these factors play in decision-making. Experiments testing models of competition are but one example of ways that empirical investigations can uncover anomalies that compel theorists to integrate concepts from psychology into our standard economic models.

In "Balancing Act: New Evidence and a Discussion of the Theory on the Rationality and Behavioral Anomalies of Choice in Credit Markets," Marieke Bos, Susan Payne Carter, and Paige Marta Skiba reflect on and contribute to the existing literature on the choice among traditional forms of credit and non-traditional forms such as payday loans.

Millions of people in the United States use payday loans, despite the fact that interest and default rates on payday loans are high relative to those on bank loans, credit card loans, and other traditional forms of credit. For these and other reasons, federal and state regulators have taken or are poised to take steps to limit or ban payday loans. The sixty-four million dollar question is whether such regulatory action is warranted.

According to the standard rational actor model, borrowers choose the cheapest form of credit available to them (rational take-up) and have no difficulty implementing their optimal borrowing and repayment choices over time (time consistency). Bos, Carter, and Skiba argue that the evidence suggests that borrowers generally are not time consistent—they tend to underpredict their intensity of borrowing and overpredict their ability to repay—which may justify regulatory action. However, say the authors, the weight of the existing evidence also suggests that borrowers generally are rational in their take up of credit, including with respect to their choices among forms of credit, and they argue that regulators should take this evidence into account before they ban or severely limit access to any one type of credit.

Bos, Carter, and Skiba add to this literature by introducing new data on observed choices of customers switching to pawnshop loans when payday loans are not available. They exploit a discontinuity in the lending decisions of the payday lender to draw inferences about a causal relationship between the availability of a payday loan and the subsequent decision to take out a pawnshop loan. The discontinuity is based on the payday lender's credit score threshold: below the threshold applicants are denied a payday loan, and above the threshold applicants are granted a loan. On the assumption that borrowers immediately above and below the threshold are otherwise similar, they analyze the effect of being denied a payday loan on the subsequent decision to take out a pawnshop loan. They find that people turn to pawnshop loans when they lack access to payday loans. Citing related work that suggests that people also turn to auto title loans when payday loans are unavailable, the authors conclude that regulators need to consider the potential substitution effects of restricting access to payday credit.

In "The Effect of Advertising on Home Equity Credit Choices," Sumit Agarwal and Brent Ambrose examine the effect of direct mail advertising (also known as junk mail) on the choice between two types of home equity loans: variable-rate revolving loans and fixed-rate term loans. Economists have long studied the impact of advertising on consumers' behavior. They have also extensively studied borrowers' choices over home loan contracts. Agarwal and Ambrose, however, are the first to combine these lines of inquiry and examine the impact of lender advertising on home equity credit choices.

Agarwal and Ambrose consider three theories of how advertising affects choices: the persuasive, informative, and complementary theories. Under the persuasive theory, advertising alters consumers' preferences. Under the informative and complementary theories, advertising does not alter preferences; instead it either provides consumers with information and lowers their search costs (informative theory) or encourages consumers to satisfy their preferences (complementary theory).

Agarwal and Ambrose exploit a natural experiment arising from a home equity lender's marketing campaign that allows them to distinguish between walk-in (WI) applicants, who were not targeted by the lender's marketing campaign, and direct mail (DM) applicants, who were targeted with a direct mail solicitation advertising either a revolving loan or a term loan. By examining the choices of the DM applicants relative to the choices made by the WI applicants, and by using the bank's pricing algorithm to precisely calculate the loan offer rate for the product not selected, the authors are able to test the persuasive view versus the informative or complementary view of advertising. If the lender's direct mail campaign is persuasive, then the authors should observe differences in how the DM and WI applicants' loan choices respond to economic factors such as the prevailing interest rates and the intended use of proceeds. However, if the advertising is informative or complementary, then they should observe DM and WI applicants responding similarly to such economic factors.

Controlling for observable differences between the WI and DM applicants using a matched sample design, Agarwal and Ambrose are able to isolate the effect of the direct mail solicitation on the applicant's loan choice. They find that DM applicants are more likely to ignore the economic factors that influenced the choices of the WI applicants.

Specifically, they find that 78 percent of the DM applicants were influenced by the lender's solicitation, while 22 percent responded to the economic factors. Further analysis of only the applicants who were clearly influenced by the lender's solicitation reveals that 74 percent were persuaded to originate a product that was opposite to the one selected by their counterparts who did not receive a direct mail solicitation. However, they also find that the direct mail solicitation could be classified as informative for 26 percent of the DM applicants. Thus, while their study reveals that lender advertising has a persuasive effect for a majority of the applicants who received a solicitation, they also find evidence consistent with the informative view of advertising for a smaller subset of applicants. Such heterogeneity in results is quite common in behavioral economics research, and legal scholars will want to take it into account when importing findings from the field.

## 2.3   Crime and Punishment

The next two chapters in the volume explore topics in crime and punishment.

A central question in law is how to design punishment schemes to maintain social order. In "Punishment, Social Norms, and Cooperation," Erte Xiao reviews recent research in behavioral economics on how punishment promotes prosocial behavior. The standard economic theory of crime and punishment focuses on how punishment can change the expected payoff of antisocial behavior (Becker 1968). It assumes that people take actions to maximize their expected utility, and posits that punishment can promote social order by increasing the expected cost of antisocial behavior. In particular, according to the standard theory, society can deter violations of the social order by increasing either the probability or the magnitude of punishment so that the expected cost of violating the social order is greater than the prospective benefit.

Controlled laboratory experiments provide evidence that punishment schemes can enforce prosocial behavior. At the same time, however, studies also show that punishment can backfire. The mixed results of punishment studies raise the questions of why punishment sometimes promotes social order but other times leads to even higher levels of violation, and how to design punishment schemes to avoid detrimental effects. In her review of the literature, Xiao considers studies of both formal punishment imposed exogenously by institutions and informal peer punishment, and she discusses factors that can lead to the detrimental effects of punishment.

Xiao first discusses research exploring the idea that people may infer negative intentions from punishment and retaliate against their punishers. She then proceeds to review research on restricted punishment mechanisms which prohibit illegitimate punishment and thereby reduce retaliatory behavior. As Xiao observes, however, implementing restricted punishment mechanisms may be difficult in the real world, where heterogeneity, uncertainty, and other factors can make it hard to decide what behavior should be punished. For example, mechanisms that require consensus from the community may be unavailable to a society in which people have substantially heterogeneous beliefs about right and wrong. And good luck can mask violations that ought to be punished.

Next, Xiao discusses research on how punishment can crowd out both the intrinsic motivation and the image motivation to conform to prosocial norms. She argues that to avoid such crowd-out effects, it is important to frame punishment as a signal of a norm violation and not as a price, and therefore a justification or excuse, for a norm violation, and to take into account the visibility of the target behavior when designing punishments.

Xiao ends the chapter by discussing research on how punishment can promote prosocial behavior by communicating social norms (the norm expression function of punishment) and by influencing people's beliefs (empirical expectations) about whether others obey prosocial norms. She also highlights research on mechanisms other than punishment, such as requiring people to justify their actions, which can promote prosocial behavior.

In "Prospect Theory, Crime and Punishment," Sanjit Dhami and Ali al-Nowaihi reexamine the standard economic theory of crime and punishment in light of cumulative prospect theory, or CPT (Tversky and Kahneman 1992). CPT is perhaps the leading alternative to expected utility theory, on which the standard economic theory of crime and punishment is based. CPT assumes, *inter alia*, that utility is defined over changes in wealth relative to a reference point which partitions the domain of outcomes into gains and losses; that the disutility of a loss is larger than the utility of an equal-sized gain (loss aversion); and that expected utility is calculated with respect to a non-linear transformation of the decumulative probability distribution over outcomes (rank-dependent probability weighting). After providing a brief introduction to CPT and setting out a simple economic model of crime, Dhami and al-Nowaihi proceed to discuss two issues in the economics of crime: the tax evasion problem and the Becker proposition.

The tax evasion problem refers to the following puzzle. Given realistic penalties and probabilities of detection and conviction, the return per tax dollar evaded is strictly positive. Hence, the standard model, which again is based on expected utility theory, predicts that every taxpayer whose tax is not withheld at the payment source should evade paying at least some of his taxes. Empirical evidence, however, suggests that many such taxpayers fully pay their taxes. Dhami and al-Nowaihi show how CPT can resolve the tax evasion puzzle (as well as a related problem, known as the Yitzhaki puzzle, concerning how tax evasion changes with tax rates). The basic idea is that loss aversion and overweighting of audit probabilities can generate the observed levels of compliance given realistic penalties for evasion. More specifically, the authors show that, for realistic levels of tax evasion and audit probabilities, the penalty rate predicted by CPT, with the loss aversion and probability weighting parameters calibrated to match estimates from the literature, is consistent with the observed penalty rate.

The Becker proposition refers to the idea that, if criminals behave according to expected utility theory, then given any nonzero probability of enforcement, no matter how small, crime can be deterred by a sufficiently large penalty. The Becker proposition suggests that society can deter crime at an arbitrarily low cost, for example *de minimis* enforcement coupled with capital punishment. It also suggests that we should not observe law-breaking in the face of a Becker-type punishment scheme (a small probability of a large penalty). However, this is not the case in the real world. Dhami and al-Nowaihi call this the Becker paradox. After considering and rejecting a number of alternative explanations, the authors show how a variant of CPT can resolve the Becker paradox. Again, their result is driven by the reference dependence and probability weighting features of CPT.

Dhami and al-Nowaihi conclude the chapter by noting several limitations of their analysis, including, for example, the lack of a distinction between actual and perceived probabilities of enforcement (and the composite treatment of the probabilities of detection and conviction); the assumption that criminals know the law and act rationally (whether according to expected utility theory or CPT); the lack of a distinction between deterrence and incapacitation and the failure to consider other theories of punishment (e.g., retribution); the abstraction from dynamic issues and group behavior; and the omission from the model of the judicial stage.

## 2.4   Torts

The two subsequent chapters focus on tort law and litigation.

In "Behavioral Models in Tort Law," Barbara Luppi and Francesco Parisi examine how behavioral phenomena can impact the economic analysis of tort law. After laying out the standard accident model developed by Shavell (1987) and others, Luppi and Parisi provide a taxonomy of behavioral biases, social biases, and memory errors drawn from the behavioral economics and psychology literatures. For example, their catalog of behavioral biases includes optimism bias, the availability heuristic, base rate fallacy, hyperbolic discounting, and loss aversion, while their lists of social biases and memory errors include the Lake Wobegon effect and hindsight bias, respectively. Importantly, their taxonomy indicates how each type of bias or error impacts the standard model. For instance, it indicates that optimism bias can affect agents' beliefs about the probability of an accident and the severity of loss in the event of an accident; that hyperbolic discounting can affect agents' beliefs about the magnitude of loss, the cost of care, and detection and enforcement, as well as their litigation and settlement decisions; and that the Lake Wobegon effect can impact agents' beliefs about the efficacy and cost of care.

After providing their taxonomy of behavior phenomena, Luppi and Parisi illustrate how each "impact class" of biases and errors—specifically, biases and errors that impact (i) beliefs about the probability of an accident, (ii) beliefs about the effectiveness of care, (iii) beliefs about the cost of care, (iv) beliefs about the severity of loss, (v) beliefs about detection and enforcement, and (vi) decisions about litigation and settlement—can be incorporated into the standard accident model. The aim of this exercise, they say, is to provide a common modeling language that law and economic scholars can use to analyze the effects of behavioral phenomena in tort law and perhaps other areas of law as well.

In "Law and Economics and Tort Litigation Institutions: Theory and Experiments," Claudia Landeo summarizes a recent and important theoretical literature related to litigation and settlement negotiations that incorporates a central concept from the field of psychology: self-serving bias. In the 1960s and 1970s, psychologists produced empirical findings suggesting that individuals tend to systematically process information in a way that is beneficial to their interests (Miller and Ross 1975). Landeo describes how theorists have modified neoclassical models of decision-making applicable to settlement negotiations to incorporate the assumption that litigants might be subject to self-serving bias. This addition to the theoretical models provides yet another explanation for settlement breakdown that leads to costly trials.

One major contribution of the chapter is its description of the interplay between theorists and empiricists—mostly experimentalists—as grounded in the scientific method. Landeo explains how experimentalists have carefully designed experimental environments not to mimic actual settlement negotiations, a clearly impossible task, but rather to incorporate all theoretical assumptions in a simple environment that rules out as many alternative explanations as possible. In this way, empiricists are able to provide theorists and policymakers with information about how much confidence they can place in particular theories and which features of the theories require revision.

Landeo also describes recent theoretical work that predicts how risk creators might alter decisions related to precaution-taking in reaction to the anticipated impacts of self-serving bias in the event an injury occurs and an injured party brings a claim for damages. The results suggest that self-serving bias can reduce social welfare and might also mitigate the intended positive effect of statutory damages caps on settlement negotiations. Presumably, the next step in the investigation of the impacts of self-serving bias on precaution-taking is to develop empirical tests to put the theory's feet to the fire.

### 2.5   Happiness and Trust

The next two chapters in the volume discuss research in happiness and trust.

In "Happiness 101 for Legal Scholars: Applying Happiness Research to Legal Policy, Ethics, Mindfulness, Negotiations, Legal Education, and Legal Practice," Peter Huang catalogs a body of literature that considers a behavioral approach to evaluations of social welfare. This branch of behavioral economics shifts our focus away from the standard economic objective of maximizing wealth and towards maximizing happiness, or at least towards some combination of the two. Huang begins by cataloging happiness studies that focus on a number of areas important for legal policymaking, including antitrust, business law, and tax. Huang then points us to works that discuss the pros and cons of government's role, if any, in optimizing happiness, different ways some countries have begun to measure happiness (and unhappiness), subjective measures governments have used to evaluate their effectiveness, and whether happiness is the be-all and end-all of life.

Huang offers an account of how modern happiness research emerged from the field of behavioral economics. He also summarizes the research that studies the difference between experienced happiness and remembered happiness, how policymaking should account for this difference and how policymakers can take advantage of the difference to increase wellbeing. Huang then draws our attention to arguments related to the potential positive impacts of increases in mindfulness, including a boost in the amount of ethical behavior people engage in. He argues that governments can best increase mindfulness by educating the polity on the positive association between mindfulness and happiness. He then turns to theories and findings related to how a focus on happiness might change how we define optimal conflict resolution and the literature's important lessons about best practices for agents who represent clients in negotiations.

Finally, Huang summarizes the state of the literature on happiness, legal education, and legal practice. Happiness research, Huang argues, has opened our eyes to the realities of the negative association between law schools and happiness and how we go about training future lawyers to reverse this correlation. The benefits of focusing on happiness can extend beyond legal training and towards efforts to improve the emotional satisfaction of practicing law. Law firms have tapped into happiness research to reform organizational culture and work environments with the goal of increasing happiness and retaining talented lawyers. In these ways, Huang shows us how the impacts of happiness research have gone well beyond conversations between economists and psychologists.

In "Trust and the Law," Benjamin Ho and David Huffman draw lessons from literatures related to economic growth, behavioral economics, and organizational economics to develop an original economic model of trust and law. Guided by empirical findings, the authors develop a principal-agent model that assumes that the agent's utility depends not only on his net monetary gain but also on the impact of his trustworthiness on the cost of effort. Specifically, the model assumes that the agent's decision over costly effort depends not only on the cost of expending effort but also on his preferences over being a trustworthy agent who resists taking advantage of the principle when given an opportunity to do so at no monetary cost to himself. To the model they add the impact of law, which can either increase or decrease the value of trustworthiness. Although some argue that strong legal enforcement of promises crowds out trust, some have found evidence from the field suggesting that trust and strong contract enforcement are positively correlated. One possible explanation is that strong contract enforcement encourages trust between contracting parties. Another is that high trust levels compel the creation of strong contract enforcement regimes. A third is that trust and strong enforcement create synergies when both are present. This empirical finding has received little attention in the theoretical literature, and Ho and Huffman strive to fill the gap.

Given that identifying the causal relationship between trust and strong enforcement is difficult using observations from the field, experimentalists have explored the question in laboratory environments. Experimentalists have stripped out contract enforcement of any type to determine whether efficiency is reduced due to a lack of trust. While simple economic models predict that agents will make choices based solely on monetary gains, experimentalists have found that factors other than monetary gains play a role in the choices of at least some. Results vary both across studies and within studies. Some evidence supports the claim that external enforcement crowds out trust. External enforcement appears to be a substitute for trust. Other studies suggest that the process of establishing external enforcement mechanisms can increase trust levels such that enforcement and trust appear to be complements.

To explain these seemingly contradictory results, the authors go back to the basics related to the mechanisms on which trust is based. From a psychological perspective, Ho and Huffman explain that trust might be driven by altruism (unconditional kindness) or by reciprocity (conditional kindness). Ho and Huffman build reciprocity into their theoretical model. It assumes that agents get utility from the beliefs of principals over the agent's level of trustworthiness. This preference to maintain one's image might drive agents to expend costly effort even when the law requires none. The level of trust exhibited by principals will depend on their level of betrayal aversion. Depending on whether trust is driven by altruism or reciprocity, the law might act as a substitute for or a complement to trust. The same sort of conditional result seems to appear in the game theory literature. Ho and Huffman present two case studies to further flesh out the complex relationship between trust and external enforcement: employment contracts and apology laws.

## 2.6   Experiments and Neuroeconomics

The penultimate set of chapters deals with experiments and neuroeconomics.

In "Law and Economics in the Laboratory," Gary Charness and Gregory DeAngelo take us on a tour of some of the many laboratory experiments that have produced results relevant for law. After arguing the benefits of laboratory studies as a valid method for testing economic theory, the authors summarize a handful of studies from three distinct literatures—experimental studies on (1) the decision-making of judges, juries and attorneys, (2) the effects of law enforcement mechanisms on behavior, and (3) the role of communication in principal-agent relationships. Many of the studies take us beyond the standard economic theories and import concepts from psychology in an effort to increase the theories' predictive value.

Charness and DeAngelo begin with the large and growing experimental literature related to the choices of actors functioning in legal environments. Many studies have examined whether judges' decisions are subject to biases and heuristics that have found support in the experimental literature. Experiments employing actual judges as subjects have found convincing evidence that judges suffer from the same errors in decision-making as non-judge subjects, including anchoring, egocentricity, and hindsight bias. In contrast, other results suggest that judges are able to overcome at least some biases. Similarly, experimentalists have found that psychological biases might influence jury decisions. For example, mock decisions over damages awards depended on how much the plaintiff's attorney requested (holding all else constant) and whether the defendant was local or not. Subjects also exhibited signs of "dissent neglect"—the tendency to down-weight opinions that differ from their own. Finally, the authors describe a set of studies that reveal potential biases in attorney decisions. Evidence suggests that biases can creep in when attorneys advise clients about plea deals and when they estimate expected awards.

The authors then summarize a handful of experiments that test theories related to legal enforcement mechanisms. Again, experiments point to the possibility of a powerful role of biases for predicting outcomes when enforcement mechanisms are applied. For example, experimental evidence suggests that litigants' expectations over trial outcomes are influenced by self-serving biases. Individuals tend to assume that uncertain issues will be resolved in their favor. This might help us explain why some cases fail to settle when standard theory predicts they will. Other studies have found counterintuitive results related to the enforcement of collusion prohibitions. The authors explain why the lab acts as a useful environment for untangling causal links between institutions designed to enforce the law and individual and group decision-making.

Finally, Charness and DeAngelo summarize a number of experimental findings related to the role of communication in achieving efficient outcomes in principal-agent relationships, where, for example, the agent promises effort and the principal cannot observe the actual effort level. Generally we look to law to act as a verification mechanism, which compels the agent to keep his promise. Recent evidence from the lab, however, suggests that judicial enforcement of contracts might not be required to reach efficient outcomes. Standard theory assumes that reputation effects are sufficient to keep agents in line, but clever experiment designs eliminate reputation effects as a driver of behavior and focus instead on guilt aversion. The findings suggest that individuals tend to follow through on promises when non-binding promises are communicated in settings where choices are made anonymously. Others have conducted experiments to study a similar problem related to the inability of principals to observe an agent's talent level. If information were perfect, principals would pay high-talent agents more than low-talent agents, and only if the agent expended the promised amount of effort. When information and actions are hidden, standard theory predicts that low-talent agents will sell themselves as high-talent agents, and all agents will promise effort but not keep their promise. Principals, therefore, will not contract with any type of agent. Behavioral economic theories, on the other hand, assume that forces other than incentives to increase monetary payouts drive choices. For example, if low-talent agents benefit when principals pay them a low-talent wage (relative to no wage), they might truthfully reveal their talent level to gain the trust of the principal and then expend effort to reward the principal's trust. The authors describe the designs of and results from experiments developed to test the standard theory against such behavioral theories. The evidence suggests that the behavior of at least some portion of the population comports with the predictions of behavioral theories. The supported theories lead to interesting implications about the legal enforcement of contracts in settings of hidden actions and hidden information.

In "What Explains Observed Reluctance to Trade? A Comprehensive Literature Review," Kathryn Zeiler summarizes the state of the experimental literatures in the fields of economics and psychology that test theories designed to explain valuation gaps and exchange asymmetries. Reluctance to trade (aka the endowment effect) is one of the most widely studied phenomena in the field of behavioral economics and one of the most widely applied behavioral economics concepts in legal scholarship. While neoclassical theory assumes indifference curves are reversible, implying that an individual's valuation of an item or a right is independent of whether the individual is endowed with the item or the right, beginning in the mid-1970s, empirical evidence seemed to support claims that valuations depend on endowment status. Despite attempts to eliminate observed reluctance to trade by, for example, reducing transactions costs, anonymizing choices, having subjects make non-hypothetical choices, and employing demand-revealing preference elicitation mechanisms, many (although not all) experimentalists continued to report observed reluctance to trade. Researchers proposed a number of theories including preference imprecision, lack of market discipline, lack of familiarity with the valuation elicitation mechanism, and endowment theory (an application of prospect theory's assumptions of reference-dependent preferences and loss aversion to contexts of riskless choice).

As Zeiler explains, the literature took a sharp turn in the late 1980s and early 1990s. Knetsch (1989) employed simple exchange experiments, ruled out a number of possible explanations, and observed reluctance to trade in the form of exchange asymmetries, with owners of goods like mugs resisting trading them for equally priced goods such as pens. Following this study, Kahneman, Knetsch, and Thaler (1990) ran a number of treatments to test a refined version of endowment theory, assuming that individuals are loss averse, but only if the owned good is not held for resale and perfect substitutes are unavailable.

Using a demand-revealing preference elicitation mechanism and allowing subjects practice with the mechanism, they observed a number of trades below the number expected in the absence of reluctance to trade, and they attributed this valuation gap to endowment theory.

Zeiler notes that legal scholars continue to cite these two studies today despite the fact that empirical results have called endowment theory into question and alternative theories have garnered strong empirical support. The chapter summarizes multiples lines of research that offer alternative theories and document support for them when tested against endowment theory. For example, reported evidence supports expectation theory, a generalized version of endowment theory that assumes that reference points are set not by endowments but by expectations over outcomes. Others report evidence against expectation theory. Researchers have reported evidence for and against a number of alternative theories including substitution theory, preference imprecision, mere ownership theory (aka attachment theory), enhancement theory, a theory of subject misconceptions, a number of theories that attempt to explain gaps in lottery valuations, transaction disutility, bad deal aversion, and regret avoidance. Today, a number of theories are alive and well in the literature. We cannot, at this stage, point with confidence to any one theory. The chapter provides a comprehensive guide to the social science literature, which has moved well beyond endowment theory and provides support for a number of theories crafted to explain observed reluctance to trade.

In "Incentives, Choices, and Strategic Behavior: A Neuroeconomic Perspective for the Law," Terrence Chorvat and Kevin McCabe offer suggestions for how legal scholarship can benefit from the importation of findings from the burgeoning field of neuroeconomics. The authors begin by offering an account of how neuroeconomics fits into the science of economics. In short, they claim that neuroscience has a role to play both in "collecting interesting facts and naming items of interest" (i.e., observing which brain regions are involved in particular decision processes) and in using discoveries from neuroscience to inform economic models of decision processes. They also note important limitations of the first role—the same neural regions are often associated with different mental processes, and it is difficult to identify which might be driving choices. In addition, both roles are hindered by the difficulties of studying long-term decisions such as retirement planning, which cannot easily be observed in the lab at one point in time. Despite this, we can learn something from correlating brain activity with choices made in the lab about the neurological bases of long-term decisions. The big-picture bottom line is that the field is new and currently limited but has great potential to add to our knowledge base and to assist in the endeavor to generate models with strong predictive value.

The chapter goes on to catalog some of what neuroeconomics has taught us about the neural basis of financial decisions. Standard economic models assume that individuals invest to maximize their returns in uncertain environments, and that we form expectations about the future based in part on histories of asset returns and discount future earnings using an exponential function. Exponential discounting assumes that marginal rates of substitution depend only on how far apart in time the two points of consumption lie. Behavioral economists have reported a large set of empirical results, suggesting that this assumption does not comport with observed behavior. In the face of this evidence, theorists have gone back to the drawing board to develop alternative assumptions related to how individuals perceive the value of amounts gained in the future. For example, one non-standard model builds in hyperbolic discounting, which assumes that the rates of substitution depend not only on the temporal distance between the two points in time but also on the temporal distance between the current period and the two points. While some have tested the predictions of exponential versus hyperbolic discounting using field data or choices made in laboratories from which inferences are drawn about motivations, neuroeconomics uses a different approach. Specifically, inferences are drawn from identification of which parts of the brain are active around the time subjects choose, or from genetic profiles or hormone levels of decision-makers. Findings suggest heterogeneity in preferences over waiting and differences in how experienced and inexperienced traders perceive information. Other findings suggest that the activation of certain neural systems make asset bubble formation more likely. The chapter summarizes a number of additional findings that help us understand behavior in financial markets. Finally, Chorvat and McCabe offer thoughts on how law scholars might apply these findings, including lessons for those interested in how tax law might impact choices in markets.

## 2.7   Cautions and Ways Forward

The final two chapters of the volume provide words of caution for behavioral law and economics scholars and thoughts on how the field could be improved.

In "The Price of Abstraction," Gregory Mitchell argues that the attempted replacement of law and economics, and its assumptions of rationality, with the assumed irrationality of behavioral law and economics is less than ideal. Mitchell offers several suggestions for legal scholars to improve on the importation of behavioral economics into their scholarship. First, Mitchell recommends a higher level of appreciation for observed heterogeneity in preferences and choices and for the practical significance (as opposed to statistical significance) of observed irrational behavior reported by behavioral economics studies. This lack of appreciation, he argues, leads to distorted descriptive and normative conclusions. Legal scholars cite scientific findings to support claims of widespread irrationality leading to negative consequences, but often the findings do not support such grand claims. The chapter includes a revealing table of findings from a series of meta-analyses that consider entire literatures rather than single studies to determine the state of the science with respect to a number of phenomena widely touted as robust, widely prevalent, and substantial. In contrast to the conventional wisdom in the literature, the table reveals small to moderate effect sizes for a majority of the observed phenomena.

Second, Mitchell argues that applications of behavioral economics findings rarely properly account for the conditional nature of the findings and points out potential problems with generalizing from the results to varied populations. Legal scholars often over-claim when they fail to account for the conditions that seem to drive anomalies. They do the same when they assume that findings from narrow studies identify common characteristics or preferences across individuals. Both of these errors result in conclusions that lack a proper dose of nuance and potentially lead readers astray.

Third, Mitchell cautions importers of behavioral economics findings to be clear about the mechanisms that cause deviations from rational choice model predictions. Consumers of behavioral economics often mistake observed phenomena for mental processes that cause the observed behavior. In fact, the literature provides very few solid conclusions about the mechanisms that actually drive choices. Without a firm understanding of this limitation of the current state of the science, importers are too quick to offer broad predictions that apply across a wide array of environments. To address this concern, along with the others, Mitchell suggests the addition of realism and theory to applications of behavioral economics in law. In this way, he takes an important step in diagnosing and offering ways to treat a number of dysfunctions in the behavioral law and economics literature.

In "Why Behavioral Economics Isn't Better, and How It Could Be," Owen Jones provides a perspective on problems with both developments and applications of developments in behavioral economics and then offers steps we can take to make them better. Jones begins by identifying four problems with the status quo: the use of "behavioral economics" as the field's name; the lack of agreement about what the field is and what its tools are designed to do; the singular focus on the tools of psychology as a way to develop better economic models; and the focus on a small subset of all that psychology has to offer. Jones then offers a theory to explain why the field is plagued by these specific problems. The upshot is that universities have not done enough to foster truly multi-disciplinary work. He points to the need to rein in our impulse to fracture disciplines by creating more and more subspecialties and to instead provide incentives for the generation of environments that allow for cross-discipline communication and collaboration. He aptly notes that many disciplines "from Sociology to Evolutionary Biology to Economics to Neuroscience to Political Science to Artificial Intelligence" aim to develop accurate models of human behavior. Despite this, Jones notes that legal scholars seem to draw almost exclusively from the fields of economics and psychology when looking to the scientific literatures for help in explaining and predicting behavior relevant for law. After laying out what he sees as the main causes of this phenomenon, he illuminates how it holds back our efforts to develop sound policymaking and informed legal analysis.

Jones offers a set of intriguing recommendations for how we can remove the blinkers and get a broader view of the relevant scientific literatures. Proposing a "converging-questions approach," Jones gives us a step-by-step guide for improving the study of human behavior. To make the proposal concrete, he walks us through how these steps might help us to better understand what causes observed valuation gaps, or so-called "endowment effects." In particular, he highlights the ways in which the field of evolutionary biology has contributed to our identification of the drivers of valuation gaps. In particular, insights from what we know about primate behaviors thought to increase reproductive success can teach us a great deal about the drivers behind the otherwise puzzling behavior of modern-day humans. In turn, these insights can help us refine models that predict behavior given specific sets of environmental conditions. Jones lists a broad array of findings from neuroeconomics that help us understand how various stimuli impact brain activity, which can help us get a handle on why we react to those stimuli in the ways that we do. Jones's main point is that no one field and no dyad of intersecting fields can bring us closer to understanding human behavior than truly multi-disciplinary efforts that span across a number of contributing fields. To us, this seems a promising avenue for expanding our knowledge base.

# REFERENCES

Becker, Gary S. 1968. Crime and Punishment: An Economic Approach. *Journal of Political Economy* 76: 169–217.

Kahneman, Daniel, Jack L. Knetsch, and Richard H. Thaler. 1990. Experimental Tests of the Endowment Effect and the Coase Theorem. *Journal of Political Economy* 98: 1325–1438.

Knetsch, Jack L. 1989. The Endowment Effect and Evidence of Nonreversible Indifference Curves. *American Economic Review* 79: 1277–1284.

Miller, Dale T. and Michael Ross. 1975. Self-Serving Biases in the Attribution of Causality: Fact or Fiction? *Psychological Bulletin* 82: 213–225.

Shavell, Steven. 1987. *Economic Analysis of Accident Law*. Cambridge, MA: Harvard University Press.

Tversky, Amos and Daniel Kahneman. 1992. Advances in Prospect Theory: Cumulative Representation of Uncertainty. *Journal of Risk and Uncertainty* 5: 297–323.

Zeiler, Kathryn. Forthcoming. Mistaken about Mistakes. *European Journal of Law and Economics.*

# PART I

# FOUNDATIONS

# 1. Conceptual foundations: a bird's-eye view
*Jonathan Baron and Tess Wilkinson-Ryan*

## 1. INTRODUCTION

The term "behavioral law and economics" was apparently coined by Jolls, Sunstein, and Thaler (1998).[1] The idea was that the economic approach to law, as represented in the field called "law and economics," had imported a kind of micro-economic theory that assumed that agents were rational in a certain sense. Yet this sort of theory itself was under challenge, at first from psychology but ultimately from economists themselves. The challenge was not so much to the concept of rationality, although that too had been challenged by philosophers. Rather, it was that, in fact, agents did not *behave* rationally much of the time. If law were going to use economic theory as the basis of analysis, then it would have to acknowledge these behavioral findings and somehow incorporate them.

In this chapter, we shall try to outline the conceptual foundations of the field that has emerged. We shall concentrate on the "behavioral" concepts, many of which have come from psychology.[2] In an effort to be concrete, we shall illustrate our points with examples, with the hope that we do not tread too much on the territory of other chapters in this book.

## 2. WHERE IS BEHAVIOR RELEVANT?

The field covers several kinds of decision makers: courts (judges and juries), individuals (bringing a lawsuit, committing a crime, making and honoring contracts, etc.), and lawmakers (regulators, legislators, and, ultimately, voters). Naturally, some of these decisions have been studied by psychologists, economists, and legal scholars who lack an interdisciplinary perspective (e.g., Dhami and Ayton 2001, for courts, and Becker 1968, for crime). Unfortunately for the student, this work cannot be ignored, but we shall not emphasize it here. We shall emphasize the general framework provided by "behavioral decision theory," also known as the field of "judgment and decision making" (JDM), which we think is a better term.

---

[1] It was analogous to "behavioral decision theory." Now we also have "behavioral public finance" and behavioral many other things.

[2] Some have come from experimental economics, which psychologists tend to regard as a subset of experimental social psychology, constrained by various rules such as forbidding deception.

## 3.   NORMATIVE, DESCRIPTIVE, PRESCRIPTIVE

JDM concerns three types of theories or models. Normative models are standards that researchers use to evaluate judgments and decisions. In some cases the model is simply "the right answer," as when people are asked to estimate quantities such as cost or frequency of mishaps. Such models are based on *correspondence* between a judgment and some real state of the world. In other cases, the right answer depends on a person's values and beliefs, so the only possible criterion is one of internal consistency, or *coherence* (Hammond 1996; Dunwoody 2009). Some judgments, such as probability judgments, can be evaluated both ways. A weather forecaster who says that the probability of precipitation is .5, rain .3, and snow .3, is incoherent. If events she says have .9 probability consistently occur with a frequency of .7, her judgment is mis-calibrated, lacking in correspondence.

Descriptive models explain judgments and decisions. Of particular interest are models that explain why judgments are systematically non-normative. Judgments can be non-normative because of random error, or because they are systematically *biased* in one direction. An example of a bias is that the sum of probabilities assigned to subsets (rain and snow) usually exceeds the probability assigned to the whole set (precipitation). Fox and Tversky (1998) have developed a mathematical model that explains this bias and other judgments, based on the idea that subjective probabilities are distorted.

Much of the tension in the JDM field concerns the issues of correspondence, coherence, and biases. One common argument is that, in real environments, the processes that lead to incoherence are sometimes best at achieving correspondence (Gigerenzer et al. 1999).

Prescriptive models are ways of fixing or avoiding non-normative judgments and decisions. Several methods are relevant here, including the design of law itself, and its implementation through the wording of jury instructions, contracts, etc. The JDM field also is concerned with tools for the formal analysis of judgments and decisions, such as aggregation of judgments to make a prediction or analysis of risk regulation in terms of costs and benefits, where the benefits are often subjective. A recent innovation in prescriptive theory is the idea of *decision architecture*, the idea of designing decisions themselves so that people are more likely to choose the best option according to normative theory (Thaler and Sunstein 2008).

We should not assume that all biases need to be corrected or worked around. Some may be side effects of psychological processes that are optimal in typical environments. Yet, on the other hand, we should not assume that relevant legal environments are typical. Processes that usually serve us well may break down when we are asked to assess tort penalties for unusual harms, for example.

## 4.   NORMATIVE MODELS

Normative models in behavioral law and economics start with economic theory itself, particularly micro-economic theory, which is concerned with choices and transactions among decision makers. Microeconomics itself, however, is a mix of all three types of models, as well as general frameworks for expressing more specific models, such as demand curves, indifference curves, elasticity, and the marginal rate of substitution. The main normative models involve maximization of utility, profit, or wealth. An important example is expected-utility theory, which applies to decisions in which outcomes are uncertain.

Often these normative models are also assumed to be descriptive models, but this is where behavioral data often says otherwise. Micro-economics also includes much of game theory, which is a normative model for strategic interaction of multiple parties, in which outcomes depend on the decisions of more than one person.

In addition to standard micro-economics, analysis often relies on welfare economics as a normative model, particularly concerning distributional questions. Welfare economics is concerned with the maximization of some measure of social welfare in a society

Here we concentrate on the models that are most useful on the behavioral side. In the psychology of judgment and decisions, other normative models include statistics and logic.

### 4.1  Utility and Probability

The most standard normative models in this area are those involving utility and probability. Utility is a numerical measure of good, or, for some, of the extent to which goals are achieved. Utility theory, actually a set of theories, specifies that the best option in a choice is the one with the highest utility. Utility is, however, a function of outcomes, and typically the outcomes of a decision are uncertain. In this case, we want the highest *expected* utility (EU). The expected utility of an option is $\sum_i p_i u_i$, that is the sum over all possible outcomes $i$ of, for each outcome, its probability times its utility. We can think of it as the average utility if the decision were repeated. Probability is a function of individual beliefs, and utility is a function of individual values, so, often, the only way we have of determining whether people follow this model is to test coherence over several decisions (see Section 5.5.1).

In EU theory, we usually assume that the utility of money is "marginally declining" or "concave." This means that a given difference in money in your bank account, say $1,000, has a bigger effect on utility when the amounts of money are small. A difference between $1,000 and $2,000 has more effect than the difference between $1,000,000 and $1,001,000, or even the difference between $2,000 and $3,000. If you plot a graph of utility against money, it is concave when viewed from the bottom; its slope is decreasing as you move to the right. A consequence of this assumption is that we are averse to risks. If you have a choice of $2,000 or a 50/50 gamble on $1,000 or $3,000, you will take the $2,000, because the potential utility loss of $1,000 is greater than the potential gain, and they are equally likely.

Formal development of utility theory (e.g., Krantz et al. 1971) shows how we can assign numbers to outcomes or options, representing their utility. Conformity to utility theory in its various forms implies conformity to several subsidiary principles. One is transitivity: if you prefer option A to B, and B to C, then you must also prefer A to C. Transitivity implies that utility is an ordinal scale: any set of utility numbers that accounts for a set of choices cannot yield different orderings of the choices in the set. Obviously, transitivity is a property of numbers themselves.

But utility theories require not only that we can order outcomes but also that we can order *differences* of pairs of outcomes. Often we are confronted with choices between, say A1 together with B1 vs. A2 with B2. We must make a trade-off. If A1 is better than A2 to a greater extent than B2 is better than B1, then we should choose the first pair.

Thus, the utility scale must be more than ordinal. It must be an interval scale, allowing the comparison of intervals. Differences must be transitive too.

Various mathematical theories have started with these principles (plus others) and have derived theorems concerning the representation of utility and its uniqueness. Uniqueness refers to what transformations can preserve the representation. An ordinal scale is preserved by any monotonic transformation. An interval scale is preserved by any linear transformation, that is, by multiplication and addition. Utility is an interval scale, but not a ratio scale. Ratio scales cannot be transformed by addition because they have unique zero points. Interval scales do not. Utility is thus a measure like time, with no natural zero point, but not like mass. Utility is always relative. That is all we need, because we are always comparing options to one another, so we need only differences.

Various theories derive the interval property in different ways. For example, one (non-obvious but important) way of deriving expected utility theory involves the sure-thing principle (Savage 1954), which is based on an analysis of decisions into options (e.g., umbrella or not), uncertain states of the world (e.g., rain or sunny), and consequences, which are a function of both the option and the state. The "sure-thing principle" states, roughly, that if, for a given state of the world, the consequence is independent of the option chosen, the nature of that consequence does not affect the choice of options. This principle implies, ultimately, that option differences in different states of the world are independent of each other, so they may be added.

Interestingly, and non-trivially, the coherence principles of probability theory can be derived from EU itself. The two main principles are the addition rule and the multiplication rule.[3]

Another relevant version of utility theory concerns decisions over time. Here the outcomes may occur at different times, and the utility of later outcomes may be discounted. We set aside the question of when such discounting is rational, and why it might not be in some cases. But we must assume that the relative utility of outcomes (or their differences) does not itself change with the passage of time alone. An implication is that, if you prefer L (a large reward) at time T2 to S (a smaller reward) at (an earlier) time T1, this preference should not change as time passes and you move closer in time to T1. Decisions are independent of when they are made, so long as the outcomes and their dates are the same. This principle of delay independence implies that discounting must be exponential: over a given interval of time (like a month), the utility of an outcome at the end of the interval is a constant percentage of its utility at the beginning of the interval. Economists often assume exponential discounting for money, even though the utility of money is not generally assumed to be a linear function of the amount.

## 4.2    Utilitarianism and Welfare Economics

A natural extension of EU is utilitarianism, a normative model for decisions that affect many people, such as laws and regulations. Utilitarianism holds that we should maximize

---

[3]    If A and B are mutually exclusive, then $p(A \text{ or } B) = p(A) + p(B)$ and $p(C \text{ and } D) = p(C|D) p(D)$. The expression $p(C|D)$ is the conditional probability of C given D, the belief we would have in C if we knew D.

utility over all people. Famously, it implies that harm is justified only if it is necessary to increase total good. This was Bentham's ([1843] 1948) justification for legal punishment, and the idea was fully incorporated into economic theories of punishment (Becker 1968; Shavell 2004).

The extension from EU to utilitarianism is natural because we can think of many decisions either as decisions affecting one random person under uncertainty or as social decisions affecting many people. For example, the decision about whether to require a vaccination involves a trade-off between disease prevention and side effects. From the individual perspective, each person has some probability of getting the disease if not vaccinated, or of side effects if vaccinated. We can use EU theory to find the best option for that random person. From the social perspective, we have numbers of people instead of probabilities, but the analysis is the same, and the results should agree.

Formally, utilitarianism treats people as independent in much the same way in which EU treats states of the world as independent. We can compare options by looking at the differences between the two options for each person, some of which can be negative, and adding up the differences.

Welfare economics has taken a broader view (Adler 2012). Instead of maximizing total utility, it seeks to maximize a *social welfare function*, a function that computes the welfare of society from the welfare of all the individuals. This theory retains the assumption that nothing else matters, but it includes utilitarianism as a special case. Almost all theories assume that the utility of money (or its contribution to social welfare) declines as the amount of individual income or wealth increases. A hundred dollars means more to a poor person than to a rich one. Thus, the general approach is consistent with some sort of redistribution.

As Shavell (2004) points out, for most legal issues, it does not matter whether we apply utilitarianism, some other social welfare function in common use, or even the most naïve method of aggregating welfare, the total of economic wealth. This argument is stronger if we assume (as Shavell does) that distributional concerns should not affect the law, except in one place, namely taxation (broadly defined so as to include negative taxation and social insurance). Thus, only in taxation does it matter whether we try to maximize (for example) utility or wealth.[4] Taking this point of view, Kaplow and Shavell (2002) analyze a number of legal principles. They point out that non-welfarist legal principles, such as those based on fairness, can generally be understood as leading to violations of ex-ante Pareto optimality, that is, the application of such rules could possibly make some people worse off, in terms of their individual expectations, while making nobody better

---

[4]   One argument for Shavell's assumption is that the attempt to craft legal rules with distributional concerns in mind is a crude tool. For example, we might tilt the balance toward plaintiffs in tort law on the grounds that they are generally poorer than defendants. But that is not always true. Another argument is that, if some otherwise-optimal law does tilt toward the rich, we can optimally correct this effect by making taxes more progressive. An argument on the other side is that such corrections do not happen in the real world, so we are stuck with a second-best system. Also, an appropriate correction through progressive taxation for one type of case might be large and thus an over-correction for another type, or it might reduce incentive enough so as to reduce total utility.

off.[5] They take their argument to support, in broad terms, the economic theory of law as a normative basis.

There are other normative models. One concerns negotiations, which are theoretically central to the analysis of contracts. All of those that we consider are consistent with utility theory in general. Some of the models for decisions with multiple parties, however, do not assume (as utilitarianism and social-welfare functions usually do) that utilities of different individuals can be compared, so they apply some weaker standard such as Pareto optimality, which holds that, if outcome A is better than B for one person and worse for nobody, then A should be preferred.

### 4.3    Game Theory

One of these weaker theories, which is quite influential, is game theory (Luce and Raiffa 1957). Game theory applies to situations in which several people make decisions. The outcome for each person depends on the decisions of several people (which may include the person in question). Games like chess and checkers are an obvious example, with two players, but many games have more players. The theory is rich and complex, with applications to many practical problems such as the design of markets (Roth 2008) and negotiation (Raiffa 1982).

Game theory has provided a set of concepts that are applied more broadly in the study of decision making. One is the distinction between cooperative and non-cooperative games. Cooperative games are of particular interest because they include prisoners' dilemma games and the extension of those to multiple players. In these games each player has a choice between two options, one of which is best for the player, defection, and the other of which is better for everyone else, cooperation. (The "better for everyone else" may mean that some good is provided to everyone if some minimal number cooperate, which could be everyone. Or it could mean that the total is larger, if we are willing to sum across people.) A great variety of games of this type have been studied and analyzed. They include what are called social dilemmas, public-goods games, n-person prisoners' dilemmas, and commons dilemmas; these terms overlap extensively in their meaning. Examples of cooperative acts are paying taxes voluntarily, respecting the property of others, restraining one's own pollution, restraining use of common resources such as water or fish, and limiting family size. Arguably, participation in democratic government (e.g., voting) is also a form of cooperation (Baron 2012). Laws often punish defection, thus reducing the self-interested benefit of defection, possibly to the point where it disappears. In some cases the law does not fully deter defection by reducing its expected benefit to zero; for example, penalties for under-paying income taxes, taking into account the chance of getting caught, rarely reduce the expected value of underpayment to zero. An interesting fact is that people often cooperate spontaneously when the cost of doing so is not too great (Dawes and Thaler 1988). Cooperation is often enforced through social norms (Bicchieri 2006).

When game theory is taken as a normative model, it typically assumes that people

---

[5]    The same principle of ex-ante Pareto optimality is also inconsistent with non-utilitarian social-welfare theories (Adler 2012), but Kaplow and Shavell do not go down this road.

act in their narrow self-interest. Thus, defection is "rational" in social dilemmas. Often defection is also justified by EU theory of a sort that considers only self-interested utility (hence ignores altruism, the utility for other people's achievement of their goals), but EU and game theory do not quite always agree. For example, suppose some good is provided only if everyone cooperates, and, in this case, each player would be worse off by defecting (because the good is large enough to make up for the cost of cooperation). Game theory in this case would typically say that the game has two equilibria: everyone cooperates or everyone defects, but it would not specify the implications of this fact for each player's choices. EU theory could do so, however, by taking into account the probabilities of each player for what the other players will do. If you think it is sufficiently likely that everyone else will cooperate, then you should cooperate.

Utilitarianism, when applied to similar cases, will usually prescribe cooperation, unless the benefit of cooperation is too small, given the number of other cooperators, or unless the theory gives special consideration to the decision maker's cost of cooperation. It could give such special consideration, for example, by assuming that an individual's willingness to sacrifice self-interest is limited and that the decision must be made so as to maximize utility for all, taking this limit into account as if it were an external fact (Baron and Szymanska 2010).

## 5. DESCRIPTIVE THEORY

Economic theory is often descriptive as well as normative. It is used to make predictions about the effects of economic interventions, and to some extent it is useful. For example, considerable evidence supports the economic theory of the relation between crime and punishment, which holds that crime is deterred more by higher penalties or higher probability of apprehension (e.g., Fisman and Miguel 2007).[6] But we concentrate here on predictions that do not follow naturally from economic theory.

### 5.1 Heuristics and Biases

Kahneman and Tversky (1972) introduced the idea of heuristics as a way of explaining biases (systematic departures from normative standards). For example, one bias is the neglect of base rates in probability judgment, which can result from the "representativeness heuristic." In a classic study (Kahneman and Tversky 1973), subjects were given a description of "Tom W," which resembled a stereotypical computer-science graduate student. They were asked to rank the probabilities that Tom was in a number of different graduate fields, including computer science and "social sciences." Another group was asked to rank Tom's similarity to the typical student in each field, that is, the extent to which Tom was representative of that field. A third group was asked to rank

---

[6] Fisman and Miguel examined parking tickets by United Nations staff, finding that national origin affected the number of tickets when penalties were absent because of diplomatic immunity, but when immunity was removed all tickets decreased dramatically. It should be noted that Robinson and Darley (2004) claimed to find minimal effects of penalties on crime, but their analysis was mostly limited to small changes in the law.

the sizes of the different fields. Of interest was that the probability rankings matched the similarity (representativeness) rankings almost perfectly and had essentially no relation to the sizes of the different fields, although the subjects judged these sizes quite accurately. Normatively, the sizes, the base rates, matter. (In the extreme case, if the field had only one student, Tom would not be very likely to be in that field even if he matched the typical student fairly well.) But people ignore these base rates. Arguably, base rates are even excluded by law when they are normatively relevant, as in the exclusion of evidence of prior convictions.

The term "heuristic" was invented by the mathematician George Polya (1945), who thought of heuristics as a weak method, something that might help in solving a problem. It is a rule that can be applied easily when we are stuck on a problem. Kahneman and Tversky recognized the value of heuristics but argued that they could also mislead, especially in cases, unlike mathematics, where the answer they yielded could not be easily checked.

Legal scholars were quick to seize on the idea of heuristics to explain various phenomena in the judicial system, but this literature has tended to rely heavily on the first few heuristics that Kahneman and Tversky and others enumerated. Many others have been proposed in the last few decades (Baron 2008).

More recently, Sunstein (2005) has argued that heuristics are used for moral judgments, and these moral heuristics often have legal implications. These heuristics cause biases, if the normative model of utilitarianism is used as a standard.[7]

An example of a moral heuristic is "do no harm," a rule against causing harm through action, even to prevent greater harm (which would result from omission) (Baron 1996). The resulting bias is called "omission bias," a bias in favor of harmful omissions over less harmful acts (Ritov and Baron 1990; Spranca, Minks, and Baron 1991; Baron and Ritov 2009). Omission bias is probably behind opposition to (and laws against) active euthanasia. It may also underlie the reluctance of regulatory agencies to approve drugs that may have harmful side effects. It is arguably built into the law, in the absence of "bad Samaritan" laws in most jurisdictions. An exception is tort law, where negligence is typically an omission, not an act. Omission bias is reduced in cases where the decision maker has responsibility for the welfare of the potential victim.

People show great variation in omission bias. Some do not show it at all in many situations. Much of this variation seems to be related to how people think about causality. A "but for" (*sine qua non*) view of causality would not show any bias. The bias is found when people think about causality in physical terms. If a vaccine causes a side effect, we can imagine a sequence of causal steps between the injection and the disease. If failure to vaccinate causes a disease, no such series of steps between behavior and outcome are apparent.

### 5.1.1   Attribute substitution and the isolation effect

Many heuristics work through what Kahneman and Frederick (2002) call "attribute substitution." The idea is that we estimate some value by using another value that is correlated with the first, usually because the latter is easier to judge. Thus, very young

---

[7]   Sunstein does not endorse this standard but almost all of his examples of biases are biases as defined by it.

children who have trouble counting beyond 5, when asked which of two rows of coins has more coins, will pick the longer row regardless of the number (Lawson, Baron, and Siegel 1974).

The "isolation effect," another general mechanism for heuristics, is that people attend to what is available "on screen" and tend to ignore what they could easily infer (Kahneman and Lovallo 1993).[8] When evaluating policies, the intended purpose of the policy is what is on screen, and people often ignore secondary effects. For example, they prefer taxes on businesses to income taxes, but when they are asked who pays the business tax, many people switch (McCaffery and Baron 2006).

Both mechanisms may be involved in judgments about risk. When people are asked how to allocate funds to reduce risks, and when they are given options in terms of the proportion of risk reduced, they tend to allocate more money when the proportion is greater, regardless of the absolute size of the risk. This results in larger allocations to large reductions in tiny risks (e.g., McDaniels 1988). This effect may account for a substantial part of the discrepancies in risk regulation noted by Breyer (1993) and others: some risks are under-regulated in terms of cost per life saved, while others are over-regulated. The latter tend to be risks that affect fewer people.

### 5.1.2   Simple heuristics and adaptive cognition

The idea of heuristics is two-sided. Presumably most heuristics exist because they have adaptive value.[9] They may be faster, easier, less demanding of information, or capable of producing an answer when nothing else is available. Gerd Gigerenzer and those he has inspired have demonstrated many cases where simple heuristics outperform more elaborate ways of making judgments (Gigerenzer et al. 1999). For example, in one famous set of experiments, German subjects were as good as Americans at saying which of two American cities was larger. The Germans knew very much less, but they could do well at the task by picking the single city that they recognized, when they recognized only one (Goldstein and Gigerenzer 2002; Hoffrage 2011).

### 5.1.3   Two-systems theory

The idea of heuristics meshes with a kind of psychological theory that has been around for centuries, based on the idea that our cognitive machinery has two ways of doing things: System 1 is fast, automatic, and perhaps impulsive and System 2 is slow and reflective (e.g., Evans 2008; Kahneman 2011). The distinction is perhaps best illustrated in trick problems, such as those used by Frederick (2005). For example, "If it takes 5 machines 5 minutes to make 5 widgets, how long would it take 100 machines to make 100 widgets?" System 1 says "100 minutes." Some people stop there. But System 2 can correct this error. Close to the idea of System 1 is the role of emotion, drives, and motives, such as sex, anger, fear, and joy. Although it is tempting to think that System 1 is the source of biases and System 2 is the source of rational thinking, the evidence for this view is weak. Biases and

---

[8]   The isolation effect is essentially the same as "focusing" (Legrenzi, Girotto, and Johnson-Laird 1993) and "choice bracketing" (Read, Loewenstein, and Rabin 1999).

[9]   Such functionalist or teleological explanations are not the only ones that can be given. Nor do they imply that adaptive value works through biological evolution. It can also work through cultural evolution, individual learning, or individual invention.

errors may well arise from difficult-to-use rules, which are applied by System 2 (insofar as the distinction is clear).

One of the questions for contemporary JDM research is when people rely on System 1 vs. System 2 (see, e.g., Milkman, Chugh, and Bazerman 2009). People are apparently more likely to rely on System 2 reasoning when they believe they will be asked to give reasons for their choices (Tetlock 1985), when they make choices about events in the far rather than the near future (Milkman, Rogers and Bazerman 2008), and when they are making judgments in a foreign language (Keysar, Hayakawa, and An 2012).

### 5.1.4    Impulsiveness, hot cognition, and self-control

Economics thinks of preferences in a very straightforward way: if you did it or chose it, then you preferred to do it or choose it. This is the theory of revealed preferences. What makes the notion of preferences complicated from a psychological standpoint is that people make all kinds of impulsive or unfortunate decisions that they would never have planned to make and that they regret almost immediately. For example, a smoker might, all things considered, prefer not to be a smoker. But when the next nicotine craving hits, he smokes a cigarette. The economic view of this behavior is that whatever his professed preference, his choice to smoke reveals that he preferred to smoke that cigarette. From a psychological view, it is not clear that we ought to identify the decision to smoke as the real preference and ignore the agent's explicit goals or subsequent regret. When a choice is made often determines how it is made, in ways that present a challenge for straightforward ideas about preference and self-control.

Impulsiveness describes the value of now, the disproportionate weighing of outcomes in the current period, such that an outcome with a smaller but sooner benefit trumps one with a later, bigger benefit (Lynch and Zauberman 2006). Smoking now has a small immediate reward; quitting smoking has a big long-term health benefit. The idea of hot vs. cold cognitive states (Metcalfe and Mischel 1999) is related to impulsiveness. A hot state is one in which the outcome is immediate and highly salient or vivid. Decisions made with the prospect of immediate gratification are made in a hotter state than those that ask people to consider future rewards, but a hot state is not just about time preference. It also describes the individual's visceral attraction to the reward, which is made greater by states of deprivation—hunger, thirst, exhaustion, and drug withdrawal cause people to reason very differently about the value of food, water, sleep, and opioids, respectively (Loewenstein 1996). Of particular importance to any discussion of legal action is the phenomenon called the "hot/cold empathy gap" (Loewnstein 1996). The hot/cold empathy gap describes the consistent failure of individuals in a cold state to predict how they will behave in a hot state. This has implications for a wide spectrum of individual decision making, from the everyday (hungry shoppers choose more junk food than sated shoppers) to the criminally offensive (men in an aroused state report greater willingness to use deception or force with a partner than men in a non-aroused state).

Behavioral law and economic studies of impulsiveness and hot cognition have focused on legal approaches to reducing the probability or harm of impulsive choices. Sin taxes and warning labels are common policy approaches for reducing poor consumption choices, but the existing studies suggest that these approaches will fail, because decision makers in a hot state are quite insensitive to the costs, financial or otherwise, of immediate gratification (Lynch and Zauberman 2006). On the other hand, cooling-off periods have gotten quite a bit of traction with behavioral law and economics scholars (Jolls and Sunstein 2006). Cooling-off laws give consumers some amount of time after a purchase to correct for decisions that now cause regret.

### 5.1.5  Outrage, retribution, and punishment

A utilitarian view of punishment is largely concerned with deterrence (and also incapacitation and rehabilitation, when these are relevant), but for most individuals the motive for punishment is retribution. The psychological study of anger, disgust, and punishment has been highly influential for legal scholars, particularly for criminal law. In some respects, this is an odd area for behavioral law and economics, insofar as it is an odd area for law and economics, too. Although Becker (1968) and Posner (1973) have written highly influential articles on optimal deterrence, many if not most legal scholars advocate an essentially deontological theory of state punishment. In other words, the most influential normative theory of punishment, at least in the criminal law context, expressly disavows utilitarianism. Psychological research suggests that such theories are supported by the intuitive judgments of many people (Robinson and Darley 2000).

**Anger and outrage**  The psychology of anger begins with the observation that anger is a physiologically intense emotion; that is, it is characterized by a high level of arousal. Cognitive appraisal (e.g., this person intends to do me harm) and physiological response (heart racing, body temperature rising) have dynamic effects—when you think you've been wronged, you experience anger arousal, but the physiological experience of anger may also drive attributions of blame. Anger is an emotion that motivates action, and often the action it motivates is retaliation. One way for an angry person to reduce the aversive aroused state is to retaliate; for example, counter-aggression noticeably reduces blood pressure (Baker and Schaie 1969).

Feelings of anger or outrage may push people to punish less carefully. Punishment, of any reasonable target, becomes the goal, at the expense of accuracy (Goldberg, Lerner, and Tetlock 1999). Angry people are more likely to attribute harm to a person rather than a situation (Keltner, Locke, and Audrain 1993), more likely to infer culpability from a set of ambiguous facts (Goldberg, Lerner, and Tetlock 1999), and more likely to rely on superficial cues or stereotypic judgments (Bodenhausen et.al.1994).

**Retaliation**  When people are mad, they retaliate. Psychological research on anger suggests that anger is a highly aversive state that people really want to stop experiencing. One of the most effective ways to dissipate angry feelings is to act on them; this is retaliation. In a classic Ultimatum game (Thaler 1988), one of two subjects is randomly chosen to receive $10. This subject can offer some amount to his partner, the Receiver, who can accept or refuse. If the Receiver refuses, the money goes back to the experimenter. Economic theory based on self-interest alone implies that the Receiver should accept any amount greater than 0. Yet many Receivers turn away stingy non-zero offers, leaving both players with nothing. One way of explaining this finding is that the Receiver sees the stingy offer, gets mad, and fights back with the only tool available. Indeed, this explanation is supported by Xiao and Houser (2011) who find that if Receivers are permitted to communicate their anger to selfish Senders, the Receivers will then take the low offers.

There are multiple theories, some complementary to each other, to explain the psychology of anger and revenge. Evolutionary psychologists argue that revenge and retaliation are adaptive, insofar as one who exacts revenge for slights against him will deter others from taking advantage (Tooby, Cosmides, and Price 2006), and indeed there is evidence that the threat of retaliation inhibits aggression (Baron 1973). Psychologists who ascribe to a theory of inequity aversion argue that "getting even" really is about restoring psychological equity (Berscheid, Boye, and Walster 1968).

Citizens can also impose punishments on one another without a legal judgment. A party to a contract who feels taken advantage of might breach knowing that expectation damages will not fully compensate the non-breaching party for the hassle, much less the insult, caused by breach (Wilkinson-Ryan 2011). Disputants in a tort suit might refuse to keep negotiating if they think the other party is being clearly unfair—even if settlement is cheaper than litigation (Babcock and Loewenstein 1997). Divorcing spouses may force litigation as a means of punishing a violation of the marriage contract (Wilkinson-Ryan and Baron 2009).

**Third-party punishment**    Third-party punishment is a response to a first person's moral violation, against a second-person victim, by a third person who did not suffer direct harm from the violation. From a behavioral point of view, the interesting point is that people will impose punishments on perceived wrongdoers, even when the punisher has no obligation to punish and when the punishment is costly to the punisher (Fehr and Gächter 2002).

Arguably, third-party punishment by a state is central to law itself. In the absence of something like a government, retaliation by individuals or groups (such as kin) is common, and the invention of a legal system is seen as a reform, preventing cycles of violence and replacing impulsive action with something like due process (Diamond 2008). However, governments, once they exist, try to prevent both second-party punishment (retaliation, "taking the law into your own hands") and third-party punishment ("vigilante justice"). Subjects in economic experiments on third-party punishment are thus in an awkward position, because of social norms against third-party punishment outside of the law. The experiments may depend on making it clear that the law has no role.

Aside from criminal law, citizens are asked to levy punishments on wrongdoers when they decide punitive damages in tort actions. From the point of view of potential parties to litigation, the ability to predict the magnitude of a damages award bears both on whether or not to take certain precautions, and, ultimately, whether or not to settle a claim (Polinsky and Shavell 1999).

Translating a sense of moral wrongfulness or outrage into an award of money is a particularly complex decision, and it leads to unusually erratic judgments (Kahneman, Schkade, and Sunstein 1998). The outrage model suggests that subjects arrive easily at an appropriate severity of punishment, and thus have a shared "punitive intent." But assigning a dollar value to the punitive intent becomes more difficult, and jurors are apt to take into account a variety of factors, including the size of the offending firm and the extent of harm suffered by the plaintiff.

**Pointless punishment and neglect of deterrence**    Baron and Ritov (1993) have described a phenomenon they call "pointless punishment," wherein people are willing to impose punitive damages on tortfeasors irrespective of the consequences of the punishment for the social good—that is, people punished misdeeds, even in scenarios in which the punishment itself would yield net harms to society. In that case, such punishment was retributive, but many subjects, in other scenarios, were sensitive to whether or not the punishment could deter future harm.

The questionnaire used by Baron and Ritov asked respondents to imagine that the United States had a legal system (much like New Zealand's), in which separate decisions were made about penalties against injurers and compensation for victims (Baron and Ritov 1993). The cases, one involving a death caused by a vaccine and the other involving sterility caused by a birth-control pill, were designed so that they would probably not meet a negligence standard for liability. Subjects (including retired judges) were asked about appropriate penalties under two conditions: a finding of liability would lead the producer to make a safer product; or it would lead the producer to remove the product from the market, which would mean that only a less safe alternative would be available. (Arguably, this is what happened in the U.S. in the 1970s and 1980s, with respect to some vaccines.)

Some subjects thought that the penalty should be less, or zero, when its deterrent effect was perverse, that is, leading to worse outcomes. Most subjects thought that the penalty should be the same. Baron and Ritov (1993) asked subjects if they had heard of the deterrence principle as a justification of punishment and, once it was briefly explained, whether they agreed with it. Some subjects had not heard of it: of these, about equal numbers accepted and rejected it once it was explained. Other subjects had heard of it: of these, some rejected it, and some accepted it. Those who rejected the principle thought that retribution was a better way to apply the law. In sum, many people who apply non-utilitarian principles do not know what they are rejecting. A brief explanation of the utilitarian approach will be persuasive to some of these people, but not to others.

· Of interest in this study were the individual differences in whether deterrent effects were considered, and in the willingness to consider them. We might conclude that "on the average, people levy pointless punishments," but that obscures the fact that the average does not represent everyone and that people are somewhat malleable.

## 5.2 Other-regarding Preferences

Economic models of human decision making often assume rational, self-interested agents. In this section we take up the latter part of that formulation for a moment, the idea that people's preferences are driven by self-interest. The assumption that people are self-interested is often an assumption of convenience, if only because there are individual differences and some people really are only self-interested, and the law must take them into account. But there may be situations in which this assumption does more harm than good, where making law for the "knaves crowds" out intrinsic virtuous motivation (Frey 1997).

### 5.2.1 Prosocial behavior and fairness

There is ample evidence that most people have other-regarding preferences. Some examples of this are very intuitive; it is quite natural to express a preference for one's children to be happy and successful, even when there is no clear material benefit to oneself. It is more difficult to explain typical results from the classic dictator game, in which a participant in an experiment is given $10 and told to allocate some or none of it to an anonymous second player. Instead of keeping all of the money, most players give away a non-trivial sum, even if the experimenter cannot identify who made which allocation, and even if the players will never know one another's identities (Forsythe et al. 1994; Engel 2011).

Unlike economics, psychology starts with the premise that empathy and prosocial behavior are adaptive and, indeed, integral to normal psychological development. The psychological study of other-regarding preferences has long been oriented around the question of when and why people help one another. Emotional accounts argue that humans have a kind of reflexive aversion to seeing other humans in need (Piliavin et al. 1981), or more generally, that the human capacity to empathize is central to prosocial behavior (Coke, Batson, and McDavis 1978). There are also norm-based explanations suggesting that people help because they prefer to follow an internalized social norm that favors helping and sharing, in turn avoiding "self-sanctions" like guilt and lowered self-esteem (Schwartz 1973). Perhaps the most influential description of the helping/sharing norm is equity theory (Walster, Walster, and Berscheid 1978) and inequity aversion (Fehr and Schmidt 1999).

The idea that people are not entirely self-interested, that they may prefer to exchange some marginal welfare of their own in order to increase the welfare of others, has been very influential for private law contexts like negotiation and contract. For example, one of the core predictions of economists for legal behavior is that a party to a contract will breach the contract when breach is cheaper than performance (including the cost of paying expectation damages). Recent work suggests that many people would not breach for small to moderate increases in profit, in large part because they are sensitive to the expectations of the promisee and prefer not to disappoint them (Wilkinson-Ryan and Baron 2009). Loewenstein, Thompson, and Bazerman (1989) used negotiation experiments to track disputants' preferences for outcomes to self and other, and found that many subjects were willing to forego gains to themselves in favor of a more equitable allocation. In short, the identification of other-regarding preferences in experimental and field settings offers evidence about when negotiators, parties to a contract, or even disputants in a settlement might choose to forgo profit in favor of equity.

### 5.2.2 Moralistic and protected values

Just as people may have preferences for the material well-being of others, there is also strong evidence that they have "moralistic" principles for others. That is, some people would prefer that others follow a particular set of moral rules even when following those rules does not have good consequences for those affected or for the adherents of the rules in question, outside of the moralistic value itself. Baron (2003) found endorsements of moralistic goals across a number of policy domains, often without regard to the consequences of the behavior and the preferences of the other. The idea of moralistic values helps explain policy debates in a variety of arenas, including same-sex marriage, contraception and abortion, environmental regulation, pornography, and drug use. Holders of moralistic values often attempt to justify them in terms of consequences for someone, but such justifications often seem too weak to justify the strength of the value itself.

Many of these moralistic values are also protected from trade-offs with other values (Baron and Spranca 1997; Baron and Ritov 2009; see also Fiske and Tetlock 1997 for a similar idea, which they called "sacred values"). People will say, for example, that abortion is always wrong no matter how great the benefits that would result from allowing a single abortion (and regardless of whether a majority of people think otherwise). Roth (2007) has argued that values of this sort, with popular support, find their way into laws and rules, such as prohibitions on selling organs. He argues that a feeling of repugnance lies behind such prohibitions, which he labels as "repugnant transactions."

## 5.3 Naïve Theories

Unfairly neglected in recent literature is another approach, which holds that people have naïve theories. The idea comes from the study of child development. Children think that the sun goes around the earth, that the earth is flat. But naïve theories are also found in adults. Some people think that a thermostat works like an accelerator, so that, if you turn it way up, the room will heat up faster (Kempton 1986). This approach is somewhat like the idea of biases, as compared to normative models. But the "true theories" to which judgments are compared are not seen so much as definitions of optimality that are good for all time but rather as just the most defensible current thinking. People undoubtedly have naïve theories of economics, of how the law works, and of their roles as citizens (Baron 2012).

One area in which naïve theories are both abundant and consequential is consumer finance. Recent debates over regulation of financial markets have cited a number of behavioral anomalies that are arguably caused by naïve theories, especially in the high-stakes context of retirement planning (see, e.g., Coates and Hubbard 2007). Benartzi and Thaler (2001) documented the phenomenon of "naïve diversification," showing that most people think that portfolio diversification is essentially an investment of 1/n into each of n funds offered—they believe that spreading out investments is good, irrespective of the attributes of the options at hand. Similarly, many investors rely on an explicit theory that favors funds with strong past performance and ignores fund fees, which are deemed too small to matter (Wilcox 2003), though in fact almost most retail investors are better off ignoring past performance and choosing the lowest-fee funds available.

## 5.4 Error

Most of the emphasis in the JDM literature is on biases, which are systematic errors, but unsystematic errors also matter in the law. One example is variability in awards of punitive damage (Sunstein, Kahneman, and Schkade 2005). Whatever the right answer about what these awards should be, juries are extremely variable, and the same happens with simulated juries. As in the case of capital punishment, questions arise about whether variable penalties are inherently unfair.

From a normative perspective, the prospective offender should consider the expected utility of the offense. For sufficient deterrence, the expected utility of the penalty should be greater—but not too much greater—than the expected utility of the gain from the offense.[10] Thus, it should not matter whether the penalty is variable; all that matters is the expected utility of all the penalties. But it is possible that the variability is skewed. Errors in punitive damages are limited on the low size by 0, but not limited on the high side, so

---

[10]   Over-deterrence has at least three disadvantages: it causes harm to offenders that is not justified by the harm prevented; it is costly; and it deters offenses that arguably should not be deterred, such as breaking into a cabin in the wilderness in order to avoid freezing to death.

that the mean of these awards is higher than the median. But the median may come closer to what is correct. If so, the variability itself creates excessive awards.

One might argue that variability is unfair even if the mean were correct. The same might be said for the variability that results from taking probability of apprehension into account when assessing penalties (one of the arguments in favor of assessing punitive damages at all). From a utilitarian point of view, however, variability does not necessarily reduce total utility, and the alternative would be worse. If we treated all offenses as if apprehension rates were 100%, under-deterrence would be massive, and unfairness would still result from the fact that some offenders would get away with no penalty at all.

## 5.5    Formal Models

JDM scholars sometimes apply formal, mathematical models to explain judgments and decisions. EU and probability theory are models of this sort, as are other models used in economics. But the emphasis in JDM is on models that explain biases.

### 5.5.1    Prospect theory and related theories

Kahneman and Tversky (1979) proposed a modification of EU that accounted for most of the known biases, which they called prospect theory (PT). The EU of a prospect is $\sum_i p_i u_i$, over the possible outcomes $i$. PT replaces $p_i$ with a transformation $\pi p_i$, where the $\pi$ function exaggerates small differences in probability near 0 and 1 and pushes other probabilities toward .5 (or something a little lower), as if people tended to think of the probability of an event in terms of three categories: "won't happen," "might happen," and "will happen." The effect is to make people overattentive to small differences in very low probabilities (and very high ones).

PT then replaces $u_i$ with $v_i$, the "value function." Economists usually think of the utility of money in terms of wealth. But $v_i$ is applied not to wealth but to gains and losses from a reference point, usually the status quo. In EU, we usually assume that wealth has declining marginal utility. The value of an additional $1,000 is greater to an average person than to a billionaire. (The billionaire thus suffers less pain from paying more in taxes, up to a point.) But, according to PT, when people make decisions involving gains and losses from the status quo, they think differently. The value function $v$ has two features. One is that "losses loom larger than gains." This is of course perfectly reasonable; EU says the same thing about wealth. But for PT, the distinction between gains and losses is psychological. It depends on what you think of as the reference point.[11]

One result is that possession can determine the reference point and increase the apparent value of an endowment. In a classic study of this "endowment effect," some Cornell students were told that they owned a Cornell mug and were asked how much money they would require to give it up. Another group was told that they could have a choice of money or the mug, and they were asked how much money they would require to take the

---

[11]    Tversky and Kahneman (1992) presented a second version of PT, which takes into account the ranking of possible outcomes, called cumulative prospect theory. For this exposition, we treat the two forms as equivalent, because they make the same major assumptions, but some of their predictions differ, with results favoring the later theory.

money rather than the mug. The only difference between the groups was thus what they were told about ownership. The "owners" demanded about twice as much money to give up (forego) the mug (Kahneman, Knetsch, and Thaler 1990).

Although PT attributes this effect to loss aversion, that is, to the shape of $\upsilon$, it is also possible that it results from a simple heuristic against change, i.e., a bias toward the status quo. Loss aversion itself has been studied in other ways and turns out to be somewhat labile, depending on how it is measured (e.g., McGraw et al. 2010; Ert and Erev 2013). Note that questions about a results explanation are not the same as questions about its reality.

The second feature of $\upsilon$ is that differences near the reference point have more of an effect than differences farther away, regardless of whether they are gains or losses. This illustrates a general psychological principle of *diminishing sensitivity*, which also applies to the $\pi$ function, particularly the decreased sensitivity to probability differences that are far from 0 or 1. Again, EU would normally imply diminishing sensitivity for gains, but not for losses. Because of the declining marginal utility of wealth, EU says the opposite for losses. The difference between losing $1,000 and losing nothing is less serious than the difference between $10,000 and $11,000 according to EU, but more serious according to PT. This is why people can be risk averse when gains are involved but risk seeking for losses. Faced with a choice of losing $100 for sure or a 50/50 gamble of losing $200 or nothing, people may choose the gamble because the difference between –$100 and 0 seems larger than that between –$200 and –$100 .

A third feature is that the reference point is malleable; it can change as a result of how a gamble is described or "framed." In the classic "Asian disease problem" (Tversky and Kahneman 1981), subjects were told that an unusual Asian disease is expected to kill 600 people. Half the subjects were told that there were two programs: one would save 200 people, and the other had a .33 chance of saving 600. The other half of the subjects were told that with the first program 400 would die, and with the second there was a .67 chance that 600 would die. The first way of presenting the problem implied a reference point of the 600 lost, so the outcomes were gains. The second way used the absence of the disease as the reference point, so outcomes were losses. Subjects were risk averse in the gain form, tending to choose the 200 lives, but risk seeking in the loss form. The two forms are, of course, equivalent. This result illustrates the effect of framing.

PT has been used to explain a number of choices and biases in the legal context. Zamir and Ritov (2010) used a set of experiments to show that loss aversion affects the preference for contingent-fee arrangements in lawyer-client relationships. Experimental "plaintiffs" preferred a contingent fee even if the expected fee was much higher in such a situation than in a non-contingent fee arrangement. Defendants, on the other hand, preferred fixed fees—because defendants choose between two purely negative gambles, and do not have the option to avoid a loss altogether. In contract, researchers have argued, and shown experimentally, that the contract serves as a reference point around which parties frame their expectations (Hart and Moore 2008; Fehr, Hart, and Zehnder 2011). Parties are willing to accept certain costs built into the contract but respond negatively when they must pay the same costs at a counterparty's discretion under a flexible contract. In other words, the moment of contract resets the status quo and provides a frame for evaluating each particular outcome as a gain or a loss.

Many of the psychological insights of PT, and the findings that support it, have survived subsequent research: the malleability of reference points and the effects of framing; different risk attitudes in gains and losses; diminishing sensitivity; and some examples of loss aversion. However, PT may be misleading in its account of how people combine information about outcome probability and utility. In particular, PT (along with many other theories) ascribes risk aversion/seeking and loss aversion to the shape of the utility (or value) function. An alternative type of model ascribes these effects to the weights rather than the utilities. The weights, psychologically, refer to the amount of attention paid to each possible consequence. Risk aversion and loss aversion result from more attention/weight to the worst possible outcomes. One such model is the transfer-of-attention exchange (TAX) model of Birnbaum (Birnbaum 2008; Birnbaum, Johnson, and Longbottom 2008), which accounts for choices among gambles in terms of differential attention to better and worse outcomes. Several results are inconsistent with PT and related models but consistent with the TAX model, for example PT does not explain some violations of stochastic dominance.[12]

As Birnbaum (2008) points out, we must be careful to distinguish phenomena from their theoretical accounts. Risk aversion is a phenomenon; concave utility is an explanation of it, but not the only explanation. Of course, true utility of money surely is concave—an additional $1,000 matters more to a poor person than to a rich one—but responses to gambles need not occur for this reason. (And the declining marginal utility of wealth cannot plausibly account for the amount of risk aversion found in laboratory experiments with small amounts of money.)

### 5.5.2   Psychophysics and psychophysical numbing

The idea of "declining marginal disutility" of losses illustrates a general psychological principle of *diminishing sensitivity*. Differences seem smaller when they are farther from a salient reference point. When we think about disasters that affect large numbers of people, such as wars, famines, hurricanes, and earthquakes, the numbers affected cease to matter so much as they get larger. This "psychophysical numbing" leads us to focus disproportionately on single victims and attend less to the great mass (Slovic 2007).

### 5.5.3   Hyperbolic discounting

Diminishing sensitivity may account for over-attention to the near future, as opposed to the distant future (Lynch and Zauberman 2006). A delay of one day from now means more to us than the difference between 7 and 8 days in the future, yet, when the 7th day arrives, our perspective will change. Whatever the cause, people's discounting of future events falls off sharply when the events are close in time, roughly in the shape of a hyperbola. Yet economic theory, for good reason, says it should fall off with exponential decay. The phenomenon of hyperbolic discounting may help to explain the sorts of impulsiveness we described in Section 5.1.4.

Anomalies in preferences over time are of particular relevance to legal decision makers. Regulation of insurance, consumer financial products, retirement savings, and even

---

[12]   Stochastic dominance says that if, for gamble G and all values of X, the probability of winning X or more is at least as great as the probability of winning X or more in (non-identical) gamble F, then G should be preferred over F.

contracting in general is often faced with evidence that individuals underweight the value of future events. Moreover, the story is not even that straightforward—recent evidence suggests intertemporal discounting is not symmetric for past and future. In a paper that brings hyperbolic discounting to prospect theory, Caruso, Gilbert, and Wilson (2008) show that people value future events more than equivalent events in the equidistant past. They demonstrate their theory with jury decision-making experiments. Subjects were asked, for example, to set damages for a person who had been injured and either had gone through a painful recovery or would undergo a painful recovery—and they awarded more when the recovery was imagined in the future rather than the past. For ordinary citizens making legal decisions and judgments, the temporal relationships of the relevant events may affect decisions even when timing should be irrelevant.

### 5.6 Myside Bias, Polarization, and Cultural Cognition

Another set of biases concern the irrational persistence of belief (Baron 2008, ch. 9).[13] *Selective exposure* is the tendency to seek evidence that will support beliefs that are already strong. *Biased assimilation* is the tendency to downgrade contradictory evidence when it arrives, while taking supporting evidence at face value. These biases, together with the tendency not to look for alternative possibilities, are together called myside bias. When people on opposite sides of some issue are subject to these biases, the result is polarization, those on each side become more extreme. Mere presentation of evidence does not help, because of biased assimilation.

Kahan et al. (2011) have recently argued that myside bias is stronger when "cultural" factors support certain beliefs. For example, those opposed to government regulation because of their social environment are more likely to deny the role of human beings in causing global warming. Thus, people are motivated to hold beliefs consistent with their overall cultural perspectives. More generally, we might suppose that bias is stronger when a belief is more central to a person's identity (in the sense of Erikson 1968), which is usually but not always related to a person's cultural milieu.

Excessive reading of the psychological literature on myside biases is a risk factor for pessimism. Before we sink into despair, we must remember a couple of things. First, the research is mostly about average effects. On the average, people have these biases. But studies of individual differences show extreme variability, to the point where we can be confident that many people do not display these biases at all (e.g., Stanovich and West 1998). The reason they show up in average effects is simply that very few people, if any, show the opposite biases, such as over-weighing evidence against one's current beliefs. The average of zero and some positive effects is positive.

Second, myside bias is correlated with people's beliefs about what good thinking is. Those who are most subject to these biases also believe that good thinkers are loyal to their beliefs, for example (Baron 1995). Such findings suggest that myside bias can be corrected

---

[13]   Much has been written about how "crazy" (or unwarranted) beliefs persist, but little about how they are first formed. People who believe that the attacks of 9/11 were a conspiracy by the U.S. government, or Israel, have persisted in this belief despite counter-arguments, but most people never formed such beliefs in the first place. Why not?

by challenging people's naïve theories about what good thinking is. People might be taught to respect thinking that is "actively open-minded" (Baron 2008).

# 6.   PRESCRIPTIVE APPROACHES

The sort of debiasing just mentioned is one kind of prescriptive approach, that is, an answer to the question of what to do about biases and errors. The behavioral law and economics literature has suggested others.

## 6.1   Decision Analysis, Cost-benefit Analysis, and Decision Aids

One approach is to provide tools to help people analyze decisions formally. Governments have taken various steps to avoid reliance on human intuitive judgments. Central banks have largely removed the setting of interest rates from the hands of politicians. Several regulatory agencies of many governments use cost-benefit analysis, to varying degrees, to decide on regulations. Breyer (1993) and (in a more moderate form) Sunstein (2002) have advocated extensions of this technocratic approach. It could, for example, reduce the problem of over-regulating some things while under-regulating others.

Other tools for decision analysis could be used for individual decisions. Some decision aids of this sort are used in the design of guidelines for diagnosis and treatment in medicine, and also for individual decisions. In principle they could also be used to aid courts, especially when technical data are involved.

A relevant example from health care is the decision about fetal testing for Down syndrome (e.g., Ganiats 1996). Some years ago, the major test for this was amniocentesis, which involves withdrawing fluid from the uterus and examining the cells. The test was not perfect, and as a side effect it sometimes caused miscarriages. But the probability of a Down syndrome birth increased with the mother's age. A widely adopted guideline for the test was that women over 35 should have it. The origin of this guideline was that, at this age, the probability of a test-caused miscarriage was equal to the probability of a Down-syndrome birth. The assumption was that a positive test result would lead to an abortion. If we apply EU theory to this decision, such a guideline would be appropriate if the disutility of a miscarriage were equal to that of a Down-syndrome birth. But that is rarely the case. Even crude assessment of individual utilities for these two outcomes would imply that some women should never have amniocentesis (even if they were willing to have abortions if the test were positive) and others should have it at much younger ages. This example shows how the use of simple decision analysis, in terms of expected utility, could yield better decisions for individuals. In this case, the incorrect decisions did not result from any particular known biases, but they were not optimal. (Now there are many more fetal tests available, and the decision is much more complicated. Individualized decision analysis would still help, but it would require a computer.)

A similar example is the allocation of funds to different investments in retirement programs. Many employers now offer default plans that are designed to be optimal for most employees, but employees with defined-contribution plans can usually choose from various options that vary in risk and expected outcome (e.g., stocks vs. bonds). Some of the companies that provide these investments attempt to measure something like the risk attitude of their customers, which utility theory would say is a function of the degree of curvature of the utility function for money. Such measurements may be less successful than those that might be used for amniocentesis (Baron 2011).

## 6.2 Libertarian Paternalism and the "Decision Architect"

Thaler and Sunstein (2008) proposed another prescriptive approach, which is to think of the design of decisions as they are presented to people, which they call decision architecture. Sometimes this involves simply changing the way in which options are presented, such as putting recommended options first on a list. It can also involve changing the options themselves. But the idea is to leave people free to choose while, at the same time, trying to shield them from the harmful effects (on others as well as themselves) of decision biases. Some changes in design require legislation or regulatory decisions. Examples are requiring that employers who offer pension plans make diversified plans the default, while giving employees the option to switch to a riskier plan. People are biased toward the default, so this idea makes use of a bias to help people choose options thought by others to be better. Other examples of decision architecture include mandatory waiting (cooling-off) periods (which counteract the tendency to make impulsive decisions), mandatory provision of options to undo bad decisions, and mandatory provision of information. In some cases, such devices could replace what amount to legal prohibitions (e.g., against giving up the right to sue, or assisting suicide), thus increasing the choices available.

Recent research on nudges has focused extensively on the use of default rules (e.g., Sunstein 2011, 2013). Perhaps that is the result of the fact that other sorts of nudges (e.g., sin taxes, cooling-off periods, and mandatory disclosure of certain kinds of information) have been known and used for some time, while the intentional use of defaults that people are free to override as a means of "light paternalism" is new. The idea of a bias toward the default should be distinguished from two other closely related biases: the status-quo bias and omission bias (Baron 2008). Default bias does not require a status quo. An example is that new motorists can be assigned to insurance policies with or without a limited tort provision. When this is done, they strongly favor whatever they are assigned (Johnson et al. 1993). Omission bias is a bias toward inaction, but the term is limited to cases in which both action and omission cause harm. When both options result in improvements, actions are often favored over omissions, but this effect is generally small compared to the effect for harms, leading to an overall bias toward the default (Baron and Ritov 1994).

Aside from the auto-insurance example, another example of an apparently successful nudge concerns organ donation. Countries where being an organ donor is the default (especially those with hospitals that are willing to enforce the rules) have much higher donation rates than those with an opt-in rule (Johnson and Goldstein 2003). Another good example is enrollment in pension plans and employer-provided health insurance by default, with the possibility of opting out (Sunstein 2011).

Thaler and Sunstein argue that their proposals mostly "nudge" people in the direction away from biases and errors, while leaving people free to make bad choices, or, ideally, choices that are better for them than the default. They thus call their approach "libertarian paternalism." But economists might argue that they are sometimes increasing the cost of some options, if only the cost of waiting. Hence the line between coercion and liberty is not sharp (Baron 2010).

### 6.3   Asymmetric Paternalism and Libertarian Welfarism

Camerer et al. (2003) suggest a different analysis that leads to most of the same conclusions. Many of the proposals favored by Sunstein and Thaler can be seen as preventing large harms to a few at the expense of very minor costs to many, hence the idea of "asymmetric paternalism." For example, compulsory waiting periods for marriage, divorce, or assisted suicide can prevent a small number of huge mistakes, for a relatively small cost to many. If the cost ratio is sufficiently extreme, measures of this sort have a utilitarian rationale.

Korobkin (2009) has extended the idea in another direction (although fully compatible with the idea of asymmetry), which is to consider social benefits as well as individual benefits.[14] He calls this libertarian welfarism. A prime example is organ donation (as noted earlier), where we can take advantage of bias toward the default in order to increase donation rates through presumed consent (Johnson and Goldstein 2003).

## 7.   CONCLUSION

The simple elegance of classical economic theory has been disrupted by findings from psychology and related fields. Note that the disruption is not in the normative application of economic theory but first in the descriptive part, and, as a result in new prescriptive ideas that do not arise from economics itself. To some it seems unfortunate that the findings of psychology seem more like a list of heuristics, biases, and models than any sort of cohesive theory like that of micro-economics. This is especially so now that the list of biases has increased several fold over the much smaller list available when legal scholars started taking this work seriously. We have tried here to point out some common themes in the research, which tie together various bunches of findings.

A general concern that often arises is that many of the prescriptions that come out of these new findings, such as those of libertarian paternalism, seem like tricks designed to manipulate irrational actors. Economic theory, by contrast, is all about incentives and is designed for rational actors. Irrational actors may not stay irrational, especially when they are repeatedly manipulated by the same tricks. An implication of this view is that we should spend more effort trying to make people more rational and not jump to the conclusion that irrationality is always with us. Indeed, large individual differences in most biases indicate that it is not universal.

Yet, the forces that produce irrational biases—still not fully understood—are likely to remain. Civilization and its army of educators will be waging a constant battle against these forces, but they will probably continue to exist. Thus, the design of the law and its application may need to consider how it can deal with irrationality for the foreseeable future.

---

[14]   Sunstein and Thaler include many examples in which the benefits are social, but they do not make a point of discussing the general idea.

# REFERENCES

Adler, Matthew D. 2012. *Well-being and Fair Distribution: A Framework for Policy Analysis*. New York: Oxford University Press.

Babcock, Linda, and George Loewenstein. 1997. Explaining Bargaining Impasse: The Role of Self-serving Biases. *Journal of Economic Perspectives* 11: 109–126.

Baker, John W., and K. Warner Schaie. 1969. Effects of Aggressing "Alone" or "With Another" on Physiological and Psychological Arousal. *Journal of Personality and Social Psychology* 12: 80–86.

Baron, Jonathan. 1995. Myside Bias in Thinking About Abortion. *Thinking and Reasoning* 1: 221–235.

Baron, Jonathan. 1996. Do No Harm. Pp. 197–213 in *Codes of Conduct: Behavioral Research into Business Ethics*, edited by David M. Messick and Ann E. Tenbrunsel. New York: Russell Sage Foundation.

Baron, Jonathan. 2003. Value Analysis of Political Behavior – Self-interested: Moralistic:: Altruistic: Moral. *University of Pennsylvania Law Review* 151: 1135–1167.

Baron, Jonathan. 2008. *Thinking and Deciding*. 4th ed. New York: Cambridge University Press.

Baron, Jonathan. 2010. Book Review, *Nudge: Improving Decisions About Health, Wealth, and Happiness*, by Richard H. Thaler and Cass R. Sunstein. *Journal of Behavioral Decision Making* 23: 224–226.

Baron, Jonathan. 2011. Risk Attitude, Investments, and the Taste for Luxuries versus Necessities. *Frontiers in Psychology: Cognition*, November 15. http://dx.doi.org/10.3389/fpsyg.2011.00329.

Baron, Jonathan. 2012. The "Culture of Honor" in Citizens' Concepts of Their Duty as Voters. *Rationality and Society* 24: 37–72.

Baron, Jonathan, and Ilana Ritov. 1993. Intuitions About Penalties and Compensation in the Context of Tort Law. *Journal of Risk and Uncertainty* 7: 17–33.

Baron, Jonathan, and Ilana Ritov. 1994. Reference Points and Omission Bias. *Organizational Behavior and Human Decision Processes* 59: 475–498.

Baron, Jonathan, and Ilana Ritov. 2009. Protected Values and Omission Bias as Deontological Judgments. Pp. 133–167 in *Moral Judgment and Decision Making*, edited by Daniel M. Bartels et al., vol. 50 of *The Psychology of Learning and Motivation*, edited by Brian H. Ross. San Diego, CA: Academic Press.

Baron, Jonathan, and Mark Spranca. 1997. Protected Values. *Organizational Behavior and Human Decision Processes* 70: 1–16.

Baron, Jonathan, and Ewa Szymanska. 2010. Heuristics and Biases in Charity. Pp. 215–236 in *The Science of Giving: Experimental Approaches to the Study of Charity*, edited by Daniel M. Oppenheimer and Christopher Y. Olivola. New York: Taylor and Francis.

Baron, Robert A. 1973. Threatened Retaliation from the Victim as an Inhibitor of Physical Aggression. *Journal of Research in Personality* 7: 103–115.

Becker, Gary S. 1968. Crime and Punishment: An Economic Approach. *Journal of Political Economy* 76: 169–217.

Benartzi, Shlomo, and Richard H. Thaler. 2001. Naive Diversification Strategies in Defined Contribution Saving Plans. *American Economic Review* 91: 79–98.

Bentham, Jeremy. [1843] 1948. *An Introduction to the Principles of Morals and Legislation*. Oxford: Blackwell Publisher.

Berscheid, Ellen, David Boye, and Elaine Walster. 1968. Retaliation as a Means of Restoring Equity. *Journal of Personality and Social Psychology* 10: 370–376.

Bicchieri, Cristina. 2006. *The Grammar of Society: The Nature and Dynamics of Social Norms*. New York: Cambridge University Press.

Birnbaum, Michael H. 2008. New Paradoxes of Risky Decision Making. *Psychological Review* 115: 463–501.

Birnbaum, Michael H., Kathleen Johnson, and Jay-Lee Longbottom. 2008. Tests of Cumulative Prospect Theory with Graphical Displays of Probability. *Judgment and Decision Making* 3: 528–546.

Bodenhausen, Galen V., Lori A. Sheppard, and Geoffrey P. Kramer. 1994. Negative Affect and Social Perception: The Differential Impact of Anger and Sadness. *European Journal of Social Psychology* 24: 45–62.

Breyer, Stephen. 1993. *Breaking the Vicious Circle: Toward Effective Risk Regulation*. Cambridge, MA: Harvard University Press.

Camerer, Colin F., Samuel Issacharoff, George Loewenstein, Ted O'Donoghue, and Matthew Rabin. 2003. Regulation for Conservatives: Behavioral Economics and the Case for "Asymmetric Paternalism." *University of Pennsylvania Law Review* 151: 1211–1254.

Caruso, Eugene M., Daniel T. Gilbert, and Timothy D. Wilson. 2008. A Wrinkle in Time: Asymmetric Valuation of Past and Future Events. *Psychological Science* 19: 796–801.

Coates, John C. IV, and R. Glenn Hubbard. 2007. Competition and Shareholder Fees in the Mutual Fund Industry: Evidence and Implications for Policy. *Journal of Corporation Law* 33: 151–222.

Coke, Jay S., C. Daniel Batson, and Katherine McDavis. 1978. Empathic Mediation of Helping: A Two-Stage Model. *Journal of Personality and Social Psychology* 36: 752–766.

Dawes, Robyn M., and Richard H. Thaler. 1988. Cooperation. *Journal of Economic Perspectives* 2: 187–197.
Dhami, Mandeep K., and Peter Ayton. 2001. Bailing and Jailing the Fast and Frugal Way. *Journal of Behavioral Decision Making* 14: 141–168.
Diamond, Jared. 2008. Vengeance is Ours. *New Yorker*, April 21.
Dunwoody, Philip T. 2009. Theories of Truth as Criteria in Judgment and Decision Making. *Judgment and Decision Making* 4: 116–125.
Engel, Christoph. 2011. Dictator Games: A Meta Study. *Experimental Economics* 14: 583–610.
Erikson, Erik H. 1968. *Identity, Youth and Crisis.* New York: Norton.
Ert, Eyal, and Ido Erev. 2013. On the Descriptive Value of Loss Aversion in Decisions under Risk: Six Clarifications. *Judgment and Decision Making* 8: 214–235.
Evans, Jonathan St. B. T. 2008. Dual-processing Accounts of Reasoning, Judgment, and Social Cognition. *Annual Review of Psychology* 59: 255–278.
Fehr, Ernst, and Simon Gächter. 2002. Altruistic Punishment in Humans. *Nature* 415: 137–140.
Fehr, Ernst, Oliver Hart, and Christian Zehnder. 2011. Contracts as Reference Points—Experimental Evidence. *American Economic Review* 101: 493–525.
Fehr, Ernst, and Klaus M. Schmidt. 1999. A Theory of Fairness, Competition, and Cooperation. *Quarterly Journal of Economics* 114: 817–868.
Fiske, Alan P., and Philip E. Tetlock. 1997. Taboo Trade-offs: Reactions to Transactions that Transgress the Spheres of Justice. *Political Psychology* 18: 255–297.
Fisman, Raymond, and Edward Miguel. 2007. Corruption, Norms, and Legal Enforcement: Evidence from Diplomatic Parking Tickets. *Journal of Political Economy* 115: 1020–1048.
Forsythe, Robert, Joel L. Horowitz, N. Eugene Savin, and Martin Sefton. 1994. Fairness in Simple Bargaining Experiments, *Games and Economic Behavior* 6: 347–369.
Fox, Craig R., and Amos Tversky 1998. A Belief-based Account of Decision under Uncertainty. *Management Science* 44: 879–895.
Frederick, Shane. 2005. Cognitive Reflection and Decision Making. *Journal of Economic Perspectives* 19: 24–42.
Frey, Bruno S. 1997. A Constitution for Knaves Crowds out Civic Virtues. *Economic Journal* 107: 1043–1053.
Ganiats, Theodore G. 1996. Justifying Prenatal Screening and Genetic Amniocentesis Programs by Cost-effectiveness Analysis. *Medical Decision Making* 16: 45–50.
Gigerenzer, Gerd, Peter M. Todd, and the ABC Research Group. 1999. *Simple Heuristics That Make Us Smart.* Oxford: Oxford University Press.
Goldberg, Julie H., Jennifer S. Lerner, and Phillip E. Tetlock. 1999. Rage and Reason: The Psychology of the Intuitive Prosecutor. *European Journal of Social Psychology* 29: 781–795.
Goldstein, Daniel G., and Gerd Gigerenzer. 2002. Models of Ecological Rationality: The Recognition Heuristic. *Psychological Review* 109: 75–90.
Hammond, Kenneth R. 1996. *Human Judgment and Social Policy: Irreducible Uncertainty, Inevitable Error, Unavailable Injustice.* New York: Oxford University Press.
Hart, Oliver, and John Moore. 2008. Contracts as Reference Points. *Quarterly Journal of Economics* 123: 1–48.
Hoffrage, Ulrich. 2011. Recognition Judgments and the Performance of the Recognition Heuristic Depend on the Size of the Reference Class. *Judgment and Decision Making* 6: 43–57.
Johnson, Eric J., and Daniel G. Goldstein. 2003. Do Defaults Save Lives? *Science* 302: 1338–1339.
Johnson, Eric J., John Hershey, Jacqueline Meszaros, and Howard Kunreuther. 1993. Framing, Probability Distortions, and Insurance Decisions. *Journal of Risk and Uncertainty* 7: 35–51.
Jolls, Christine, and Cass R. Sunstein. 2006. Debiasing through Law. *Journal of Legal Studies* 35: 199–241.
Jolls, Christine, Cass R. Sunstein, and Richard H. Thaler. 1998. A Behavioral Approach to Law and Economics. *Stanford Law Review* 50: 1471–1550.
Kahan, Dan M., Maggie Wittlin, Ellen Peters, Paul Slovic, Lisa Larrimore Ouellette, Donald Braman, and Gregory N. Mandel. 2011. The Tragedy of the Risk-perception Commons: Culture Conflict, Rationality Conflict, and Climate Change. Temple University Legal Studies Research Paper No. 2011-26. http://dx.doi.org/10.2139/ssrn.1871503.
Kahneman, Daniel. 2011. *Thinking, Fast and Slow.* New York: Farrar, Strauss and Giroux.
Kahneman, Daniel, and Shane Frederick. 2002. Representativeness Revisited: Attribute Substitution in Intuitive Judgment. Pp. 49–81 in *Heuristics and Biases: The Psychology of Intuitive Judgment*, edited by Thomas Gilovich, Dale Griffin, and Daniel Kahneman. New York. Cambridge University Press.
Kahneman, Daniel, Jack L. Knetsch, and Richard H. Thaler. 1990. Experimental Tests of the Endowment Effect and the Coase Theorem. *Journal of Political Economy* 98: 1325–1348.
Kahneman, Daniel, and Daniel Lovallo. 1993. Timid Choices and Bold Forecasts—A Cognitive Perspective on Risk-taking. *Management Science* 39: 17–31.
Kahneman, Daniel, David Schkade, and Cass R. Sunstein. 1998. Shared Outrage and Erratic Awards: The Psychology of Punitive Damages. *Journal of Risk and Uncertainty* 16: 49–86.

Kahneman, Daniel, and Amos Tversky. 1972. Subjective Probability: A Judgment of Representativeness. *Cognitive Psychology* 3: 430–454.

Kahneman, Daniel, and Amos Tversky. 1973. On the Psychology of Prediction. *Psychological Review* 80: 237–251.

Kahneman, Daniel, and Amos Tversky. 1979. Prospect Theory: An Analysis of Decision under Risk. *Econometrica* 47: 263–291.

Kaplow, Louis, and Steven Shavell. 2002. *Fairness Versus Welfare*. Cambridge, MA: Harvard University Press.

Keltner, Dacher, Kenneth D. Locke, and Paul C. Audrain. 1993. The Influence of Attributions on the Relevance of Negative Emotions to Personal Satisfaction. *Personality and Social Psychology Bulletin* 19: 21–29.

Kempton, Willett. 1986. Two Theories of Home Heat Control. *Cognition* 10: 75–90.

Keysar, Boaz, Sayuri L. Hayakawa, and Sun Gyu An. 2012. The Foreign-language Effect: Thinking in a Foreign Tongue Reduces Decision Biases. *Psychological Science* 23: 661–668.

Korobkin, Russell. 2009. Libertarian Welfarism. *California Law Review* 97: 1651–1685.

Krantz, David H., R. Duncan Luce, Patrick Suppes, and Amos Tversky. 1971. *Foundations of Measurement, Volume 1: Additive and Polynomial Representations*. New York: Academic Press.

Lawson, Glen, Jonathan Baron, and Linda S. Siegel. 1974. The Role of Length and Number Cues in Children's Quantitative Judgments. *Child Development* 45: 731–736.

Legrenzi, Paulo, Vittorio Girotto, and Philip N. Johnson-Laird. 1993. Focusing in Reasoning and Decision Making. *Cognition* 49: 36–66.

Loewenstein, George F. 1996. Out of Control: Visceral Influences on Behavior. *Organizational Behavior and Human Decision Processes* 65: 272–292.

Loewenstein, George F., Leigh Thompson, and Max H. Bazerman. 1989. Social Utility and Decision Making in Interpersonal Contexts. *Journal of Personality and Social Psychology* 57: 426–441.

Luce, R. Duncan, and Howard Raiffa. 1957. *Games and Decisions: Introduction and Critical Survey*. New York: Wiley.

Lynch, John G., and Gal Zauberman. 2006. When Do You Want It? Time, Decisions, and Public Policy. *Journal of Public Policy and Marketing* 25: 67–78.

McCaffery, Edward J., and Jonathan Baron. 2006. Isolation Effects and the Neglect of Indirect Effects of Fiscal Policies. *Journal of Behavioral Decision Making* 19: 1–14.

McDaniels, Tim L. 1988. Comparing Expressed and Revealed Preferences for Risk Reduction: Different Hazards and Question Frames. *Risk Analysis* 8: 593–604.

McGraw, A. Peter, Jeff T. Larsen, Daniel Kahneman, and David Schkade. 2010. Comparing Gains and Losses. *Psychological Science* 21: 1438–1445.

Metcalfe, Janet, and Walter Mischel. 1999. A Hot/Cool System Analysis of Delay of Gratification: Dynamics of Willpower. *Psychological Review* 106: 3–19.

Milkman, Katherine L., Dolly Chughy, and Max H. Bazerman. 2009. How Can Decision Making Be Improved? *Perspectives on Psychological Science* 4: 379–383.

Milkman, Katherine L., Todd Rogers, and Max H. Bazerman. 2008. Harnessing Our Inner Angels and Demons: What We Have Learned About Want/Should Conflicts and How That Knowledge Can Help Us Reduce Short-sighted Decision Making. *Perspectives on Psychological Science* 3: 324–338.

Piliavin, Jane A., J. F. Dovidio, Samuel L. Gaertner, and Russel D. Clark. 1981. *Emergency Intervention*. New York: Academic Press.

Polinsky, A. Mitchell, and Steven Shavell. 1999. On the Disutility and Discounting of Imprisonment and the Theory of Deterrence. *Journal of Legal Studies* 28: 1–16.

Polya, George. 1945. *How To Solve It: A New Aspect of Mathematical Method*. Princeton: Princeton University Press.

Posner, Richard A. 1973. *Economic Analysis of Law*. Boston: Little Brown.

Raiffa, Howard. 1982. *The Art and Science of Negotiation*. Cambridge, MA: Harvard University Press.

Read, Daniel, George L. Loewenstein, and Matthew Rabin. 1999. Choice Bracketing. *Journal of Risk and Uncertainty* 19: 171–197.

Ritov, Ilana, and Jonathan Baron. 1990. Reluctance to Vaccinate: Omission Bias and Ambiguity. *Journal of Behavioral Decision Making* 3: 263–277.

Robinson, Paul H., and John M. Darley. 2000. Testing Lay Intuitions of Justice: How and Why? *Hofstra Law Review* 28: 611–634.

Robinson, Paul H., and John M. Darley. 2004. Does Criminal Law Deter? A Behavioral Science Investigation, *Oxford Journal of Legal Studies* 24: 173–205.

Roth, Alvin E. 2007. Repugnance as a Constraint on Markets. *Journal of Economic Perspectives* 21: 37–58.

Roth, Alvin E. 2008. What Have We Learned from Market Design? *Economic Journal* 118: 285–310.

Savage, Leonard J. 1954. *The Foundations of Statistics*. New York: Wiley.

Schwartz, Shalom H. 1973. Normative Explanations of Helping Behavior: A Critique, Proposal, and Empirical Test. *Journal of Experimental Social Psychology* 9: 349–364.

Shavell, Steven. 2004. *Foundations of Economic Analysis of Law*. Cambridge, MA: Belknap Press.

Slovic, Paul. 2007. "If I Look at the Mass I Will Never Act": Psychic Numbing and Genocide. *Judgment and Decision Making* 2: 79–95.

Spranca, Mark, Elisa Minsk, and Jonathan Baron. 1991. Omission and Commission in Judgment and Choice. *Journal of Experimental Social Psychology* 27: 76–105.

Stanovich, Keith E., and Richard F. West. 1998. Individual Differences in Rational Thought. *Journal of Experimental Psychology: General* 127: 161–188.

Sunstein, Cass R. 2002. *Risk and Reason: Safety, Law, and the Environment*. New York: Cambridge University Press.

Sunstein, Cass R. 2005. Moral Heuristics. *Behavioral and Brain Sciences* 28: 531–573.

Sunstein, Cass R. 2011. Empirically Informed Regulation. *University of Chicago Law Review* 78: 1349–1429.

Sunstein, Cass R. 2013. Deciding by Default. *University of Pennsylvania Law Review* 162: 1–57.

Sunstein, Cass R., Daniel Kahneman, and David Schkade. 2005. Assessing Punitive Damages (With Notes on Cognition and Valuation in Law). *Yale Law Journal* 107: 2071–2153.

Tetlock, Phillip E. 1985. Accountability: A Social Check on the Fundamental Attribution Error. *Social Psychology Quarterly* 48: 227–236.

Thaler, Richard H. 1988. The Ultimatum Game. *Journal of Economic Perspectives* 2: 195–206.

Thaler, Richard H., and Cass R. Sunstein. 2008. *Nudge: Improving Decisions About Health, Wealth, and Happiness*. New Haven, CT: Yale University Press.

Tooby, J., Leda Cosmides, and Michael E. Price. 2006. Cognitive Adaptations for n-person Exchange: The Evolutionary Roots of Organizational Behavior. *Managerial and Decision Economics* 27: 103–129.

Tversky, Amos, and Daniel Kahneman. 1981. The Framing of Decisions and the Psychology of Choice. *Science* 211: 453–458.

Tversky, Amos, and Daniel Kahneman. 1992. Advances in Prospect Theory: Cumulative Representations of Uncertainty. *Journal of Risk and Uncertainty* 5: 297–323.

Walster, Elaine, G. William Walster, and Ellen Berscheid. 1978. *Equity: Theory and Research*. Boston: Allyn and Bacon.

Wilcox, Ronald T. 2003. Bargain Hunting or Star Gazing? Investors' Preferences for Stock Mutual Funds. *Journal of Business* 76: 645–664.

Wilkinson-Ryan, Tess. 2011. Breaching the Mortgage Contract: The Behavioral Economics of Strategic Default. *Vanderbilt Law Review* 64: 1547–1583.

Wilkinson-Ryan, Tess, and Jonathan Baron. 2009. Moral Judgment and Moral Heuristics in Breach of Contract. *Journal of Empirical Legal Studies* 6: 405–423.

Xiao, Erte, and Daniel Houser. 2011. Punish in Public. *Journal of Public Economics* 95: 1006–1017.

Zamir, Eyal, and Ilana Ritov. 2010. Revisiting the Debate over Attorneys' Contingent Fees: A Behavioral Analysis. *Journal of Legal Studies* 38: 246–288.

# 2.   Behavioral probability
*Alex Stein*

## 1.   INTRODUCTION

This chapter examines experimental studies that identify misalignments between ordinary people's decisions under uncertainty and the rules of mathematical probability.[1] These studies use mathematical probability as a criterion for rational decisions. Based on this criterion, the studies tag people's deviations from mathematical probability as irrational (or as boundedly rational). The studies also identify those deviations' recurrent patterns and develop a taxonomy for describing people's probabilistic mistakes. Under this taxonomy, those mistakes include "representativeness," "availability," "base-rate neglect," and suppression of the product rule.

Representativeness is a person's preference of familiar scenarios over statistical data (Kahneman 2011, pp. 146–55). Availability is an individual's overestimation of the probabilities attaching to events that fall within her experience or easily come to mind (Kahneman 2011, pp. 129–36). Base-rate neglect is a probability assessment that fails to consider general distributions of relevant events (Kahneman 2011, pp. 166–74). Suppression of the product rule is a person's failure to treat a compound event (events *A* and *B* occurring simultaneously) as less probable than each of its components (*A* or *B*) (Kahneman 2011, pp. 156–65).

Arguably, these mistakes lead to erroneous decisions that adversely affect people's welfare. Behavioral economists[2] argue that the government should step in to prevent these erroneous decisions. Specifically, they recommend the following legal reforms: mandatory supply of information to error-prone individuals,[3] soft choice-architecture,[4] and regulatory intervention that will prevent and correct people's probabilistic mistakes.[5] Areas targeted by these recommendations include accidents and risk regulation, consumer

---

[1]   The most significant of those studies are reported and analyzed in Kahneman (2011). Written by the discipline's founding father, this book is sure to become a canonical text on behavioral probability.

[2]   This designation includes not only economists, but also psychologists investigating the ways in which people reason and make decisions.

[3]   See, e.g., Bar-Grill and Stone (2009) using behavioral economics to propose expansive disclosure requirements in connection with cellular service agreements. But see Ben-Shahar and Schneider (2011) criticizing the ongoing expansion of disclosure requirements.

[4]   See Thaler and Sunstein (2008) introducing the "choice architecture" method, understood as governmental manipulation of individuals' menu of choices in a manner that nudges those individuals to take the desired action.

[5]   For a summary of regulatory initiatives driven by behavioral economics and an analytical framework for regulation premised on subjects' bounded rationality, see Vandenbergh, Carrico and Schultz Bressman (2011, pp. 763–78).

agreements, business contracts, credit and lending, employment, insurance, prenuptial agreements, and adjudicative fact-finding.[6]

Studies surveyed herein have been carried out by Daniel Kahneman, Amos Tversky and other behavioral economists. These studies form a distinct field of inquiry, identified here as "behavioral probability." Behavioral probability is part of a more comprehensive area of study: behavioral economics. Behavioral economics is a discipline that encompasses behavioral probability along with experimental and empirical studies of people's assessments of utility. Behavioral economics has been immensely successful as a general discipline: it has influenced many studies of economics, finance, and law (Vandenbergh, Carrico, and Schultz Bressman 2011; Bar-Gill and Warren 2008; Eisenberg 1995; Jolls, Sunstein, and Thaler 1998; Kahan 2010; Rachlinski 1998; Sunstein 1986; Williams 2009; Zamir 1998).

This chapter is organized as follows. Section 2 examines the rules of mathematical probability that the studies surveyed herein use as a benchmark for rationality. Section 3 juxtaposes these rules against people's hardwired habit of understanding the world in terms of causes and effects. This juxtaposition identifies a serious tension between mathematical probability and people's causal understanding of the world. I show that this causal understanding is not indicative of people's irrationality (or bounded rationality). Far from irrational, people's causal understanding of the world has its own probabilistic framework, identified as inductive, or Baconian, probability. Section 4 uses these insights to revisit the experiments carried out by Kahneman, Tversky, and other behavioral economists and tendered as a proof of people's probabilistic failures. I demonstrate that these experiments do not establish that people are probabilistically irrational (or boundedly rational). In fact, I show that some of these experiments are methodologically flawed.

---

[6]    See, e.g., Bar-Gill and Warren (2008) identifying and calling for regulatory correction of people's over-optimism in consumer credit agreements; Eisenberg (1995) identifying over-optimism in people's liquidated damage undertakings, prenuptial agreements and other areas of contract and commending a regime that authorizes courts to modify contractually prearranged payments and waivers; Jolls, Sunstein and Thaler (1998, pp. 1522–28) identifying and calling for regulatory correction of hindsight biases in courts' determinations of negligence, environmental torts, punitive damages, and non-obviousness of patented inventions; Kahan (2010, pp. 1623–25) describing the effect of hindsight bias on fact-finding in adjudication; Rachlinski (1998) identifying the presence of hindsight bias in courts' ascertainments of parties' compliance with ex-ante norms and commending legal rules that counteract this bias; Sunstein (1986, pp. 1167–68) identifying and calling for regulatory correction of base-rate neglects in people's decisions about risk and insurance, contractual undertakings, and their own employment termination prospects; Williams (2009) identifying and calling for regulatory correction of people's base-rate neglects and resulting overconfidence in marriage-related and employment agreements and in credit card borrowing; Zamir (1998, pp. 269–70) identifying and calling for regulatory correction of people's base-rate neglects and availability bias in savings and credit decisions.

## 2.   MATHEMATICAL PROBABILITY: LANGUAGE AND EPISTEMICS[7]

The best way to understand mathematical probability is to perceive it as a language that describes the facts relevant to a person's decisions. Like all languages that people use in their daily interactions, the probability language has a set of conventional rules. These rules determine the meanings, the grammar, and the syntax of probabilistic propositions. Compliance with these rules enables one person to form meaningful propositions about probability and communicate them to other people.

The probability language differs from ordinary languages in three fundamental respects: scope, parsimony, and abstraction. First, ordinary languages have a virtually unlimited scope, as they promote multiple purposes in a wide variety of ways. People use those languages in communicating facts, thoughts, ideas, feelings, emotions, sensations, and much else. The probability language, in contrast, has a much narrower scope because it only communicates the reasoner's epistemic situation or balance of knowledge versus ignorance. The reasoner uses this language to communicate what facts she considers relevant to her decision and the extent to which those facts are probable. Second, ordinary languages have rich vocabularies.[8] The probability language, by contrast, is parsimonious by design: it uses a small set of concepts to describe multifarious events in a standardized mode. This mode establishes a common metric for all propositions about the probabilities of uncertain events. This metric creates syntactical uniformity in the probability language and makes it interpersonally transmittable. Finally, because a person usually needs to deal with more than one uncertain event, she needs a uniform set of abstract concepts by which to relate one probability estimate to another and to integrate those estimates into a comprehensive assessment of probability.

These attributes of the probability language account for its high level of abstraction, uncharacteristic of any ordinary language. To maintain the required parsimony and conceptual uniformity, the probability language uses mathematical symbols instead of words. Those symbols allow a person to formulate her assessments of probability with precision. This precision, however, is purchased at a price: the comprehensive trimming of particularities and nuances that characterize real-world facts. The scope of each assessment's meaning and applicability thus becomes opaque and at times indeterminable. This tradeoff—precise language for a weak epistemic grasp—is a core characteristic and the core problem of mathematical probability. The two components of this tradeoff stand in an inverse relationship to each other. To be able to formulate her probability assessments with precision, a person must get rid of untidy concepts, downsize her vocabulary, and abstract away the multifaceted nuances of the real world. All this weakens the person's epistemic grasp of the real world. As a result, her abstract, numerical estimates will say hardly anything informative about concrete events that unfold on the ground. To have a strong epistemic grasp of the factual world, a person has to be wordy: she must utilize a rich vocabulary and loosen her conceptual precision.

---

[7]   This section is based on Stein (2011).

[8]   See, e.g., *The Oxford English Dictionary* (1989) a 20-volume dictionary that explains the meanings of over 600,000 words originating from approximately 220,000 etymological roots.

## 2.1   The Language of Mathematical Probability

The mathematical probability system designates the numerical space between 0 and 1 (the algebraic equivalents of 0% and 100%) to accommodate every factual scenario that exists in the world:[9]

---

0                                               1

This space accommodates two propositions that are factually certain:

**Proposition A:** The probability that one of all the possible scenarios will materialize equals 1.

**Proposition B:** Correspondingly, the probability that none of all the possible scenarios will materialize equals 0.

These propositions are tautological. The first proposition essentially says, "Something will certainly happen." The second makes an equally vacuous attestation: "There is no way that nothing will happen." All other propositions occupying the probability space are meaningful because they describe concrete events that unfold in the real world. These meaningful propositions are inherently uncertain. There is no way of obtaining complete information that will verify or refute what they say. Consequently, the probability of any concrete scenario is always greater than zero and less than one. More precisely, the probability of any concrete scenario, $P(S)$, equals one minus the probability of all factual contingencies in which the scenario does not materialize: $P(S) = 1 - P(\text{not} - S)$. This formula is called the "complementation principle."[10]

To illustrate that principle, consider a random toss of a coin. The coin is unrigged: its probability of landing on heads is the same as its probability of landing on tails. Each of these probabilities thus equals 0.5. The two probabilities divide the entire probability space among themselves. The coin's probability of landing on either heads or tails equals 1, and we already know that this proposition is vacuous or tautological.

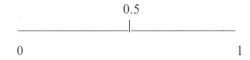

0.5

0                                               1

This illustration does not address the key question about the coin. What does "unrigged" mean? How does one know that this specific coin is equally likely to land on heads or on tails? This important question focuses on the epistemics of mathematical probability,

---

⁹   My discussion simplifies Kolmogorov's classic definition of the "probability space" (Kolmogorov 1956).

¹⁰   See Cohen (1989, pp. 17–18, 56–57) stating and explaining the complementation principle.

discussed in Section 2.2 below. My present discussion only addresses mathematical probability's syntax and semantics. For that reason, I assume for now that the two probabilities are equal. The coin's probability of landing on tails, as opposed to heads, or vice versa, is deemed to be 0.5.

We are now in a position to grasp the second canon of mathematical probability: the "multiplication principle" or the "product rule" (see Cohen [1989, pp. 18–21], stating and explaining the multiplication principle). The multiplication principle holds that the probability of a joint occurrence of two mutually independent events, $S_1$ and $S_2$, equals the probability of one event multiplied by the probability of the other. Formally: $P(S_1 \& S_2) = P(S_1) \times P(S_2)$.

My coin example makes this principle easy to understand. Consider the probability of two successive tosses of an unrigged coin landing on heads. The probability that the first toss will produce heads, $P(S_1)$, equals 0.5. The probability that the second toss will produce heads, $P(S_2)$, equals 0.5 as well. The first probability occupies half of the entire probability space, while the second—as part of the compound, or conjunctive, scenario we are interested in—occupies half of the space taken by the first probability. The diagram below shows this division of the probability space:

The complementation and multiplication principles are the pillars of the mathematical system of probability. All other probability rules derive from these principles. Consider the "disjunction rule" (see Kneale [1949, pp. 125–26] stating and explaining the disjunction rule) that allows a person to calculate the probability of alternative scenarios, denoted again as $S_1$ and $S_2$. This probability equals the sum of the probabilities attaching to those scenarios, minus the probability of the scenarios' joint occurrence. Formally: $P(S_1$ or $S_2)$ $= P(S_1) + P(S_2) - P(S_1 \& S_2)$. Here, the deduction of the joint-occurrence probability, $P(S_1 \& S_2)$, prevents double counting of the same probability space. The probability of each individual scenario, $P(S_1)$ and $P(S_2)$, occupies the space in which the scenario unfolds both alone as well as in conjunction with the other scenario: $P(S_1)$ occupies the space in which $S_1$ occurs together with $S_2$, and $P(S_2)$ occupies the space in which $S_2$ occurs together with $S_1$. There is, however, only one space for $S_1 \& S_2$ as a combined scenario, and hence the deduction.

A joint occurrence of two (or more) events is not always factually possible. For example, a single toss of a coin can yield either heads or tails, but not both: that is, $P(S_1 \& S_2)$ $= 0$. The coin's probability of landing on heads or, alternatively, on tails consequently equals 1 (0.5 + 0.5 – 0). But in real-life situations, events often occur in conjunction with each other. For example, a medical patient's permanent disability may originate from his preexisting condition, from his doctor's malpractice, or from both. If so, then $P(S_1 \& S_2) > 0$.

A conjunctive occurrence of two events can also be perceived as a compound scenario in which one event ($H$) unfolds in the presence of another ($E$). The probability of any such scenario is called "conditional" because it does not attach unconditionally to a single event, $H$, but rather to event $H$ given the presence, or occurrence, of $E$, which is denoted as $P(H|E)$.

This formulation allows me to present another core component of the mathematical probability system: Bayes' Theorem.[11] This theorem establishes that when I know the individual probabilities of $E$ and $H$ and the probability of $E$'s occurrence in the presence of $H$, I can calculate the probability of $H$'s occurrence in the presence of $E$. Application of the multiplication principle (the product rule) to the prospect of a joint occurrence of two events, $E$ and $H$, yields $P(E \& H) = P(E) \times P(H|E)$. Under the same principle, the conjunctive probability of $E$ and $H$, restated as $P(H \& E)$, also equals $P(H) \times P(E|H)$. This inversion sets up a probabilistically important equality: $P(E) \times P(H|E) = P(H) \times P(E|H)$.[12] Bayes' Theorem is derived from this equality: $P(H|E) = P(H) \times P(E|H) \div P(E)$.

My labeling of the two events as $E$ and $H$ is not accidental. Under the widely accepted terminology, $H$ stands for a reasoner's *hypothesis*, while $E$ stands for her *evidence*. Both $E$ and $H$ are events, but the reasoner is not considering those events individually. Rather, she is examining the extent to which evidence $E$ confirms hypothesis $H$. A Bayesian formulation consequently separates between the probability of hypothesis $H$ before the arrival of the evidence ($P(H)$); the general probability of the evidence's presence in the world ($P(E)$); and the probability of the evidence being present in cases in which hypothesis $H$ materializes ($P(E|H)$). These three factors allow the reasoner to compute the posterior probability of her hypothesis: the probability of hypothesis $H$ given evidence $E$. The reasoner must process every item of her evidence sequentially by applying this procedure. She must perform a Bayesian calculation time and time again until all of her evidence is taken into account. Each of those calculations will update the hypothesis's prior probability by transforming it into a new posterior probability. The posterior probability will become final after the reasoner had exhausted all of the available evidence.[13]

Notice the significance of the evidence-based multiplier, $P(E|H) \div P(E)$. This multiplier is called the "likelihood ratio" (Schum 1994, p. 218) or—as I prefer to call it—the "relevancy coefficient."[14] The relevancy coefficient measures the frequency with which $E$ appears in cases featuring $H$, relative to the frequency of $E$'s appearance in all possible cases. If $P(E|H) \div P(E) > 1$ ($E$'s appearance in cases of $H$ is more frequent than its general appearance), the probability of hypothesis $H$ goes up. Formally: $P(H|E) > P(H)$, which means that evidence $E$ confirms hypothesis $H$. On the other hand, when $P(E|H) \div P(E) < 1$ ($E$'s appearance in cases of $H$ is less frequent than its general appearance), the probability of hypothesis $H$ goes down. Formally: $P(H|E) < P(H)$, which means that evidence $E$ makes hypothesis $H$ less probable (or disconfirms it). Finally, if $P(E|H) = P(E)$ ($E$'s appearance in cases of $H$ is as frequent as its general appearance), the presence of $E$ does not influence the probability of $H$. This makes evidence $E$ altogether irrelevant.[15]

To illustrate, consider a tax agency that uses internal fraud-risk criteria for auditing

---

[11]   See Bayes (1763) for a modern statement of the theorem, see Cohen (1989, p. 68).

[12]   Because of this inversion, some call Bayes' Theorem the "Inversion Theorem." See, e.g., Kneale (1949, p. 129).

[13]   For a good explanation of this updating, see Schum (1994, pp. 215–22).

[14]   Schum (1994, p. 219) associating the likelihood ratio with the "force of evidence".

[15]   Cf. Lempert (1977, pp. 1025–27) offering similar formulation of relevancy coefficients.

firms.[16] By applying those criteria, the agency singles out for auditing one firm out of ten. This ratio is public knowledge. Firms do not know anything about the agency's criteria for auditing (nor does anyone else outside the agency). Under the information available to firms, their prior probability of being audited equals 0.1.

Now consider an individual firm whose reported expenses have doubled relative to past years. Does this evidence change the probability of being audited? The answer to this question depends on whether a steep increase in a firm's reported expenses appears more frequently in cases in which it was audited than in general. Assume that experienced accountants formed an opinion that increased expenses are three times more likely to appear in auditing situations than generally. This relevancy coefficient triples the prior probability of the firm's audit. The firm's posterior probability of being audited thus turns into 0.3.

But how do we know that these evidential effects are brought about by *causes* and are more than a mere correlation? We do not know it for sure, and I address this issue below in Section 2.2. My current goal, as I already mentioned, is quite narrow: in the present section, I only articulate the semantics and syntax of mathematical probability. Bayes' Theorem is part of those semantics and syntax: it tells us how to conceptualize our epistemic situations by using mathematical language. However, as I demonstrate below in Section 2.2, the theorem itself provides no instructions on how to understand causes and effects of the outside world and relate them to each other.

Mathematical language creates a uniform conceptual framework for all probability assessments that rely on instantial multiplicity or frequency of events. For those who base their estimates of probability on events' frequency, this language is indispensable.[17] This language is also necessary for formulating probability assessments on the basis of propensity—a disposition of a given factual setup to produce a particular outcome over a series of cases or experiments.[18] Finally, people basing their decisions upon intuited or "subjective" probabilities[19] might also benefit from using the mathematical language. This language introduces conceptual precision and coherence into a reasoner's conversion of her experience-based beliefs into numbers. Those numbers must more or less correspond to the reasoner's empirical situation. A mismatch between the numbers and empirical reality will produce a bad decision (Cohen 1989, p. 60).

Proper use of the mathematical language, however, does not guarantee that a person's probability assessments will be accurate. This language only helps a person conceptualize her raw information in numerical terms and communicate it to other people. Before using this language, a person must properly perceive and understand this information. This basic cognitional task is an antecedent to a person's mathematical assessment of

---

[16]  A good real-world example of this practice is the secret "Discriminant Index Function" (DIF), used by the IRS in selecting taxpayers for audits. See, e.g., *Gillin v. Internal Revenue Serv.* (980 F.2d 819, 822 1st Cir. [1992]) "The IRS closely guards information concerning its DIF scoring methodology because knowledge of the technique would enable an unscrupulous taxpayer to manipulate his return to obtain a lower DIF score and reduce the probability of an audit."; Lawsky (2009, pp. 1068–70) describing the DIF method used by the IRS.

[17]  See Cohen (1989, pp. 47–48) explaining frequency as a rate of relevant instances.

[18]  Cohen (1989, pp. 53–58) explaining propensity as a rate of relevant instances.

[19]  Cohen (1989, pp. 58–70) explaining subjective probability in terms of reasoners' betting odds.

probability. Bayes' Theorem and other mathematical rules of probability do not tell people how to go about this task.

Proper use of mathematical probability therefore can only guarantee a gambling kind of accuracy: accuracy in ascribing probability estimates to perceived generalities, as opposed to individual events. If so, granted that a person properly conceptualizes her experiences in mathematical language, will her probability assessments be accurate if she commits no mathematical errors in making those assessments? This question is fundamental to the entire probability theory, and the answer to it depends on what "accurate" means. The mathematical system offers reasoners only one sort of guarantee. Absent information about relevant causes and effects, a reasoner will do well to follow that system, which would then enable her to achieve the maximal level of accuracy. Failure to follow that system will lead the reasoner astray.

This virtue of mathematical probability is best illustrated by a gambling scenario known as "Dutch Book." Consider a gambler who accepts two $100 bets at odds of 1 to 2 that a particular tennis player will win and, respectively, lose her upcoming match. This combination of bets is fundamentally irrational. Should the player win the match, the gambler would win $100 on the first bet, but would lose $200 on the second; and in the event the player loses the match, the gambler would lose $200 on the first bet and win only $100 on the second. Hence, the gambler is sure to lose $100.

This outcome has a simple explanation: the gambler ascribed an identical probability $(0.667)$[20] to factual propositions that negate one another, which was a bad idea. If the gambler's acceptance of the first bet was a good decision, the player's probability of winning the match would then be 0.667, as estimated by the gambler. Under that probability, however, the gambler could not rationally accept the second bet, which assumed that the player had a 0.667 probability of losing the match. Given that the gambler was right to accept the first bet, this probability could only be 0.333 $(1 - 0.667)$. Any other probability assessment in placing bets would make the gambler lose his money.

Based on this insight, Frank Ramsey and Bruno de Finetti have demonstrated (independently of each other) that failure to follow the rules of mathematical probability engenders irrational decisions (Cohen 1989, pp. 60–61). This demonstration, however, holds true only in gambling situations in which decision-makers have no information about causes and effects that determine the course of specific events. Economists do not pay much attention to this limitation (Stein 2011, pp. 223–34), and I now turn to discuss it.

## 2.2   The Epistemics of Mathematical Probability

John Stuart Mill sharply criticized the use of instantial multiplicity as a basis for inference (Mill [1843] 1980, pp. 549–53). He described it as "the natural induction of uninquiring minds, the induction of the ancients, which proceeds *per enumerationem simplicem*: 'This, that, and the other A are B, I cannot think of any A which is not B, therefore every A is B'" (Mill [1843] 1980, p. 549).

This sentence succinctly identifies the core problem of the mathematical probability

---

[20]   This probability reflects the gambler's belief that the player wins two matches out of three under given conditions, which makes him accept the bet at the odds of 1 to 2.

system: this system, says Mill, is epistemologically fragile, if not empty. The system's mathematical rules only instruct the reasoner on how to convert her information into cardinal numbers. These rules have no epistemic ambition. They do not tell the reasoner what counts as information upon which she ought to rely. This task is undertaken by the system's rules of inference that are not as rigorous and intuitive as Boolean algebra. I examine those rules of inference in the paragraphs ahead.

One of those rules holds that any scenario not completely eliminated by existing evidence is a factual possibility that must occupy some of the probability space. The reasoner must consequently assign some probability to any such scenario, and this probability must be greater than zero. I call this rule "the uncertainty principle."

The second rule—"the principle of indifference"—is a direct consequence of the first. This rule determines the epistemic implications of the unavailable information for the reasoner's probability decision. The rule postulates that unavailable information is not slanted in any direction, meaning that the reasoner has no reasons for considering one unevidenced scenario as more probable than another unevidenced scenario (Cohen 1989, pp. 43–44). In other words, the reasoner ought to be epistemically indifferent between those scenarios, and this indifference makes the unevidenced scenarios equally probable.

The third rule logically derives from the second. It presumes that statistical distributions are extendible. To follow Mill's formulation, if 70% of events exhibiting feature *A* exhibit feature *B* as well, then presumptively any future occurrence of *A* has a 70% chance of occurring together with *B*. I call this rule "the extendibility presumption." This presumption is tentative and defeasible: new information showing, for example, that *B* might be brought about by *C*—a causal factor unassociated with *A*—would render it inapplicable. Absent such information, however, the extendibility presumption applies with full force. The presumption's mechanism relies on the indifference principle as well. This principle treats all indistinguishable occurrences of *A*, past and future, as equivalents. The same principle marks any missing information that could identify *B*'s causal origins as unslanted. The reasoner consequently must treat this unknown information as equally likely to both increase and decrease the rate of *B*'s appearance in cases of *A*. Every future occurrence of *A* thus becomes statistically identical to *A*'s past occurrences that exhibited *B* at a 70% rate.

The uncertainty principle seems epistemologically innocuous, but this appearance is misleading. Any factual scenario that existing evidence does not completely rule out must, indeed, be considered possible. This scenario therefore must have *some* probability on a 0–1 scale. All of this is undoubtedly correct. The uncertainty principle, however, also suggests that the reasoner *can* assign concrete probabilities to such unevidenced scenarios. This "can" is epistemologically unwarranted because the reasoner does not know those probabilities. Any of her probability estimates will be pure guesswork: a creation of knowledge from ignorance.

The principle of indifference is a pillar of the entire system of mathematical probability.[21] It stabilizes the reasoner's information in order to make it amenable to mathematical calcu-

---

[21] See Keynes (1921, pp. 41–42) describing the indifference principle as essential for establishing equally probable possibilities—a preliminary condition for all mathematical assessments of probability.

lus.[22] The principle's information-stabilizing method is best presented in Bayesian terms. Take a reasoner who considered all available information and determined the probability of the relevant scenario, $P(S)$. The reasoner knows that her information is incomplete and turns to estimating the implications of the unavailable information ($U$). The reasoner tries to figure out whether this unavailable information could change her initial probability estimate, $P(S)$. In formal terms, the reasoner needs to determine $P(S|U)$. Under Bayes' Theorem, this probability equals $P(S) \times [P(U|S) \div P(U)]$. With the prior probability, $P(S)$, already known, the reasoner needs to determine the relevancy coefficient, $P(U|S) \div P(U)$. To this end, she needs to obtain two probabilities: the probability of $U$'s appearance in general and the probability of $U$'s appearance in cases of $S$. Because the reasoner has no information upon which to make that determination, the indifference principle tells her to assume that $U$ is equally likely to confirm and to disconfirm $S$: $P(U|S) = P(U)$. The relevancy coefficient consequently equals 1, and the reasoner's prior probability, $P(S)$, remains unchanged. The indifference principle essentially instructs the reasoner to deem missing information altogether irrelevant to her decision.

This instruction is epistemologically invalid. The reasoner can treat unavailable information as irrelevant to her decision only if she has no reason to believe that it might be relevant (Keynes 1921, pp. 55–56). Whether those reasons are present or absent depends on the reasoner's known information. When this information indicates that the unavailable information might be relevant, $P(U|S)$ and $P(U)$ can no longer be considered equal to each other. The indifference principle consequently becomes inapplicable. On the other hand, when the known information indicates that the unavailable information is irrelevant to the reasoner's decision, something else happens. The known information establishes that $P(U|S)$ actually equals $P(U)$. The proven, as opposed to postulated, equality between $P(U|S)$ and $P(U)$ makes the indifference principle redundant. From the epistemological point of view, therefore, there are no circumstances under which this principle can ever become applicable.[23]

The indifference principle thus does not merely purport to manage unavailable information. Instead, it forces itself on the available information by requiring the reasoner to interpret that information in a particular way. Effectively, the principle instructs the reasoner to proceed on the assumption that all the facts necessary for her probability assessment are specified in the available information. This artificially created informational closure sharply contrasts with the causative probabilistic reasoning that I discuss in Section 3.[24]

From an epistemological standpoint, the extendibility presumption is an equally problematic device. This presumption bypasses the question of causation, which makes

---

[22]   As Keynes explains, "In order that numerical measurement may be possible, we must be given a number of *equally* probable alternatives" (Keynes 1921, p. 41).

[23]   See Cohen (1989, pp. 45–46) showing that the indifference principle is either circular or redundant; Keynes (1921, pp. 45–47) demonstrating that the indifference principle is arbitrary and epistemologically unsustainable.

[24]   See Cohen (1979, p. 389), "Baconian [causative] probability-functions ... grade probabilification ... *by the extent to which* all relevant facts are specified in the evidence."

it epistemologically deficient.[25] As Mill's quote suggests, an occurrence of feature *B* in numerous cases of *A* does not, by and of itself, establish that *B* might occur in a future case of *A*. Only evidence of causation can establish that this future occurrence is probable. This evidence needs to identify the causal forces bringing about the conjunctive occurrence of *A* and *B*. Identification of those forces needs to rely on a plausible causal theory demonstrating that *B*'s presence in cases of *A* is law-bound rather than accidental (Cohen 1986, p. 177). This demonstration involves proof that *B* is or tends to be uniformly present in cases of *A* for reasons that remain the same in all cases (Cohen 1986, pp. 177–79). Those invariant reasons make the uniformity law-bound (Cohen 1986, p. 179). Their absence, in contrast, indicates that *B*'s presence in cases of *A* is possibly accidental. The observed uniformity consequently becomes non-extendible. Decision-makers who choose to rely on this uniformity will either systematically err or arrive at correct probability assessments by sheer accident. They will never base those assessments upon knowledge.[26]

To illustrate, consider again the basic factual setup of my tax-audit example: the tax agency audits one firm out of ten. Assuming that no other information is available, will it be plausible to estimate that each firm's probability of being audited equals 0.1? This estimate's plausibility depends on whether the "one-to-ten" distribution is extendible. This distribution could be extendible if the agency were to make its audit decisions by some randomized procedure, such as a draw. This randomization would then give every firm an equal chance of being audited by the agency. The agency, however, does not select audited firms by a draw. Instead, it applies its secret fraud-risk criteria. This fact makes the observed distribution of audits non-extendible. Consequently, the 0.1 estimate of a firm's probability of being audited is completely implausible. Relying on it would be a serious mistake.[27]

To rebut this critique, adherents of mathematical probability might invoke the long-run argument, mistakenly (but commonly) grounded upon Bernoulli's law of large numbers (Bernoulli [1713] 2006, pp. 315–40).[28] This argument concedes that the 0.1 estimate of a firm's probability of being audited is not a reliable predictor of any specific auditing event. The argument, however, holds that repeat-players—firms that file tax reports every year—should rely on this estimate because at some point it will transform into a real audit. With some firms, it will happen sooner than with others, but eventually the agency will audit every firm.

This argument recommends that every person perceive her epistemic state of uncertainty as an actual experience of a series of stochastic events that can take her life in any

---

[25] Another problem with extendibility is its dependence on a reference class—a statistical generalization that can be gerrymandered in numerous ways (Allen and Pardo 2007, pp. 111–14).

[26] For classic accounts of why accidentally true beliefs do not constitute knowledge, see Gettier (1963), which explains that accidentally acquired justification for a true belief is not knowledge; and Goldman (1967) attesting that a knower's true belief must be induced by the belief's truth. See also Nozick (1993, pp. 64–100) defining knowledge as a true belief supported by the knower's truth-tracking reasons.

[27] Taxpayers' responses to an increase in the general probability of audit are difficult to measure. For one such attempt, see Slemrod, Blumenthal and Christian (2001, p. 465), which finds that audit rates are positively correlated with reported income of low-income and middle-income taxpayers and are negatively correlated with reported income of high-income taxpayers.

[28] For a superb account of the law's intellectual history, see Hacking (1990, pp. 95–104).

direction. This recommendation fills every informational gap with God playing dice. However, neither God nor the tax agency will actually throw a die to identify firms that require an audit. Whether a particular firm will be audited will be determined by causal forces, namely, the tax officers who will apply the agency's fraud-risk criteria to what they know about each firm. Each firm therefore should rely on its best estimate of how those officers will evaluate its tax return. If, instead of relying on this estimate, a firm chooses to base its actions on the 10% chance of being audited, it will sooner or later find itself on the losing side.[29] This firm will either take wasteful precautions against liability for tax evasion or expose itself to that liability by acting recklessly.[30]

---

[29]   This point was famously made by Samuelson (1963).

[30]   To mitigate this problem, statisticians often use "confidence intervals." See, e.g., Wonnacott and Wonnacott (1990, pp. 253–86). A confidence interval is essentially a second-order probability: an estimate of the chances that the reasoner's event-related (first-order) probability is accurate. Conventionally, those chances must not go below 95%—a confidence level that promises that the reasoner's estimate of the event-related probability will be accurate in 95 cases out of 100 (Wonnacott and Wonnacott 1990, pp. 254–55). The reasoner must conceptualize her estimate of the event-related probability not as a fixed figure, but rather—more realistically—as an average probability deriving from a sample of probabilities attaching to factual setups similar to hers. The reasoner should expand her sample of setups by relying on her experience or by conducting a series of controlled observations. If she obtains a sufficiently large sample, the setups' probabilities will form a "normal" bell-shaped distribution curve. Subsequently, in order to obtain a 95% confidence level in her estimate of the probability, the reasoner must eliminate the curve's extremes and derive the estimate from the representative middle. Technically, she must shorten the distribution curve by trimming away 2.5% from each tail. This trimming will compress the reasoner's information and narrow the range of probabilities in her sample. The average probability calculated in this way will then have a high degree of accuracy. The chances that it will require revision in the future as a result of the arrival of new information are relatively low. This feature will make the probability estimate resilient or, as some call it, robust or invariant. See Logue (1995, pp. 78–95) associating strength of probability estimates with resiliency; Nozick (2001, pp. 17–19, 79–87) associating strength of probability estimates with their invariance across cases. The 95% confidence-interval requirement undeniably improves the quality of probabilistic assessments. The fact that those assessments stay invariant across many instances makes them dependable (Cohen 1989, p. 118). This improvement, however, does not resolve the deep epistemological problem identified in this section. Resilience of a probability estimate only indicates that the estimate is statistically stable. For example, a resilient probability of 0.7 can only identify the number of cases—70 out of 100—in which the underlying event will actually occur. This assurance, however, does not determine the applicability of the 0.7 probability to individual events. Whether this (or other) probability attaches to an individual event does not depend on the availability of this assurance; rather, it depends on the operation of the indifference principle and the extendibility presumption. These inferential rules apply to an individual event in the absence of information accounting for the difference between the cases in which the event occurs and the cases in which it does not occur. The reasoner will thus always make an epistemically unwarranted assumption that the unavailable information is not slanted in any direction. The mathematical system may try to adopt a more demanding informational criterion: one that differentiates between probability estimates on the basis of their epistemic weights (Keynes 1921, pp. 71–77). For contemporary analyses of Keynes's "weight" criterion, see Cohen (1989, pp. 102–109); Schum (1994, pp. 251–57); Stein (2005, pp. 80–91); Cohen (1985). Charles Peirce also endorsed this criterion when he observed that "to express the proper state of our belief, not *one* number but *two* are requisite, the first depending on the inferred probability, the second on the amount of knowledge on which that probability is based" (Peirce 1872–1878). Under this criterion, the weight of a probability estimate will be determined by the comprehensiveness of what the reasoner does and does not know about her case (Keynes 1921, pp. 71, 77). The decisional

## 3.   CAUSAL PROBABILITY AND COMMON SENSE

Consider the following scenario:

> Peter undergoes a brain scan by MRI, and the scan is analyzed by a radiologist. The radiologist tells Peter that the lump that appears on the scan is benign to the best of her knowledge. She clarifies that she visually examined every part of Peter's brain and found no signs of malignancy. Peter asks the radiologist to translate the "best of her knowledge" into numbers, and the radiologist explains that 90% of the patients with similar-looking lumps have no cancer and that indications of malignancy are accidentally missed in 10% of the cases. The radiologist also tells Peter that only complicated brain surgery and a biopsy can determine with certainty whether he actually has cancer. According to the radiologist, this surgery involves a 15% risk of severe brain damage; in the remaining 85% of the cases, it successfully removes the lump and the patient recovers. Peter's primary care physician subsequently informs him that MRI machines have varying dependability. Specifically, he tells Peter that about 10% of those machines fail to reproduce images of small-size malignancies in the brain.

Under the mathematical system, Peter's probability of not having cancer equals 0.81. This number aggregates two probabilities of 0.9: the probability of correctness that attaches to the radiologist's diagnosis and the machine's probability of properly reproducing the image of Peter's brain. Peter's probability of having cancer consequently equals 0.19 $(1 - 0.81)$.[31] This probability is greater than the 0.15 probability of sustaining severe brain damage from the surgery. Should Peter opt for the surgery?

Under the mathematical system, he should. The fatalities to which the two probabilities attach are roughly identical. If so, Peter should choose the course of action that reduces the fatality's probability. Under the mathematical system of probability, this choice will improve Peter's welfare (by 4% of the value of his undamaged brain).

Common sense, however, would advise Peter to rely on the causative probability instead. Specifically, it would tell Peter to rely on the radiologist's negative diagnosis and pay little or no attention to the background statistics. The radiologist's diagnosis is the only empirically-based causal account that concerns Peter's *individual* condition.[32] The radiologist informs Peter about what she saw and what did she not see in his brain.[33] This diagnosis is the only information compatible with the causal nature of Peter's

---

synergy between probability and weight will create a serious problem of incommensurability. Consider a reasoner who faces a high but not weighty probability, on the one hand, and a weighty but low probability, on the other hand. Which of the two probabilities is more dependable than the other? This question does not have a readily available answer. There is simply no metric by which to compare the two sets of probabilities. This problem may not be insurmountable, but why tolerate it in the first place? Why try hard to undo the damage caused by the mathematical system's epistemological outlaws, instead of barring them? Sections 3 and 4 below respond to this question.

[31]   This calculation applies the negation rule. The same probability can be calculated by aggregating Peter's 10% chance of having a small malignancy missed by the MRI machine with his 10% chance of being one of the radiologist's false negatives. Peter's probability of falling into *either* of these misfortunes equals $(0.1 + 0.1) - (0.1 \times 0.1) = 0.19$. This calculation follows the disjunction rule.

[32]   Cf. Cohen (1980) arguing that patient-specific diagnoses are superior to statistical ones.

[33]   See, e.g., Mavroforakis et al. (2005) specifying malignancy and benignancy indicators that a radiologist should evaluate qualitatively in each patient and developing a quantitative tool to make those evaluations more robust.

physical environment. The general statistic extrapolated from the radiologist's and the MRI machine's history of errors is incompatible with this environment. This statistical information identifies no causal factors relevant to Peter's brain.

This common sense (that gets philosophical support from Francis Bacon [Bacon 1889] and John Stuart Mill [Mill [1843] 1980, pp. 549–53]) is impeccable. Peter should rely on the radiologist's diagnosis of his brain. Peter will make a serious and potentially fatal mistake if he chooses to undergo the brain surgery instead. Evidence that the radiologist erred in the past in ten diagnoses out of 100 reduces the general reliability of her diagnoses. This evidence, however, is causally irrelevant to the question of whether Peter has cancer. Whether Peter has cancer is a matter of empirical fact that the radiologist tried to ascertain. Her ascertainment of this fact relied on a series of patient-specific observations and medical science. While doing her job, the radiologist does not proceed stochastically by randomly distributing ten false-negative diagnoses across one hundred patients. Rather, she does her best for each and every patient, but, unfortunately, fails to identify cancer in 10 patients out of 100.

These errors had patient-specific or scan-specific causes: invisible malignancies, malfunctioning MRI machines, accidental oversights, and so forth. Those causes are unidentifiable, which means that Peter may still find himself among the afflicted patients. As an empirical matter, however, the unknown status of those causes does not equalize the chances of being misdiagnosed for each and every patient. Consequently, Peter has no empirical basis to discount the credibility of the radiologist's diagnosis of his brain by 10%.[34] This diagnosis is not completely certain, but it gives Peter qualitatively the best information that he can depend upon. This information is qualitatively the best because it is supported by an established causal theory: the radiologist's application of medical science to what she saw in Peter's brain. By contrast, no causal theory can ever support the view that the radiologist's patients are equally likely to be misdiagnosed as cancer-free.[35]

With this in mind, consider how ordinary people reason about their daily affairs. People are born into the world of causes and effects. Their daily affairs encompass events and phenomena that bring about other events and phenomena. As people accumulate their experiences and education, they internalize the idea of causation and the corresponding belief that things always happen for a reason and never without a reason.[36] Causal mechanisms underlying events and phenomena that people experience in their lives are not always known, but they are always present in the world. This causal understanding of the world drives most of ordinary people's decisions. These decisions therefore virtually always focus on some discrete, individual event and its underlying cause, as opposed to general distributions of similar-looking events. The same goes for generalizations that

---

[34] The same holds true for a possible malfunctioning of the MRI machine that scanned Peter's brain. There is no reason to believe that the risk of malfunction is distributed evenly across all machines and patients.

[35] Error statistics are not immaterial: if many (say, 30%) of the radiologist's diagnoses were false, Peter would have a good reason to doubt her credibility. This factor, however, would still be causatively irrelevant to whether he actually has cancer. Under these circumstances, Peter would have to find a credible specialist or endure the uncertainty. Cf. Thomson (1984, pp. 127–33) distinguishing between "external" evidence that derives from naked statistics and "internal" case-specific evidence that fits into a causal generalization.

[36] See generally Lagnado (2011).

ordinary people use in their decisions. These generalizations explain the world as governed by causal laws. They are akin to law-like generalities investigated by modern scientists.[37]

For that reason, when a person decides under conditions of uncertainty whether a certain event will (or did) occur, she articulates the available scenarios and selects the most plausible of those scenarios. More precisely, the person tries to figure out which of the available scenarios makes most sense in terms of coherence, consilience, causality, and evidential coverage (Allen and Stein 2013, pp. 567–71). This reasoning to the "best explanation" generally aligns with the common sense that people use in their daily affairs (Allen and Stein 2013, pp. 575–77).

This mode of reasoning rejects the indifference principle that animates mathematical probability. As I already explained, the indifference principle instructs reasoners to ignore the uncertainties in their evidence on the assumption that those uncertainties cancel each other out (Keynes 1921).[38] This assumption converts the reasoners' ignorance into the actual knowledge of probabilities, which it deems to be equal; and it has no epistemic warrant for that. Under the "best explanation" criterion, the decision-maker must select the best evidenced set of causes and effects, while rejecting all unevidenced hypotheses. She cannot assume that those hypotheses are equally probable—and thus cancel out—just because they are completely unevidenced. This epistemological injunction also does not allow the decision-maker to translate her reasons into mathematical fractions occupying a 0–1 scale. Because the decision-maker's information is incomplete, she has no epistemically justified reason to postulate that she knows the probabilities of all relevant scenarios. The decision-maker must consequently use words, rather than numbers, in evaluating the coherence, consilience, causal fit, and evidential coverage of competing scenarios.

To properly understand how ordinary people reason, one also needs to separate their "beliefs" from "acceptances," as recommended by philosophers of rationality.[39] Under this taxonomy, "acceptance" is a mentally active process that includes application of decisional rules to available information (Kahneman 2011, pp. 16–20). "Belief," by contrast, is a person's feeling, sensation, or hunch: an intellectually passive state of mind generated by unanalyzed experiences (Kahneman 2011, pp. 16–20).

Many of people's actions are driven by beliefs that people do not bother to reflect upon until it becomes necessary. For example, a person may form a belief that all medications sold by drugstores across the United States are as safe and as effective as advertised. Acting upon this unexamined belief is rational up to a point. For example, a person can rationally rely on this experience-based belief when she takes care of minor aches and discomforts. However, in serious health matters, a person will do well to discuss the

---

[37]  See generally Lange (1993) defining law-bound regularities as separate from accidental events.
[38]  See Keynes (1921, pp. 41–42) describing the indifference principle as essential for establishing equally probable possibilities—a preliminary condition for all mathematical assessments of probability; as Keynes explains, "In order that numerical measurement may be possible, we must be given a number of *equally* probable alternatives" Keynes (1921, p. 41, original emphasis); see Cohen (1989, 45–46) showing that the indifference principle is either circular or redundant; Keynes (1921, 45–47) demonstrating that the indifference principle is arbitrary and epistemologically unsustainable; see also Cohen (1979, p. 389) "Baconian [causative] probability-functions . . . grade probabilification . . . *by the extent to which* all relevant facts are specified in the evidence."
[39]  See Cohen (1992, pp. 1–27, 100–108) delineating the differences between "belief" and "acceptance".

pros and cons of every relevant medication with a qualified professional. Her decisions in such matters must rely upon rigorous and well-articulated criteria for assessing the medication's effects, as in my radiologist example. In other words, instead of simply relying on her beliefs, the person must form an "acceptance" based upon rules of reasoning.

Importantly, "belief" and "acceptance" are not analogs of what psychologists call "System 1" and "System 2" (Kahneman 2011, pp. 19–30). The "System 1/System 2" taxonomy only captures the intensity of a person's brainwork. To this end, it focuses on whether the person puts deliberative effort into her decisions (System 2) or decides quickly and unreflectively by using her intuition (System 1) (Kahneman 2011, pp. 1–30). By contrast, the belief–acceptance taxonomy captures the brainwork's normative content by separating the person's rule-free decisions (beliefs) from his rule-driven decisions (acceptances). System 1 and System 2 can, however, generate both beliefs and acceptances, depending on whether the person follows decisional rules—intuitively or reflectively. To be sure, a rule follower will use System 2 more often than System 1. Many people, however, also develop rule-driven instincts: drivers following the "two-second rule" to avoid colliding with a vehicle ahead of them are a good example of persons making rule-driven decisions that fall under System 1. On the other hand, some people may expend their deliberative efforts (System 2) on the formation of rule-free beliefs.

Behavioral economists systematically ignore these perfectly rational characteristics of ordinary people's reasoning. In Section 4 below, I evaluate the consequences of that omission. Before conducting that evaluation, I complete my discussion of causal probability by taking a closer look at its virtues. Specifically, I develop an analytical tool for separating cases that call for the application of mathematical probability from cases in which mathematical probability leads reasoners astray and where they will do well to use causal probability instead.

## 4.   BOUNDED PROBABILISTIC RATIONALITY REVISITED[40]

In the following paragraphs I revisit the flagship experiments that helped behavioral economists to establish the bounded probabilistic rationality theory (BPR). My critique of BPR is twofold. First, I show that BPR and its supporting experiments suffer from insurmountable methodological problems. Subsequently, I demonstrate that BPR is flawed from the standpoint of conventional probability theory as well.

### 4.1   Belief vs. Acceptance

Behavioral experiments underlying the bounded rationality thesis uniformly miss the belief–acceptance distinction. People who participate in these experiments develop no rule-based acceptances, nor are they asked to form such acceptances by the experimenters. All they do is report their pre-analytical beliefs because this is what the experimenters ask them to do. People's rationality, however, can only be evaluated by reference to their

---

[40]   This section draws on Stein (2013).

acceptances that apply rules of reasoning.[41] Identifying the criteria, or rules, that people apply in their evaluations of probability consequently becomes crucial.

Behavioral economists systematically fail to investigate people's acceptances, as distinguished from their beliefs. As I explain below, this omission undermines BPR. Failure to separate rule-driven acceptances from rule-free beliefs has also led behavioral economists to conflate people's cognitive performance with cognitive competence.[42] This conflation makes the resulting behavioral accounts deficient. The fact that a person systematically makes statistical errors in forming her beliefs does not establish that she would also commit those errors in forming her acceptances, in which case she would familiarize herself with and reflectively apply the requisite statistical rules. In fact, empirical studies of statistical education report considerable success of the various learning methods through which students acquire understandings of statistical inference.[43]

Behavioral economists' failure to separate beliefs from acceptances looms large in the "Linda Problem"—a celebrated experiment of Kahneman and Tversky (Kahneman 2011, pp. 156–58). Linda was described to participants as a 35-year-old woman, who was "single," "outspoken," "very bright," and deeply concerned with "issues of discrimination and social justice." Linda's college life included majoring in philosophy and participating in anti-nuclear demonstrations. Participants were asked to select Linda's occupation and social identity from the list provided by Kahneman and Tversky. "Bank teller" and "feminist bank teller" were among the options on that list. Most participants ranked Linda's being a "feminist bank teller" as more probable than Linda's simply being a "bank teller."

This assessment of probability defies mathematical logic. Linda's feminism was a probable, but still uncertain, fact. Her occupation as a bank teller was a merely probable, rather than certain, fact as well. The probability of each of those characteristics was somewhere between 0 and 1. Hence, the probability that these two characteristics would be present simultaneously must be lower than the probability that attached to each individual characteristic. Linda was more likely to have only the "bank teller," or only the "feminist," characteristic than to possess both characteristics at once. Assuming that the characteristics are mutually independent and that the probability of each characteristic is, say, 0.6, Linda's probability of being a feminist bank teller would equal 0.36. Remarkably, the Linda results were replicated with doctorate students at Stanford Business School.

To verify this important finding, Kahneman and Tversky conducted another experiment that featured a simple question: "Which alternative is more probable? Linda is a bank teller. Linda is a bank teller and is active in the feminist movement." Once again, the participants ranked the second joint-event scenario as more probable than the first single-event scenario.

Kahneman reports that after completing one such experiment, he asked the participants, "Do you realize that you have violated an elementary logical rule?" In response,

---

[41]   Stein (2013, p. 88) "Nor would [a belief] deserve praise or blame in the way that a responsible act of acceptance deserves it."

[42]   This conflation was first spotted by Cohen (1981, pp. 328–29).

[43]   See, e.g., Arnold et al. (2011) reporting success with teaching statistical inference to 14-year-old students with the help of hands-on physical simulations; Hall and Vance (2010), reporting success in teaching introductory statistics with the help of students' self-explanation and peer feedback.

a graduate student said "I thought you just asked for my opinion." Kahneman cites this response to illustrate the stickiness of people's probabilistic irrationality: the student who gave this response believed that her *opinion* on factual matters could defy mathematical logic.

The student's response, however, ought to have moved Kahneman in a different direction. What the student was actually saying was "Had I known that you were expecting me to give you not just my best hunch about Linda's job and social identity, but rather a rule-based evaluation of the relevant probabilities, my answer might have been different." The student, in other words, understood the experiment as asking her to express her belief, rather than articulate and apply her criteria for acceptances. In forming this belief, she felt free to rely on her common sense and experience rather than on statistical rules. Her reasoning aligned with that of scientists who begin their inquiries with intuitive beliefs that they subsequently accept or reject (Cohen 1989, pp. 89–90).

Similar to many other experiments carried out by behavioral economists, the Linda Problem could only elicit the beliefs that participants intuitively formed. Those beliefs do not reveal much about the participants' probabilistic rationality. Forming a rule-free belief, as opposed to a rule-driven acceptance, does not commit the believer to any specific reason, or rule, that she will follow in her other decisions.[44] Acceptances driven by rules of reasoning are different. Most medical patients, for example, would attest that having spinal surgery followed by a coronary bypass operation is riskier than undergoing spinal surgery alone. This attestation correctly applies the product rule for conjunctive probabilities to facts that the patient deeply cares about. Unsurprisingly, it expresses the patient's acceptance rather than belief.

As far as beliefs are concerned, the participants' prevalent reaction to Linda was far from irrational. Formation of a person's belief always calls on the experience that a person has accumulated throughout her life.[45] This experience cannot be artificially blocked by statistical rules, unless the person is expressly told to suppress all of her beliefs that do not conform to those rules and to base her decision on acceptance.[46] From the standpoint of an ordinary person's belief, the single-event scenario "Linda is a bank teller" was incomplete because bank tellers' work does not normally occupy their entire lives. The absence of information about Linda's social identity and afterwork engagements thus created a gap fillable by experience. Hence, it was entirely rational for participants to make an experience-based assumption that Linda must have *some* social identity or afterwork engagement. This assumption made the participants focus on the following question: is it more probable that, "Linda is a feminist bank teller" or that "Linda is a bank teller whose social identity and afterwork engagements are feminism free"?[47]

Based on Linda's background information, the participants were absolutely (and

---

[44]   Cf. Schauer (1995) associating official reasons with commitment to apply similar reasons in future cases.

[45]   See, e.g., Hume (1739) famously explaining "belief" as a consequence of the believer's "number of past impressions and conjunctions."

[46]   Cf. Cohen (1991) arguing that jurors should suppress their beliefs and determine facts through "acceptance."

[47]   Cf. Gigerenzer (2005, pp. 8–9) criticizing Linda and similar experiments for their reliance on a "content-blind" norm for rationality.

unsurprisingly) correct in forming a belief that ranked Linda's feminism above other afterwork engagements. In technical terms, Linda's probability of being a bank teller and a feminist, $P(T\&F)$, equaled $P(T) \times P(F)$. Correspondingly, Linda's probability of being a bank teller while having a non-feminist afterwork engagement, $P(T\&NF)$, equaled $P(T) \times P(NF)$. Under the factual setup that the participants were asked to consider, Linda was more likely to be a feminist than a non-feminist: $P(F) > P(NF)$. Hence, $P(T\&F) > P(T\&NF)$.

To preclude the formation of this rational belief, Kahneman and his associates ought to have asked the participants a simple question, suggested by Gerd Gigerenzer: "There are 100 persons who fit the description above (that is, Linda's). How many of them are: Bank tellers? Bank tellers and active in the feminist movement?" (Gigerenzer 2005, p. 10). This question would have elicited predominantly the statistically correct response (Gigerenzer 2005).

Kahneman's anticipated reply to this critique might fall along the following lines. The participants' real task was to cut through the "noise" (the statistically meaningless information) and see what the experimenters asked them to do. The participants, so goes the argument, ought to have noticed that their task was to compare the probabilities of a single and a compound, or conjunctive, event. Had the participants noticed that, they also would have noticed that Linda's probability of being a feminist bank teller was no different from the proverbial coin's probability of revealing *heads* in two successive throws. On a 0 to 1 scale, this probability equals $0.5 \times 0.5 = 0.25$.

The coin analogy, however, is untidy because Linda's social identity and afterwork engagement were not an unrigged coin. Linda's background information made her engagement in feminist causes the most probable afterwork scenario. Arguably, this scenario was more probable than the case in which Linda's work as a bank teller— surprisingly fulfilling or unduly exhaustive—represented everything she did in her life.

The upshot of my preceding discussion is straightforward. Studies of people's probabilistic decisions are not very fruitful when they focus on intuitive beliefs. Focusing on people's rule-driven acceptances in settings that call for statistical reasoning—as in my double-surgery example—could give Kahneman and other behavioral economists a much better sense of people's probabilistic rationality.

Behavioral economists, however, have chosen not to go along this route. Instead of adopting a simple all-statistics setup for their experiments, they mix statistical data with case-specific information. This informational mix can be found not only in the Linda Problem. Almost every experiment associated with the Kahneman and Tversky school of thought uses this mix, and there is a reason for that as well. Kahneman explains that causal associations corrupt people's decisions: people try to find causal connections where none exists, while irrationally discounting important statistical information (Kahneman 2011, pp. 74–78). This cognitive malfunction has shaped Kahneman's and his associates' experimental agenda. Kahneman and his associates seek to uncover how people's "causation illusion" drives them to ignore statistical data and depart from statistical reasoning. As I demonstrated in Section 3, however, there is nothing wrong in people's attempt to understand the outside world as a series of causes and effects. In fact, people will do well to rely on that understanding in most decisions they make during their lifetime.

**4.2    BPR vs. Probability Theory**

BPR also encounters difficulties in the realm of probability theory. Responsible for those difficulties is the statistical–causative mix of information on which behavioral economists often base their experiments. Consider one of Kahneman and Tversky's most famous experiments: the "Blue Cab Problem." Kahneman, Tversky, and their collaborators told their participants about a hit-and-run accident that occurred at night in a city in which 85% of cabs were blue and 15% were green (Kahneman 2011, pp. 166–70; Bar-Hillel 1980, pp. 211–12). They also told the participants that the hit-and-run victim filed a lawsuit against the companies operating those cabs—identified respectively as "Blue Cab" and "Green Cab"—and that an eyewitness testified in the ensuing trial that the cab that hit the victim was green. Another piece of information that the participants received concerned a rather unusual procedure that took place at this trial. The experimenters told the participants that "[t]he court tested the witness' ability to distinguish between Blue and Green cabs under nighttime visibility conditions [and] found that the witness was able to identify each color correctly about 80% of the time, but confused it with the other color about 20% of the time" (Bar-Hillel 1980, pp. 211–12). Based on this information, most participants in the experiments assessed the probability that a green cab hit the victim at 0.8, presumably because they believed this was the probability that the eyewitness's testimony was correct (Kahneman 2011, p. 167).

This assessment of probability aligned with the given credibility of the witness, but not with Bayes' Theorem.[48] The prior odds that the responsible cab was green as opposed to blue, $P(G)/P(B)$, equaled 0.15/0.85. To calculate the posterior odds, $P(G|W)/P(B|W)$, with $W$ denoting the credibility of the witness, these odds had to be multiplied by the likelihood ratio. This ratio is equal to the odds attaching to the scenario in which the witness identified the cab's color correctly, rather than incorrectly: $P(W|G)/P(W|B)$. The posterior odds consequently equaled $(0.15 \times 0.8)/(0.85 \times 0.2)$—that is, 12/17. The probability that the victim's allegation against the Green Cab is true thus amounted to 12/(17 + 12) or 0.41—far below the "preponderance of the evidence standard" ($> 0.5$) that applies in civil litigation. The experiment thus seems to provide an elegant and robust demonstration of individuals' total neglect of base rates.

This and similar experimental vignettes have a serious flaw that I call unspecified causality. The experimenters did not tell the participants that the relative frequency of blue and green cabs' appearances on the streets of the city could somehow affect the witness's capacity to tell blue from green. This causal effect is quite unusual: an ordinary person can tell blue from green even when they see one green cab and many blue cabs.[49] The experimenters therefore ought to have told the participants that the witness's ability to distinguish between blue and green cabs might have been affected by the frequency with which those cabs appeared on the streets. Alternatively, the experimenters ought to have told the participants that in cases in which the witness failed to give the correct

---

[48]    For exposition and proof of Bayes' Theorem, see Stein (2011, pp. 211–13).

[49]    See Cohen (1986, p. 329) "[I]f the green cab company suddenly increased the size of its fleet relative to that of the blue company, the accuracy of the witness's vision would not be affected, and the credibility of his testimony would therefore remain precisely the same in any particular case of the relevant kind."

identification of the cab's color, he might have made this mistake randomly rather than for some specific reason (Stein 2011, pp. 253–55).

The experimenters, in other words, ought to have ruled the causality factor in or out. Instead, they allowed the participants to deal with the unspecified causality as they deemed fit, and the participants rendered an unsurprising—albeit not watertight—verdict that the distribution of cabs' colors in the city did not affect the witness's ability to tell blue from green. Absent a causal connection between these two factors, the errant cab's probability of being green as opposed to blue was indeed 0.8.

Unspecified causality is a serious flaw also because it makes the relevant reference class malleable.[50] To see how this malleability affected the Blue Cab Problem, factor in the preponderance requirement that a plaintiff in a civil suit needs to satisfy in order to win the case.[51] Under this requirement, the victim was certainly entitled to win her suit against Green Cab when the errant cab's probability of being green, given the testimony of the witness—$P(G|W)$—was greater than 0.5. The victim, however, was equally entitled to win the suit when the probability of the scenario in which the witness correctly identifies a green cab—$P(W|G)$—was greater than 0.5. The relevant reference class, in other words, could have been either the cab's color or the witness's accuracy.[52] The participants therefore could not be wrong in selecting the witness's accuracy as the relevant reference class. This perfectly rational choice allowed the participants to treat the probability of the witness's accuracy (0.8) as a dominant factor in their decision.

More fundamentally, the mix of statistical and causative information brings into consideration the normative openness of the "probability" concept (Stein 2011, pp. 200–204). As a normative matter, the Blue Cab Problem can be analyzed under two distinct analytical frameworks: mathematical (Pascalian) and causative (Baconian) (Stein 2011, pp. 253–56). The mathematical framework uses Bayes' Theorem, whose application gives the victim's case a 0.41 probability (if we ignore the unspecified causality and the reference-class problem). This probability represents the errant cab's chances of being green rather than blue, with a cab-identifying witness scoring 80 out of 100 on similar identifications in a city in which 85% of the cabs are blue and 15% are green.

The causative framework, on the other hand, yields an altogether different result, close to the mathematical probability of the witness's accuracy (0.8). Under this framework, which I explained in more detail in Section 3, an event's probability corresponds to the quantum and variety of the evidence that confirms the event's occurrence while eliminating rival scenarios (Stein 2011, pp. 243–46). This qualitative evidential criterion separates causative probability from the mathematical calculus of chances (Stein 2011, pp. 235–46). Under this criterion, the eyewitness's testimony that the errant cab was green was credible enough to rule out the "errant blue cab" scenario as causatively implausible. On the other hand, the distribution of blue and green cabs in the city had no proven effect on the eyewitness's capacity to tell blue from green. The eyewitness's testimony consequently overrode the cabs' distribution evidence and removed it from the fact-finding process.

---

[50] For an outstanding analysis of reference-class malleability, see Allen and Pardo (2007, pp. 111–14).

[51] See Stein (2005, pp. 143–48, 219–25) explaining the preponderance requirement and its underlying justifications.

[52] This insight belongs to Owen (1987, p. 199).

This eliminative method (favored by Francis Bacon and John Stuart Mill [Stein 2011, pp. 204–206, 236–40]) allowed the participants to evaluate the probability of the victim's case at 0.8. This fact-finding method is not devoid of difficulties, but it is also far from being irrational (Stein 2011, pp. 236–40).

Contrary to Kahneman's view, the Blue Cab Problem and similar experiments do not establish that people's probability judgments are irrational.[53] These judgments *are* predominantly rational. The legal system need not do more than remedy people's informational shortfalls—not cognitive incapacities—by applying the conventional doctrines of foreseeability, disclosure, informed consent, unconscionability, and consumer protection.

## 4.3   Causation vs. Chance

Behavioral economists often criticize people for putting too much faith in causation (Kahneman 2011, pp. 74–78, 114–18). This criticism presupposes that incomplete causal indicators can only create an associative illusion of causation (Kahneman 2011). At the same time, behavioral economists believe that incomplete statistical indicators—the chances that surround us—are real and hence dependable (Kahneman 2011, pp. 71–78, 166–74).

This unexplained normative asymmetry is best illustrated by another milestone experiment of Kahneman and Tversky. Aimed at identifying the "representativeness" bias, the "Steve Problem" featured Steve, described to participants as "very shy and withdrawn, invariably helpful, but with little interest in people, or in the world of reality. A meek and tidy soul, he has a need for order and structure, and a passion for detail" (Kahneman 2011, p. 420). The experimenters asked the participants to choose Steve's most probable occupation from a list that included "farmer, salesman, airline pilot, librarian, [and] physician" (Kahneman 2011). According to Kahneman and Tversky, the participants used familiar (i.e., "representative") stereotypes to identify Steve as a likely librarian, while ignoring the fact that librarians are vastly outnumbered by farmers (Kahneman 2011).

Kahneman and Tversky assume that there was only one correct way to answer the question about Steve's job (Kahneman 2011, pp. 420–21). According to them, the participants had to find out the percentage of farmers, salesmen, airline pilots, librarians, and physicians in the general pool of working males. This percentage determined Steve's probability of being a farmer, a salesman, an airline pilot, a librarian, or a physician. Kahneman and Tversky believe that trying to identify Steve's profession through his personality traits is doomed to fail, as these traits are rather weak causal indicators of a person's professional identity. The general statistic representing an average working male's chances of having one of the above-mentioned professions was a far more dependable indicator. This indicator therefore ought to have trumped the uninformative individual traits. The participants' failure to notice this statistical indicator, and their

---

[53]   Cf. Gigerenzer (1996, p. 593) criticizing Kahneman and Tversky for testing people's ascriptions of probabilities to single events not amenable to such assessments.

consequent reliance on Steve's individual traits was a cognitive error (Kahneman 2011, pp. 420–21).

I posit that this experiment was poorly designed. Steve's personality traits did not make him a librarian, but they were certainly relevant to his choice of profession. If so, the participants should have been looking for a different, and more refined, statistic. Specifically, they should have been looking for the percentage of farmers, salesmen, airline pilots, librarians, and physicians in the general pool of working males who are shy, withdrawn and helpful, have meek and tidy souls and a passion for detail, and also need order and structure, while exhibiting little interest in people and the world of reality. Of course, this investigation would have been futile because general employment statistics do not single out the subcategory of working males formulated by Kahneman and Tversky. However, the fact that this investigation would have been futile does not make it inconsequential. Information revealing Steve's job preferences was material. Distribution of professions across working males generally was a rough and potentially misleading substitute for that information. This distribution was informative, but its evidential value did not outweigh the evidential value of Steve's personality traits. Kahneman and Tversky evidently think that it did, but this is just an opinion rather than empirical fact. People participating in the Steve Problem were entitled to use their opinions instead.

The Steve Problem's design incorporates unspecified causality. This feature opened two decisional routes for the experiment's participants. One could rationally estimate Steve's probability of being a librarian as a matter of chance. Alternatively, one could estimate this probability as a question of Steve's choice. Under the framework of chance, decision-makers would rely on the distribution of relevant professions across working males in general. Under the framework of choice, they would consider a probable bargaining equilibrium between Steve and prospective employers. This equilibrium solution would practically remove from the list the physician, the pilot, and the salesman. Arguably, as between being a farmer and being a librarian, Steve would choose to be a librarian. Finding a librarian position might be difficult—given the scarcity of such positions, relative to the many jobs available on a farm—but Steve could succeed in getting it.

Kahneman and Tversky disapprove of the participants' preference for the choice framework. Notwithstanding their disapproval, this preference is perfectly rational. The choice framework is not problem-free, given the scarcity of case-specific information about Steve, but extrapolating Steve's probable occupation from the general pool of working males is equally problematic. Both modes of reasoning rely heavily on speculation, and there is consequently no way to tell which of them is epistemically preferable. Calling one of these modes of reasoning "rational" and another "irrational" is simply wrong.

Unspecified causality in an experiment's design *always* makes the relevant reference class malleable. Consider again Steve's case. Individuals participating in this experiment could perceive their task in two completely different ways. They could ask themselves whether Steve's personality traits separate him from the average working male. According to Kahneman and Tversky, this was the right question to ask. However, an alternative—and equally rational—way to define the reference class was to focus on a narrower category of working males who have Steve's characteristics. The relevant reference class, in other words, could be either of the following: (1) males, as distributed across different professions; or (2) professions, as distributed across different males. The first of these categories emphasizes chance, while the second centers on choice. There is no way to determine which of those categories is more dependable than the other as a basis for statistical inference. Kahneman and Tversky evidently prefer chance over choice. The participants in their experiments did the opposite. As for myself, I remain undecided.

Behavioral economists criticize people's reliance on case-specific knowledge as a "law of small numbers" (Kahneman 2011, pp. 109–18). This criticism is far removed from how most people—including judges and juries[54]—ascertain facts in their day-to-day lives. Behavioral economists' skepticism about case-specific knowledge also cannot be justified as a wholesale proposition, for it brushes aside a distinct mode of probabilistic reasoning, known as causative or Baconian reasoning (Stein 2011, pp. 204–206, 235–46). Behavioral economists' disregard of Baconian probability is perplexing. This mode of probabilistic reasoning is perfectly rational (Stein 2011), and it also could explain—and, indeed, justify—people's decisions that behavioral economists describe as erroneous.[55]

Under the causative system outlined in Section 3, a combination of credible case-specific evidence and experience can develop a single causal explanation for the relevant event that will override the competing statistical explanations (Stein 2011, pp. 235–46). This override is the essence of the Baconian elimination method (Stein 2011, pp. 204–206). For example, in the Blue Cab Problem, participants were entitled to assign overriding probative value to the witness's testimony that the errant cab was green. This testimony was not watertight, but it was credible and event-specific. The event's causal impact on the witness's perceptive apparatus qualitatively differed from the city's cab-color statistics. This impact might have been epistemically superior to those statistics and therefore properly overrode them in the participants' minds.

This override was likely at work in the Steve Problem as well. There, participants used Steve's personality traits to eliminate from their list every profession that did not fit the stereotype associated with these traits. "Librarian" was the only item that survived this elimination procedure, which led the participants to estimate that Steve must be a librarian. Kahneman and Tversky correctly observe that this estimate was unfounded.[56] They are, however, too quick to denounce the participants' reasoning for failing to account for Steve's prior probability of being a farmer, as opposed to a librarian. Under the causative system of probability, the elimination method that the participants chose to use was valid. The participants simply did not have enough evidence for choosing the "librarian" over the "farmer." They would have had enough evidence for this assessment had they been informed, for example, that Steve is a connoisseur of literature. The addition of this information would have allowed the participants not to factor the statistical prevalence of farmers into their assessment.

---

[54]   See Stein (2005, pp. 80–106) explaining case-specificity requirements in the law of evidence.

[55]   See Cohen (1986, pp. 165–68) explaining why it is rational for people to rely on causative probabilities instead of naked statistics.

[56]   They explained that "In the case of Steve . . . the fact that there are many more farmers than librarians in the population should enter into any reasonable estimate of the probability that Steve is a librarian rather than a farmer" (Kahneman 2011, p. 420).

# 5.  CONCLUSION

Throughout their long history, humans have worked hard to tame chance.[57] They adapted to their uncertain physical and social environments by using the method of trial and error. This evolutionary process made humans reason about uncertain facts the way they do. Behavioral economists argue that humans' natural selection of their prevalent mode of reasoning wasn't wise. They censure this mode of reasoning for violating the canons of mathematical probability that a rational person must obey.

In this chapter, I have challenged both parts of this claim. Based on the insights from probability theory and the philosophy of induction, I have argued that a rational person need not apply mathematical probability in making decisions about individual causes and effects. Instead, she should be free to use common-sense reasoning that generally aligns with causative (Baconian) probability. I also have shown that behavioral experiments uniformly miss their target when they ask reasoners to extract probability from information that combines causal evidence with statistical data. Because it is perfectly rational for a person focusing on a specific event to prefer causal evidence to general statistics, those experiments establish no deviations from rational reasoning. Those experiments are also flawed in that they do not separate the reasoners' unreflective beliefs from rule-driven acceptances. The behavioral economists' claim that people are probabilistically challenged consequently remains unproven.

# REFERENCES

Allen, Ronald J., and Michael S. Pardo. 2007. The Problematic Value of Mathematical Models of Evidence. *Journal of Legal Studies* 36: 10–40.

Allen, Ronald J., and Alex Stein. 2013. Evidence, Probability, and the Burden of Proof. *Arizona Law Review* 55: 557–602.

Arnold, Pip, Maxine Pfannkuch, Chris J. Wild, Matt Regan, and Stephanie Budgett. 2011. Enhancing Students' Inferential Reasoning: From Hands-On to "Movies". *Journal of Statistics Education* 19. http://www.amstat.org/publications/jse/v19n2/pfannkuch.pdf (last visited May 13, 2015).

Bacon, Francis. 1889. Novum Organum. P. 191 in *Bacon's Novum Organum*, 2nd edn, edited by Thomas Fowler. Oxford: Clarendon Press.

Bar-Grill, Oren, and Rebecca Stone. 2009. Mobile Misperceptions. *Harvard Journal of Law & Technology* 23: 49–118.

Bar-Grill, Oren, and Elizabeth Warren. 2008. Making Credit Safer. *University of Pennsylvania Law Review* 157: 1–101.

Bar-Hillel, Maya. 1980. The Base-Rate Fallacy in Probability Judgments. *Acta Psychologica* 44: 211–33.

Bayes, Thomas. 1763. An Essay Towards Solving a Problem in the Doctrine of Chances. http://www.stat.ucla.edu/history/essay.pdf (last visited Jan. 25, 2014).

Ben-Shahar, Omri, and Carl E. Schneider. 2011. The Failure of Mandated Disclosure. *University of Pennsylvania Law Review* 159: 647–749.

Bernoulli, Jacob. [1713] 2006. *The Art of Conjecturing*. Trans. Edith Dudley Sylla. Baltimore, MD: Johns Hopkins University Press.

Cohen, L. Jonathan. 1979. On the Psychology of Prediction: Whose Is the Fallacy? *Cognition* 7: 385–407.

Cohen, L. Jonathan. 1980. Bayesianism Versus Baconianism in the Evaluation of Medical Diagnoses. *British Journal for the Philosophy of Science* 31: 45–62.

Cohen, L. Jonathan. 1981. Can Human Irrationality Be Experimentally Demonstrated? *Behavioral and Brain Sciences* 4: 317–70.

---

[57]  See generally Hacking (1990).

Cohen, L. Jonathan. 1985. Twelve Questions About Keynes's Concept of Weight. *British Journal for the Philosophy of Science* 37: 263–78.

Cohen, L. Jonathan. 1986. *The Dialogue of Reason: An Analysis of Analytical Philosophy*. New York, NY: Oxford University Press.

Cohen, L. Jonathan. 1989. *An Introduction to the Philosophy of Induction and Probability*. New York, NY: Oxford University Press.

Cohen, L. Jonathan. 1991. Should a Jury Say What It Believes or What It Accepts? *Cardozo Law Review* 13: 465–83.

Cohen, L. Jonathan. 1992. *An Essay on Belief and Acceptance*. Oxford: Clarendon Press.

Eisenberg, Melvin Aron. 1995. The Limits of Cognition and the Limits of Contract. *Stanford Law Review* 47: 211–59.

Gettier, Edmund L. 1963. Is Justified True Belief Knowledge? *Analysis* 23: 121–23.

Gigerenzer, Gerd. 1996. On Narrow Norms and Vague Heuristics: A Reply to Kahneman and Tversky (1996). *Psychological Review* 103: 592–98.

Gigerenzer, Gerd. 2005. I Think, Therefore I Err. *Social Research* 72: 195–218.

Goldman, Alvin I. 1967. A Causal Theory of Knowing. *Journal of Philosophy* 64: 357–72.

Hacking, Ian. 1990. *The Taming of Chance*. Cambridge: Cambridge University Press.

Hall, Simin, and Eric A. Vance. 2010. Improving Self-Efficacy in Statistics: Role of Self-Explanation & Feedback. *Journal of Statistics Education* 18. https://ww2.amstat.org/publications/jse/v18n3/hall.pdf (last visited May 13, 2015).

Hume, David. 1739. A Treatise of Human Nature. Pp. 1–102 in Vol. 1 of *A Treatise on Human Nature*, edited by David Fate Norton and Mary J. Norton. Oxford: Oxford University Press.

Jolls, Christine, Cass R. Sunstein, and Richard Thaler. 1998. A Behavioral Approach to Law and Economics. *Stanford Law Review* 50: 1471–550.

Kahan, Dan M. 2010. The Economics—Conventional, Behavioral, and Political—of "Subsequent Remedial Measures" Evidence. *Columbia Law Review* 110: 1616–53.

Kahneman, Daniel. 2011. *Thinking, Fast and Slow*. New York, NY: Farrar, Straus and Giroux.

Keynes, John Maynard. 1921. *A Treatise on Probability*. London: Macmillan and Co.

Kneale, William. 1949. *Probability and Induction*. Oxford: Clarendon Press.

Kolmogorov, A. N. 1956. *Foundations of the Theory of Probability*. 2nd English edn. Translation edited by Nathan Morrison. New York, NY: Chelsea Publishing Company.

Lagnado, David A. 2011. Causal Thinking. Pp. 129–46 in *Causality in the Sciences* edited by Phyllis McKay-Illari, Federica Russo, and Jon Williamson. New York, NY: Oxford University Press.

Lange, Marc. 1993. Lawlikeness. *Noûs* 27: 1–27.

Lawsky, Sarah B. 2009. Probably? Understanding Tax Law's Uncertainty. *University of Pennsylvania Law Review* 157: 1017–74.

Lempert, Richard O. 1977. Modeling Relevance. *Michigan Law Review* 75: 1021–57.

Logue, James. 1995. *Projective Probability*. Oxford: Clarendon Press.

Mavroforakis, Michael, Harris Georgiou, Nikos Dimitropoulos, Dionisis Cavuras, and S. Theodoridis. 2005. Significance Analysis of Qualitative Mammographic Features, Using Linear Classifiers, Neural Networks and Support Vector Machines. *European Journal of Radiology* 54: 80–89.

Mill, John Stuart. [1843] 1980. *A System of Logic, Ratiocinative and Inductive: Being a Connected View of the Principles of Evidence and the Methods of Scientific Investigation*. 8th edn. New York: Harper.

Nozick, Robert. 1993. *The Nature of Rationality*. Princeton, NJ: Princeton University Press.

Nozick, Robert. 2001. *Invariances: The Structure of the Objective World*. Cambridge, MA: Harvard University Press.

Owen, David. 1987. Hume Versus Price on Miracles and Prior Probabilities: Testimony and Bayesian Calculation. *Philosophical Quarterly* 37: 187–202.

*Oxford English Dictionary, The*. 1989. 2nd edn. New York, NY: Oxford University Press.

Peirce, Charles Sanders. 1872–1878. The Probability of Induction. P. 295 in vol. 3 of *Writings of Charles S. Peirce, A Chronological Edition*, edited by Christian J. W. Kloesel. Bloomington, IN: Indiana University Press.

Rachlinski, Jeffrey J. 1998. A Positive Psychological Theory of Judging in Hindsight. *University of Chicago Law Review* 65: 571–625.

Samuelson, P. A. 1963. Risk and Uncertainty: A Fallacy of Large Numbers. *Scientia* 98: 108–13.

Schauer, Frederick. 1995. Giving Reasons. *Stanford Law Review* 47: 633–59.

Schum, David A. 1994. *The Evidential Foundations of Probabilistic Reasoning*. New York, NY: John Wiley & Sons, Inc.

Slemrod, Joel, Marsha Blumenthal, and Charles Christian. 2001. Taxpayer Response to an Increased Probability of Audit: Evidence from a Controlled Experiment in Minnesota. *Journal of Public Economics* 79: 455–83.

Stein, Alex. 2005. *Foundations of Evidence Law*. New York, NY: Oxford University Press.

Stein, Alex. 2011. The Flawed Probabilistic Foundation of Law & Economics. *Northwestern University Law Review* 105: 199–260.

Stein, Alex. 2013. Book Review: Are People Probabilistically Challenged? *Michigan Law Review* 111: 855–75.

Sunstein, Cass R. 1986. Legal Interference with Private Preferences. *University of Chicago Law Review* 53: 1129–74.

Thaler, Richard H., and Cass R. Sunstein. 2008. *Nudge: Improving Decisions About Health, Wealth, and Happiness*. New York, NY: Penguin Books.

Thomson, Judith Jarvis. 1984. Remarks on Causation and Liability. *Philosophy and Public Affairs* 13: 101–33.

Vandenbergh, Michael, Amanda R. Carrico, and Lisa Schultz Bressman. 2011. Regulation in the Behavioral Era. *Minnesota Law Review* 95: 715–81.

Williams, Sean Hannon. 2009. Sticky Expectations: Responses to Persistent Over-Optimism in Marriage, Employment Contracts, and Credit Card Use. *Notre Dame Law Review* 84: 733–91.

Wonnacott, Thomas H., and Ronald J. Wonnacott. 1990. *Introductory Statistics*. 5th edn. New York, NY: John Wiley & Sons.

Zamir, Eyal. 1998. The Efficiency of Paternalism. *Virginia Law Review* 84: 229–86.

# PART II

# ANTITRUST AND CONSUMER FINANCE

# 3. Exclusionary vertical restraints and antitrust: experimental law and economics contributions
*Claudia M. Landeo[1]*

## 1. INTRODUCTION

Vertical restraints refer to arrangements between firms at different levels of the vertical chain that restrict the conditions under which these firms may operate. They often serve legitimate and value-enhancing business goals. On the other hand, vertical restraints may be anticompetitive.[2] These business practices have been the subject of lively policy and academic discussions. Scholars associated with the Chicago School (Director and Levi 1956; Posner 1976; Bork 1978) challenged early foreclosure doctrines[3] by arguing that vertical restraints primarily reflected efficiency considerations. More recently, industrial organization economists (Aghion and Bolton 1987; Rasmusen et al. 1991; Ordover, Salop, and Saloner 1990; Hart and Tirole 1990; Whinston 1990; Bolton and Whinston 1991, 1993; Spier and Whinston 1995; Segal and Whinston 2000; Nalebuff 2004) have used the tools of game theory and information economics to show that these practices might actually serve anticompetitive purposes.[4]

Legal scholars recognize the important role of economic theory in the design of non-arbitrary and effective antitrust policies. Without economic theories, antitrust institutions might be vulnerable to the instabilities generated by interest groups. As a result, the likelihood of achieving welfare-enhancing goals with those policies might be uncertain (Hovenkamp 2011). However, the influence of the new economic theories on antitrust

[1] I acknowledge research support from the National Science Foundation (Award No. SES-1155761). Part of this research was conducted at Yale Law School and Harvard Law School, where I served as a Visiting Senior Research Scholar in Law. I am grateful to both institutions for their hospitality. I thank Kathy Spier and Kathy Zeiler for insightful comments.

[2] As Whinston (2006) notes, the economics of antitrust broadly encompasses two main important categories: exclusion and collusion. Exclusion refers to the firm's attempt to preserve its market power through the exclusion of rival firms using exclusionary practices. These practices involve market foreclosure through vertical integration, exclusive dealing contracts, and tying and bundling, among other practices. Collusion refers to the firm's attempt to raise prices through collaboration with rival firms. Examples of these practices are price fixing and horizontal merger. Extensive experimental literature on collusion has been developed (see surveys by Engel 2007; Holt 1995; Davis and Holt 2008; Normann 2008). The focus of this chapter is on the more recent experimental literature on exclusionary practices.

[3] Early foreclosure doctrines suggest that incumbent firms can use contracts to exclude potential entrants, and, hence, reduce competition.

[4] Bolton and Whinston (1991) state that the early foreclosure doctrines were not based on solid theoretical foundations. Hence, the Chicago School critics of the foreclosure arguments deserve credit for "pointing out [their] logical flaws" (p. 207).

policies has been limited.[5] This might reflect the scarce empirical evidence of the robustness of these theories (Lafontaine and Slade 2008).[6] In the field, contractual agreements between firms and negotiation processes are typically conducted in private. Then, the factors that affect these processes and outcomes are not easily observed by policy-makers. Importantly, the low impact of economic theories on antitrust institutions might be due to the complexity of the economic models. Hovenkamp (2011, p. 82) argues that

> Antitrust writers who are untrained in economics rely heavily on noneconomic values because this enables them to have an antitrust policy without undertaking the (sometimes difficult) task of learning how the market system works. That approach may be easier in the short run, but it is calculated to have painful consequences in the long run.

We argue that experimental law and economics might strengthen the contributions of economic theories of vertical restrains to the design and implementation of antitrust law and policies. First, experimental law and economics serves to test economic theories of antitrust. Hence, it provides empirical evidence of the robustness of these theories. Second, the combination of economic theories of antitrust and experimental law and economics represents the application of scientific research methods. As a result, the likelihood of admissibility in court of economic expert testimony based on economic theories of antitrust might be strengthened. Third, experimental law and economics studies of antitrust are characterized by the construction of simple numerical implementations of more complex and abstract economic theories. These simple environments might facilitate policy-makers' understanding of economic theories of antitrust and their implications.

We start our analysis by characterizing the legal environment in which vertical restraints operate. We then outline the main components of the methods of experimental economics applied to the study of law, and discuss the contributions of experimental law and economics.

Finally, we assess the validity of our claims regarding the contributions of experimental law and economics by investigating the methodological characteristics of seminal experimental work on vertical restraints and the outcomes produced by these studies. Although the experimental literature on exclusionary vertical restraints is relatively recent, our analysis of this work supports our claims: (1) these studies identify relevant modeled and previously non-modeled factors, such as fairness considerations, and provide empirical evidence of the anticompetitive effects of these business practices; (2) the combination of theoretical and experimental work implemented in these studies follows scientific research

---

[5]    Baker (2013) argues that, "Exclusionary conduct is commonly relegated to the periphery in contemporary antitrust discourse, while price-fixing, market division and other forms of collusion are placed at the core of competition policy . . . Exclusion is routinely described as having a lesser priority than collusion *even though exclusion is well established as a serious competitive problem in both antitrust law and industrial organization economics*" (pp. 1–3; emphasis added).

[6]    Lafontaine and Slade (2008) state that "Empirical evidence [regarding vertical restraints] is somewhat fragmented . . . Given the small number of available studies, it is difficult to make definite claims about robust empirical regularities . . . In particular, some of the studies yield . . . ambiguous effects from restraints" (pp. 13, 14, 21). They conclude "Further empirical work might reveal more systematically the sets of circumstances under which particular restraints tend to be undesirable" (p. 23). See also Lafontaine and Slade (2007, 2012).

methods and, hence, might increase the likelihood of court admissibility of evidence originated on economic models of vertical restraints; and, (3) the simple environments implemented in these experimental studies certainly facilitate practitioners' understanding of the more complex economic models of vertical restraints.

Although this chapter is motivated by vertical restraint environments, the analysis presented here applies to other environments as well. Consider, for instance, the design of mechanisms to facilitate judicial resolution of business deadlocks. Game-theoretic models have been constructed to assess the equity and efficiency properties of different partnership dissolution mechanisms such as Shotguns and Auctions (see for instance Landeo and Spier 2013; Brooks et al. 2010; de Frutos and Kittsteiner 2008).[7] Experimental work on these mechanisms has facilitated practitioners' understanding of these theoretical models and their effects by providing simple numerical examinations of these theories (see Landeo and Spier 2013, 2014c, 2014d; Kittsteiner, Ockenfels, and Trhal 2012).[8]

The chapter is organized as follows. Section 2 discusses the current antitrust policies regarding vertical restraints. Section 3 describes the main components of experimental economics methods applied to the study of law, and discusses the applications of experimental law and economics to the study of vertical restraints. Section 4 is devoted to the analysis of seminal experimental law and economics studies on vertical restraints. Section 5 discusses the contributions of experimental law and economics work on vertical restraints, and concludes the chapter.

## 2. ANTITRUST LAW AND VERTICAL RESTRAINTS

The Sherman and Clayton Antitrust Acts, and the Federal Trade Commission Act encompass the main U.S. federal antitrust provisions. The Sherman Act, passed in 1890, represents the first attempt to promote healthy competition. Sections 1 and 2 of the Sherman Act contain the main provisions regarding vertical restraints. Specifically, section 1 establishes prohibition on any "contract, combination ... or conspiracy in restraint of trade." Section 2 condemns "monopolization." Commentators argue that the Sherman Act makes illegal certain acts of monopolizing, not monopoly itself. The passage of the Clayton Act in 1914 reflects an attempt to clarify the business practices that might be considered illegal. Section 3 of the Clayton Act forbids contracts imposing restraints under which customers "shall not use or deal in the goods, supplies, or other commodities of the lessor or seller," where the effect "may be substantially to lessen competition or tend to create a monopoly." This section regulates tying, bundling, and exclusive dealing.[9] Section 7 of the Clayton Act has been used to challenge vertical mergers.

---

[7] In the Shotgun mechanism, one owner proposes a price, and the other owner decides whether to buy the other party's assets or to sell her assets to the other party at that price.

[8] See also JTA LE ROUX PTY LTD as trustee for the FLR FAMILY TRUST -V- LAWSON [2013] WASC 293 for an illustration of the impact of economic theories of business deadlock resolution (Brooks, Landeo, and Spier 2010; Landeo and Spier 2014c) on Australian judicial deadlock resolution institutions (Supreme Court of Western Australia, Justice Edelman).

[9] Bundling refers to the practice of selling two products together. Tying is a form of bundling. It refers to the practice of conditioning the sale of one product (the tied product) on the buyer's

Antitrust laws are enforced by the Federal Trade Commission and the Department of Justice Antitrust Division. The Federal Trade Commission Act, passed in 1914, created the Federal Trade Commission. Section 5 of the Act represents the fundamental enforcement provision. Commentators argue that this section applies not only to the violations included in the Sherman and Clayton Acts, but also to lesser acts that might violate the "spirit of those laws" (Hovenkamp 2011). The Department of Justice Antitrust Division shares jurisdiction over civil antitrust cases with the Federal Trade Commission. However, the Antitrust Division also has the power to file criminal cases against violations of the antitrust laws.[10]

The vagueness of the Sherman and Clayton Acts explains the important role of courts in interpreting their provisions.[11] Courts evaluate vertical integration and exclusive dealing contracts using a case-by-case rule of reason. Under this rule, economic efficiencies are balanced against possible anticompetitive harm (*Continental T.V., Inc. v. GTE Sylvania, Inc.*).[12] The current antitrust policies regarding vertical integration are reflected in *Port Dock & Stone Corp. v. Oldcastle Northeast, Inc.*:[13]

> [A] complaint pleading that a defendant expanded vertically and as a result, decided to discontinue doing business with its erstwhile trading partners at the next level down, does not plead an actionable refusal to deal. Such allegations are equally consistent with the idea that the monopolist expected to perform the second level service more efficiently than the old trading partners and thus undertook the vertical integration for a valid business reason, rather than for an anticompetitive one.

The legal standard in cases of exclusive dealing contracts follows *Tampa*'s suggested rule of reason approach (*Tampa Elect. Co. v. Nashville Coal Co.*).[14] Under this rule, foreclosure on the order of 30–40 percent of market share is generally necessary to avoid judgment for the defendant. This standard has been especially relevant for cases decided after *Jefferson Parish Hosp. Dist. No. 2 v. Hyde*.[15] When the foreclosed market share is sufficiently high, *Tampa*'s rule of reason requires courts to examine additional factors, such as contract duration, likelihood of collusion in the industry and the degree to which other firms in the market also use exclusive dealing practices, nature of the distribution system and

---

agreement to purchase a second product (the tying product). Exclusive dealing contracts refer to arrangements that state that one party to the contract will deal only with the other party for some set of transactions.

[10]    The Hart-Scott-Rodino Antitrust Improvements Act, passed in 1976, represents an amendment to the Clayton Act. It requires pre-merger notification to the Department of Justice and to the Federal Trade Commission in case of large mergers.

[11]    For instance, even though promotion of healthy competition has become the center of the antitrust policy, the economic meaning of healthy competition is not well defined in the antitrust law (Whinston 2006).

[12]    433 US 36, 97 S.Ct. 2549, 53 L. Ed. 2d 568 – Supreme Court, 1977.

[13]    507 F3d 117, 125, 2d Cir., 2007.

[14]    365 U.S. 320, 81 S.Ct. 623, 1961; on remand, 214 F. Supp. 647, M.D.Tenn., 1963.

[15]    466 U.S. 2, 44, 104 S.Ct.; Note 22, 466 U.S. at 45, 97 S.Ct. at 1575, O'Connor, J., concurring: "Exclusive dealing is an unreasonable restraint on trade only when a significant fraction of buyers or sellers are frozen out of a market by the exclusive deal." The concurrers concluded that 30 percent coverage was inadequate because they could not find evidence of anticompetitive effects (Hovenkamp 2011).

distribution alternatives remaining available after exclusive dealing, and other pro- and anticompetitive factors.

Tying practices, on the other hand, are assessed using a modified *per se* rule approach. Courts have developed tests for assessing whether tying arrangements are *per se* unlawful. Evidence of coercion, sufficient economic power in the tying market, and anticompetitive effects in the tied market are the main factors considered in these tests. For instance, in *Yentsch v. Texaco, Inc.*,[16] the court applied a five-part test (Hovenkamp 2011, p. 435):

(1)   There must be separate tying and tied products.
(2)   There must be "evidence of actual coercion by the seller that in fact forced the buyer to accept the tied product."
(3)   The seller must possess "sufficient economic power in the tying product market to coerce purchaser acceptance of the tied product."
(4)   There must be "anticompetitive effects in the tied market."
(5)   There must be "involvement of a 'not substantial' amount of interstate commerce in the tied product market."

An exception to the application of the modified *per se* rule in cases of tying practices is represented by the D.C. Circuit in *United States v. Microsoft Corp.* case.[17] The court concluded that the bundling of software applications into a software computer operating system qualified for a rule of reason treatment. They stated that "applying *per se* analysis ... creates risks of error and of deterring welfare-enhancing innovation" (Hovenkamp 2011, pp. 89–90).

An adequate application of the case-by-case and *per se* rules by courts requires good knowledge of the factors that affect the anticompetitive effects of vertical restraints. Economic models certainly contribute to the understanding of the effects of vertical restraint institutions. As we discuss in the next section, experimental law and economics might strengthen the influence of economics models of vertical restraints on the design and implementation of antitrust law and policies.

## 3.   EXPERIMENTAL LAW AND ECONOMICS AND ANTITRUST

Experimental law and economics refers to the application of experimental economics methods to the study of legal institutions and business practices relevant to the design of legal institutions.[18] As Falk and Heckman (2009) argue, "[c]ausal knowledge requires

---

[16]   630 F2d. 46, 56–57, 2d Cir., 1980.
[17]   253 F.3d 34. 90, D.C.Cir.; cert, denied, 534 U.S. 952, 122 S.Ct. 350, 2001.
[18]   See Smith (1976), Plott (1982), Roth (1986, 1995), and Davis and Holt (1993) for seminal discussions about experimental economics methods. See Croson (2005), Croson and Gächter (2010) for more recent excellent discussions of experimental economics methods. See Roth (2008) for a discussion of the contributions of experimental economics methods to market design. See Hoffman and Spitzer (1985), McAdams (2000), Croson (2002, 2009), Talley and Camerer (2007), and Arlen and Talley (2008) for surveys regarding the application of experimental economics methods to law and economics.

controlled variation" (p. 537). Controlled laboratory experiments provide an optimal "methodology for advancing causal knowledge" (p. 535). The combination of experimental economics methods and economic modeling represents the application of scientific research methods.

## 3.1   Types of Studies

Three basic types of experimental law and economics studies might be applied to the analysis of antitrust institutions:[19] (1) experimental studies that test economic theories of antitrust; (2) experimental work that assesses the effectiveness of specific antitrust policies before these policies are implemented in the field (testbed policy experiments);[20] and, (3) experiments that test economic anomalies (for instance cognitive biases) that might impede the effectiveness of antitrust policies.[21]

Experimental law and economics work on vertical restraints involves studies conducted to test theoretical models of antitrust.[22] The main features that these studies should encompass are as follows. First, the experimental settings must capture the theoretical assumptions.[23] However, the environments should be simple enough to ensure subjects' understanding of the environments and tasks. Second, economic theories involve choices and economic consequences of these choices. The relationship between subjects' payoffs and choices in the experimental settings (i.e., the pay-for-performance schemes) should be aligned with the incentives encompassed in the theoretical models.[24]

Third, economic theories consist of abstract representations applicable to different

---

[19]   This classification follows Roth (1986) and Croson (2002). Roth (1986) presents a general classification of experimental economics studies. Croson (2002) applies Roth's (1986) classification to experimental law and economics studies.

[20]   For instance, in their seminal work on testbed policy experiments, Hong and Plott (1982) experimentally assess the effects of a policy change proposed by the Interstate Commerce Commission. (See Plott (1994) for a general discussion of testbed experiments.) The experimental design used in these types of studies involves a degree of context and draws from subject pools that are aligned with the environments in which the policies will be implemented. The information provided by these studies might help to improve the design of antitrust institutions.

[21]   "[A]n economic anomaly is a result inconsistent with the present economics paradigm . . . An empirical result is anomalous if it is difficult to 'rationalize,' or if implausible assumptions are necessary to explain it within the paradigm" (Thaler 1987, p. 198). In these types of studies, the degree of context and subject pools should be aligned with the real-life settings that trigger these anomalies. See for instance, Babcock et al.'s (1995) study on self-serving bias and pretrial bargaining, and Landeo's (2009) study of cognitive biases and tort reform. See Thaler (1992) for more general applications of these types of experiments.

[22]   Although the other two types of experimental work have not been used to study anticompetitive vertical restraints, their contributions might be significant.

[23]   This implies an experimental environment with a high degree of internal validity.

[24]   As noted by Smith (1976, p. 275), the experimental design should ensure control over the "[subjective] values [associated with the possible choices] . . . Such control can be achieved by using a reward structure to induce prescribed monetary value on actions." This concept is referred to as "induced valuation." A common criticism of experimental economics methods is related to the size of subjects' payments, and the degree of parallelism with the economic consequences of choices in the field. As noted by Falk and Heckman (2009, p. 537), "The effects of varying stake size are mixed and seem to depend on concrete experimental contexts." The implementation of additional

situations and individuals. Although the experimental settings should involve minimal context, the degree of context and labels should guarantee subjects' understanding of the experimental environment, tasks, choices, and consequences of these choices.[25] In addition, no specific requirements are imposed on the subject pools. Experiments in economics generally involve undergraduate students.[26] Fourth, experiments in economics do not use deception. As Croson (2005) states, this requirement is aligned with the theoretical assumption that agents understand and believe the relationship between their actions and their payoffs.[27]

### 3.1.1 Experimental law and economics contributions

We argue that experimental law and economics studies of vertical restraints might strengthen the influence of economic theory on the design and implementation of antitrust policies. First, experimental law and economics studies might advance the knowledge of the factors that affect the anticompetitive effects of these business practices. Specifically, experimental studies conducted to test the theoretical predictions of economic models of antitrust might provide evidence of the robustness of these theories. If the economic theories do not work in these carefully controlled experimental settings (which replicate the theoretical assumptions and strategic environments), there is little hope that these theories would work in more complex field environments (Plott 1999). These studies might also reveal previously non-modeled factors that influence the impact of vertical restraints, and hence provide useful feedback to theorists.

Second, experimental law and economics might increase the likelihood of admissibility in court of the evidence provided by economic experts.[28] Under the *Frye* standard (*Frye v. United States*),[29] the admissibility of expert evidence was based on whether or not the particular opinion of a testifying expert was generally accepted. Kobayashi (1997) argues that "[i]n practical terms, this often meant that the theory has been published in a peer reviewed journal, a standard that game theory easily passes" (p. 414). However, in 1993, the Supreme Court rejected the *Frye* test (*Daubert v. Merrell Dow Pharmaceuticals, Inc.*).[30] A reliability standard under Rule 702 of the Federal Rules of Evidence was then established. This new test requires that the evidence (i) is "scientific knowledge" (i.e.,

---

experimental treatments that allow for different payoff levels might be recommended to test the robustness of findings related to certain research questions. See also Camerer and Hogarth (1999).

[25] The lab implementation of a theoretical setting generally involves the use of a simple context, that is, a simple environment where the theory applies. For instance, the experimental environment might resemble a simple market setting. Labels such as player A and player B might be used to describe the roles played by the subjects. The use of minimal context ensures control over subjective interpretations of labels, and allows for replicability of the study by other researchers.

[26] Findings from experimental studies devoted to analyzing the effects of subject pools suggest that the behavior of undergraduate students and other populations, in context-free experimental environments, are not significantly different (Fréchette 2015).

[27] This element represents a fundamental difference between experiments in psychology and economics.

[28] See Kirkwood (1988).

[29] 293 F. 1013, 1923.

[30] 509 U.S. 579, 1993.

generated through scientific methods), and (ii) "will assist the trier of fact to understand or determine a fact in issue."

Economic testimony based solely on theoretical models (without empirical or experimental evidence) might fail the scientific method requirement of the *Daubert* test. In fact, this test has been previously applied to exclude or limit expert economic testimony (see for instance, *Ohio v. Louis Trauth Dairy, Inc.*, 925 F. Supp. 1247, 1996). Hence, the combination of experimental work with economic modeling might strengthen the contributions of economic theory to the formulation of antitrust law and policies.

Finally, we claim that experimental law and economics might facilitate policy-makers' understanding of economic theories of antitrust. Regarding courts' knowledge of economic models of antitrust, Langenfeld and Alexander (2011, p. 25) indicate that:

> experts need to educate the court about standard economic methodologies. For example, in *Concord Boat*, the court stated that it did not find references to the Cournot economic model in previous cases. Virtually all economists or lawyers versed in antitrust are at least aware that the Cournot model is well recognized.

This is, of course, an extreme example of the divorce between policy-making and academic work on antitrust. However, the complexity of the new economic theories of antitrust might preclude policy-makers from understanding these frameworks. We argue that experimental law and economics represents an effective tool to educate policy-makers on economic theories of antitrust. Experimental economics studies involve replications of theoretical environments using simple numerical examinations. Hence, these settings might facilitate practitioners' understanding of the contributions of complex mathematical models of antitrust.

## 4.   EXPERIMENTAL STUDIES ON EXCLUSIONARY VERTICAL RESTRAINTS

This section assesses the validity of our claims regarding the contributions of experimental law and economics by examining seminal experimental work on exclusionary vertical restraints.

### 4.1   Vertical Integration and Market Foreclosure

Vertical integration involves situations in which vertically-related activities that could be located in separate businesses are combined and integrated "under one roof"' in a single business.[31] Perfectly legitimate purposes might explain vertical integration. Vertical integration might allow firms to exploit technological complementarities,

---

[31]   A wide range of vertical arrangements are alternatives to vertical integration. In these environments, legally enforceable contracts limit the behavior of the parties. These arrangements are termed *vertical restraints*. By giving one party some control over the other party's actions, these arrangements are a form of partial vertical integration. These practices include exclusive dealing contracts, and tying and bundling, among others, and are discussed next.

reduce transaction costs (Coase 1937), gain control over production processes and preclude opportunistic behavior, overcome informational imperfections, and internalize externalities.[32] Profit-maximizing goals will determine the firm's decision regarding "making" (vertically integration) or "buying." Vertical integration might also serve anticompetitive purposes. It might be used by a firm as a tool to create or maintain market power.

The leverage theory of foreclosure states that vertical integration might be used by firms to extend their market power to other markets. As a result, vertical integration might harm downstream firms by precluding access to inputs. Similarly, this business practice might negatively affect upstream firms by removing supply opportunities. The insights from this theory have been applied in important antitrust cases. For instance, in *Brown Shoe Company v. United States*,[33] Brown (a manufacturer of shoes) wanted to integrate with a shoe retailer. The Supreme Court concluded that the merger reduced competition by precluding access by competitors to the share of the market served by the acquired retailer. As a result, this merger was held illegal. The Chicago School (Bork 1978; Posner 1976) criticized this Court ruling by stating that market power in one market could not profitably be extended into other markets. Specifically, Bork (1978) argued that it would not be profitable for Brown to exclude rivals in the downstream market because the benefits from this exclusion to Brown would be offset by the losses to the shoe retailer.[34]

More recently, economists have used game-theoretic models to show that vertical integration might serve to protect rather than extend market power, and lead to market foreclosure (Ordover, Salop, and Saloner 1990; Hart and Tirole 1990; Bolton and Whinston 1991, 1993).[35] In these settings, a monopolist in an upstream market, faced with competition in the downstream market, may not be fully able to exploit its monopoly power because it may not be able to credibly commit to downstream firms that it will restrict output. Anticipating this situation, downstream firms will not accept contracts that allow the producer to fully extract monopoly profits.[36] Vertical integration resolves

---

[32] Consider, for instance, the case of "double marginalization" (Tirole 1988). Double marginalization refers to a situation in which two independent firms (upstream and downstream), with market power in their respective markets, apply markups in their prices (i.e., set prices above their marginal costs). Pricing above the marginal cost generates a deadweight loss. Due to the application of markups by both firms, deadweight losses occur twice. See also Riordan (2008).

[33] 370 U.S. 294, 1962.

[34] Forcing the shoe retailer to exclusively sell Brown's product (i.e., to stop doing business with upstream firms that offer less costly products) would generate losses in profits to the shoe retailer. Brown, on the other hand, would obtain gains related to increased sales in the downstream market. Bork (1978) argues that the retailer's losses would exceed the upstream firm's benefits. As a result, it would not be in the interest of the vertically integrated firm to foreclose upstream rivals.

[35] See also Riordan and Salop (1995) and Riordan (1998). See Rey and Tirole (2001) for more recent work.

[36] The insights derived from these theories can be illustrated with a simple example. Consider an upstream monopolist and two downstream firms, firms A and B. The monopolist cannot credibly commit not to serve firm A's rival (firm B). This is because, after contracting with firm A, the monopolist will benefit from serving firm B as well. Anticipating the increase in competition and the lower profits, firm A will be willing to pay less to the monopolist. As a result, the upstream firm will not be able to make full monopoly profits.

the monopolist's commitment problem,[37] and, hence, enables the upstream monopolist to fully exploit its market power.[38]

### 4.1.1   Experimental evidence

Martin, Normann, and Snyder (2001) experimentally assess the anticompetitive effects of vertical integration.[39] Their experimental environment replicates Rey and Tirole's (2001) theoretical model of vertical integration involving an upstream monopoly producer of an essential input and two downstream firms that compete in the final good market. In their simple experimental setting, a manufacturer (the monopolist) and one or two retailers (the downstream firms) play a bargaining game: the manufacturer proposes a contract and the retailers decide whether to accept or reject the contract.

The following experimental treatments are implemented. First, the integration treatments include integration and no-integration settings. The no-integration environment encompasses a single upstream firm that produces an input at constant average and marginal costs and two downstream firms that convert each unit of input into a unit of a homogeneous final good. The upstream monopolist can simultaneously make take-it-or-leave-it contract offers to each of the downstream firms specifying the quantity and fixed payment demanded. In the next stage, downstream firms simultaneously decide whether to accept or reject the offers. The integration environment involves an integrated firm (upstream and downstream units) and a non-integrated downstream firm. Theory predicts that the integrated firm will commit to selling the monopoly quantity through its downstream subsidiary and not supplying the other downstream firm. Hence, market foreclosure against the non-integrated downstream firm will occur in equilibrium.

Second, the contract type treatments involve public and private contracts. In the case of public contracts, the contract offers become publicly known before downstream firms make a decision. Public contracts might serve as a commitment device (the upstream monopolist can earn the monopoly profit by publicly offering half the monopoly output at half the monopoly profit to each downstream firm). If, however, the contracts are negotiated privately (downstream firms do not observe the contract offered to other downstream firms), theory predicts that the upstream monopolist will not be able to earn the monopoly profit without vertical integration.[40]

---

[37]   Consider vertical integration between the upstream firm and downstream firm A. The integrated firm will internalize firm A's losses associated with more competition. Then, the integrated firm will have an incentive not to serve downstream firm B.

[38]   An important assumption in Hart and Tirole (1990) is that contracts are both bilateral and private.

[39]   See Mason and Phillips (2000) for an interesting experimental study regarding the effects of vertical integration on collusion.

[40]   Under secret contracts, there are multiple perfect Bayesian equilibria. The theoretical predictions depend on the out-of-equilibrium beliefs of downstream firms concerning the contract offered to their rivals. Under passive beliefs (i.e., when receiving an out-of-equilibrium offer, each downstream firm believes that its rival receives the equilibrium offer), output is higher, and the upstream monopolist's profits are lower than in the joint-profit-maximizing outcome. Under symmetric beliefs (i.e., when receiving an out-of-equilibrium offer, each downstream firm believes that its rival received the same out-of-equilibrium offer), output is set at the monopoly level and the joint-profit-maximizing outcome is achieved.

Third, the interaction treatments include one-shot and finite repetitions. The authors claim that finite repetitions might act as a commitment device for the monopolist, and hence, generate market foreclosure even in the case of private contracts.[41] The interaction treatments are implemented using random and fixed groupings, respectively.[42]

Martin, Normann, and Snyder's (2001) findings suggest that vertical integration might induce market foreclosure. These results also indicate the presence of a monopolist's commitment problem, and that vertical integration and public contracts might serve as commitment devices. In fact, the total output and profit are similar and close to the monopoly level in the integrated and non-integrated/public contract environments.

Interestingly, Martin, Normann, and Snyder's experimental results differ from the theoretical predictions regarding the division of profits between upstream and downstream firms. Theoretically, it is expected that the upstream firm will have all the bargaining power (by making take-it-leave-it offers), and hence, will get all of the industry profits. However, their findings under the two non-integrated settings, with public and private contracts, suggest that the upstream monopolist obtains only a fraction of the industry profits. These results are aligned with the presence of non-monetary preferences observed in previous experimental work on ultimatum environments.[43] In these settings, the strategic anticipation of the receiver's rejection of inequitable offers (due to non-monetary preferences) induces the proposer to make more generous offers (Hoffman et al. 1994). These findings are also consistent with recent work on more general bargaining environments, where non-monetary preferences might induce more equitable allocations of the pie (Landeo and Spier 2014a). The unpredicted bargaining effects observed by Martin, Normann, and Snyder (2001) provide an additional rationale for the choice of vertical integration by monopolists.

Their experimental design also allows them to indirectly investigate the nature of out-of-equilibrium beliefs under private offers by assessing the downstream acceptance decision as a function of the contract offer. Their findings suggest that the beliefs of non-integrated downstream firms are heterogeneous (between passive and symmetric beliefs). This finding leads to the development of an empirically relevant extension to the theory. Finally, Martin, Normann, and Snyder's (2001) results do not provide support for reputational effects elicited by finitely-repeated interactions.[44] Extensions of this work

---

[41]   If the game is played repeatedly, the upstream firm might be able to form a reputation for low output (i.e., to convince downstream firm A that it will not serve downstream firm B). Downstream firm A will then accept higher prices. As a result, the upstream monopolist will have an incentive to restrict its output, and hence, credibly commit to output restriction.

[42]   All treatments involve 10 rounds. In the random grouping treatments, groups of three people are randomly chosen every round; in the fixed grouping treatments, grouping is decided at the beginning of the first round and stays fixed throughout all rounds.

[43]   Ultimatum games involve two players, a proposer and a receiver. The proposer makes an offer to the receiver (i.e., he proposes an allocation of 10 dollars between the two players). After observing the offer, the receiver decides whether to accept or reject it. In case of rejection, each player receives zero dollars. Under standard preferences, the theory predicts that the proposer will offer zero dollars plus a penny to the receiver and the receiver will accept the offer. See Güth, Schmittberger, and Schwartz (1996) for seminal work on ultimatum games.

[44]   In theory, finite repetitions allow the formation of reputation, and hence, solve the monopolist's commitment problem (see footnote 41). It is then expected that the findings from the one-shot

might involve the implementation of the reputation conditions under infinitely-repeated interactions.[45]

Normann (2011) experimentally investigates whether reputational considerations and the vertical integration institution might act as informal commitment devices for the upstream firm, and hence, induce market foreclosure. His experimental setting replicates Ordover, Salop, and Saloner's (1990) theoretical environment. This theoretical framework involves four players, two upstream firms and two downstream firms. The sequence of moves is as follows: the upstream firms decide whether to vertically integrate, the upstream firms simultaneously set input prices, and the downstream firms simultaneously set good prices (after observing input costs). Vertical integration would be profitable for the upstream firm if it could commit not to compete in the upstream market. This strategy would induce higher input prices, and hence, raise downstream rivals' cost.[46] Given that this strategic setting does not involve formal commitment (in the form of incentives), market foreclosure should not be observed in equilibrium.[47]

Normann's experimental design focuses on the behavior of the upstream firms. Hence, it abstracts from the downstream market. The following treatments are implemented. The vertical integration treatments encompass vertically integrated and non-vertically integrated environments. In both environments, two upstream firms simultaneously decide the upstream price. In the integration treatment, the payoffs for the players include an additional component related to the downstream unit. Following Martin, Normann, and Snyder (2001), the reputational treatments involve one-shot and finite repetition environments. In theory, it is expected that neither the vertical integration institution nor the presence of finitely-repeated interactions will solve the commitment problem of the upstream firm. In fact, a Bertrand equilibrium in which each firm charges the minimum price should hold.

Normann's (2011) findings suggest that prices are significantly higher in markets where vertical integration is allowed (compared to non-integrated settings), that is, the integrated firm's pricing behavior is less competitive than that of a non-integrated firm.

---

and finite-repetition treatments will be different. Martin, Normann and Snyder's (2001) results do not suggest significant differences between these two treatments.

[45]   The authors argue that Selten and Stoecker's (1988) findings on prisoner's dilemma settings suggest that infinitely-repeated interactions do not have a strong impact on subjects' behavior (compared to finitely-repeated interactions). However, recent studies indicate that infinitely-repeated interactions actually have significant effects (Dal Bó 2005). See also Landeo and Spier (2014b).

[46]   If the integrated firm withdraws from the upstream market (i.e., the integrated firm stops serving downstream firms), competition in the upstream market would be reduced. As a result, downstream rival firms would face higher input prices.

[47]   Ordover, Salop, and Saloner (1990) present this argument. Hart and Tirole (1990) and Reiffen (1992) demonstrate that, even though foreclosure would be a profitable strategy for the integrated firm in Ordover, Salop, and Saloner's (1990) environment, it is not an optimal strategy. The integrated firm still has an incentive to compete in the input market. Given that Ordover, Salop, and Saloner's (1990) setting does not endogenously elicit commitment, their claims hold only by imposing the assumption that commitment is present. Hart and Tirole (1990) argue, however, that this assumption is strong: "Commitment is unlikely to be believable" in these environments. Normann (2011) provides a refined analysis of Ordover, Salop, and Saloner's (1990) theoretical environment.

However, integrated firms do not completely foreclose the input market (i.e., firms do not completely refrain from competing in the input market). These results hold in both the one-shot and finitely-repeated environments. The lack of evidence for market foreclosure indicates that the commitment problem of the upstream firm (pointed out by Hart and Tirole 1990, and Reiffen 1992) cannot be resolved by implementing informal commitment devices such as a vertical integration institution without a formal commitment or reputational considerations elicited through finite interactions.[48] These findings are aligned with previous experimental studies on commitment (Huck and Müller 2000; Reynolds 2000; Cason and Sharma 2001; Martin, Normann, and Snyder 2001).[49]

## 4.2 Anticompetitive Effects of Exclusive Dealing Contracts

Exclusive dealing contracts encompass arrangements that state that one party to the contract will deal only with the other party for some set of transactions and include transfers of money from one party to the other in exchange for exclusivity. The literature on exclusive dealing contracts underscores the use of such contracts as a market foreclosure mechanism.

Beginning in the 1950s, scholars identified with the Chicago School argued that exclusive dealing contracts could not be profitably employed by incumbents to exclude more efficient rivals (Director and Levi 1956; Posner 1976; Bork 1978).[50] Hence, exclusive dealing arrangements would be adopted only when they served legitimate business purposes, such as preventing free riding and protecting relationship-specific investment.[51] Recently, scholars have used the tools of game theory and information economics to show that exclusive contracts may be adopted for purely anticompetitive reasons. In fact, rational firms would, in some circumstances, use such contracts to exclude rivals and reduce competition.

Rasmusen, Ramseyer and Wiley (1991) and Segal and Whinston (2000) demonstrate that an incumbent monopolist can use exclusive contracts (modeled as transfers from the incumbent to a buyer in exchange for the buyer's promise not to buy from any other seller) to deter efficient entry when there are economies of scale in production.[52] Entry becomes

---

[48]   See Martin, Normann, and Snyder (2001) regarding the elicitation of reputational considerations through finite interactions.

[49]   Although the findings are not aligned with the equilibrium predictions, they are consistent with a quantal-response equilibrium analysis of the game (McKelvey and Palfrey 1998), a behavioral game-theory concept. Quantal response equilibrium takes decision errors into account, so that players do not choose the best response with probability one but choose better choices more frequently. In the context of this study, quantal-response equilibrium implies that integrated firms do indeed price less competitively than non-integrated ones. Integrated firms still compete in the input market (that is, there is no market foreclosure).

[50]   Although the incumbent seller would want to discourage the entry of competitors in order to protect market share and profits, buyers would prefer to facilitate entry (since entry would lead to lower prices). Given the amount of money that the monopolist would need to pay to convince the buyers to agree on exclusive deals (their increased consumer surplus from entry), this strategy would be unprofitable for the monopolist.

[51]   See Kaplow (1985) for a comprehensive discussion of this literature.

[52]   The theoretical environment involves three main stages: the contracting stage (where the monopolist makes offers to both buyers, and, after observing both offers, the buyers simultaneously

unprofitable when a sufficiently high number of buyers accept the contracts.[53] When the incumbent seller cannot discriminate and must make the same offer to all buyers, there is multiplicity of equilibria: both exclusion and entry might occur in equilibrium. When the incumbent monopolist can discriminate and make better offers to some buyers than to others, Segal and Whinston (2000) demonstrate that the unique equilibrium involves exclusion.

Important antitrust cases involve exclusive dealing practices. For instance, in *In re Beer Distribution Antitrust Litigation*,[54] Anheuser-Bush was accused of requiring distributors to exclusively distribute Anheuser-Bush products. More recently, Microsoft was accused of requiring computer manufacturers, internet service providers, and software producers to exclude, at least partially, Netscape's Navigator Web browser in favor of its own Internet Explorer browser.[55]

### 4.2.1   Experimental evidence
Landeo and Spier (2009) experimentally study the factors that affect the anticompetitive effects of exclusive dealing contracts. They replicate Rasmusen, Ramseyer, and Whiley's (1991) and Segal and Whinston's (2000) strategic environments in a laboratory setting.[56] Their simple experimental environment involves a two-stage game with three players (an incumbent monopolist and two downstream buyers). The exclusive dealing setting consists of transfers from the monopolist to the buyers in exchange for exclusivity. Specifically, in the first stage, the incumbent monopolist offers a transfer to each buyer. In the second stage, each buyer decides whether to accept or reject the offer. When the monopolist cannot discriminate and is constrained to propose equal offers to both buyers, the strategic environment resembles a coordination game with endogenous payoffs, in which equilibrium with exclusion, and equilibrium with entry might occur.[57] When the

---

decide whether to accept their respective offers); the entry stage (where the potential entrant decides whether to enter the market); and the pricing stage (where market prices are determined).

[53]   Kaplow (1985) critiqued the Chicago School using a similar logic.

[54]   188 F.R.D. 557, 1999.

[55]   253 F.3d 34, 2001. Additional cases involving exclusive contracts include *United States v. Visa U.S.A.* (344 F.3d 229 (2003)), in which Visa was attacked for its agreements with banks that prohibited them from distributing rival credit cards, including American Express and Discover; *United States v. Dentsply* (399 F.3d 181 (2001)), in which Dentsply, the dominant maker of artificial teeth, was accused of illegally excluding rival manufacturers through exclusive agreements with dental wholesalers; and *Conwood v. United States Tobacco* (290 F.3d 768 (2002)), in which United States Tobacco, the dominant producer of moist snuff, was accused of illegally excluding rivals using exclusive contracts with retailers. See Kwoka and White (2009).

[56]   Landeo and Spier (2009) focus their experimental design on Rasmusen, Ramseyer, and Wiley's (1991) and Segal and Whinston's (2000) contracting stage. This design strategy is aligned with the purpose of the study (to assess the factors that influence the determinants of exclusion) with the goal of minimizing subjects' cognitive effort.

[57]   Specifically, the strategic setting resembles a stag-hunt game (also called "an assurance game"). Strategic uncertainty arises in this environment: although both buyers are better off by coordinating on rejection (which allows the potential entrant to enter the market, to compete with the monopolist, and to bring the prices down to the monopolist's marginal cost), each buyer will reject the contract only if he is sufficiently sure the other buyer will also reject the contract. See Ochs (1995) for a survey of seminal experimental work on coordination games. See Harsanyi and

incumbent monopolist can discriminate and make a better offer to one of the buyers, the strategic environment involves a unique equilibrium with exclusion. Divide-and-conquer strategies allow the incumbent seller to exploit the negative externalities between the buyers and foreclose the market.[58]

Landeo and Spier (2009) first study the effects of discriminatory strategies (strategies under which the incumbent monopolist makes different offers to the two buyers in an attempt to induce market foreclosure). Two offer treatments are implemented, no discrimination (where the incumbent is constrained to make equal offers) and discrimination (where the incumbent's offers can be different). Second, building on previous findings from experimental economics and social psychology regarding fairness (Loewenstein, Thompson, and Bazerman 1989),[59] reciprocity (Sobel 2005), and the role of intentionality on triggering social preferences (Blount 1995), Landeo and Spier (2009) explore the effect of payoff endogeneity (operationalized through the comparison between contracts designed by other human subjects versus contracts exogenously provided) on exclusion. Two buyer-payoff treatments are implemented, endogenous and exogenous. Under the endogenous conditions, a human seller chooses the offers. The seller gets a payoff equal to zero in the case of rejection by both buyers. Under the exogenous-payoffs conditions, a computer exogenously makes the offers.[60] Subjects are informed that the computer makes the offers.

Third, they assess the effects of non-binding communication between buyers (Aumann 1990; Farrell and Rabin 1996; Duffy and Feltovich 2002; Cooper et al. 1992; Crawford 1998; Blume and Ortmann 2007). Two communication treatments are implemented, no-communication and two-way buyer-buyer communication (where the buyers state their intentions before deciding whether to accept or reject the exclusive deals). The theoretical predictions suggest that divide and conquer strategies will increase the likelihood of market foreclosure. In theory, neither communication nor intentionality will affect the exclusion rate.

Landeo and Spier's (2009) findings indicate that exclusion may be surprisingly easy for incumbent firms to achieve. Even in the absence of discrimination, when adequate communication channels were not available, subjects failed to coordinate on their preferred equilibria and entry was deterred. Second, coordination was particularly elusive when the incumbent seller had a human identity. The human face of a sales representative (an agent for the seller) might elicit fairness and reciprocity from the agents representing the buyers, and facilitate the exclusion of faceless rivals (in the event of contracts perceived as fair). These results underscore the importance of the seller's intentionality. Third, their

---

Selten (1988) for a theoretical discussion of equilibrium selection mechanisms in coordination games.

[58]  In this setting, entry occurs if both buyers reject the contract. Hence, the acceptance of the contract by one buyer negatively affects the likelihood of entry and the payoff of the other buyer. In the literature, this is referred to as a negative externality between the buyers.

[59]  See Fehr and Schmidt (1999) and Bolton and Ockenfels (1998, 2000) for theoretical studies of social preferences.

[60]  Each exogenous session is matched with a previously run endogenous session, and the computer is programmed to follow the pattern of offers made by the human seller in the corresponding endogenous session.

experimental analysis suggests that, better communication among the buyers induces more generous offers from the seller and a higher likelihood of entry, when discrimination is not allowed. Hence, communication among non-competing buyers might serve the public interest by facilitating entry. Fourth, as predicted by Segal and Whinston (2000), their results indicate that the ability of the incumbent to discriminate in the contract terms offered to the buyers enhances the effectiveness of exclusionary practices, when buyers are allowed to communicate.

Landeo and Spier (2012) assess the robustness of Landeo and Spier's (2009) findings regarding the effects of payoff endogeneity to the explicit presence of a potential entrant, and explore the effects of communication between the potential entrant and the buyers about the incumbent seller's offers and the likelihood of exclusion.[61] Their strategic environment involves a four-player, two-stage game. In addition to the roles of seller and buyers, their experimental environment includes the role of a potential entrant (a fourth passive player). The potential entrant is a captive player because her payoff depends on the decisions of the incumbent monopolist (the contract designer) and the two buyers. The explicit presence of a potential entrant might induce the buyers and the strategic seller to consider this fourth party, and hence it might affect the exclusionary power of exclusive dealing contracts. The entrant gets a payoff greater than zero only in the case of rejection by both buyers. Thus, the explicit presence of an entrant might act as a focal point device, that is, "a signal that coordinates [buyers' mutual] expectations" (Schelling 1960, p. 54).[62] Hence, it might induce buyers to choose their preferred equilibrium (the entry equilibrium).

Their experimental design encompasses two buyer-payoff treatments, endogenous payoffs (contract offers decided by a human seller), and exogenous payoffs (contract offers exogenously administered by the computer). They also consider two communication treatments; no-communication and one-way unstructured entrant-buyers communication (where the potential entrant sends unstructured messages to both buyers after the buyers receive the proposal from the seller but before the buyers make their decisions).

Landeo and Spier's (2012) results indicate that Landeo and Spier's (2009) findings regarding the effect of endogeneity are robust in terms of the explicit presence of a potential entrant. In fact, endogeneity significantly increases the likelihood of exclusion. Buyers are more likely to accept exclusive contracts when they are endogenously designed by a human seller (rather than exogenously generated). Second, communication between the entrant and the buyers reduces the likelihood of exclusion, and induces more generous sellers' offers. Third, Landeo and Spier's findings suggest that the explicit presence

---

[61]    See Bohnet and Frey (1999) and Andreoni and Rao (2011) for evidence of the effects of communication on enhancing social proximity. Although Landeo and Spier's (2012) experimental environment is characterized by anonymity, communication might still reduce social distance by allowing buyers to learn more about the potential entrants. Schelling (1968), as cited in Bohnet and Frey (1999, p. 339), states that "the more we know, the more we care." See also Hoffman et al. (1996) and Charness, Haruby, and Sonsino (2007).

[62]    Schelling argues that "[coordination problems] provide some focal point for a concerted choice, some clue to coordination, some rationale for the convergence of the participants' mutual expectations" (Schelling 1960, p. 90). He also states that "[a] prime characteristic of . . . focal points is some kind of prominence or conspicuousness" (Schelling 1960, p. 57).

of an entrant might act as a focal-point mechanism in exogenous-payoffs environments, facilitating buyers' coordination on their preferred equilibrium (entry equilibrium).

Smith (2011) and Boone, Müller, and Suetens (2014) provide additional experimental tests of Rasmusen, Ramseyer, and Wiley's (1991) and Segal and Whinston's (2000) environments. Smith's (2011) experimental design involves a multi-player three-stage game. Specifically, she studies the effects of the number of buyers, size of the minimum efficient scale (percentage of buyers required to exclude), and non-binding communication between buyers in a non-discriminatory offer setting (i.e., in a setting in which the incumbent seller is restricted to make the same offers to all buyers). Smith's (2011) findings suggest that, while the number of buyers is not shown to significantly impact exclusion rates, a higher fraction of signed buyers necessary for exclusion significantly decreases the exclusion rate. These findings might suggest that industries with larger fixed costs, smaller technological advantages of the potential entrant, and larger-scale efficiencies would be more likely to elicit foreclosure effects due to exclusive dealing. Consistent with Landeo and Spier's (2009) findings, her results suggest that exclusion rates are lower when buyers engage in non-binding communication. Boone, Müller, and Suetens (2014) study the effects of sequential offers, private contracting, and discrimination, implementing Segal and Whinston's (2000) environment in the lab. They find that discrimination increases exclusion rates only when offers are both sequential and private. Contrary to the theoretical predictions, their results suggest that exclusion through sequential offers is a costly strategy. Buyers more frequently reject low offers, which induces sellers to be more generous in their offers.

### 4.3  The Leverage Theory of Tying and Bundling

Bundling refers to the practice of selling two products together. Pure bundling implies that the products are available only as a bundle. Under mixed bundling, the products are available on both a stand-alone basis and as a bundle. Furthermore, the price of the bundle is lower than the sum of the two individual prices. Tying is a form of mixed bundling. It refers to the practice of conditioning the sale of one product (the tied product) on the buyer's agreement to purchase a second product (the tying product).[63]

Tying and bundling practices can be used to ensure quality and improve overall performance of a product or a service. These practices might also serve to price discriminate (*Illinois Tool Works Inc. v. Independent Ink, Inc.*),[64] and to raise prices for the combined package (*Eastman Kodak Co. v. Image Technical Services, Inc.*).[65] Importantly, tying and bundling might be used to raise rivals' costs, and create barriers to entry (*United Stated v. Microsoft*).[66]

Courts have condemned tying practices under the leverage theory, which states that a

---

[63]  For instance, if a printer is compatible with only the seller's ink cartridges, then the seller conditions the sale of the ink cartridges (the tied product) on the purchase of a printer (the typing product).

[64]  547 U.S. 28, 2006.

[65]  504 U.S. 451, 112 S.Ct. 2072, 1992.

[66]  253 F.3d 34, 2001. An additional antitrust case involving tying and bundling is *LePage's Inc. v. 3M* (324 F.3d 141, 2003).

firm with monopoly power in one market can use its leverage to engage in tying in order to monopolize a second market. Chicago School scholars (Director and Levi 1956; Bowman 1957; Posner 1976; Bork 1978) challenged this view.[67] They claimed that leveraging could not increase the monopolist's profits. Hence, if a monopolist did employ tying, his motivation could not be to leverage his market power. Instead, the motivation could be related to efficiency or to price discrimination. Whinston (1990) demonstrates that the Chicago School's criticism of the leveraging theory holds only if the competition level in the tied market is not affected. By tying, Whinston argues, the monopolist can reduce sales of its tied-good market competitor, and, hence, lower the competitor's profits below the level that would justify continued operation. Hence, tying can lead to monopolization of the tied-good market, and exclusion of the competitor.

More recently, Nalebuff (2004) analyzed the effects of bundling practices in an oligopolistic environment. He shows that bundling might also act as an effective entrant-deterrent mechanism. Specifically, a company that has market power in two goods can, by bundling them together, make it harder for a rival wishing to sell only one of these goods to enter the market. Bundling allows the incumbent to defend both products without having to price low in each market. Nalebuff's (2004) analysis also demonstrates that bundling is an effective tool even if entry deterrence fails. Since bundling mitigates the impact of competition on the incumbent, an entrant can expect the bundling strategy to persist, even without any commitment. In contrast to Whinston's (1990) model, in which tying commits the monopolist to being more aggressive against an entrant and this commitment discourages entry, Nalebuff's (2004) finds that bundling reduces the entrant's potential profits while mitigating the profit loss to an incumbent if entry occurs. Thus, bundling is credible even without any commitment device.[68]

### 4.3.1    Experimental evidence

Hinloopen et al. (2014) examine the market foreclosure effects of product bundling by implementing a simple experimental environment in which a firm with monopoly power in one market faces competition by a second firm in another unrelated market. This experimental environment replicates the general features of the oligopoly model of bundling presented by Martin (1999).[69] Two bundle treatments are included, pure bundle and no-bundle environments.[70] Two sequence-of-moves treatments are also included; simultaneous moves (both firms simultaneously decide their output levels) and sequential moves (a leader makes a first move; after observing the output decision of the leader, the follower makes an output decision). The sequence-of-moves treatments are implemented

---

[67]    See Kaplow (1985) for a criticism of the Chicago School position.

[68]    Choi and Stefanadis (2001) also rely on a commitment to bundle as a way to deter entry. In their setting, bundling decreases the expected returns for the potential entrant, and, therefore, may lead to foreclosure and reduction of the total welfare. See also Carlton and Waldman (2002). See Simpson and Wickelgren (2007a) for more recent work.

[69]    Martin's (1999) findings suggest that bundling can allow a firm with a monopoly in one market to leverage the market power in other markets, to strategically disadvantage rivals in those markets, and to reduce social welfare. He shows that bundling by a firm with a monopoly over one product has a strategic effect because it changes the substitution relationships among the goods that consumers choose.

[70]    Mixed bundling is not allowed in this environment.

to examine the commitment value of product bundling. Specifically, under simultaneous-move Cournot competition, the bundling firm trades off reduced sales in its monopoly market to increase output in the duopoly market. The bundling strategy might operate as a commitment device to sell more in the second market. Under a Stackelberg setting, when both markets have identical demand and cost structures, an additional commitment is not required as the monopolist is the first mover. Hence, in theory, bundling should not affect optimal quantities. Previous experimental work on Stackelberg settings without bundling, however, suggests that non-monetary preferences such as inequity-aversion considerations (Huck, Müller, and Normann 2001, 2002; Fonseca, Huck, and Normann 2005; Müller 2006) might preclude Stackelberg leaders from exercising their first-mover advantage. Hence, the sequence-of-moves treatments might support the claim that bundling provides additional commitment power to the Stackelberg leader.

Their findings suggest that bundling represents an effective mechanism for transferring market power from one market to another market. Bundling successfully works as a commitment device, across sequence-of-moves treatments. With simultaneous moves (bundling, no-bundling), the monopolist offers the number of units predicted by the theory. Interestingly, when the monopolist is the Stackelberg leader, the predicted equilibrium is better attained with bundling and average outputs are significantly closer to the theoretical predictions. These findings might indicate the presence of non-modeled behavioral factors. Under bundling, the followers might understand that any output reduction of the Stackelberg leader would generate larger costs. Hence, they might infer that the decisions of the leaders do not involve intentionality to hurt the followers.[71] These results are aligned with Landeo and Spier's (2009, 2012) findings regarding the effects of sellers' intentionality on buyers' (receivers') acceptance, in the context of exclusive dealing contracts. Importantly, bundling negatively affects consumer surplus and total surplus.

Caliskan et al. (2007) experimentally study whether bundling and the addition of fringe competition in an originally monopoly market affect market foreclosure and social welfare in strategic settings that allow for mixed bundling. Their experimental environments involve posted-offer markets with two sellers in the first market, a dominant seller and a second seller representing the fringe competition. The dominant seller also participates in the second market, where he faces three identical competitors. A computer performs the role of buyer.[72] In theory, it is profitable for the multiproduct firm to offer a pure bundle, which results in a residual stand-alone demand in the second market too small to support independent sellers in that market. Bundling is an optimal price strategy even in the absence of a competitor in the first market. Hence, in theory, the multiproduct firm bundles, deters entry in the second market, and reduces consumer and total surplus.

---

[71]  Specifically, followers might infer that the output choice of the bundling firm simply reflects the leader's need to maximize profits in the first market. Hence, the intentions of the monopolist might be perceived as less hostile.

[72]  Each session involves several five-second rounds. A posted-offer market is implemented every round as follows: computer-buyers arrive at the marketplace in random order, and a buyer searches for the best price offer (the one that maximizes her surplus). A purchase occurs only when the buyer's surplus from the best offer is non-negative, and the seller providing the offer has available capacity. If two or more sellers make the same best offer, the buyer randomly chooses one of them.

The following experimental treatments are implemented. First, three fringe treatments are considered: fringe competition with 8 percent of the dominant seller's capacity, fringe competition with 5 percent of the dominant seller's capacity, and no-fringe competition. Second, two bundling treatments are studied: bundling (where pure and mixed bundling practices are allowed) and no-bundling.

Caliskan et al.'s findings regarding the effects of fringe competition with eight percent of the dominant seller's capacity suggest that a fringe seller in the first market increases the total consumer surplus realized from the first and second markets, and decreases the total seller surplus. However, the effects of fringe competition on total welfare (consumer and seller surpluses), relative to no-fringe competition, are not significant. In this environment, bundling does not induce exclusion, and does not affect consumer surplus or total welfare. Similarly, fringe competition does not change the exclusionary and welfare implications of bundling (even though this competition decreases the bundle transaction price). Their results under fringe competition with 5 percent of the dominant seller's capacity confirm the theoretical prediction regarding exclusion: bundling helps the dominant seller exclude his competitors in the second market, generating complete foreclosure in 30 percent of the cases. However, the effects of bundling on consumer surplus or total welfare are not significant. Contrary to the theoretical predictions, their findings suggest that monopolists also use mixed bundling (separate units of first-market products are sold in addition to the bundled products). In this environment, fringe competition increases the total consumer surplus in the first and second markets, decreases the total seller surplus (a weaker effect, compared to the effect of fringe competition with eight percent of the dominant seller's capacity), and increases total welfare. In addition, fringe competition does not affect the exclusionary and welfare effects of bundling (despite decreasing the bundle price).

A final experimental environment is implemented. It consists of fringe competition with 5 percent of the dominant seller's capacity and higher efficiency in producing first-market products (lower fixed cost of the dominant seller in the first market). Their findings suggest that the higher efficiency of the dominant firm in the first market induces a transfer of the consumer surplus that the fringe seller originally generated back to the dominant firm. Specifically, this higher efficiency in production for the dominant firm decreases the consumer surplus and increases the seller surplus. However, the effect on total welfare is not significant.

Although this study provides evidence of the effects of bundling on market foreclosure, Caliskan et al.'s (2007) findings do not suggest that the seller's ability to bundle harms consumers.

## 5.   DISCUSSION AND CONCLUSIONS

This chapter argues that experimental law and economics might strengthen the contributions of economic theory to the design and implementation of antitrust law and policies. Although the experimental literature on exclusionary vertical restraints is relatively recent, our analysis of these studies supports our claims. Specifically, our analysis of experimental work on vertical restraints suggests that these studies: (1) generate empirical evidence of the anticompetitive effects of these business practices; (2) apply scientific research methods (i.e., combine theoretical and experimental tools) and, hence, might increase the likelihood of admissibility in a court of economic expert testimony; and (3) provide simple numerical representations of complex economic models, and, hence, might enhance practitioners' understanding of relevant economic theories.

Consider first the case of vertical integration. Martin, Normann, and Snyder's (2001) and Normann's (2011) experimental environments represent simple replications of the more complex theoretical models developed by Rey and Tirole (2001) and Ordover, Salop, and Saloner (1990), respectively. Importantly, their experimental settings allow them to study the effects of modeled and previously non-modeled factors. Martin, Normann, and Snyder's (2001) findings provide conclusive evidence of the foreclosure effects of vertical integration. Interestingly, their findings suggest that publicly observed vertical contracts might also induce market foreclosure by acting as a commitment device for the monopolist. Normann's (2011) study deepens our understanding of the role of extrinsic incentives associated with vertical integration in solving the upstream firm's commitment problem, and, hence, allowing it to foreclosure the market. Although these studies generally support the theoretical predictions, they also suggest the presence of previously non-modeled behavioral regularities, and, hence, provide useful feedback for theorists. For instance, Martin, Normann, and Snyder's (2001) experimental results in the non-integrated settings differ from the theoretical predictions regarding the division of profits between upstream and downstream firms. More equitable allocations are observed in these environments, suggesting the presence of non-monetary preferences and/or the monopolist's strategic anticipation of others' non-monetary preferences. The strategic monopolist might anticipate other actors' non-monetary preferences, and, hence, be even more inclined to vertically integrate.

Regarding exclusive contracts and market foreclosure, Landeo and Spier's (2009) environment represents a simple numerical implementation of Rasmusen, Ramseyer, and Wiley's (1991) and Segal and Whinston's (2000) theoretical frameworks. Landeo and Spier's study provides strong evidence of the exclusionary power of exclusive dealing contracts. Their findings suggest that divide-and-conquer strategies from monopolists are effective foreclosure mechanisms. Importantly, their results also indicate that market foreclosure may be surprisingly easy for incumbent firms to achieve. Even in the absence of discrimination, when adequate communication channels are not available, buyers might fail to coordinate on their preferred outcome and entry might be deterred. These findings are robust to the presence of an actual potential entrant (Landeo and Spier 2012), and to an increase in the number of buyers (Smith 2011). Smith's (2011) findings also suggest that industries with larger fixed costs, smaller technological advantages of the potential entrant, and larger-scale efficiencies might strengthen the exclusionary power of exclusive dealing contracts.

Although Landeo and Spier's (2009) results are aligned with the theoretical predictions, they also reveal the presence of previously non-modeled behavioral factors. For instance, their results indicate that coordination between buyers is particularly elusive when the incumbent seller proposes contract offers that are perceived as unfair. In fact, the human face of a sales representative (an agent for the incumbent monopolist) might elicit fairness and reciprocity from the agents representing the buyers, and facilitate the exclusion of faceless rivals. The presence of social preferences (i.e., buyers' fairness and reciprocity considerations) and the importance of the seller's intentionality might explain these findings.

Landeo and Spier's (2009) and Smith's (2011) findings also suggest that better communication among the buyers might lead to more generous offers from the seller and a greater likelihood of entry. Hence, communication among non-competing buyers might serve the public interest by facilitating entry. Finally, Landeo and Spier's (2012) results indicate that communication between the potential entrant and the buyers reduces the likelihood of exclusion. These results might be explained by the presence of social preferences (which are elicited by the increase in the social proximity between the buyers and the potential entrant) and/or the role of the explicit presence of an entrant as a focal-point coordination mechanism.

Regarding bundling practices, Hinloopen, Müller, and Normann's (2014) study nicely replicates Martin's (1999) theoretical framework using a simple experimental setting. Their results indicate that these business strategies represent an effective mechanism for transferring market power from one market to another market. Moreover, Caliskan et al.'s (2007) study suggests that these results are robust to the presence of fringe competition in the upstream market. A lower fringe competition's market share strengthens the anticompetitive effects of bundling. Although Hinloopen et al.'s (2014) findings suggest a negative effect on consumer welfare, Caliskan et al.'s (2007) results do not indicate that the seller's ability to bundle harms consumers. More experimental investigation is therefore necessary. Interestingly, Hinloopen et al.'s (2014) results suggest the importance of intentionality, a previously non-modeled factor, on the outcomes of market interactions in sequential settings.

The analysis presented in this chapter suggests that the combination of theoretical work and experimental analysis might enhance the policy implications of the economic theories of antitrust, and, hence, the welfare effects of this theoretical work.

## REFERENCES

Aghion, P., and P. Bolton. 1987. Contracts as a Barrier to Entry. *American Economic Review* 77: 388–401.
Andreoni, P., and J. Rao. 2011. The Power of Asking: How Communication Affects Selfishness, Empathy, and Altruism. *Journal of Public Economics* 95: 513–520.
Arlen, J., and E. Talley. 2008. *Experimental Law and Economics*. Cheltenham, UK: Edward Elgar.
Aumann, R. J. 1990. Nash Equilibria Are Not Self-Enforcing. Pp. 201–206 in *Economic Decision-Making: Games, Econometrics and Optimization: Contributions in Honour of Jacques H. Dreze*, edited by J. J. Gabszewicz, J. F. Richard, and L. A. Wolsey. Amsterdam: Elsevier Science.
Babcock, L., G. Loewenstein, S. Issacharoff, and C. Camerer. 1995. Biased Judgments of Fairness in Bargaining. *American Economic Review* 11: 109–126.
Baker, J. B. 2013. Exclusion as a Core Competition Concern. *Antitrust Law Journal* 78: 527–590.
Blount, S. 1995. When Social Outcomes Aren't Fair: The Effect of Causal Attributions on Preferences. *Organizational Behavior and Human Decision Processes* 63: 131–144.
Blume, A., and A. Ortmann. 2007. The Effects of Costless Pre-Play Communication: Experimental Evidence from Games with Pareto-Ranked Equilibria. *Journal of Economic Theory* 132: 274–290.
Bohnet, I., and B. S. Frey. 1999. Social Distance and Other-Regarding Behavior in Dictator Games: Comment. *American Economic Review* 89: 335–339.
Bolton, G. E., and A. Ockenfels. 2000. ERC: A Theory of Equity, Reciprocity, and Competition. *American Economic Review* 90: 166–193.
Bolton, G. E., and A. Ockenfels. 1998. Strategy and Equity: An ERC-Analysis of the Güth–van Damme Game. *Journal of Mathematical Psychology* 42: 215–226.
Bolton, P., and M. D. Whinston. 1993. Incomplete Contracts, Vertical Integration, and Supply Assurance. *Review of Economic Studies* 60: 121–148.
Bolton, P., and M. D. Whinston. 1991. The "Foreclosure" Effects of Vertical Mergers. *Journal of Institutional and Theoretical Economics* 147: 207–226.
Boone, J., W. Müller, and S. Suetens. 2014. Naked Exclusion in the Lab: The Case of Sequential Contracting. *The Journal of Industrial Economics* 62: 137–166.

Bork, R. H. 1978. *The Antitrust Paradox: A Policy at War by Itself*. New York: Basic Books.

Bowman, W. S. 1957. Tying Arrangements and the Leverage Problem. *Yale Law Journal* 67: 19–36.

Brodley, J., and C. A. Ma. 1993. Contract Penalties, Monopolizing Strategies, and Antitrust Policy. *Stanford Law Review* 45: 1161–1213.

Brooks, R., C. M. Landeo, and K. E. Spier. 2010. Trigger Happy or Gun Shy: Dissolving Common-Value Partnerships with Texas Shootouts. *RAND Journal of Economics* 41: 649–673.

Caliskan, A., D. Porter, S. Rassenti, V. L. Smith, and B. J. Wilson. 2007. Exclusionary Bundling and the Effects of a Competitive Fringe. *Journal of Institutional and Theoretical Economics* 163: 109–132.

Camerer, C. F., and J. Hogarth. 2002. The Strategic Use of Tying to Preserve and Create Market Power in Evolving Industries. *RAND Journal of Economics* 33: 194–220.

Camerer, C. F., and J. Hogarth. 1999. The Effects of Financial Incentives in Experiments: A Review and Capital-Labor-Production Framework. *Journal of Risk and Uncertainty* 19: 7–42.

Carlton, D. W., and M. Waldman. 2002. The Strategic Use of Tying to Preserve and Create Market Power in Evolving Industries. *RAND Journal of Economics* 33: 194–220.

Cason, T., and T. Sharma. 2001. Durable Goods, Coasian Dynamics and Uncertainty: Theory and Experiments. *Journal of Political Economy* 109: 1311–1354.

Charness, G., E. Haruby, and D. Sonsino. 2007. Social Distance and Reciprocity: An Internet Experiment. *Journal of Economic Behavior and Organization* 63: 88–103.

Choi, J. P., and C. Stefanadis. 2001. Tying, Investment, and the Dynamic Leverage Theory. *RAND Journal of Economics* 32: 52–71.

Coase, R. 1937. The Nature of the Firm. *Economica* 4: 386–405.

Cooper, Russell W., Douglas V. DeJong, Robert Forsythe, and Thomas W. Ross. 1992. Communication in Coordination Games. *Quarterly Journal of Economics* 107: 739–771.

Crawford, V. P. 1998. A Survey of Experiments on Communication via Cheap Talk. *Journal of Economic Theory* 78: 286–298.

Croson, R. 2009. Experimental Law and Economics. *Annual Review of Law and Social Sciences* 5: 17.1–17.20.

Croson, R. 2005. The Method of Experimental Economics. *International Negotiation* 10: 131–148.

Croson, R. 2002. Why and How to Experiment: Methodologies from Experimental Economics. *University of Illinois Law Review* 4: 921–945.

Croson, R., and Simon Gächter. 2010. The Science of Experimental Economics. *Journal of Economic Behavior and Organization* 73: 122–131.

Dal Bó, P. 2005. Cooperation under the Shadow of the Future: Experimental Evidence from Infinitely Repeated Games. *American Economic Review* 95: 1591–1604.

Davis, D., and C. A. Holt. 2008. The Effects of Collusion in Laboratory Experiments. Pp. 170–176 in *Handbook of Experimental Economic Results*, edited by C. Plott and V. Smith. New York: Elsevier Press.

Davis, D., and C. Holt. 1993. *Experimental Economics*. New Jersey: Princeton University Press.

de Frutos, M. A., and T. Kittsteiner. 2008. Efficient Partnership Dissolution under Buy-Sell Clauses. *RAND Journal of Economics* 39: 184–198.

Diamond, P.A., and E. Maskin. 1979. An Equilibrium Analysis of Search and Breach of Contract, I: Steady States. *Bell Journal of Economics* 10: 282–316.

Director, A., and E. H. Levi. 1956. Law and the Future: Trade Regulation. *Northwestern University Law Review* 51: 281–296.

Duffy, J., and N. Feltovich. 2002. Do Actions Speak Louder than Words? An Experimental Comparison of Observation and Cheap Talk. *Games and Economic Behavior* 39: 1–27.

Engel, C. 2007. How Much Collusion? A Meta-Analysis of Oligopoly Experiments. *Journal of Competition Law and Policy* 4: 491–549.

Falk, A., and J. J. Heckman. 2009. Lab Experiments Are a Major Source of Knowledge in the Social Sciences. *Science* 326: 535–538.

Farrell, J. 2005. Deconstructing Chicago on Exclusive Dealing. *Antitrust Bulletin* 50: 465–480.

Farrell, J. and M. Rabin. 1996. Cheap Talk. *Journal of Economic Perspectives* 10: 103–118.

Fehr, E. and K. M. Schmidt. 1999. A Theory of Fairness, Competition, and Cooperation. *Quarterly Journal of Economics* 114: 817–868.

Fonseca, M. A., S. Huck, and H. T. Normann. 2005. Playing Cournot although They Shouldn't: Endogenous Timing in Experimental Duopolies with Asymmetric Costs. *Economic Theory* 2: 669–677.

Fréchette, G. R. 2015. Laboratory Experiments: Professionals versus Students. Pp. 360–390 in *Handbook of Experimental Economic Methodology*, edited by Guillaume Fréchette and Andrew Schotter. Oxford: Oxford University Press.

Fumagallli, C., and M. Motta. 2006. Exclusive Dealing and Entry When Buyers Compete. *American Economic Review* 96: 785–795.

Güth, W., R. Schmittberger, and B. Schwartz. 1996. An Experimental Analysis of the Ultimatum Bargaining. *Journal of Economic Behavior and Organization* 3: 367–388.

Harsanyi, J. C., and R. Selten. 1988. *A General Theory of Equilibrium Selection in Games*. Cambridge, MA: MIT Press.

Hart, O., and P. Tirole. 1990. Vertical Integration and Market Foreclosure. *Brookings Papers on Economic Activity: Microeconomics* 1990: 205–276.

Hinloopen, J., W. Müller, and H. T. Normann. 2014. Output Commitment through Product Bundling: Experimental Evidence. *European Economic Review* 67: 228–229.

Hoffman, E., K. McCabe, K. Shachat, and V. L. Smith. 1994. Preferences, Property Rights, and Anonymity in Bargaining Games. *Games and Economic Behavior* 7: 346–380.

Hoffman, E., K. McCabe, and V. L. Smith. 1996. On Expectations and the Monetary Stakes in Ultimatum Games. *International Journal of Game Theory* 25: 289–301.

Hoffman, E., and M. L. Spitzer. 1985. Experimental Law and Economics: An Introduction. *Colorado Law Review* 85: 991–1024.

Holt, C. A. 1995. Industrial Organization: A Survey of Laboratory Research. Pp. 349–443 in *Handbook of Experimental Economics* edited by J. Kagel and A. Roth. Princeton, NJ: Princeton University Press.

Hong, J. T., and C. R. Plott. 1982. Rate Filing Policies for Inland Water Transportation: An Experimental Approach. *Bell Journal of Economics* 13: 1–19.

Hovenkamp, H. 2011. *Federal Antitrust Policy: The Law of Competition and Its Practice*. St. Paul, MN: West Publishing.

Huck, S., and W. Müller. 2000. Perfect Versus Imperfect Observability—An Experimental Test of Bagwell's Result. *Games and Economic Behavior* 31: 174–190.

Huck, S., W. Müller, and H. T. Normann. 2002. To Commit or Not to Commit: Endogenous Timing in Experimental Duopoly. *Games and Economic Behavior* 38: 240–264.

Huck, S., W. Müller, and H. T. Normann. 2001. Stackelberg Beats Cournot: On Collusion and Efficiency in Experimental Markets. *Economic Journal* 111: 749–765.

Innes, R., and R. J. Sexton. 1994. Strategic Buyers and Exclusionary Contracts. *American Economic Review* 84: 566–584.

Kaplow, L. 1985. Extension of Monopoly Power through Leverage. *Columbia Law Review* 85: 515–556.

Kittsteiner, T., A. Ockenfels, and N. Trhal. 2012. Heterogeneity and Partnership Dissolution Mechanisms: Theory and Lab Evidence. *Economic Letters* 117: 394–396.

Kirkwood, J. B. 1988. Antitrust Implications of the Recent Experimental Literature on Collusion. *Journal Reprints Antitrust Law and Economics* 18: 605–622.

Kobayashi, B. H. 1997. Game Theory and Antitrust: A Post-Mortem. *George Mason Law Review* 5: 411–421.

Kwoka, Jr., J. E., and L. J. White. 2009. *The Antitrust Revolution*. New York: Oxford University Press.

Lafontaine, F., and M. Slade. 2012. Inter-Firm Contracts: Evidence. Pp. 958–1013 in *The Handbook of Organizational Economics*, edited by R. Gibbons and J. Roberts. Princeton, NJ: Princeton University Press.

Lafontaine, F., and M. Slade. 2008. Exclusive Contracts and Vertical Restraints: Empirical Evidence and Public Policy. Pp. 391–414 in *The Handbook of Antitrust Economics*, edited by P. Buccirossi. Cambridge, MA: MIT Press.

Lafontaine, F., and M. Slade. 2007. Vertical Integration and Firm Boundaries: The Evidence. *Journal of Economic Literature* 65: 629–685.

Landeo, C. M. 2009. Cognitive Coherence and Tort Reform. *Journal of Economic Psychology* 24: 69–89.

Landeo, C. M., and K. E. Spier. 2016. Stipulated Damages as a Rent-Extraction Mechanism: Experimental Evidence. *Journal of Institutional and Theoretical Economics* 172: 235–273.

Landeo, C. M., and K. E. Spier. 2015. Incentive Contracts for Teams: Experimental Evidence. *Journal of Economic Behavior and Organization* 119: 496–511.

Landeo, C. M., and K. E. Spier. 2014a. Contracts as a Rent-Extraction Mechanism: An Experimental Study of Stipulated Damages under Social Preferences. Mimeo, University of Alberta and Harvard Law School.

Landeo, C. M., and K. E. Spier. 2014b. Incentive Contracts for Teams. Mimeo, University of Alberta and Harvard Law School.

Landeo, C. M., and K. E. Spier. 2014c. Shotguns and Deadlocks. *Yale Journal on Regulation* 31: 143–187.

Landeo, C. M., and K. E. Spier. 2014d. Irreconcilable Differences: Judicial Resolution of Business Deadlocks. *University of Chicago Law Review* 81: 203–229.

Landeo, C. M., and K. E. Spier. 2013. Shotgun Mechanisms for Common-Value Partnerships: The Unassigned-Offeror Problem. *Economics Letters* 121: 390–394.

Landeo, C. M., and K. E. Spier. 2012. Exclusive Dealing and Market Foreclosure: Further Experimental Results. *Journal of Institutional and Theoretical Economics* 168: 150–170.

Landeo, C. M., and K. E. Spier. 2009. Naked Exclusion: An Experimental Study of Contracts with Externalities. *American Economic Review* 99: 1850–1877.

Langenfeld, J., and C. Alexander. 2011. *Daubert* and Other Gatekeeping Challenges of Antitrust Experts. *Antitrust* 25: 21–28.

Loewenstein, G. F., L. Thompson, and M. H. Bazerman. 1989. Social Utility and Decision Making in Interpersonal Contexts. *Journal of Personality and Social Psychology* 57: 426–441.

Martin, S. 1999. Strategic and Welfare Implications of Bundling. *Economic Letters* 62: 371–376.

Martin, S., H. T. Normann, and C. M. Snyder. 2001. Vertical Foreclosure in Experimental Markets. *RAND Journal of Economics* 32: 466–496.

Mason, C. F., and O. R. Phillips. 2000. Vertical Integration and Collusive Incentives: An Experimental Analysis. *International Journal of Industrial Organization* 18: 471–496.

Masten, S. E., and E. A. Snyder. 1989. The Design and Duration of Contracts: Strategic and Efficiency Considerations. *Law and Contemporary Problems* 52: 63–85.

McAdams, R. H. 2000. Experimental Law and Economics. Pp. 539–561 in *Encyclopedia of Law and Economics*, edited by B. Bouckaert and G. DeGeest. Cheltenham: Edward Elgar.

McKelvey, R. D., and T. R. Palfrey. 1998. Quantal Response Equilibria for Extensive Form Games. *Experimental Economics* 1: 9–41.

Müller, W. 2006. Allowing for Two Production Periods in the Cournot Duopoly: Experimental Evidence. *Journal of Economic Behavior and Organization* 60: 100–111.

Nalebuff, B. 2004. Bundling as an Entry Barrier. *Quarterly Journal of Economics* 119: 159–187.

Normann, H. T. 2011. Vertical Mergers, Foreclosure and Raising Rivals' Costs: Experimental Evidence. *Journal of Industrial Economics* 59: 506–527.

Normann, H. T. 2008. Experimental Economics for Antitrust Law and Policy. Pp. 773–800 in *Issues in Competition Law and Policy*, edited by W. Collins. Chicago: American Bar Association.

Ochs, J. 1995. Coordination Problems. Pp. 195–252 in *The Handbook of Experimental Economics*, edited by John H. Kagel and Alvin E. Roth. Princeton, NJ: Princeton University Press.

Ordover, J., S. Salop, and G. Saloner. 1990. Equilibrium Vertical Foreclosure. *American Economic Review* 80: 127–142.

Plott, C. R. 1999. Policy and the Use of Laboratory Experimental Methodology in Economics. Pp. 303–307 in *Uncertain Decisions: Bridging Theory and Experiments*, edited by L. Luini. Norwell, MA: Kluwer Academic Publishers.

Plott, C. R. 1994. Market Architectures, Institutional Landscapes and Testbed Experiments. *Economic Theory* 1: 3–10.

Plott, C. R. 1982. Industrial Organization Theory and Experimental Economics. *Journal of Economic Literature* 20: 1485–1527.

Posner, R. A. 1976. *Antitrust Law: An Economic Perspective*. Chicago: University of Chicago Press.

Rasmusen, E. B., J. M. Ramseyer, and J. S. Wiley, Jr. 1991. Naked Exclusion. *American Economic Review* 81: 1137–1145.

Reiffen, D. 1992. Equilibrium Vertical Foreclosure: Comment. *American Economic Review* 82: 694–697.

Rey, P., and J. Tirole. 2007. A Primer on Foreclosure. Pp. 2145–2220 in *The Handbook of Industrial Organization*, edited by M. Armstrong and R. Porter. North Holland: Amsterdam.

Rey, P., and J. Tirole. 2001. A Primer on Foreclosure. Mimeo, University of Toulouse.

Reynolds, S. 2000. Durable-Goods Monopoly: Laboratory Market and Bargaining Experiments. *RAND Journal of Economics* 31: 375–394.

Riordan, M. H. 2008. Competitive Effects of Vertical Integration. Pp. 145–182 in *The Handbook of Antitrust Economics*, edited by P. Buccirossi. Cambridge, MA: MIT Press.

Riordan, M. H. 1998. Anticompetitive Vertical Integration by a Dominant Firm. *American Economic Review* 88: 1232–1248.

Riordan, M., and S. Salop. 1995. Evaluating Vertical Mergers: A Post-Chicago Approach. *Antitrust Law Journal* 63: 513–568.

Roth, A. E. 2008. What Have We Learned from Market Design? *Economic Journal* 118: 285–310.

Roth, A. E. 1995. Bargaining Experiments. Pp. 253–348 in *The Handbook of Experimental Economics*, edited by J. H. Kagel and A. E. Roth. Chicago, IL: The University of Chicago Press.

Roth, A. E. 1986. Laboratory Experimentation in Economics. *Economics and Philosophy* 2: 245–273.

Roth, A. E., and J. Murnighan. Information and Aspirations in Two-Person Bargaining. Pp. 91–103 in *Aspiration Levels in Bargaining and Economic Decision Making*, edited by R. Tietz. Heidelberg, Germany: Springer-Verlag.

Schelling, T. C. 1968. The Life You Save May Be Your Own. Pp. 127–162 in *Problems in Public Expenditure Analysis*, edited by S. Chase. Washington, DC: Brookings Institution.

Schelling, T. 1960. *The Strategy of Conflict*. Cambridge, MA: Harvard University Press.

Segal, I. R. 2003. Coordination and Discrimination in Contracting with Externalities: Divide and Conquer. *Journal of Economic Theory* 113: 147–181.

Segal, I. R. 1999. Contracting with Externalities. *Quarterly Journal of Economics* 114: 337–388.

Segal, I. R., and M. D. Whinston. 2000. Naked Exclusion: Comment. *American Economic Review* 90: 296–309.

Selten, R., and R. Stoecker. 1988. End Behavior in Sequences of Finite Prisoner's Dilemma Supergames: A Learning Theory Approach. *Journal of Economic Behavior and Organization* 7: 47–70.

Simpson, J., and A. Wickelgren. 2007a. Bundled Discounts, Leverage Theory, and Downstream Competition. *American Economic Review* 9: 1–14.

Simpson, J., and A. Wickelgren. 2007b. Naked Exclusion, Efficient Breach, and Downstream Competition. *American Economic Review* 97: 1305–1320.

Sloof, R., H. Oosternbeek, A. Riedl, and J. Sonnemans. 2006. Breach Remedies, Reliance and Renegotiation. *International Review of Law and Economics* 26: 263–296.

Smith, A. M. 2011. An Experimental Study of Exclusive Contracts. *International Journal of Industrial Organization* 29: 4–13.

Smith, V. L. 1976. Experimental Economics: Induced Value Theory. *American Economic Review* 66: 274–279.

Sobel, J. 2005. Interdependent Preferences and Reciprocity. *Journal of Economic Literature* 63: 392–436.

Spier, K. E., and M. D. Whinston. 1995. On the Efficiency of Privately Stipulated Damages for Breach of Contract: Entry Barriers, Reliance, and Renegotiation. *RAND Journal of Economics* 26: 180–202.

Talley, E. L. 1994. Contract Renegotiation, Mechanism Design, and the Liquidated Damages Rule. *Stanford Law Review* 46: 1195–1243.

Talley, E., and C. Camerer. 2007. Experimental Law and Economics. Pp. 1619–1650 in *The Handbook of Law and Economics*, edited by M. Polinsky, and S. Shavell. Amsterdam: Elsevier.

Thaler, R. H. 1992. *The Winners Curse: Paradoxes and Anomalies of Economic Life*. Princeton, NJ: Princeton University Press.

Thaler, R. H. 1987. Anomalies: The January Effect. *Journal of Economic Perspectives* 1: 197–201.

Thompson, L. 1990. Negotiation Behavior and Outcomes: Empirical Evidence and Theoretical Issues. *Psychological Bulletin* 108: 515–532.

Tirole, J. 1988. *The Theory of Industrial Organization*. Cambridge, MA: MIT Press.

Whinston, M. D. 2006. *Lectures on Antitrust Economics*. Cambridge, MA: MIT Press.

Whinston, M. D. 1990. Tying, Foreclosure, and Exclusion. *American Economic Review* 80: 837–859.

## Legal Cases

*Ayres v. Robinson*, 887 F. Supp. 1049, 1995.

*Brown Shoe v. United States*, 370 U.S. 294, 1962.

*Concord Boat Corporation v. Brunswick Corporation*, 207 F.3d 1039 (8th Cir. 2000), 2000.

*Continental T.V., Inc. v. GTE Sylvania, Inc.*, 433 US 36, 97 S.Ct. 2549, 53 L. Ed. 2d 568 – Supreme Court, 1977.

*Conwood v. United States Tobacco*, 290 F.3d 768, 2002.

*Daubert v. Merrell Dow Pharmaceuticals, Inc.*, 509 U.S. 579, 1993.

*Frye v. United States*, 293 F. 1013, 1923.

*Illinois Tool Works Inc. v. Independent Ink, Inc.*, 547 U.S. 28, 2006.

JTA LE ROUX PTY LTD as trustee for the FLR FAMILY TRUST -V- LAWSON [2013] WASC 293.

*Jefferson Parish Hosp. Dist. No. 2 v. Hyde*, 466 U.S. 2, 7, 104 S.Ct. 1551, 1556, 1984.

*LePage's Inc. v. 3M*, 324 F.3d 141, 2003.

*Port Dock & Stone Corp. v. Oldcastle Northeast, Inc.*, 507 F.3d 117, 125, 2d Cir., 2007.

*In re Beer Distribution Antitrust Litigation*, 188 F.R.D. 557, 1999.

*Tampa Elect. Co. v. Nashville Coal Co.*, 365 U.S. 320, 81 S.Ct. 623, 1961; on remand, 214 F. Supp. 64, M.D.Tenn., 1963.

*United States v. Dentsply*, 399 F.3d 181, 2001.

*United States v. Microsoft Corp.*, 253 F.3d 34. 90, D.C.Cir., cert, denied, 534 U.S. 952, 122 S.Ct. 350, 2001.

*United States v. Visa U.S.A.*, 344 F.3d 229, 2003.

*Yentsch v. Texaco, Inc.*, 630 F2d. 46, 56–57, 2d Cir. 1980.

# 4. Balancing act: new evidence and a discussion of the theory on the rationality and behavioral anomalies of choice in credit markets

*Marieke Bos, Susan Payne Carter, and Paige Marta Skiba\**

## 1. INTRODUCTION

Millions of people in the United States use alternative forms of credit like payday loans and pawnshop loans.[1] According to the 2011 FDIC report from their survey of unbanked and underbanked individuals in the United States, over 5.6 million people had used payday loans and 8.9 million had used pawnshop loans (Burhouse and Osaki 2012).

We analyze choices in these high-cost credit markets to argue that the choice of credit take-up is often a decision made rationally considering the choices available. However, the subsequent use of alternative forms of credit is characterized by failure to anticipate either future time preferences or future spending needs (consumption shocks).

We add to the literature on consumers' credit use by analyzing the influence of the introduction of payday credit on pawn credit uptake. By exploiting a discontinuity in the approval process used by payday lenders, we are able to study the causal effect of being rejected for a payday loan. Perhaps not surprisingly, we find that those who receive a payday loan are less likely to use pawnshop loans within the immediate future; however, the effect is economically small. Previous researchers have shown that individuals who have payday loans often do not have access to other forms of credit. Our results show that pawnshops might, therefore, be used rationally since they are likely the only available alternative to an individual who is denied a payday loan.

We start our paper by providing an overview of how consumers choose between forms of credit by drawing on the traditional microeconomics literature. We summarize recent empirical evidence on how people use credit and provide a description of relevant behavioral economics issues including time inconsistency, financial literacy, and loss aversion. We then turn to our own empirical results on how people choose between alternative credit types before concluding with a discussion.

---

\* The views expressed herein are those of the authors and do not represent the U.S. Military Academy, the Department of the Army, or the Department of Defense.

[1] Payday loans typically last two weeks, are collateralized by a personal check and have an annualized interest rate of about 300 percent. Borrowers are required to have a job to obtain a loan. Pawnshop loans merely require a borrower to have some personal property to use as collateral, typically jewelry or electronics, usually last 30 days and also come with triple-digit annualized interest rates. We describe in more detail how these markets work in Section 3.

## 2. THE THEORETICAL FOUNDATIONS OF CONSUMER CREDIT INTERACTIONS

In this section, we provide an overview of theories from traditional and behavioral economics that help illuminate: (1) how consumers choose among different credit products; (2) how consumers make repayment decisions conditional on entering a credit contract; and (3) the stickiness of credit choices. We argue that the weight of evidence suggests borrowers are, for the most part, rational in their take-up of credit and their tradeoffs between and among forms of credit, conditional on their ex-ante predictions for their future consumption. However, borrowers appear to under-predict their intensity of borrowing and over-predict their ability to repay. While the rational model has simple predictions about borrowers minimizing costs, the task of quantifying the non-pecuniary costs is important and subtle.

### 2.1 Rational Model

We start with a description of the rational choice model in economics. This model, often describing a rational actor as *homo economicus*, predicts this actor will simply choose the credit contract that maximizes his or her utility from among the contracts for which she is eligible by minimizing monetary and other costs associated with the different types of borrowing. Furthermore, the actor is assumed to use all of the available information and process that information correctly in accordance with Bayesian updating. Finally, borrowers are assumed to have rational expectations about their future spending needs and ability to repay. That is not to say they need to be able to accurately predict the future, but the assumption is that they will have a good idea, for example, of the process (probability, mean, and variance) by which they receive both good and bad shocks to their spending.

This model also employs strict assumptions about how people make tradeoffs over time. Consumers' choices are each associated with a utility measure that represents the consumer's preferences (such as being risk averse, risk seeking, etc.). This function is maximized at each point in time, trading off consumption choices today with the capacity for either more or less consumption tomorrow. For example, saving today means less consumption today but increased consumption at some future date. In concrete terms, an individual may decide when to pay her phone bill by comparing the utility of doing it today (time $t$) with the utility of doing it on any possible future date so long as it meets certain constraints, like paying the bill before the phone is disconnected. Certain time periods may come with an extra cost: paying the bill before a new paycheck arrives may come with the extra disutility of not having enough money to also buy groceries. These choices regarding how utility is traded off over time depend not just on such opportunity costs, but also in part on the extent to which borrowers discount future utilities.

In the traditional model, when economists take discounting into account, they assume that borrowers are *time consistent*—meaning a borrower's preferences about plans in the future do not change at different points in time. For example, if a time-consistent borrower plans on the 1st of the month to pay her utility bill on the 15th of the month, her plan will not change once the 14th of the month rolls around. In other words, the discount between each future period is the same: from period one's perspective, she discounts period two by some factor (for example, $\delta$). From period two's perspective, she discounts period three by the same factor, δ. From period three's perspective, she again discounts the next period by the same factor, δ, and so on. Returning to the original time period's perspective, the time-consistent borrower discounts each future period by δ raised to the number of periods in the future so that her total discounted utility will be the sum of all the discounted instantaneous utilities (example: $U_1 = u_1 + \delta u_2 + \delta^2 u_3 + \delta^3 u_4 + \ldots$). This behavior over time translates into discount factors that exponentially grow over time, which is why it is called exponential discounting, and can account for very impatient behavior as individuals may discount the future heavily.

A drawback of exponential discounting is the strong assumption that individuals exhibit time consistency which is often at odds with the way people make choices in the real world.[2] The exponential model assumes a consumer's discount rate between any two periods is constant, whether those two periods are today and tomorrow or 365 days and 365-plus-one days from now,[3] and further assumes that consumers know the rate at which they will discount any of these periods. Time consistency precludes *any* kind of misprediction about future discounting rates. Such a misprediction could manifest itself as procrastination and self-control problems. We turn to these possibilities later.

A second drawback of exponential discounting is how quickly utility gets discounted very heavily. Even for a high value of the discount factor, say 0.99, which indicates a generally patient person, if one examines discounting at the daily level (which would be a reasonable way to consider the choices we explore here in credit markets), the borrower would care almost nothing about utility in one year. That utility would be discounted by $0.99^{365}$, which equals approximately 0.02, implying that borrowers care about utility in one year fifty times *less* than utility today![4] For example, this consumer would be indifferent between receiving $10 today and $500 in one year. Exponential discounting, therefore, may work well in theory (the time consistency aspect helps significantly in calculating the tradeoffs that consumers face) and in some real-world contexts, but not as well when shorter time frames are concerned.

Like all models, exponential discounting is a useful simplification of the real world, and, though not always realistic in its predictions about behavior, it can be a nice starting point for thinking about choices over time. There is, however, overwhelming evidence refuting the exponential model. Even Paul Samuelson, writing the canonical paper that works through the exponential discounting model, was forthcoming about its drawbacks and unrealistic predictions for behavior. Recent alternatives do a good job of capturing the factors that, realistically, affect individuals' tradeoffs over time—such as self-control problems, procrastination, and a combination of long-run patience with short-run impatience that we will discuss below in more detail. The manner in which consumers discount the future is paramount to how consumers decide whether to borrow, and if so, from which source.

In sum, the rational actor model says simply that potential borrowers choose the cheapest form of credit and do not have any difficulties implementing their choices over

---

[2]  See O'Donoghue and Rabin (1999) for an overview.

[3]  Frederick, Loewenstein, and O'Donoghue (2002, p. 358), "Constant discounting entails an even handedness in the way a person evaluates time. It means that delaying or accelerating two dated outcomes by a common amount should not change preferences between the outcomes."

[4]  This is because $1/.02 = 50$.

time in terms of repaying debt and taking on additional debt. With these ideas in hand, we next proceed to outline concepts from the behavioral economics literature that relax some of the rational choice model's assumptions within the context of the consumption credit market.

## 2.2   Rational Model and Credit Choice

Assume a consumer enters the credit market with an exogenous need to borrow and is eligible for both mainstream credit sources like credit cards and alternative sources like payday and pawn credit. The next section outlines the important tradeoffs consumers face within this framework.

### 2.2.1   Credit, no credit

A consumer first weighs the current and future utility of having access to money now with the disutility associated with the immediate and future costs of taking out the loan. Here we emphasize that the borrowing costs go beyond the interest and fee payments. These costs can entail, for example, the opportunity cost of the time it takes to get the loan (search and travel time; delivering heavy or otherwise unwieldy items to the pawnshop; etc.). Other types of non-monetary costs are important as well. For example, a consumer will incur costs when surrendering possession of a pawned object during the loan period: a singer-songwriter in Nashville having pawned her guitar, for example. The risk of defaulting is also an important potential cost. Defaulting on a loan in the mainstream credit market has consequences for future credit access vis-à-vis the individual's credit score and credit report,[5] and potentially even for endeavors beyond the credit market such as being hired or obtaining a real estate rental contract or phone subscription.

For pawn and payday loans, such a default will certainly have concomitant consequences for future credit access since, after default, the borrower will relinquish ownership of the pawned object, or in the case of payday lending, incur severe damage to her subprime credit score as a result of the collateral check bouncing. In both cases future access to credit will be restricted after default since one cannot pawn an object one no longer owns and one's damaged credit score will almost surely no longer meet the threshold for payday lenders to grant a new payday loan.

### 2.2.2   Mainstream vs. alternative credit

Interest rates on payday and pawnshop loans are high relative to the average interest rate of mainstream credit sources like a bank loan or a credit card.[6]

In Texas, where our data are from, the legal limit on the interest rate for a pawnshop loan is 20 percent per 30-day loan, equivalent to a 240 percent APR. Payday lenders in our study charged 18 percent fees (essentially, interest). Unlike interest rates on traditional

---

[5]   For more on delinquency, see Bos and Nakamura (2014) on credit arrears and forgiveness.

[6]   Other forms of alternative credit, including title lending, are becoming increasing popular as well. Title lending is potentially an important alternative to payday loans (see Fritzdixon, Hawkins and Skiba (2014) for more on title lending). Because we know of no large dataset illuminating title lending choices, we restrict our analysis of alternative sources of credit to payday lending and pawnshops.

forms of credit, interest rates on payday loans are per loan, regardless of the duration of the loan or the credit score of the borrower.

Given the large difference between the pecuniary cost of a payday loan and that of a pawn loan, how, if at all, does the choice between a pawn loan and a payday loan fit into the rational model? For starters, as one might expect, research has shown that for the vast majority of pawn and payday borrowers, mainstream credit is not likely part of their choice set any longer. Recent research documenting the types of borrowers that use pawn and payday loans supports this idea: Agarwal and Bos (2014) find that 74 percent of the pawn borrowers in Sweden are simply excluded from mainstream credit at the time they take out a pawn loan. Similarly, Bhutta, Skiba, and Tobacman (2015) find that 80 percent of borrowers applying for their first payday loan have precisely $0 available in credit card liquidity.

The most detailed demographics on pawnshop borrowers comes from Sweden. The typical Swedish pawn borrower (described in Agarwal and Bos (2014)) is more likely to be young, female, and living in a big city than the average Swede. She may be currently married, but is more likely to have experienced a divorce or widowhood in the year before taking the pawn loan. She is twice as likely to be an immigrant. Her income is lower, and she is less likely to have investment income or own a house. If she does own a house, it is likely to be of below-average value. Her history with regular banks looks worse, with more loan denials, a higher debt-to-income ratio, and more arrears on her credit file. In addition, she is also more likely to have used at least 90 percent of her existing credit lines at mainstream banks or to have no credit line available.

The population in the payday loan data used in the analysis below is typically low-income (median annual income of just $20,000). The median balance on the individuals' most recent checking account statement is just $66. Sixty-two percent of payday loan applicants are female and the median age is 36 years old. Fifty percent of individuals in the data are black and 30 percent are Hispanic.

For liquidity-constrained individuals, like those in these datasets, high-cost borrowing can facilitate consumption smoothing when unexpected income shocks occur. For example, a pawn loan might enable the borrower to buy food for her kids until payday or to pay an electricity bill before the company disconnects the electricity, thereby avoiding subsequent high reconnection fees, etc.

The daily interest on a typical 30-day pawnshop loan would match the daily interest on a payday loan with an interest rate of 15 percent (18 percent) where the payday loan is 22.5 (27) days.[7] If the payday loan lasted any longer, the daily interest rate would be cheaper on the payday loan, and if the payday loan were any shorter, the daily interest rate on the payday loan would be more expensive. In other words, the longer a payday loan is, the cheaper it is relative to the typical pawnshop loan. The average length of a payday loan in our sample is only 15.1 days, suggesting that it would typically be cheaper for borrowers to use pawnshop loans. However, to the extent that the borrower incurs a cost in connection with forfeiting the use of the collateralized item, the effective cost of a

---

[7]  The daily interest rate on a pawnshop loan is 20 percent per 30 days $= (0.2)/30$ per day. The daily interest rate on a payday loan of length $x$ and with interest rate $r$ is $r/x$. When $r = 0.15$, $x$ must be 22.5 and when $r = 0.18$, $x$ must be 27.

pawnshop loan rises, potentially making a payday loan the cheaper option—a conceivable explanation for why some individuals with jobs and bank accounts would prefer to use payday loans when they are available.

Nevertheless, research also finds that a smaller fraction of the payday/pawn borrowers use both mainstream and alternative forms of credit simultaneously. Agarwal and Bos (2014) find that nearly 5 percent of their pawn borrowers do so. Agarwal, Skiba, and Tobacman (2009), explore a dataset of customers at a large credit card issuer who also use payday loans. They find, surprisingly, that these borrowers have on average "substantial credit card liquidity" when they apply for a payday loan. Borrowers, however, have decreasing credit card liquidity leading up to their first payday loan transaction, suggesting that borrowers are waiting to enter the alternative credit market for as long as possible.[8]

Finally, research identifies an even smaller fraction of borrowers that theoretically have access to mainstream credit but only use pawn credit. As described below in the section on substitutes or complements, there are specific loan features beyond pecuniary characteristics that can influence consumers' choices between pawn and payday credit.

### 2.2.3  Payday, pawn

In order to evaluate whether borrowers make rational choices, one must somehow observe, measure, and compare the perceived utility induced by the specific loan characteristics for the different borrowers. Utility is a theoretical construct, and measurement issues are always prevalent. However, in our case, we might be especially concerned about measuring welfare when studying the choice between a pawn loan and a payday loan. As we described in the previous section, there are numerous reasons beyond pecuniary differences why a specific borrower may prefer a pawn loan over a payday loan or vice versa.

That said, we document in our empirical analysis below that consumers, when denied access to a payday loan, are more likely to take out a subsequent pawn loan. Of course, while our empirical design is well suited for such analysis in the sense that we know precisely when a borrower is denied or allowed access to payday loans, we cannot observe previous pawnshop behavior. Borrowers may have been borrowing on pawn loans, sought a payday loan to repay a pawn loan, and then returned to the pawn market.

One obvious reason borrowers may prefer a payday loan over a pawn loan is the difference in loan size. In our data we see that an average payday loan is $275 and the average pawnshop loan around $75. The size of a pawn loan is determined by the resale value of the item and the size of a payday loan is capped at half of a borrower's take-home pay (and subject to state-mandated caps, typically $500 or $1,000). This size difference could be offset by the relative price difference. Pawn and payday loans may also have differential stigma attached to them. Both are generally abhorred in mainstream media. We do not have a measure to capture such other costs that may differ by loan type.

---

[8]   This finding coincides with a line of research documenting debt puzzles such as consumers holding credit card debt and savings accounts simultaneously. See Telyukova (2013) for a review.

### 2.2.4 Limitations to welfare analysis

One aspect that potentially undermines the validity of the rational model with exponential discounting in the context of the credit market is the assumption that borrowers are able to employ the available information correctly. Limited financial literacy has been well documented, not merely among low-income borrowers, or those using alternative credit sources, but across the income and education distribution. Recent work by Lusardi, Mitchell, and Curto (2009) asks three basic financial literacy questions with multiple choice answers:

(1) "Suppose you had $100 in a savings account and the interest rate was 2% per year. After 5 years, how much do you think you would have in the account if you left the money to grow?"
(2) "Imagine that the interest rate on your savings account was 1% per year and inflation was 2% per year. After one year, would the money in the account buy more than it does today, exactly the same or less than today?"
(3) "Do you think the following statement is true or false? Buying a single company stock usually provides a safer return than a stock mutual fund."

They find that only one-third of respondents could answer all three questions correctly. Of particular interest to us are the responses to question 1 on interest rates. Two-thirds of survey respondents answered correctly, but one-third were unaware whether the balance in the interest-bearing account would increase or decrease.

Many other authors have found substantial limitations in financial literacy more broadly (Lusardi and Mitchell 2009; Lusardi, Mitchell and Curto 2009, 2014) and among payday borrowers specifically (Lusardi and Scheresberg 2013). While lenders must and do post APRs, it has been shown that APRs are not well understood because of biases in understanding exponential growth (Stango and Zinman 2009) or the existence of other parts of the credit contract that may not be salient or easily understood. For example, Bertrand and Morse (2011) have shown that reminding borrowers of the cost of a payday loan (i.e., giving the APR) and also providing, for comparison, APRs for other sources of credit (car loans, credit cards, and subprime mortgages) reduces the amount that individuals borrow from a payday lender.

All of these limitations would make it difficult for borrowers to effectively make the tradeoffs in utility described above. In addition to it being hard for individuals to accurately understand the true costs of these loans, there is mixed evidence on whether payday loans have positive or negative welfare effects.[9] Melzer (2011) finds that payday loan use is associated with a decrease in individuals' well-being, and Skiba and Tobacman (2011) find that payday loan access leads to an increased incidence of personal bankruptcy filing. Alternatively, other work has shown that payday loans help borrowers manage expenses (Morgan, Strain and Seblani 2012; Morse 2011; Zinman 2010). Bhutta, Skiba and Tobacman (2015) find no effect of payday loan access on a number of financial measures.

While the research on the consequences of borrowing on payday loans is mixed, what is certain is that payday borrowers do not use a payday loan once, only for unexpected

---

[9] Caskey (2010) provides a nice review of this research.

expenses. Such expenses may be how consumers entered into the market in the first place, but several researchers have shown that once they begin borrowing, people use payday loans in a serial manner (see Carter, Skiba, and Sydnor 2013; Skiba and Tobacman 2011; and Burke et al. 2014). We argue that most benefits or costs of payday loans stem from the subsequent repayment behavior, not the mere access to or one-time use of such a loan. As described in the next section, borrowers tend to mis-predict their future borrowing behavior, and hence the relative utility of either borrowing or not borrowing and of borrowing on different credit products.

### 2.3    Repayment Behavior of Payday Borrowers

The rational model with exponential discounting described above assumes that, after the initial choice to take out or not take out a pawn or payday loan, borrowers are time-consistent, i.e., they correctly predict their future discounting.

#### 2.3.1    Hyperbolic discounting

Self-control and procrastination problems are not in line with the assumptions of the exponential model. Remember that a rational model assumes people trade off utilities over time using exponential discounting, whereby the discount rate between any two periods, be it today and tomorrow or a day 365 days from now and a day 365+1 days from now, is constant. The constant discounting comes with the assumption that people are time-consistent: if I predict I will discount a day next week by some factor $x$, I will in fact exhibit that discount factor. But much research, and intuition, suggests that people do not always follow these time-consistent patterns, and that people exhibit self-control problems and are biased toward the present.

As such, a main alternative has emerged, hyperbolic discounting (Laibson 1997). This model adds an additional discount factor while leaving the other components of exponential discounting intact. The extra discount factor captures the idea that people discount the current period more heavily than other future periods—a "present bias." The discounting that occurs between today and tomorrow is manifestly different than the discounting that occurs between any two future consecutive days. This model captures behaviors such as smokers swearing off smoking but beginning tomorrow, and dieters deciding they will cut back next week. Today is different from any other day, and we plan to be time-consistent *tomorrow*.

Hyperbolic discounters can be either *naive* or *sophisticated* about their self-control problems. "Naïfs" fail to realize that they will have different discount rates in the short and long runs and expect to be more patient in the future than they end up being (demonstrating time inconsistency, a form of irrational behavior). "Sophisticates," on the other hand, realize they will have differing discount rates in the short run and long run and may seek commitment devices to combat their procrastination.

Much evidence and intuition supports the theoretical validity of hyperbolic discounting in consumer finance as well as other fields. Behaviors like simultaneously saving for retirement and borrowing on credit cards are, for example, accurately captured by this model (Laibson, Repetto, and Tobacman 2000). The repeated use and delaying of default on payday loans has been documented by Skiba and Tobacman (2008). For an overview on the evidence see DellaVigna (2009). Of course, hyperbolic discounting, while it improves on the realism of exponential discounting, is also a very stylized theory of decision-making and can fail to capture many critical factors of decision-making. It should be noted that recent research (Andreoni and Sprenger 2012) has investigated the extent to which preferences that appear to exhibit aspects of hyperbolic discounting may in fact be expressing aspects of uncertainty and risk related to future outcomes, rather than some irrational behavior with regard to choice over time.

### 2.3.2 Loss aversion

Another behavioral anomaly that is especially important in the context of collateralized loans is loss aversion (Kahneman and Tversky 1984). Loss aversion is the effect whereby losses (relative to some reference point) "loom larger" than gains. For example, the utility loss associated with losing $10 is larger than the utility gain of winning $10. Typically, this gap is measured to be about two, meaning losing $10 feels about twice as bad as winning $10 feels good.

Recent evidence suggests that different types of items are more likely to trigger loss aversion than others. If borrowers are pawning sentimental items, those items might be more likely to be subject to loss aversion than items whose value is purely consumption value (see Carter and Skiba (2012) for information on borrowers pawning sentimental items).

We believe loss aversion may play a role in the weighing of the potential costs and benefits of using a collateralized loan such as a pawnshop loan. Next we describe in more detail how people actually use payday loans and pawnshop loans, and which of the theories described above can best account for those behaviors.

## 3. PAYDAY AND PAWN CREDIT INTERACTIONS

### 3.1 How do Pawn Loans and Payday Loans Work?

Pawnshop loans are short-term (30- to 90-day) loans for which personal possessions are used as collateral. The borrower, showing a valid ID, leaves a possession, or "pledge," in exchange for a loan, typically around $75. If the borrower does not return to repay the principal plus interest after the set time, the pledge is forfeited and resold by the pawnbroker. No job, bank account, or credit check is required to borrow from a pawnshop.

Payday loans are also short-term, but they are backed with the promise of a future paycheck rather than being collateralized in the traditional sense. Borrowers must write a check postdated for their next payday; therefore, steady employment and a checking account are prerequisites for borrowing. Payday lenders often use a subprime credit score to determine eligibility. Individuals with scores below the cutoff are almost always rejected, and those with scores above the threshold are almost always approved (for more on this type of credit scoring see Agarwal, Skiba, and Tobacman (2009) and Skiba and Tobacman (2011)).

### 3.2   Substitutes or Complements?

Looking only at the short-term nature of both payday and pawn credit, the two forms of credit may be considered substitutes and/or complements. Carter (2015) shows that low-income borrowers sometimes use the two in conjunction rather than as alternatives and uses data from the FDIC survey in 2009 to show that in the preceding year, conditional on someone using a payday loan, there was a 13.8 percent chance that that individual also used a pawnshop loan in the prior year. Just over 3 percent of all households had used payday loans in the preceding year, and around 2 percent of all households had visited a pawnshop in the preceding year.[10]

Beyond the traditional pecuniary aspects, there are inherent differences and similarities between pawn and payday borrowing and mainstream borrowing that should be taken into consideration when we analyze the use of, and/or the choice between, the two kinds of credit. Agarwal and Bos (2014, p. 7) summarize one view:

> First, compared with payday lending pawn credit is less likely to lead borrowers into a downward spiral of increased financial distress. The fact that the borrower physically hands over the collateral to the pawnbroker eliminates—if the collateral is adequately appraised—most of the credit risk in case of a default. This near absence of risk has eliminated the need for credit scoring or an information-sharing system among pawnbrokers or, for that matter, information-sharing between pawnbrokers and regular banks. As a result, beyond the loss of the collateral the consequences of defaulting on a pawn loan for future credit access are absent in the mainstream credit market. Therefore, it is possible that risk-averse agents use pawn credit because they value the option to access bank credit in the future. Another possibility is that risk-averse agents use pawn credit because the cost of defaulting is known a priori. The consequences of defaulting on pawn credit are clear: one loses ownership of the pledged collateral.

A second dimension for comparison is the speed of obtaining pawn and payday credit compared to that of obtaining mainstream credit. Typically, after one has arrived at the pawnshop, or at the storefront of a payday lender for that matter, the time from appraisal to the dispensing of cash is 5–10 minutes. Hence, consumers might use pawn or payday credit because it is relatively fast. A difference that holds between pawn credit and both payday and mainstream bank credit is that the pawnbroker does not request any additional information from the customer beyond her identification and collateral. Therefore, consumers might choose pawn credit over other types of credit because they value their privacy. Payday lenders need to be able to verify the validity of the applicant's employment/paycheck because the paycheck serves as the collateral.

Beyond the influence of the current institutional environment on the choice of form of credit, individuals might be influenced by the institutional setting in their country of origin or by their cultural heritage; see, for example, Guiso, Sapienza, and Zingales (2006) on the influence of culture on, among other things, saving decisions, as well as Osili and Paulson (2008) on the influence of formal and informal constraints on U.S. immigrants' financial decisions. Hence, cultural attitudes and habits might lead some consumers to choose pawn credit instead of bank loans.

---

[10]   The question in the FDIC survey is "Have you or anyone in your household ever sold items at a pawn shop?"; thus, a positive response does not necessarily indicate that the individual actually took out a pawnshop loan.

The last reason we will mention, which is not to say that there are not more, is the idea that individuals use pawn and/or payday credit because they are not well informed about either their outside options or the compounded costs of these forms of credit, or both. These kinds of issues are dealt with in a fast-growing literature on financial literacy; see, for example, Agarwal et al. (2011), Bertrand and Morse (2011) and Lusardi and Scheresberg (2013).

### 3.3 Cost

Interest rates on payday and pawnshop loans vary by state but are, in general, high relative to the average interest rate charged by a mainstream bank for a credit card or an uncollateralized line of credit. In Texas, where our data are from, the legal limit on the interest rate for pawn credit is 20 percent for a loan with a duration of 30 days. (This rate amounts to a 240 percent APR (20 percent*12 weeks with no compounding).) The payday lender in our study charged 15 percent interest until May 2001, when it began charging 18 percent. Unlike with traditional forms of credit, interest rates on payday loans are per loan, meaning that regardless of the length of the loan or the credit score of the borrower, the interest paid on any loan of a given size would be the same. For example, if someone took out a $200 loan at an interest rate of 18 percent for 15 days, she would pay the same, $36, as someone with a different credit score who took out a 30-day $200 loan. In our sample, the average loan duration was 15.1 days. A loan with this duration and an interest rate of 18 percent would have an implied APR of 438 percent.[11]

### 3.4 Data

We use administrative records from a large national lender that offers both payday and pawn credit in the United States. Our data cover all of the lender's operations in Texas from 1997 to 2004, containing the universe of loan records. Payday loans were not offered in the lender's stores until 2000. In our sample we have 1,226,386 payday loans taken out between 2000 and mid-2004, and for each loan we observe the size, origination date, due date, repayment status (repayment, default, or rollover), and interest amount. We also observe records on people who applied for but were denied a payday loan. Additionally we observe characteristics about each individual: gender, age, subprime credit score, race, home ownership status, and payment frequency (paid once a month, twice a month, once every two weeks, or once every week).

The data consist of 398,722 pawn loans taken out between 1997 and 2004 and for each of these loans, similarly, we observe the size, total loan duration, and status of the loan (eventual default or repayment), and the item used as collateral. Pledges are categorized into: jewelry, electronics, tools/equipment, household items, sporting equipment, guns, musical instruments, and camera equipment.[12]

Finally, we merge these payday data and pawn data at the individual level to examine

---

[11]  Interest rates on payday loans and pawnshop loans are not compounded.

[12]  These same data on payday loans have been studied in other papers, including Agarwal, Skiba, and Tobacman (2009) and Skiba and Tobacman (2011).

the interplay between these two forms of credit. The major drawback of these data is that we only have records from one lender (albeit the universe of those records). We cannot therefore observe the entire credit portfolio for people in our sample, but we interpret our results as lower bounds on the importance of the interactions between these types of credit.

### 3.5    Aggregate Trends Over Time

Caskey (2005) documents that while the number of pawnshops grew through the 1990s, that number decreased between 2000 and 2002 after payday loans became more popular in the late 1990s. Pawnshop borrowers often have bank accounts and are employed (a requirement for taking out a payday loan), making them eligible for payday loans as well; this suggests that pawnshop borrowers may turn to payday loans at the expense of more pawnshop borrowing. Around this time, many large pawnshop operators also began offering payday loans in their stores and opening new stores focused solely on payday loans.

Our data does not predate the arrival of payday loans to the market in general, but we can observe when payday loans started being offered in the same stores as pawnshop loans.

Figure 4.1 tracks the monthly average total amount pawned in each store at which both payday loans and pawnshop loans were offered, as well as the monthly average total amount stores lent in payday loans, by the number of months since the store began offering payday loans. As the graph shows, the general trajectory for pawnshop lending

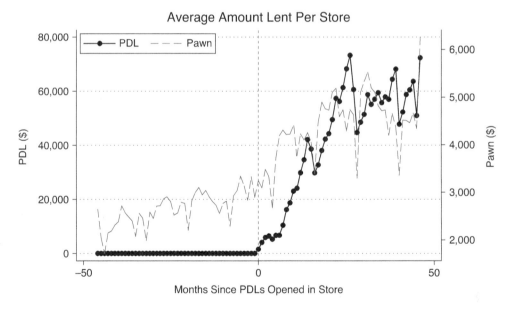

*Note:*    This figure shows the monthly average total amount pawned in each store where both payday loans and pawnshop loans were offered, as well as the monthly average total amount lent in payday loans per store, by the number of months since the store began offering payday loans.

*Figure 4.1    Average load amount per store*

was positive and continued to increase over time after payday loans became available. However, the use of pawnshop loans begins to level off, suggesting that their growth was stabilized by the influx of payday credit—although the leveling off could also be the result of other macroeconomics factors, such as unemployment rates at the time.

Next we explore the consequences of not being able to borrow on a payday loan. By exploiting a discontinuity in the lending decisions of the payday lender, we are able to draw certain inferences about a causal relationship between the availability of a payday loan and the subsequent decision to take out a pawn loan.

### 3.6 Identification Strategy: Regression Discontinuity Design

The discontinuity is based on the lender's credit score threshold: below the threshold applicants are denied a payday loan, and above the threshold applicants are granted a loan.[13] Based on the assumption that borrowers just below and just above the threshold are similar in all other relevant dimensions, we are able to compare their respective outcomes and analyze the effect of failing to obtain a payday loan on the subsequent decision to take out a pawn loan. This regression-discontinuity approach permits us not only to look at the pawnshop use of those who are denied a payday loan, but to also explore the counterfactual: what would have happened if the payday loan was actually granted?

#### 3.6.1 Regression discontinuity

We use the sample of payday lending storefronts that offer both payday loans and pawnshop loans. All of our results hold (but are muted) if we also include shops that offer either payday loans or pawnshop loans but not both. We estimate the following regressions by ordinary least squares:[14]

$$y_i = \alpha + \beta_1 x_1 + \beta_2 f(x_2) + \beta_3 Z + e \tag{1}$$

where the dependent variable $y$ denotes the probability someone takes out a loan ($y_1$) or the amount ($y_2$) pawned. $\alpha$ is a constant and $x_1$ is a dummy for being above the cutoff. $f(x_2)$ is a second order polynomial of the credit score below and above the threshold and is included to control for any effects of credit score on pawnshop use that might not be linear. $Z$ is a vector with borrower characteristics including age, gender, and race.

The coefficient on the indicator for being above the threshold measures the change in the amount or likelihood of taking out a pawnshop loan if the borrower was able to obtain a payday loan relative to someone who was not. We analyze the subsequent pawn credit use over a number of time horizons following an individual's first payday loan application: 2 days, 1 week, 2 weeks, and 1 month.

---

[13]  Skiba and Tobacman (2011) document this discontinuity in approval ratings along the same cutoff and provide evidence that individuals on either side of the cutoff are similar except with respect to their ability to get a loan; 99.6 percent of applicants with scores below the cutoff are rejected and 96.9 percent of loans with scores above the cutoff are approved.
[14]  In addition to this linear probability model, we also run a probit model. Results are similar so we present OLS here.

### 3.6.2   Graphical representation of discontinuity regressions

Figure 4.2 and Figure 4.3 show the fraction of people that take out a pawnshop loan and the average amount that someone takes out for each of four different time periods: 2 days, 1 week, 2 weeks, and 1 month after the date that an individual first borrows. In the figures, the credit scores are split into 100 bins and the fraction of people who take out a pawnshop loan (Figure 4.2) and the average amount of the loan from a pawned item (Figure 4.3) for that bin are plotted as dots on the graph. The line shows the predicted results from the regression-discontinuity regressions described in Equation (1) without the demographic characteristics.

If payday loans and pawnshop loans are substitutes, we expect borrowers who are precluded from getting a payday loan (borrowers who are below the credit score cutoff) to be more likely to take out a pawnshop loan afterward. If they are complements, we would expect that individuals who obtain access to payday loans to be likely to then take out a pawnshop loan. If the difference between the two groups on either side of the threshold decreases over time, it might be that borrowers who obtain payday loans are then turning to pawnshop loans if payday loans are not meeting their credit needs. Alternatively they could be having trouble making their payday loans payments and thus turning to pawnshops to help pay off the loan.

### 3.7   Results

In general, we can see that in all figures there is a drop in both the number and size of pawnshop loans taken out for those that are able to take out a payday loan relative to those who are denied a payday loan.

We can see in Figure 4.2 and Table 4.1 that in the two days following approval for a payday loan, individuals have a three-percentage-point decrease in their likelihood of taking out a pawnshop loan. The magnitude of the increase in the amount pawned for that same time period is $3 (shown in Figure 4.3 and reported in Table 4.2). These results generally hold with little variation in the probability of taking a loan or in the amount of the loan when we expand the time horizon out past two days after the denial or approval of the payday loan (looking across the columns in Tables 4.1 and 4.2).

While the decrease in the use of pawnshop loans around the threshold is statistically significant, suggesting some substitution, the amount of the decrease is economically very small. The average size of a payday loan is around $275, while the average size of a pawnshop loan is only $75; thus, it may not be surprising that borrowers who are rejected for a payday loan are not pawning significantly more. It may be either that payday loan applicants have already pawned the items they are willing and able to pawn prior to applying for the payday loan, that payday borrowers who are rejected are turning to other lenders rather than pawnshop loans, or that pawnshop and payday loans are not strong substitutes.

As noted before, in order to take out a pawn loan one has to have something that actually can be pawned as collateral. As gold constitutes the largest share of pawned items in the US pawn industry it might explain the slight increased likelihood for women to take out a pawn loan after payday denial compared to men. Moreover, as single-mother households in the US have been rapidly growing, it is also true that women become more vulnerable if a health/income shock hits their household. That again increases

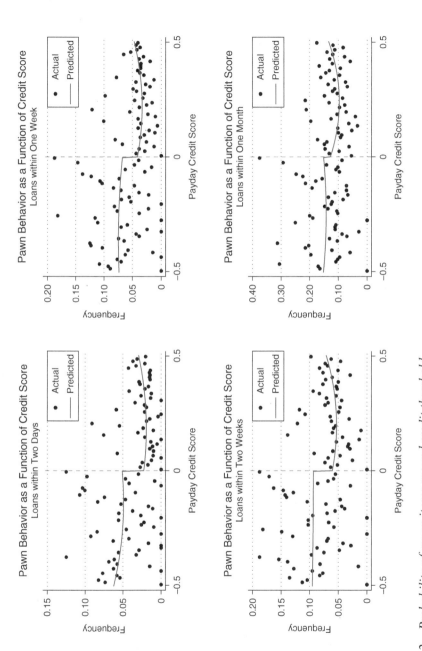

*Figure 4.2   Probability of pawn items around credit threshold*

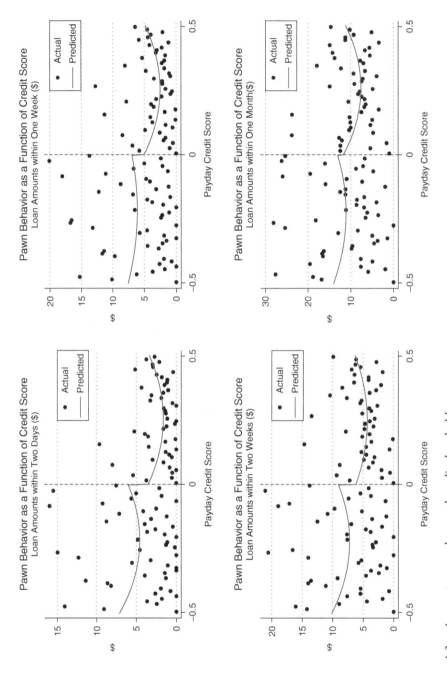

*Figure 4.3    Amount pawned around credit threshold*

*Table 4.1 Taking out a pawnshop loan*

|  | (1) | (2) | (3) | (4) | (5) | (6) | (7) | (8) |
|---|---|---|---|---|---|---|---|---|
|  | 2 Days Following PDL Application | | 1 Week Following PDL Application | | 2 Weeks Following PDL Application | | 1 Month Following PDL Application | |
| Above Threshold | -0.029*** | -0.032*** | -0.035*** | -0.033*** | -0.036*** | -0.044*** | -0.038*** | -0.042* |
|  | (0.003) | (0.010) | (0.004) | (0.012) | (0.005) | (0.015) | (0.007) | (0.022) |
| Controls Included |  | X |  | X |  | X |  | X |
| N | 23,195 | 23,195 | 23,195 | 23,195 | 23,141 | 23,141 | 22,938 | 22,938 |
| R-Squared | 0.0035 | 0.0361 | 0.0033 | 0.0452 | 0.0022 | 0.0537 | 0.0011 | 0.0687 |

*Notes:* Table 4.1 shows the coefficient from an RD regression on the decision to use a pawnshop. Columns (1) and (2) show the decision to take out a pawnshop loan two days following a payday loan applications; Columns (3) and (4) look one week after the payday loan application; Columns (5) and (6), 2 weeks following; and Columns (7) and (8), one month following. In the odd columns, the only independent variable included is an indicator for being above the payday loan credit approval threshold. In the even columns, there are controls for: squared function of credit score on either side of the cut-off, the frequency an individual is paid (semi-monthly, weekly, every two weeks, monthly), months they have lived in a location, whether they are paid by direct deposit, monthly pay, homeownership, tenure at job, age, race, gender, checking account balance, dummies for missing demographics, and month dummies. Regressions are run for credit scores within a standard deviation of the credit score on either side of the cut-off. ***, **, and * indicate statistical significance at the 0.01, 0.05, and 0.1 level respectively. Standard errors are included in parentheses.

117

*Table 4.2  Pawnshop amount*

| | (1) | (2) | (3) | (4) | (5) | (6) | (7) | (8) |
|---|---|---|---|---|---|---|---|---|
| | 2 Days Following PDL Application | | 1 Week Following PDL Application | | 2 Weeks Following PDL Application | | 1 Month Following PDL Application | |
| Above Threshold | -2.82*** | -2.95** | -3.11*** | -2.70* | -2.89*** | -4.04** | -2.99*** | -3.35 |
| | (0.462) | (1.445) | (0.514) | (1.604) | (0.622) | (1.936) | (0.870) | (2.686) |
| Controls Included | | X | | X | | X | | X |
| N | 23,195 | 23,195 | 23,195 | 23,195 | 23,141 | 23,141 | 22,938 | 22,938 |
| R-Squared | 0.0016 | 0.0179 | 0.0015 | 0.0224 | 0.0009 | 0.0248 | 0.0005 | 0.0340 |

*Notes*: Table 4.2 shows the coefficient from an RD regression on the amount pawned. Columns (1) and (2) show the amount ($) pawned two days following a payday loan applications. Columns (3) and (4) look one week after the payday loan application; Columns (5) and (6), 2 weeks following; and Columns (7) and (8), one month following. In the odd columns, the only independent variable included is an indicator for being above the payday loan credit approval threshold. In the even columns, there are controls for: squared function of credit score on either side of the cut-off, the frequency and individual is paid (semi-monthly, weekly, every two weeks, monthly), months they have lived in a location, whether they are paid by direct deposit, monthly pay, homeownership, tenure at job, age, race, gender, checking account balance, dummies for missing demographics, and month dummies. Regressions are run for credit scores within a standard deviation of the credit score on either side of the cut-off. ***, **, and * indicate statistical significance at the 0.01, 0.05, and 0.1 level respectively. Standard errors are included in parentheses.

the likelihood of needing short-term credit compared to men. As we cannot appraise the items ourselves, we cannot determine whether men versus women (or blacks versus whites) are treated differently in their use of pawnshop loans. We do see that blacks are generally less likely than whites to get a pawnshop loan.

To explore potential heterogeneity, we reran our regression for separate subsamples. For females, the results were similar to those for the full sample. For the male sample, we no longer reached statistical significance, but the coefficient remained negative. We have data on race for just 34 percent of the sample, but some interesting facts emerge when splitting the sample by race. Statistical significance remains when we run regressions separately for blacks for the time period up until one month, although the magnitudes are larger, suggesting even more substitution for this group. However, when we split the sample into whites and Hispanics only, the statistical significance disappears in the regressions that include demographics, but they remain negative.

One of the pitfalls in our analysis is the prevalence of other payday and pawnshop lenders in the area around the source of our data; since we lack data from these competitors we will not be able to present a complete picture of pawn and payday credit use in the area at the time.

## 4.   SUMMARY AND DISCUSSION: REGULATION

In this chapter we have summarized existing evidence on how people make important, and sometimes costly, choices in credit markets and presented some new evidence on the substitution between payday and pawn credit. Because people substitute among alternative forms of credit, it is important for regulators to document how, when, and why people substitute among forms of credit. With the inception of the Dodd Frank Act,[15] we have seen changes to regulation in credit markets, and attention has increasingly fallen on alternative sources of credit, like payday loans. In March 2015, the Consumer Financial Protection Bureau (CFPB) announced that it would seek to "end payday debt traps." The CFPB is poised to make major changes, likely restricting payday lending (CFPB 2015).

Above we have outlined both theory and evidence on how and why people transition between forms of alternative and traditional credit. Regulators should consider these factors before they ban or severely limit access to any one type of credit. Pawnshops can be a good alternative for those without access to payday loans, and even for those who do have access. But there are alternative sources of credit that are more risky than pawnshops. Remember that default in the pawn market does not come with much cost, beyond the loss of the pawned item.

We have seen in the empirical section that people turn to pawnshops when they lack access to payday loans. Previous work also suggests that in states where payday loans are banned, auto title lending is becoming an important source of credit for low-income Americans (Fritzdixon et al. 2014). Title loans are becoming increasingly popular and have incurred little regulatory scrutiny to date. Fritzdixon et al. (2014) argue that the loans

---

[15]   Dodd–Frank Wall Street Reform and Consumer Protection Act of 2010 § 312(b)(2)(B)(i); 12 U.S.C. §5412(b)(2)(B)(i) (Supp. V 2011).

have obfuscated terms, which often leads to unexpectedly long (nine months and longer) periods of indebtedness and unexpectedly high costs due to hidden fees and confusing interest rate calculations.

When payday loans were banned in 13 states, the question of where borrowers would go was never an important part of regulators' calculus. We hope more research on choices between credit products will allow data on these transitions to be part of the conversation.

# REFERENCES

Agarwal, Sumit, and Marieke Bos, 2014. Rationality in the Consumer Credit Market: Choosing between Alternative and Mainstream Credit (June 1, 2014). Available at SSRN: http://ssrn.com/abstract=1978574 (last accessed June 2015).

Agarwal, Sumit, John C. Driscoll, Xavier Gabaix, and David Laibson. 2011. Learning in the Credit Card Market. Working Paper No. 13822. National Bureau of Economic Research, Cambridge, Mass.

Agarwal, Sumit, Paige Marta Skiba, and Jeremy Tobacman. 2009. Payday Loans and Credit Cards: New Liquidity and Credit Scoring Puzzles? *American Economic Review Papers and Proceedings* 99: 412–17.

Andreoni, James, and Charles Sprenger. 2012. Risk Preferences Are Not Time Preferences. *American Economic Review* 102: 3357–76.

Bertrand, Marianne, and Adair Morse. 2011. Information Disclosure, Cognitive Biases and Payday Borrowing. *Journal of Finance* 66: 1865–93.

Bhutta, Neil, Paige Marta Skiba, and Jeremy Tobacman. 2015. Payday Loan Choices and Consequences. *Journal of Money, Credit, and Banking* 47: 223–60.

Bos, Marieke, Susan Payne Carter, and Paige Marta Skiba. 2012. The Pawn Industry and Its Customers: The United States and Europe. Vanderbilt Law & Economics Research Paper No. 12-26. Vanderbilt Law School, Nashville, TN.

Bos, Marieke, and Leonard I. Nakamura, 2014. Should Defaults Be Forgotten? Evidence from Variation in Removal of Negative Consumer Credit Information (July 1, 2014). FRB of Philadelphia Working Paper No. 14-21.

Burhouse, Susan, and Yazmin Osaki. 2012. 2011 FDIC National Survey of Unbanked and Underbanked Households. https://www.fdic.gov/householdsurvey/2011/index.html

Burke, Kathleen, Jonathan Lanning, Jesse Leary, and Jialan Wang. 2014. *CFPB Data Point: Payday Lender*. The CFPB Office of Research. http://files.consumerfinance.gov/f/201403_cfpb_report_payday-lending.pdf

Carrell, Scott, and Jonathan Zinman. 2014. In Harm's Way? Payday Loan Access and Military Personnel Performance. *Review of Financial Studies* 27: 2805–40.

Carter, Susan Payne. 2015. Payday Loan and Pawnshop Usage: The Impact of Allowing Payday Loan Rollovers. *Journal of Consumer Affairs* 49: 436–56.

Carter Susan Payne, and Paige Marta Skiba. 2012. Pawnshops, Behavioral Economics, and Self-Regulation. *Review of Banking & Financial Law* 32: 193–220.

Carter Susan Payne, Paige Marta Skiba, and Justin Sydnor. 2013. The Difference a Day (Doesn't) Make: Does Giving Borrowers More Time to Repay Break the Cycle of Repeated Payday Loan Borrowing? http://www.law.northwestern.edu/research-faculty/colloquium/law-economics/documents/Skiba%20Payday.pdf (last accessed June 2015).

Caskey, John. 2005. Fringe Banking and the Rise of Payday Lending. In Patrick Bolton and Howard Rosenthal (eds) *Credit Markets for the Poor*. New York: Russell Sage Foundation.

Caskey, John. 2010. Payday Lending: New Research and the Big Question. Working Paper No. 10-32. Research Department, Federal Reserve Bank of Philadelphia, Philadelphia, PA.

Consumer Financial Protection Bureau 2015. CFPB Fact Sheet: The CFPB Considers Proposal to End Payday Debt Traps. http://files.consumerfinance.gov/f/201503_cfpb-proposal-under-consideration.pdf (last accessed June 2015).

DellaVigna, Stefano. 2009. Psychology and Economics: Evidence from the Field. *Journal of Economic Literature* 47: 315–72.

Frederick, Shane, George Loewenstein, and Ted O'Donoghue. 2002. Time Discounting and Time Preference: A Critical Review. *Journal of Economic Literature* 40: 351–401.

Fritzdixon, Kathryn, Jim Hawkins, and Paige Marta Skiba. 2014. Dude, Where's My Car Title? The Law, Behavior, and Economics of Title Lending Markets. *University of Illinois Law Review* 1013–58.

Gerardi, Kristopher, Lorenz Goette, and Stephan Meier. 2010. Financial Literacy and Subprime Mortgage

Delinquency: Evidence From a Survey Matched to Administrative Data. Working Paper 2010-10. Federal Reserve Bank of Atlanta, Atlanta, GA.

Guiso, Luigi, Paola Sapienza, and Luigi Zingales. 2006. Does Culture Affect Economic Outcomes? *Journal of Economic Perspectives* 20: 23–48.

Kahneman, Daniel and Amos Tversky. 1984. Choices, Values, and Frames. *American Psychologist* 39: 341–50.

Laibson, David. 1997. Golden Eggs and Hyperbolic Discounting. *Quarterly Journal of Economics* 112: 443–77.

Laibson, David, Andrea Repetto, and Jeremy Tobacman. 2000. A Debt Puzzle. Working Paper No. w7879. National Bureau of Economic Research, Cambridge, Mass.

Linardi, Sera and Tomomi Tanaka. 2013. Competition as a Savings Incentive: A Field Experiment at a Homeless Shelter. *Journal of Economic Behavior & Organization* 95: 240–51.

Lusardi, Annamaria, and Carlo de Bassa Scheresberg. 2013. Financial Literacy and High Cost Borrowing in the United States. Working Paper No. 18969. National Bureau of Economic Research, Cambridge, Mass.

Lusardi, Annamaria, and Olivia S. Mitchell. 2009. How Ordinary Consumers Make Complex Economic Decisions: Financial Literacy and Retirement Readiness. Working Paper No. 15350. National Bureau of Economic Research, Cambridge, Mass.

Lusardi, Annamaria, Olivia S. Mitchell, and Vilsa Curto. 2009. Financial Literacy and Financial Sophistication Among Older Americans. Working Paper No. 15490. National Bureau of Economic Research, Cambridge, Mass.

Lusardi, Annamaria, Olivia S. Mitchell, and Vilsa Curto. 2014. Financial Literacy and Financial Sophistication in the Older Population. *Journal of Pension Economics & Finance* 13(4): 347–366.

Meier, Stephan, and Charles Sprenger. 2010. Present-Biased Preferences and Credit Card Borrowing. *American Economics Journal: Applied Economics* 2: 193–210.

Melzer, Brian. 2011. The Real Costs of Credit Access: Evidence from the Payday Lending Market. *Quarterly Journal of Economics* 126: 517–55.

Morgan, Donald P., Michael R. Strain, and Ihab Seblani. 2012. How Payday Credit Access affects Overdrafts and Other Outcomes. *Journal of Money, Credit, and Banking* 44: 519–31.

Morse, Adair. 2011. Payday Lenders: Heroes or Villains? *Journal of Financial Economics* 102: 28–44.

O'Donoghue, Ted, and Matthew Rabin. 1999. Doing it Now or Later. *The American Economic Review* 89: 103–24.

Osili, Una Okonkwo, and Anna Paulson. 2008. What Can We Learn about Financial Access from U.S. Immigrants? The Role of Country of Origin Institutions and Immigrant Beliefs. *World Bank Economic Review* 22: 431–55.

Skiba, Paige, and Jeremy Tobacman. 2008. Payday Loans, Uncertainty and Discounting: Explaining Patterns of Borrowing, Repayment, and Default. Vanderbilt Law & Economics Research Paper No. 08-33. Vanderbilt Law School, Nashville, TN.

Skiba, Paige, and Jeremy Tobacman. 2011. Do Payday Loans Cause Bankruptcy? Vanderbilt Law & Economics Research Paper No. 11-13. Vanderbilt Law School, Nashville, TN.

Stango, Victor, and Jonathan Zinman. 2009. Exponential Growth Bias and Household Finance. *Journal of Finance* 64: 2807–49.

Telyukova, Irina. 2013. Household Need for Liquidity and the Credit Card Debt Puzzle. *Review of Economic Studies* 80: 1148–77.

Zinman, Jonathan. 2010. Restricting Consumer Credit Access: Household Survey Evidence on Effects Around the Oregon Rate Cap. *Journal of Banking and Finance* 34: 546–56.

# 5. The effect of advertising on home equity credit choices

*Sumit Agarwal and Brent W. Ambrose**

## 1. INTRODUCTION

Advertisers spend billions of dollars on marketing across all forms of media. For example, in 2005, over \$55 billion was spent on direct mail advertisements, making "junk mail" second only to television (at \$68 billion) in dollars expended on advertising.[1] Financial institutions spent over \$8.4 billion marketing a wide variety of investment and credit products (e.g., mutual funds, insurance contracts, bank accounts, credit cards, and mortgage loans, to name just a few of the major categories), making the financial services the fourth highest industry by dollars spent on advertising.[2]

Obviously, one of the roles of advertising is to persuade the consumer to purchase a good or service. Thus, a natural question arises: to what extent does advertising or persuasion impact consumer financial decisions? We answer this question by examining the effect of direct advertising on one of the most important financial decisions facing households—the choice of mortgage contract type.

Financial economists now recognize that marketing and persuasion can affect consumer investment decisions. For example, studies of consumer investments in mutual funds indicate that marketing plays an active role in determining the money flow into funds.[3] In addition to evidence from mutual fund trading, Grullon, Kanatas, and Weston (2004)

\* We thank Jan Brueckner; Richard Buttimer; Souphala Chomsisengphet; Dimitris Christelis (European University Institute Discussant); Henrik Cronqvist (AEA Discussant); Jim Follain; Fu Yuming; Bert Higgins; Andrew Karolyi; David Laibson; Ken Lusht; Donna Nicholson; George Pennacchi; Devin Pope (NBER Discussant); John Quigley; Stuart Rosenthal; Josh Teitelbaum; Nancy Wallace; and the seminar participants at 2008 American Economic Association meeting in New Orleans, the 2008 NBER Summer Institute, Baruch College, the Federal Reserve Bank of Chicago, the National University of Singapore, Ohio State University, Syracuse University, the University of California-Berkeley, the University of North Carolina at Charlotte, and the 2007 Conference on Behavioral Approaches to Consumption, Credit, and Asset Allocation at the European University Institute in Florence, Italy, for helpful discussions and comments. Research assistance was ably provided by Lauren Gaudino and Cosmin Lucaci. We also thank Luca Benzoni and Olena Chyruk for providing us with the bond risk premium data.

[1] Source: *Advertising Age*, June 26 2006. (http://adage.com/images/random/lna2006.pdf).

[2] To put this in perspective, automotive, retail, and telecom were the top three industries in terms of advertising expenditures at \$20.9 billion, \$18.6 billion, and \$9.9 billion, respectively (source: *Advertising Age*, June 26, 2006).

[3] In one of the first studies to examine mutual fund marketing, Sirri and Tufano (1998) suggest that mutual fund advertising lowers consumer search costs and that this can explain the link between advertising and fund flow. Similarly, Jain and Wu (2000) and Barber, Odean, and Zheng (2005) show that mutual fund advertising is related to money flow (investment). More recently, Cronqvist (2006) shows that mutual fund advertising impacts investors' choices, even though it

find evidence linking firm product market advertising and investor interest. Furthermore, Barber and Odean (2008) document that exogenous factors calling attention to particular stocks can affect investor purchase decisions.[4] Thus, these studies reinforce the idea that marketing can and does impact financial decisions.

While previous research in economics and marketing indicates that advertising is effective, little is known about the impact that advertising has on altering consumer evaluation of financial decisions.[5] That is, can advertising lead consumers to ignore important financial factors when faced with an economic decision? In one of the few studies to examine this question, Bertrand et al. (2006) conducted a field experiment in South Africa, using personal loan contracts. Their experiment presents evidence showing that variations in the psychological features of the advertisement, as well as traditional economic variables such as interest rates, impact consumer loan take-up rates. The results from this field experiment are consistent with the findings of Russo, Carlson, and Meloy (2006) that persuasive information can lead decision-makers to choose inferior alternatives.[6] At the theoretical level, Mullainathan, Schwartzstein, and Shliefer (2008) built a simple model of persuasion that helps explain certain aspects of marketing—branding, advertisement, and product attributes (also see Mullainathan and Shliefer 2005)—while Shapiro (2006) theoretically demonstrates that advertisements can be persuasive rather than informative.

To the best of our knowledge, little research has examined the impact that advertising and persuasion can have on consumer choice in the mortgage market.[7] Yet, for most households, their mortgage is their single largest financial liability and the choice of mortgage contract type can have a substantial impact on the overall cost of home financing (Campbell, 2006).

We examine the consumer choice of mortgage contract type by focusing on the home equity lending market in the presence of direct mail advertising. Our data comes from a large financial institution (the data are proprietary in nature) that accepted home equity credit applications from a large number of branch offices. Furthermore, we utilize a natural experiment arising from the bank's marketing campaign that allows us to determine whether an applicant was exposed to a direct mail solicitation prior to applying for a loan. During the marketing campaign, applicants arrived at the bank's branch locations via

---

provides little information. In addition, Reuter and Zitzewitz (2006) find that mutual fund flows are positively related to positive news articles in the financial press.

[4]  Although Barber and Odean (2008) do not explicitly examine the role of advertising, they do note that news events, excessive trading volume, and extraordinary returns can affect investment decisions.

[5]  The economics literature traditionally classifies advertising as being persuasive, informative, or complementary (Bagwell, 2007). The informative view assumes that advertising simply conveys information, (e.g., Stigler 1961; Nelson, 1974, 1975), while the persuasive view assumes that advertising can alter consumer preferences.

[6]  In a related area of the literature, numerous studies have focused on the role that information framing has on individual decision choices (see, e.g. Kahneman and Tversky, 1979; Tversky and Kahneman 1981, 1986, among others.)

[7]  Recently, Perry and Motley (2008) explore the differences in newspaper print advertising message content in the Washington, D.C. metropolitan area aimed at the prime and subprime mortgage markets. Their analysis reveals that newspaper print mortgage advertisements having persuasive elements were more common than print advertisements containing informative elements.

one of two methods. First, applications were accepted at local branches from customers who were not targeted by the bank's marketing campaign. We refer to these applicants as "walk-in" (WI) customers. Second, the lender received applications at the branch locations from customers who were targeted with a direct mail solicitation advertising a home equity product. We refer to these applicants as "direct mail" (DM) customers. We are able to test the persuasive view versus the informative or complementary view of advertising by examining the choices of the DM customers relative to the choices made by the WI customers and by using the bank's pricing algorithm to precisely calculate the loan offer rate for the product not selected. If the lender's direct mail campaign is persuasive, then we should observe differences between the DM and WI customers' mortgage choices. However, if the advertising is informative or complementary, then we should observe DM and WI customers responding similarly to changes in economic conditions.

Our empirical method allows us to control for all observable differences between the WI and DM customers that are captured by the bank's underwriting process. As a result, we are able to isolate the effect of the direct mail solicitation on the customer's mortgage decision. In particular, we show that consumers who receive a direct mail solicitation are more likely to ignore the important economic and interest rate environment factors that influenced the decisions of the WI customers. Examining the applicant choices reveals that 78 percent of the DM customers were influenced by the bank's solicitation, while 22 percent responded to signals present in the economic environment. Further analysis of only the applicants who were clearly influenced by the bank's solicitation reveals that 74 percent were persuaded to originate a product that was opposite to the one selected by their counterparts who did not receive a direct mail solicitation. However, we also find that the direct mail solicitation could be classified as informative for 26 percent of the DM customers.

Interestingly, for the borrowers that our analysis indicates were likely persuaded by the bank's marketing campaign, we find that their three-month prepayment rate is almost four times higher than the corresponding prepayment rates on borrowers who were informed by the bank's solicitation. These results are consistent with evidence of consumer learning.[8] Thus, while our study reveals that bank advertising has a persuasive effect on consumer financial decisions for a majority of the applicants who received a solicitation, we also find evidence that is consistent with the informative role of advertising for a smaller subset of consumers.

Finally, we believe that our findings are not the result of sample selection issues arising from possible correlation between the customer's decision to respond to the bank's marketing campaign and the mortgage choice decision. First, we note that contract choice is a function of a borrower's expected tenure.[9] As a result, we expect that if sample selection is present it should bias our analysis toward observing a higher probability of selecting the fixed-rate product, weakening the effect of a line solicitation and biasing our estimated coefficients away from statistical significance. Second, we find no differences in location patterns between WI and DM customers. Third, we use a variety of econometric

---

[8]    See Agarwal et al. (2005).
[9]    See Rosenthal and Zorn (1993) for a discussion of borrower tenure and mortgage choice preferences.

methods to control for possible borrower self-selection bias—all of which point to the same conclusion. Thus, we do not believe that sample selection is biasing our findings of a persuasive advertising effect.

The findings from this study support the growing literature revealing that consumers are highly influenced by the presentation of information that frames financial decisions. For example, Madrian and Shea (2001) present evidence showing that the design of a firm's retirement contribution plan has a meaningful impact on the participation choices of employees.[10] In another example outside of economics, Kressel, Chapman, and Leventhal (2007) demonstrate that the format of survey questions has a direct impact on an individual's end-of-life treatment choice. In addition, in an area more closely related to the mortgage choice decision examined in this chapter, Shiller (2008) discusses anecdotal evidence that many subprime borrowers accepted mortgage terms that were probably not in their best interests, simply because the information about the contract appeared to come from an expert—such as a financial institution. Thus, our result indicating that advertising has a strong influence on consumer choice of mortgage product is consistent with this growing body of evidence showing that the way information is presented or that the way financial choices are framed can have a significant impact on the decision outcome.

Our chapter proceeds as follows. In the next section, we outline the previous theoretical and empirical studies of borrower mortgage choice and the role of advertising. We describe the data and empirical strategy in Section 3. In Section 4, we present our primary empirical test designed to show the effect of the bank's solicitation. Then in Section 5, we discuss several robustness checks. We summarize our conclusions in Section 6.

## 2.  MORTGAGE CHOICE AND THE ROLE OF ADVERTISING

The theoretical literature on mortgage choice is well developed and offers a number of testable hypotheses. For example, Alm and Follain (1987) and Brueckner (1986) suggest that borrower risk aversion is a primary factor determining mortgage choice. These models indicate that borrowers with low risk aversion and high discount rates should prefer the higher interest rate risk associated with adjustable contracts, while borrowers with relatively high risk aversion and/or lower discount rates should prefer fixed-rate contracts. Thus, the trade-off between fixed-rate mortgages (FRMs) and adjustable-rate mortgages (ARMs) should depend upon the prevailing interest rate environment and risk premiums at the time of origination.[11]

Extending the earlier work on mortgage choice, Brueckner (1993) and Rosenthal and Zorn (1993) focus on the role that borrower expected mobility plays in determining the selection of adjustable-rate versus fixed-rate debt. The comparative statistics derived from these models indicate that the borrower's propensity to choose an adjustable-rate contract is inversely related to her expected tenure. Furthermore, the comparative statistics in

---

[10]  Brown, Liang, and Weisbenner (2007) also show that the menu of investment options has a significant impact on participant portfolio choice.

[11]  See Dhillion, Shilling, and Sirmans (1987) for empirical verification.

Brueckner (1993) also support earlier theoretical models by indicating that the level of interest rates are inversely related to the attractiveness of the adjustable-rate debt.

More recently, a number of researchers have recognized the complexity and importance of the optimal mortgage choice problem within the context of household life-cycle consumption models. For example, Campbell and Cocco (2003) solve a dynamic model of mortgage choice and consumption assuming that borrower income is risky. Their analysis implies that borrowers with high risk aversion will prefer fixed-rate mortgages and that mortgage choice may reveal unobserved heterogeneity in borrower risk profiles.[12] In a novel empirical test that takes advantage of the discontinuity in the U.S. mortgage market resulting from the distinction between "conforming" and "non-conforming" mortgages, Vickery (2006) finds that borrower mortgage choices are highly sensitive to changes in FRM interest rates.[13] For example, Vickery (2006) estimates that a 10 basis point increase in fixed-rate mortgage rates corresponds to a 10.4 percentage point decline in the FRM market share.[14]

While the theoretical literature clearly shows that borrower choice of mortgage type should depend upon the prevailing financial conditions at origination, the prior empirical research has relied on the use of originated loans, necessitating the use of econometric models to infer borrower sensitivity to the interest rate environment.[15] Yet, a recent analysis of the home equity lending market by Agarwal et al. (2011) reveals that lenders can and do alter loan contract terms during the underwriting process and thus effect the observed "choice" of contract type. In this study, we focus on the borrower's initial choice as revealed on the credit application. Thus, we are able to isolate the factors impacting borrower choice, free of any bias introduced through subsequent lender screening and underwriting.

While our brief review of the literature demonstrates that borrower mortgage choice has received considerable attention, no study has examined the impact of lender advertising on this choice. Economists have long considered the effect of advertising on consumer behavior. In a recent survey of the previous century of economic research on advertising, Bagwell (2007) notes that economists generally view advertising as falling into one of three categories: persuasive, informative, or complementary. Under the persuasive

---

[12]    See also Sa-Aadu and Shilling (1994); Sa-Aadu and Sirmans (1995); and Chiang, Chow, and Liu (2002). Campbell (2006) confirms this result by finding that the share of ARMs to total mortgage origination is directly proportional to both the FRM–ARM interest rate differential and the level of the FRM interest rate. In addition, borrower mobility (see Chan, 1996; and Gabriel and Rosenthal, 1993) and borrower perceptions of default risk (see Posey and Yavas, 2001) may play a role in contract choice. Recent theoretical work by van Hemert, de Jong, and Driessen (2005) and van Hemert (2006) also reinforces the link between borrower risk aversion and ARM preference.

[13]    Conforming mortgages are loans that are eligible for purchase by the housing government sponsored enterprises (GSEs); Fannie Mae and Freddie Mac. In contrast, non-conforming mortgages are ineligible for purchase by the GSEs. In general, conforming mortgages have loan balances below the conforming loan limit (updated annually) and meet other underwriting risk criteria set by the GSEs.

[14]    Recent work by Koijen, van Hemert, and van Nieuwerburgh (2007) using aggregate ARM/FRM market shares indicates that the inflation risk premium and prepayment option value are primary factors in determining ARM market shares.

[15]    See Brueckner and Follain (1988), for example.

view, economists assume that "advertising alters consumers' tastes."[16] According to the persuasive theory, firms advertise with the goal of altering consumers' preferences so that they purchase the good or service being advertised.[17] In the context of our mortgage choice problem, the persuasive view of advertising suggests that a lender's direct mail solicitation causes consumers to ignore their evaluation of the economic environment and thus select the advertised product.

In contrast, the informative view, based on the work of Ozga (1960) and Stigler (1961), concludes that advertising provides consumers with information and lowers consumer search costs. In the context of the mortgage choice problem, the informative view of advertising suggests that the lender's direct mail solicitation provides information to the consumers (for example, reminding them that attractive interest rates exist on home equity products). As a result, direct mail solicitations lower search costs but do not alter preferences for a particular product based on the prevailing economic environment. Under this view, the consumer's choice should coincide with the type of product advertised in the solicitation.

Finally, the complementary view assumes that consumers' tastes and preferences are stable and advertising complements them to encourage consumption.[18] Under this view, the direct mail solicitation encourages prospective customers to want a home equity product from the lender, but the choice of product type still reflects their individual tastes and preferences.

Our study of home equity product choice has the potential to differentiate these competing economic views of advertising. First, if the persuasive view of advertising is correct, then we should observe the direct mail customers ignoring economic and interest rate environment factors and selecting the mortgage product suggested in the solicitation. However, if the informative view is correct, then we should observe the consumer's product choice coinciding with the product advertised in the solicitation, and this choice should be consistent with our theoretical expectations for product choice given the economic and interest rate environment prevailing at the time of application. Finally, if the complementary view is correct, then we should observe the direct mail customers selecting products in line with the theoretical predictions, given the economic and interest rate environment, without regard to the type of product listed on the solicitation.

Empirically differentiating between the three competing views of advertising is difficult. Thus, we first compare DM customers with a matched sample of WI customers in order to eliminate any spurious comparisons. Second, we use information provided by the borrowers about their intended use of the funds to identify borrowers most likely to be informed by the advertising and those most likely to be complemented by it.

---

[16]  Bagwell (2007), p. 3.
[17]  Bagwell (2007) documents that the persuasive view developed from early research by Robinson (1933) and Braithwaite (1928). Bagwell (2007, p. 10) comments that Braithwaite suggested that "advertising's effect is to induce consumers to purchase the wrong quantities of goods that are not well adapted to their true needs . . ."
[18]  See Bagwell (2007) for a discussion of the development of the complementary view.

## 3.   DATA AND EMPIRICAL METHODS

The data used in this study are the same as those discussed in Agarwal et al. (2011) and Agarwal et al. (2006). The data were provided by a large financial institution and consist of variable-rate home equity lines-of-credit (HELOCs) and fixed-rate home equity loans (HELs) issued to owner-occupants from March 2002 through December 2002.[19] The credit lines are open for the first five years, and the borrower is only required to make interest payments on the utilized line balance during this period. After the fifth year, the line is closed and is converted to a fully amortizing, fixed-rate term loan with a remaining term of five to 15 years.

The lender received applications from customers via two channels. First, the majority of applications were from customers walking into their local branch and requesting a home equity credit application. At this point, the local loan officer provided the customer with a menu of various home equity products—with the primary choice being a variable rate line-of-credit or fixed-rate loan.[20] As previously mentioned, we refer to these customers as "walk-in" (WI) customers. Between March 2002 and December 2002, the lender received over 108,000 applications by WI customers.

Second, the lender also received applications from customers who had received a direct mail solicitation advertising either a line-of-credit or home equity loan.[21] Between March 2002 and May 2002, the bank sent out over 3 million direct mail solicitations in 12 equally distributed waves (or campaigns) to potential customers (or households) with credit (FICO) scores above 640.[22] Across these 12 campaigns, approximately 2.1 million customers were targeted with a line-of-credit solicitation while 981,000 received a home equity loan solicitation. Conditional on maintaining the approximately two-to-one ratio of line to loan mailings, the bank randomly selected customers to receive the line-of-credit or loan offer.[23] That is, the bank did not specifically target individuals for a line or loan

---

[19]   During the sample period, this institution had operations primarily in the New England, Mid-Atlantic, and Florida regions and was ranked among the top five commercial banks and savings institutions by the FDIC.

[20]   Each product also contained a variety of pricing options based on the requested loan-to-value ratio.

[21]   By matching names, addresses, and solicitation mailing date from the bank's direct mail database with customer names, addresses, and application dates from the bank's home equity application database, we are able to identify the home equity customers that received a solicitation prior to their application for credit.

[22]   In designing the marketing program, the bank requested that the credit bureau provide a random sample of households in the target area that had credit scores above 640 for the purpose of conducting a direct mail campaign. By law, the bank cannot request information from the credit bureau and then screen the households again prior to mailing the solicitation. That is, once the bank pulls a credit score for a household, it is obligated to send that household a solicitation. The solicitation does not indicate that the households are "pre-approved" for credit. Since the solicitation is based only on credit score, some households that ultimately respond to the offer may be denied credit by the bank based on other household characteristics that are not in line with the bank's underwriting standards. In addition, the bank did not specifically target existing customers or non-customers. Rather, it requested a large random sample of eligible households residing in its geographic target market.

[23]   We confirmed the bank's random assignment of the line-of-credit and loan offers through discussions with representatives at the bank. Furthermore, we note that the random assignment is

*Table 5.1   Summary statistics for direct mail customers*

| Variables | Bank Solicitations | | | | Consumer Response | | | |
|---|---|---|---|---|---|---|---|---|
| | Loans Mean Std | | Lines Mean Std | | Loans Mean Std | | Lines Mean Std | |
| FICO Score | 722.6 | 42.8 | 729.7 | 48.6 | 714.8 | 37.0 | 726.8 | 44.8 |
| State MA | 22.7% | 30.2% | 20.8% | 28.6% | 24.7% | 28.6% | 21.0% | 27.2% |
| State CT | 10.8% | 37.3% | 13.0% | 33.6% | 10.8% | 15.7% | 14.9% | 13.7% |
| State ME | 5.7% | 8.7% | 6.7% | 9.7% | 6.1% | 6.2% | 6.1% | 4.9% |
| State NH | 4.4% | 20.4% | 4.7% | 21.2% | 5.0% | 14.7% | 4.4% | 14.7% |
| State NJ | 8.4% | 27.7% | 10.3% | 11.2% | 7.1% | 14.8% | 10.7% | 7.7% |
| State NY | 35.5% | 47.6% | 33.0% | 37.5% | 33.7% | 38.5% | 30.7% | 35.5% |
| State PA | 4.9% | 9.6% | 4.2% | 5.2% | 4.5% | 4.7% | 4.5% | 7.5% |
| State RI | 7.2% | 25.7% | 6.8% | 25.0% | 6.8% | 24.7% | 6.9% | 17.6% |
| Frequency | .981 Million | | 2.072 Million | | 11,249 | | 20,500 | |

*Note:*   This table shows the mean credit scores (FICO) for the recipients of the bank's direct mail soliciation and the customers who responded to the solicitation. The table also reports the frequency distribution of mailings and responses by customer location (State).

offer; rather, the bank randomly sent the line and loan mailings to customers with FICO scores greater than 640.[24] The bank's solicitation was essentially an "informational" type of advertisement in that it was designed to alert potential customers to the existence of the home equity type of credit offered by the bank. Although the solicitation "featured" one type of contract (either the HELOC or HEL), the solicitation clearly indicated that the featured product was not exclusive.[25]

Table 5.1 shows the mean FICO scores and geographic distribution of the customers sent the direct mail solicitations. Consistent with the bank's practice of randomly selecting customers for the two product solicitations, we see that the average FICO scores of the line and loan groups do not differ economically.[26] Table 5.1 also shows the average credit scores and geographic distribution for the customers who responded to the bank's solicitation. As is typical in direct mail marketing campaigns, the response rate is low. For example, 20,500 customers responded to the bank's line-of-credit solicitation for a 0.99 percent response rate and 11,249 customers responded to the loan solicitation for a

---

consistent with industry practice in financial product marketing campaigns. For example, Ausubel (1999) reports a similar random assignment of direct mail solicitations in credit card offers.

[24]   The bank's two-to-one targeting of lines-of-credit versus loans likely reflects the underlying profitability of these contracts and responses to competitive pressures. For example, Agarwal et al. (2006) show that home equity lines-of-credit and home equity loans have significantly different default rates, implying substantial differences in potential regulatory capital requirements under Basel II.

[25]   Consistent with industry practice regarding these types of solicitations, the solicitation did not offer a "discount" but stated that rates were subject to change and borrower underwriting guidelines.

[26]   The precision underlying consumer credit scoring models is such that the bank would not distinguish between borrowers with FICO scores of 729 and 722.

response rate of 1.15 percent. We also see that the credit scores for responding customers are lower than the credit quality of the population receiving the solicitation; this is consistent with the experience reported in other consumer loan research.[27] Although the customers received a solicitation for a specific product (either a line-of-credit or a loan), at the time of application the local loan officer showed them the same product menu as the WI customers and they were free to choose either product. Additionally, the solicitation for a line offer provided the option for the customer to choose a loan offer (and vice versa). As previously mentioned, we refer to the customers who responded to this advertisement as "direct mail" (DM) customers.

Table 5.2 shows the descriptive statistics for the DM and WI customer groups. A com-

*Table 5.2  Summary statistics for walk-in and direct mail customers*

| Variables | Walk-In | | Direct Mail | |
|---|---|---|---|---|
| | Mean | Std | Mean | Std |
| Customer LTV | 61.88 | 25.49 | 70.31 | 19.98 |
| Appraised LTV | 64.68 | 28.21 | 71.40 | 19.08 |
| Borrower Estimated Home Value | $329,521 | $236,802 | $299,334 | $221,874 |
| Appraised Home Value | $318,491 | $202,334 | $286,330 | $189,785 |
| Requested Loan Amount | $66,664 | $50,431 | $60,291 | $40,428 |
| Loan Amount Approved | $67,279 | $51,631 | $61,123 | $40,592 |
| APR | 5.46 | 1.06 | 5.45 | 1.06 |
| FICO Score | 728.02 | 50.50 | 724.40 | 41.03 |
| Debt to Income | 38.17 | 18.99 | 27.89 | 14.49 |
| Consumption | 30% | 42% | 28% | 42% |
| Refinancing | 46% | 48% | 48% | 48% |
| Years on the Job | 7.85 | 9.01 | 4.57 | 2.81 |
| Income | $122,241 | $160,425 | $110,694 | $71,919 |
| Borrower Age | 46.51 | 12.57 | 46.52 | 11.25 |
| First Mortgage Balance | $143,361 | $110,230 | $132,991 | $108,955 |
| Months at Address | 99.20 | 129.26 | 86.14 | 26.62 |
| Self-Employed | 7% | 26% | 6% | 23% |
| Retired | 8% | 27% | 2% | 13% |
| Home Maker | 1% | 11% | 1% | 10% |
| Married | 53% | 50% | 48% | 50% |
| Frequency | 108,117 | | 31,749 | |

*Note:*  Customer LTV is the loan-to-value ratio based on the requested loan amount and the borrower's self-reported house value. Appraised LTV is the bank's loan-to-value ratio based on the approved loan amount and independent property appraisal. APR is the effective contract interest rate on the loan product selected. FICO is the borrower's credit quality score at application. Debt-to-income is the ratio of the borrower's debt to total income. Income is the borrower's income at date of application. Consumption is a dummy variable indicating that the borrower intends to use the loan/line proceeds for consumption purposes. Refinancing is a dummy variable indicating that the borrower is using the loan/line proceeds to refinance existing debt. Home improvement is the omitted use of funds. Self-Employed, Retired, Home Maker, and Married are dummy variables indicating the borrower's respective employment and marriage status.

---

[27]  Ausubel (1999) reports a similar result for responses to direct mail credit card solicitations.

*Table 5.3 Demographic characteristics of walk-in and direct mail customers' locations*

|  | Direct Mail | (Mailings) | Direct Mail | (Response) | Walk-In | |
|---|---|---|---|---|---|---|
|  | Loans | Lines | Loans | Lines | Loans | Lines |
| Median Age | 37.71 | 37.70 | 37.58 | 37.41 | 37.53 | 37.90 |
|  | (5.38) | (5.19) | (5.33) | (5.24) | (5.26) | (5.34) |
| Median Income | $50,400.83 | $50,677.17 | $50,698.97 | $50,595.60 | $50,337.68 | $50,597.95 |
|  | ($19,266.53) | ($19,540.89) | ($19,617.34) | ($19,436.17) | ($19,622.13) | ($19,829.23) |
| % Female | 50.86% | 50.15% | 50.32% | 50.40% | 50.32% | 50.08% |
|  | (2.57%) | (2.56%) | (2.53%) | (2.53%) | (2.50%) | (2.50%) |
| % Black | 6.99% | 7.00% | 7.08% | 7.02% | 7.05% | 7.13% |
|  | (13.65%) | (13.55%) | (13.70%) | (13.66%) | (13.69%) | (13.96%) |
| Number of Zip Codes | 4,622 | 4,668 | 4,577 | 4,605 | 4,833 | 4,792 |

*Note:* This table reports the demographic characteristics' means and standard deviations (in parentheses) for the zip codes corresponding to the resident locations of the walk-in customers and the direct mail recipients based on whether the borrower selected a line-of-credit or a loan. The statistics are calculated by weighting by the number of customers in each zip code. The columns under "Direct Mail (Mailings)" refer to the zip codes (neighborhoods) associated with recipients of the bank's direct mail solicitation. The columns under "Direct Mail (Response)" refer to the zip codes (neighborhoods) of the customers who responded to the solicitation. The columns under "Walk-Ins" refer to the zip codes (neighborhoods) of the walk-in customers.

parison of the sample means between the WI and DM customers clearly suggests that the two groups are different. For example, on average the WI customers have higher estimated home values, greater income, more job seniority, and longer tenure at the present address. Furthermore, WI customers request greater loan amounts (consistent with having higher average house values) but lower loan-to-value ratios. Combined, these risk factors suggest that WI loans are lower risk.[28]

Although the DM and WI customer groups are distinct, the bank did not systematically target the line or loan solicitation to individuals who were more likely to respond to such solicitations. To confirm this, we report the summary statistics for location (neighborhood) demographic characteristics in Table 5.3. As we know the zip code for all walk-in customers as well as all recipients of the bank's direct mail solicitation, we aggregated census tract demographic information from the 2000 census to the zip code

---

[28]  Although it is possible that the WI customers were exposed to the bank's direct mail marketing campaign through contact with the DM recipients (see Hong, Kubik, and Stein (2005) or Shiller and Pound (1989) for evidence of informal information transfer about financial products), we are unable to control or measure this possibility. However, if the WI customers did systematically respond to the bank's direct mail campaign via "word-of-mouth" contact with the DM recipients, then this contamination should bias our analysis away from finding an effect for the advertisement. In our empirical analysis, we use the WI customers as the control group and thus any spillover from contact with the DM customers would bias downward our estimates of the direct mail effect on the DM customers' choice. This implies that any positive effect may actually be stronger than reported in our analysis. Furthermore, as part of our process for matching the direct mail customers with the home equity credit application database, we confirmed that the customers identified as direct mail applicants applied for the credit after the mailing date of the direct mail solicitation.

level.[29] The columns under "Direct Mail (Mailings)" show the mean values of the zip codes for all recipients of the bank's solicitation. The columns associated with "Direct Mail (Response)" show the mean values of the zip codes for the customers who actually responded to the bank's solicitation. Finally, the "Walk-In" columns show the mean values for the zip codes corresponding to the WI customers. If the bank systematically targeted areas based on demographic characteristics, then we should see differences in the demographic characteristics of the "Direct Mail (Mailings)" zip codes and the "Walk-In" zip codes. Similarly, if the customers who responded to the solicitation are concentrated in areas that are demographically distinct, then we should observe differences between the "Direct Mail (Response)" zip codes and both the "Direct Mail (Mailings)" and "Walk-In" zip codes. Comparing the mean values reported in Table 5.3 clearly shows that the WI and DM customers reside in demographically similar neighborhoods. For example, the median neighborhood income for persons who received a line-of-credit solicitation is $50,677; the median neighborhood income for walk-in customers who selected lines-of-credit is $50,598; and the median neighborhood income for DM customers who received a line-of-credit solicitation and responded is $50,596. As a result, it does not appear that meaningful systematic differences exist in the neighborhoods of WI and DM customers.

Our empirical analysis focuses on identifying the effect that lender advertising has on financial decisions. As discussed previously, identifying advertising's effect is challenging. Complicating this challenge, there are potential selection issues arising from differences in the response sensitivity of individuals to the bank's advertisement. Thus, we propose a consumer choice model under the assumption that consumers select the contract that maximizes their personal utility function and that this utility is maximized subject to a variety of economic and personal factors. Analogous to studies that examine the effect of social programs or medical treatments, we include a shift variable that identifies the type of direct mail solicitation received.

We face two, somewhat related, potential sample selection issues arising from the consumer's choice of mortgage product as well as the consumer's decision to apply to our particular bank. The first issue is that the consumer's response to the bank's marketing effort may not be exogenous. That is, the household's decision to respond to the offer may be correlated with the factors that impact the mortgage choice decision. The nature of the correlation arises from the fact that the choice of loan versus line-of-credit is a function of expected borrower tenure. For example, analysis by Rosenthal and Zorn (1993) suggests that borrowers with relatively higher expected mobility should prefer adjustable-rate loans over fixed-rate loans. Since our study involves home equity credit (not first mortgages), it is reasonable to assume that applicants seeking home equity credit have low expected mobility—which indicates a high tenure expectation. As a result, home equity credit applicants should have an unbiased preference for a home equity loan, all else being equal. Thus, any bias introduced as a result of applicant self-selection should be skewed toward observing a higher probability of selecting the fixed-rate product, weakening the effect of a line solicitation, and biasing our estimate of the shift variable downward. As a result, the presence of applicant self-selection should

---

[29]   The statistics are calculated by weighting by the number of customers in each zip code.

bias the estimated coefficients away from our hypothesis that advertising will affect consumer choices. Thus, any finding of a persuasive effect from advertising would be stronger than indicated.

The second sample selection issue is the possibility that the individuals who responded to the bank's solicitation already had a preference for a particular credit product and the direct mail solicitation simply reminded them that credit was available at the bank. That is, the household's decision to respond to the bank's offer could be correlated with unobserved factors affecting their preference for one product over the other. We control for this possibility by creating a matched sample design that controls for all observable differences between borrowers exposed to the bank's solicitation letter and those who applied for credit without having prior contact from the bank (Section 4). We match the direct mail respondents to the walk-in customers using all the information contained on the credit applications—in effect creating a subset of WI customers who are identical to the DM customers across all key demographic, economic, and geographic variables. If the sample selection issue is present, then we should observe the DM customers' choices coinciding with the matched WI customers.

Although our matched sample design uses all observable information about the customers, it is not perfect in being able to isolate whether customers who received a solicitation were "pre-disposed" to one form of credit or the other. Thus, we designed two alternative econometric methods to control for this potential sample selection issue as a robustness check. The results from these alternative methods are consistent with the results from our primary econometric method presented here and thus give us confidence that we have pinpointed the effect of the bank's marketing campaign. To save space, we report the results from these tests in an on-line appendix.[30]

# 4. AN ANALYSIS USING A MATCHED SAMPLE DESIGN

## 4.1 Sample Design

In order to control for potential sample selection bias, we implemented a matched sample design. The matched sample method utilized all observable information captured on the customer's credit application to create a control sample that was not exposed to the bank's solicitation. Thus, by comparing the product choices between the matched samples, we were able to isolate the effect of the bank's advertisement.

Since the bank targeted a subsample of the WI population to receive a direct mail solicitation (those with credit scores greater than 640), our analysis concentrates on the subset of WI customers identical to the DM customers with the exception that they did not receive a solicitation. In this context, the direct mail solicitation is the experimental "treatment", and our goal is to assess whether it has any impact on mortgage choice. Under the null hypothesis that consumers choose debt contracts based on the prevailing economic environment, we should not observe a difference in the factors affecting the mortgage choice between the two groups. In other words, by directly matching customers

---

[30]  See http://www.ushakrisna.com/arm_appendix.pdf

across demographic, geographic, and time dimensions, we effectively remove any observable differences used in underwriting between the two groups.

We begin by matching the 108,117 walk-in consumers with the 31,749 direct mail consumers, using the nearest centroid sorting algorithm based on the Euclidean distances computed over all demographic and financial variables within a zip code.[31, 32] Once we obtain the probability of the distance to the centroid, we rank order the 108,117 WI observations and choose the closest 31,749 accounts. Thus, the clustering procedure produces a sample of WI consumers that matches the DM consumers along these financial, demographic, and geographic variables.

Table 5.4 reports the descriptive statistics for the DM customers and the matched WI sample. It is clear from examining the mean values in Table 5.4 that the matching algorithm produces a WI sample that closely resembles the DM customers in terms of credit quality, loan amount, house value, income, and borrower age. For example, the average FICO scores and loan-to-value ratios of the two groups are within approximately 1 point of each other, and the difference in the average borrower incomes is about 2 percent ($2,462). Comparing the mean values for the WI and DM customers based on the selected product reveals little economic difference between the two groups.

Let $Y_i$ represent applicant $i$'s choice of mortgage type ($Y = 1$ denotes the line-of-credit and $Y = 0$ denotes the home equity loan), we estimate the following probit models of credit choice:

$$Pr[Y_i^{DM} = 1] = \Phi(\beta X_i + \alpha I_i^y) \qquad (1)$$

for the DM customers, and

$$Pr[Y_i^{WI} = 1] = \Phi(\beta X_i) \qquad (2)$$

for the matched WI customers. In equations (1) and (2) $\Phi$ represents the standard normal distribution; $X_i = [x_i^R, x_i^E, x_i^D]$ is a matrix of explanatory variables describing the individual's risk ($x_i^R$), the interest rate environment ($x_i^E$), and other individual demographic and geographic factors ($x_i^D$); and $I_i^y$ indicates whether the applicant received a direct mail line-of-credit solicitation, and zero otherwise. Thus, $\alpha$ captures the differential effect of receiving a line-of-credit solicitation on the probability that the applicant selects a line-of-credit. Equations (1) and (2) are estimated via maximum likelihood.

## 4.2  Results

Table 5.5 presents the estimated coefficients for the probit models of borrower choice for the matched walk-in and direct mail samples. We compare the marginal effects to

---

[31]    See Anderberg (1973) and Hartigan (1985) for details on this method. In addition, see Brown and Goetzmann (1997) and Brown, Goetzmann, and Grinblatt (1998) for applications in finance of the Euclidean distance algorithm.

[32]    As a robustness check, we also computed the Euclidean distances over a set of five predetermined key variables. The sorting algorithm produced an approximately 99 percent overlap between the respective WI subsamples. As a result, the results reported later are not qualitatively different.

Table 5.4  Summary statistics for the matched sample walk-in (W1) and direct mail (DM) customers based on credit choice

| | Home Equity Loans | | | | Home Equity Lines | | | |
| | Walk-In | | Direct Mail | | Walk-In | | Direct Mail | |
| Variables | Mean | Std | Mean | Std | Mean | Std | Mean | Std |
|---|---|---|---|---|---|---|---|---|
| Customer LTV | 72.9 | 25.2 | 75.25 | 20.77 | 70.7 | 23.5 | 69.10 | 19.79 |
| Appraised LTV | 72.5 | 26.2 | 76.20 | 19.90 | 72.3 | 26.6 | 70.22 | 18.88 |
| Borrower Estimated Home Value | $216,922 | $133,379 | $213,621 | $156,538 | $324,164 | $138,623 | $320,339 | $237,885 |
| Appraised Home Value | $208,924 | $148,383 | $204,998 | $129,894 | $312,367 | $159,017 | $306,261 | $204,462 |
| Requested Loan Amount | $48,102 | $18,981 | $47,916 | $30,309 | $60,585 | $19,372 | $63,324 | $42,908 |
| Loan Amount Approved | $46,579 | $19,724 | $45,417 | $26,856 | $62,432 | $16,725 | $64,972 | $43,958 |
| APR | 7.85 | 1.13 | 8.15 | 1.17 | 5.09 | 1.15 | 4.79 | 1.03 |
| FICO Score | 715.3 | 43.1 | 713.94 | 35.33 | 725.8 | 38.0 | 728.02 | 45.93 |
| Debt to Income | 33.7 | 19.0 | 31.53 | 11.88 | 30.4 | 20.7 | 26.99 | 15.14 |
| Consumption | 17% | 33% | 18% | 38% | 30% | 43% | 30% | 43% |
| Refinancing | 77% | 44% | 78% | 41% | 40% | 48% | 41% | 50% |
| Years on the Job | 3.7 | 8.5 | 3.23 | 2.49 | 4.7 | 7.5 | 4.90 | 2.89 |
| Income | $97,020 | $69,009 | $92,805 | $63,801 | $118,414 | $71,895 | $115,077 | $73,908 |
| Borrower Age | 48.8 | 11.8 | 46.27 | 12.10 | 46.6 | 11.3 | 46.58 | 11.04 |
| First Mortgage Balance | $109,717 | $63,618 | $105,244 | $83,168 | $134,547 | $69,539 | $139,790 | $115,274 |
| Months at Address | 80.1 | 117.4 | 79.79 | 83.74 | 90.6 | 106.4 | 88.24 | 92.98 |
| Self-Employed | 5% | 22% | 5% | 23% | 8% | 27% | 6% | 24% |
| Retired | 4% | 20% | 3% | 16% | 5% | 22% | 2% | 12% |
| Home Maker | 1% | 7% | 1% | 9% | 1% | 9% | 1% | 10% |
| Married | 53% | 50% | 47% | 50% | 49% | 50% | 49% | 50% |
| Frequency | 9,021 | | 11,249 | | 22,728 | | 20,500 | |

*Note:*  The walk-in sample was created using the nearest centroid sorting algorithm based on the Euclidean distances computed over all demographic and financial variables within a zip code. Customer LTV is the loan-to-value ratio based on the requested loan amount and the borrower's self-reported house value. Appraised LTV is the bank's loan-to-value ratio based on the approved loan amount and independent property appraisal. APR is the effective contract interest rate on the loan product selected. FICO is the borrower's credit quality score at application. Debt-to-income is the ratio of the borrower's debt to total income. Income is the borrower's income at date of application. Consumption is a dummy variable indicating that the borrower intends to use the loan/line proceeds for consumption purposes. Refinancing is a dummy variable indicating that the borrower is using the loan/line proceeds to refinance existing debt. The omitted category is "home improvement". Self-Employed, Retired, Home Maker, and Married are dummy variables indicating the borrower's respective employment and marriage status.

135

*Table 5.5   Consumer choice between home equity loans and lines-of-credit*

| | Walk-in Consumers | | | |
|---|---|---|---|---|
| | Coefficient Value | Standard Error | P-value | Marginal Impact |
| Intercept | −9.6299 | 1.4418 | <.0001 | |
| Economic Environment Variables: | | | | |
| Outside Option (Rate Diff FRM-ARM) | 0.3587 | 0.0478 | <.0001 | 11.65% |
| Outside Option FRM APR | 0.1365 | 0.0251 | <.0001 | 14.59% |
| Loan-to-Value Variables: | | | | |
| Ln (Borrower Estimate of the House Value) | 0.0024 | 0.0002 | <.0001 | 1.94% |
| Ln (Loan Amount Requested) | 0.0014 | 0.0002 | <.0001 | 1.83% |
| Borrower Stated Use of Funds | | | | |
| Consumption | 0.8127 | 0.0888 | <.0001 | 12.83% |
| Refinancing | −1.2024 | 0.0639 | <.0001 | −19.98% |
| Borrower Characteristics: | | | | |
| FICO | 0.0063 | 0.0007 | <.0001 | 0.06% |
| Debt to Income | −0.0168 | 0.0020 | <.0001 | −0.04% |
| Ln (Income) | 0.0752 | 0.0184 | <.0001 | 8.71% |
| Borrower Age | 0.0037 | 0.0012 | <.0001 | 0.28% |
| Years on the Job | 0.0205 | 0.0033 | <.0001 | 0.27% |
| Ln (First Mortgage Balance) | 0.1983 | 0.0417 | <.0001 | 6.86% |
| Ln (Months at Address) | 0.2133 | 0.0296 | <.0001 | 5.01% |
| Self-Employed | 0.0470 | 0.0865 | 0.9037 | 3.92% |
| Retired | −0.3308 | 0.1485 | 0.0176 | −1.45% |
| Home Maker | −0.1379 | 0.0327 | <.0001 | −0.43% |
| Married | −0.2473 | 0.0561 | <.0001 | −1.71% |
| Line Solicitation $(I^v)$ | | | | |
| Month Loan Origination Dummies | Yes | | | |
| State Location Control Dummies | Yes | | | |
| Number of Observations | 31,749 | | | |
| Pseudo R-sq | 14.82% | | | |

*Notes:*  This table reports the maximum-likelihood parameter estimates, relevant marginal impacts, and P-values (in parentheses) for the probit model of whether the customer selected the home equity line-of-credit (HELOC). The dependent variable is a dummy variable equal to 1 if the customer selected the HELOC and 0 otherwise. Outside Option Rate Difference is between the borrower's selected contract rate and the "outside" option contract rate. The "outside" option is the contract not selected and the rate is the contract rate that would have been offered to the borrower at origination. Outside Option FRM APR% is the fixed-rate home equity loan interest rate in effect at the time of origination. FICO is the borrower's credit quality score at application. Debt-to-income is the ratio of the borrower's debt to total income. Income is the borrower's income at date of application. Consumption is a dummy variable indicating that the borrower intends to use the loan/line proceeds for consumption purposes. Refinancing is a dummy variable indicating that the borrower is using the loan/line proceeds to refinance existing debt. The omitted category is "home improvement". Self-Employed, Retired, Home Maker, and Married are dummy variables indicating the borrower's respective employment and marriage status. Line Solicitation $(I^v)$ indicates whether the individual received a HELOC solicitation. The Standard Errors are corrected using the two-dimensional clustering procedure (across months and state location) of Petersen (2009).

| Direct Mail Consumers | | | | Direct Mail Consumers | | | |
|---|---|---|---|---|---|---|---|
| Coefficient Value | Standard Error | P-value | Marginal Impact | Coefficient Value | Standard Error | P-value | Marginal Impact |
| −4.0453 | 0.5265 | <.0001 | | −4.4211 | 0.5179 | <.0001 | |
| −0.0876 | 0.3490 | 0.9423 | −1.81% | −0.2137 | 0.3649 | 0.5435 | −2.79% |
| −0.1014 | 0.1486 | 0.5555 | −0.94% | −0.2093 | 0.1564 | 0.4697 | −1.96% |
| 0.0022 | 0.0008 | <.0001 | 1.68% | 0.0022 | 0.0008 | <.0001 | 1.74% |
| 0.0024 | 0.0003 | <.0001 | 1.22% | 0.0024 | 0.0003 | <.0001 | 1.29% |
| 1.0376 | 0.0881 | <.0001 | 8.81% | 1.0311 | 0.0951 | <.0001 | 9.84% |
| −0.7175 | 0.0429 | <.0001 | −8.27% | −0.7438 | 0.0454 | <.0001 | −8.95% |
| 0.0013 | 0.0005 | <.0001 | 0.04% | 0.0013 | 0.0005 | <.0001 | 0.04% |
| −0.0265 | 0.0023 | <.0001 | −0.04% | −0.0267 | 0.0023 | <.0001 | −0.04% |
| 0.3390 | 0.0866 | 0.0002 | 3.91% | 0.3677 | 0.0941 | 0.0002 | 4.05% |
| 0.0048 | 0.0020 | 0.0117 | 0.27% | 0.0050 | 0.0022 | 0.0108 | 0.29% |
| 0.0092 | 0.0061 | 0.1923 | 0.39% | 0.0096 | 0.0064 | 0.1766 | 0.41% |
| 0.0720 | 0.0330 | 0.0272 | 5.65% | 0.0747 | 0.0363 | 0.0253 | 5.88% |
| 0.0336 | 0.0027 | <.0001 | 4.00% | 0.0364 | 0.0028 | <.0001 | 4.07% |
| 0.2729 | 0.0712 | <.0001 | 1.29% | 0.2943 | 0.0745 | <.0001 | 1.31% |
| −0.6170 | 0.1269 | <.0001 | −1.24% | −0.6240 | 0.1383 | <.0001 | −1.27% |
| −0.0620 | 0.0323 | 0.04 | −0.22% | −0.0680 | 0.0341 | 0.0373 | −0.23% |
| −0.1184 | 0.0720 | 0.0844 | −0.86% | −0.1234 | 0.0769 | 0.0756 | −0.92% |
| 2.1446 | 0.5726 | <.0001 | 45.27% | | | | |
| Yes | | | | Yes | | | |
| Yes | | | | Yes | | | |
| 31,749 | | | | 31,749 | | | |
| 15.92% | | | | 14.78% | | | |

determine the sensitivity of borrowers to the independent variables based on whether or not they received a solicitation.[33] Effectively, this method is equivalent to estimating a single model over both samples and interacting a dummy variable for direct mail with each variable.

The marginal effects indicate that WI borrowers are sensitive to the interest rate environment. For example, a one point increase in the fixed-rate reference interest rate results in a 14.6 percent jump in the probability that the borrower will select the line-of-credit. In addition, every one point increase in the FRM rate over the ARM rate (*Outside Option Rate Difference*) increases the odds of selecting the line-of-credit contract by 11.7 percent. Furthermore, we also see that the borrower's intended use of funds significantly impacts

---

[33] We calculate the marginal effects following Ai and Norton (2003).

their product choice. Borrowers intending to use the home equity funds for consumption are 12.8 percent more likely to choose the line-of-credit, while borrowers indicating that they are refinancing existing debt are 20.0 percent more likely to select the fixed-rate loan.

Table 5.5 also shows the estimated coefficients and marginal effects for the borrower choice model estimated on the direct mail sample. In contrast to the WI borrowers, we first notice that none of the independent financial and demographic variables have marginal effects above 10 percent. Furthermore, many of the key variables identified in the WI sample are no longer statistically significant. For example, neither the outside option rate difference nor the FRM reference interest rate are statistically significant. It is important to reinforce that these variables are the actual prices being offered to the borrower at the time of application. Thus, in contrast to the WI borrowers, the insignificant coefficients for these loan pricing terms implies that the direct mail customers are not basing their mortgage choice decision on the key interest rate factors identified by theory. This result is all the more striking given the relative importance of these factors in explaining the walk-in control group choice.

Comparing the marginal effects indicates that the intended use of the loan funds affects both the WI and DM customer choice. However, we see that the DM customer choice is less sensitive to their stated use of funds. For example, DM borrowers indicating that they are refinancing are 8.3 percent more likely to select the home equity loan product, while the refinancing WI customers are 20.0 percent more likely to select the home equity loan. Borrowers intending to use their home equity funds for consumption also display a similar, but less dramatic, difference.

The dummy variable $I^v$ in the direct mail model isolates the impact of the type of direct mail offer sent to the customer. The marginal effect clearly indicates that this variable has the largest impact on the customer's choice. Customers who receive a line-of-credit direct mail solicitation are 45.3 percent more likely to select the line of credit than the loan product. The impact of this variable far exceeds the effect of any of the other variables. Thus, it appears that the bank's solicitation even significantly dampens the effect of the customer's intended use of the funds.

Finally, to demonstrate that the DM customers do respond differently from the WI customers to the economic environment, we estimate equation (2) for the DM sample. In other words, we do not include the $I^v$ dummy variable. The last four columns of Table 5.5 show the estimated coefficients for this model. Again, the lack of significance in the coefficients for the outside option rate difference and interest rate level clearly indicate that the DM customer group is not responding to the prevailing interest rate environment. If the inclusion of $I^v$ in (1) were biasing the results for the DM customers, then the estimated coefficients and marginal effects of the model without this variable should mirror those of the WI customers. We explore the accuracy of this conclusion further in the following sections.

The results presented here make a compelling case against the informative view of advertising. Under the informative view, we should observe similar sensitivities to changes in the interest rate environment for the WI and DM customers. Thus, the insignificant interest rate parameters for the DM customers are inconsistent with the informative view and suggest that the lender's solicitation was persuasive.

### 4.2.1 Persuasive versus complementary advertising

In order to ascertain whether the bank's solicitation was persuasive or complementary, we examine the choice of borrowers who received a direct mail solicitation, but chose the product not advertised. As discussed previously, during the application process, all customers are presented with the full loan contract menu. Thus, even though the DM customer may have received a solicitation advertising a line-of-credit, the customer also had the option of applying for a home equity loan. By matching the database that tracked the customers who received a direct mail solicitation with the database of applications, we can identify instances when the borrower switched products. For example, if the borrower received a line-of-credit (or loan) solicitation, but applied for a home equity loan (or line-of-credit), then we classify that borrower as a "switcher." However, if the borrower received a line-of-credit (loan) solicitation and also applied for a line-of-credit (loan), then we classify that borrower as a "non-switcher." We note that out of the 31,749 customers who received a direct mail solicitation, 22 percent selected a product that was different from the one in the solicitation. Furthermore, 2,375 (21 percent) of the applicants who selected the loan product received a direct mail offer for a line-of-credit product, while 4,623 (23 percent) of the applicants who selected the line-of-credit product received the loan solicitation.

By analyzing the switchers and non-switchers, we can draw distinctions between borrowers who were potentially persuaded (the non-switcher) versus those who were complemented (the switchers). In other words, did the switchers ignore the bank's direct marketing cue and select the product consistent with prior theoretical predictions? We answer this question by estimating the walk-in model for the direct mail switchers. Table 5.6 reports the results from this model. Again, we compare the marginal effects to the baseline WI customers to identify any differences in sensitivity.

The results clearly indicate that the DM customers who switched are similar to the WI customers in that they are sensitive to the interest rate environment. The marginal impact of a one point increase in the outside option rate difference results in a 12.2 percent increase in the probability that they will select the line-of-credit product. This result compares favorably with the 11.7 percent effect observed for the WI customers. Similarly, we see that a one point increase in the reference fixed-rate mortgage rate increases the probability of selecting the line-of-credit by 8.4 percent (compared with 14.6 percent for the WI customers). Finally, we also note that consumption and refinancing motivations have the same effects on the DM switching customers as the WI customers. Thus, the results are consistent with the complementary view of advertising. The DM customers who switched responded to the bank's offer letter, but still reacted to the economic environment in selecting the product.

The results in Tables 5.5 and 5.6 revealing that switchers appear to respond to economic environmental cues in a similar fashion to the walk-in customers raises an interesting question: do observable differences exist between the switchers and non-switchers? In other words, can we identify the customers who are more likely to be persuaded by the bank's solicitation? Obviously, customers who switched away from the product highlighted on the solicitation were not persuaded, by definition. Thus, by systematically examining the differences between customers who switched versus those who did not switch, we are able to obtain insights about the characteristics of customers who are most likely to be persuaded by the bank's solicitation (i.e., those who did not switch).

*Table 5.6   Analysis of direct mail switcher choice*

| | Coefficient Value | Standard Error | P-value | Marginal Impact |
|---|---|---|---|---|
| Intercept | | −5.02870 | 1.52845 | <.0001 |
| Economic Environment Variables: | | | | |
| Outside Option (Rate Diff FRM-ARM) | 0.27212 | 0.04620 | <.0001 | 12.15% |
| Outside Option FRM APR | 0.17237 | 0.01282 | <.0001 | 8.43% |
| Loan-to-Value Variables: | | | | |
| Ln (Borrower Estimate of the House Value) | 0.00613 | 0.00018 | <.0001 | 1.96% |
| Ln (Loan Amount Requested) | 0.00385 | 0.00014 | 0.0201 | 1.06% |
| Borrower Stated Use of Funds: | | | | |
| Consumption | 1.10815 | 0.11210 | <.0001 | 10.28% |
| Refinancing | −0.71249 | 0.05458 | <.0001 | −11.95% |
| Borrower Characteristics: | | | | |
| FICO | 0.00151 | 0.00059 | <.0001 | 0.02% |
| Debt to Income | −0.02870 | 0.00269 | <.0001 | −0.03% |
| Ln (Income) | 0.19226 | 0.05149 | <.0001 | 3.98% |
| Borrower Age | 0.00407 | 0.00249 | 0.0959 | 0.11% |
| Years on the Job | 0.01625 | 0.00769 | 0.0189 | 0.12% |
| Ln (First Mortgage Balance) | 0.08561 | 0.03627 | 0.024 | 2.03% |
| Ln (Months at Address) | 0.00275 | 0.00075 | <.0001 | 0.93% |
| Self-Employed | 0.00899 | 0.08236 | 0.92 | 0.29% |
| Retired | −0.45621 | 0.18234 | 0.0143 | −1.30% |
| Home Maker | −0.19746 | 0.19411 | 0.398 | −0.24% |
| Married | −0.06336 | 0.08427 | 0.569 | −0.24% |
| Month Loan Origination Dummies | Yes | | | |
| State Location Control Dummies | Yes | | | |
| Number of Observations | 6998 | | | |
| Pseudo R-sq | 18.97% | | | |

*Notes:*   This table reports the maximum-likelihood parameter estimates for the probit model of whether the direct mail customers selected the line-of-credit (HELOC) product. The dependent variable is a dummy variable equal to 1 if the customer selected the line-of-credit and 0 otherwise. Outside Option Rate Difference is between the borrower's selected contract rate and the "outside" option contract rate. The "outside" option is the contract not selected and the rate is the contract rate that would have been offered to the borrower at origination. Outside Option FRM APR% is the fixed-rate home equity loan interest rate in effect at the time of origination. FICO is the borrower's credit quality score at application. Debt-to-income is the ratio of the borrower's debt to total income. Income is the borrower's income at date of application. Consumption is a dummy variable indicating that the borrower intends to use the loan/line proceeds for consumption purposes. Refinancing is a dummy variable indicating that the borrower is using the loan/line proceeds to refinance existing debt. The omitted category is "home improvement". Self-Employed, Retired, Home Maker, and Married are dummy variables indicating the borrower's respective employment and marriage status. The Standard Errors are corrected using the two-dimensional clustering procedure (across months and state location) of Petersen (2009).

In order to focus on the explicit differences between customers who switched from the solicited product and those who did not, we estimate a simple logit model for switch versus no switch. Table 5.7 reports the estimated coefficients. The results indicate the customers having the characteristics of being more financially sophisticated (higher incomes and higher credit scores) are more likely to switch away from the advertised product. For example, the marginal effects imply that a customer with a FICO score of 774 is 24 percent more likely to switch than a customer with a FICO score of 724.[34] Interestingly, we also see that older customers are less likely to switch than younger customers. For example, the marginal effects indicate that a 56-year-old customer is 33 percent less likely to switch than a 46-year-old customer.[35] This result is consistent with the findings of Agarwal et al. (2009) that financial sophistication declines with age. We also see that the customer's indicated intended use of the funds has a direct effect on the probability of switching. For example, borrowers using the loan proceeds for refinancing are 2.7 percent more likely to switch, while borrowers using the funds for consumption are 5.6 percent less likely to switch than borrowers using the funds for home improvements.

The results in Table 5.7 clearly indicate a significant difference between customers who switched and thus were not persuaded, versus those who did not switch (and thus may have been persuaded.) For example, the results are consistent with the idea that customers seeking to rate refinance are sufficiently sophisticated that they respond to incentives present in the economic environment and are not persuaded to accept the offer presented in the solicitation. The implications from this analysis is that consumers more susceptible to advertising persuasion appear to be less financially sophisticated.

### 4.2.2 Persuasive versus informative advertising

In the previous section we focused on the switchers to show that they were most likely informed or complemented by the bank's solicitation. We also saw that the switchers are systematically different from the non-switchers. In this section, we examine the non-switchers to separate the persuaded from the informed.

We focus our analysis on the 24,751 customers (78 percent of the direct mail customers) who selected the product that was advertised (i.e., those who did not switch products), as these were the individuals most likely to be persuaded or informed by the bank's advertising campaign. By definition, the 6,998 customers who selected the product opposite to the one that was advertised in their solicitation letter could not have been persuaded. For the advertisement to be persuasive, the customer would have to select the product that was featured on the solicitation. In order to determine the product that would have been selected absent any advertising effect, we use the estimated coefficients from the matched walk-in sample model (Table 5.5) to generate a prediction of whether the customer would select the line-of-credit or home equity loan product.[36] We then compare the customer's model prediction to her actual selection.

Table 5.8 reports the frequency of persuaded versus informed consumers. Based on our

---

[34]   The mean FICO score for the DM customers is 724.
[35]   The mean customer age at date of application is 46.5 years.
[36]   We use a 50 percent cutoff criteria to determine whether the customers should select the line-of-credit product.

*Table 5.7    Analysis of decision to switch away from product offered in direct mail solicitation*

|  | Coeff. Val. | Std. Err. | P-value | Marg Impact |
|---|---|---|---|---|
| Intercept | 8.2849 | 0.0701 | <.0001 |  |
| Loan-to-Value Variables: |  |  |  |  |
| Ln (Borrower Estimate of the louse Value) | −0.0040 | 0.0006 | <.0001 | 1.45% |
| Ln (Loan Amount Requested) | 0.0020 | 0.0004 | <.0001 | 0.10% |
| Borrower Stated Use of Funds: |  |  |  |  |
| Consumption | −0.2410 | 0.0450 | <.0001 | −5.64% |
| Refinancing | 0.0042 | 0.0141 | 0.7722 | 2.71% |
| Borrower Characteristics: |  |  |  |  |
| FICO | 0.0209 | 0.0014 | <.0001 | 0.48% |
| Debt to Income | −0.0238 | 0.0026 | <.0001 | 0.00% |
| Ln (Income) | 0.0220 | 0.0098 | 0.0258 | 2.07% |
| Borrower Age | −0.1259 | 0.0123 | <.0001 | −3.29% |
| Years on the Job | 0.3505 | 0.0109 | <.0001 | 0.10% |
| Ln (First Mortgage Balance) | −0.0132 | 0.0095 | 0.1694 | −1.97% |
| Ln (Months at Address) | −0.1035 | 0.0080 | <.0001 | −0.63% |
| Self-Employed | −0.0744 | 0.0024 | <.0001 | −0.04% |
| Retired | −0.0382 | 0.0050 | <.0001 | −0.17% |
| Home Maker | −0.0006 | 0.0002 | 0.0002 | −0.06% |
| Married | 1.4110 | 0.0076 | <.0001 | 0.00% |
| Month Loan Origination Dummies | Yes |  |  |  |
| State Location Control Dummies | Yes |  |  |  |
| Number of Observations | 31,749 |  |  |  |
| Pseudo R-sq | 7.93% |  |  |  |

*Notes:* This table reports the maximum-likelihood parameter estimates for the logit model of whether the customer selected the alternative product from the one contained in the direct mail solicitation. The dependent variable is a dummy variable equal to 1 if the customer switched and 0 otherwise. FICO is the borrower's credit quality score at application. Debt-to-income is the ratio of the borrower's debt to total income. Income is the borrower's income at date of application. Consumption is a dummy variable indicating that the borrower intends to use the loan/line proceeds for consumption purposes. Refinancing is a dummy variable indicating that the borrower is using the loan/line proceeds to refinance existing debt. The omitted category is "home improvement". Self-Employed, Retired, Home Maker, and Married are dummy variables indicating the borrower's respective employment and marriage status. Standard Errors are corrected using the two-dimensional clustering procedure (across months and state location) of Petersen (2009).

classification scheme, we see that 18,292 (74 percent) of the 24,751 non-switching customers were effectively "persuaded" by the bank's direct mail solicitation. That is, these borrowers selected the product that was featured on the solicitation but was opposite the one predicted by the model. However, we also note that 26 percent (6,459 out of 24,751) of the customers were "informed" by the bank's solicitation, since they selected the product predicted by the model and it was also featured on the solicitation.

Although the analysis in Table 5.8 suggests that 74 percent of the DM customers were persuaded to select a product that was counter to the one predicted by our model, it is possible that our model has a high predictive error rate resulting in a large Type II error.

*Table 5.8   Analysis of persuaded versus informed consumers*

| | Number Mailed | Predicted HELOAN | | Predicted HELOC | |
|---|---|---|---|---|---|
| | | Selected HELOAN | Selected HELOC | Selected HELOAN | Selected HELOC |
| Mailed HELOC | 15,877 | ... | **12,336** **50%** | ... | *3,541* *14%* |
| Mailed HELOAN | 8,874 | *2,918* *12%* | ... | **5,956** **24%** | ... |

*Notes:*  This table reports the frequency of customers identified as either persuaded or informed. For all direct mail borrowers who did not switch products, we estimated the predicted product that they should select based on the coefficients from the walk-in mortgage choice model (Table 5.5). We then compared the predicted choice to the actual choice based on whether the borrower received a HELOC or HELOAN solicitation. The persuaded borrowers selected the product opposite to the one predicted and are noted in bold. Informed borrowers selected the product that is consistent with the one predicted and are noted in italics. Borrowers following into the (···) cells selected the predicted product and thus ignored the bank's advertising.

Thus, to gain a greater appreciation for whether model predictive error can explain these results, we examine the model predictive accuracy using a hold-out sample of customers who were not exposed to the bank's direct mail solicitation. Recall that the previous analysis is based on the borrower choice model for the matched sample of 31,749 walk-in customers, leaving 76,386 walk-in customers as a de facto hold-out sample. Thus, by estimating the predicted product choice for the hold-out walk-in customers, we are able to observe an unbiased estimate of the model's predictive accuracy. Table 5.9 reports the results of this test. The results clearly indicate that the model's predictive accuracy (using the 50 percent cutoff criteria) is very high. Table 5.9 shows that the model is able to predict the actual product choice for 85 percent of the customers, implying a Type II error rate of 15 percent. In contrast, the predictive error rate for the direct mail customers is 74 percent. We feel that this is compelling evidence that the bank's marketing campaign did have a persuasive effect.

As a final check, we also report in Table 5.9 the estimated prediction rate for the direct mail customers who switched products. Table 5.9 shows that the WI model is able to predict the actual product choice for 72 to 75 percent of the DM switchers implying Type II error of 28 to 25 percent. Recall from the previous analysis, we found that the product choice model coefficients and marginal effects for the direct mail switchers are similar to those for the walk-in borrowers. Thus, it is not surprising that we find the predictive error rate for the DM switchers is similar to the error rate for the WI hold-out sample.

## 4.3   Summary

To summarize, our analysis reveals that borrower mortgage choice is sensitive to the economic environment. Yet, we also observe that a subset of borrowers who received solicitations or "cues" from the bank did not select a mortgage product in a manner consistent with theoretical expectations. Overall, the results suggest that the lender's

*Table 5.9   Walk-in and direct mail customer prediction error rates*

| Actual Selection | Walk-in Customer | | | Direct Mail Customer | | |
| --- | --- | --- | --- | --- | --- | --- |
| | Predicted Selection | | | Predicted Selection | | |
| | HELOC | HELOAN | Total | HELOC | HELOAN | Total |
| HELOC | 48,345 | 8,167 | 56,512 | 3,481 | 1,142 | 4,623 |
| | 85.5% | 14.5% | | 75% | 25% | |
| HELOAN | 3,056 | 16,800 | 19,856 | 668 | 1,707 | 2,375 |
| | 15.4% | 84.6% | | 28% | 72% | |
| Total | 51,401 | 24,967 | 76,386 | 4,149 | 2,849 | 6,998 |

*Notes:*   This table reports the predicted walk-in and direct mail customer selection error rate. For all walk-in customers who were not included in the matched sample analysis and all direct mail customers who switched products, we estimated the predicted product that they would have selected based on the coefficients from the matched sample walk-in mortgage choice model (Table 5.5). We then compare the predicted choice to the actual choice. Effectively, this test provides an indication of the predictive accuracy of the estimated mortgage choice model using a hold-out sample.

advertising campaign had a persuasive effect for a subset of borrowers who are less financially sophisticated.[37]

## 5.   ROBUSTNESS TESTS

One concern with our conclusion is that we may be attributing a persuasive effect to the bank's marketing campaign for borrowers who may not care about the product they selected simply because the costs associated with making an "incorrect" decision are trivial. For example, our analysis could classify borrowers as being "persuaded" even if

---

[37]   A natural question arises as to whether the bank's advertising had an "economic" impact on the borrower. Unfortunately, we are unable to calculate a direct cost. However, we note that fixed-rate products have higher interest rates than variable-rate products, and thus, borrowers who were steered to fixed-rate loans but who should have selected the variable-rate line-of-credit did bear a higher interest cost. Greenspan (2004) has suggested that many borrowers may have incorrectly preferred fixed-rate products. However, it is also not the case that all borrowers persuaded to select the variable-rate contract benefited from such steering. Variable-rate products do expose borrowers to greater future interest rate risk, and as discussed in Section 2, theoretical models show that fixed-rate contracts should be preferred by some borrowers depending upon economic and demographic factors. As a result, borrowers who were persuaded to select the variable-rate line-of-credit were exposed to greater interest rate risk than appropriate, since they should have selected the fixed-rate contract as suggested by the theoretical predictions based upon the prevailing economic conditions at the time of origination.

A second concern is that it is possible that we are attributing the DM borrowers' product selection to the affect of the bank's solicitation when it could also be the result of the bank's loan officers. If the bank loan officers perceive that DM customers are less sophisticated, then they might attempt to "push" them toward less desirable products. However, as will be demonstrated in the next section, DM customers have higher prepayment rates and thus the bank would have an economic incentive to train the loan officers to not engage in such activities.

*Table 5.10   Average line-of-credit takedown rate*

|             | Month 0 | Month 12 | Month 24 |
|-------------|---------|----------|----------|
| Walk-in     | 58.9%   | 63.2%    | 67.1%    |
| Direct Mail | 60.3%   | 63.7%    | 66.0%    |

*Note:*   This table reports the average line-of-credit takedown (utilization) rate at origination, month 12, and month 24. The utilization rate is the amount of funds drawn expressed as a percentage of total credit line available.

they originated a line-of-credit in order to have ready access to funds in the future. These borrowers would clearly not select a home equity loan product, even if the economic environment pointed to it as the optimal choice, since they would not be utilizing the funds immediately. In order to test whether this effect could be responsible for our results, Table 5.10 takedown shows the average takedown (or utilization) rates at origination, month 12, and month 24 for the matched WI and DM customers who selected and originated the line-of-credit. If the DM customers viewed the costs associated with the line-of-credit as trivial, then we would expect to find their utilization rates substantially lower than those of the WI customers. The results clearly reveal that the average utilization rates for WI and DM customers are comparable and thus do not support the hypothesis that the costs associated with selecting the line-of-credit are trivial.

As a final robustness check of whether the advertising was persuasive or informative, we examine the *ex post* origination performance of the applications that were actually booked. If the advertising was persuasive such that it caused borrowers to select a product inconsistent with their needs, then we would expect to observe these customers making adjustments over time. To test for this effect, we examine the loan prepayment rates over the one-month, three-month, and six-month periods after origination. These windows are sufficiently short such that exogenous factors (such as changes in interest rates or household mobility) should have a minimal impact on borrower prepayment decisions. If the persuaded borrowers learn that they selected an inappropriate product, then we should observe a higher prepayment rate for these borrowers than for borrowers that we identified as being informed or complemented.[38]

To examine the differences in prepayment, we identified all applications that ultimately resulted in loans or lines being booked. We note that approximately 89 percent of the DM and WI matched sample applications that resulted in booked loans or lines (for 28,099 DM customers and 28,256 WI customers, respectively). For the customers identified by our model as being persuaded by the bank's solicitation, we note that approximately 90 percent of the applications resulted in booked loans or lines. Similarly, approximately 86 percent and 87 percent of the complemented and informed customer applications, respectively, resulted in booked loans or lines.

Turning first to the persuaded customers, we observed that 707 prepaid during the three months after origination, implying an unconditional prepayment rate of 4.3 percent. In

---

[38]   We note again that the home equity loans and lines were "no fee" products. Thus, the borrowers were able to repay their loans and lines without penalty.

contrast, we observed an unconditional three-month prepayment rate of 2.9 percent for the complemented (switchers) and informed customers.[39] Furthermore, the unconditional three-month prepayment rate for the walk-in customers is 1.7 percent.[40]

Table 5.11 reports the estimated coefficients for a simple logistic prepayment model.[41] Using the empirical mortgage performance literature to provide guidance in specifying the independent variables in the prepayment model, we estimated the following model:

$$Pr(h_i = 1) = \Lambda(\beta X_i + \alpha L_i + \gamma A_i + \pi[L_i * A_i]), \tag{3}$$

where $h_i$ equals one if the mortgage is prepaid during the three-month period following origination, and zero otherwise; $\Lambda$ represents the logistic cumulative distribution function; $X_i$ is a matrix of explanatory variables; $L_i$ is a dummy variable, with $L_i = 1$ if the contract is a line-of-credit and $L_i = 0$ if the contract is a loan; and $A_i = [A_i^P, A_i^I, A_i^C]'$ with $A_i^k(k = P, I, C)$ equaling one if borrower $i$ was identified as being persuaded $(P)$, informed $(I)$, or complemented $(C)$.[42] We interact the product type dummy variable $(L_i)$ with $A_i$ in order to assess whether the prepayment rates differ across product and borrower type. Following Agarwal et al. (2006), we include in the set of explanatory variables $(X)$, a series of variables designed to capture the financial incentives to repay the loan. The variables include the value of the borrower's prepayment option $(OPTION)$, an indicator of whether the prepayment option is "in-the-money" $(InMoney)$, and a variable $(DSpread)$ that captures the interaction of between $InMoney$ and $OPTION$.[43] Not surprising, given that we examine relatively short periods after origination, none of the financial variables are significant in the one-month and three-month models, indicating that changes in the economic environment in the months immediately following origination did not impact borrower prepayment behavior. In the six-month model, the borrower's prepayment option value $(OPTION)$, LTV, and FICO scores are positive and significant. Thus, the results from the six month prepayment model indicate that as the length of time since origination increases, changes in economic conditions and borrower heterogeneity begin to explain differences in prepayment rates. For example, the results show that after six-months, higher quality borrowers (borrowers with higher loan-to-value ratios at origination) and borrowers with a greater financial incentive to prepay have a greater probability of exercising their prepayment option. In addition, the line-of-credit dummy variable $(L)$

---

[39]   We observed 172 prepayments made among the 6,018 complemented borrowers (or switchers) and 163 prepayments made among the 5,619 informed borrowers.

[40]   We observed that 491 out of the 28,256 walk-in loans booked were prepaid within the first three months after origination.

[41]   Given the short time horizon of our prepayment model, we estimated the prepayment model using a logistic framework rather than with a hazard rate model.

[42]   The walk-in customers are the reference category.

[43]   The *OPTION* variable follows Deng, Quigley, and Van Order (2000) and is calculated as

$$OPTION_i = \frac{V_i - V_i^*}{V_i}$$

where $V_i$ is the present value of the remaining mortgage payments at the current market interest rate and $V_i^*$ is the present value of the remaining mortgage payments at the contract interest rate.

*Table 5.11 Prepayment behavior of home equity loans and lines*

| | 1-Month Prepay Model | | 3-Month Prepay Model | | 6-Month Prepay Model | |
|---|---|---|---|---|---|---|
| | Coefficient (Std. Error) | Marginal Effects | Coefficient (Std. Error) | Marginal Effects | Coefficient (Std. Error) | Marginal Effects |
| Intercept | −2.1375*** (0.24) | | −2.9068** (0.30) | | −2.2516*** (0.28) | |
| Log (FICO) | 0.1102 (0.10) | 1.41 | 0.1179 (0.11) | 1.40 | 0.1474*** (0.06) | 2.03 |
| LTV | 0.0275 (0.02) | 0.11 | 0.0206 (0.03) | 0.17 | 0.0858*** (0.03) | 0.18 |
| OPTION | 0.0148 (0.02) | 0.22 | 0.0126 (0.02) | 0.33 | 0.0325*** (0.01) | 0.27 |
| InMoney | −0.0216 (0.08) | −0.15 | −0.0231 (0.09) | −0.13 | −0.0228 (0.10) | −0.13 |
| DSpread | 0.0119 (0.04) | 0.04 | 0.0115 (0.06) | 0.06 | 0.0212 (0.05) | 0.05 |
| Lines (L) | 0.1127 (0.13) | 0.57 | 0.1748 (0.10) | 0.38 | 0.1365*** (0.06) | 1.89 |
| Persuaded $(A^p)$ | 0.2964*** (0.12) | 1.90 | 0.4554*** (0.13) | 3.18 | 0.3674*** (0.13) | 3.90 |
| Informed $(A^I)$ | 0.1474 (0.14) | 0.51 | 0.1481 (0.12) | 0.85 | 0.1314 (0.15) | 0.83 |
| Complemented $(A^c)$ | 0.0872 (0.17) | 0.58 | 0.1453 (0.18) | 0.47 | 0.1218 (0.15) | 0.54 |
| Lines $(L)$*Persuaded $(A^p)$ | 0.2883*** (0.14) | 1.94 | 0.3845*** (0.18) | 3.47 | 0.3388*** (0.13) | 4.75 |
| Lines (L)*Informed $(A^I)$ | 0.1171 (0.14) | 0.49 | 0.1244 (0.11) | 0.82 | 0.1237 (0.14) | 1.33 |
| Lines (L)*Complemented $(A^c)$ | 0.0956 (0.17) | 0.54 | 0.1106 (0.19) | 0.55 | 0.1167 (0.14) | 0.86 |
| Other Controls | Yes | | Yes | | Yes | |
| State Dummies | Yes | | Yes | | Yes | |
| Time Dummies | Yes | | Yes | | Yes | |
| Number of Prepay | 947 | | 1,533 | | 3,717 | |
| Number of Obs. | 56,355 | | 56,355 | | 56,355 | |
| Pseudo $R^2$ | 1.48% | | 1.73% | | 1.92% | |

*Notes:* This table reports the maximum-likelihood parameter estimates for the logistic one-month, three-month, and six-month prepayment models. The dependent variable equals one if the borrower prepaid the mortgage during the one-month, three-month, or six-month period following origination and zero otherwise. FICO is the borrower's credit quality score at application; LTV is the loan-to-value ratio at application; OPTION is the value of the borrower's prepayment option reflecting the difference between the market rate of interest and the contract interest rate; InMoney indicates whether the prepayment option is 'in-the-money'; DSpread is the interaction of InMoney and OPTION; Persuaded, Informed, and Complemented are indicator variables denoting whether the borrower was persuaded, informed, or complemented by the bank's direct mail solicitation (walk-in customers are the reference category). (L) indicates whether the individual received a line-of-credit solicitation. Standard Errors are reported in parentheses and are corrected using the two-dimensional clustering procedure (across months and state location) of Petersen (2009). *** indicates significance at the 1% level.

is positive and significant indicating a divergence of prepayment speeds based on product type six months after origination.

For the purposes of our study the most interesting results are the positive and significant coefficients associated with the variables indicating that the borrower was persuaded ($A^P$ and $L*A^P$). This finding is consistent with the theory that persuaded borrowers may have recognized that they selected an inappropriate product. The marginal effects for $A^P$ suggest that the prepayment rate for a borrower persuaded to originate a line or loan is over three times as high as the prepayment rate experienced by the walk-in customers over the three months following origination. Over the six-month window following origination, these borrowers have a prepayment rate that is almost four times greater than the walk-in group. In addition, the marginal effects for the interaction term ($L*A^P$) indicate that borrowers persuaded to originate lines-of-credit have higher prepayment speeds than the persuaded loan borrowers. Furthermore, the coefficients indicating whether the borrower was informed or complemented are insignificant, suggesting that the three-month prepayment rate for these borrowers is not statistically different from the prepayment rate for the walk-in customers. Thus, our analysis shows that the borrowers most likely to have made a mistake by following the bank's advertising cue (i.e., the borrowers identified as being persuaded) are significantly more likely to quickly prepay out of this product than the typical walk-in customer not exposed to the bank's solicitation.

## 6.   CONCLUSIONS

Financial economists now recognize that marketing and persuasion can have important effects on consumer decisions. In this chapter, we examine the effect of direct mail (or junk mail) advertising on individual financial decisions by studying consumers' choice of debt contracts.

The results from our analysis suggest that financial variables underlying the relative pricing of debt contracts are the leading factors explaining consumer debt choice. Furthermore, we also find that the intended use of the debt proceeds significantly affects consumer choice. In particular, we find that borrowers who intend to use the debt proceeds for consumption are 13 percent more likely to select the line-of-credit and borrowers who are refinancing existing debt are approximately 20 percent less likely to choose the line-of-credit than the borrowers who intend to use the funds for home improvements.

With respect to the impact of advertising on borrower choice, we find evidence that the lender's advertising campaign had a persuasive effect on consumer contract choice. We arrive at this conclusion based on a variety of tests. First, we performed an analysis based on a matched sample design. This method reveals that none of the financial and demographic variables that are important for the control group's product selection have an impact on the product choice decision for the direct mail sample. In fact, the customers who received a direct mail line-of-credit solicitation are 45.3 percent more likely to select the line-of-credit product than the fixed-rate loan product. Furthermore, analysis of the product choice model coefficients for the group of borrowers who ignored the bank's direct mail solicitation and selected the product not advertised reveals that the key financial and demographic variables have the same signs and magnitude as the control group.

This finding suggests that the advertisement had a complementary effect for this set of borrowers. For the group of borrowers we identified as likely to be persuaded, we find that the odds of prepayment over the three-month period after loan origination is almost four times higher than the prepayment rate experienced by the control group and over six times higher over the six months following origination. Finally, we note that a substantial (one-third) portion of the consumers who received a direct mail solicitation did not view the offer as persuasive because they remained sensitive to the economic environment as theory predicts. Thus, the evidence indicates that these consumers viewed the direct mail advertisement as complementary to their decision-making process.

The results from this study suggest that further research is needed in order to understand the reactions of individuals to various information cues. For example, in the wake of the ongoing financial crisis in the mortgage and housing markets, banking and consumer regulatory agencies are exploring the issue of information disclosure in the residential mortgage market.[44] Thus, being able to identify individuals who are most susceptible to financial advertisements may aid in identifying the type of information that is critical to making informed financial decisions. Yet, the results from this study indicate that the responses to bank marketing campaigns vary among individuals, implying that any regulatory action should reflect the heterogeneous responses of individuals to financial information.

# REFERENCES

Agarwal, S., B. W. Ambrose, S. Chomsisengphet, and C. Liu. 2006. An Empirical Analysis of Home Equity Loan and Line Performance. *Journal of Financial Intermediation*, 15: 444–469.

Agarwal, S., B. W. Ambrose, S. Chomsisengphet, and C. Liu. 2011. The Role of Soft Information in a Dynamic Contract Setting: Evidence from the Home Equity Credit Market. *Journal of Money, Credit and Banking*, 43(4): 633–655.

Agarwal, Sumit, Souphala Chomsisengphet, Chunlin Liu, and Nicholas S. Souleles. 2005. Do Consumers Choose the Right Credit Contracts? Mimeo, The Wharton School, University of Pennsylvania.

Agarwal, Sumit, John Driscoll, Xavier Gabaix, and David Laibson, 2009. Age of Reason: Financial Decisions over the Life Cycle, Brookings Papers on Economic Activity, 51–117.

Ai, C. and E. C. Norton. 2003. Interaction Terms in Logit and Probit Models. *Economic Letters*, 80: 123–129.

Alm, J. R. and J. R. Follain. 1987. Consumer Demand for Adjustable-Rate Mortgages. *Housing Finance Review*, 6: 1–16.

Anderberg, M. R. 1973. *Cluster Analysis for Applications*, New York: Academic Press, Inc.

Ausubel, L. 1999. Adverse Selection in the Credit Card Market. Working Paper, University of Maryland.

Bagwell, Kyle. 2007. The Economic Analysis of Advertising. In *Handbook of Industrial Organization, Vol. 3* edited by M. Armstrong and B. Porter, North-Holland: Amsterdam.

Barber, B. M. and T. Odean. 2008. All that Glitters: The Effect of Attention and News on the Buying Behavior of Individual and Institutional Investors. *Review of Financial Studies*, 21(2): 785–818.

Barber, B. M., T. Odean, and L. Zheng. 2005. Out of Sight, Out of Mind: The Effects of Expenses on Mutual Fund Flows. *Journal of Business*, 78(6): 2095–2119.

Bertrand, M., D. Karlan, S. Mullainathan, E. Shafir, and J. Zinman. 2006. What's Psychology Worth? A Field Experiment in Consumer Credit Markets. Working Paper, Harvard University.

Braithwaite, D. 1928. The Economic Effects of Advertisement. *Economic Journal*, 38: 16–37.

---

[44]   For example, the Federal Trade Commission Bureau of Economics held a conference ("Consumer Information and the Mortgage Market," May 29, 2008) in order to explore issues associated with consumer mortgage knowledge and consumer understanding of mortgage disclosures.

Brown, J. R., N. Liang, and S. Weisbenner. 2007. Individual Account Investment Options and Portfolio Choice: Behavioral Lessons From 401(k) Plans. *Journal of Public Economics*, 91(10): 1992–2013.

Brown, S. J. and W. N. Goetzmann. 1997. Mutual Fund Styles. *Journal of Financial Economics*, 43(3): 373–399.

Brown, S. J., W. N. Goetzmann, and M. Grinblatt. 1998. Positive Portfolio Factors. NBER Working Paper #6412.

Brueckner, J. 1986. The Pricing of Interest Rate Caps and Consumer Choice in the Market for Adjustable-Rate Mortgages. *Housing Finance Review*, 16: 119–136.

Brueckner, J. 1993. Why Do We Have Arms? *Journal of the American Real Estate and Urban Economics Association*, 21(3): 333–345.

Brueckner, J. and J. Follain J. 1988. The Rise and Fall of the Arm: An Econometric Analysis of Mortgage Choice. *Review of Economics and Statistics*, 70(1): 93–102.

Brueckner, J. and J. Follain. 1989. Arms and the Demand for Housing. *Regional Science and Urban Economics*, 19(2): 163–187.

Campbell, J. Y. 2006. Household Finance. *Journal of Finance*, LXI: 1553–1604

Campbell, J. Y. and Joao F. Cocco, 2003, Household Risk Management and Optimal Mortgage Choice, *Quarterly Journal of Economics*, 118: 1449–1494.

Chan, S. 1996. Residential Mobility and Mortgages. *Regional Science and Urban Economics*, 26(3–4): 287–311.

Chiang, R., Y. Chow, and M. Liu. 2002. Residential Mortgage Lending and Borrower Risk: The Relationship Between Mortgage Spreads and Individual Characteristics. *Journal of Real Estate Finance and Economics*, 25(1): 5–32.

Cronqvist, H. 2006. Advertising and Portfolio Choice. Working Paper, The Ohio State University.

Deng, Y., J. M. Quigley, and R. Van Order, 2000. Mortgage Terminations, Heterogeneity and the Exercise of Mortgage Options. *Econometrica*, 68(2): 310–331.

Dhillon, U., S., J. Shilling, and C. F. Sirmans. 1987. Choosing Between Fixed and Adjustable Rate Mortgages. *Journal of Money, Credit and Banking*, 19: 260–267.

Gabriel, S. and S. Rosenthal. 1993. Adjustable-Rate Mortgages, Household Mobility, and Homeownership: A Simulation Study. *Journal of Real Estate Finance and Economics*, 7(1): 29–41.

Greenspan, A. 2004. *Understanding Household Debt Obligations* at the Credit Union National Association 2004 Governmental Affairs Conference, Washington, D.C. (February 23, 2004) [http://www.federalreserve.gov/boardDocs/speeches/2004/20040223/default.htm].

Grullon, G., G. Kanatas, and J. P. Weston. 2004. Advertising, Breadth of Ownership, and Liquidity. *Review of Financial Studies*, 17(2): 439–461.

Hartigan, J. A. 1985. Statistical Theory in Clustering. *Journal of Classification*, 2: 63–76.

Hong, H., J. D. Kubik, and J. C. Stein. 2005. Thy Neighbor's Portfolio: Word-of-Mouth Effects in the Holdings and Trades of Money Managers. *Journal of Finance*, 60(6): 2801–2824.

Jain, P. C. and J. S. Wu. 2000. Truth in Mutual Fund Advertising: Evidence on Future Performance and Fund Flows. *Journal of Finance*, 55(2): 937–958.

Kahneman, D. and A. Tversky. 1979. Prospect Theory: An Analysis of Decision under Risk. *Econometrica*, 47(2): 263–292.

Koijen, R. S. J., Otto van Hemert, and Stign van Nieuwerburgh. 2007. Mortgage Timing. NBER Working Papers #13361.

Kressel, L. M., G. G. Chapman, and E. Leventhal. 2007. The Influence of Default Options on the Expression of End-of-Life Treatment Preferences in Advance Directives. *Journal of General Internal Medicine*, 22(7): 1007–1010.

Madrian, B. C. and D. F. Shea. 2001. The Power of Suggestions: Inertia in 401(k) Participation and Savings Behavior. *Quarterly Journal of Economics*, 116(4): 1149–1187.

Mullainathan, S. and A. Shliefer. 2005. Persuasion in Finance. NBER Working Paper #11838.

Mullainathan, S., J. Schwartzstein, and A. Shliefer. 2008. Coarse Thinking and Persuasion. *Quarterly Journal of Economics*, 123(2): 577–619.

Nelson, P. 1974. Advertising as Information. *The Journal of Political Economy*, 82(4): 729–754.

Nelson, P. 1975. The Economic Consequences of Advertising. *The Journal of Business*, 48(2): 213–241.

Ozga, S. A. 1960. Imperfect Markets Through Lack of Knowledge. *Quarterly Journal of Economics*, 74: 29–52.

Perry, V. G. and C. M. Motley. 2008. Reading the Fine Print: An Analysis of Mortgage Advertising Messages. Working Paper, George Washington University.

Petersen, M. A. 2009. Estimating Standard Errors in Finance Panel Data Sets: Comparing Approaches. *Review of Financial Studies*, 22(1): 435–480.

Posey, L. and A. Yavas. 2001. Adjustable and Fixed Rate Mortgages as a Screening Mechanism for Default Risk. *Journal of Urban Economics*, 49(1): 54–79.

Reuter, J. and E. Zitzewitz. 2006. Do Ads Influence Editors? Advertising and Bias in the Financial Media. *Quarterly Journal of Economics*, 121(1): 197–227.

Robinson, J. 1933. *Economics of Imperfect Competition*, London: Macmillan and Co.

Rosenthal, S. and P. Zorn. 1993. Household Mobility, Asymmetric Information, and the Pricing of Mortgage Contract Rates. *Journal of Urban Economics*, 33: 235–253.

Russo, J. E., K. A. Carlson, and M. G. Meloy. 2006. Choosing an Inferior Alternative. *Psychological Science*, 17(10): 899–904.

Sa-Aadu, J. and J. Shilling. 1994. Tests of Borrower Perceptions in the Adjustable-Rate Mortgage Market: Do Borrowers View Arm Contracts as Distinct? *Journal of Urban Economics*, 36(1): 8–22.

Sa-Aadu, J. and C. F. Sirmans. 1995. Differentiated Contracts, Heterogeneous Borrowers, and the Mortgage Choice Decision. *Journal of Money Credit and Banking*, 27(2): 498–510.

Shapiro, J. 2006. A "Memory-Jamming" Theory of Advertising. Working Paper, University of Chicago.

Shiller, R. J. 2008. *The Subprime Solution*. Princeton, NJ: Princeton University Press.

Shiller, R. J., and J. Pound. 1989. Survey Evidence on Diffusion of Interest and Information Among Investors. *Journal of Economic Behavior and Organization*, 12: 47–66.

Sirri, E. R. and P. Tufano. 1998. Costly Search and Mutual Fund Flows. *Journal of Finance*, 53(5): 1589–1622.

Stigler, G. 1961. The Economics of Information. *Journal of Political Economy*, 69: 213–225.

Tversky, A. and D. Kahneman. 1981. The Framing of Decisions and the Psychology of Choice. *Science*, 211(4481): 453–458.

Tversky, A. and D. Kahneman. 1986. Rational Choice and the Framing of Decisions. *The Journal of Business*, 59(4): S251–S278.

van Hemert, O. 2006. Life-Cycle Housing and Portfolio Choice with Bond Markets. Working Paper, New York University.

van Hemert, O., F. de Jong, and J. Driessen. 2005. Dynamic Portfolio and Mortgage Choice for Homeowners. Working Paper, New York University.

Vickery, J. 2006. Interest Rates and Consumer Choice in the Residential Mortgage Market. Working Paper, Federal Reserve Bank of New York.

# PART III

# CRIME AND PUNISHMENT

# 6. Punishment, social norms, and cooperation
## Erte Xiao

Cooperation in human society is driven by incentives, both material and nonmaterial. Material incentives can be positive, such as reward, or negative, such as punishment. Both can be implemented formally by law or informally by peers. Nonmaterial incentives are often related to emotions, such as guilt, pride, esteem, or shame. These nonmaterial incentives can often motivate individuals to take cooperative actions even if they are inconsistent with material incentives. While nonmaterial incentives can be intrinsic institutions that constrain individuals from engaging in socially undesirable activities, external interventions that manipulate material incentives are often needed to promote social order in modern societies. A central question in law is how to establish effective external intervention mechanisms, such as punishment, by changing material incentives of the targeted adverse behavior.

Standard economic theory of punishment has focused on how it can change the payoff of the target behavior and thereby influence outcomes. Assuming that people seek to maximize their profit, punishment promotes cooperation by increasing the expected cost of non-cooperative behavior (Becker 1968). According to the normative theory of punishment, we can deter violations by increasing either the probability or the magnitude of punishment so that the expected cost of violation is greater than the benefit. Results from controlled laboratory experiments also provide evidence that introducing punishment institutions can enforce cooperation (e.g., Fehr and Gächter 2000; Andreoni, Harbaugh, and Vesterlund 2003; Dickinson 2001; Ostrom, Walker, and Gardner 1992; Yamagishi 1986, 1988). On the other hand, studies also show that punishment can backfire (e.g., Fehr and Falk 2002; Fehr and List 2004; Frey and Oberholzer-Gee 1997; Kreps 1997; Tenbrunsel and Messick 1999; Gneezy and Rustichini 2000; Fehr and Rockenbach 2003; Houser et al. 2008), which is inconsistent with the predictions of the standard economic theory of punishment. The mixed results of punishment studies raise the questions of why punishment promotes cooperation sometimes but leads to even higher levels of violation in other settings, and how to design punishment mechanisms to avoid detrimental effects.

In this chapter, I discuss how punishment influences behavior by reviewing experimental research providing negative evidence on the punishment effect. To provide a more complete overview, I discuss studies of both formal punishment imposed exogenously by institutions and informal peer punishment. I discuss several factors that can lead to the detrimental effects of punishment, and for each factor I suggest solutions. The factors I discuss are not a complete list. Rather, I focus on the factors highlighted by the existing literature that inform the design of effective punishment mechanisms. Further, I argue that the effectiveness of punishment is closely connected to its ability to express norms. I conclude this chapter by reviewing recent research on social norms and suggesting that institutions that enhance the salience of social norms might be especially effective in influencing behavior.

## 1.   NEGATIVE PUNISHMENT INTENTIONS

People are strongly disposed to infer intentions when trying to understand a person's actions (see e.g., Gibbs 1999; Taylor 1979; Kahneman, Knetsch, and Thaler 1986). As a result, many economic models now include intention effects. Rabin (1993) is an early approach to incorporating perceived kindness into one's own preferences. Another example is Dufwenberg and Kirchsteiger (2004), who develop a theory of reciprocity for extensive form games. Substantial experimental research also suggests that intentions can play an important role in shaping decisions (see, e.g., McCabe, Rigdon, and Smith 2003; Falk and Kosfeld 2006; Nelson 2002; Charness and Haruvy 2002; Charness and Levine 2007; Charness 2004; Brandts and Solà 2001; Greenberg and Frisch 1972; Gordon and Bowlby 1989; Blount 1995; Offerman 2002).

The use of punishment can be viewed as an unfair act and can create a hostile atmosphere (e.g., Bewley 1999; Falk and Kosefeld 2006; Frey 1993). Consequently, imposing punishment can lead to retaliation and reduce cooperation. Previous research provides evidence that those receiving punishment are likely to retaliate against their punishers (see Casari and Luin 2009; Cinyabuguma, Page, and Putterman 2006; Denant-Boemont, Masclet, and Noussair 2007; Dreber et al. 2008; Falk, Fehr, and Fischbacher 2005; Nikiforakis 2008). For example, Nikiforakis (2008) shows that in a public goods game when peer punishment is allowed, retaliation occurs with about one quarter of all punishments when there are opportunities for counter-punishment. The result is that cooperation breaks down and group-level earnings are also lower compared with the case when no punishment opportunity is available. The author also argues that counter-punishments seem to be driven partly by a desire to reciprocate punishment. This retaliation can also lead to antisocial punishment, which has a detrimental effect on cooperation (e.g., Herrmann, Thöni, and Gächter 2008).

The findings from the above research suggest the importance of designing more restricted punishment mechanisms in which illegitimate punishment is not allowed. Restricted punishment is a feature of many real-world settings. For example, in formal contractual relationships, when one individual reneges on his obligation, the legal system provides the victim with the right to punish the defector.

For this reason, attention has recently focused on how to design effective restricted punishment mechanisms. Casari and Luini (2009) investigated a "consensual institution" in a public goods game whereby a request to punish a specific group member will be implemented only if at least two agents request such a punishment. Ertan, Pageb, and Putterman (2009) studied a public goods game where subjects can vote on who should be punished and found that this mechanism can promote cooperation, compared with a procedure where no restrictions are placed on who should be punished. Faillo, Grieco, and Zarri (2013) conducted a repeated public goods experiment where a person could only punish those who contributed less than he or she had contributed. They found that the level of cooperation doubled in relation to treatments with unrestricted punishment.

These controlled laboratory studies suggest that placing constraints on punishment can significantly improve its effectiveness in promoting cooperation. However, implementing such restricted punishment mechanisms may be difficult in naturally occurring environments. For example, a restricted punishment mechanism that requires consensus from the community may be too costly to implement when it is not clear what is the best for the group. One reason this might occur is that people's beliefs regarding what is right and what is wrong may be substantially heterogeneous. Further, in some societies bad norms exist and good ones do not. In such societies, adverse behavior is acceptable and people even inflict punishment on people who act with integrity. For example, in a society with widespread bribery and kickbacks, people may not punish corrupt behavior, and idiosyncratic honest behavior may instead be punished by the group. In cases such as these, punishment that requires agreement by the group may not be effective in promoting honesty.

Other features of naturally occurring environments, such as uncertainty, may also prevent bad behavior from being punished in the presence of restricted punishment mechanisms. One example is the airline security problem. When one airline invests in baggage security, it still faces the risk of dangerous luggage being transferred from other airlines unless it inspects all transferred bags (see Heal and Kunreuther 2005). In this case, if agents don't undertake protective measures, they may not suffer a loss due to the stochastic nature of the negative event. In fact, total payoffs would be the highest if everyone defected by choosing not to invest and, by chance, the negative outcome never occurred. This uncertainty related to the payoffs makes non-cooperative behavior less likely to be punished than when outcomes are deterministic, since agents may be spared losses even if they do not undertake protective measures.

For example, some people may be risk-seekers and view the decision not to cooperate as optimal, regardless of whether other agents decide to cooperate. Xiao and Kunreuther (2015) investigate how a restricted punishment mechanism affects cooperation in a stochastic prisoner's dilemma environment representing this type of situation. In this stochastic prisoner's dilemma, each person can decide whether to cooperate, and the outcomes of alternative strategies are specified probabilistically. Under the restricted punishment mechanism, only cooperators can punish non-cooperators. The data from this experiment provide evidence that the restricted punishment mechanism is less effective in an environment where the outcomes are stochastic than when they are known with certainty. The reason is that non-cooperators are less likely to be punished when outcomes are impacted by uncertainty.

When a third party is involved in the punishment decision process, such sanction systems can be less effective because offenders may be less likely to be punished even though illegitimate punishment is constrained. For example, Tan and Xiao (2012) find that in a prisoner's dilemma experiment, an independent third party vetoes not only punishment to the cooperators but punishment to the defectors as well. Compared with the case where the implicated parties are allowed to punish each other, both the cooperation rate and the earnings are lower when the enforcement of punishment requires approval from an independent third party.

Thus, for punishment mechanisms to be effective, it may not be enough to place constraints on the right to punish. It is important to create social norms for cooperation and to establish well-enforced regulations. Communication may help in this regard. In addition to helping coordinate cooperation (e.g., Balliet 2010), communication when accompanied by punishment can help recipients understand that punishment is imposed to deter certain types of behavior that harm the group, and thereby it mitigates the negative intention that the recipients may infer from the sanction. When bad norms prevail, in addition to relying on punishment, institutions should be built to send clear messages to the community regarding what is socially desirable behavior and why certain behavior should be punished. An interesting study by Janssen et al. (2010) shows that, when punishment is combined with communication, the group performs best in a common-pool resource problem. The authors argue the reason is that without communication, receiving a sanction does not carry a clear message about why punishment is imposed, especially when the decision environment is complicated.

## 2.    CROWDING OUT EFFECT OF PUNISHMENT INCENTIVES

### 2.1    Crowding Out Intrinsic Motivation

Punishment can backfire even absent negative intentions. Houser et al. (2008) conducted a controlled laboratory experiment, based on Fehr and Rockenbach (2003), to compare how cooperative behavior is affected when subjects face the threat of punishment imposed by their partner (i.e., intentional punishment) and when the punishment threat is imposed by nature (i.e., nonintentional punishment). Participants play a one-shot investment experiment in pairs (see also Berg, Dickhaut, and McCabe 1995). Investors transfer an amount to trustees, and trustees receive triple the transfer amount. Investors can also request a return on this investment and, in some treatments, can threaten sanctions to enforce their requests. The authors compare how trustee decision-making is influenced by whether they face threats from investors or from nature. When not threatened, trustees typically decide to return a positive amount less than the investor requested. When threatened, this decision becomes least common. If the request is large relative to the sanction, then most trustees return nothing. If the request is small, trustees typically return the requested amount. Interestingly, these results do not vary with investors' intentions. The authors argue the results are consistent with previous studies that find negative incentive effects due to cognitive dissonance and self-serving bias.

Cognitive dissonance is a psychological term describing the uncomfortable tension that comes from holding two conflicting thoughts at the same time. It is the perception of incompatibility between two cognitions, where "cognition" is defined as any element of knowledge, including attitude, emotion, belief, or behavior. Cognitive dissonance theory (Festinger 1957) posits that people desire to keep their behavior and beliefs consistent. Absent external incentives, people justify their behavior through an appeal to internal motivations. However, when present, an external incentive can become a salient behavioral justification, and this can, in principle, crowd out norm-based conduct when individuals perceive the external intervention to be controlling (Deci, Koestner, and Ryan 1999; Lepper and Greene 1978). In principle, the salience of incentives in justifying behavior does not necessarily lead to selfish acts. As I discuss later, punishment can also signal disapproval of the targeted behavior. However, if people's judgments are biased toward self-interest (Babcock and Loewenstein 1997), then they are likely to interpret the punishment as a price they can pay to support selfish behavior (Gneezy and Rustichini 2000; Falk, Gächter, and Kovács 1999). Thus, absent threats, people will make decisions within an ethical context, and selfish decisions will be relatively infrequent. When threatened by punishment, people will cooperate to avoid punishment when a sanction's cost exceeds the benefit of defection. When the sanction's cost is lower than this benefit, however, people will pay the fine and maximize their earnings. Tenbrunsel and Messick (1999) propose a similar model on the impact of sanctions that provides similar predictions.

Li et al. (2009) conducted an fMRI (functional magnetic resonance imaging) study and provided neural data that support this model of incentive effects. Using a similar experiment design as in Houser et al. (2008), they found that trustees reciprocate relatively less when facing sanction threats, and that the presence of sanctions significantly reduces trustee brain activities involved in social reward valuation (in the ventromedial prefrontal cortex, lateral orbitofrontal cortex, and amygdala) while it simultaneously increases brain activities in the parietal cortex, which has been implicated in rational decision-making.[1]

Even considering these negative results, in my view punishment is still needed as it has a positive impact on some types of individuals, although it can be counterproductive for other types. The key is how to design punishment to avoid its potential detrimental effects. Proceeding along this line, we can classify people roughly into three types in any specific decision-making context based on the strength of their intrinsic motive to cooperate: (1) purely selfish—those who do not have intrinsic motivation to cooperate and will behave selfishly absent punishment; (2) weakly cooperative—those who do have intrinsic motivation and behave cooperatively when punishment is absent but adopt profit-maximizing strategies when they can find an excuse for selfish behavior (e.g., excuses provided by the presence of punishment); (3) strongly cooperative—those who have a strong intrinsic motivation to cooperate and who would not use punishment as an excuse for not cooperating. Based on the findings from the studies discussed above, punishment can potentially reduce the cooperation rate of the weakly cooperative type. However, punishment is necessary to deter bad behavior among the purely selfish type, and introducing punishment will not reduce the cooperation rate of either the purely selfish type or the strongly cooperative type. Therefore, the key question is how we can minimize the detrimental effect of punishment on the weakly cooperative type. This question is especially important to consider when there is a significant proportion of weakly cooperative types in the population. In this case, any detrimental effect of punishment can significantly diminish the overall efficacy of punishment.

If punishment leads to profit-maximizing behavior among weakly cooperative types, one might think that imposing strong punishment may reduce opportunistic behavior (i.e., the cost of receiving punishment becomes higher than the cost of cooperating). Nevertheless, as a practical matter, severe punishment usually requires costly monitoring. It can also be extremely time-consuming to implement. In addition, mechanisms based exclusively on severe sanctions may also suffer from an absence of marginal deterrence for serious crimes (see, e.g., Stigler 1970). Consequently, punishment incentives used to promote cooperation are often weak in the sense that the expected cost of a violation is less than the expected benefit of cooperating (Tyler 2006).

An alternative solution is to design the punishment mechanism so that it is hard for the weakly cooperative to perceive selfish behavior as acceptable as long as one pays the penalty. One implication is that, when designing institutions to maintain social order

---

[1]   This finding suggests that monetary incentives will engage System 2 in decision-making that requires more cognitive effort. See more discussions on System 1 and System 2 in Kahneman (2011).

and cooperation, punishment should not be the only mechanism applied. For example, we may need to combine material punishment with nonmaterial punishment or reward. Studies have shown that nonmonetary informal sanctions, such as expressing disapproval or approval, can also reduce selfish behavior (e.g., Masclet et al. 2003; Noussair and Tucker 2005; Ellingsen and Johannesson 2008; Xiao and Houser 2009).

It is also important to make the norm of cooperation transparent to the community so that paying a penalty cannot excuse one's misbehavior. As I elaborate later, the effectiveness of punishment is affected by whether the punishment signals a norm violation. We may avoid the detrimental effect of punishment by moving people away from the perspective that punishment (e.g., a fine) is a price (and therefore an excuse for violation), toward the alternative perspective that punishment is a signal of a norm violation. Further empirical studies are needed to determine how different punishment designs may induce or mitigate the disutility associated with norm violations.

## 2.2    Crowding Out Image Motivation

Image motivation refers to the desire to be liked and respected by others and by oneself. Image motivation can lead to cooperative behavior as people seek approval from others (see, e.g., Akerlof 1980; Hollander 1990; Bénabou and Tirole 2006; Andreoni and Bernheim 2009; Ellingsen and Johannesson 2011). For example, a person may be willing to pay the cost of recycling, especially in public, because the act can signal to others that this person has good traits and cares about the welfare of the community.

The introduction of incentives can potentially crowd out image motives. Bénabou and Tirole (2006) construct a theory arguing that when incentives are present, they reduce the signaling value of good deeds and therefore reduce prosocial behavior. For example, to promote recycling norms, some cities, such as Philadelphia, have enacted laws that punish households that fail to recycle. Although enforcing such a law increases the cost of failure to recycle, it can potentially reduce image motives for recycling. The reason is that people may question whether the individual recycles because he cares about the environment or because he is simply trying to avoid the penalty.

Experiments have provided evidence for the crowding out effect of incentives on image motivation. For example, Ariely, Bracha, and Meier (2009) find that in the absence of monetary incentives, subjects significantly increase their effort in a charitable giving task when they perform the task in public rather than in private. In contrast, when monetary incentives are introduced, these incentives have no effect on efforts made in public, while they do increase efforts made in private. They conclude that "private monetary incentives seem to interact negatively with image concerns, leading to the result that monetary incentives are more effective in motivating private prosocial decisions than ones made in a public setting" (p. 546).

Although these findings are in the domain of monetary rewards, such detrimental effects may also extend to the domain of punishment. On the other hand, "doing good" is not equivalent to "not doing bad". Compared with doing good things, not to engage in misconduct is often less salient and less visible. In addition, "not doing good" is not the same as "doing bad". Doing bad is often viewed much more negatively than not doing good. In criminal law, an omission is judged as a guilty act, and thus gives rise to liability, only when the law imposes a duty to act and the defendant is in breach of that duty. More studies are needed to identify how punishment affects image motivation.

Nevertheless, findings regarding crowding out call attention to the importance of taking into account the visibility of the target behavior when designing punishment mechanisms. While incentives can be effective in promoting non-visible compliance, such as tax compliance, it might be counterproductive when used to promote visible conformity, such as following traffic rules on the road. To promote visible compliance without crowding out image motivation, it may help to introduce other types of interventions. For example, when enforcing traffic rules, it is helpful to address that following the rule is desirable both for one's own and others' safety. These public normative messages can help to maintain the image function of obedience and highlight that disobedience can have a negative impact on the violator's image.

The discussion so far suggests the importance of establishing social norms of cooperation even when punishment mechanisms can be imposed. Next I discuss how punishment can be used to signal norms, and how to design punishment mechanisms to enhance their norm expressive functions.

## 3.   THE NORM EXPRESSIVE FUNCTION OF PUNISHMENT

Punishment promotes compliance not only by changing incentives but also by communicating social norms. Research in law and economics has argued that norm expression is an important function of punishment (see, e.g., Kahan 1998; Cooter 1998; Sunstein 1996; Tyran and Feld 2006; Masclet et al. 2003; Galbiati and Vertova 2008; Bénabou and Tirole 2011). For example, laws that forbid the sale of children send a message to the public that children should be valued in a way that forbids the acceptance of cash as a reason for taking them out of parental care. Punishment is used to inform violators and the public that the targeted behavior is not approved, and that it violates a social norm. By nature, the social norms that punishment enforces are often inconsistent with people's self-interest (see Bicchieri 2006); yet, as I will discuss in more detail in the next section, norms can substantially affect people's decisions. It follows that the norm expression function of punishment can have a significant effect on behavior. For example, Galbiati and Vertova (2008) reported data from a public goods experiment supporting the idea that punishment informs people what they should or should not do, and this established obligation has a significant effect on cooperation. The experiment showed that the expressive power of punishment can influence behavior independent of the incentive mechanism.

The effectiveness of the norm expressing function of punishment is particularly important where good norms do not exist and bad ones do. In these situations, laws can help reconstruct existing norms and change the social meaning of the targeted behavior (see Sunstein 1996). For example, as the number of accidents related to mobile phone use while driving increases, many states have outlawed certain types of cell phone use. "Currently, 44 states, D.C., Puerto Rico, Guam and the U.S. Virgin Islands ban text messaging for all drivers" (Governors Highway Safety Association n.d.).[2] Enforcing such

---

[2]   http://www.ghsa.org/html/stateinfo/laws/cellphone_laws.html (last accessed July 2014).

laws not only increases the cost of disobedience but also signals to the public that using a mobile phone while driving is inappropriate and is disapproved of by the society.

Given the role of punishment in expressing social norms, it is important to ask what factors may interfere with the communication function of punishment. At first glance, the norm expressive function of punishment argument seems to contradict the crowding out effect of punishment discussed earlier. There, the evidence shows how punishment crowds out norm-based decision-making and induces egocentric decisions. I argue that both are important aspects of the punishment effect. It is important to learn under what conditions punishment can signal norms and thereby promote cooperation rather than be interpreted as the price for non-cooperative behavior. I have discussed that self-serving bias can lead people to interpret punishment as a price they pay for selfish behavior. People are more likely to engage in selfish behavior because paying the price (the penalty) can reduce their negative feelings about acting selfishly. This suggests that the punishment should be designed so that it does not become a reasonable excuse for noncompliance. I argue here that when a law is perceived as legitimate, people are more likely to be averse to violating the norms enforced by punishment and thus less likely to perceive the penalty as the price for violating.

### 3.1 Legitimacy of Punishment

People who view the law as legitimate are more likely to comply, even though it might contradict their interests (Easton 1965). As written in Tyler (2006), "citizens may comply with the law because they view the legal authority they are dealing with as having a legitimate right to dictate their behavior; this represents an acceptance by people of the need to bring their behavior into line with the dictates of an external authority" (p. 25).

In empirical studies that test the correlation between legitimacy and compliance, researchers often ask participants questions such as, "If a police officer asks you to do something that you think is wrong, should you do it anyway?" It is reasonable to assume that when people answer "yes" to those questions, indicating they believe that laws should be obeyed simply because that is the right thing to do, they are more likely to perceive the law as signaling social norms and feel guilt or shame when breaking the law rather than viewing punishment as the price for misconduct and accepting it as a way to mitigate the negative feeling associated with selfish behavior. Thus any instruments that improve the legitimacy of the law can potentially promote the norm expression function of punishment. This knowledge can help in designing effective punishment mechanisms.

The legitimacy of law refers to the respect that people show to the authorities, the sense of obligation to obey authorities, or a shared sense that the existing legal arrangements are as they ought to be (Tyler 2006). Thus, the legitimacy of law is correlated with people's perception of the authorities. According to procedural justice theory (Lind and Tyler 1988), views on authority are strongly connected to how people view the fairness of the procedures through which authorities make decisions. The theory suggests that how the law is originated and enforced and people's perception of enforcers' motivations can affect people's views about the authority and thereby the legitimacy of the law. Because the studies I reviewed examined the outcome of different ways of originating or implementing punishment, I focused my discussion on procedural justice theory. It is worth noting, however, that substantive justice of the law does clearly matter. When an individual views a law as substantively fair he/she may be more likely to view the procedures that originate or enforce the law as also fair. While separately identifying the impact of substantive and distributive fairness can be difficult in the field, studies using controlled laboratory experiment can in principle do so. In particular, by holding fixed the punishment incentives while varying only the procedures determining how punishment is selected or implemented, one is able to provide clean evidence informing the role and importance of procedural justice (e.g. Tyran and Feld 2006; Xiao 2013, discussed below).

Tyran and Feld (2006) showed that, in a public goods environment, compliance improves greatly when mild punishment is imposed by group members rather than exogenously. The reason is that voting for punishment expresses support for a cooperation norm. Exogenously imposed punishment, on the other hand, lacks such a signaling function. Expected compliance further promotes cooperation as people are conditional cooperators, that is, people are more likely to cooperate when they expect others will do so. In related work, Baldassarri and Grossman (2011) conducted a public goods experiment involving 1,543 Ugandan farmers from 50 producer cooperatives to investigate the effectiveness of centralized punishment. In the experiment, after two primary rounds of a public goods game, one player is selected and is given the power to punish group members in the following four rounds. The authors found that when the punisher is selected by the group members, the contribution rate is significantly higher than when the punisher is randomly selected by a lottery. The authors argue that the results "demonstrate the causal effect of legitimacy on cooperation: participants are more responsive to the authority of an elected monitor than a randomly chosen monitor" (p. 11023).

It is worth noting that elected authorities promote cooperation more effectively than randomly selected ones, not only when they apply monetary punishment but also when they merely communicate to group members. Levy et al. (2011) conducted a public goods experiment to investigate how leaders influence group members' cooperative behavior by communication. In one treatment, group members select a leader after five rounds of a public goods game and the leader can send a message "Let's contribute . . . to the group account" to the group members in the following ten rounds. The authors find that the cooperation level is significantly higher when the messages are sent by the elected leader than from a randomly selected leader, even though the suggested contribution levels do not differ between the two conditions.

Thus, people seem more likely to conform when the authority is elected, regardless of whether the order is in the form of punishment or simply solicitation. An implication is that it is easier to promote social order when citizens have the opportunity to take part in the decision-making process, present their arguments, be heard, and have their views considered by authorities.

The perception of legitimacy is also impacted by how a law is enforced. For example, using interview materials, He (2005) studies why there are prevalent violations of discriminatory licensing legislation in Beijing. Under the legislation, it is much more difficult for rural-urban migrants to obtain the licenses they need to conduct business lawfully. The author argues that the law is not followed because it is not consistently enforced. For example, sporadic campaigns are launched to enforce the laws during politically sensitive periods, such as the meeting period of the national people's congress. As a result, migrants do not respect the law and commonly rent licenses illegally from the locals. The inconsistency in law enforcement may be observed in other societies where legal systems are corrupt. If the law is not enforced consistently, people will doubt whether it is in the best interest of the society or rather is purely a tool for authorities to pursue their own interests. As a result, people may be more likely to interpret punishment as the price that authorities charge for violations.

One reason the law may not be enforced consistently is that enforcers' self-interest intervenes. Since punishment typically involves depriving violators of resources they own, such as money or labor, resources can become revenue for authorities. This can create temptation for authorities to profit from enforcement, especially if their power is not regulated, as is often the case in corrupt societies. Xiao (2013) provides experimental evidence indicating that if people know that enforcers can benefit monetarily by punishing, they no longer view punishment as signaling a norm violation.

In the experiment reported by Xiao (2013), an enforcer both observes whether an agent tells the truth and can decide whether to punish the agent. The principal, who does not know the truth, can observe the enforcer's punishment decisions and decide whether to trust the agent. The author finds the principals are significantly less likely to trust the agent when punishment is imposed. However, this effect disappears when the principal knows that the enforcer can profit from imposing punishment. As a result, dishonest behavior is significantly more frequent under profitable punishment mechanisms than under non-profitable punishment mechanisms.

The experiment setting in that paper also reflects the naturally occurring environments where punishment records can signal the punishee's type and therefore affect the chance of being trusted by others in the future. For example, background checks, such as driving or criminal record checks, are often part of the process used to determine whether a job candidate is qualified for a position. However, a candidate's record may have less weight in hiring decisions if employers believe legal systems are corrupt and that enforcers can profit from creating violations. Future research is needed to examine cross-country correlations between the extent of corruption in legal systems and the impact of backgrounds on hiring decisions.

The relationship between profitable punishment and norm violations suggests a potential causal relationship between corrupt legal systems and pervasive norm violations. By definition, corrupt societies include persistent and pervasive norm violations. Scholars have highlighted the importance of punishment in curbing corruption (Abbink 2006). Unfortunately, in corrupt societies, authorities who enforce punishments are typically also perceived as highly corrupt (Hunt 2006; Transparency Internal 2007). Rather than corrupt societies simply reflecting a culture of norm disobedience, legal institutions that embed corrupting temptations (e.g., profitable punishment) may be causally connected to systemic patterns of norm violations in society. Therefore it is important to establish institutions that signal intolerance for corruption in the legal system. Such institutions have proven effective in natural environments. For example, during the economic growth period in Hong Kong, the Independent Commission Against Corruption (ICAC) was established to clean up its endemic corruption in law enforcement and many other government departments. The ICAC ultimately proved vital in transforming Hong Kong from a graft-ridden city into a metropolis known for cleanliness and lawfulness. Indeed, such organizations may be a necessary first step toward mitigating pervasive norm violations in severely corrupt societies, and doing so might help set the stage for rapid and peaceful economic expansion.

Another important question is how to design the enforcer's compensation package. How an enforcer is paid can significantly influence the expressive function and the outcome of punishment. Some scholars have suggested the importance of paying a high salary to officials to reduce their temptation to earn extra money from their power (Abbink 2006). However, a fixed guaranteed salary has the downside that it does not motivate the enforcers to work hard to catch violators. In principle, profitable punishment that links enforcers' performance to their payment could motivate prosecutors to put more effort into catching offenders. On the other hand, this opportunity for punishers to profit may lead them to choose to further their own revenue interests rather than pursuing the goals of norm conformity and promoting socially desirable behavior. It may be argued that we can maintain the expressive function of punishment, and also motivate the enforcers to work hard, when the enforcers are rewarded if and only if they punish the violators.

However, in naturally occurring environments, the opportunity to profit from punishment may motivate authorities to change the rules so that it is easier for people to violate them and receive punishment. For example, in Pittsburgh, hourly rates at many parking meters were almost doubled in 2011 as part of the city's effort to raise revenue to save its ailing pension funds from state takeovers. In addition to increasing hourly rates, the Pittsburgh city council also lengthened the enforcement time of meters and hired more employees to write tickets.[3] Motorists.org also reports that in 2008 six cities in the United States shortened yellow light time on stoplights to increase violations and thus increase tickets issued for profit.[4] Thus profitable punishment may still have detrimental effects on the expressive function of punishment, even when enforcers are rewarded only if they punish rule violators. This may be especially true when the appropriateness of a rule is ambiguous (e.g., it might be unclear how long a stop light should remain yellow to promote safe driving). Consequently, it remains an open question how different enforcer compensation mechanisms affect the outcomes of punishment.

The discussion on the importance of legitimacy may also explain why punishment has negative effects in some studies (e.g., Gneezy and Rustichini 2000; Fehr and Rockenbach 2003; Houser et al. 2008) but not in others (e.g., Fehr and Gächter 2000; Andreoni, Harbaugh, and Vesterlund 2003; Ostrom, Walker, and Gardner 1992; Yamagishi 1986, 1988). In the former studies, the punishment is often imposed by one party, who is also the only one who benefits from the punishee's cooperative behavior. In contrast, in the latter group, the punishment is often imposed by more than one individual in the group, and thus people are more likely to view punishment as signaling norm violations which incur negative emotions when receiving punishment.

### 3.2   Implementation of Punishment

While legitimate punishment can influence behavior by signaling norms, how the punishment is implemented can affect the salience of the norm message sent by punishment. As I discuss in the next section, a norm might not influence behavior when people are

---

[3]   See http://www.wpxi.com/news/news/pittsburgh-parking-rates-to-increase-tomorrow/nD6wk/
[4]   See http://www.motorists.org/blog/6-cities-that-were-caught-shortening-yellow-light-times-for-profit/ for details.

not focusing on the norm. Xiao and Houser (2011) conducted public goods experiments suggesting that publicly implemented punishment can promote the salience of the social norm and therefore is more effective in promoting cooperation than privately implemented punishment, even absent shame and information effects. In the experiment, subjects form a group of four and decide how to allocate their endowment. Every dollar they invest in the public goods account generates two dollars that will be split equally among the group members. Since the profit from the investment to the group account is always less than the investment, a profit-maximizing strategy is never to invest. However, the group benefits most if everyone invests. The authors then examine the effect of a weak punishment mechanism. In each round, there is a 50 percent chance that the round will be monitored and, if so, the one who contributes least to the public account receives a small punishment. The punishment amount is so small that the dominant strategy remains not to invest. The authors compare the outcome of two types of enforcement. In one, punishment is implemented privately so that only the lowest contributor who receives the punishment sees the implementation of punishment. In another, when punishment is implemented everyone in the group is informed. In both cases, punishment is common knowledge and decisions are anonymous. Thus, the experiment design ensures that any treatment difference cannot be attributed to shame or differences in information.[5] They find that privately implemented punishment does not increase contribution compared with the baseline, in which a punishment mechanism is not introduced. However, when the same punishment mechanism is implemented publicly, the contribution level is significantly higher than both the baseline and the private punishment treatment. The data suggest that the ability to observe the punishment of free riders promotes the effectiveness of punishment.

It is worth noting that public punishment absent of shame is observed in the real world. For example, to enforce the honor code, many organizations (e.g., West Point and Kellogg Graduate School of Management) announce to the community when an honor-code violation occurs and is punished. Such public implementation can remind people to follow the norm and thus can enhance the effectiveness of punishment.

## 4.   SOCIAL NORM INTERVENTIONS

We often observe voluntary social cooperation even when there is no punishment for violation or reward for compliance. Scholars have argued that norms can substantially affect people's decisions, and social norms are recognized as important motivations behind individual decision-making in several economic models (see, e.g., Elster 1989; Lewis 1969; Rabin 1993; Fehr and Schmidt 1999; Bolton and Ockenfels 2000; Camerer and Fehr 2004; Fehr and Fischbacher 2004; Young 2008). The earlier discussion suggests that the effectiveness of punishment is also closely related to the extent that punishment communicates social norms. Thus, an understanding of the role of social norms in decision-making can both provide additional instruments to enforce cooperation and help in the design of effective punishment mechanisms.

---

[5]   For discussion on shame punishment, see Posner (2000).

Empirical studies of norm conformity show that focusing people on an existing norm is important for social norms to influence behavior (e.g., Schultz 1998; Keizer et al. 2008; Goldstein, Cialdini, and Griskevicius 2008; Schultz et al. 2007). For example, Cialdini, Kallgren, and Reno (1990) hypothesized that focusing people on the idea that one ought not to litter should decrease littering. To test this, the experimenters tucked handbills with different messages under windshield wipers of cars in a library parking lot. Supporting their hypothesis, they found that subjects littered less when the message was "April is Keep Arizona Beautiful Month. Please Do Not Litter" than when the message was "April is Arizona's Fine Arts Month. Please Visit Your Local Art Museum."

Recent research has pointed out the importance of expectations in social norms. An individual's tendency toward norm conformity is affected by what she believes others would do in a similar situation (i.e., empirical expectations of norm compliance) and what she believes others think she ought to do (i.e., normative expectations of norm compliance) (see Bicchieri 2006; Bicchieri and Xiao 2009; Paprzycka 1999; Cason and Mui 1998; Bardsley and Sausgruber 2005; Krupka and Weber 2009; Sugden 1998, 2004). The expectation-based social norms theory provides researchers with a nice tool to measure and study social norms. It suggests that we can identify social norms by eliciting people's beliefs (Bicchieri and Xiao 2009; Krupka and Weber 2009), and information on these beliefs provides explicit evidence on the role of social norms in decision-making (e.g., Gächter, Nosenzo, Sefton 2013; Xiao 2015).

The expectation-based social norm theory suggests the importance of differentiating two types of expectations. When norm obedience is prevalent, one's expectation regarding what people will do is often in line with one's expectation regarding what people think one ought to do. In this case, normative and empirical expectations work in the same direction and motivate the same behavior. For example, when most of your neighbors recycle, you form the empirical expectation that people do recycle. At the same time, your normative expectation is also that people think you should recycle. Thus, the presence of both expectations makes it more likely that you will recycle.

On the other hand, when noncompliance is pervasive, we may experience an inconsistency between normative and empirical expectations. Thus, the understanding of how each type of expectation influences behavior can help us design institutions to enforce conformity, especially when they are in conflict. One example is corruption. Even in the presence of laws and social norms condemning corruption, the widespread occurrence of bribery and kickbacks can induce people to form empirical expectations that most people are corrupt, while simultaneously holding the normative expectation that most people disapprove of corruption. In cases such as this, to design efficient institutions to enforce prosocial norms we must learn which expectation might have a greater effect on decisions. While it may not be easy to address such a question in the field, laboratory experiments provide an opportunity to compare the effects of these two types of expectations.

Bicchieri and Xiao (2009) conducted an experiment where a dictator can decide how to split between herself and the matched receiver the money given to her by the experimenter. In the experiment, the authors exogenously manipulate dictators' expectations in the direction of either selfishness or fairness by providing dictators' data from certain previous sessions. They find that when dictators are given only information about what other dictators did or thought one should do, their normative expectations are consistent with empirical expectations and both are in line with the dictators' behavior. When presenting conflicting information (for example, most dictators in one session thought that one should be fair, but a majority of dictators in another session thought that one should behave selfishly), the normative expectation deviates from the empirical expectation. Importantly, the empirical expectation about other dictators' choices significantly predicts a dictator's own choice. However, dictators' normative expectations regarding what other dictators think ought to be done do not have a significant impact on their decisions after controlling for empirical expectations. These findings suggest that when designing institutions or policies to discourage undesirable behavior, it is important to change people's empirical expectations about whether others also follow the norms. Punishment that only signals normative messages without shaping people's empirical expectations of majority norm compliance may not be effective in promoting cooperation.

I discussed how punishment sends a signal of what is not approved, which means punishment can influence people's normative expectations. Punishment can also signal the punisher's belief about the target group's behavior. It has been argued that the principal's choice of incentives reveals her beliefs about the trustworthiness of the target group (see Bénabou and Tirole 2003; Sliwka 2007; Ellingsen and Johannesson 2008; Van Der Weele 2012). When the authority decides to increase punishment severity, it probably sends a signal to people that the number of violations is increasing, which requires more severe punishment. Thus, punishment may fail sometimes because it signals that many people are violating that norm. It is therefore important to balance the incentive effect and signaling effect of punishment when designing the mechanism.

In addition to punishment, other institutions can be designed to highlight social norms and enforce cooperation. One common practice is to require justification for one's decision. For example, the Department of Health and Human Services (HSS) announced that health insurance providers needed to justify rate increases of 10 percent or more starting September 1, 2011.[6] How the justification requirement influences judgment and choices has been discussed in psychology literature on accountability. Tetlock (1985) proposed a social contingency model of judgment and choice to understand how accountability influences behavior. In this model he assumes that people tend to be "cognitive misers," in that they rely on simple heuristics to make judgments quickly. When people believe they will have to justify their views, if they are unconstrained by past commitments they will try to anticipate the possible objections from the audience and adopt the salient, socially acceptable position. This process of thinking can promote the salience of social norms (normative expectations here). Xiao (2015) studies how pure justification pressure can promote cooperation in economic exchange environments. The author finds that, in a one-shot anonymous interaction, compared with the case when the behavior is simply observed by the audience, individuals are more likely to act on what they believe the audience thinks they should do when they also have to explain the decisions to the audience. When it is salient that the audience thinks one should cooperate, justification pressure significantly promotes cooperation, even absent negative consequences for non-cooperative behavior. One implication of this finding for the HSS justification policy is that, in addition to promoting transparency, the pure pressure of justification imposed by HSS's new policy may motivate health insurance providers to set reasonable prices for consumers.

---

[6]    See https://www.healthcare.gov/health-care-law-protections/rate-review/

## 5.   SUMMARY

How to design punishment mechanisms to maintain social order is a central question in law. In the past, researchers have focused on models that assume people are profit maximizing and punishment can be designed to enforce conformity by increasing the expected cost of noncompliance. Recent research in behavioral economics draws attention to other aspects of punishment. This research points out that punishment can backfire. One reason is that the recipient may infer negative intentions from punishment and thus retaliate. I review recent research on how to design restricted punishment mechanisms to restrict retaliatory punishment and promote cooperation. Such restricted punishment may still have limited power when the complexity of the real world makes it hard to decide what behavior should be punished. Communication is important to convey what is socially disapproved and to create social norms for cooperation. Punishment can backfire even absent intention effects. I discussed research showing how punishment may be detrimental because it crowds out the intrinsic motivation of conformity, and non-monetary incentives may need to be combined with monetary incentives to avoid this crowding out effect. Research on incentives crowding out self-image motives suggests that whether punishment should be visible or not depends on the nature of the targeted behavior.

Another important function of punishment is as a signal of social norms. I discussed the importance of establishing legitimacy to enhance the norm expression function of punishment and to avoid crowding out. This behavioral research suggests that punishment and social norm instruments are complements in altering human behavior. Punishment can facilitate changes when bad norms prevail. Understanding how punishment and social norms influence behavior can help us to design effective incentive mechanisms to promote cooperation. Punishment is more effective in enforcing cooperation when it can signal social disapproval of noncompliance. The more salient are the norm messages sent by punishment, the more effective punishment can be in enforcing cooperation.

## REFERENCES

Abbink, Klaus. 2006. Laboratory Experiments on Corruption. Pp. 418–37 in *International Handbook on the Economics of Corruption*, edited by S. Rose-Ackerman. Cheltenham: Edward Elgar Publishing.

Akerlof, George A. 1980. A Theory of Social Custom, of Which Unemployment May Be One Consequence. *Quarterly Journal of Economics* 94(4): 749–75.

Andreoni, James, and B. Douglas Bernheim. 2009. Social Image and the 50-50 Norm: A Theoretical and Experimental Analysis of Audience Effects. *Econometrica* 77(5): 1607–36.

Andreoni, James, William Harbaugh, and Lise Vesterlund. 2003. The Carrot or Stick: Reward, Punishment and Cooperation. *The American Economic Review* 93(3): 893–902.

Ariely, Dan, Anat Bracha, and Stephan Meier. 2009. Doing Good or Doing Well? Image Motivation and Monetary Incentives in Behaving Prosocially. *American Economic Review* 99(1): 544–55.

Babcock, Linda, and George Loewenstein. 1997. Explaining Bargaining Impasse: The Role of Self-serving Biases. *Journal of Economic Perspective* 11(1): 109–26.

Baldassarri, Delia and Guy Grossman. 2011. Centralized Sanctioning and Legitimate Authority Promote Cooperation in Humans. *Proceedings of the National Academy of Sciences* 108(27): 11023–27.

Balliet, Daniel. 2010. Communication and Cooperation in Social Dilemmas: A Meta-Analytic Review. *Journal of Conflict Resolution* 54(1): 39–57.

Bardsley, Nicholas and Rupert Sausgruber. 2005. Conformity and Reciprocity in Public Good Provision. *Journal of Economic Psychology* 26(5): 664–81.

Becker, Gary. 1968. Crime and Punishment: An Economic Approach. *The Journal of Political Economy* 76(2): 169–217.

Bénabou, Roland and Jean Tirole. 2003. Intrinsic and Extrinsic Motivation. *Review of Economic Studies* 70: 489–520.

Bénabou, Roland and Jean Tirole. 2006. Incentives and Prosocial Behavior. *American Economic Review* 96(5): 1652–78.

Bénabou, Roland and Jean Tirole. 2011. Laws and Norms. Working Paper No. 17579. National Bureau of Economic Research, Cambridge, Mass.

Berg, Joyce, John Dickhaut, and Kevin McCabe. 1995. Trust, Reciprocity and Social History. *Games Economic Behavior* 10: 122–42.

Bewley, Truman. 1999. *Why Wages Don't Fall During a Recession*. Cambridge, Mass.: Harvard University Press.

Bicchieri, Cristina. 2006. *The Grammar of Society: The Nature and Dynamics of Social Norms*. New York: Cambridge University Press.

Bicchieri, Cristina and Erte Xiao. 2009. Do the Right Thing: But Only If Others Do So. *Journal of Behavioral Decision Making* 22(2): 191–208.

Blount, Sally. 1995. When Social Outcomes Aren't Fair: The Effect of Causal Attributions on Preferences. *Organizational Behavior and Human Decision Process* 63(2): 131–44.

Bolton, Gary E. and Axel Ockenfels. 2000. ERC: A Theory of Equity, Reciprocity, and Competition. *American Economic Review* 90: 166–93.

Brandts, Jordi and Carles Solà. 2001. Reference Points and Negative Reciprocity in Simple Sequential Games. *Games and Economic Behavior* 36(2): 138–57.

Camerer, Colin. 2003. *Behavioral Game Theory: Experiments in Strategic Interaction*. Princeton, N.J.: Princeton University Press.

Camerer, Colin and Ernst Fehr. 2004. Measuring Social Norms and Preferences Using Experimental Games: A Guide for Social Scientists. Pp. 55–95 in *Foundations of Human Sociality*, edited by J. Henrich, S. Bowles, R. Boyd, C. Camerer, E. Fehr, and H. Gintis. New York: Oxford University Press.

Casari, Marco and Luigi Luini. 2009. Group Cooperation under Alternative Punishment Institutions: An Experiment. *Journal of Economic Behavior and Organization* 71(2): 273–82.

Cason, Timothy and Vai-Lam Mui. 1998. Social Influence in the Sequential Dictator Game. *Journal of Mathematical Psychology* 42: 248–65.

Charness, Gary. 2004. Attribution and Reciprocity in an Experimental Labor Market. *Journal of Labor Economics* 22: 665–68.

Charness, Gary and Ernan Haruvy. 2002. Altruism, Equity, and Reciprocity in a Gift-Exchange Experiment: An Encompassing Approach. *Games and Economic Behavior* 40: 203–31.

Charness, Gary and David Levine. 2007. Intention and Stochastic Outcomes: An Experimental Study. *Economic Journal* 117: 1051–72.

Cialdini, Robert B., Carl A. Kallgren, and Raymond R. Reno. 1990. A Focus Theory of Normative Conduct: A Theoretical Refinement and Reevaluation of the Role of Norms in Human Behavior. *Advances in Experimental Social Psychology* 24: 201–34.

Cinyabuguma, M., T. Page, and L. Putterman. 2006. Can Second-order Punishment Deter Perverse Punishment? *Experiment Economics* 9(3): 265–79.

Cooter, Robert D. 1998. Expressive Law and Economics. *Journal of Legal Studies* 27(2): 585–608.

Deci, Edward L., Richard Koestner, and Richard M. Ryan. 1999. A Meta-analytic Review of Experiments Examining the Effect of Extrinsic Rewards on Intrinsic Motivation. *Psychological Bulletin* 125: 627–68.

Denant-Boemont, Laurent, David Masclet, and Charles N. Noussair. 2007. Punishment, Counterpunishment, and Sanction Enforcement in a Social Dilemma Experiment. *Economic Theory* 33: 145–67.

Dickinson, David. 2001. The Carrot vs. the Stick in Work Team Motivation. *Experimental Economics* 4: 107–24.

Dreber, Anna, David G. Rand, Drew Fudenberg, and Martin A. Nowak. 2008. Winners Don't Punish. *Nature* 452: 348–51.

Dufwenberg, Martin, and George Kirchsteiger. 2004. A Theory of Sequential Reciprocity. *Games and Economic Behavior* 47: 268–98.

Easton, David. 1965. *A Framework for Political Analysis*. Englewood Cliffs: Prentice-Hall.

Ellingsen, Tore, and Magnus Johannesson. 2008. Anticipated Verbal Feedback Induces Pro-social Behavior. *Evolution and Human Behavior* 29(2): 100–105.

Ellingsen, Tore, and Magnus Johannesson. 2011. Conspicuous Generosity. *Journal of Public Economics* 95(9): 1131–43.

Elster, J. 1989. Social Norms and Economic Theory. *Journal of Economic Perspectives* 3(4): 99–117.

Elster, Jon. 1999. *Alchemies of the Mind: Rationality and the Emotions*. Cambridge: Cambridge University Press.

Ertan, Arhan, Talbot Pageb, and Louis Putterman. 2009. Who to Punish? Individual Decisions and Majority Rule in Mitigating the Free Rider Problem. *European Economic Review* 53: 495–511.

Faillo, Marco, Daniela Grieco, and Luca Zarri. 2013. Legitimate Punishment, Feedback, and the Enforcement of Cooperation. *Games and Economic Behavior* 77(1): 271–83.

Falk, Armin, and Michael Kosfeld. 2006. The Hidden Cost of Control. *American Economic Review* 96(5): 1611–30.

Falk, Armin, Ernst Fehr, and Urs Fischbacher. 2005. Driving Forces Behind Informal Sanctions. *Econometrica* 7(6): 2017 30.

Falk, Armin, Simon Gächter, and Judit Kovács. 1999. Intrinsic Motivation and Extrinsic Incentives in a Repeated Game with Incomplete Contracts. *Journal of Economic Psychology* 20(3): 251–84.

Fehr, Ernst, and Armin Falk. 2002. Psychological Foundation of Incentives. *European Economic Review* 46: 687–724.

Fehr, Ernst, and Urs Fischbacher. 2004. Social Norms and Human Cooperation. *TRENDS in Cognitive Sciences* 8(4): 185–90.

Fehr, Ernst, and Simon Gächter. 2000. Cooperation and Punishment in Public Goods Experiments. *American Economic Review* 90(4): 980–94.

Fehr, Ernst, and John List. 2004. The Hidden Costs and Rewards of Incentives. *Journal of the European Economic Association* 2(5): 743–71.

Fehr, Ernst, and Bettina Rockenbach. 2003. Detrimental Effects of Sanctions on Human Altruism. *Nature* 422: 137–40.

Fehr, Ernst, and Klaus Schmidt. 1999. A Theory of Fairness, Competition, and Cooperation. *Quarterly Journal of Economics* 114: 817–68.

Festinger, Leon. 1957. *A Theory of Cognitive Dissonance*. Stanford, Calif.: Stanford University Press.

Frey, Bruno. 1993. Does Monitoring Increase Work Effort? The Rivalry between Trust and Loyalty. *Economic Inquiry* 31: 663–70.

Frey, Bruno, and Felix Oberholzer-Gee. 1997. The Cost of Price Incentives: An Empirical Analysis of Motivation Crowding-Out. *American Economic Review* 87: 746–55.

Gächter, Simon, Daniele Nosenzo, and Martin Sefton. 2013. Peer Effects in Pro-Social Behavior: Social Norms or Social Preferences? *Journal of the European Economic Association* 11(3): 548–73.

Galbiati, Roberto, and Pietro Vertova. 2008. Obligations and Cooperative Behaviour in Public Good Games. *Games and Economic Behavior* 64(4): 146–70.

Gibbs, Raymond. 1999. *Intentions in the Experience of Meaning*. New York: Cambridge University Press.

Gneezy, Uri, and Aldo Rustichini. 2000. A Fine Is a Price. *Journal of Legal Studies* 29(1): 1–17.

Goldstein, Noah J., Robert B. Cialdini, and Vladas Griskevicius. 2008. A Room with a Viewpoint: Using Social Norms to Motivate Environmental Conservation in Hotels. *Journal of Consumer Research* 35(3): 472–82.

Gordon, Michael, and Roger L. Bowlby. 1989. Reactance and Intentionality Attribution as Determinants of the Intent to File a Grievance. *Personal Psychology* 42: 309–29.

Governors Highway Safety Association. n.d. "Distracted Driving Laws" http://www.ghsa.org/html/stateinfo/laws/cellphone_laws.html (last accessed July 2014).

Greenberg, Martin S., and David M. Frisch. 1972. Effect of Intentionality on Willingness to Return a Favor. *Journal of Experimental Social Psychology* 8: 99–111.

He, Xin. 2005. Why Do They Not Comply with the Law? Illegality and Semi-legality among Rural-Urban Migrant Entrepreneurs in Beijing. *Law & Society Review* 39(3): 527–62.

Heal, Geoffrey M., and Howard Kunreuther. 2005. IDS Models of Airline Security. *Journal of Conflict Resolution* 41: 201–17.

Herrmann, Benedikt, Christia Thöni, and Simon Gächter. 2008. Antisocial Punishment Across Societies. *Science* 319: 1362–67.

Hollander, Heinz. 1990. A Social Exchange Approach to Voluntary Cooperation. *American Economic Review* 80(5): 1157–67.

Houser, Daniel, Erte Xiao, Kevin McCabe, and Vernon Smith. 2008. When Punishment Fails: Research on Sanctions, Intentions and Non-cooperation. *Games and Economic Behavior* 62(2): 509–32.

Hunt, Jennifer. 2006. Why Are Some Public Officials More Corrupt Than Others? Pp. 323–51 in *International Handbook on the Economics of Corruption Northampton*, edited by Susan Rose-Ackerman. Northampton, Mass.: Edward Elgar Publishing.

Janssen, Marco A., Robert Holahan, Allen Lee, and Elinor Ostrom. 2010. Lab Experiments for the Study of Social-Ecological Systems. *Science* 328: 613–17.

Kahan, Dan M. 1998. Social Meaning and the Economic Analysis of Crime. *Journal of Legal Studies* 27(2): 661–72.

Kahneman, Daniel. 2011. *Thinking, Fast and Slow*. New York: Farrar, Straus and Giroux.

Kahneman, Daniel, Jack Knetsch, and Richard Thaler. 1986. Fairness as a Constraint on Profit-seeking: Entitlements in the Market. *American Economic Review* 76: 728–41.

Keizer, Kees, Siegwart Lindenberg, and Linda Steg. 2008. The Spreading of Disorder. *Science* 322(5908): 1681–85.

Kreps, David. 1997. Intrinsic Motivation and Extrinsic Incentives. *American Economic Review Papers and Proceedings* 87(2): 359–64.

Krupka, Erin, and Roberto Weber. 2009. The Focusing and Informational Effects of Norms on Pro-social Behavior. *The Journal of Economic Psychology* 30: 307–20.

Lepper, Mark, and David Greene. 1978. *The Hidden Cost of Reward: New Perspectives on the Psychology of Human Motivation.* New York: Wiley.

Levy, David, Kail Padgitt, Sandra Peart, Daniel Houser, and Erte Xiao. 2011. Leadership, cheap talk, real cheap talk. *Journal of Economic Behavior and Organization* 77: 40–52.

Lewis, David K. 1969. *Convention: A Philosophical Study.* Cambridge, Mass.: Harvard University Press.

Li, Jian, Erte Xiao, Daniel Houser, and Read Montague. 2009. Neural Responses to Sanction Threats in Two-party Economic Exchange. *Proceedings of the National Academy of Sciences of the United States of America* 106(39): 16835–40.

Lind, Allan E., and Tom. R. Tyler. 1988. *The Social Psychology of Procedural Justice.* New York: Plenum Press.

Masclet, David, Charles Noussair, Steven Tucker, and Marie-Claire Villeval. 2003. Monetary and Non-monetary Punishment in the Voluntary Contributions Mechanism. *American Economic Review* 93: 366–80.

McCabe, Kevin, Mary Rigdon, and Vernon Smith. 2003. Positive Reciprocity and Intention in Trust Games. *Journal of Economic Behavior and Organizations* 52(2): 267–75.

National Motorists Association Blog. 2008. 6 Cities That Were Caught Shortening Yellow Light Times For Profit. http://blog.motorists.org/6-cities-that-were-caught-shortening-yellow-light-times-for-profit/#sthash. W3GiZkPl.dpuf (last accessed March 2008).

Nelson, William Robert. 2002. Equity and Intention: It's the Thought that Counts. *Journal of Economic Behavior and Organizations* 48(4): 423–30.

Nikiforakis, Nikos. 2008. Punishment and Counter-punishment in Public Good Games: Can We Really Govern Ourselves? *Journal of Public Economics* 92(1–2): 91–112.

Noussair, Charles, and Steven Tucker. 2005. Combining Monetary and Social Sanctions to Promote Cooperation. *Economic Inquiry* 43(3): 649–60.

Offerman, Theo. 2002. Hurting Hurts more than Helping Helps. *European Economic Review* 46: 1423–37.

Ostrom, Elinor, James Walker, and Roya Gardner. 1992. Covenants With and Without a Sword: Self-governance is Possible. *The American Political Science Review* 86(2): 404–17.

Paprzycka, Katarzyna. 1999. Normative Expectations, Intentions and Beliefs. *The Southern Journal of Philosophy* 37(4): 629–52.

Posner, Eric A. 2000. *Law and Social Norms,* 5th edn. Cambridge, Mass.: Harvard University Press.

Rabin, Matthew. 1993. Incorporating Fairness into Game Theory and Economics. *American Economic Review* 83: 1281–302.

Schultz, P. Wesley. 1998. Changing Behavior with Normative Feedback Interventions: A Field Experiment on Curbside Recycling. *Basic and Applied Social Psychology* 21(1): 25–36.

Schultz, P. Wesley, Jessica M. Nolan, Robert B. Cialdini, Noah J. Goldstein, and Vladas Griskevicius. 2007. The Constructive, Destructive, and Reconstructive Power of Social Norms. *Psychological Science* 18(5): 429–34.

Sliwka, Dirk. 2007. Trust as a Signal of a Social Norm and the Hidden Costs of Incentive Schemes. *American Economic Review* 97(3): 999–1012.

Stigler, George G. 1970. The Optimum Enforcement of Laws. *Journal of Political Economy* 78: 526–36.

Sugden, Robert. 1998. Normative Expectations: The Simultaneous Evolution of Institutions and Norms. Pp. 73–100 in *Economics, Value, and Organization,* edited by Avner Ben-Ner and Louis Putterman. Cambridge, Mass.: Cambridge University Press.

Sugden, Robert. 2004. *The Economics of Rights, Cooperation and Welfare,* 2nd edn. Chippenham: Palgrave Macmillan.

Sunstein, Robert. 1996. On the Expressive Function of Law. *University of Pennsylvania Law Review* 144: 2021–31.

Tan, Fangfang, and Erte Xiao. 2012. Peer Punishment with Third Party Approval in a Social Dilemma Game. *Economic Letters* 117(3): 589–91.

Taylor, Charles. 1979. Action as Expression. Pp. 73–89 in *Intention and Intentionality: Essays in honor of G. E. M. Anscombe,* edited by C. Diamond, and J. Teichman. Ithaca, N.Y.: Cornell University Press.

Tenbrunsel, Ann E., and David M. Messick. 1999. Sanctioning Systems, Decision Frames, and Cooperation. *Administrative Science Quarterly* 44: 684–707.

Tetlock, Phillip E. 1985. Accountability: A Social Check on the Fundamental Attribution Error. *Social Psychology Quarterly* 48(3): 227–36.

Transparency Internal. 2007. Report on the Transparency International Global Corruption Barometer 2007. http://www.transparency.org/content/download/27256/410704/file/GCB_2007_report_en_02-12-2007.pdf (last accessed April 2015).

Tyler, Tom R. 2006. *Why People Obey the Law.* Princeton, N.J.: Princeton University Press.

Tyran, Jean-Robert, and Lars P. Feld. 2006. Achieving Compliance when Legal Sanctions are Non-deterrent. *Scandinavian Journal of Economics* 108(1): 135–56.

Van der Weele, J. 2012. The Signaling Power of Sanctions in Social Dilemmas. *Journal of Law, Economics and Organization* 28(1): 103–26.

Wenzel, Michael. 2005. Misperceptions of Social Norms about Tax Compliance: From Theory to Intervention. *Journal of Economic Psychology* 26: 862–83.

Xiao, Erte. 2013. Profit-seeking Punishment Corrupts Norm Obedience. *Games and Economic Behavior* 77: 321–44.

Xiao, Erte. 2015. Justification and Conformity. Working Paper, Monash University. Available at SSRN: http://ssrn.com/abstract=1989463

Xiao, Erte, and Daniel Houser. 2005 Emotion Expression in Human Punishment Behavior. *Proceedings of the National Academy of Sciences of the United States of America* 102(20): 7398–401.

Xiao, Erte, and Daniel Houser. 2009. Avoiding the Sharp Tongue: Anticipated Written Messages Promote Fair Economic Exchange. *Journal of Economic Psychology* 30(3): 393–404.

Xiao, Erte, and Daniel Houser. 2011. Punish in Public. *Journal of Public Economics* 95: 1006–17.

Xiao, Erte, and Howard Kunreuther. 2015. Punishment and Cooperation in Stochastic Prisoner's Dilemma Game. *Journal of Conflict Resolution.* doi: 10.1177/0022002714564426.

Yamagishi, Toshio. 1986. The Provision of a Sanctioning System as a Public Good. *Journal of Personality and Social Psychology* 51(1): 110–16.

Yamagishi, Toshio. 1988. Seriousness of Social Dilemmas and the Provision of a Sanctioning System. *Social Psychology Quarterly* 51(1): 32–42.

Young, Peyton H. 2008. Social Norms. In *The New Palgrave Dictionary of Economics*, 2nd edn, edited by Steven N. Durlauf and Lawrence E. Blume. London: Macmillan.

*WPXI News*. 2011. Pittsburgh Parking Rates to Increase Tomorrow. May 31 http://www.wpxi.com/news/news/pittsburgh-parking-rates-to-increase-tomorrow/nD6wk/

# 7. Prospect theory, crime and punishment
*Sanjit Dhami and Ali al-Nowaihi**

## 1. INTRODUCTION

Traditional models of crime and punishment adopt an *expected utility* (EU) analysis. EU has two main features: (1) the objective function is linear in probabilities; and (2) utility is defined over final levels of wealth. Over the last 60 years considerable empirical evidence has refuted both features.[1]

*Rank dependent utility* (RDU) relaxes the first feature of EU, namely, linearity in probabilities. It is thereby able to explain several sources of evidence much better, for example it can explain the Allais paradox (Allais, 1953) while EU cannot.[2]

*Cumulative prospect theory* (CP) relaxes both features of EU. Thus, CP assumes non-linearity in probabilities as in RDU. But in addition, under CP, decision makers derive utility from changes (in say, consumption or wealth) relative to some *reference point*. This partitions the domain of outcomes into *gains* and *losses*. Furthermore, CP incorporates several psychologically important features, based on empirical evidence, that substantially increases its predictive power relative to RDU and EU. These features include *loss aversion*, concavity of the utility function in gains and convexity in losses. This leads to a rich *four-fold pattern of attitudes to risk*.[3] CP has increasingly established itself in the literature and provides, to our minds, the most satisfactory decision theory available.

The purpose of this chapter is to examine the basic theory of crime and punishment when criminals are rational and when they use CP.[4] By rational we mean "rational" in the legal, medical and psychological senses of this term.[5]

---

* We are immensely grateful to Professor Teitelbaum for the very careful and thorough reading of our manuscript and for excellent suggestions. All errors are our own.

[1] See, for instance, Kahneman and Tversky (1979), Quiggin (1982), Starmer (2000) and Wakker (2010).

[2] As an illustration of the Allais paradox, consider Problems 3 and 4 from Kahneman and Tversky (1979) given to the same 95 subjects. Problem 3: Choose between the lottery A that pays 4,000 (Israeli pounds) with probability 0.80 and the lottery B that pays 3,000 for sure. Eighty percent of subjects chose B over A. Problem 4: Choose between the lottery C that pays 4,000 with probability 0.20 and the lottery D that pays 3,000 with probability 0.25. Sixty-five percent of subjects chose C over D. Thus, some subjects must have simultaneously chosen B over A and C over D. But it can be shown that this is impossible under EU.

[3] Under CP, the four-fold pattern is as follows; see Tversky and Kahneman (1992) and Kahneman and Tversky (2000, p. 56). In the domain of gains, individuals are risk seeking for low probability high gains and risk averse for high probability low gains. In the domain of losses individuals are risk seeking for large probability small losses and risk averse for small probability large losses.

[4] We omit a discussion of judgment heuristics despite their obvious importance because they are not properly a part of CP although some heuristics might be used in the editing phase of prospect theory; see subsection 2.5 below.

[5] Unfortunately, in mainstream economics the term "rational" is used to describe a decision maker who follows EU and standard game theory.

Section 2 gives a brief, self-contained treatment of EU, RDU and CP that is relevant for this chapter. Subsection 2.2 introduces the concept of a *probability weighting function* (PWF) that is used to relax the linearity in probabilities assumption in EU. We focus on the Prelec (1998) probability weighting function that is axiomatically founded and is consistent with the evidence, at least for probabilities that are bounded away from the end-points of the probability interval [0,1]. Subsections 2.1, 2.3 and 2.4 introduce the reader, respectively, to the basics of EU, RDU and CP. The first generation (non-cumulative) prospect theory is considered in subsection 2.5.

Section 3 sets out a basic model of crime that is simple and tractable, yet is able to handle a range of different kinds of crimes.

Section 4 considers the application of CP to the problem of tax evasion. For actual penalty rates and probabilities of detection and conviction, the return per dollar evaded is strictly positive. EU then predicts that every taxpayer whose tax is not withheld at source should evade at least some tax.[6] However, empirical evidence shows that at least 20% of such taxpayers fully pay their taxes.[7] Furthermore, under decreasing absolute risk aversion, EU predicts that a taxpayer who evades some but not all tax will evade less as the tax rate increases. This result, known as the Yitzhaki (1974) puzzle, is rejected by the bulk of empirical evidence. Using a simplified version of the model in Dhami and al-Nowaihi (2007, 2010) we show how prospect theory can easily explain these tax evasion puzzles. This provides a useful tutorial in the application of all elements of CP to an important issue in the economics of crime and punishment.

In a seminal contribution, Becker (1968) opened the way to a rigorous formal analysis of crime. However, he assumed that decision makers follow EU. Becker (1968) showed that the most *efficient* way to deter crime is to impose the *severest possible penalty with the lowest possible probability* (this we will call a *Becker-type punishment*). We shall call this result the *Becker proposition*. The intuition is simple and compelling. By reducing the probability of detection and conviction, society can economize on costs of enforcement such as policing and trial costs. But by increasing the severity of the punishment (monetary and non-monetary), the deterrence effect of the punishment is maintained.

The Becker proposition takes a particularly stark form if we add two assumptions: (1) risk neutrality or risk aversion; and (2) the availability of infinitely severe (monetary and

---

[6]   This is a special case of modern portfolio theory. Given a risk-free asset and a risky asset with a higher expected return, then, according to EU theory, the optimal portfolio will include a positive amount of the risky asset, however risk averse an investor is. In our case the risky asset is the evaded tax and the risk-free asset is fully paid up tax.

[7]   The following is a small sample, but appears fairly typical. Andreoni, Erard and Feinstein (1998) report that for 1988 US data, 53% of taxpayers report the correct amount of tax due and 7% over report (in error). They assume that 7% under report in error. Thus they estimate that 67% do not intend to evade. Allowing for tax being withheld at source for 50% of taxpayers, this means that about one third of taxpayers do not evade. The experimental work of Choo, Fonseca and Myles (2013) for the UK showed that 60% fully comply; those who do not comply declare about 80% of their income. Only 2% completely hide their income. In a field experiment in Germany, Dwenger et al. (2014) found that 21% fully comply even in the zero deterrence treatment. In their experiment, Buhren and Kundt (2013) compare three treatments: high effort, moderate effort and no effort. The percentages of subjects who never evaded were 14% (high effort), 30% (moderate effort) and 18% (no effort).

non-monetary) punishments, for example capital punishment. With these extra assumptions, the Becker proposition implies that crime would be deterred completely however small the probability of detection and conviction. Kolm (1973) succinctly phrased the main insight of the Becker proposition as *hang offenders with probability zero*.

In Section 5 we derive the *Becker proposition* under EU and show that it also holds under RDU. We derive conditions under which the implementation of the Becker proposition is welfare improving.

Section 6 considers the Becker proposition under CP. We consider a range of reference points that encompass plausible psychological principles. In each case we find that the Becker proposition holds.

The Becker proposition is a general result that applies to many different situations in which decision makers could potentially take an action that with some *very small probability* leads to *very large losses or punishments*. These we call *Becker-type punishments*, for instance, committing a crime in the presence of capital punishment, driving and talking on a mobile phone, not wearing seat belts or running a red light. The Becker proposition predicts that humans will not engage in such actions that lead to Becker-type punishments. However if humans do engage in such actions then the Becker proposition is violated—this we call the *Becker paradox*. We do observe humans committing a crime even in the face of capital punishment, running red traffic lights, driving and talking on mobile phones, not wearing seat belts, etc.[8] What accounts for the Becker paradox?

Section 7 explores several explanations of the Becker paradox that have been proposed, and argues that none of these survive in the case of red traffic light running or driving and talking on mobile phone.

Section 8 considers a newer explanation put forward by al-Nowaihi and Dhami (2010b). They argue that the reason the Becker proposition holds under RDU and CP is the behavior of the probability weighting function near zero probability. RDU and CP use *standard probability weighting functions*. These functions (the Prelec (1998) function is an example) have the property that they become extremely steep as $p \rightarrow 0$. Hence, decision makers who use these functions are extremely sensitive to Becker-type punishments (i.e., too sensitive to the "large losses" that arise with "very small probability"). Based on the available evidence they conjecture the presence of two kinds of individuals.[9] A fraction $1-\mu \in [0,1]$ of the decision makers use the standard probability weighting function that we alluded to above. The complementary fraction, $\mu$, of individuals simply ignores events of very low probability as suggested by the evidence. This al-Nowaihi and Dhami (2010b) achieve by proposing a new probability weighting function, the *composite Prelec weighting function* (CPF). The CPF is similar to the Prelec (1998) function except for probabilities close to the endpoints of the probability interval [0,1]. In particular, and unlike the standard probability weighting functions, the CPF is quite flat near the origin (in a sense that we shall make precise). Decision makers who use the CPF give very low salience to low probability events. Al-Nowaihi and Dhami (2010b) show that under CP

---

[8]   See al-Nowaihi and Dhami (2010b) for other examples in a non-crime context.
[9]   See the experimental results from Kahneman and Tversky (1979), the evidence from the take up of insurance for natural hazards in Kunreuther et al. (1978) and models of bimodal perception of risk; see Viscusi (1998).

the fraction μ will not be dissuaded by Becker-type punishments, hence, explaining the Becker paradox.[10]

Finally in Section 9 we consider some of the limits of our analysis. Individuals may not correctly perceive actual probabilities of detection and conviction. They could be overconfident or pessimistic. Individuals might not be sure about the legality of their actions, relying on their own sense of legitimacy or fairness rather than the law. These considerations do not invalidate our models so long as the subjectively perceived probabilities satisfy the standard axioms of probability theory. However, the next two limitations are more serious and require the development of alternative models. (1) At the time of committing the crime, criminals may be under the influence of drugs, calling their rationality into question. (2) The standard model supposes that individuals act singly to commit crimes. However, this ignores the behavior of criminals in gangs, which is of considerable importance.

## 2.   PROSPECT THEORY AND ITS VARIANTS

We regard cumulative prospect theory (CP) to be the most successful decision theory under risk (even uncertainty) available. CP can explain everything that rank dependent utility theory (RDU) can explain, but the converse is not true. RDU can explain everything that expected utility theory (EU) can explain, but the converse is not true. Here we review EU, probability weighting functions (PWF), RDU and the original (non-cumulative) prospect theory (PT).

### 2.1   Expected Utility Theory (EU)

Let $Y = \{y_1, y_2, \ldots, y_n\}$ be a fixed, finite, set of real numbers such that $y_1 \leq y_2 \leq \ldots \leq y_n$. We interpret $Y$ as the set of all possible levels of wealth of the decision maker or, more generally, *outcomes*. We define a *lottery* (or *gamble*), $L$, as

$$L = (y_1, p_1; y_2, p_2; \ldots; y_n, p_n),  \tag{1}$$

where $p_1, p_2, \ldots, p_n$, are the probabilities with which the corresponding outcomes, $y_1, y_2, \ldots, y_n$, occur. So, $p_i \geq 0$ and $\sum_{i=1}^{n} p_i = 1$. Let the set of all lotteries of the form given in (1) be denoted by $\mathcal{L}$. In general, an action by the decision maker does not result in a definite outcome but in a lottery. Let $u(y_i) \in \mathbb{R}$ be the utility to the decision maker when the outcome is $y_i$. The *expected utility* to the decision maker from lottery (1) is

$$EU(L) = \sum_{i=1}^{n} p_i u(y_i).  \tag{2}$$

---

[10]   Posner (2004) reconsidered some basic results in the economic analysis of tort law and contract law under the assumption that there is a floor below which the relevant probability is so small that the relevant agent treats it as if it were zero. In the case of unilateral accidents in tort law, for example, the relevant probability is the probability of an accident and the relevant agent is the injurer (we are grateful to Joshua Teitelbaum for drawing our attention to this).

The fundamental assumption of EU is that a decision maker chooses from all feasible actions that action that maximizes his expected utility (2). Because of the linearity of (2) in $p_i$, the attitude to risk of an expected utility maximizer is entirely captured by the shape of his utility function, $u$. For example, he is risk averse if, and only if, $u$ is strictly concave. He is risk seeking if, and only if, $u$ is strictly convex. The utility function, $u$, can either be strictly concave or strictly convex but not both. However, risk aversion and risk seeking behavior are often seen together in the same individual. Kunreuther et al. (1978) show that EU is unable to explain the poor take up of insurance against earthquakes, floods and hurricanes. Rabin (2000) shows that a reasonable degree of risk aversion for low stake gambles implies an absurdly high degree of risk aversion for high stake gambles. For example, it follows from his "calibration theorem" that an individual who (quite reasonably) would reject the gamble lose 9c with probability half or win 10c with probability half, at all levels of wealth, would also, necessarily, reject the following gamble: lose $1 with probability half or win an infinite amount of wealth with probability half; which is absurd.

As we shall see in Section 4, below, in the context of tax evasion, the predictions of EU are both quantitatively incorrect (by factors of up to 100) and qualitatively incorrect. By contrast, the evidence on tax evasion is easily explained by CP.

These are just some examples from the large literature that has documented the systematic and robust failure of EU. As long ago as 1957, Luce and Raiffa (two of the founders of decision theory and game theory) described the then available evidence against EU as "bolstered by a staggering amount of empirical data."[11] More recently, Camerer and Loewenstein (2004, p. 20) wrote ". . . the statistical evidence against EU is so overwhelming that it is pointless to run more studies testing EU against alternative theories . . .". Comprehensive reviews of the violation of EU can be found in Kahneman and Tversky (2000), Starmer (2000) and Wakker (2010). It is surprising, therefore, that the bulk of the research in economics in general and law and economics in particular is still conducted in an EU framework.

The most successful of the alternatives to EU are RDU and CP. Both employ non-linear transformation of probability by the device of a probability weighting function, which we turn to next.

## 2.2   Probability Weighting Functions (PWF)

**Definition 1:** *A probability weighting function (PWF) is a strictly increasing function* $w : [0,1] \overset{onto}{\rightarrow} [0,1]$.

A simple proof, that we omit, can be used to derive the following Proposition.

**Proposition 1:** *A PWF, $w(p)$, has the following properties: (a) $w(0) = 0$, $w(1) = 1$. (b) $w$ has a unique inverse, $w^{-1}$, and $w^{-1}$ is also a strictly increasing function from $[0,1]$ onto $[0,1]$. (c) $w$ and $w^{-1}$ are continuous.*

---

[11]   See Luce and Raiffa (1957, p. 37).

Since the Becker proposition hinges on the behavior of decision makers as $p \to 0$, we now offer some definitions that establish the relevant terminology. Definition 2 clarifies the sense in which a PWF is extremely steep as $p \to 0$.

**Definition 2**: *For $\sigma > 0$, $w(p)$ $\sigma$-infinitely-overweights infinitesimal probabilities if $\lim_{p \to 0} \frac{w(p)}{p^\sigma} = \infty$.*

**Definition 3**: *(Standard probability weighting functions): We shall call the entire class of PWFs that satisfy Definition 2, for empirically relevant values of $\sigma$, the class of standard probability weighting functions. All the main PWFs used in RDU and CP are of this form.*

Some well known examples of standard PWFs are Tversky and Kahneman (1992), Lattimore, Baker and Witte (1992), Wu and Gonzalez (1996), Prelec (1998) and Gonzalez and Wu (1999).[12]

**Example 1** *(Prelec's probability weighting function): The Prelec (1998) probability weighting function, $w : [0,1] \xrightarrow{onto} [0,1]$, is one of the most popular and satisfactory probability weighting functions. It is parsimonious, consistent with the stylized facts and has an axiomatic foundation.[13] It is given by $w(0) = 0$ and*

$$w(p) = e^{-\beta(-\ln p)^\alpha}, 0 < p \leq 1, 0 < \alpha < 1, \beta > 0. \tag{3}$$

*The Prelec function is strictly concave for low probabilities but strictly convex for high probabilities, i.e., it is inverse-S shaped as, for example, in $w(p) = e^{-(-\ln p)^{\frac{1}{2}}}$ ($\alpha = 0.5$, $\beta = 1$), sketched in Figure 7.1 as the bold curve. In Figure 7.1, the point of inflection is on the $45^o$ line. This arises because $\beta = 1$.[14] Furthermore, it can be easily shown that in the special case $\alpha = \beta = 1$, we get $w(p) = p$, as under expected utility theory.*

**Proposition 2**: *(a) The Prelec function is a PWF in the sense of Definition 1.*
*(b) For all $\sigma > 0$, the Prelec function $\sigma$-infinitely-overweights infinitesimal probabilities, i.e., $\lim_{p \to 0} \frac{w(p)}{p^\sigma} = \infty$. Thus, the Prelec function is a standard PWF (Definition 3).*

*Proof of Proposition 2*: See al-Nowaihi and Dhami (2010a, 2011).

---

[12]   However, Ingersoll (2008) showed that the Tversky and Kahneman and the Wu and Gonzalez probability weighting functions are not increasing for all parameter values. Hence, their use should be restricted to the set of parameter values for which they are strictly increasing. In this respect, as well as others, the Prelec probability weighting function is superior (we are grateful to Joshua Teitelbaum for drawing our attention to this).

[13]   For the axiomatic foundations, see Prelec (1998), Luce (2001) and al-Nowaihi and Dhami (2006).

[14]   For $\beta < 1$ the inflection point is above the $45^\circ$ line while for $\beta > 1$ the inflection point is below the $45^\circ$ line. The interested reader can consult al-Nowaihi and Dhami (2011) for further details on these and other related issues on the Prelec function.

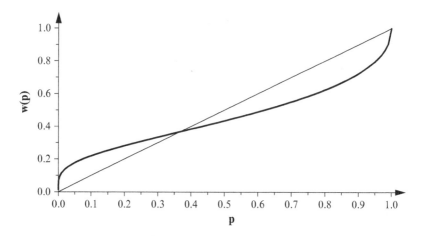

*Figure 7.1    The Prelec probability weighting function*

The bulk of the empirical evidence points to individuals having an inverse-S shaped weighting function (as in the Prelec curve) for probabilities bounded away from the endpoints of the probability interval $[0,1]$; see for instance, Wakker (2010).[15]

## 2.3    Rank Dependent Utility (RDU)

The refutations of EU such as the Allais paradox,[16] which violates the well-known independence axiom,[17] have led to the relaxation of the assumption of linearity in probabilities. The main alternative to EU in decision theory that has resulted from work in this direction is *rank dependent expected utility* (RDU). Machina (2008) describes RDU as the most popular alternative to EU. The objective function under RDU is described in Definition 4, below.

**Definition 4** (*Quiggin, 1982*): *Consider the lottery* $L = (y_1, p_1; y_1, p_1; \ldots; y_n, p_n)$ *where* $y_1 \leq y_2 \leq \ldots \leq y_n$. *For RDU, the decision weights,* $\pi_j$, *are defined by*

$$\pi_i = w(\Sigma_{j=i}^n p_j) - w(\Sigma_{j=i+1}^n p_j), \tag{4}$$

---

[15]    We shall argue below that the behavior of decision makers at the endpoints of the probability interval $[0,1]$ is more nuanced and this has important implications for the explanation of the Becker proposition.

[16]    Recall footnote 2.

[17]    Consider three lotteries $L_1$, $L_2$ and $L$ and a probability $p \in [0,1]$. Consider the two compound lotteries $(L_1, p; L, 1 - p)$ and $(L_2, p; L, 1 - p)$. The first compound lottery gives a subject the chance to play lottery $L_1$ with probability $p$ and lottery $L$ with probability $1 - p$; and similarly for the second compound lottery. The independence axiom states that a subject will prefer $L_2$ to $L_1$ if, and only if, she prefers the second compound lottery to the first compound lottery.

*where w is a 'standard probability weighting function' (see Definition 3). The decision maker's rank dependent utility, RDU, of the lottery L, is*

$$RDU(L) = \Sigma_{j=1}^{n} \pi_j u(y_j), \tag{5}$$

*where u is a utility function (as under EU).*

The main difference between (2) and (5) is that RDU replaces probabilities with decision weights. With this modification to EU, RDU can explain everything that EU can, but the converse is false (e.g., RDU can explain the Allais paradox while EU cannot).[18] The construction of decision weights in (4) shows the sense in which *cumulative transformations of probabilities* are made under RDU. This construction ensures that stochastically dominated choices are never made by the decision maker;[19] see Quiggin (1982) and Starmer (2000).[20]

The decision weights in (4) are very intuitive. It can be shown that if, for instance, the probability weighting function is convex (concave) throughout then a decision maker who uses (4) places much greater (smaller) decision weight on smaller outcomes as compared to larger outcomes. Such a decision maker appears to an outside observer as *pessimistic* (*optimistic*).[21] Thus, while (4) may appear to be cognitively challenging, it encapsulates simple psychological principles of optimism and pessimism.

## 2.4 Cumulative Prospect Theory (CP)

In addition to the non-linear weighting of probabilities, which we have described above, extensive empirical evidence shows that decision makers behave in the following manner.[22] (i) They derive utility from changes in wealth relative to some reference point and not final wealth levels (*reference dependence*). This partitions the domain of outcomes into *the domain of gains and the domain of losses* relative to the reference point. (ii) Losses bite more than equivalent gains (*loss aversion*). (iii) The utility function is concave in the domain of gains but convex in the domain of losses. These features are incorporated in prospect theory (PT) according to Kahneman and Tversky (1979) and cumulative prospect theory (CP) according to Tversky and Kahneman (1992). We now outline CP, which has axiomatic foundations and has better explanatory power relative to EU and RDU.[23] Consider a lottery of the form

---

[18] When $w(p) = p$, RDU collapses to EU.

[19] A crucial assumption needed here is that the probability weighting function is increasing, as in Definition 1, above. But this is violated by the Tversky and Kahneman and the Wu and Gonzalez probability weighting functions for some parameter values; recall footnote 12 (we are grateful to Joshua Teitelbaum for drawing our attention to this).

[20] This insight was the major impetus to the development of cumulative prospect theory (CP) according to Tversky and Kahneman (1992).

[21] See Wakker (2010) for the details.

[22] See Kahneman and Tversky (1979), Starmer (2000) and Wakker (2010).

[23] Readers interested in the axiomatic developments can follow up the references in Wakker (2010). The empirical success of CP is highlighted and described in several places; see for instance Kahneman and Tvesky (2000), Starmer (2000) and Wakker (2010).

$$L - (y_{-m}, p_{-m}; y_{-m+1}, p_{-m+1}; \ldots; y_{-1}, p_{-1}; y_0, p_0; y_1, p_1; \ldots; y_n, p_n),$$

where $y_{-m} \leq \ldots \leq y_0 \leq \ldots \leq y_n$ are the outcomes, possibly wealth levels, and $p_{-m}, \ldots, p_n$ are the corresponding probabilities, such that $p_i \geq 0$ and $\sum_{i=-m}^{n} p_i = 1$. The reference point for wealth is denoted by $y_0$.[24] Thus, we have $m$ outcomes in the domain of losses and $n$ outcomes in the domain of gains for a total of $m + n + 1$ outcomes.

In CP, decision makers derive utility from wealth relative to a reference point, $y_0$. In order to capture this fact, we define lotteries in incremental form (or "prospects").

**Definition 5** *(Lotteries in incremental form or prospects): Let $x_i = y_i - y_0, i = -m, \ldots, n$ be the increment in wealth relative to $y_0$ when the outcome is $y_i$. Hence $x_{-m} \leq \ldots \leq x_0 = 0 \leq \ldots \leq x_n$. Then, a lottery in incremental form (or a prospect) is:*

$$L = (x_{-m}, p_{-m}; x_{-m+1}, p_{-m+1}; \ldots; x_{-1}, p_{-1}; x_0, p_0; x_1, p_1; \ldots; x_n, p_n), \qquad (6)$$

*or, in more compact form,*

$$L = (\mathbf{x}, \mathbf{p}). \qquad (7)$$

Denote by $\mathcal{L}_P$ the set of all *prospects* of the form (6).

**Remark 1**: *An outcome is in the domain of gains if $x_i \geq 0$ and in the domain of losses if $x_i \leq 0$.*[25]

**Definition 6**: *(Kahneman and Tversky, 1979):* A *utility function,* $\upsilon(x)$, *under CP is a continuous strictly increasing mapping* $\upsilon : \mathbb{R} \to \mathbb{R}$ *that satisfies:*
1. $\upsilon(0) = 0$ *(reference dependence).*
2. $\upsilon(x)$ *is concave for $x \geq 0$ (declining sensitivity for gains).*
3. $\upsilon(x)$ *is convex for $x \leq 0$ (declining sensitivity for losses).*
4. $-\upsilon(-x) > \upsilon(x)$ *for $x > 0$ (loss aversion, e.g., the disutility from a loss of \$1 is more painful than the utility from a gain of \$1).*

Tversky and Kahneman (1992) propose the following utility function which has different shapes in the domains of gains and losses.

$$\upsilon(x) = \begin{cases} x^{\gamma_+} & \text{if } x \geq 0 \\ -\theta(-x)^{\gamma_-} & \text{if } x < 0 \end{cases}, \qquad (8)$$

where $\gamma_{\pm}, \theta$ are constants satisfying $0 < \gamma_{\pm} < 1, \theta \geq 1$. $\theta$ is known as the *coefficient of loss aversion*. The utility function in (8) fits well the data in Kahneman and Tversky (1979).

---

[24]   $y_0$ could be initial wealth, status-quo wealth, average wealth, desired wealth, rational expectations of future wealth, etc. depending on the context. See Kahneman and Tversky (2000), Köszegi and Rabin (2006), and Schmidt, Starmer and Sugden (2008).

[25]   The reference outcome, $x_0 = 0$, is typically considered to be in both domains.

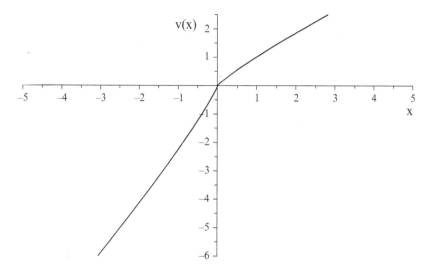

*Figure 7.2    The utility function under CP*

Tversky and Kahneman (1992) estimated that $\gamma_{\pm} \simeq 0.88$ and $\theta \simeq 2.25$. See Figure 7.2, above.

Tversky and Kahneman (1992) assert (but do not prove) that the axiom of *preference homogeneity* generates the value function in (8).[26] Al-Nowaihi, Bradley and Dhami (2008) give a formal proof, as well as some other results, for example that, necessarily, $\gamma_{+} = \gamma_{-}$. Henceforth, we shall set $\gamma_{\pm} = \gamma$ (although none of our results depend on this).

We now show how the decision weights are constructed under CP. This is the analogue of the construction of decision weights under RDU (see Definition 4). The main difference from RDU, in this respect, is that under CP one computes decision weights separately in the domains of gains and losses. In principle, one could use a probability weighting function, $w_{+}$, for the domain of gains, and a different weighting function, $w_{-}$, for the domain of losses. However, the empirical evidence indicates that these functions are very similar so, as in Prelec (1998), we set $w_{+} = w_{-} = w$.[27] Moreover, none of our results depend on $w_{+} = w_{-}$.

**Definition 7:** *For CP, the decision weights, $\pi_{i}$, are defined as follows. In the domain of gains,*

---

[26]    Letting $\sim$ be the binary indifference relation, *preference homogeneity* is the condition $(\mathbf{x}, \mathbf{p}) \sim x \Rightarrow (k\mathbf{x}, \mathbf{p}) \sim kx$, for any $k > 0$.

[27]    Abdellaoui (2000) and Abdellaoui, Vossmann and Weber (2005) find that there is no significant difference in the curvature of the weighting function for gains and losses. For the Prelec function (see Example 1), we know that the parameter $\alpha$ controls the curvature. However, the elevation (which in the Prelec function is controlled by the parameter $\beta$) can be different in the domain of gains and losses. Empirically, however, it appears that $\beta$ is close to 1; see Stott (2006). Fehr-Duda and Epper (2012) report $\beta$ to be, respectively, 0.868 and 0.958 for the student population and a representative population.

$$\pi_i = w(\Sigma_{j=i}^n p_j) - w(\Sigma_{j=i+1}^n p_j), \ i = 1, \ldots, n,$$

*while in the domain of losses,*

$$\pi_j = w(\Sigma_{i=-m}^j p_i) - w(\Sigma_{i=-m}^{j-1} p_i), \ j = -m, \ldots, -1.$$

*As in RDU, w is a standard probability weighting function (see Definition 3).*[28]

**Definition 8** *(Value function): A decision maker using CP maximizes the following value function defined over $\mathcal{L}_P$,*

$$V(L) = \Sigma_{i=-m}^n \pi_i \upsilon(x_i), \ L \in \mathcal{L}_P. \tag{9}$$

*where $\upsilon$ is defined in Definition 6 and $\pi$ is defined in Definition 7.*

Recall that under EU a decision maker is risk averse (seeking) if, and only if, the utility function is strictly concave (convex).[29] However, the overweighting of the low probabilities, recall Figure 7.1, can override the mild concavity (convexity) of the CP utility function for gains (losses), recall Figure 7.2. Thus CP, but not EU, can explain how a decision maker can simultaneously gamble for a low probability high gain and insure against a low probability large loss.[30]

### 2.4.1 How serious is the problem of specifying reference points?
Some may view the inability of CP to specify the reference point as a weakness of the theory. A range of reference points has been considered, for example the status quo, a fair entitlement, expected value of the gamble, aspiration level, norms and even a rational expectations outcome. Human behavior is sufficiently rich and context-dependent that the specification of a single reference point for all behaviors and contexts is likely to be rejected by the evidence. However, a sensible reference point may suggest itself in applications. For instance, in Dhami and al-Nowaihi (2007, 2010), the reference point for a potential tax evader is legal after-tax income. This is a natural reference point because for any level of declared income, the taxpayer is in the domain of gains if not caught and in the domain of losses if caught. In Köszegi and Rabin (2006, 2007), the reference point is the rational expectations of the actual outcomes; such a reference point is self-fulfilling.

In the model of tax evasion presented in Section 4 below, Dhami and al-Nowaihi (2007) show that the "legal after tax income" (the status quo income in this case) is the unique reference income such that for any level of declared income, the taxpayer is in the domain of gains if not caught evading and in the domain of losses if caught. Any other reference point would not be satisfactory on this criteria. On the other hand, if the government is

---

[28] Note that a value for $\pi_0$ is not specified by Definition 7. Since $\upsilon(x_0) = \upsilon(0) = 0$, we see, from (9), that a value for $\pi_0$ can be assigned in any convenient way. A natural normalization is for $\pi_0$ to be assigned a value so that $\Sigma_{i=-m}^n \pi_i = 1$. But other normalizations have also been suggested, for example, in Wakker (2010), a value to $\pi_0$ is assigned so that $\Sigma_{i=-m}^n \pi_i = 2$.

[29] Recall the discussion just after (2) in subsection 2.1

[30] Recall the four-fold pattern of attitudes to risk and footnote 3.

offering income support to $n$ identical, poor individuals then it would be natural for poor individuals to have a reference income such that each expects to get $1/n$ of the available fund (this would be the fair entitlement).

One can explore the implications of alternative reference points on the predictions of the model (see, e.g., Section 6). One can also empirically test assumptions made about alternative reference points. In this respect, CP is no different from any other theory in economics.[31] Empirical evidence shows that reference-dependence is very important.[32] If we eliminate reference points then we would typically need to introduce other auxiliary assumptions to compensate for the reduced explanatory power. This seems more serious than testing for the appropriate reference point.

## 2.5   First Generation (Non-cumulative) Prospect Theory (PT)

The first generation of prospect theory (PT) laid out given by Kahneman and Tversky (1979). PT distinguishes between two phases of decision making: *editing* and *evaluation*. In the editing phase, a decision maker "simplifies" a real-world problem to make it amenable to formal analysis. The various operations of simplification are consistent with many known psychological principles. In the evaluation phase, a value (a real number) is attached to each feasible lottery from the set $\mathcal{L}_P$. The lottery with the highest numerical value is chosen. Analogous to (9), the decision maker maximizes the following objective function in the evaluation phase

$$V(L) = \Sigma_{i=-m}^{n} w(p_i)\upsilon(x_i), \, L \in \mathcal{L}_P. \tag{10}$$

The objective functions under PT and CP are similar. The utility function $\upsilon$ (Definition 6) is common. Under CP the decision weights are formed as in Definition 7. However, under PT, $\pi_i = w(p_i)$, which has the implication that the decision maker could choose first-order stochastically dominated options, even when such dominance is obvious.[33] PT came under intense attack for this feature. The publication of RDU by Quiggin (1982) showed that this problem could be solved by cumulative transformations of probabilities. This insight was incorporated into the second generation of prospect theory, CP (see Definition 7). However, a major casualty of the transition from PT to CP was that the psychologically rich editing phase was jettisoned.

---

[31]   Assuming a particular functional form under EU calls for similar testing of the appropriateness of that functional form. Use of the Bayes rule in economic theory or of Bayesian econometrics requires similar testing with respect to the priors assumed in the model, and so on.

[32]   There is now extensive evidence for loss aversion. A reference point is a prerequisite to defining loss aversion, hence, evidence for loss aversion is also evidence for reference dependence. The evidence for loss aversion comes from many diverse contexts, such as from disparities in willingness to pay and willingness to accept, labour supply of New York taxi drivers, status-quo bias, equity premium puzzle, etc. See the excellent collection of papers in Kahneman and Tversky (2000) for the relevant citations. More recently, there is growing evidence that contracts themselves may embed a reference point in the minds of the contracting parties and influence post-contractual behavior. Indeed, this channel has been used to provide an alternative theory of the firm; see Hart and Moore (2008) for the theoretical apparatus and Fehr, Hart and Zehnder (2011) for the evidence.

[33]   See Quiggin (1982), Kahneman and Tversky (1984) and Starmer (2000).

There are several potential simplifications of lotteries that might be undertaken in the editing phase (e.g., the *availability heuristic*[34] and the *isolation effect*[35]). For our purposes the most important aspect of the editing phase is that many people code events of extremely small probability as zero probability events, a feature that we consider in more detail below.

## 3.   A SIMPLE MODEL OF CRIME

Consider an individual who can receive income $y_0$ from a legal activity or income $y_1 > y_0$ from an illegal activity. Hence, the benefit, $b$, to the individual from the illegal activity is

$$b = y_1 - y_0 > 0. \tag{11}$$

The law and economics approach to crime typically focuses on two main instruments of deterrence: (1) *the probability of detection and conviction*, $p$, $0 \leq p \leq 1$; and (2) *the severity of the punishment*, $F$. The former can be enhanced, for instance, by hiring more police officers, improving their training and equipment. The latter includes monetary fines as well as non-monetary punishments such as imprisonment or barring offenders from certain activities. We use $F$ for the monetary value of all punishments, which is not innocuous but simplifies the analysis considerably.[36] We assume that,

$$F \in [0,\infty]. \tag{12}$$

In particular, it is feasible to levy a fine at least equal to the benefit from crime, $b$. This is true of Examples 2–4 that we give below.[37] Given the enforcement parameters $p$ and $F$, the individual makes only one choice, to commit the crime or not.

---

[34]   The availability heuristic was described by Tversky and Kahneman (1974) as follows: "There are situations in which people assess the frequency of a class or the probability of an event by the ease with which instances or occurrences can be brought to mind. For example, one may assess the risk of heart attack among middle-aged people by recalling such occurrences among one's acquaintances."

[35]   The following example illustrates the isolation effect (Kahneman and Tversky, 1979, Problem 10). Consider again lotteries A to D of Problems 3 and 4 in Kahneman and Tversky 1979 (recall footnote 2). Consider the following two lotteries, $L_1$ and $L_2$. In $L_1$ there is a 0.25 chance to play A. In $L_2$ there is a 0.25 chance to play B. Seventy-eight percent chose $L_2$ over $L_1$. EU implies that lottery $L_1$ is equivalent to $C$ and that $L_2$ is equivalent to $D$. Hence, 78% should also choose D over C. However, we know from Problem 4 that only 35% chose D over C (recall footnote 2).

The explanation is that subjects ignore the probability 0.25 that is common to $L_1$ and $L_2$ and decide simply by comparing A and B. This is consistent with the outcome of Problem 3, where 80% of subjects chose B over A, consistent with the 78% who chose $L_2$ over $L_1$ here (recall footnote 2).

[36]   Typically, $p$ and $F$ are taken to be substitutes. However, under certain conditions these instruments might become complements; see, for instance, Garoupa (2001). Our model is consistent with both. In actual practice the relative deterrence abilities of each of these can be quite different; see Section 9 below.

[37]   It is also consistent with real-world practice (e.g., the death penalty or lifetime punishments)

**Example 2** *(Theft or robbery): Engaging in theft gives a monetary reward $b \geq 0$. If the thief is caught (with probability $p \geq 0$), he is made to pay a fine, $F \geq b$.*

**Example 3** *(Tax evasion): Consider the following widely used model (Allingham and Sandmo, 1972; Yitzhaki, 1974). A taxpayer has taxable incomes $z_1 > 0$ and $z_2 > 0$ from two economic activities, both of which are taxed at the rate $t > 0$. Income $z_1$ cannot be evaded (for instance, it could be wage income with the tax withheld at source). However, the individual can choose to evade or declare income $z_2$.*[38] *It follows that $y_0 = (1 - t)(z_1 + z_2)$. Suppose that the taxpayer chooses to evade income $z_2$. Hence, $y_1 = (1 - t)z_1 + z_2 > y_0$ and the benefit from tax evasion is $b = tz_2 \geq 0$. If caught evading, the individual is asked to pay back the tax liabilities owed, $b = tz_2$, and an additional penalty, $\delta t z_2$, where $\delta > 0$ is the penalty rate. Hence, $F = (1 + \delta)tz_2$.*

**Example 4** *(Pollution): Consider a firm that produces a fixed level of output that is sold for a profit, $\pi$. As a by-product, and conditional on the firm's existing technology, the firm creates a level of emissions, $E$, that is greater than the legal limit, $\overline{E}$. With probability $p \geq 0$ the firm's emissions are audited by the appropriate regulatory authority. Emissions can be reduced at a cost of $c > 0$ per unit by making changes to existing technology. Hence, $y_0 = \pi - c(E - \overline{E})$ and $y_1 = \pi$ so that $b = c(E - \overline{E}) \geq 0$ is the benefit arising from not lowering emissions to the legal requirement. If caught, the firm is made to pay $b = c(E - \overline{E})$ as well as a penalty $k \geq 0$. Hence, $F = k + c(E - \overline{E})$.*

### 3.1 The Social Costs of Crime and Law Enforcement

Let $C(p, F) \geq 0$ be the *cost to society of law enforcement*. Let $D(p, F)$ be the *damage to society caused by crime*. We assume that $C(0,0) = 0$, i.e., in the absence of any law enforcement, costs of such enforcement are zero. If crime is deterred completely by $p = p_0$ and $F = F_0$ then there are no damages from crime, i.e., $D(p_0, F_0) = 0$.

We also assume that $C$ and $D$ are continuous functions of $p$ and $F$ with continuous first and second partial derivatives, i.e., $C, D \in C^2$.[39] We denote partial derivatives with subscripts, e.g., $C_p = \frac{\partial C}{\partial p}$ and $C_{pF} = \frac{\partial^2 C}{\partial p \partial F}$. We assume that

$$C_p > 0, \ C_F \geq 0. \tag{13}$$

Thus, the cost of law enforcement is a strictly increasing function of the probability of detection and conviction, $p$, and a non-decreasing function of the level of punishment.

---

for many kinds of crimes. It is an assumption made in standard models of crime and punishment; see, for instance, Polinsky and Shavell (2007).

[38] Examples include income from several kinds of financial assets, domestic work, private tuition, private rent and income from overseas. In actual practice, tax evasion often takes the form of completely hiding certain taxable activities; see Dhami and al-Nowaihi (2007).

[39] Using standard notation, $C^n$ is the class of continuous functions with continuous partial derivatives up to, and including, order $n$. The class of functions $C^n$ is not to be confused with the cost of law enforcement function, $C$.

**Definition 9** *(Ideal fine: A special case): The case $C_F = 0$ can be thought of as that of an ideal fine, which has a fixed administrative cost and involves a transfer from the offender to the victim or society (so there is no aggregate loss to society other than the fixed administrative cost).*

## 3.2   Society's Objective

Let the total cost to society of crime be

$$T(p, F) = C(p, F) + D(p, F). \tag{14}$$

We assume that for $p > 0$,

$$[T_F]_{F=0} < 0. \tag{15}$$

Society aims to choose the instruments $p$ and $F$ so as to minimize $T(p, F)$. The condition (15) ensures that $F = 0$ is not the optimal fine.

## 3.3   Punishment Functions

The objective of minimizing $T(p, F)$ with respect to $p, F$ can be broken down into two stages. First, we ask whether, for each $p$, there is a level of punishment, $F = \varphi(p)$, that minimizes $T(p, F)$ given $p$. If the existence of such an *optimal punishment function* is assured, then we can ask whether there exists a probability, $p$, that minimizes $T(p, \varphi(p))$.

**Definition 10** *(Punishment function): A punishment function, $\varphi(p): [0,1] \to [0,\infty]$ assigns to each $p \in [0,1]$, a punishment $\varphi(p) \in [0,\infty]$.*

**Definition 11** *(Optimal punishment function): Let $\varphi : [0,1] \to [0,\infty]$ be a punishment function. We call $\varphi$ an optimal punishment function if, for al $p \in [0,1]$ such that $\varphi(p) < \infty$, and for all $F \in [0,\infty)$, $T(p, \varphi(p)) \leq T(p, F)$.*

**Proposition 3** *(Existence of optimal punishment functions):*
*(a)   An optimal punishment function, $\varphi(p) : [0,1] \to [0,\infty]$, exists.*
*(b)   If $\varphi(p) < \infty$ then $[T_F(p, F)]_{F=\varphi(p)} = 0$ and $[T_{FF}(p, F)]_{F=\varphi(p)} \geq 0$.*
*(c)   If $\varphi(p) < \infty$ and $[T_{FF}(p, F)]_{F=\varphi(p)} > 0$ then $\varphi'(p) = -[\frac{T_{pF}}{T_{FF}}]_{F=\varphi(p)}$.*
*(d)   If $\varphi(p) < \infty$, $[T_{FF}(p, F)]_{F=\varphi(p)} > 0$ and $[T_{pF}(p, F)]_{F=\varphi(p)} > 0$ then $\varphi'(p) < 0$.*

*Proof of Proposition 3:* For the proofs of (a) and (b) see Proposition 1 in al-Nowaihi and Dhami (2012). Part (c) then follows using the identity

$$\frac{d}{dp}[T_F(p, F)]_{F=\varphi(p)} = [T_{FF}(p, F)\varphi'(p) + T_{pF}(p, F)]_{F=\varphi(p)} = 0.$$

Finally, (d) is an immediate consequence of (c).

**Definition 12** *(Cost and fine elasticities): $\eta_p^C = \frac{p}{C}C_p$ is the probability elasticity of cost, $\eta_F^C = \frac{F}{C}C_F$ is the punishment elasticity of cost and $\eta_p^F = -\frac{p}{\varphi(p)}\frac{d\varphi}{dp}$ is the probability elasticity of punishment.*

**Lemma 4:** $\frac{d}{dp}C(p,\varphi(p)) > 0$ *if, and only if,* $\eta_p^C > \eta_p^F\eta_F^C$ *at* $F = \varphi(p)$.

> *Proof of Lemma 4:* By straightforward calculation. See al-Nowaihi and Dhami (2012). The condition $\eta_p^C > \eta_p^F\eta_F^C$ holds, for instance, for an *ideal fine* (see Definition 9).

### 3.4 The Hyperbolic Punishment Function

A popular and tractable punishment function that we shall make use of in this paper is the hyperbolic punishment function (HPF), $H(p)$, defined below.

**Definition 13:** *A hyperbolic punishment function, HPF is defined by*

$$H(p) = b/p, \tag{16}$$

*where b is a positive constant.*

In $p,F$ space, the HPF plots as a rectangular hyperbola. Note that, for (16), $\varphi(0) = \infty$.

The HPF has been widely used in the law and economics field.[40] In many cases of interest the optimal punishment function may be quite intractable and the researcher might not be interested in deriving an *optimal punishment function* but rather in using a sensible and tractable punishment function. The tractability of the HPF is clear. Suppose we have a model for which the HPF is an upper bound for the optimal punishment function. In other words, for any feasible level of $p$, the punishment recommended by the HPF is at least as high as the optimal punishment function. Then, if the HPF cannot deter crime for that model, then neither can the optimal punishment function. And, conversely, if the HPF is a lower bound to the optimal punishment function, and if the HPF can deter crime, then so can the optimal punishment function. These considerations reduce the need to compute an optimal punishment function (a non-trivial exercise) in many cases. We shall use this argument in our proof of Proposition 11(a), below.

**Proposition 5:** *Suppose the punishment, F, enters the social cost function, $T(p,F)$, only as a product with the probability of detection, $p$, i.e.,*

$$T(p,F) = \Phi(p,pF). \tag{17}$$

*We assume that $\Phi$ is $C^2$ and that*

$$\frac{\partial \Phi}{\partial y}(p,y) = 0, \frac{\partial^2 \Phi}{\partial y^2}(p,y) \geq 0 \text{ for exactly one } y = b \in \mathbb{R}^+. \tag{18}$$

---

[40]   The following quote from Polinsky and Shavell (2007, p. 413 n. 17) testifies to the importance of the HPF: "[The HPF] or its equivalent, was put forward by Bentham (1789, p. 173), was emphasized by Becker (1968) and has been noted by many others since then."

*Then the optimal punishment function (Definition 11 and Proposition 3) is the HPF,*
$H(p) = \frac{b}{p}.$

*Proof of Proposition 5*: By Proposition 3(a), an optimal punishment function, $\varphi(p)$, exists. From Proposition 3(b) and (17) we get $[T_F(p,F)]_{F=\varphi(p)} = p[\frac{\partial \Phi}{\partial y}(p,y)]_{y=pF} = 0$ and $[T_{FF}(p,F)]_{F=\varphi(p)} = p^2[\frac{\partial^2 \Phi}{\partial y^2}(p,y)]_{y=pF} \geq 0$, hence, from (18), we get $pF = b$, i.e., $F = \frac{b}{p}$. Thus the optimal punishment function is the hyperbolic punishment function, $H(p) = \frac{b}{p}.$

## 4.   TAX EVASION: CP VERSUS EU

Issues of tax evasion are extremely important. For the US, for example, based on the most recent data, a conservative estimate of the tax gap (difference between taxes paid and taxes owed) is of the order of $300 billion per year (Slemrod, 2007). Most traditional analysis of tax evasion is largely based on an EU framework. Dhami and al-Nowaihi (2007, 2010) used CP instead to model the tax evasion decision.

Theoretical work, based on EU, has struggled to cope with the stylized facts:

1)   The audit probability, $p$, for an amateur tax evader lies between 0.01 to 0.03, while the penalty rate, $\lambda$, that is levied in addition to the payment of the evaded tax liabilities, ranges from 0.5 to 2.0.[41] The seminal applications of EU to the tax evasion problem, by Allingham and Sandmo (1972) and Yitzhaki (1974), show that a taxpayer will evade some tax if the expected return per dollar on evading the tax, $1 - p - p\lambda$, is positive. Using observed values of $p$ and $\lambda$, the expected return on tax evasion is between 91% and 98.5%. However, experimental evidence suggests that at least 20% of taxpayers fully declare all their income, even when $p = 0$.[42]

2)   To square the predicted extent of tax evasion under expected utility with the evidence, taxpayers should be risk averse to an absurd degree.[43]

3)   Yitzhaki (1974) showed that under decreasing absolute risk aversion, EU predicts that a taxpayer who evades some but not all tax will evade less as the tax rate increases. In a large majority of the cases, experimental, econometric and survey evidence rejects this result. This we call the *Yitzhaki puzzle*.

4)   Under EU obligatory advance tax payments should not influence the taxpayer's evasion decision. However, empirical and experimental evidence shows that obligatory advance tax payments reduce tax evasion; see, for example, Yaniv (1999).

Dhami and al-Nowaihi (2007, 2010) show that these qualitative and quantitative paradoxes can be explained using CP. They also give the comparative static results with respect

---

[41]   See Skinner and Slemrod (1985) and other references in Dhami and al-Nowaihi (2007).

[42]   Recall footnote 7.

[43]   Skinner and Slemrod (1985) report a coefficient of relative risk aversion (CRRA) of 70 for EUT to explain the evidence on the extent of tax evasion. Realistic magnitudes of CRRA lie much closer to 1; see Chetty (2006). Consider the gamble to win $50,000 or win $100,000, with equal probability. For a coefficient of relative risk aversion of 30, the certainty equivalent of this gamble is $51,209 (Kahneman and Tversky, 2000, p. 304).

to the parameters of CP. We give a simplified version of their model below.[44] The main simplification is that they consider an endogenous probability of detection that depends on the amount evaded while we consider here an exogenous probability.

## 4.1 The Basic Set-up

Each taxpayer has some exogenous taxable income $W > 0$ and can choose to declare some amount $D \in [0, W]$. The government levies a tax at some constant marginal rate $t \in [0, 1]$ on declared income. The taxpayer is audited with probability $p \in [0, 1]$ subsequent to the filing of tax returns and the audit reveals the true taxable income which leads to a certain conviction.[45] If caught, the dishonest taxpayer must pay the outstanding tax liabilities $t(W - D)$ and a penalty $\lambda t(W - D)$ where $\lambda > 0$ is the penalty rate. If evasion is discovered, the taxpayer also suffers some stigma $s(W - D)$ where $s > 0$ is the stigma rate on evaded income. Stigma is distributed over taxpayers in the interval $s \in [\underline{s}, \bar{s}]$ with density $\varphi(s)$ and distribution function $\Phi(s)$, denoting by $Y_A$ and $Y_{NA}$, respectively, the income of the taxpayer when he is audited and when he is not,

$$Y_{NA} = W - tD, \tag{19}$$

$$Y_A = W - tD - t(1 + \lambda)(W - D) - s(W - D). \tag{20}$$

The government moves first, making an announcement of $p$ and $\lambda$. The taxpayer then makes the decision to either fully report his or her income or evade a fraction of it. Finally, the government audits each taxpayer with a probability $p$ and dishonest taxpayers are required to give up a fraction $t(1 + \lambda)$ of their unreported income in addition to suffering stigma at the rate of $s$ for each dollar of tax evaded.

## 4.2 The Tax Evasion Decision under EU

Under EU, the carrier of utility is the final wealth level. In order to facilitate comparison with the power form of the utility function under CP (see 8), the utility of any outcome is defined as follows:[46]

$$u(Y_i) = Y_i^\gamma, \gamma \in (0, 1). \tag{21}$$

---

[44] The interested reader can look up their papers for the references, the justification behind the assumptions, robustness tests, etc.

[45] Dhami and al-Nowaihi (2007) consider an endogenous probability of detection that depends on the amount of income declared. The lower is the income declared by the taxpayer, the greater is the probability of an audit.

[46] Note that (21) is valid only for $Y_A \geq 0$. However, from (20), it is possible that $Y_A < 0$. The simplest way to deal with this case is to define $u(Y_A) = 0$ for $Y_A < 0$. Other possibilities are $v(Y_A) = -u(-Y_A)$ and $v(Y_A) = -\infty$. None of our results depend on which specification we use for $u(Y_A)$ when $Y_A < 0$.

Given $p$ and $\lambda$, the taxpayer chooses declared income $D \in [0, W]$ in order to maximize expected utility, which, using (19) and (20), is given by

$$E[U] = (1 - p)(Y_{NA})^\gamma + p(Y_A)^\gamma. \tag{22}$$

Differentiating (22) in the region $Y_A > 0$, the f.o.c. with respect to $D$ is

$$\frac{\partial E[U]}{\partial D} = -t\beta(1-p)(Y_{NA})^{\gamma-1} + p\beta(t\lambda + s)(Y_A)^{\gamma-1} \le 0, \; D\frac{\partial E(U)}{\partial D} = 0, \; D \ge 0, \tag{23}$$

where $Y_A$ and $Y_{NA}$ are defined in (19) and (20) respectively. The second order condition can be easily checked to hold. Hence, (23) is sufficient to find a maximum value. Thus, necessary and sufficient conditions for the maximization of EU in the region $Y_A > 0$, are given by

$$\frac{\partial E(U)}{\partial D} \ge 0 \text{ for } D = W, \tag{24}$$

$$\frac{\partial E(U)}{\partial D} = 0 \text{ for } 0 < D < W, \tag{25}$$

$$\frac{\partial E[U]}{\partial D} \le 0 \text{ for } D = 0. \tag{26}$$

If the taxpayer does not evade ($D = W$) then $Y_A = Y_{NA} = W - tD > 0$ and, hence, (23) and the first row of (24) all apply. In particular, $\frac{\partial E(U)}{\partial D} \ge 0$ gives $-t(1 - p) + p(t\lambda + s) \ge 0$ and, hence,

$$\lambda p \ge \frac{1-p}{p} - \frac{s}{t}. \tag{27}$$

In $(\lambda, p)$ space, (27) gives the set of $(\lambda, p)$ points such that a taxpayer with stigma $s \in [\underline{s}, \overline{s}]$ reports the full amount of income. At all points below this set, the taxpayer chooses to evade some strictly positive fraction of income. Using (27), in the absence of stigma costs, i.e., $s = 0$, the taxpayer will evade some positive fraction of income when

$$1 - p - p\lambda > 0, \tag{28}$$

as claimed earlier. Solving (25) for an interior solution to the declared income, one obtains the relevant comparative static effects summarized in Proposition 6 below.

**Proposition 6:** *Under EU, tax evasion is decreasing in $p$, $\lambda$, and $s$. If preferences exhibit decreasing absolute risk aversion, then tax evasion is decreasing in the tax rate.*

## 4.3 The Tax Evasion Decision under Prospect Theory

We now compute the utility of an outcome under CP. Denote the reference income of the taxpayer as $R$ and the income relative to the reference point as $X_i = Y_i - R, i = A, NA$. Hence, the utility associated with any outcome $X_i$ is defined as $\upsilon(X_i)$ where $\upsilon$ is defined in (8), so

$$\upsilon(X_i) = \begin{cases} X_i^\gamma & if \quad X_i \geq 0 \\ -\theta(-X_i)^\gamma & if \quad X_i < 0 \end{cases} \tag{29}$$

Although PT/CP does not provide sufficient guidance to determine the reference point in each possible situation, in several cases there are natural and plausible candidates for a reference point. We take the *legal after-tax income*, $(1 - t)W$, as the reference point, $R$. This is the *unique* level of reference income such that, for any level of $D$, if the taxpayer is caught he is in the domain of losses and if he is not caught he is in the domain of gains. For this reason, this seems to be a sensible and natural choice for reference income.

Substituting $R = (1 - t)W$, (19) and (20) into $X_A, X_{NA}$ we get

$$X_{NA} = t(W - D) \geq 0, \text{ and} \tag{30}$$

$$X_A = -(\lambda t + s)(W - D) \leq 0. \tag{31}$$

Hence, the taxpayer is in the *domain of gains* in the 'No Audit' state and the magnitude of the gains is the amount of the tax evaded. In the complementary 'Audit' state, the taxpayer is in the *domain of losses*; the magnitude of the loss per unit of tax evaded equals the penalty on the evaded tax plus stigma costs. The taxpayer faces the following lottery or *prospect* denoted by $L$,

$$L = [-(\lambda t + s)(W - D), p; t(W - D), 1 - p].$$

Since there is only one outcome in the domain of gains and only one in the domain of loss, the lottery $L$ is evaluated in the same way under PT and CP.[47] The *value function* under CP is given in Definition 8, which in this case is $V(L) = \pi(1 - p)\upsilon(X_{NA}) + \pi(p)v(X_A)$. Substituting (30) and (31) in the value function, we get

$$V(f) = \pi(1 - p)\upsilon(t(W - D)) + \pi(p)\upsilon(-(\lambda t + s)(W - D)). \tag{32}$$

Using the definition of $\upsilon(X_i)$ in (29), this allows (32) to be written as

$$V(f) = w(1 - p)[t(W - D)]^\gamma + w(p)(-\theta)[(\lambda t + s)(W - D)]^\gamma. \tag{33}$$

The taxpayer maximizes the value equation in (33) by an appropriate choice of $D$, given the probability weighting function $w(p)$. Rewriting (33),

---

[47] Provided that the lottery $L$ has passed through the editing phase under PT.

$$V(f) = (W - D)^\gamma h(\theta, p, s, t, \lambda, \alpha, \gamma), \tag{34}$$

where

$$h = h(\theta, p, s, t, \lambda, \alpha, \gamma) = t^\gamma \left( w(1 - p) - \theta \left( \lambda + \frac{s}{t} \right)^\gamma w(p) \right) \gtreqless 0. \tag{35}$$

For calibration purposes we use the Prelec PWF (Definition 1) with $\beta = 1$. Since the value equation in (34) is monotonic in $D$, the solution is given by:

$$
\begin{aligned}
D &= 0 & \text{if} \quad h > 0 \\
D &\in [0, W] & \text{if} \quad h = 0 \\
D &= W & \text{if} \quad h < 0.
\end{aligned}
\tag{36}
$$

The solution is a *bang-bang solution* and might be descriptive of several forms of tax evasion which take the form of hiding certain activities completely from the tax authorities.[48]

Using (36), the following is immediate

$$
\begin{aligned}
\text{Case: I} \quad & D = 0 & \text{if} \quad \left(\tfrac{1}{\theta}\right)\tfrac{w(1-p)}{w(p)} > (\lambda + \tfrac{s}{t})^\gamma \\
\text{Case: II} \quad & D \in [0, W] & \text{if} \quad \left(\tfrac{1}{\theta}\right)\tfrac{w(1-p)}{w(p)} = (\lambda + \tfrac{s}{t})^\gamma \\
\text{Case: III} \quad & D = W & \text{if} \quad \left(\tfrac{1}{\theta}\right)\tfrac{w(1-p)}{w(p)} < (\lambda + \tfrac{s}{t})^\gamma.
\end{aligned}
\tag{37}
$$

The comparative static results in Proposition 7 follow directly from (37).

**Proposition 7:** *The following factors are conducive to completely eliminating tax evasion (i.e. $D = W$). (1) Low tax rates, $t$, (2) high levels of stigma, $s$, and high penalties for tax evasion, $\lambda$, (3) high levels of loss aversion, $\theta$ and (4) overweighting of the probability of a loss, $p$, which leads to a decrease in $\frac{w(1-p)}{w(p)}$.*

Comparing the results under EU and CP (Propositions 6 and 7), both predict that tax evasion decreases with an increase in $p$, $\lambda$, and $s$.[49] However, while EU predicts that individuals evade less income as the tax rate increases (Yitzhaki puzzle), CP predicts the opposite, which is consistent with most of the evidence. This is formally shown in Proposition 8 below (we omit the simple proof).

**Proposition 8:** *Ceteris-paribus, $\exists\ t = t_c \in [0, 1]$ such that the individual does not evade taxes if $t < t_c$ but evades taxes if $t > t_c$.*

Proposition 8 is simplest to understand when $s = 0$ (although it also holds for $s > 0$). Because the penalty paid on undeclared income, $t\lambda(W - D)$, is proportional

---

[48]    For the general case considered in Dhami and al-Nowaihi (2007) in which the probability of detection depends on the amount declared, one gets continuous dependence of the solution on the parameters of the model. The bang-bang solution arises in the special case of an exogenous probability of detection.

[49]    Dhami and al-Nowaihi (2007, 2010) show that one would need unreasonably high levels of stigma to reconcile the extent of actual evasion with the predictions of EU.

to the tax rate, $t$, a change in the tax rate has no substitution effect, just an income effect. An increase in the tax rate makes the taxpayer poorer. Hence, under decreasing absolute risk aversion (the empirically correct assumption), EU predicts that a taxpayer would become more risk averse, and so evade less. By contrast, under CP, the utility function is convex for losses. An increase in the tax rate causes an audited taxpayer to be poorer and in the domain of losses where he is risk seeking. So he evades more.

### 4.4   Model Calibration

From estimates in Tversky and Kahneman (1992) they get $\gamma \approx 0.88$ and $\theta \approx 2.25$. A tax rate of 30%, i.e., $t = 0.3$ is used. The stigma rate from the detection of tax evasion is assumed to be distributed uniformly over the unit interval, i.e., $s \in [0,1]$.[50]
 From Proposition 8, we know that all individuals characterized by $s > s_c$ do not evade taxes, while all those with $s < s_c$ evade taxes.[51] Given the assumption that stigma is uniformly distributed over $[0,1]$, the stylized fact that approximately 30% of taxpayers evade taxes corresponds to $s_c = 0.3$, which is the value we shall use for the calibration exercise.[52]
 We ask the following question. Given realistic magnitudes of tax evasion, i.e., 30%, how close are the predicted $\lambda, p$ values under EU and CP, respectively, to their actual values, i.e., $p$ between 1 and 5 percent and $\lambda$ between 0.5 and 2?[53]
 Under EU, using (24)–(27), the locus of $(\lambda, p)$ combinations that need to be consistent with the actual data is given by[54]

$$\lambda^{EU}(p) = \frac{1-p}{p} - \frac{0.3}{0.3}, \tag{38}$$

where the superscript $EU$ refers to expected utility theory. Using (37), and the Prelec weighting function, a similar $(\lambda, p)$ locus under CP is given by

$$\lambda^{CP}(p) = \left(\frac{1}{2.25}\right)^{\frac{1}{0.88}} \Gamma(p)^{\frac{1}{0.88}} - \frac{0.3}{0.3}, \tag{39}$$

where superscript $CP$ refers to cumulative prospect theory, and

$$\Gamma(p) = \exp[(-\ln p)^{0.35} - (-\ln(1-p))^{0.35}].$$

---

[50]   Dhami and al-Nowaihi (2007) explain the reasons and check that the results are robust for other values of stigma.
[51]   A similar result can easily be seen to hold for EU.
[52]   Recall footnote 7.
[53]   We could have equivalently posed our question in many different ways. For example, given actual $(\theta, p)$ combinations, what level of tax evasion does each theory predict?
[54]   At $D = W$ it can be checked that

$$\frac{\partial EU}{\partial D} < 0 \text{ for } s < s_c; \quad \frac{\partial EU}{\partial D} = 0 \text{ for } s = s_c; \quad \frac{\partial EU}{\partial D} > 0 \text{ for } s > s_c.$$

The condition in (38) is derived from $\frac{\partial EU}{\partial D} = 0$.

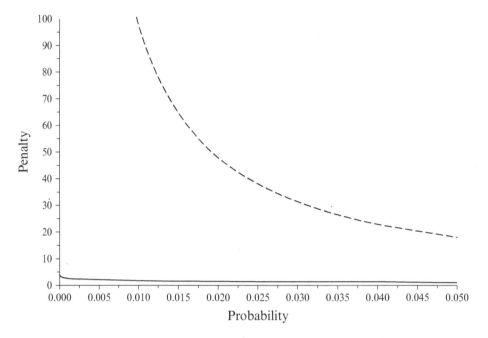

*Figure 7.3*   θ, *p values under EU and CP consistent with the evasion data*

We have substituted the value of $\alpha = 0.35$ in $\Gamma(p)$.[55]

In Figure 7.3, the horizontal axis represents $p$ and the vertical axis represents $\lambda$. Since $p \approx 0.01 - 0.03$ the horizontal axis is shown up to a maximum value of 0.05.[56] The upper, dashed, curve plots the $(\lambda, p)$ locus for expected utility in (38) and the lower, unbroken, curve plots the $(\lambda, p)$ locus for prospect theory in (39).[57]

The numerical magnitudes of $(\lambda, p)$ that correspond to the two loci are shown in Table 7.1.

$\lambda^{EU}(p)$ and $\lambda^{CP}(p)$ are the penalty rates consistent with a given $p$, and a tax evasion rate of 30%, under EU and CP, respectively. For most realistic audit probabilities, i.e., $p \in [0.01, 0.03]$ the estimate of the penalty rate under CP, $\lambda^{CP}(p)$, ranges from 0.66 to 1.21. This is consistent with actual values for the audit probabilities, which range from 0.5 in the USA to 2.0 in Italy; see Bernasconi (1998) for these figures. On the other hand, EU

---

[55]   Dhami and al-Nowaihi (2007) check that the results are robust for other plausible values of α.

[56]   Here we follow Skinner and Slemrod (1985) and we quote "In 1981 a total of 2% of private returns were audited in the United States. While the IRS has established elaborate methods of flagging suspicious returns, it is unlikely that the probability of audit, $p$, for the amateur tax evader exceeds 5% depending on the kind of evasion." Suppose that only 2% of returns are audited. Even if taxes are only withheld at source for 60% of the population, the effective probability of audit for the remaining 40% who have an opportunity to evade is no more than 5%.

[57]   Note that in Figure 7.3, the vertical axis gives the penalty rate. Hence, a penalty rate of 50, for instance, means that for each pound of tax evaded, the penalty is 50 pounds. Actual magnitudes of penalty rates range from 50 pence to 2 pounds for every pound evaded.

*Table 7.1   Comparison of l under expected utility and prospect theory*

| $p$ | .005 | .010 | .015 | .020 | .025 | .030 | .035 | .040 | .045 | .050 |
|---|---|---|---|---|---|---|---|---|---|---|
| $\lambda^{EU}(p)$ | 197.7 | 97.7 | 64.3 | 47.7 | 37.7 | 31.0 | 26.2 | 22.7 | 19.9 | 17.7 |
| $\lambda^{CP}(p)$ | 1.6 | 1.2 | 1.0 | 0.9 | 0.8 | 0.7 | 0.6 | 0.5 | 0.5 | 0.4 |

predicts a penalty rate, $\lambda^{EU}(p)$, that is up to 100 times larger in this range and on average about 60 times higher! The above is summarized by the following Proposition (see Dhami and al-Nowaihi, 2007).

**Proposition 9:** *For realistic magnitudes of tax evasion (approximately 30 percent) and audit probabilities (1 to 3 percent), the penalty rate predicted by prospect theory is 0.66 to 1.21 while that predicted by EUT is 31 to 98. The penalty rate predicted by prospect theory is consistent with observed rates.*

This provides strong vindication for the choice of CP in explaining actual parameters of policy choice relevant for the tax evasion problem. It is remarkable that the predicted magnitudes of $(\lambda, p)$ are so close to the actually observed values when one considers that the parameter values used for the calibration exercise were obtained from independent experimental evidence applied to generic situations of risk. Furthermore, all aspects of CP (reference dependence, diminishing sensitivity, loss aversion, non-linear probability weighting) were needed in order to arrive at a good fit that matched the data.

Dhami and al-Nowaihi (2010) extend this analysis to an endogenous determination of the tax rate. They find that in order to explain, simultaneously, the tax rate, the budget deficit, and the level of government expenditure the world is best described by a normative social planner following EU and taxpayers following prospect theory.

## 5.   THE BECKER PROPOSITION UNDER EU AND RDU

The Becker (1968) proposition (BP) describes the most efficient punishment that would completely deter crime under the assumption of rational criminals who follow EU.

### 5.1   The Becker Proposition under EU

We now consider the BP under EU.[58] Consider an individual with continuously differentiable and strictly increasing utility of income, $u$. Using the model in Section 3, if the criminal does not engage in crime, his payoff, $U_{NC}$, is given by $U_{NC} = u(y_0)$. On the other hand, if the individual engages in crime, his expected utility from crime, $EU_C$, is

---

[58]   In Becker (1968), the first order conditions are given with equality. When the optimum lies on the boundary this poses obvious problems. An intuitive argument is then given in Becker (1968) to justify this approach. We provide the formal underpinning to Becker's informal argument.

given by $EU_C - pu(y_1 - F) + (1 - p)u(y_1)$. The individual does not engage in crime if the *no-crime condition (NCC)* $EU_C \leq U_{NC}$ is satisfied. Thus, the NCC is

$$NCC: pu(y_1 - F) + (1 - p)u(y_1) \leq u(y_0). \tag{40}$$

**Proposition 10** *(Becker, 1968): Under EU, if the utility function is unbounded below, so that $u(y_1 - F) \rightarrow -\infty$ as $F \rightarrow \infty$, then, for any $p > 0$, no matter how small, crime can be deterred by a sufficiently high punishment, $F$*

*Proof of Proposition 10:* Immediate from the NCC (40).

**Proposition 11** *(Becker, 1968): Under EU,*
(a)    *If the individual is risk neutral or risk averse, so that $u$ is concave, then the HPF $H(p) = \frac{b}{p}$ will deter crime. It follows that given any $p > 0$, no matter how small, crime can be deterred by a sufficiently large punishment.*
(b)    *If, in addition, $\eta_p^C > \eta_F^C$ (Definition 12), then reducing $p$ reduces $T(p, F)$.*

*Proof of Proposition 11:* See al-Nowaihi and Dhami (2012).

Note the subtle difference between Propositions 10 and 11(a). The former requires that utility is unbounded below while the latter requires that utility be concave. While Proposition 11(a) is well known from Becker (1968), Proposition 11(b) is, as far as we know, a new result.

In contrast to these results, Levitt (2004, p. 175) argues ". . . given the rarity with which executions are carried out in this country and the long delays in doing so, a rational criminal should not be deterred by the threat of execution." That might well be true as an empirical finding, however, it is not consistent with the decision maker following EU, under the conditions of Proposition 11. The probability of capital punishment can be made arbitrarily small but it will certainly deter crime under EU (Becker proposition).

### 5.2    Risk-loving Behavior and the Becker Proposition

We now consider the role of risk for the BP in the following two examples.

**Example 5:** *Consider the utility function $u(y) = e^y$. Note that $u'(y) = e^y > 0$, $u''(y) = e^y > 0$, hence, this utility function exhibits risk seeking behavior. Thus, Proposition 11(a) does not apply. In fact, substituting $u(y) = e^y$ in the NCC (40), and allowing infinitely large fines, gives that crime is deterred if, and only if, $p > p_{\min} = 1 - \frac{u(y_0)}{u(y_1)} > 0$. Hence, even if infinite punishments were available, it would be possible to deter crime only if the probability of conviction was above a certain minimum. Thus, the BP need not hold in the case of risk seeking behavior.*

**Example 6:** *Consider a simple version of the utility function in (8).*

$$u(y) = \begin{cases} y^\gamma & if \quad y \geq 0 \\ -(-y)^\gamma & if \quad y < 0 \end{cases}, 0 < \gamma < 1. \tag{41}$$

*Here we have risk seeking behavior in the region $y < 0$. In this case, the NCC, (40), holds for any $p \in (0,1]$, if the punishment function is given by $F = \varphi(p) = y_1 + q(y_1, y_0)$, where $q(y_1, y_0) = (\frac{y_1^\gamma - y_0^\gamma}{p})^{\frac{1}{\gamma}}$. Thus, the BP holds despite the utility function exhibiting risk seeking behavior for $y < 0$. Thus, risk seeking behavior is not sufficient to explain the Becker paradox.*

### 5.3 The Becker Proposition under RDU

Suppose that the decision maker uses RDU. Using Definition 4, the payoff from no-crime is $U_{NC} = u(y_0)$. The payoff from crime is

$$RDU_C = [1 - w(1 - p)]u(y_1 - F) + w(1 - p)u(y_1). \tag{42}$$

Hence, under RDU the no-crime condition (*NCC*), $RDU_C \leq U_{NC}$, holds if, and only if,

$$[1 - w(1 - p)]u(y_1 - F) + w(1 - p)u(y_1) \leq u(y_0). \tag{43}$$

**Proposition 12:** *(a) Under RDU, if the utility function is unbounded below, so that $u(y_1 - F) \to -\infty$ as $F \to \infty$, then, for any $p > 0$, no matter how small, crime is deterred by a sufficiently high F. In other words, the BP holds.*

*Proof of Proposition 12*: Immediate from the NCC (43).

**Proposition 13:** *Under RDU and for any PWF, $w(p)$:*
*(a) If the utility function, u, is concave, then, given any $p > 0$, no matter how small, crime is deterred by choosing the punishment function $\varphi(p) = \frac{b}{1 - w(1 - p)}$, and*
*(b) If, in addition, $\eta_p^C > \frac{pw'(1 - p)}{1 - w(1 - p)}\eta_F^C$ (Definition 12 and Lemma 4), then reducing p reduces the total social cost of crime and law enforcement, $T(p, F)$.*

*Proof of Proposition 13*: See al-Nowaihi and Dhami (2012).

## 6. THE BECKER PROPOSITION UNDER CP

Under CP, the reference point is exogenous. Schmidt, Starmer and Sugden (2008) and Köszegi and Rabin (2006), have advocated the endogenous determination of the reference point. We allow for both possibilities. We now state our first assumption in this section.

A1. *Constant reference point for no-crime:* If the decision maker decides not to commit the crime, take reference income, $y_{nc}$, to be constant.

Let $y_c$ and $y_{nc}$ be, respectively, the reference points if the decision maker decides to commit the crime or not. Then, under CP, the payoff from not committing crime is

$$V_{NC} = v(y_0 - y_{nc}). \tag{44}$$

We assume that a criminal is in the domain of losses if caught but in the domain of gains if not caught. Thus, if caught (with probability $p$), the outcome, $y_1 - F$, is in the domain of losses (i.e., $y_1 - F - y_c \leq 0$). If not caught (with probability $1 - p$), the outcome, $y_1$, is in the domain of gains (i.e., $y_1 - y_c \geq 0$). Thus, we have one outcome each in the domains of losses and gains.[59] Using Definition 7, the respective decision weights are $w(p)$ and $w(1 - p)$. Then, under CP, the individual's payoff from committing a crime is given by

$$V_C = w(p) v(y_1 - F - y_c) + w(1 - p) \upsilon(y_1 - y_c). \tag{45}$$

The no-crime condition (*NCC*) in the case of CP is $V_C \leq V_{NC}$, which is equivalent to

$$w(p) \upsilon(y_1 - y_c - F) + w(1 - p) \upsilon(y_1 - y_c) \leq \upsilon(y_0 - y_{nc}). \tag{46}$$

## 6.1   Reference Points Independent of $p$ and $F$

We begin with fixed reference points $y_c$ and $y_{nc}$ that can be distinct (i.e., state dependent) but are independent of $p, F$. Proposition 14 establishes that the BP holds under CP in this case.

**Proposition 14:** *Assume that the reference incomes, $y_{nc}$ and $y_c$, are independent of $p$ and $F$ and the utility function, $\upsilon$, is unbounded below. Then, given any $p > 0$, no matter how small, crime can be completely deterred with a sufficiently high punishment, $F$. Thus, the BP holds under CP in this case.*

*Proof of Proposition 14:* Immediate from the NCC (46).

## 6.2   Reference Point for Crime is Expected Income from Crime

Proposition 14, above, assumed that reference points are independent of $p$ and $F$. Assumptions, A2 and A3, relax this feature.

A2.   *Reference point for crime is expected income from crime*: The reference income, $y_c$, from the criminal act is the *expected income from crime*, i.e.,

$$y_c = y_1 - pF. \tag{47}$$

If income is higher (lower) than expected, then the decision maker is in gains (losses).[60]

A3.   *Power form utility*: The utility function is as in (8) with $\gamma_\pm = \gamma$.

---

[59]   In the context of tax evasion, Example 3, Dhami and al-Nowaihi (2007, 2010), show that the *legal after-tax income* is the unique reference point such that for all levels of declared income the taxpayer is in the domain of loss if caught and in the domain of gains if not caught.

[60]   The recent literature has considered the reference income to be expected income; see, for instance, Koszegi and Rabin (2006, 2007), Crawford and Meng (2011).

Suppose that the decision maker uses CP and A1–A3 hold. We get three cases:

C1. *Socially responsible individuals ($y_0 > y_{nc}$):* The individual is in the domain of gains from not committing the crime so feels positively rewarded on account of his honesty.

C2. *Regretful individuals ($y_0 < y_{nc}$):* The individual is in the domain of losses by being honest, so experiences *regret* in foregoing the higher income from crime.

C3. *Individuals whose legal income is their reference point ($y_{nc} = y_0$).*

**Lemma 15:** *Under A1, A2, A3, the NCC for CP, (46), takes the following forms.*
C1. *Socially responsible individuals, $y_0 > y_{nc}$:*

$$p^\gamma (1-p)^\gamma F^\gamma \left[ \frac{w(1-p)}{(1-p)^\gamma} - \theta \frac{w(p)}{p^\gamma} \right] \le (y_0 - y_{nc})^\gamma. \tag{48}$$

C2. *Regretful individuals, $y_0 < y_{nc}$:*

$$p^\gamma (1-p)^\gamma F^\gamma \left[ \frac{w(p)}{p^\gamma} - \frac{w(1-p)}{\theta (1-p)^\gamma} \right] \ge (y_{nc} - y_0)^\gamma. \tag{49}$$

C3. *Individuals whose legal income is their reference point, $y_{nc} = y_0$:*

$$\frac{w(p)}{p^\gamma} \ge \frac{w(1-p)}{\theta (1-p)^\gamma}. \tag{50}$$

*Proof of Lemma 15:* Substitute $y_c = y_1 - pF$, from A2, into the NCC (46) to get

$$w(p)\upsilon(-(1-p)F) + w(1-p)\,v(pF) \le \upsilon(y_0 - y_{nc}). \tag{51}$$

Using A3, (8) and (51) we get the three cases (48), (49) and (50).

### 6.3 Comparative Static Results

Proposition 16, below, gives three results, R1, R2 and R3, corresponding to cases C1, C2 and C3 of Lemma 15, above.

**Proposition 16:** *(Comparative static results):*
R1. *For the case of socially responsible individuals, C1, the NCC (48) is more likely to hold: (i) the larger the legal income, $y_0$, (ii) the larger the parameter of loss aversion, $\theta$, and (iii) the smaller the fine, F, provided that $\frac{w(1-p)}{(1-p)^\gamma} > \theta \frac{w(p)}{p^\gamma}$.[61]*
R2. *For the case of regretful individuals, C2, the NCC (49) is more likely to hold: (i) the larger is $y_0$, (ii) the larger is $\theta$, (iii) the larger the fine, F, provided that $\frac{w(p)}{p^\gamma} > \frac{w(1-p)}{\theta (1-p)^\gamma}$.[62]*

---

[61]  In particular, no crime will occur if there is no punishment, $F = 0$. If $\frac{w(1-p)}{(1-p)^\gamma} \le \theta \frac{w(p)}{p^\gamma}$, then no crime will occur.
[62]  If $\frac{w(p)}{p^\gamma} < \frac{w(1-p)}{\theta (1-p)^\gamma}$, then no level of punishment, F, however high, will deter crime.

*R3.    For the case, C3, of individuals whose legal income is their reference point, the NCC
(50) is more likely to hold the larger is* $\theta$. *But* $y_0$, *F have no effect on the NCC.*

*Proof of Proposition 16:* Immediately follows from Lemma 15.

According to Proposition 16, for individuals, C1 and C2, the *greater* the legal income, $y_0$, the *less* likely a person is to commit a crime. For socially responsible individuals (C1), an increase in $y_0$ increases the gain from not committing the crime, hence, increasing the incentive to be honest. For regretful individuals (C2) an increase in $y_0$ reduces the regret from not committing the crime, increasing the incentive to be honest. In the next two subsections we examine the comparative static implications of Proposition 16 for loss aversion, $\theta$, and fines, *F*.

## 6.4   Loss Aversion and the Extent of Crime

An important consideration is the effect of risk aversion on the decision to commit a crime. Under EU, attitudes to risk are entirely captured by the shape of the utility function. By contrast, under RDU and CP (see Definitions 4 and 7), risk aversion is determined *jointly* by the shapes of the utility function *and* the probability weighting function. Indeed, in CP it can be shown that there is a rich four-fold pattern of attitudes to risk, and this is supported by the evidence.[63] Thus, potentially, all parameters of the utility function and probability weighting function control attitudes to risk.

However, empirically, it appears that the parameter of loss aversion, $\theta$, is the dominant parameter. Novemsky and Kahneman (2005) show that there is "no risk aversion beyond loss aversion." In other words, it is quite possible that what empirical researchers, using EU, are picking up as risk aversion is really caused by loss aversion instead.[64] Thus, the comparative static effects of $\theta$ assume great importance. Proposition 16 shows that in all three cases, C1, C2 and C3, greater loss aversion (higher $\theta$) reduces crime because it magnifies the deterrence effect of fines.

## 6.5   Fines and Crime

Proposition 16 gives two kinds of comparative static results with respect to fines, *F*.

1.   From result R2(iii), regretful individuals, C2, are *less* likely to commit the crime, the *larger* the fine, *F* (provided $\frac{w(p)}{p^\gamma} > \frac{w(1-p)}{\theta(1-p)^\gamma}$), which is as expected.
2.   But from result R1(iii), socially responsible individuals, C1, are *more* likely to commit the crime, the *larger* the fine, *F* (provided $\frac{w(1-p)}{(1-p)^\gamma} > \theta\frac{w(p)}{p^\gamma}$).

To explain these results, we return to the no-crime condition (46). The quantity, $\upsilon(y_1 - y_c)$, on the left-hand-side of (46), is the utility from committing a crime, getting the reward, but not being caught. This merits a definition.

---

    63    Recall footnote 3.
    64    See also, for instance, Kahneman and Tversky (2000), Kahneman (2003), Marquis and Holmer (1996) and Rizzo and Zeckhauser (2004).

**Definition 14** *(Elation):* We call, $\upsilon(y_1 - y_c)$, *the elation from committing a crime and not being caught.*

Suppose that increasing the fine, $F$, reduces the reference point for crime, $y_c$. This is the case if the reference point for crime is expected income from crime, $y_c = y_1 - pF$, as under our assumption, A2. In this case, the elation from committing a crime and not being caught, $\upsilon(y_1 - y_c)$, will increase. Hence, the term $w(1 - p)\upsilon(y_1 - y_c)$, on the left-hand-side of (46) will increase. But increasing the fine, $F$, will reduce the utility from crime if caught, $\upsilon(y_1 - y_c - F)$ and, hence, the other term on the left-hand-side of (46), $w(p)\upsilon(y_1 - y_c - F)$, will decline. If the former effect outweighs the latter, then an *increase* in $F$ will make it *more* likely that an individual will commit a crime. This case arises under the conditions of Proposition 16 R1(iii).

Such unusual comparative static results may potentially explain some paradoxical behaviors such as participation in dangerous sports, for example walking a tightrope over a canyon. The more dangerous the activity, the more attractive it is for some individuals.[65]

### 6.6 The Becker Proposition Holds under CP

We now introduce two further assumptions: A4 and A5.

A4. The punishment function is the hyperbolic punishment function (HPF), $F = \varphi(p) = b/p$ (Definition 13), where $b = y_1 - y_0$ is the benefit from crime.

**Lemma 17:** *Under assumptions A1–A4, the NCC for CP, (46), takes the following forms for the three different kinds of individuals.*
C1. *Socially responsible individuals,* $y_0 > y_{nc}$:

$$\frac{w(p)}{p^\gamma} \geq \frac{1}{\theta(1-p)^\gamma}\left[w(1-p) - \left(\frac{y_0 - y_{nc}}{y_1 - y_0}\right)^\gamma\right]. \tag{52}$$

C2. *Regretful individuals,* $y_0 < y_{nc}$:

$$\frac{w(p)}{p^\gamma} \geq \frac{1}{(1-p)^\gamma}\left[\frac{w(1-p)}{\theta} + \left(\frac{y_{nc} - y_0}{y_1 - y_0}\right)^\gamma\right]. \tag{53}$$

C3. *Individuals whose reference point for no-crime is income from no-crime,* $y_{nc} = y_0$:

$$\frac{w(p)}{p^\gamma} \geq \frac{w(1-p)}{\theta(1-p)^\gamma}. \tag{54}$$

A5. The probability weighting function $w(p)$ is a standard weighting function (see Definition 3). In particular, the weighting function $\sigma$-infinitely-overweights infinitesimal probabilities for $\sigma = \gamma$, where $\gamma$ is as in *A3* and so $\lim_{p \to 0} \frac{w(p)}{p^\gamma} = \infty$ (e.g., the Prelec (1998) function, Example 1).

---

[65] Such activities, though legal, nevertheless fit our framework. The punishment, $F$, is here self-inflicted.

**Proposition 18:** *If the decision maker follows CP and Assumptions A1–A5 hold then the Becker proposition holds for all three kinds of decision makers, C1, C2, C3.*

*Proof of Proposition 18:* Take the limit, $p \to 0$, in each of (52)–(54), and use assumption A5, to get, respectively, for individuals C1, C2, C3 that

$$\infty \geq \frac{1}{\theta}\left[1 - \left(\frac{y_0 - y_{nc}}{y_1 - y_0}\right)^\gamma\right]. \tag{55}$$

$$\infty \geq \frac{1}{\theta} + \left(\frac{y_{nc} - y_0}{y_1 - y_0}\right)^\gamma. \tag{56}$$

$$\infty \geq \frac{1}{\theta}. \tag{57}$$

The NCCs (55)–(57) clearly all hold. Hence, the BP holds in all three cases.

We have argued that CP is the most satisfactory decision theory among the mainstream alternatives. It can explain everything that EU or RDU can explain but the converse is false. Proposition 18 demonstrates the resilience of the Becker proposition under CP even when a wide range of reference points is allowed for.

## 7. THE COMPETING EXPLANATIONS OF THE BECKER PARADOX

The *Becker paradox* arises when observed behavior is contrary to the *Becker proposition*, i.e., when contrary to expectations we observe people engaging in actions that lead to Becker-type punishments. Our main focus will be on crime and punishment. However, the Becker paradox is quite general. Let $A$ be the set of all actions for which a decision maker faces a Becker-type punishment (*a small probability of a very large loss*). Then each act in the set $A$ belongs to the *class of Becker paradoxes*. We consider three examples below from a law and economics context: jumping red traffic lights, talking on mobile phones while driving and wearing seat belts. Al-Nowaihi and Dhami (2010b) consider several other examples from non-crime contexts, such as not taking up a voluntary breast cancer examination and not buying insurance against low probability natural hazards.

We first critically discuss alternative explanations of the Becker paradox. Subsection 7.1 then argues that these explanations are insufficient, singly or jointly, to explain the general class of Becker paradoxes.

1.  *Risk seeking behavior:* If decision makers are risk seekers (compare Examples 5, 6 above) then the BP need not hold. This potential explanation is given in Becker (1968) but it creates great difficulties for other explanations of human behavior that require some form of risk aversion (e.g., insurance, investment, saving, risk management, principal-agent theory and mechanism design). Moreover, risk seeking behavior is not sufficient, as shown by Example 6.

2. *Bankruptcy issues:* Bankruptcy issues put an upper bound on the level of possible fines.[66] There are several objections to this explanation. First, it takes fines literally rather than the more general interpretation as the monetary equivalent of punishment. Second, even when interpreted literally, fines can be backed up by other punishments such as imprisonment (which is currently the case) or penal slavery (which used to be the case) for those (and their descendants) unwilling or unable to pay the fine. Third, the historic trend has been to limit the consequences of declaring bankruptcy, for example the emergence of the limited company; see Friedman (1999).

3. *Differential punishments:* The argument for a system of differential punishments is unassailable. However, it does not explain why the whole portfolio of punishments cannot be made more severe while maintaining differentiation. For example, we could combine imprisonment and capital punishment with various degrees of torture. In fact, the historic trend is to make prisons (and capital punishment, where it still remains) more humane. See Polinsky and Shavell (2000b) for a discussion.

4. *Errors in conviction:* To our minds, this is one of the two most persuasive explanations (the other is rent seeking behavior). The penal system may fail to convict an offender (a type I error), or might falsely convict an innocent person (a type II error).[67] The possibility of falsely convicting an innocent person causes a loss to society. Unboundedly severe punishments then cause potentially unbounded losses to society. This destroys one of the fundamental assumptions of the economic model of crime, i.e., increasing $p$ is more costly to society than increasing $F$; see Polinsky and Shavell (2000b).

5. *Rent seeking behavior:* The possibility of a false conviction and the availability of out of court settlements, encourages malicious accusations. This temptation increases with increasing $F$, thus undermining the basic assumption that increasing $F$ is less costly than increasing $p$. The possibility of failing to convict an offender encourages payments by offenders to lawyers to defend them or (even worse) to pay police (and other monitoring authorities) to "turn a blind eye." Again this possibility undermines the assumption that increasing $F$ is less costly to society than increasing $p$; see, for instance, Friedman (1999). Explanations 4 and 5 seem persuasive but fail for the general class of Becker paradoxes; see subsection 7.1, below.

6. *Abhorrence of severe punishments:* Society may not, for reasons of norms, fairness, etc., accept severe punishments.[68] This provides a strong potential explanation for the Becker paradox, but leaves open the question of an explanation of these norms. However, our focus is on examining the purely economic case for the Becker paradox. This explanation, like most others in this section is found wanting when we consider the general class of Becker paradoxes in subsection 7.1, below.

7. *Objectives other than deterrence:* Punishment might have objectives other than deterrence, for example incapacitation and retribution. Incapacitation is easily incorporated into an economic model of crime because it has measurable monetary

[66]  See, for example, Polinsky and Shavell (1991) and Garoupa (2001).

[67]  See, for instance, Andreoni (1991) and Feess and Wholschlegel (2009).

[68]  For a model in which preferences for fairness ensure that fines are bounded away from their upper bound, see Polinsky and Shavell (2000a).

benefits and costs.[69] It may be possible to give an evolutionary-economic explanation to the emergence of the desire by individuals for retribution. Such a desire, if publicly known, would clearly add another instrument of deterrence for potential criminals.

8. *Risk aversion with bounded punishments:* Suppose that criminals are risk averse and differ in their benefits, $b$, from crime. Consider an increase in fines. On the one hand, the imposition of the fine acts as a deterrent for some individuals (depending on their level of $b$). But on the other hand, for those who are not deterred, an increase in fines reduces the risk-averse criminals' income, if caught. If the utility of all citizens enters the social welfare function, then fines have opposing effects, leading to an interior solution where these marginal effects balance out.[70]

9. *Pathological traits of offenders:* Colman (1995) shows how the persistence of "criminal types" (the most notorious being psychopaths) can be part of an evolutionary stable Nash equilibrium. These individuals are predisposed to commit crime irrespective of the enforcement parameters $p, F$. Although this explains why the Becker proposition fails when applied to the most heinous crimes, it does not explain other members in the general class of Becker paradoxes; see subsection 7.1, below.

### 7.1   Why Might These Explanations Not Suffice?

We now argue that the above explanations, either singly or in conjunction, cannot explain the *general class of Becker paradoxes* (recall first paragraph of Section 7).

#### 7.1.1   Evidence from jumping red traffic lights

Consider an individual act of running red lights. There is (at least) a *small probability* of an accident with possibly infinite losses ($F$ in our framework), for example loss of life. Hence, this problem belongs to the general class of Becker paradoxes. However, the consequences are *self-inflicted*.

Bar-Ilan and Sacerdote (2001, 2004) estimate that there are approximately 260,000 accidents per year in the US caused by red-light running with implied costs of car repair alone in the order of $520 million per year. Clearly, this is an activity of economic significance and it is implausible to assume that running red traffic lights are simply "mistakes". Bar-Ilan (2000) and Bar-Ilan and Sacerdote (2001, 2004) provide, what is to our minds, near decisive evidence that the explanations above cannot provide a satisfactory explanation of the Becker paradox within an EU framework.

Using Israeli data, Bar-Ilan (2000) calculated that the expected gain from jumping one red traffic is, at most, one minute (the length of a typical light cycle). Given the known probabilities he finds that if a slight injury causes a loss greater or equal to 0.9 days, a risk neutral person will be deterred by that risk alone. But, the corresponding numbers for the additional risks of serious and fatal injuries are 13.9 days and 69.4

---

[69]   Although empirically its effect is a more elusive problem; see Section 9 below.

[70]   This explanation is according to Polinsky and Shavell (1979) and Kaplow (1992) but it is subsumed within our point 6, abhorrence of severe punishments, above.

days respectively, which should deter red traffic light running completely, but clearly does not.[71]

Clearly EU combined with risk aversion would find it difficult to explain this evidence. Explanations 2–8 above do not apply here, because the punishment is *self-inflicted*.[72] Explanation 9 is also inadequate, for Bar-Ilan and Sacerdote (2004, p. 1) report "We find that red-light running decreases sharply in response to an increase in the fine . . . Criminals convicted of violent offences or property offences run more red lights on average but have the same elasticity as drivers without a criminal record". This leaves explanation 1, i.e., risk seeking, but we have already noted the problems with it above.

### 7.1.2   Driving while talking on hand-held mobile phones
Consider the usage of hand-held mobile phones in moving vehicles. A user of mobile phones faces potentially *infinite punishment* (e.g., loss of one's and/or the family's life) with *low probability*, in the event of an accident.[73] Hence, this problem belongs to the general class of Becker paradoxes. The BP applied to this situation suggests that drivers will not use mobile phones while driving. But evidence is to the contrary.

Various survey evidence in the UK indicates that up to 40% of individuals drive and talk on mobile phones; see, for example, the RSPA (2005).[74] Pöystia, Rajalina and Summala (2005) report that two thirds of Finnish drivers and 85% of American drivers use their phone while driving, which increases the risk of an accident by two to six fold.[75]

### 7.1.3   Not wearing seat belts
Although the probability of an accident may be quite low for the average driver, not wearing seat belts could turn potentially low losses into infinite losses, for example a loss of life. Individuals have a choice of wearing a seat belt and the evidence indicates that seat belts save lives. Hence, this problem belongs to the general class of Becker paradoxes. People were reluctant to use non-mandatory seat belts despite publicly available evidence that seat belts save lives. Prior to 1985, in the US, only 10–20% of motorists wore seat belts voluntarily; see Williams and Lund (1986).

---

[71]   To these costs, should be added the time lost due to auto-repairs, court appearances, fines, increase in car insurance premiums and the cost and pain of injury and death.

[72]   For instance, one cannot argue along the lines of Explanation 6 that there are any norms or fairness considerations involved in jumping red traffic lights.

[73]   Extensive evidence suggests that the perceived probability of an accident might be even lower than the actual probability because drivers are *overconfident* of their driving abilities. Taylor and Brown (1998) suggest that up to 90% of car accidents might be caused by overconfidence. The overconfidence finding is pervasive in behavioral economics and arises from many diverse contexts. In each case, the individual's perceived probability of a loss is lower than the actual probability, which further strengthens our argument for the general class of Becker paradoxes.

[74]   The Royal Society for the Prevention of Accidents.

[75]   Hands-free equipment, although now obligatory in many countries, seems not to offer essential safety advantages. This suggests that it is the mental distraction that is dangerous, rather than the physical act of holding a mobile phone.

# 8.   A NEW EXPLANATION OF THE BECKER PARADOX?

This section considers a recently proposed explanation of the Becker paradox by al-Nowaihi and Dhami (2010b).

## 8.1   Some Stylized Facts on Non-linear Weighting of Probabilities

Given the nature of the Becker paradoxes (Section 7), the attitudes to low probability events are crucial. Extensive evidence suggests the following stylized facts.

S1.   For probabilities in the interval $[0,1]$ that are bounded away from the end-points, decision makers overweight small probabilities and underweight large probabilities. This is reflected in the shape of standard probability weighting functions, for example the Prelec function (see Figure 7.1).[76]

S2.   For probabilities close to the endpoints of $[0,1]$ two types of behaviors are observed:
S2a: A fraction $\mu \in [0,1]$ of decision makers (i) ignore events of extremely low probability and/or (ii) treat extremely high probability events as certain.[77]
S2b: The remaining fraction $1-\mu$ places great salience on the size of the outcomes (particularly losses), even if the probabilities are very small or very large.

EU does not take account of S1, S2a or S2b. By contrast, S1 is incorporated into almost all *non-linear weighting models*, including RDU, PT and CP. RDU and CP incorporate S1 and S2b (but not S2a). Hence, they use probability weighting functions that are extremely steep near the origin (see Definition 3). Decision makers using such models place very high subjective weight, $w(p)$, on the probability, $p$, of facing the Becker-type punishments. Thus, for the class of Becker paradoxes (Section 7) such individuals would always be deterred by Becker-type punishments. Therefore, one would expect that the Becker paradox would be even stronger under RDU and CP. This intuition turns out to be correct, as we proved above in subsection 5.3 and Section 6. These individuals will always be deterred by capital punishment, will never run red traffic lights, will always buy insurance for low probability natural hazards, will never talk on mobile phones while driving, etc.; see al-Nowaihi and Dhami (2010b). But then, the Becker paradox remains unresolved under most mainstream decision theories.

## 8.2   Resolution of the Becker Paradoxes

In order to explain the Becker paradoxes one needs a decision theory that simultaneously accounts for S1, S2a, S2b. There are two alternative theories that do so. The first is prospect theory, PT that we described in subsection 2.5 above. However, the downside is that PT can violate monotonicity. We consider the PT explanation in subsection 8.3 below.

---

[76]   The evidence for stylized fact S1 is well documented and we do not pursue it further; see, for instance, Kahneman and Tversky (1979), Kahneman and Tversky (2000) and Starmer (2000).

[77]   The actual fraction $\mu$ could be affected by many factors. In the context of buying insurance against low probability natural hazards, in one set of experiments (Chapter 7 in Kunreuther et al., 1978) one can infer that $\mu=0.8$; see al-Nowaihi and Dhami (2010b).

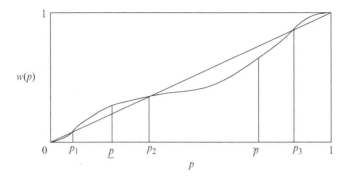

*Figure 7.4   A composite Prelec probability weighting function (CPF)*

The second theory that simultaneously accounts for S1, S2a, S2b is al-Nowaihi and Dhami's (2010b) *composite cumulative prospect theory*, CCP. CCP is formal, axiomatically founded, and respects monotonicity (i.e., decision makers will not choose stochastically dominated options). Before explaining CCP, and showing how it is able to explain the Becker paradoxes, we shall introduce the *composite Prelec probability weighting function* (CPF), which is of fundamental importance in CCP.

Figure 7.4 gives the general shape of the CPF. Let $p_1, p_2, p_3$ be objective probabilities.[78] From Figure 7.4 we see that a CPF overweights probabilities in the range $(p_1, p_2)$ and underweights probabilities in the range $(p_2, p_3)$, thus S1 holds in $(p_1, p_3)$. On the other hand, the CPF underweights probabilities in the range $(0, p_1)$ and overweights probabilities in the range $(p_3, 1)$, so much so that the CPF is almost flat very near 0 and very near 1. This reflects the fact that decision makers who use a CPF ignore events of extremely low probability and treat extremely probable events as certain.[79] Thus S2a holds in the interval $(0, p_1) \cup (p_3, 1)$.

**Remark 2:** *Under CPF,* $\lim_{p \to 0} w(p)/p = 0$ *and* $\lim_{p \to 1} \frac{1 - w(p)}{1 - p} = 0$ *(compare with Definition 2).*

We now define CCP and *composite rank dependent utility* (CRDU) in the following two remarks.

**Remark 3** *(CCP; al-Nowaihi and Dhami, 2010b): Under CCP, a fraction* $1 - \mu$ *of the population uses Tversky and Kahneman's (1992) CP with its standard probability weighting function (see Definition 3). Such individuals satisfy stylized fact S2b. The remaining fraction* $\mu$ *uses CP but replaces the standard probability weighting function with the CPF. Such individuals satisfy stylized fact S2a.*

**Remark 4:** *(CRDU; al-Nowaihi and Dhami, 2010b): Composite rank dependent utility (CRDU) is defined analogously with rank dependent utility, RDU, replacing CP in Remark 3. We argue, however, that CCP is more satisfactory than CRDU.*

---

[78]   We could also allow for subjective probabilities so long as they are non-negative and add up to one across the set of all possible outcomes.
[79]   Recall footnote 10.

Given Remarks 2, 3, 4, it follows that:

1.  In each of CCP and CRDU, a fraction $1-\mu$ of the individuals follows respectively, CP and RDU. They infinitely overweight infinitesimal probabilities (Definition 2) and, thus, they avoid acts that lead to Becker-type punishments. But then the Becker paradox remains for such individuals.
2.  In each of CCP and CRDU, a fraction $\mu$ follows respectively, CP and RDU, with one important difference. They use the CPF rather than any of the standard weighting functions (Definition 3) and, so, place very low subjective weights on very low probabilities (Remark 2). Hence, one might conjecture that they would *not* be dissuaded from acts that lead to Becker type punishments, thus, resolving the Becker paradox. This intuition is only partially correct because in Becker type punishments, against the 'very low probability' must be set the 'very high level of punishment'. Al-Nowaihi and Dhami (2010b) show that for the fraction $\mu$ of individuals, CRDU is unable to explain the Becker paradox while CCP can explain it.
3.  In conjunction, the previous two remarks explain why, in the face of Becker type punishments, a fraction $\mu$ of the population run red traffic lights, do not wear non-mandatory seat belts, drive and simultaneously talk on mobile phones and commit other sorts of crimes. It also explains why another fraction, $1-\mu$, is deterred in the face of Becker-type punishments.

So why is CCP successful when all other theories fail? The main reason is that in addition to more reasonable behavior for low probabilities (in the region $[0, p_1]$ in Figure 7.4) CCP shares other empirically important features with CP that are absent in CRDU. In particular, al-Nowaihi and Dhami (2010b) show that the *reference dependence* feature of CCP turns out to be necessary to address the problem (a feature that RDU and CRDU lack). Due to reference points, criminals derive *elation* in the state of the world where they are not caught (see Definition 14). The higher the level of punishment, the higher is the elation from escaping it. In conjunction with Remark 2, elation ensures that such decision makers will not be dissuaded by Becker type punishments, hence, explaining the Becker paradox.

### 8.3    The Resolution of the Becker Paradox under PT

*First generation (non-cumulative) prospect theory*, PT, also attempts to incorporate S1 and S2. As noted earlier, PT makes a distinction between an *editing* and an *evaluation* phase. From our perspective, the most important aspect of the editing phase takes place when decision makers decide which improbable events to treat as impossible and which probable events to treat as certain. As noted earlier, in subsection 2.5, under PT, the decision weights and the probability weighting function are identical, i.e., $\pi_i = w(p_i)$. Kahneman and Tversky (1979) drew $\pi(p)$ as in Figure 7.5, which is *undefined* at both ends, reflecting the vexed issue of how decision makers behave over these ranges of probabilities.

Kahneman and Tversky (1979, pp. 282–283) wrote the following to summarize the evidence for S2, which is worth reading carefully.

> The sharp drops or apparent discontinuities of $\pi(p)$ at the end-points are consistent with the notion that there is a limit to how small a decision weight can be attached to an event, if it is

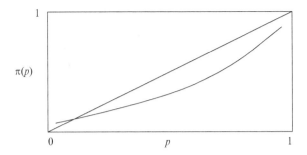

*Source:* *Kahneman and Tversky (1979, p. 283).*

*Figure 7.5* *Ignorance at the endpoints*

given any weight at all. A similar quantum of doubt could impose an upper limit on any decision weight that is less than unity . . . the simplification of prospects can lead the individual to discard events of extremely low probability and to treat events of extremely high probability as if they were certain. Because people are limited in their ability to comprehend and evaluate extreme probabilities, highly unlikely events are either ignored or overweighted, and the difference between high probability and certainty is either neglected or exaggerated. Consequently $\pi(p)$ is not well-behaved near the end-points.

In Kahneman and Tversky's words, low probability events are either *ignored* (S2a) or *overweighted* (S2b). After the prospects are "psychologically cleaned" in this manner in the *editing phase*, the decision maker then applies (10) in the *evaluation phase*. If low probabilities are ignored by any individual then Becker-type punishments will not work to deter the individual from crime, hence, explaining the Becker paradox too.

## 9.   LIMITATIONS OF THE STANDARD MODEL

This section notes several limitations of the analysis conducted in the above sections.

We have not drawn a distinction between actual and perceived probabilities of detection. However, in actual practice these might be different due to overconfidence, pessimism or lack of awareness on the part of criminals. This can reduce or even increase the effectiveness of deterrence; see Klick and Tabarrok (2005), Teitelbaum (2007) and Lawsky (2013). If opportunities for learning are limited then actual and perceived probabilities may not converge.

Jolls, Sunstein and Thaler (1998) remark that the market for crime is very different from, say, financial markets. Suppose that individuals have very different perceptions of the probabilities of detection. Then, unlike financial markets, individuals cannot necessarily bet that the perceptions of the others are incorrect. Thus there may be no mechanism that ensures that perceptions of probabilities arrive at the true values. Furthermore, learning opportunities are limited. Once an individual decides to commit a crime and is imprisoned then, insofar as prisons are criminogenic, the opportunities to reverse an earlier mistake are limited.

Robinson and Darley (2004) list several chastening factors for the classical analysis of crime. Criminals might not be aware of the law. They could use their own personal sense of right and wrong to predict the legality of their actions.

These factors might give another reason why the Becker paradox arises: people do not perceive the deterrence parameters appropriately.

One way in which perceived probability of detection can be rased is to make use of the *availability heuristic*. For instance, large and brightly colored parking tickets may increase the perceived probability of being caught following a parking offense; see, for instance, Jolls, Sunstein and Thaler (1998).

In most of our models deterrence is predicted to work. The one exception is Proposition 16, in which result R 1(iii), for the case of socially responsible individuals, C1, shows that the *larger* the fine, $F$, the *more* likely an individual is to commit a crime. Dölling et al. (2009) conduct a meta study that takes account of a very large number of published studies on deterrence. This meta study involved 700 studies with 7,822 effect estimates. They found only a weak confirmation of the deterrence hypothesis (that increased deterrence reduces crime). The expected sign was found in 73.8% of the studies but about half of all estimates were found to be insignificant. A very thorough survey of the alternative forms of deterrence and their effectiveness can be found in Durlauf and Nagin (2010).

We have made no distinction between deterrence and incapacitation. One way in which deterrence may benefit society is by reducing the incentive of potential criminals to commit a crime. However, the beneficial effects of deterrence may be overstated because one could be picking up a second effect on account of the incapacitation of some of the offenders who are incarcerated and so are removed from the population of potential criminals.[80] This has made the estimation of deterrence elasticities a difficult job. Using the Italian Clemency Act of 2006, Drago, Galbiati and Vertova (2009) found that the deterrence elasticity was −0.74 at the 7 month interval and −0.45 at the 12 month interval. By contrast, much lower elasticities of the order of −0.07 were found by Iyengar (2008) using data from California's three-strike law. Buonanno and Raphael (2013, p. 2462) also analyze the consequences of the Italian Clemency Act of 2006 and find that ". . . most of the crime-preventing effects of incarceration operate through incapacitation rather than deterrence."

A natural experiment to separate the deterrence and incapacitation effects is to look at the behavior of young criminals as they approach the age of 18 in Florida. Reaching the age of 18 moves potential offenders from juveniles to adults. Presuming that other relevant factors change continuously, the discontinuous jump in deterrence can be used to identify the effects of deterrence on crime. Using this methodology, Levitt (1998) finds the deterrence elasticity to be −0.40 for violent crime. However, using the same methodology, Lee and McCrary (2009) found a much smaller deterrence elasticity of increased penalties of the order of −0.13. They conjecture that the difference in their findings from Levitt (1998) arises because the latter use annualized data.

Our model makes no predictions about which of the two instruments, $p$ or $F$, is more effective. However, increasing $p$ may be a far more effective means of deterrence compared to an increase in $F$; see, for instance, Pogarsky (2002) and Durlauf and Nagin (2010). If the initial level of punishment is 20 years in prison then an increase in imprisonment to 25

---

[80]    Incapacitation is sometimes a stated objective of criminal sentencing.

years for the same offense might not be very effective. One reason is the *present bias in preferences* caused by hyperbolic discounting. Thus a marginal increase in the probability of detection might be more effective than an increase in punishment. A review of the major studies leads Doob and Webster (2003) to conclude that there was no conclusive evidence that stronger sentences reduce crime. We have sidestepped this problem by assuming that it is possible to compute the exact monetary equivalent of all possible punishments.

We have assumed that criminals are rational. If drugs and alcohol are involved in criminal offenses, then individuals might not be making the "rational" decisions that are required in classical theories of deterrence, whether they be EU, RDU, PT or CP. Similar comments apply to crimes committed by individuals with mental problems. Darley (2005, p. 196) cites the findings of The Center on Addiction and Substance Abuse: ". . . substance abuse and addiction have shaped the criminal histories of 80 percent of prisoners today. . ." Pogarsky (2002) divides the population of potential criminals into three types: acute conformists, the incorrigible and the deterrable. The incorrigible are not affected by the deterrence parameters but the deterrable are deterred. If true, these factors undermine the standard models of crime based on rational calculation.

Our model does not consider dynamic issues, but these are potentially very important. Supermax prisons in which prisoners face greater hardship than normal imprisonment (such as physical isolation) do not seem to cut the rate of re-offending relative to normal imprisonment; see, for instance, Mears and Bales (2009). There is also some evidence that imprisonment can cause a criminogenic effect, i.e., increase the likelihood that criminals might reoffend. Several channels may work to facilitate the criminogenic effect. These include stigmatization of offenders and loosening of ties with family and friends. A dynamic model would need to incorporate these effects.

An important omission from our model is the judicial stage, where a range of behavioral factors could be at play. The evidence indicates that even lawyers and judges are not immune from behavioral biases such as hindsight bias; see, for instance, Rachlinski (2011). This raises important ethical issues for criminal law. Juries may be asked to judge the probability that a defendant's action caused harm after having been told that the action did indeed cause harm. Juries may be subject to the hindsight bias, thus influencing their awards of damages; see, for instance, Rachlinski (1998). Defendants might be subject to overoptimism so they might discount the larger probability of being found guilty by juries subject to the hindsight bias. However, these factors would need to be taken into account by a rational criminal prior to committing a crime. These considerations show the danger of assuming a probability of detection and conviction, $p$ known to the criminal without any ambiguity.

Models of criminal behavior typically assume that crime is committed by "individuals." However, in actual practice crime is often the handiwork of gangs. This requires us to have a theory of behavior in groups and teams. Decision theory designed for a single individual might not be appropriate to the behavior of groups where peer effects and team incentives may play important roles. Given the refutations of mainstream game theory (not reviewed here), what is needed is a behavioral game theory (still in its infancy).

Most models of crime, neoclassical or behavioral, incorporate a composite probability of detection and conviction. If, say, these respective probabilities are 0.3 and 0.5, and these events are independent, then the composite probability is assumed to be 0.15. The experiments of Feldman and Teichman (2009) cast doubts on this practice. They consider two sources of risk from a potentially illegal action: (1) the risk of detection and (2) the risk of their action being found illegal. The main finding is that there is reduced compliance with the law when the second type of risk is increased relative to the first type, even when the composite probability is held fixed. One possible reason that the authors give is *motivated reasoning*, namely, that individuals feel more comfortable making choices that they think could be justified, ex-post, in front of a dispassionate observer. In this case, individuals could have a self-serving bias to justify their actions as being legal.

We have assumed that the only role of punishment is to deter crime. However, a related aim could be retribution. These issues are nicely separated in Bronsteen, Buccafusco and Masur (2010). They use two insights from happiness economics. (1) Humans adapt quickly and quite well in terms of their well-being to events of a positive or negative nature. (2) Humans suffer from a form of projection-bias in which they underestimate how quickly they will adapt to negative future events. They also underestimate the pain they suffered from past negative events. These insights have interesting implications. For a potential offender, future punishment might be aversive. However, a repeat offender who has been incarcerated before, might underestimate the disutility from past prison experiences. The fact that humans adapt well to the prison environment, and quite quickly, has implications for the actual levels of deterrence and retribution achieved by punishments.

# REFERENCES

Abdellaoui, Mohammed. 2000. Parameter-free elicitation of utility and probability weighting functions. *Management Science* 46: 1497–1512.

Abdellaoui, Mohammed, Frank Vossmann and Martin Weber. 2005. Choice-based elicitation and decomposition of decision weights for gains and losses under uncertainty. *Management Science* 51: 1384–1399.

Allais, Maurice. 1953. Le comportement de l'homme rationnel devant le risque: critique des postulats et axiomes de l'école Américaine. *Econometrica* 21: 503–546.

Allingham, Michael G. and Agnar Sandmo. 1972. Income tax evasion: A theoretical analysis. *Journal of Public Economics* 1: 323–38.

al-Nowaihi, Ali, Ian Bradley and Sanjit Dhami. 2008. The utility function under Prospect Theory. *Economics Letters* 99: 337–339.

al-Nowaihi, Ali and Sanjit Dhami. 2006. A simple derivation of the Prelec probability-weighting function. *Journal of Mathematical Psychology* 50: 521–524.

al-Nowaihi, Ali and Sanjit Dhami. 2010a. Probability-weighting functions. Discussion Paper No. 10/10. Department of Economics, University of Leicester.

al-Nowaihi, Ali and Sanjit Dhami. 2010b. Composite Prospect Theory. Discussion Paper No. 10/11. Department of Economics, University of Leicester.

al-Nowaihi, Ali and Sanjit Dhami. 2011. Probability-weighting functions. In *Wiley Encyclopedia of Operations Research and Management Science*, edited by James J. Cochran, Louis Anthony Cox, Jr., Pinar Keskinocak, Jeffrey P. Kharoufeh and J. Cole Smith. John Wiley and Sons. DOI: 10.1002/9780470400531. eorms0681.

al-Nowaihi, Ali and Sanjit Dhami. 2012. Hyperbolic punishment functions. *Review of Law and Economics* 8(3): 759–787.

Andreoni, James. 1991. Reasonable doubt and the optimal magnitude of fines: Should the penalty fit the crime? *RAND Journal of Economics* 22: 385–395.

Andreoni, James, Brian Erard and Jonathan Feinstein. 1998. Tax compliance. *Journal of Economic Literature* 36: 818–860.

Bar Ilan, Avner. 2000. The response to large and small penalties in a natural experiment. Unpublished manuscript. University of Haifa, Department of Economics, 31905 Haifa, Israel.

Bar Ilan, Avner and Bruce Sacerdote. 2001. The response to fines and probability of detection in a series of experiments. Working Paper No. 8638. National Bureau of Economic Research, Cambridge, Mass.

Bar Ilan, Avner and Bruce Sacerdote. 2004. The response of criminals and non-criminals to fines. *Journal of Law and Economics* 47: 1–17.

Becker, Gary. 1968. Crime and punishment: An economic approach. *Journal of Political Economy* 76: 169–217.

Bentham, J. 1789. An introduction to the principles of morals and legislation. In *The Utilitarians*. Garden City, NY: Anchor Books, 1973.

Bernasconi, Michele. 1998. Tax evasion and orders of risk aversion. *Journal of Public Economics* 67: 123–134.

Bronsteen, John, Christopher J. Buccafusco and Jonathan S. Masur. 2010. Welfare as happiness. *Georgetown Law Journal* 98: 1583–1641.

Buhren, Christoph and Thorben Kundt. 2013. Worker or shirker: Who evades more taxes? A real effort experiment. Working Paper No. 26-2013. Philipps-University Marburg.

Buonanno, Paolo and Steven Raphael. 2013. Incarceration and incapacitation: Evidence from the 2006 Italian Collective Pardon. *American Economic Review* 103: 2437–2465.

Camerer, Colin F. and George Loewenstein. 2004. Behavioral economics: Past, present and future. Pp. 3–51 in *Advances in Behavioral Economics*, edited by Colin F. Camerer, George Loewenstein and Matthew Rabin. New York: Princeton University Press.

Chetty, Raj. 2006. A new method of estimating risk aversion. *American Economic Review*: 96(5): 1821–1834.

Choo, Lawrence, Miguel A. Fonseca and Gareth Myles. 2013. Lab experiment to investigate tax compliance: Audit strategies and messaging. Research Report No. 308. HM Revenue and Customs.

Colman, Andrew M. 1995. Prisoner's dilemma, chicken, and mixed-strategy evolutionary equilibria. *Behavioral and Brain Sciences* 18: 550–551.

Crawford, Vincent P. and Juanjuan Meng. 2011. New York City cabdrivers' labor supply revisited: Reference-dependence preferences with rational-expectations targets for hours and income. *The American Economic Review* 101: 1912–1932.

Darley, John M. 2005. On the unlikely prospect of reducing crime rates by increasing the severity of prison sentences. *Journal of Law and Policy* 13: 181–247.

Dhami, Sanjit and Ali al-Nowaihi. 2007. Why do people pay taxes? Prospect theory versus expected utility theory. *Journal of Economic Behavior and Organization* 64: 171–192.

Dhami, Sanjit and Ali al-Nowaihi. 2010. Optimal income taxation in the presence of tax evasion: Expected utility versus prospect theory. *Journal of Economic Behavior and Organization* 75: 313–337.

Dölling, Dieter, Horst Entorf, Dieter Hermann and Thomas Rupp. 2009. Is deterrence effective? Results of a meta-analysis of punishment. *European Journal of Criminal Policy and Research* 15: 201–224.

Doob, Anthony N. and Cheryl M. Webster. 2003. Sentence severity and crime: Accepting the null hypothesis. Pp. 143–195 in *Crime and Justice: A Review of Research*, edited by Michael H. Tonry. Chicago: University of Chicago Press.

Drago, Francesco, Roberto Galbiati and Pietro Vertova. 2009. The deterrent effects of prison: Evidence from a natural experiment. *Journal of Political Economy* 117(2): 257–280.

Durlauf, S. N. and D. S. Nagin. 2010. The deterrent effect of imprisonment. Pp. 43–94 in *Controlling Crime: Strategies and Tradeoffs*, edited by P. J. Cook, J. Ludwig and J. McCrary. Chicago: University of Chicago Press.

Dwenger, Nadja, Henrik Kleven, Imran Rasul and Johannes Rincke. 2014. Extrinsic and intrinsic motivations for tax compliance: Evidence from a field experiment in Germany. Working Paper. FAU Friedrich-Alexander Universitat Erlangen-Nurnberg.

Feess, Eberhard and Ansgar Wohlschlegel. 2009. Why higher punishments may reduce deterrence. *Economics Letters* 104: 69–71.

Fehr, Ernst, Oliver Hart and Christian Zehnder. 2011. Contracts as Reference Points—Experimental Evidence. *American Economic Review* 101: 493–525.

Fehr-Duda, Helga and Thomas Epper, 2012. Probability and Risk: Foundations and Economic Implications of Probability-Dependent Risk Preferences. *Annual Review of Economics*, Annual Reviews, 4(1): 567–593.

Feldman, Yuval and Doron Teichman. 2009. Are all legal probabilities created equal? *NYU Law Review* 84: 980–1022.

Friedman, David. 1999. Why not hang them all: The virtues of inefficient punishment. *Journal of Political Economy* 107: S259–S269.

Garoupa, Nuno. 2001. Optimal magnitude and probability of fines. *European Economic Review* 45: 1765–1771.

Gonzalez, Richard and George Wu. 1999. On the shape of the probability weighting function. *Cognitive Psychology* 38: 129–166.

Hart, Oliver and John Moore. 2008. Contracts as Reference Points. *Quarterly Journal of Economics* 123: 1–48.

Ingersoll, Jonathan. 2008. Non-monotonicity of the Tversky-Kahneman probability-weighting function: A cautionary note. *European Financial Management* 14: 385–390.

Iyengar, Radha. 2008. I'd rather be hanged for a sheep than a lamb: The unintended consequences of three-strikes laws. Working Paper No.13784. National Bureau of Economic Research, Cambridge, Mass.

Jolls, Christine, Cass R. Sunstein and Richard Thaler. 1998. A behavioral approach to law and economics. *Stanford Law Review* 50(5): 1471–1550.

Kahneman, Danicl. 2003. Maps of bounded rationality: Psychology for behavioral economics. *American Economic Review* 93: 1449–1475.

Kahneman, Daniel and Amos Tversky. 1979. Prospect theory: An analysis of decision under risk. *Econometrica* 47: 263–291.

Kahneman, Daniel and Amos Tversky. 1984. Choices, values and frames. *American Psychologist* 39(4): 341–350.

Kahneman, Daniel and Amos Tversky. 2000. *Choices, Values and Frames.* Cambridge: Cambridge University Press.

Kaplow, Louis. 1992. The optimal probability and magnitude of fines for acts that definitely are undesirable. *International Review of Law and Economics* 12: 3–11.

Klick, Jonathan and Alexander Tabarrok. 2005. Using terror alert levels to estimate the effect of police on crime. *Journal of Law and Economics* 48: 267–279.

Kolm, Serge-Christophe. 1973. A Note on optimum tax evasion. *Journal of Public Economics* 2: 265–270.

Köszegi, Botond and Matthew Rabin. 2006. A model of reference-dependent preferences. *Quarterly Journal of Economics* 121: 1133–1165.

Köszegi, Botond and Matthew Rabin. 2007. Reference-dependent risk attitudes. *American Economic Review* 97: 1047–1073.

Kunreuther, Howard, Ralph Ginsberg, Louis Miller, Philip Sagi, Paul Slovic, Bradley Borkan and Norman Katz. 1978. *Disaster Insurance Protection: Public Policy Lessons.* Wiley: New York.

Lattimore, Pamela M., Joanna R. Baker and Ann D. Witte. 1992. The influence of probability on risky choice: A parametric investigation. *Journal of Economic Behavior and Organization* 17: 377–400.

Lawsky, Sarah B. 2013. Modelling uncertainty in tax law. *Stanford Law Review* 65: 241–278.

Lee, David S. and Justin McCrary. 2009. The deterrence effect of prison: Dynamic theory and evidence. Working Paper. Berkeley Program in Law and Economics, Working Paper Series, UC Berkeley, University of California.

Levitt, Steven D. 1998. Juvenile crime and punishment. *Journal of Political Economy* 106: 1156–1185.

Levitt, Steven D. 2004. Understanding why crime fell in the 1990s: Four factors that explain the decline and six that do not. *Journal of Economic Perspectives* 18: 163–190.

Luce, R. Duncan. 2001. Reduction invariance and Prelec's weighting functions. *Journal of Mathematical Psychology* 45: 167–179.

Luce, R. Duncan and Howard Raiffa. 1957. *Games and Decisions: Introduction and Critical Survey.* New York: Wiley.

Machina, Mark. J. 2008. Non-expected utility theory. Pp. 74–84 in *The New Palgrave Dictionary of Economics.* 2nd ed., edited by Steven N. Durlauf and Lawrence E. Blume. New York: Macmillan.

Marquis, M. Susan and Martin R. Holmer. 1996. Alternative models of choice under uncertainty and demand for health insurance. *The Review of Economics and Statistics* 78: 421–427.

Mears, Daniel P. and William D. Bales. 2009. Supermax incarceration and recidivism. *Criminology* 47(4): 1131–1166.

Novemsky, Nathan and Daniel Kahneman. 2005. The boundaries of loss aversion. *Journal of Marketing Research* XLII: 119–128.

Pogarsky, Greg. 2002. Identifying deterrable offenders: Implications for deterrence research. *Justice Quarterly* 19(3): 431–452.

Polinsky, Mitchell and Steven Shavell. 1979. The optimal trade-off between the probability and magnitude of fines. *American Economic Review* 69: 880–891.

Polinsky, Mitchell and Steven Shavell. 1991. A note on optimal fines when the wealth varies among individuals. *American Economic Review* 81: 618–621.

Polinsky, Mitchell and Steven Shavell. 2000a. The fairness of sanctions: Some implications for optimal enforcement policy. *American Law and Economics Review* 2: 223–237.

Polinsky, Mitchell and Steven Shavell. 2000b. The economic theory of Public enforcement of law. *Journal of Economic Literature* 38: 45–76.

Polinsky, Mitchell and Steven Shavell. 2007. The theory of public enforcement of law. Pp. 403–454 in vol. 2 of *Handbook of Law and Economics*, edited by Mitchell Polinsky and Steven Shavell. Amsterdam: Elsevier.

Posner, Eric A. 2004. Probability errors: Some positive and normative implications for tort and contract law. *Supreme Court Economic Review* 11: 125–141.

Pöystia, Leena, Sirpa Rajalina and Heikki Summala. 2005. Factors influencing the use of cellular (mobile) phone during driving and hazards while using it. *Accident Analysis & Prevention* 37: 47–51.

Prelec, Drazen. 1998. The probability weighting function. *Econometrica* 60: 497–528.

Quiggin, John. 1982. A theory of anticipated utility. *Journal of Economic Behavior and Organization* 3: 323–343.

Rabin, Matthew (2000). Risk aversion and expected-utility theory: A calibration theorem. *Econometrica* 68: 1281–1292.

Rachlinski, Jeffrey. 1998. A positive psychological theory of judging in hindsight. *The University of Chicago Law Review* 65: 571–625.

Rachlinski, Jeffrey J. 2011. The psychological foundations of behavioral law and economics. *University of Illinois Law Review*: 1677–1696.

Rizzo, John A. and Richard J. Zeckhauser. 2004. Reference incomes, loss aversion and physician behavior. *Review of Economics and Statistics* 85: 909–922.

Robinson, Paul H. and John M. Darley. 2004. Does criminal law deter? A behavioral science investigation. *Oxford Journal of Legal Studies* 24: 173–205.

Schmidt, Ulrich, Chris Starmer and Robert Sugden. 2008. Third-generation prospect theory. *Journal of Risk and Uncertainty* 36: 203–223.

Skinner, Jonathan and Joel Slemrod. 1985. An economic perspective on tax evasion. *National Tax Journal* 38: 345–353.

Slemrod, Joel. 2007. Cheating ourselves: The economics of tax evasion. *Journal of Economic Perspectives* 21(1): 25–48.

Starmer, Chris. 2000. Developments in non-expected utility theory: The hunt for a descriptive theory of choice under risk. *Journal of Economic Literature* 38: 332–382.

Stott, Henry P. 2006. Choosing from cumulative prospect theory's functional menagerie. *Journal of Risk and Uncertainty* 32: 101–130.

Taylor, Shelley E. and Jonathon D. Brown. 1998. Illusion and well-being: A social psychological perspective on mental health. *Psychological Bulletin* 103: 193–210.

Teitelbaum, Joshua C. 2007. A unilateral accident model under ambiguity. *Journal of Legal Studies* 431–477.

The Royal Society for the Prevention of Accidents. 2005. The risk of using a mobile phone while driving. www.rospa.com.

Tversky, Amos and Daniel Kahneman. 1974. Judgment under uncertainty: Heuristics and biases. *Science* 185: 1124–1131.

Tversky, Amos and Daniel Kahneman. 1992. Advances in prospect theory: Cumulative representation of uncertainty. *Risk and Uncertainty* 5: 297–323.

Viscusi, W. Kip. 1998. *Rational Risk Policy: The 1996 Arne Ryde Memorial Lectures*. Oxford: Oxford University Press.

Wakker, Peter P. 2010. *Prospect Theory for Risk and Ambiguity*. Cambridge: Cambridge University Press.

Williams, Allan F. and Adrian K. Lund. 1986. Seat belt use laws and occupant crash protection in the United States. *American Journal of Public Health* 76: 1438–1442.

Wu, George and Richard Gonzalez. 1996. Curvature of the probability-weighting function. *Management Science* 42: 1676–1690.

Yaniv Gideon, 1999. Tax compliance and advance tax payments: A prospect theory analysis. *National Tax Journal* 52: 753–764.

Yitzhaki, Shlomo. 1974. A note on income tax evasion: A theoretical analysis. *Journal of Public Economics* 3: 201–202.

# PART IV

# TORTS

# 8.  Behavioral models in tort law
*Barbara Luppi and Francesco Parisi*

## 1.  INTRODUCTION

Legal rules create incentives expecting that people will rationally respond to legal sanctions and institutional constraints. However, biases and imperfections in human cognition alter people's response to legal incentives, undermining the effectiveness of legal intervention (Sunstein 2000; Parisi and Smith 2005). A number of psychological biases alter people's assessment of their own skills and of the risks they face, jeopardizing their ability to act optimally in their daily activities. As pointed out by a number of scholars, behavioral biases and cognitive imperfections pose a distinctive problem in the design of tort rules (Posner 2003; Grady 2005; Jolls 2005; Ulen 2005). As such, tort law may fail to deter certain activities because the human response to these rules may be hindered by the same biases and cognitive shortcomings that affect the tortious behavior.

This chapter examines how problems identified by behavioral literature become relevant in the case of a tort action. Section 2 considers the existing taxonomy of behavioral problems and suggests how such problems could be modeled in the context of a tort problem. This exercise aims to provide a common modeling language that can be utilized by law and economic scholars when considering the effect of behavioral biases and cognitive imperfections in tort and other areas of law. Through this exercise we intend to show how different behavioral problems can be incorporated into the standard tort model and expressed in algebraic form. Our formulation is one demonstration of the many possible expressions of behavioral problems and tort action concepts. The models we present are applicable to a wide range of tort law and have the potential for application to a broad range of legal problems. Given the limited scope of this chapter, Section 2 derives only basic results based on our formulations through comparison of simple first-order conditions of the standard tort problem. Section 3 discusses instruments useful in determining the extent to which de-biasing and insulating strategies can be employed in tort policy.

## 2.  MODELING BEHAVIORAL BIASES AND COGNITIVE IMPERFECTIONS IN TORT LAW

The social sciences model human choices through an operational set of working hypotheses and conjectures. Over time, many of these hypotheses and conjectures crystalize and advance in status to self-evident axioms of human choice, providing a set of operational rules in the analytical toolbox of the field or discipline. Economic analysis, for example, starts from a set of fundamental rules regarding human choice. It includes a description of how human beings value their actions, how they perceive the environment in which they act, how they gather and process information regarding themselves and others, and how they choose to act to satisfy their objectives. The standard operational assumption widely adopted by economic theory is the so-called "rational actor" model, a stylized view of human choice within which the "economic man" is able to perfectly process information and choose the action that maximizes his objectives. Despite the social sciences' ability to develop a set of operation rules, this does not necessarily guarantee their accuracy. Over the past decades, research at the intersection of economics and psychology has revealed the inadequacy and predictive shortcomings of the economic assumption of rationality. Behavioral and experimental economics research has shown the behavioral regularities of real human beings depart from the behavioral patterns of the "economic man" acting within the paradigms of economic rational choice.

The attempt to open the "black box" of human reasoning and adopt a description of man behavior more aligned with reality is especially important to the fields of law and applied economics. These fields derive policy implications from economic models in order to assess the efficiency of legal rules and institutions. In carrying out this task, law and economics relies on a description of human behavior to assess how individuals react to changes in law or legal institutions. Behavioral law and economics contributes to this task by utilizing the findings of psychological and behavioral decision research. The resulting, empirically based, models of human behavior lend greater accuracy to the analysis of law and legal institutions and deliver more robust policy implications.

## 2.1   A Simple Tort Model Under Full Rationality

We start our analysis by recasting the standard bilateral care model of tort law, in which both parties are assumed to be fully rational. The full rationality assumption in a tort model implies that both the tortfeasor and the prospective victim correctly assess the riskiness of their actions, the effectiveness of their care, the gravity of the potential loss, and the cost of care. Parties in the standard tort model are thus assumed to be free from the behavioral biases that affect ordinary humans. Understanding the structure of the tort problem under full rationality serves as a stepping-stone for understanding the tort problem when behavioral problems are introduced. Based on the requirements of the standard bilateral care model, we consider below a general full-rationality setting under which we model the enforcement and settlement opportunities for the tortfeasor and the victim.

The tortfeasor carries out an activity, denoted by $w$, which generates a value $V_T(w)$ to the tortfeasor. Similarly, the victim carries out an activity, denoted by $z$, which produces a value $V_V(z)$ to the victim. The activity values $V_T(w)$ and $V_V(z)$ share similar properties; $V_V(z)$ increases with the activity level in the relevant range at a decreasing rate, i.e., $V_i > 0$ and $V_{ii} < 0$ for $i = w,z$. Both parties contribute to the likelihood of an accident. Parties can, however, invest in precautions to reduce the probability of an accident. Denote respectively with $x$ and $y$ the tortfeasor's level of precaution, where $x \in [0,\infty)$, and the victim's level of precaution, where $y \in [0,\infty)$. Precautions depend positively on activity levels.[1] The probability of an accident decreases proportionally to the tortfeasor's and/

---

[1]   We present here a general analytical framework. The total amount of precautions $x$ and $y$ are assumed to be an increasing function of activity levels, respectively $w$ and $z$, i.e. $x_w > 0$ and $y_z > 0$. In many models, total precautions are assumed to be in a multiplicative relationship, i.e. $wx$ and $zy$, where $x$ and $y$ are the per-unit of activity level of care.

or the victim's precautions ($x$ and $y$) at a decreasing rate. Analytically, an accident occurs with probability $p(x,y)$, where $p(x,y) \in (0,1)$, $p_i < 0$, $p_{ii} > 0$, for $i = x,y$. In most tort problems, parties' precautions are assumed to be substitutes, i.e., $p_{xy} < 0$. When an accident occurs, it creates an (exogenous) loss denoted by $L$, where $L > 0$. Total expected harm is equal to $wzp(x,y)L$.[2]

Following Shavell (1987), total welfare is defined as the sum of the value of the activities of the tortfeasor and the victim, and both parties' net expected accident and precaution costs. Analytically, the social welfare function takes the following form:

$$max_{(x,y,w,z)}S = V_T(w) + V_V(z) - wzp(x,y)L - x(w) - y(z)$$

The socially optimal levels of precaution $x^{**}$ and $y^{**}$ are defined by the following first order conditions:

$$-wzp_x(x^{**},y)L = 1 \tag{1}$$

$$-wzp_y(x,y^{**})L = 1 \tag{2}$$

At the social optimum, the marginal reduction in the expected accident loss equals the marginal cost of care.

The socially optimal levels of activity $w^{**}$ and $z^{**}$ satisfy the following first order conditions:

$$V_w = zp(x,y)L + x_w \tag{3}$$

$$V_z = wp(x,y)L + y_z \tag{4}$$

According to these conditions, the marginal benefit from an increase in activity level equals the marginal cost of the activity, given an increase in expected accident loss.

Social and private incentives may differ. In order to investigate the optimal private incentives of the parties, we must characterize the private problems of the tortfeasor and the victim under alternative liability regimes. Setting the stage for the subsequent analysis, we enrich the model by allowing for imperfect enforcement and/or out-of-court settlement, which may affect precaution and activity incentives. Assume that when an accident occurs, enforcement occurs with probability $e$. Enforcement is perfect when $e = 1$ and imperfect in all those cases when $e < 1$. When an accident occurs and enforcement ensues, parties can sue and the court awards damages equal to $D$. However, parties may prefer to opt for an out-of-court settlement in which the tortfeasor agrees to pay $S$. Assume the parties litigate with probability $\alpha$ and choose an out-of-court settlement with probability $1 - \alpha$, where $0 < \alpha < 1$.

---

2    The multiplicative relationship of the activity levels, $w$ and $z$, in the production of an accident captures the intuition that both tortfeasor and victim need to carry out the activity for the accident to occur.

The tortfeasor's private objective function takes the following form:

$$max_{(x,w)}F = V_T(w) - ewzp(x,y)[\alpha D + (1 - \alpha)S] - x(w)$$

The private optimal levels of precaution $x^*$ and activity $w^*$ are defined by the following first-order conditions:

$$-ewzp_x(x,y)[\alpha D + (1 - \alpha)S] = 1 \tag{5}$$

$$V_w = ezp(x,y)[\alpha D + (1 - \alpha)S] + x_w \tag{6}$$

The victim's private objective function takes the following form:

$$max_{(y,z)} = V_V(z) - wzp(x,y)L + ewzp(x,y)[\alpha D + (1 - \alpha)S] - y(z)$$

The private optimal levels of precaution $y^*$ and activity $z^*$ are defined by the following first-order conditions:

$$-wzp_y(x,y^*)\{L - e[\alpha D + (1 - \alpha)S]\} = 1 \tag{7}$$

$$V_z = wp(x,y)\{L - e[\alpha D + (1 - \alpha)S] + y_z \tag{8}$$

In Section 2.2, we build on this setup by considering possible ways to model behavioral departures from full rationality due to cognitive, behavioral, and social biases. We will demonstrate that these biases can affect the perception of each and every component of a risk-creating activity as well as the perception of enforcement and settlement opportunities after the tort occurs. We will use these models to illustrate how such biases may affect the familiar results of efficiency in tort law.

## 2.2    What About Making It Real?

Behavioral law and economics attempts to bridge the analytical gap between the paradigms of rational choice and the observations of how humans actually choose. The resulting models account for the way in which individuals process information and choose their behavior. We contribute to this literature by developing a tort model that embeds a more complex and realistic description of human decision-making legal analysis. To start, we use the classification of behavioral biases drawn from experimental and psychological evidence. Experimental and psychological research has identified behavioral regularities and cognitive biases that lead to departures from the standard paradigm of rational choice. For example, people tend to adopt simplifying decisional procedures that reduce or completely suppress relevant information. This may stem from individuals' false perceptions of the likelihood of events based on their optimistic or pessimistic disposition, lack of knowledge, or inability to accurately process available information. Individuals tend to make decisions not on a "neutral" interpretation of evidence, but rather base their choices on cognitive factors, affecting their ability to correctly process available information. We have identified a handful of biases that affect an individual's overall decision-making capabilities and beliefs, and list them in Tables 8.1 and 8.2. As this list is drawn from the ever-growing number of biases identified by behavioral scientists, it is by necessity tentative and incomplete. In Table 8.1, we introduce behavioral biases in decision-making.

In addition to the behavioral biases discussed in Table 8.1, other biases become relevant in the context of tort law. Some of these biases arise through social interactions with other human beings and cause distortions in self-esteem, self-perception, consensus estimation, and causal attribution. For example, individuals may regard themselves as being more popular than they actually are, or think of themselves as better (or worse) at carrying out some activity than the average person. These social biases, listed in Table 8.2(a), substantially affect individual decision-making and should be properly taken into account when analyzing the effectiveness of law. Biases may also be driven by memory errors (listed in Table 8.2(b)) affecting an individual's ability to store information and events in his or her memory, or to retract and correctly process information stored in the memory.

Each of these biases affects the results of the standard model of tort law. In a standard setting, a potential tortfeasor engages in some risky activity. The tortfeasor and a prospective victim may take precautions in order to reduce the probability and/or the gravity of an accident. A behavioral model of tort law should capture the effects of these biases on the parties' choices in a tort situation. Specifically, we will consider the effect of biases on the parties' perceptions of the probability of an accident, the severity of the harmful consequences, or on the parties' misperception of their individual skill level, to attain a false estimation of the cost or effectiveness of care. In an attempt to capture the complexity of human behavior in a manageable way, the taxonomy of biases in Tables 8.1 and 8.2 list the most direct effects of biases on choice. Biases, however, often operate on more than one level, affecting multiple or all variables of the tort problem. Our focus is on the behavioral regularities and biases that appear to undermine the standard design of tort law based on the standard rationality framework. Our effort to model behavioral irregularities and biases will hopefully offer a common modeling language aimed at capturing a wide variety of behavioral phenomena in a tort model.

### 2.2.1 Biases affecting the perceived probability of an accident

Inside the rational-person paradigm, individuals are able to perfectly assess the objective probability of an event and to infer information correctly from the available evidence. Behavioral and experimental research has shown that people inaccurately estimate the riskiness of their actions and of the environment in which they operate. When individuals underestimate or overestimate the likelihood of events, legal rules may fail to deliver efficient care and activity-level incentives. Here, we illustrate how to model biases that affect individuals' assessment of the riskiness of their actions and/or estimation of the likelihood of events.

As a first example, consider optimism bias. Optimism alters people's estimates of the likelihood of future events, making them overestimate the chances of positive or desirable events and underestimate the chances of negative or undesirable events (Coleman 2001).[3] Analytically, an optimistic person systematically underestimates the objective

---

[3]  See, among others, Lund (1925), Cantril (1938), and Weinstein (1980).

*Table 8.1*  *Behavioral biases in decision-making*

| | Perceived accident probability | Perceived efficacy of care on accident probability | Perceived loss | Perceived cost of care | Enforcement | Litigation and settlement |
|---|---|---|---|---|---|---|
| | Decision-making and belief biases | | | | | |
| • Unrealistic optimism/ optimism bias | ✓ | ✓ | ✓ | ✓ | ✓ | ✓ |
| • Pessimism bias | ✓ | ✓ | ✓ | ✓ | ✓ | ✓ |
| • Moral pessimism | | | | | | |
| • Zero-risk bias | ✓ | ✓ | ✓ | ✓ | ✓ | ✓ |
| • Neglect probability | | | | | | |
| • Ambiguity effect | ✓ | ✓ | ✓ | ✓ | ✓ | ✓ |
| • Anchoring heuristic | ✓ | ✓ | ✓ | ✓ | ✓ | ✓ |
| • Availability heuristic | | | | | | |
| • Availability bias | | | | | | |
| • Primacy effect/ recency effect/recency bias | | | | | | |
| • Representativeness heuristic | | | | | | |
| • Base rate fallacy | | | | | | |
| • Regressive bias/ Conservatism | ✓ | ✓ | ✓ | ✓ | ✓ | ✓ |
| • Illusion of control bias | ✓ | ✓ | ✓ | ✓ | ✓ | ✓ |
| • Restraint bias | ✓ | ✓ | ✓ | ✓ | ✓ | ✓ |
| • Planning fallacy | ✓ | ✓ | ✓ | ✓ | ✓ | ✓ |
| • Curse of knowledge | ✓ | ✓ | ✓ | ✓ | ✓ | ✓ |
| • Duration neglect | ✓ | ✓ | ✓ | ✓ | ✓ | ✓ |
| • Confirmation bias | ✓ | ✓ | ✓ | ✓ | ✓ | ✓ |
| • Choice supportive bias | | | | | | |
| • Pluralistic ignorance | ✓ | ✓ | ✓ | ✓ | ✓ | ✓ |
| • Bandwagon effect | | | | | | |
| • Attentional bias | ✓ | ✓ | ✓ | ✓ | ✓ | ✓ |
| • Bias blind spot | ✓ | ✓ | ✓ | ✓ | ✓ | ✓ |
| • Omission bias | ✓ | ✓ | ✓ | ✓ | ✓ | ✓ |
| • Hyperbolic discounting | ✓ | ✓ | ✓ | ✓ | ✓ | ✓ |
| • Discounting-cost effect | ✓ | ✓ | ✓ | ✓ | ✓ | ✓ |
| • Inflating-benefit effect | ✓ | ✓ | ✓ | ✓ | ✓ | ✓ |
| • Impact bias | ✓ | ✓ | ✓ | ✓ | ✓ | ✓ |
| • Endowment effect | ✓ | ✓ | ✓ | ✓ | ✓ | ✓ |
| • Loss aversion | | | | | | |
| • Status quo bias | | | | | | |

*Table 8.2 Social biases and memory errors*

| | Perceived accident probability | Perceived efficacy of care on accident probability | Perceived loss | Perceived cost of care | Enforcement | Litigation and settlement |
|---|---|---|---|---|---|---|
| **(a) Social biases** | | | | | | |
| • Placement bias (or illusory superiority or above-average effect) | | ✓ | | ✓ | | |
| • Worse-than-average effect | | ✓ | | ✓ | | |
| • Social projection bias | | | | | ✓ | ✓ |
| • Self-serving bias | | | | ✓ | ✓ | ✓ |
| • False consensus bias | | | | | ✓ | ✓ |
| • Egocentric bias | | | | | ✓ | ✓ |
| • Defensive attribution hypothesis | | | | | ✓ | ✓ |
| **(b) Memory errors** | | | | | | |
| • Bizarreness effect | | | | | | ✓ |
| • Persistence | | | | | | ✓ |
| • Misinformation effect | | | | | | ✓ |
| • Context effect | | | | | | |
| • False memory | | | | | | |
| • Illusion-of-truth effect | | | | | | |
| • Hindsight bias | ✓ | | ✓ | | | ✓ |

probability of an accident, denoted by $p(x,y)$. This can be expressed in a tort model by denoting:

$$\underline{p}(x,y) < p(x,y) \text{ for any } (x,y) \tag{9}$$

Optimistic individuals distort the probability of an accident, perceiving a lower risk, $\underline{p}$, than the true risk they face, $p$. Contrary to intuition, the sole presence of an optimism bias does not distort the marginal incentive to undertake precautions. Hence, the first-order conditions for the tortfeasor and the victim, respectively in (5) and (7), will not change. In the absence of any enforcement error and with perfect damage awards, private and social incentives are perfectly aligned in the presence of an optimism bias. The reason why is that the optimism bias introduces a distortion on the perceived level of uncertainty, but not on the effectiveness of care. The optimism bias, however, will cause a suboptimal high level of activity for both the tortfeasor and the victim. The deflated perception of activity riskiness drives each subject to underestimate the expected costs of the activity, thereby increasing the activity level above the socially optimal level.

Optimistic individuals may, in some cases, inaccurately estimate the riskiness of an event only for a subset of circumstances. For example, in some situations, individuals tend to disregard risks that are perceived to be very small, such as in the so-called zero-risk bias (Baron, Gowda, and Kunreuther 1993). In more extreme cases, individuals act as though uncertainty does not exist and make decisions believing one circumstance is certain and disregarding all other possible outcomes of their choice, such as in the neglect probability bias (Redelmeier and Kahneman 1996).

Posner (2003) analyzed the zero-risk bias as a special form of optimism bias. The individual perceives the probability so that:

$$\underline{p}(x) = \begin{cases} 0 \ if \ p < \hat{p} \\ p(x) \ if \ p \geq \hat{p} \end{cases} \tag{10}$$

According to Posner's (2003) analytical specification, the individual correctly assesses the probability of an accident when the probability is above a given threshold, $\hat{p}$, but sets accident probabilities to zero when the probability falls below the given threshold. Posner (2003) examined the effectiveness of alternative liability regimes in a unilateral care model. Posner shows that under both strict liability and negligence, individuals employ an inefficient level of care—too much or too little—for sufficiently high levels of probabilities, falling above the threshold values of zero-risk bias, and employ optimal care for intermediate values. Posner additionally shows the tendency for the difference in probability level assessment on activity levels between strict liability and negligence to disappear in these cases, due to the fact that the optimistic agent treats rare events as zero-probability events.

Beliefs regarding event likelihood may be distorted upward as well as downward. This occurs when individuals are affected by a pessimism bias or a moral pessimism bias (Alloy and Ahrens 1987). People affected by a pessimism bias tend to overestimate the likelihood of negative events and perceive the environment to be riskier than it actually is. Moral pessimism bias entails a negative expectation of the moral attitude of other individuals in society and the expectation that others violate legal and social norms more frequently than is actually observed.

Analytically, a pessimistic person systematically overestimates the objective probability of an accident, throughout the range of probability values. In a tort law setting, this can be modeled as a shifted probability function, as follows:

$$\bar{p}(x,y) > p(x,y) \text{ for any } (x,y) \tag{11}$$

A pessimism bias operates symmetrically to the optimism bias. The private marginal incentive to undertake care is not necessarily distorted and first-order conditions for the tortfeasor and the victim will coincide respectively with (5) and (7). However, the pessimism bias, resulting in an inflated perception of the activity riskiness, drives the parties to decrease their activity level below the socially efficient one, other things being equal.

Individuals may also face decisions under uncertainty, when information on alternative outcomes may be missing or ambiguous. Ellsberg (1961) identified the ambiguity effect, which describes how people tend to choose outcomes with known probability over those outcomes with unknown probability. The ambiguity effect may thus shift accident probability either downward or upward. This result can be explained by the psychological tendency to include only those options for which information is available in the strategy set (see Frisch and Baron 1988).

Teitelbaum (2007) models ambiguity using Choquet's (1954) expected utility model and examines optimal care and activity incentives in a unilateral tort setting. According to Teitelbaum (2007), the tortfeasor's optimal care decreases with ambiguity if she is ambiguity-loving, or increases if she is ambiguity-averse. Negligence-based rules appear more robust to ambiguity and may therefore be superior to strict liability in unilateral accident cases.[4]

When faced with a decision, individuals tend to adopt decisional procedures called *heuristics* to simplify the decision-making process (Kahneman, Slovic, and Tversky 1982). The adoption of a decisional heuristic allows a person to save time when processing information or to reduce the amount of calculations required by reducing the information set. Psychological studies show that individuals tend to adopt the anchoring heuristic, which is an assessment of the subjective estimation of the likelihood of a specific event, by focusing on a single piece of available information and over-relying (anchoring) on that sole piece of information. The anchoring heuristic produces biased estimations of the likelihood of an event toward the anchor value (see Epley and Gilovich 2001, discussing the tendency of anchoring with insufficient adjustment). This bias may be either upward or downward, depending on the anchor value chosen. Analytically, a person adopting an anchoring heuristic will estimate the probability of an event in the following way:

$$p^A(x,y) = a + T(x,y) \qquad (12)$$

where $a$ indicates the anchor value and $T(x,y)$ is the adjustment of the anchoring value, which may be either negative or positive. It follows that the estimated likelihood of an event may be either greater or less than the objective probability of that event, i.e.,

$$p^A(x,y) \, p \gtreqless (x,y) \qquad (13)$$

The anchoring heuristic will not affect the marginal incentives to undertake precaution, and first-order conditions for the parties will coincide with equation (5) for the tortfeasor and (7) for the victim. However, the direction of the distortion induced by the anchor will affect the perceived riskiness of the activity, thereby causing the parties to engage in a suboptimally low or high level of activity.[5]

---

[4]   For analysis of the impact of legal ambiguity in tort law, see also Geistfeld 2011 and Chakravarty and Kelsey 2012.

[5]   The anchor value may be suggested by a counterparty when signing a contract (for example, when an insurance company allows the customer to self-select a contract type), or may be part of a training program to reduce accident mortality (for example, in the workplace or for automobile

Similar effects are generated by a number of other behavioral patterns identified by psychological research. An availability bias occurs when an individual estimates the likelihood of an event on how easily he recalls that specific event (Tversky and Kahneman 1974; Reyes, Thompson and Bower 1980; Johnson and Tversky 1983). The availability bias produces estimations skewed toward more vivid events stored in the memory, events that appeared frequently in the media, or unusual or sensational events, which are easier to recall. For this reason, people tend to think that traveling by aeroplane is riskier than traveling by car, even though the death rate for car accidents is actually higher. Similarly, a primacy or recency bias (Nickerson 1998) produces a skewed estimation of the likelihood of an event toward more recent events or those with a higher emotional impact. Overestimation or underestimation of the accident likelihood may be caused by the inability of the individual to estimate correctly the impact of the prior probability of an event when assessing its conditional probability. This is the so-called base-rate fallacy (Nisbett et al. 1976; Kahneman and Tversky 1982). Similarly, the conjunction fallacy (Tversky and Kahneman 1983) occurs when the probability of a conjunct event is assessed as higher than the likelihood of the single events. The regressive bias or conservatism (Fischhoff, Slovic, and Lichtenstein 1977) tends to alter the frequency distribution of (positive or negative) events, by treating more (less) frequent events as less (more) likely than they actually are. Based on the regressive bias, individuals tend to have normal or less concentrated probability distribution of the events.

### 2.2.2   Biases affecting the effectiveness of care

Behavioral biases do not only affect the perception of riskiness but may also influence individual perception of one's own abilities and comparison of oneself with other individuals in society. In a tort setting, a distortion in perceived personal ability may affect the effectiveness of care. Individuals invest in precautions and are required to think about how much each unit of care will reduce accident probability. More skilled individuals will achieve the same reduction in accident probability by investing fewer units of care. A distorted perception of individual ability compared to the rest of society may therefore introduce inefficiency in care incentives. In this section, we discuss several behavioral biases and investigate how we can model such distortions.

Individuals tend to display "positive illusions," i.e., they may hold "unrealistically favorable perceptions about themselves" (Taylor and Brown 1988). Positive illusions include, among other biases, the above-average effect and the illusion of control bias.[6]

The above-average effect (also known as the "illusory superiority bias" or "placement bias") is a cognitive social bias that leads people to overestimate their positive qualities and underestimate their defects (Alicke, Dunning and Krueger 2005). Evidence of the above-average effect is quite robust with respect to common abilities and tasks (e.g., driving, parenting, managerial skills) but weaker with respect to unusual tasks. The above-average effect operates in conjunction with the bias blind spot (Pronin and Kugler 2007),

---

drivers). The law may affect the choice of the anchor, thereby reducing the inefficient activity level chosen by parties.

[6]   Positive illusions include also unrealistic optimism (which we discussed in subsection 2.2.1).

according to which an individual perceives herself less vulnerable to the psychological biases compared to the average person.

The illusion of control bias (Langer 1975; Langer and Roth 1975) identifies situations where an individual believes she is able to influence the realization of a desirable positive outcome, or avoid an undesirable negative outcome, even if she has no real ability to control the final outcome of her actions.

Both the above-average effect and the illusion of control biases have great relevance in legal analysis, especially in a tort context. Positive illusion biases produce an inflated perception of the effectiveness of one's care. In the presence of an illusion bias, denote with $\bar{p}$ the subjective probability of an accident and with $\bar{p}_i = \frac{\partial \bar{p}}{\partial i}, i = x, y$, the distorted marginal effectiveness of care for the tortfeasor and the victim. As suggested by Parisi (2013), even if based on different psychological explanations, these biases can be modeled in the following way:

$$|\bar{p}_i| > |p_i|, i = x, y \tag{14}$$

In the presence of positive illusions, individuals perceive their care as more effective than it actually is. The first-order conditions for the tortfeasor and the victim will become respectively:

$$-ewz\bar{p}_x(x,y)[\alpha D + (1 - \alpha)S] = 1 \tag{15}$$

$$-wz\bar{p}_y(x,y^*)\{l - e[\alpha D + (1 - \alpha)S]\} = 1 \tag{16}$$

where $\bar{p}_i, i = x, y$ behaves according to equation (9). An inflated perception of care effectiveness induces individuals to underinvest in care, due to a false perception of their abilities.

According to empirical psychological studies, the illusion of control bias tends to appear in conjunction with the optimism bias. Luppi and Parisi (2009) analyze the conjunct effect of an optimism bias and the illusion of control bias in a bilateral care tort setting and investigate the care and activity incentives under different liability regimes. Depending on the liability regime, a moral hazard problem may arise either for the tortfeasor or the victim, when the law fails to incorporate the presence of positive illusions in individual behavior. Comparative negligence regimes are superior in contrasting the moral hazard problem created by positive illusion. Additionally, they show that the traditional equivalence between contributory and comparative negligence does not hold.

Inflated perceptions of care effectiveness may also be explained on the basis of other behavioral regularities, such as the restraint bias and the planning fallacy. People may overestimate their capacity to refrain from temptation, and consequentially, their ability to undertake effective care. For example, a young college student may think he can drive to a party and avoid drinking alcohol, but he may succumb to the temptation. Prior to the drink, his perceived care effectiveness is inflated because he may not sufficiently weigh the difficulties of restraining his behavior. On a similar note, an individual may fail to correctly estimate the amount of time needed to complete a task while meeting the due care standard. This may also produce an inflated perception of care effectiveness that can be illustrated using equation (9).

Ex-post effectiveness of care may also be reduced when individuals are not able to process the intensity of their current activity. Duration neglect bias (Redelmeier and Kahneman 1996) identifies those situations where individuals cannot correctly perceive the length or intensity of the risky activity. Such individuals do not have a biased perception of their own care before exerting the activity, but during the activity, they cannot correctly assess the activity's length or intensity, thereby causing an upward distortion of their perceived care, as modeled in equation (9). A biased perception of the duration of the activity may thus lead to diminishing care effectiveness, as the duration of the activity increases. For example, a person may underestimate the need to take breaks while driving on a long trip, and her false perception of having driven for less time may induce suboptimal levels of care or less effective quality of care.

The curse of knowledge (Camerer, Loewenstein, and Weber 1989) refers to skilled and trained individuals who tend to be less creative and accurate when performing activities in which they have accumulated knowledge. The reason behind this bias is that the emotional perception of self-assurance increases the perceived effectiveness of their care (as modeled by equation (9)). However, this mental attitude may actually decrease the accuracy of a knowledgeable individual's care with respect to a less-informed person. One explanation is that trained people tend to devote less attention to routine activities and thus the precaution undertaken may be less effective.

A number of behavioral biases operate in the opposite direction, so that the perceived effectiveness of care is decreased. The worse-than-average effect (Kruger 1999) is a clear example. Individuals perceive themselves as less capable than other people in society. This implies that they feel less able to complete tasks or to perform well when facing a specific task. This induces a deflated perception of the effectiveness of their actions. Analytically, denote with $p$ the subjective probability of an accident and with $p_i = \frac{\partial p}{\partial i}, i = x,y$, the distorted marginal effectiveness of care for the tortfeasor and the victim. Analytically, the worse-than-average effect causes a downward distortion in the perceived effectiveness of care. This can be expressed as follows:

$$|\underline{p_i}| < |p_i|, i = x, y \tag{17}$$

In the presence of a worse-than-average effect, individual care is less effective than perceived. The first-order conditions for the tortfeasor and the victim will become respectively:

$$-ewz\underline{p_x}(x,y)\,[\alpha D + (1 - \alpha)S] = 1 \tag{18}$$

$$-wz\underline{p_y}(x,y^*)\,\{L - e[\alpha D + (1 - \alpha)S]\} = 1 \tag{19}$$

where $\underline{p_i}, i = x,y$ behaves according to equation (17). A deflated perception of care effectiveness induces individuals to overinvest in care, adhering to a false downward-biased perception of their abilities.

Behavioral biases may also affect care effectiveness in both directions, depending on the context where a specific bias arises. An example is the attentional bias, which affects the way individuals process available information (Nisbett and Ross 1980). People affected by an attentional bias tend to focus only on a subset of relevant information, disregarding wholly or in part other relevant information that has a correlation to their current decision. Empirical evidence suggests that drug users and, more generally, addicted individuals display attentional biases towards addiction-related events. This may help explain the frequency of relapses following treatments. In such cases, addicted individuals perceive the effectiveness of their care as higher than it actually is (as in equation (14)) and undertake less care toward their health than is socially optimal. In the presence of an attentional bias, anxious individuals focus on information more closely related to their concerns (Nisbett and Ross 1980). This is an example where attentional bias causes a lower perceived effectiveness of care (as in equation (17)), leading individuals to focus on the relevant information above the socially optimal level.

### 2.2.3 Biases affecting the cost of care

A crucial parameter when choosing the optimal precaution level is care costs. Several biases may induce a distorted perception of precaution costs, thereby affecting the incentive to undertake care.

Among the social biases, the self-serving bias creates a shield to protect and reinforce personal self-esteem (Sloan, Taylor, and Smith 2003). An individual exhibiting a self-serving bias tends to attribute a greater share of a success to himself and attribute a greater share of his failures to others, based on his own personal merits and qualities. The self-serving bias may, therefore, induce people to overestimate the opportunity costs of their precautions, since they feel their efforts are better invested in other higher-valuing activities because of their higher ability.[7] Analytically, the self-serving bias can be modeled as a higher marginal precaution cost. Denote with $c(x)$ and $c(y)$ the perceived precaution costs for the tortfeasor and the victim, respectively. Under a self-serving bias, the marginal cost perceived by the individual, denoted with $c_i = \frac{dc}{di}, i = x, y$, is higher than in the absence of any bias (which is set equal to one with no lack of generality):

$$c_i > 1, i = x, y \tag{20}$$

The privately optimal levels of precaution $x^*$ and $y^*$ are defined by the following first order conditions:

$$-ewzp_x(x, y)\left[\alpha D + (1 - \alpha)S\right] = c_x \tag{21}$$

$$-ewzp_y(x, y^*)\left[\alpha D + (1 - \alpha)S\right] = c_y \tag{22}$$

Since $p_i < 0$ and $p_{ii} > 0$, for $i = x, y$, the self-serving bias dilutes precaution incentives, causing the individual to undertake suboptimally low levels of precaution.

Behavioral biases may affect multiple dimensions. A number of other biases, listed in Tables 8.1 and 8.2(a) and discussed in the previous subsections, may influence the individual perception of precaution costs in the same direction as the self-serving bias.

The restraint bias (Nordgren, van Harreveld, and van der Pligt 2009) creates

---

[7]  For an application to litigation theory, see Babcock, Loewenstein, and Issacharof (1997).

higher precaution costs due to the individual's inability to avoid engaging in risky activities. The planning fallacy (Kahneman and Tversky 1977) instead creates higher precaution costs due to the individual's inability to correctly process the information associated with the avoidance of risky activities. The illusion of control bias (Begg, Anas, and Farinacci 1992), the above-average effect (Alicke, Dunning, and Krueger 2005), and the curse of knowledge (Camerer, Loewenstein, and Weber 1989) induce the individual to perceive a higher opportunity cost for each unit of care, because the individual feels she is better, more skilled, or more trained in a specific task. This can be modeled according to equation (20) and such phenomena may arise either for the tortfeasor, the victim, or both. The psychological mechanisms that give rise to higher precaution costs (perceived or real) or the higher opportunity costs of taking precautions are specific to each bias, but in all such situations, they cause a dilution of care incentives.

People tend to exhibit time-inconsistent choices when facing a decision between a more immediate, but smaller, reward (or cost) versus a delayed, but larger, gain (or cost). Following the findings of Chung and Herrnstein (1967) and Ainslie (1974, 1975), individual time-inconsistent choices that produce a preference reversal over time can be explained by invoking hyperbolic, rather than exponential, discounting. Contrary to exponential discounting, where evaluations decay at a constant rate, hyperbolic discounting captures the idea that valuations decay at a higher rate for small delay periods, but at a lower rate over longer periods. Hyperbolic discounting thus produces a dynamic preference inconsistency where short-term preferences are inconsistent with long-term preferences. This relationship of inverse proportionality of delay over time can be applied both to rewards and costs decisions. Individual preferences affected by hyperbolic discounting are also said to be "present-biased."

Although hyperbolic discounting has been studied in economics, a proper understanding of its consequences in legal applications is lacking. Hyperbolic discounting has been used to explain self-control problems, such as drug addiction or procrastination (O'Donoghue and Rabin 1999, 2000). It has also been used to explain retirement savings (Diamond and Koszegi 2003) or credit card borrowings (Kuchler 2012) in economic settings. In the legal context, hyperbolic discounting has been used to explain criminal behavior, which appears to be strongly correlated with high levels of self-control problems. Jolls, Sunstein, and Thaler (1998) suggest the higher effectiveness of short over long punishment, because of preferences biased toward the present. Kleiman (1997) promotes "coerced abstinence" for drug users, associated with automatic short punishment in the case of the violation of probation.

In a tort law context, we suggest that hyperbolic discounting may also explain the choice of inefficient care levels. In this setting, hyperbolic discounting may induce an upward bias in the perception of immediate precaution costs in response to a "potential" loss faced in the future. To model hyperbolic discounting bias, we need to extend the model in Section 2.1 to consider time-inconsistent preferences. When individual preferences are biased toward the present, precaution involves immediate costs for a later uncertain reward, represented by a reduction in the expected liability in the event of an accident. Adopting the quasi-hyperbolic approximation proposed by Laibson (1997), the tortfeasor's private objective function is changed as follows to account for the presence of hyperbolic discounting:

$$max_{(x,w)}F = V_T(w) - ewzp(x,y)\beta\delta^d[\alpha D + (1 - \alpha)S] - x(w)$$

where $\beta\delta^d$ identifies the discount factor applied to the expected liability after $d$ periods. A similar analysis applies for the victim.

The private optimal levels of precaution $x^*$ and $y^*$ are defined by the following first order conditions:

$$-ewzp_x(x,y)\beta\delta^d[\alpha D + (1 - \alpha)S] = 1 \qquad (23)$$

$$-wzp_y(x,y^*)\{L - e\beta\delta^d[\alpha D + (1 - \alpha)S]\} = 1 \qquad (24)$$

In such situations, the tortfeasor has diluted incentives to undertake care, given that the immediate costs of precaution are weighted against delayed and discounted benefits. The opposite holds for the victim. The victim faces two immediate costs (precautions and accident loss), receiving a delayed and hyperbolically discounted compensation.

An interesting and specific application of behavioral bias in a tort law context is the discount-cost effect, identified by Porat and Tabbach (2011). After death, an individual associates a utility equal to zero to her wealth. This zero utility value produces a divergence between private and social incentives ex-ante and ex-post. The individual discounts the probability that she will die in any case with the cost of reducing her risk of death when deciding how much to invest in saving her own life. The discount-cost effect generates a deflated perception of precaution costs and leads individuals to overinvest in precautions above a socially efficient level.[8]

### 2.2.4 Biases affecting the severity of an accident

Biases affect the perception of the environment in which individuals operate and make their decisions, including their perception of the severity of a loss if an accident occurs. It is not surprising to imagine that an optimistic person will likely have a downward bias regarding accident gravity and a dilution of care incentive. Analytically, the perceived loss $\underline{L}$ is lower than the objective one, $L$, i.e.,

$$\overline{L} < L \qquad (25)$$

and the private optimal level of precaution $x^*$ for the tortfeasor is defined by the following first order condition:

$$-ewzp_x(x,y)[\alpha\overline{L} + (1 - \alpha)S] = 1 \qquad (26)$$

A deflated gravity of accident produces a dilution of incentives, as can be easily seen from inspecting equation (26). A similar result is attained in the presence of hyperbolic

---

[8]  The divergence between private versus social incentives ex-ante and ex-post death can be equally explained when individual preferences are modeled using a state-dependent utility function, i.e. when the utility assigned to any given level of wealth depends on the state of nature (Karni 1985).

discounting. Individuals with preferences biased toward the present would discount the expected benefit of a loss reduction in the future, thereby leading to a dilution of incentives.

The opposite distortion occurs for a pessimistic person, facing an upward bias regarding accident gravity and excessive care incentives. Analytically, the perceived loss $\bar{l}$ is higher than the objective loss, $L$, i.e.,

$$\bar{L} > L \tag{27}$$

and the privately optimal level of precaution $x^*$ for the tortfeasor is defined by the following first order condition:

$$-ewzp_x(x,y)\,[\alpha\bar{L} + (1 - \alpha)S] = 1 \tag{28}$$

The omission bias identifies situations where an individual evaluates a harmful action as worse than an omission producing the same negative consequence. In a tort context, this would mean that a person would view driving over the speed limit and causing the death of a pedestrian crossing the street to be morally worse than failing to slow down in time to avoid a car accident. This bias may induce an overestimation of accident gravity (according to equation (27)) and has very important implications for the estimation of damages and punitive damages.

An inflated perception of accident gravity may also occur in the presence of the inflating-benefit effect, identified by Porat and Tabbach (2011). This effect stems from the recognition that individuals assign a private value to the possibility of consuming their wealth while alive. This value, however, is not reflected in a social evaluation, since others may be willing to consume a specific individual's wealth in the case of his death. The divergence between private and social evaluation of consumption of individual wealth may induce an overestimation of accident gravity and a resulting overinvestment of precautions above the socially optimal level.

There are a number of other biases that may also affect the perception of accident gravity in a less predictable way. A relevant psychological heuristic for the assessment of accident gravity is the anchoring heuristic, which may result in so-called hindsight bias (Fischoff 1992, 2002; Hawkins and Hastie 1990). Individuals may anchor their estimates of the likelihood of an event or the size of a loss on the basis of the information available in their memory. In a tort context, an individual may overestimate or underestimate the size of an accident on the basis of information available from a similar accident they experienced or witnessed. When affected by a hindsight bias, individuals read ex-ante events in the light of ex-post events and information. This may lead them to distort the accuracy of their predictions, feeling reinforced on the basis of the information they have observed recently. This bias may induce either an underestimation or an overestimation of the gravity of the event, thereby inducing either diluted or excessive care or activity level incentives.

Other biases may produce uncertain consequences on care incentives. For example, the attentional bias (Nisbett and Ross 1980) may produce opposite effects, depending on which information subset the individuals use to estimate the loss gravity. In some cases, the attentional bias causes excessive care, while in other contexts it may undermine the incentive to take efficient precautions. A similar logic applies when individuals adopt an anchoring heuristic (Tversky and Kahneman 1974) or are affected by any other bias (listed in Table 8.1) involving the choice of an anchor. Depending on the anchor chosen in the decision-making process, the individual may underestimate or overestimate the loss gravity, thereby diluting or reinforcing precaution incentives.

### 2.2.5   Biases affecting detection and enforcement

In any legal problem, law provides efficient incentives only when paired with an efficient enforcement mechanism. In the absence of any enforcement mechanism, the effects of the law could vanish or be greatly reduced.[9] This line of reasoning also applies in the tort law setting. As pointed out by Jolls (2005), psychological biases pose a distinct problem with respect to legal enforcement. In the absence of a perfect enforcement, behavioral biases may affect the perception of enforcement likelihood and introduce distortions in precaution choices. This is especially true when properly taking into account the contexts where people interact.

Conformity (Asch 1955) may undermine the effectiveness of enforcement and cause a dilution of precaution incentives. Bandwagon effects (Asch 1955) describe situations where people tend to conform to the observed behavior of others.[10] A bandwagon effect is more likely to occur when the percentage of people who adopt the same behavior is higher. Individuals do not process the available evidence, but adopt the same behavior as others. For example, drivers tend to drive above the speed limit when other drivers do, independently of whether a speed control or a police patrol monitors the area. This may occur because individuals infer information from other people's behavior. For example, each driver thinks that the other drivers are experienced on that route and know that speed limits are mildly enforced. Bandwagon effects may also occur because individuals prefer to conform. For example, a driver may dislike having drivers passing him and flashing their lights, and may increase his speed to conform to others. Independent of the psychological mechanism that originates conformity, bandwagon effects may determine a dilution of precaution incentives.

Among social biases, pluralistic ignorance (Katz and Allport 1931; Prentice and Miller 1993) identifies situations where a group of individuals conform to a (social) norm without rejecting it publicly, even if the majority of the individuals in the group privately reject it. Pluralistic ignorance is based on the false belief that the majority of the group accepts the norm, and single individuals conform to it in order to avoid being ostracized or excluded from the group. Krech and Crutchfield (1948, pp. 388–89) described the phenomenon of pluralistic ignorance as the situation in which "no one believes, but everyone thinks that everyone believes." Prentice and Miller (1993) used pluralistic ignorance to explain the excessive alcohol consumption among young students in parties at Princeton University. Students there tended to drink more alcohol than they would otherwise. Rather than openly express their disagreement, students adapted to the norm, basing their judgment

---

[9]   On the expressive effect of laws and the resulting levels of compliance in the absence of enforcement, see Cooter, Feldman, and Feldman (2008).

[10]   See Bikhchandani, Hirshleifer, and Welch (1992) for an economic application of bandwagon behavior.

on the false belief that since everyone else was doing the same, it was the social norm. In such situations, the perception of the enforcement of drinking laws is perceived as less important than social acceptance among the students, and, hence, this induces a dilution of incentives to comply with the law. Pluralistic ignorance also helps explain the higher tendency of individuals not to intervene in emergency cases when in a group than when facing the same situation alone. Seeing the other individuals not intervening induces the false belief that there is no necessity to intervene, rather than evaluating the opportunity to intervene on the basis of the gravity of the emergency. Highway speeding in mildly congested areas can also be used as an illustration of pluralistic ignorance, when each driver infers from the behavior of others that it is safe and acceptable to drive above the speed limit.[11]

False consensus bias (Ross, Green, and House 1977) occurs when a person assumes incorrectly that he or she has more consensus than he or she actually has among peers in a group. This occurs despite an open disagreement expressed by others in the group. Hence, false consensus bias describes the opposite situation to pluralistic ignorance. False consensus bias may lead to underestimation of enforcement likelihood, based on the false perceived support in the community. This may cause a dilution of precaution incentives.[12] Similar effects may be produced in the presence of other social biases, such as a social projection bias, a self-serving bias, or an egocentric bias (Gilovich, Husted Medvec, and Sativsky 2000).

A dilution of precaution incentives may also occur when individuals have present-biased preferences. Enforcement can be perceived as distant in time and individuals prefer avoiding actions entailing an immediate cost to avoid bearing costs in the future, associated with their liability.

Omission bias (Ritov and Baron 1990; Baron and Ritov 2004) works in opposite directions for harmful actions and harmful omissions. Since harmful actions are judged more severely than harmful omissions, the perceived enforcement should be higher for the former and looser for the latter. This implies that a potential tortfeasor may prefer to engage in harmful omissions rather than undertake equally harmful actions.[13] This may induce an individual to undertake a suboptimal mix of precautionary activities.[14]

Anchoring heuristics may produce ambivalent effects on the perception of enforcement, depending on the anchor value chosen in the judgment. An individual who saw a police patrol on the way to work in the morning would more easily think that speed controls are

---

[11]   An alternative explanation of the same phenomenon is the safety-in-numbers effect of having multiple speed-limit violators, each decreasing the probability of detection and enforcement for the others in the group (Brown 1985).

[12]   False consensus bias may play a role in the justification of antisocial sexual behavior for sex tort perpetrators (see McAdams 1997). See also Kahan (1997) for an analysis of the role of false consensus bias in gang activity.

[13]   See Chamallas and Wriggins (2010) for an application of omission bias to gender and minority discrimination in tort settings.

[14]   Zamir and Ritov (2012) examine how the combined effect of loss aversion and omission bias affects optimal litigation in civil settings, since a burden of proof is imposed on the plaintiff. The authors note that the omission bias raises de facto the actual standard of proof above the 51% threshold. Additionally, the authors suggest the standard of proof should be set higher than 51% because of loss aversion.

enforced on the route he chose, thereby exerting more precautions in the afternoon on the way back from work. However, by the same logic, the same driver may think that speed controls are not enforced if he never sees police on the route to work.

### 2.2.6 Biases affecting litigation and settlement

After an accident occurs, parties have incentives to file for litigation and, once in litigation, to opt for an out-of-court settlement solution. The expected outcome of an out-of-court settlement operates like an expected damage award in the tortfeasor's ex-ante incentives. Behavioral biases affecting the likelihood of contestants to win the litigation and/or the legal grounds of the litigation substantially influence the choice of whether to enter litigation.

Loss aversion (Kahneman and Tversky 1979; Tversky and Kahneman 1991) may severely affect victims' litigation incentives. Loss aversion occurs when an individual perceives a higher disutility from a loss than the utility increase from a same-sized gain. In a tort law context, the (emotional and/or material) loss imposed on the victim may be perceived as bigger because of loss aversion, thereby increasing the incentive to litigate or the amount $S$ for an out-of-court settlement. Loss aversion interacts with a number of psychological biases, such as the status quo bias (according to which individuals take the status quo as a reference point and exhibit a preference toward the status quo, perceiving any deviation from it as a loss) and the endowment effect (according to which individuals assign a higher value to the things they own). Status quo bias and endowment effect[15] operate exactly in the same direction. This bias only affects the victim.[16]

The confirmation bias (Nickerson 1998) identifies the tendency for individuals to interpret evidence and available information in a selective way, in order to support their own viewpoint or confirm their own beliefs. Individuals affected by a confirmation bias tend to refute any evidence contradicting their beliefs. For example, a victim involved in an accident tends to analyze the events that led to the accident in such a way as to minimize his own fault and to support more strongly his entitlement to damages. This may affect the individual's incentives to enter litigation and the willingness to settle out-of-court. It is more likely that in the presence of a confirmation bias, individuals will file for higher compensation damages $D$ or expect a higher out-of-court settlement opportunity $S$, in order to drop the case. This will lead to a contraction of the settlement opportunities set and an expansion of the litigation set.[17]

The impact bias (Gilbert et al. 1998) identifies the tendency of individuals to overestimate the length or intensity of future feeling states. When faced with a negative event,

---

[15] A number of studies incorporate the endowment effect in a legal setting. Kahneman, Knetsch, and Thaler (1990) examine the validity of the Coase Theorem in the presence of an endowment effect. Rachlinksi and Jourden (1998) focus on remedies, while Arlen, Spitzer, and Talley (2002) study a corporate agency setting when the endowment effect is present.

[16] See Zamir (2012) for an application of the loss aversion in a law context.

[17] The choice supportive bias operates in a similar direction (see Mather and Johnson 2000). People affected by this bias tend to remember their own choices as better than they actually were, thereby overattributing positive features to what they chose and negative features to options not chosen. In the presence of a choice supportive bias, individuals will more likely enter litigation or will tend to overestimate compensation damages or be less inclined to settle out-of-court.

individuals may overestimate the negative present effects on their future well-being. For example, they anchor their future states with current emotional feelings and may fail to adjust their predictions. The impact bias will more likely lead to an expansion of the litigation set and a reduction of the settlement opportunities set.

The choice of entering litigation can be substantially influenced by the perception of self in society. People who regard themselves as highly supported by the other individuals in the group they belong to (at work, in the family, in their religious community, etc.) may have a higher tendency to enter litigation, basing their choice on the false beliefs that their reasons or emotional states are widely accepted and shared by others. People affected, for example, by a false consensus bias (Marks and Miller 1987), an egocentric bias (Gilovich, Husted Medvec, and Sativsky 2000), a self-serving bias (Sloan, Taylor, and Smith 2003), or a social projection bias (Loewenstein, O'Donoghue, and Rabin 2003) may engage in more litigation than is rationally optimal.

Hindsight bias (Fischoff 1992, 2002; Hawkins and Hastie 1990) creates pervasive problems in the court's or jury's assessment of the ex-ante probability of an accident or level of care undertaken by the parties. The fact that the accident has de facto occurred leads a decision-maker to infer that the ex-ante probability of occurrence must be higher and/or that the parties must have failed to do what was necessary to avoid the accident. This may lead to the ex-ante excessive precautions and other distortions in the standard tort problem.[18]

The anchoring heuristic (Tversky and Kahneman 1974) may affect the incentive to enter litigation or settlement in opposite directions. Consider a tortfeasor involved in an accident. He may recall a recent case from the news, where the jury awarded punitive damages in a very similar context.[19] In such a situation, a tortfeasor may overestimate the damage award he faces, and may be more willing to settle out-of-court. A different tortfeasor may have been involved in a similar accident before and not held liable.[20] This may induce the tortfeasor to face litigation rather than to offer a settlement.[21] Ambiguous effects on litigation and settlement choices may also be caused by conformity with the behavior of other individuals in society (due to pluralistic ignorance or bandwagon effects). For example, a person could file against the plaintiff in a class action, even though he would never file alone. Symmetrically, a contestant could accept a settlement offer that he would have never agreed upon otherwise, if others do.

Litigation and settlement opportunities may be substantially affected by the presence

---

[18]   See Peters (1999) for an application of hindsight bias in tort liability. See also Stallard and Worthington (1998) for the strategic use of hindsight bias in the attorney closing statements to affect jurors' recall of evidence.

[19]   See Sunstein, Kahneman, and Schkade (2000) for an analysis of the impact of psychological biases on the assessment of punitive damages.

[20]   See Collins et al. (1985) for the tendency of individuals to anchor with past, retrospective bias. See also Epley et al. (2004) for the individual tendency of anchoring with themselves, adopting an egocentric anchor.

[21]   The defensive attribution hypothesis affects litigation in an indirect way. It becomes especially relevant in a jury context or for a witness's performance at trial. Eye-witnesses to a different accident than the one at trial tend to attribute responsibilities not on the basis of an objective evaluation of what they have observed directly or the evidence brought to trial. On the contrary, they are more severe in their judgments, depending on the size of the loss caused by the accident and the more similar they are to the victim (see Burger 1981; Salminen 1992; Bornstein 1998).

of memory biases in the individuals. People may have memory lapses or selective memories that affect their perception of the events that led to the accident, thereby changing their perceived entitlement to damages (van der Kolk and Fisler 1995). For example, after an accident, most people experience the recurrence of memories of the accident, even if unwanted. The persistence of traumatic memories may reinforce the victim's feelings that he deserves substantial compensation or the rightness of his desire to punish the tortfeasor. This may lead to increased litigation incentives and reduced settlement opportunities. After traumatic events, people may also experience false memory, perceiving imagination as a memory (Loftus 1980). This memory misattribution may increase, for example, the victim's perception of damage entitlement, making the victim more inclined to litigate or less willing to accept a settlement out-of-court.

Some biases may produce opposite effects, depending on whether the memory retained will induce the person to perceive that he or she has a weaker claim or, on the contrary, deserves justice and due compensation in tort. Among others, bizarreness leads individuals to remember more easily highly unlikely events rather than ordinary or more frequent daily events (Lamay and Riefer 1998). Memory may fail to retain the sequence of events depicting the accident dynamics. This may occur, for example, because of the so-called context effect (Schwarz and Sudman 1992), according to which people are less able to retrieve correct memories, when they are recalled out of the context where those memories were generated. Memory mistakes may also arise due to a misinformation effect (Loftus and Hoffman 1989), when people report incomplete or false memories due to misinformation. People may also be misled by the illusion-of-truth effect (Begg, Anas, and Farinacci 1992). Independently of the truthful or false content of a statement, individuals are more inclined to believe in familiar statements (which they have heard previously and repetitively) than in a statement heard for the first time.

## 3.   CONCLUSIONS

A growing body of law and economics literature focuses on the departure of human behavior from full rationality and the attempt to explain the positive and normative implications of bounded rationality in the formulation of legal policy. Sunstein (1997) and Jolls, Sunstein, and Thaler (1998) point to the need for a more accurate understanding of behavior and individual choice in the legal context in order to take into account shortcomings in human behavior when structuring the law.

In this chapter, we contribute to the field of behavioral law and economics, considering how to represent the impact of behavioral, cognitive, and social biases on the behavior of parties in a tort problem. This exercise provides two useful building blocks for a more systematic development of the field of behavioral tort law. In the first building block, we highlighted the most relevant ways in which biases affect decisions in the context of a tort. To this end, we have identified several categories of effects, ranging from biases that affect the parties' ex-ante perceptions of probabilities, accident loss, effectiveness or cost of care, and probability of detection and enforcement, to biases that affect the parties' ex-post evaluations of the merits of their case, gravity of the loss, and settlement opportunities.

The second building block consists of a stylized algebraic representation of the biases in the context of a tort problem. Most of the results in the law and economics literature build on the standard tort model developed by Shavell (1980, 1987). In this chapter, we have shown how behavioral, cognitive, and social biases can be incorporated in the standard model. For each group of cases, we have derived the first-order conditions to obtain a first glance at the effects of biases on incentives. This exercise aims at offering a uniform modeling language to capture the important findings of the behavioral literature within the standard model of tort law.

# BIBLIOGRAPHY

Ainslie, George W. 1974. Impulse Control in Pigeons. *Journal of the Experimental Analysis of Behavior* 21(3): 485–89.

Ainslie, George W. 1975. Specious Reward: A Behavioral Theory of Impulsiveness and Impulse Control. *Psychological Bulletin* 82(4): 463–96.

Alicke, Mark D., David A. Dunning, and Joachim I. Krueger, eds. 2005. *The Self in Social Judgment.* New York: Psychology Press.

Alloy, Lauren B., and Anthony H. Ahrens. 1987. Depression and Pessimism for the Future: Biased Use of Statically Relevant Information in Predictions for Self Versus Others. *Journal of Personality and Social Psychology* 52: 366–78.

Arlen, Jennifer, Matt Spitzer, and Eric Talley. 2002. Endowment Effects Within Corporate Agency Relationships. *Journal of Legal Studies* 31: 1–37.

Armour, David, and Shelley E. Taylor. 2002. When Predictions Fail: The Dilemma of Optimism. Pp. 334–47 in *Heuristics and Biases: The Psychology of Intuitive Judgment,* edited by Thomas Gilovich, Dale Griffin, and Daniel Kahneman. New York: Cambridge University Press.

Asch, Solomon E. 1955. Opinions and Social Pressure. *Scientific American* 193: 31–35.

Babcock, Linda, George Loewenstein, and Samuel Issacharoff. 1997. Creating Convergence: Debiasing Biased Litigants. *Law & Social Inquiry* 22: 913–25.

Babcock, Linda, George Loewenstein, Samuel Issacharoff, and Colin Camerer. 1995. Biased Judgments of Fairness in Bargaining. *American Economic Review* 85: 1337–43.

Bar-Gill, Oren. 2006. The Evolution and Persistence of Optimism in Litigation. *Journal of Law, Economics, and Organization* 22: 490–507.

Baron, Jonathan, Rajeev Gowda, and Howard Kunreuther. 1993. Attitudes toward Managing Hazardous Waste: What Should Be Cleaned Up and Who Should Pay for It. *Risk Analysis* 13: 183–92.

Baron, Jonathan, and Ilana Ritov. 2004. Omission Bias, Individual Differences and Normality. *Organizational Behavior and Human Decision Processes* 94: 74–85.

Begg, Ian M., Ann Anas, and Suzanne Farinacci. 1992. Dissociation of Processes in Belief: Source Recollection, Statement Familiarity, and the Illusion of Truth. *Journal of Experimental Psychology* 121: 446–58.

Bigus, Jochen. 2006. Tort Liability and Probability Weighting Function According to Prospect Theory. Unpublished manuscript. University of California, Berkeley, Sixteenth Annual Meeting, American Law and Economics Association, May.

Bikhchandani, Sushil, David Hirshleifer, and Ivo Welch. 1992. A Theory of Fads, Fashion, Custom, and Cultural Change as Informational Cascades. *Journal of Political Economy* 100: 992–1026.

Bornstein, Brian H. 1998. From Compassion to Compensation: The Effect of Injury Severity on Mock Jurors' Liability Judgments. *Journal of Applied Social Psychology* 28: 1477–502.

Brown, Craig. 1985. Deterrence in Tort and No-Fault: The New Zealand Experience. *California Law Review* 73(3): 976–1002.

Brown, John P. 1973. Toward an Economic Theory of Liability. *Journal of Legal Studies* 2: 323–49.

Burger, Jerry M. 1981. Motivational Biases in the Attribution of Responsibility for an Accident: A Meta-Analysis of the Defensive Attribution Hypothesis. *Psychological Bulletin* 90(3): 496–512.

Camerer, Colin, Samuel Issacharoff, George Loewenstein, Ted O'Donoghue, and Matthew Rabin. 2003. Regulation for Conservatives: Behavioral Economics and the Case for "Asymmetric Paternalism". *University of Pennsylvania Law Review* 151: 1211–44.

Camerer, Colin, George Loewenstein, and Martin Weber. 1989. The Curse of Knowledge in Economic Settings: An Experimental Analysis. *Journal of Political Economy* 97: 1232–54.

Cantril, Hadley. 1938. The Prediction of Social Events. *Journal of Abnormal and Social Psychology* 33: 364–89.

Chakravarty, Surajeet, and David Kelsey. 2012. Ambiguity and Accident Law. Unpublished manuscript, University of Exeter, Department of Economics, March.

Chamallas, Martha, and Jennifer B. Wriggins. 2010. *The Measure of Injury: Race, Gender and Tort Law*. New York: New York University Press.

Choquet, Gustave. 1954. Theory of Capacities. *Annales de l'institut Fourier* 5: 131–295.

Chung, Shin-Ho, and Richard J. Herrnstein. 1967. Choice and Delay of Reinforcement. *Journal of the Experimental Analysis of Behavior* 10(1): 67–74.

Coleman, Andrew W. 2001. Unrealistic Optimism. In *A Dictionary of Psychology*. Oxford: Oxford University Press.

Collins, Linda N., John W. Graham, William B. Hansen, and C. Anderson Johnson. 1985. Agreement Between Retrospective Accounts of Substance Use and Earlier Reported Substance Use. *Applied Psychological Measurement* 9: 301–309.

Cooter, Robert D., Michal Feldman, and Yuval Feldman. 2008. The Misperception of Norms: The Psychology of Bias and the Economics of Equilibrium. *Review of Law and Economics* 4(3): 889–911.

DeJoy, David M. 1989. The Optimism Bias and Traffic Accident Risk Perception. *Accident Analysis & Prevention* 21: 333–40.

Diamond, Peter and Botond Koszegi. 2003. Quasi-hyperbolic Discounting and Retirement. *Journal of Public Economics* 87: 1839–72

Eder, Andreas B., Klaus Fiedler, and Silke Hamm-Eder. 2011. Illusory Correlations Revisited: The Role of Pseudocontingencies and Working-Memory Capacity. *Quarterly Journal of Experimental Psychology* 64: 517–32.

Eide, Erling. 2007. Accident Liability with Rank Dependence. *Kritische Vierteljahresschrift für Gesetzgebung und Rechtswissenschaft* 1/2: 160–71.

Ellsberg, Daniel. 1961. Risk, Ambiguity, and the Savage Axioms. *Quarterly Journal of Economics* 75: 643–99.

Epley, Nicholas, and Thomas Gilovich. 2001. Putting Adjustment Back in the Anchoring and Adjustment Heuristic: Differential Processing of Self-Generated and Experimenter-Provided Anchors. *Psychological Science* 12: 391–96.

Epley, Nicholas, Boaz Keysar, Leaf Van Boven, and Thomas Gilovich. 2004. Perspective Taking as Egocentric Anchoring and Adjustments. *Journal of Personality and Social Psychology* 87: 327–39.

Finn, Peter, and Barry W. E. Bragg. 1986. Perception of the Risk of an Accident by Younger and Older Drivers. *Accident Analysis and Prevention* 18: 289–98.

Fischhoff, Baruch. 1992. Debiasing. Pp. 422–44 in *Judgment under Uncertainty, Heuristics and Biases*, edited by Daniel Kahneman, Paul Slovic, and Amos Tversky. New York: Cambridge University Press.

Fischhoff, Baruch. 1996. The Real World: What Good Is It? *Organizational Behavior and Human Decision Processes* 65: 232–48.

Fischhoff, Baruch. 2002. Heuristics and Biases in Application. Pp. 730–48 in *Heuristics and Biases: The Psychology of Intuitive Judgment*, edited by Thomas Gilovich, Dale Griffin, and Daniel Kahneman. New York: Cambridge University Press.

Fischhoff, Baruch, Paul Slovic, and Sarah Lichtenstein. 1977. Knowing with Certainty: The Appropriateness of Extreme Confidence. *Journal of Experimental Psychology: Human Perception and Performance* 3: 552–564.

Forsythe, Robert, Thomas A. Rietz, and Tom W. Ross. 1999. Wishes, Expectations and Actions: A Survey on Price Formation in Election Stock Markets. *Journal of Economic Behavior and Organization* 39: 83–110.

Frisch, Deborah, and Jonathan Baron. 1988. Ambiguity and Rationality. *Journal of Behavioral Decision Making* 1: 149–57.

Geistfeld, Mark. 2011. Legal Ambiguity, Liability Insurance and Tort Reform. *DePaul Law Review* 60: 539–71.

Gilbert, Daniel T., Elizabeth C. Pinel, Timothy D. Wilson, Stephen J. Blumberg, and Thalia P. Wheatley. 1998. Immune Neglect: A Source of Durability Bias in Affective Forecasting. *Journal of Personality and Social Psychology* 75: 617–38.

Gilovich, Thomas, Nicholas Epley, and Karlene Hanko. 2005. Shallow Thoughts About the Self: The Automatic Components of Self-Assessment. Pp. 67–84 in *The Self in Social Judgment*, edited by Mark D. Alicke, David A. Dunning, and Joachim I. Krueger. New York: Psychology Press.

Gilovich, Thomas, Victoria Husted Medvec, and Kenneth Sativsky. 2000. The Spotlight Effect in Social Judgment: An Egocentric Bias in the Estimation of Salience of One's Own Actions and Appearance. *Journal of Personality and Social Psychology* 78(2): 211–22.

Grady, Mark. 2005. The Free Radicals of Tort. Pp. 425–55 in *The Law and Economics of Irrational Behavior*, edited by Francesco Parisi, and Vernon L. Smith. Stanford: Stanford University Press.

Guppy, Andrew. 1992. Subjective Probability of Accident and Apprehension in Relation to Self-Other Bias, Age, and Reported Behavior. *Accident Analysis and Prevention* 25: 375–82.

Hamilton, David, and Robert Gifford. 1976. Illusory Correlation in Interpersonal Perception: A Cognitive Basis of Stereotypic Judgments. *Journal of Experimental Social Psychology* 12: 392–407.

Hanson, Jon D., and Douglas A. Kysar. 1999a. Taking Behavioralism Seriously: Some Evidence of Market Manipulation. *Harvard Law Review* 112: 1420–572.

Hanson, Jon D., and Douglas A. Kysar. 1999b. Taking Behavioralism Seriously: The Problem of Market Manipulation. *New York University Law Review* 74: 630–749.

Hastie, Reid, and Robyn M. Dawes. 2010. *Rational Choice in an Uncertain World, The Psychology of Judgment and Decision-Making.* Thousand Oaks, C.A.: Sage Publications Inc.

Hastie, Reid, and Nancy Pennington. 2000. Explanation-Based Decision-Making. Pp. 212–28 in *Judgment and Decision-Making: An Interdisciplinary Reader,* edited by Terry Connolly, Hal R. Arkes, and Kenneth R. Hammond. Cambridge: Cambridge University Press.

Hawkins, Scott A., and Reid Hastie. 1990. Hindsight: Biased Judgments of Past Events After the Outcomes are Known. *Psychological Bulletin* 107: 311–27.

Jenni, Karen E., and G. Loewenstein. 1997. Explaining the Identifiable Victim Effect. *Journal of Risk and Uncertainty* 14(1): 235–57.

Johnson, Eric J., and Amos Tversky. 1983. Affect, Generalization, and the Perception of Risk. *Journal of Personality and Social Psychology* 45(1): 20–31.

Jolls, Christine. 1998. Behavioral Economic Analysis of Redistributive Legal Rules. *Vanderbilt Law Review* 51: 1653–77.

Jolls, Christine 2005. On Law Enforcement with Boundedly Rational Actors. Pp. 268–86 in *The Law and Economics of Irrational Behavior,* edited by Francesco Parisi and Vernon L. Smith. Stanford: Stanford University Press.

Jolls, Christine, and Cass R. Sunstein. 2006. Debiasing through Law. *Journal of Legal Studies* 35: 199–241.

Jolls, Christine, Cass R. Sunstein, and Richard Thaler. 1998. A Behavioral Approach to Law and Economics. *Stanford Law Review* 50: 1471–550.

Kahan, Dan M. 1997. Social Influence, Social Meaning, and Deterrence. *Virginia Law Review* 83: 349–95.

Kahneman, Daniel, Jack L. Knetsch, and Richard H. Thaler. 1990. Experimental Tests of Endowment Effect and the Coase Theorem. *Journal of Political Economics* 98: 1325–48.

Kahneman, Daniel, Paul Slovic, and Amos Tversky, eds. 1982. *Judgment under Uncertainty, Heuristics and Biases.* New York: Cambridge University Press.

Kahneman, Daniel, and Amos Tversky. 1977. *Intuitive Prediction: Biases and Corrective Procedures.* Technical Report.

Kahneman, Daniel, and Amos Tversky. 1979. Prospect Theory: An Analysis of Decision under Risk. *Econometrica* 47: 263–91.

Kahneman, Daniel, and Amos Tversky. 1982. On the Study of Statistical Intuitions. *Cognition* 11: 123–41.

Kaplan, Todd R., and Bradley J. Ruffle. 2004. The Self-Serving Bias and Beliefs about Rationality. *Economic Inquiry* 42: 237–46.

Karni, Edi. 1985. *Decision Making under Uncertainty: The Case of State-Dependent Preferences.* Cambridge: Harvard University Press.

Katz, D., and F. H. Allport. 1931. *Student Attitudes.* Syracuse, N.Y.: Craftsman.

Kleiman, Mark A. R. 1997. Coerced Abstinence: A Neopaternalist Drug Policy Initiative. Pp. 182–208 in *The New Paternalism,* edited by Lawrence M. Mead. Washington, D.C.: Brookings Institution.

Krech, David, and Richard S. Crutchfield. 1948. *Theory and Problems of Social Psychology.* New York: McGraw-Hill.

Kruger, Justin 1999. Lake Wobegon Be Gone! The "Below-Average Effect" and the Egocentric Nature of Comparative Ability Judgments. *Journal of Personality and Social Psychology* 77: 221–32.

Kuchler, Theresa. 2012. Sticking to Your Plan: Hyperbolic Discounting and Credit Card Debt Paydown. Discussion Paper No. 12-025. Stanford Institute for Economic Policy Research, Stanford, C.A.

Laibson, David. 1997. Golden Eggs and Hyperbolic Discounting. *Quarterly Journal of Economics* 112(2): 443–77.

Lamay, Mary L., and David M. Riefer. 1998. Memory for Common and Bizarre Stimuli: A Storage-Retrieval Analysis. *Psychonomic Bulletin Review* 5: 312–17.

Langer, Ellen J. 1975. The Illusion of Control. *Journal of Personality and Social Psychology* 32: 311–28.

Langer, Ellen J., and Jane Roth. 1975. Heads I Win, Tails Is Chance: The Illusion of Control Is a Function of the Sequence of Outcomes in a Purely Chance Task. *Journal of Personality and Social Psychology* 32: 951–55.

Loewenstein, George, Ted O'Donoghue, and Matthew Rabin. 2003. Projection Bias in Predicting Future Utility. *Quarterly Journal of Economics* 118(4): 1209–48.

Loftus, Elizabeth F. 1980. *Memory: Surprising New Insights Into How We Remember and Why We Forget.* Reading, Mass.: Addison-Wesley.

Loftus, Elizabeth F., and H. G. Hoffman. 1989. Misinformation and Memory: The Creation of New Memories. *Journal of Experimental Psychology* 188: 100–104.

Lichtenstein, Sarah, Paul Slovic, B. Frischhoff, M. Layman, and B. Combs. 1978. Judged Frequency of Lethal Events. *Journal of Experimental Psychology: Human Learning and Memory* 4: 551–78.

Lund, Frederick H. 1925. The Psychology of Belief. *Journal of Abnormal and Social Psychology* 20: 174–96.

Luppi, Barbara, and Francesco Parisi. 2009. Beyond Liability: Correcting Optimism Bias Through Tort Law. *Queen's Law Journal* 47: 47–66.

Marks, Gary, and Norman Miller. 1987. Ten Years of Research on the False-Consensus Effect: An Empirical and Theoretical Review. *Psychological Bulletin* 102: 72–90.

Mather, Mara, and Marcia K. Johnson. 2000. Choice-Supportive Source Monitoring: Do Our Decisions Seem Better to Us as We Age? *Psychology and Aging* 15: 596–606.

Matthews, Michael L., and Aidan R. Moran. 1986. Age Differences in Male Drivers' Perception of Accident Risk: The Role of Perceived Driving Ability. *Accident Analysis and Prevention* 18: 299–313.

McAdams, Richard H. 1997. The Origin, Development, and Regulation of Norms. *Michigan Law Review* 96: 338–433.

McKenna, Frank P., Rudolf A. Stanier, and Clive Lewis. 1991. Factors Underlying Illusory Self-Assessment of Driving Skill in Males and Females. *Accident Analysis and Prevention* 23: 45–52.

Mitchell, Gregory. 2002. Why Law and Economics' Perfect Rationality Should Not Be Traded for Behavioral Law and Economics' Equal Incompetence. *Georgetown Law Journal* 91: 67–167.

Muren, Astri. 2004. Unrealistic Optimism about Exogenous Events: An Experimental Test. Unpublished manuscript, Stockholm University, Department of Economics, March.

Nickerson, Raymond S. 1998. Confirmation Bias: A Ubiquitous Phenomenon in Many Guises. *Review of General Psychology* 2: 175–220.

Nisbett, Richard E., Eugene Borgida, Richard Crandall, and Harvey Reed. 1976. Popular Induction: Information Is Not Always Informative. Pp. 113–34 in *Cognition and Social Behavior*, edited by John S. Carroll and John W. Payne. New York: Wiley.

Nisbett, Richard E., and Lee Ross. 1980. *Human Inference: Strategies and Shortcomings of Social Judgment*. Englewood Cliffs, N.J.: Prentice-Hall.

Nordgren, Loran F., Frenk van Harreveld, and Joop van der Pligt. 2009. Restraint Bias: How the Illusion of Self-Restraint Promotes Impulsive Behavior. *Psychological Science* 20(12): 1523–28.

O'Donoghue, Ted and Matthew Rabin. 1999. Doing It Now or Later. *American Economic Review* 89(1): 103–24.

O'Donoghue, Ted and Matthew Rabin. 2000. The Economics of Immediate Gratification. *Journal of Behavioral Decision Making* 13: 233–50.

Parisi, Francesco. 2013. *The Language of Law and Economics: A Dictionary*. Oxford: Oxford University Press

Parisi, Francesco, and Vernon L. Smith. 2005. *The Law and Economics of Irrational Behavior*. Stanford: Stanford University Press.

Peters Jr., Philip G. 1999. Hindsight Bias and Tort Liability: Avoiding Premature Conclusions. *Arizona State Law Review* 31: 1227–314.

Porat, Ariel, and Avraham Tabbach. 2011. Willingness to Pay, Death, Wealth, and Damages. *American Law and Economics Review* 13: 45–102.

Posner, Eric A. 2003. Probability Errors: Some Positive and Normative Implications for Tort and Contract Law. *Supreme Court Economic Review* 11: 125–41.

Prentice, Deborah A., and Dale T. Miller. 1993. Pluralistic Ignorance and Alcohol Use on iCampus: Some Consequences of Misperceiving the Social Norm. *Journal of Personality and Social Psychology* 64(2): 243–56.

Pronin, Emily 2007. Perception and Misperception of Bias in Human Judgment. *Trends in Cognitive Sciences* 11: 37–43.

Pronin, Emily, and Martin B. Kugler. 2007. Valuing Thoughts, Ignoring Behavior: The Introspection Illusion as a Source of the Bias Blind Spot. *Journal of Experimental Social Psychology* 43: 565–78.

Rachlinksi, Jeffrey, and Forest Jourden. 1998. Remedies and the Psychology of Ownership. In Symposium: The Legal Implications of Psychology: Human Behavior, Behavioral Economics and the Law. *Vanderbilt Law Review* 51: 1541–82.

Redelmeier, Donald A., and Daniel Kahneman. 1996. Patients' Memories of Painful Medical Treatments: Real-Time and Retrospective Evaluations of Two Minimally Invasive Procedures. *Pain* 116: 3–8.

Reyes, Robert M., William C. Thompson, and Gordon H. Bower. 1980. Judgmental Biases Resulting From Differing Availabilities of Arguments. *Journal of Personality and Social Psychology* 39: 2–12.

Ritov, Ilana, and Jonathan Baron. 1990. Reluctance to Vaccinate: Omission Bias and Ambiguity. *Journal of Behavioral Decision Making* 3: 263–77.

Ross, Lee, David Green, and Pamela House. 1977. The "False Consensus Effect": An Egocentric Bias in Social Perception and Attribution Processes. *Journal of Experimental Social Psychology* 13(3): 279–301.

Salminen, Simo. 1992. Defensive Attribution Hypothesis and Serious Occupational Accidents. *Psychological Reports* 70(3): 1195–99.

Sanna, Lawrence, Norbert Schwarz, and Shevaun L. Stocker. 2002. When Debiasing Backfires: Accessible Content and Accessibility Experiences in Debiasing Hindsight. *Journal of Experimental Psychology: Learning, Memory, & Cognition* 28: 497–502.

Schwarz, Norbert, and Seymour Sudman, eds. 1992. *Context Effects in Social and Psychological Research*. New York: Springer Verlag.

Shavell, Steven. 1980. Strict Liability Versus Negligence. *Journal of Legal Studies* 9: 1–26.

Shavell, Steven. 1987. *Economic Analysis of Accident Law*. Cambridge, Mass.: Harvard University Press.

Sherman, Steven J., Robert B. Cialdini, Donna F. Schwartzman, and Kim D. Reynolds. 2002. Imagining Can Heighten or Lower the Perceived Likelihood of Contracting a Disease: The Mediating Effect of Ease of Imagery. Pp. 98–103 in *Heuristics and Biases: The Psychology of Intuitive Judgment*, edited by Thomas Gilovich, Dale Griffin, and Daniel Kahneman. New York: Cambridge University Press.

Sloan, Frank A., Donald H. Taylor Jr., and V. Kerry Smith. 2003. *The Smoking Puzzle: Information, Risk Perception and Choice*. Cambridge, Mass.: Harvard University Press.

Slovic, Paul, Baruch Frischhoff and Sarah Lichtenstein. 1982. Facts Versus Fears: Understanding Perceived Risk. Pp. 463–92 in *Judgment under Uncertainty: Heuristics and Biases*, edited by Daniel Kahneman, Paul Slovic, and Amos Tversky. Cambridge, Mass.: Cambridge University Press.

Small, Deborah A., and George Loewenstein. 2003. Helping a Victim or Helping the Victim: Altruism and Identifiability. *Journal of Risk and Uncertainty* 26(1): 5–16.

Stallard, Merrie Jo, and Debra L. Worthington. 1998. Reducing the Hindsight Bias Utilizing Attorney Closing Statements. *Law and Human Behavior* 22: 671–83.

Sunstein, Cass R. 1997. Behavioral Analysis of Law. *University of Chicago Law Review* 64: 1175–95.

Sunstein, Cass R., ed. 2000. *Behavioral Law and Economics*. Cambridge: Cambridge University Press.

Sunstein, Cass R. 2002. Probability Neglect: Emotions, Worst Cases and Law. *Yale Law Journal* 114: 61–107.

Sunstein, Cass R. 2005. On the Psychology of Punishment. Pp. 339–57 in *The Law and Economics of Irrational Behavior*, edited by Francesco Parisi and Vernon L. Smith. Stanford: Stanford University Press.

Sunstein, Cass R., Daniel Kahneman, and David Schkade. 2000. Assessing Punitive Damages. Pp. 232–58 in *Behavioral Law and Economics*, edited by Cass R. Sunstein. Cambridge: Cambridge University Press.

Svenson, Ola. 1981. Are We All Less Risky and More Skillful Than Our Fellow Drivers? *Acta Psychologica* 47: 143–48.

Svenson, Ola, Fischhoff Baruch, and Donald MacGregor. 1985. Perceived Driving Safety and Seatbelt Usage. *Accident Analysis and Prevention* 17: 119–33.

Taylor, Shelley, and Jonathan Brown. 1988. Illusion and Well-Being: A Social Psychological Perspective on Mental Health. *Psychological Bulletin* 103: 193–210.

Teitelbaum, Joshua C. 2007. A Unilateral Accident Model under Ambiguity. *Journal of Legal Studies* 36: 431–77.

Tversky, Amos, and Daniel Kahneman. 1974. Judgments under Uncertainty: Heuristics and Biases. *Science* 185: 1124–31.

Tversky, Amos, and Daniel Kahneman. 1983. Extension Versus Intuitive Reasoning: The Conjunction Fallacy in Probability Judgment. *Psychological Review* 90: 293–315.

Tversky, Amos, and Daniel Kahneman. 1991. Loss Aversion in Riskless Choice: A Reference-Dependent Model. *Quarterly Journal of Economics* 106(4): 1039–61.

Ulen, Thomas 2005. Human Fallibility and the Forms of Law: The Case of Traffic Safety. Pp. 398–421 in *The Law and Economics of Irrational Behavior*, edited by Francesco Parisi, and Vernon L. Smith. Stanford: Stanford University Press.

van der Kolk, Bessel A., and Rita Fisler. 1995. Dissociation and the Fragmentary Nature of Traumatic Memories: Overview and Exploratory Study. *Journal of Traumatic Stress* 8: 505–25.

Viscusi, W. Kip 1992. *Fatal Tradeoffs: Public and Private Responsibilities for Risk*. New York: Oxford University Press.

Viscusi, W. Kip 2002. *Smoke-Filled Rooms*. Chicago: University of Chicago Press.

Viscusi, W. Kip, and Wesley A. Magat. 1987. *Learning about Risk: Consumer and Worker Responses to Hazard Warnings*. Cambridge, Mass.: Harvard University Press.

Weinstein, Neil D. 1980. Unrealistic Optimism about Future Life Events. *Journal of Personality and Social Psychology* 39: 806–20.

Weinstein, Neil D., and William M. Klein. 2002. Resistance of Personal Risk Perceptions to Debiasing Interventions. Pp. 313–23 in *Heuristics and Biases: The Psychology of Intuitive Judgment*, edited by Thomas Gilovich, Dale Griffin, and Daniel Kahneman. New York: Cambridge University Press.

Zamir, Eyal. 2012. Loss Aversion and Law. *Vanderbilt Law Review* 65: 829–94.

Zamir, Eyal, and Ilana Ritov. 2012. Loss Aversion, Omission Bias and the Burden of Proof in Civil Litigation. *Journal of Legal Studies* 41(1): 165–207.

# 9.   Law and economics and tort litigation institutions: theory and experiments
*Claudia M. Landeo**

## 1.   INTRODUCTION

In tort litigation, delayed settlement or impasse imposes high costs on the parties and society.[1] Litigation institutions might influence social welfare by affecting the likelihood of out-of-court settlement and the potential injurers' investment in product safety. An appropriate design of litigation institutions and tort reform requires good knowledge of the factors that affect litigants' behavior. The combination of theoretical and experimental law and economics, which represents the cornerstone of the application of the scientific method, might enhance our understanding of the effects of litigation institutions and tort reform on settlement and deterrence.

This chapter assesses the interaction between theoretical and experimental law and economics in the study of tort litigation institutions. Special attention is devoted to liability, litigation and tort reform institutions, and to behavioral factors that might affect impasse.

We start our analysis by identifying the methodological aspects of seminal law and economics work on litigation institutions. Law and economics scholars have studied the properties of tort litigation institutions by constructing economic models. The theoretical literature on settlement and litigation has identified two important sources of impasse. First, impasse is attributed to the presence of litigants' divergent beliefs about the trial outcome (Landes 1971; Gould 1973; Posner 1977; Shavell 1982; Priest and Klein 1984). The high degree of uncertainty that characterizes judicial adjudication might be the source of this divergence. The possibility of systematic egocentric biases in the litigants' beliefs is not considered in these frameworks.[2] A second source of impasse is related to asymmetries of information between the litigants about the strength of the plaintiff's case. Using game-theoretic tools, scholars have demonstrated that asymmetric information might generate impasse even in the absence of divergent beliefs (Cooter, Marks, and Mnookin 1982; Png 1983; Bebchuck 1984; Reinganum and Wilde 1986; Schweizer 1989;

*   I acknowledge research support from the National Science Foundation (Award No. SES-1155761). Part of this research was conducted at Yale Law School and Harvard Law School, where I served as a visiting Senior Research Scholar in Law. I am grateful to both institutions for their hospitality. I wish to thank Kathy Zeiler for insightful comments.

[1]   The direct costs of tort litigation in the U.S. reached $247 billion in 2006 (Towers Perrin Tillinghast 2007). Tort costs in the U.S. (as a percentage of the gross domestic product) were double the cost in Germany and more than three times the cost in France or the United Kingdom in 2004 (Towers Perrin Tillinghast 2005).

[2]   Hence, the cognitive processes that originate these divergent beliefs are not studied in these models.

Spier 1992, 1994; Hylton 1993).[3] Whether litigants exhibit divergent beliefs and the nature of this divergence are ultimately empirical questions. Motivated by these empirical concerns, law and economics scholars have applied experimental economics methods in the study of litigation institutions.[4]

We extend our analysis by assessing the components of the experimental environments used in more recent law and economics work of litigation and identifying the main findings of these studies. Experimental economics work has investigated the behavioral factors that might generate litigants' divergent beliefs in litigation environments. Babcock et al. (1995a, 1995b, 1997, Babcock and Loewenstein 1997) and Loewenstein et al. (1993) identify an important source of divergence that rests on a judgment error called self-serving bias. In legal contexts, self-serving bias refers to the litigant's biased belief that the court decision will favor his case. This bias is posited to originate from the egocentric interpretation of facts associated with the legal dispute. As a result of the litigants' self-serving beliefs, a higher likelihood of impasse might be observed. Babcock and Pogarsky (1999), Pogarsky and Babcock (2001) and Landeo (2009) provide experimental evidence of the effects of tort reform in the presence of self-serving bias.[5] Importantly, empirical work by Babcock et al. (1996, 1997; Babcock and Loewenstein 1997) and Eisenberg (1994) suggest that self-serving bias is generally robust in terms of debiasing interventions and litigants' experience. In response to the experimental evidence regarding litigants' self-serving beliefs, new theoretical models of liability and litigation have been developed.

Finally, we evaluate the main elements of recent theoretical studies on litigation and the contributions of this work. Building upon Bebchuk's (1984) framework, Farmer and Pecorino (2002) study settlement and litigation under self-serving bias and asymmetric information. They find that self-serving bias operates as a commitment device for the recipient of a settlement offer. As a result, the likelihood of impasse increases.[6] Landeo, Nikitin, and Izmalkov (2013) extend Reinganum and Wilde's (1986) signaling model to investigate the effects of self-serving bias on the potential injurer's incentives for care, litigation outcomes, and social welfare. Their findings suggest that self-serving bias negatively affects the defendant's expenditures on accident prevention, and, hence, increases the likelihood of an accident. Their results also indicate that self-serving bias increases the likelihood of impasse and might be welfare-reducing. Next, Landeo, Nikitin and Izmalkov (2013) use their framework to assess the effects of damage caps. Their model predicts that caps might reduce the incentives for care and increase the likelihood of an accident. Importantly, their results suggest that self-serving bias might reverse the positive

---

[3]   See Png (1987), Hylton (2002), Landeo and Nikitin (2006), and Landeo et al. (2007b) for models of liability and litigation.

[4]   Empirical studies of legal institutions can be broadly classified as follows: (1) econometric analysis of naturally generated data; (2) experimental law and economics studies (lab and field experiments); and (3) experimental social psychology studies. This chapter focuses on the interaction between experimental law and economics (lab experiments) and theoretical law and economics in the analysis of tort litigation institutions.

[5]   See Glöckner and Engel (2013) for experimental evidence of cognitive limitations in interactions between defense attorneys and prosecutors, and Eigen and Listokin (2012) for evidence of cognitive limitations of legal advocates in moot court competitions.

[6]   Deffains and Langlais (2009) provide a different extension of Bebchuk's (1984) framework that allows for self-serving bias and risk aversion.

effect of damage caps on impasse observed in theoretical environments that do not allow for litigants' egocentric biases.[7]

Our analysis suggests a productive interaction between theoretical and experimental law and economics in the study of litigation institutions. Specifically, seminal theoretical law and economics work on litigation institutions has indeed guided empirical research. The new experimental economics studies have provided empirical evidence of decision-making processes and behavioral factors that might affect litigants' beliefs and litigation outcomes. This recent knowledge regarding litigants' cognitive biases has motivated the construction of economic models of litigation involving more empirically relevant assumptions regarding litigants' beliefs.

Regarding the contributions of empirical legal studies to law and economics, Professor Cooter (2011, pp. 1475 and 1483; emphasis added) states that

> Empirical Legal Studies . . . is the maturation of law and economics . . . into normal science . . . Together they constitute the long-awaited science of law.[8] The peripheral influence of [law and economics] on law's content is sobering. To make [empirical legal studies and law and economics] central to law's content, scholars must show that correct legal reasoning often requires *scientific prediction* of law's effects.

The analysis presented in this chapter indicates that, by complementing theoretical analysis with experimental economics and more traditional empirical methods, law and economics scholars are contributing to the construction of the science of law. Importantly, as a result of the application of the scientific method, the contributions of law and economics to law's content and to the design of legal institutions might be strengthened.

Although this chapter is motivated by tort litigation institutions, we believe that the insights presented here apply to other contexts as well. Bargaining and impasse are prevalent in environments such as labor contract negotiations (Farber 1978; Kennan and Wilson 1989, 1992; Babcock and Olson 1992; Babcock, Wang and Loewenstein 1996) and partnership dissolution procedures (Brooks, Landeo and Spier 2010; Landeo and Spier 2013, 2014a, 2014b). Given that individuals run firms and human agents negotiate contracts, it is reasonable to expect that cognitive biases might also be present in these settings.[9] Hence, experimental work on the behavioral factors that affect impasse in these environments might contribute to the construction of more empirically relevant theories.

The chapter is organized as follows. Section 2 outlines seminal theoretical work on litigation. Section 3 evaluates experimental economics work on tort litigation institutions and cognitive biases. Section 4 discusses new theoretical frameworks motivated by this experimental work. Section 5 presents concluding remarks.

---

[7] See Watanabe (2010) for a recent model of filing and litigation under divergent beliefs and complete information; and Bar-Gill (2007) for a theoretical analysis of the persistence of optimistic beliefs under an evolutionary game-theoretic approach. See Yildiz (2003) for a more general bargaining model with divergent beliefs.

[8] In contrast to revolutionary science, normal science evolves by incremental improvements of theories, motivated by empirical tests of hypotheses (Kuhn 1996). See Cooter (2011) for an extensive discussion of the scientific method applied to the study of law.

[9] Marital dissolution environments (Wilkinson-Ryan and Small 2008) represent an additional interesting application.

## 2.   SEMINAL THEORETICAL WORK ON LITIGATION

Seminal law and economics work has used economic models to study the properties of tort litigation institutions. The theoretical literature on settlement and litigation has identified two important sources of impasse: divergence beliefs and asymmetric information.

First, impasse is attributed to the presence of litigants' divergent beliefs about the trial outcome. For instance, Shavell (1982) studies settlement and litigation using a theoretical framework that allows for divergent beliefs about the outcome at trial and risk-aversion.[10] In this setting, litigants' estimates of their chances of prevailing at trial, their estimated judgment of amounts, the legal costs, and their attitudes toward risk, influence the likelihood of an out-of-court settlement. Shavell's model predicts that a trial occurs if the plaintiff's estimate of the expected award at trial exceeds the defendant's estimate by at least the sum of their legal costs.[11] Priest and Klein (1984) investigate the selection of cases that proceed to trial by using a framework that allows for errors in the litigants' estimates of the trial outcome.[12] The errors are assumed to be independent, random variables with zero expectation and identical standard errors. In other words, the authors assume that the litigants form independent, unbiased estimates of the true value of the dispute. Trial occurs when the plaintiff's estimate of the award at trial exceeds the defendant's estimate by enough to offset the incentive for settlement generated by trial costs.[13] Their findings also suggest that the cases that go to trial are characterized by a 50 percent chance of the plaintiff's success at trial regardless of the applied substantive standard of law (negligence or strict liability).[14] More generally, these theoretical frameworks: (1) allow for uncertainty but do not allow for asymmetric information; (2) allow for divergent litigants' assessments of the expected trial outcome but do not allow for biased beliefs (i.e., do not consider role-specific biases), and do not explicitly model the possible sources of divergence; and (3) do not explicitly model the bargaining process.

Second, impasse is attributed to information asymmetries. Using game-theoretic environments that explicitly model the bargaining process and common beliefs (also known as common priors), law and economics scholars study how the likelihood of impasse might be affected by asymmetric information between the litigants about the trial

---

[10]   Specifically, this framework allows for divergent beliefs about the likelihood of prevailing at trial and the amount of the judgment in the event the plaintiff succeeds at trial.

[11]   In other words, trial occurs if the plaintiff's estimate of his expected award at trial net of litigation costs exceeds the defendant's estimate of his expected total loss at trial including litigation costs. The model also predicts that risk aversion increases the likelihood of out-of-court settlement. Settlement allows the parties to avoid the risk associated with going to trial.

[12]   See also Landes (1971), Gould (1973), and Posner (1977).

[13]   More general bargaining models (Crawford 1981, p. 208) predict that, in the presence of uncertainty and divergent beliefs, "[T]he existence of the contract zone [i.e., the set of mutually beneficial outcomes] is guaranteed unless the beliefs are relatively too 'optimistic.'" See Coursey and Stanley (1988) and Babcock and Landeo (2004) for experimental evidence on the effects of the size of the contract zone on the likelihood of impasse in litigation environments.

[14]   This result holds when the amount the loser pays is equal to the amount the winner gains (i.e., when the stakes are symmetric). Asymmetric stakes might occur in situations in which the resolution of the dispute affects the defendant beyond the payment at trial. Consider, for instance, the reputational costs for the defendant (firm) in the case of a verdict in favor of the plaintiff (consumer) in a products liability case. See Priest and Klein (1984) for details.

outcome. For instance, Bebchuk (1984) constructs a model of settlement and litigation in which the defendant has private information about the probability of the plaintiff's prevailing at trial (i.e., known as the defendant's type).[15] The sequence of moves is as follows. First, the uninformed plaintiff makes a settlement offer. After observing the offer, the informed defendant decides whether to accept or reject it. Rejection induces a costly trial. In this framework, impasse occurs in equilibrium.[16] Bebchuk's (1984) findings also suggest that an increase in the size of the potential award at trial, a reduction in litigation costs, or an expansion of uncertainty (i.e., an expansion in the range of defendant's types) increases the likelihood of trial. Reinganum and Wilde (1986) study a litigation game between an informed plaintiff and an uninformed defendant, in which the informed plaintiff makes the out-of-court settlement proposal. After observing the proposal, the uninformed defendant decides whether to accept or reject the offer. As in Bebchuk (1984), rejection results in a costly trial. In Reinganum and Wilde's (1986) setting, the plaintiff's settlement demand can serve as a signaling device because the cost of disputes is lower for a more severely damaged plaintiff, who can expect to get a higher award at trial. Reinganum and Wilde's (1986) findings suggest that, even in cases in which both parties share common beliefs about the likelihood of a judgment in favor of the plaintiff, asymmetric information about the damages suffered by the plaintiff suffices to generate impasse.[17]

The next two sections discuss experimental work and new theoretical developments motivated by these experimental findings. We evaluate the interaction between theoretical and experimental economics by focusing on litigation institutions and cognitive biases.

## 3. EXPERIMENTAL LAW AND ECONOMICS WORK ON LITIGATION

This section first outlines the main components of the method used in experimental law and economics. It then discusses experimental work on litigation institutions and cognitive biases. Finally, it presents empirical evidence on the robustness of the self-serving bias.

---

[15] The defendant's type indicates the strength of the plaintiff's case: defendants who are low types face plaintiffs with a relatively low probability of prevailing at trial.

[16] The presence of information asymmetries explains this result. Specifically, if the plaintiff knew the probability of prevailing at trial, then the plaintiff would make a settlement demand that the defendant would be willing to accept. The optimal settlement demand for the uninformed plaintiff, however, will be an amount that a low-type defendant (the defendant for which the case is associated with a low probability of the plaintiff's prevailing at trial) will reject.

[17] Perfect Bayesian equilibrium is the equilibrium concept applied in these settings. See also Cooter, Marks and Mnookin (1982), Png (1983), Schweizer (1989), Spier (1992, 1994), and Hylton (1993) for seminal work on pretrial bargaining. Png (1987), Hylton (2002), Landeo and Nikitin (2006), and Landeo et al. (2007b) extend these models by analyzing the potential injurer's investment in product safety. See Waldfogel (1998) for an empirical test of models of divergent (but unbiased) beliefs and asymmetric information.

### 3.1 Methodological Aspects

Experimental law and economics refers to the application of experimental economics methods to the study of legal institutions and business practices relevant to the design of legal institutions.[18]

Controlled laboratory experiments represent an optimal methodology for causality assessment (Falk and Heckman 2009) in litigation environments. In settings outside the laboratory, although researchers might be able to observe the final outcomes of pretrial bargaining and the impact of tort reform, the processes associated with pretrial bargaining negotiations and the factors that affect those processes are generally private information. In fact, data that would permit researchers to perfectly isolate the causal connection between impasse and various behavioral factors (such as cognitive limitations) and institutional interventions (such as tort reform) are scarce or inexistent. Conducting experiments to assess the predictions from theoretical models is, therefore, a valuable complement to more traditional empirical analysis.

#### 3.1.1 Types of studies

Experimental law and economics work on litigation institutions includes: (1) experiments that study behavioral factors such as cognitive limitations that might affect litigation outcomes and the effectiveness of tort reform;[19] and (2) studies that test the predictions from economic models of liability and litigation.[20] Both types of studies involve experimental environments aligned with the theoretical frameworks, and pay-for-performance schemes that replicate the incentives considered in the theory.[21] These studies do not involve deception.[22]

---

[18]  See Smith (1976), Plott (1982), Roth (1986, 1995), and Davis and Holt (1993) for seminal discussions about experimental economics methods. See Croson (2005) and Croson and Gächter (2010) for more recent excellent discussions of experimental economics methods. See Roth (2008) for a discussion of the contributions of experimental economics methods to market design. See Hoffman and Spitzer (1985), McAdams (2000), Croson (2002, 2009), Talley and Camerer (2007), and Arlen and Talley (2008) for surveys regarding the application of experimental economics methods to law and economics. See Landeo (2015) for a discussion of experimental economics methods applied to the study of antitrust institutions, and an analysis of the contributions of experimental law and economics to the study of vertical restraints and antitrust.

[19]  See Thaler (1987) for a discussion of behavioral anomalies. This chapter focuses on this type of study.

[20]  For instance, Croson and Johnson (2000) experimentally study the power of institutional rules on pretrial bargaining in environments in which inappropriate taking might occur. Babcock and Landeo (2004) experimentally study the effects of asymmetric information and a settlement escrows institution on settlement and litigation. Landeo et al. (2007a) experimentally assess the effects of tort reform on liability and litigation in the presence of asymmetric information. Although the findings from these studies support the predictions of the standard theories under investigation, they also suggest the presence of behavioral factors such as fairness considerations and cognitive limitations.

[21]  See Smith (1976). Experimental economics methods are generally criticized because of the size of subjects' payments, and the degree of alignment of these incentives with the economic consequences of choices in settings outside the laboratory. Evidence regarding the effects of the size of payoffs is inconclusive and seems to depend on the experimental environment (Falk and Heckman 2009; Camerer and Hogarth 1999).

[22]  The fields of economics and psychology fundamentally differ on the use of deception. Economics forbids deception while psychology sometimes employs it.

While these two types of studies are similar in many ways, they differ fundamentally along two dimensions: context and the population from which subjects are drawn. Economic theories consist of abstract representations applicable to different situations and individuals. Experiments that test economic models generally involve minimal context[23] and the use of university students as subjects.[24] As mentioned by Croson (2002), although both types of studies must have a high degree of internal validity (i.e., their experimental environments should be aligned with the theoretical frameworks), the experimental environments used in studies devoted to investigating behavioral anomalies should also allow for the elicitation of these anomalies. The degree of context deemed acceptable is related to this point. In particular, studies devoted to assessing cognitive biases should encompass a degree of context necessary to trigger these anomalies (if they exist).[25] In addition, if the anomalies are expected to occur in specific groups of individuals, these groups should be used as subjects. Finally, studies that evaluate cognitive biases generally include post-experimental questionnaires to explore the sources of the anomalies.[26]

---

[23] The lab implementation of a theoretical setting generally involves the use of a simple context, i.e., a simple environment where the theory applies. For instance, the experimental environment associated with a pretrial bargaining model might resemble a simple bilateral bargaining setting. Labels such as player A (representing the plaintiff) and player B (representing the defendant) might be used to describe the roles played by the subjects. The use of minimal contextual features ensures control over subjects' subjective interpretations of labels. Control facilitates replicability, i.e., the replication of the study by other researchers with the purpose of assessing the robustness of findings.

[24] Experimental studies devoted to studying the effects of subject pools in context-free experiments do not suggest significant differences in the behavior of undergraduate students and other populations (Fréchette 2015).

[25] Croson (2002) argues that "the conditions in the experiment should be such that the traditional theory can make a behavioral prediction. However, the experiment should be designed to create the anomaly as well" (p. 932). In particular, if the experiment is motivated by the results observed in a previous experimental economics lab study, then the experimental environment (including the use of context) used in the previous experiment should be replicated. If, on the other hand, the experiment is motivated by regularities observed in naturally occurring settings that challenge a theoretical framework (i.e., non-random behavioral deviations), the features of the theory should be implemented in the lab *and* the experimental environment should allow for the elicitation of the anomalies. A simple example might illustrate this point. Suppose that the anomaly refers to divergent and biased beliefs of the parties involved in bargaining negotiations. Suppose also that these cognitive limitations are role-specific biases and are elicited in environments characterized by rich context and ambiguity. Finally, suppose that these cognitive limitations challenge previous bargaining theories that assume divergent but unbiased beliefs. The experimental environment used to assess these anomalies should implement the components of the bargaining theory. In addition, the experimental environment should include rich context and ambiguity. The lab implementation might then result in an environment where the theory applies and where the anomaly might be elicited.

[26] A third type of experimental studies is devoted to assessing the effectiveness of specific policies before these policies are implemented (testbed policy experiments). Hong and Plott (1982) present seminal work on the effects of a policy change proposed by the Interstate Commerce Commission. (See Plott 1994, for a general discussion of testbed experiments.) Although this type of experimental study has not been used in liability and litigation settings yet, the information provided by these experiments might also provide good feedback to theorists and contribute to the improvement of litigation institution design. The previous classification follows Roth (1986) and

### 3.1.2   Contributions

Important contributions are derived from the application of experimental economics methods to the study of litigation institutions. Experimental law and economics work can help advance the knowledge of the factors that affect litigation processes and outcomes. Specifically, studies devoted to investigating cognitive biases in litigation environments might provide evidence of the importance of these previously non-modeled behavioral factors and, hence, contribute to the construction of more empirically relevant models of litigation. Experimental studies conducted to test the theoretical predictions of economic models of liability and litigation might provide evidence of the robustness of the theories. These studies might also reveal the presence of previously non-modeled factors that influence the impact of tort litigation institutions, and hence, might provide useful feedback to theorists. Finally, experimental studies involve the laboratory implementation of simplified versions of complex theories. These simple environments might facilitate policy-makers' understanding of the theories, and hence, might strengthen the contributions of law and economic theories to the design of litigation institutions and tort reform.

### 3.2   Experimental Evidence on Pretrial Bargaining and Cognitive Biases

As previously mentioned, seminal models of settlement and litigation (Shavell 1982; Priest and Klein 1984) predict that, in the presence of uncertain but symmetric information, litigants' divergent (but unbiased) beliefs regarding the expected outcomes at trial might preclude settlement.[27] More recently, game-theoretic models with common beliefs (Bebchuck 1984; Reinganum and Wilde 1986) find that asymmetric information between the litigants about the outcome at trial might generate impasse even in the absence of divergent beliefs. The importance of litigants' divergent beliefs on impasse and the nature of this divergence are empirical questions.

Babcock et al. (1995a, 1995b), Loewenstein et al. (1993), and Babcock et al. (1997; Babcock and Loewenstein 1997) experimentally investigate the behavioral factors that might generate litigants' divergent beliefs, and, hence, might influence the likelihood of out-of-court settlement agreements.[28] They propose an explanation for impasse that rests on a judgment error called self-serving bias. Self-serving bias, as applied in this context, refers to the litigant's biased beliefs that the court decision will favor his case due to the interpretation of the facts of the dispute in an egocentric manner. This work builds on seminal research in social psychology regarding cognitive biases (Messick and Santis 1979; Ross and Sicoly 1982; Danitioso et al. 1990; Kunda 1987, 1990; Thompson and Loewenstein 1992). In this literature, self-serving bias is attributed to motivated reasoning, which can be understood as individuals' propensity to reason in a way that supports their subjectively favored propositions by attending only to some of the available information. In particular, Kunda's (1990) experimental work suggests that "[p]eople rely on cognitive processes and representations to arrive at their desired conclusions, but

---

Croson (2002). Roth (1986) presents a general classification of experimental economics studies. Croson (2002) applies Roth's (1986) classification to experimental law and economics studies.

[27]   Settlement will occur if there is a non-empty contract zone (a set of mutually beneficial agreements).

[28]   See also Babcock and Loewenstein (1997) for a survey of their work on self-serving bias.

motivation plays a role in determining which of these will be used on a given occasion" (p. 481). "[S]elf-serving biases are best explained as resulting from cognitive processes guided by motivation because they do not occur in the absence of motivational pressures" (Kunda 1987, p. 636).

Babcock and colleagues hypothesize that, in complex environments characterized by ambiguity, even when the parties are exposed to the exact same information, they might arrive at expectations of an adjudicated settlement that are biased in a self-serving manner. As a result, the likelihood of impasse might be negatively affected by the magnitude of self-serving bias. Importantly, given that litigation outcomes might influence the decisions of potential injurers regarding their expenditures on accident prevention (Png 1987; Hylton 2002; Landeo and Nikitin 2006, 2007a, 2007b), self-serving bias might also negatively affect social welfare and the effectiveness of tort reform.[29]

For instance, Babcock et al. (1995a) provides a test of the existence of the self-serving bias in litigation environments, and the causal relation between the self-serving bias and impasse. The authors manipulate the magnitude of the self-serving bias by informing subjects of their roles at different points of the experimental session, and then analyze the effects of this manipulation on the likelihood of out-of-court settlement. Their experimental environment replicates a pretrial bargaining game between a plaintiff and a defendant. Structured bargaining with face-to-face communication, rich but symmetric information (i.e., the same complex information about a legal case is provided to both subjects), and human subjects paid according to their performance are used in this experiment. An experimental currency, the experiment dollar, is adopted. The conversion rate of experiment dollars/U.S. dollars is 10,000 experimental dollars to 1 U.S. dollar. The subject pool consists of public policy and law students.

The authors' full-context experimental environment is motivated by an actual legal case in Texas. It refers to a claim for damages resulting from an accident in which a motorcyclist and an automobile driver are involved. In this legal case, the plaintiff (the motorcyclist) is suing the defendant (the car driver) for $100,000. The material provided to the subjects includes witnesses' testimony, police reports, maps, and litigants' testimony. Subjects playing the roles of plaintiff and defendant are given the same exact information and are informed that their partners will receive the same information.[30] They are also

---

[29] The core features of the experimental environments Babcock and colleagues used are as follows: (1) an informational structure aligned with seminal theoretical models of litigation, i.e., uncertain but symmetric information; (2) a structured bargaining process (a sequence of negotiation rounds with predetermined length and unstructured face-to-face communication); (3) contextual features motivated by a simplified version of an actual legal case; (4) elicitation of judgments and choices; (5) pay-for-performance incentive schemes; and (6) university students used as subjects. Multiple experiments are conducted using the same basic experimental design. This feature of Babcock and colleagues' work allows them to test the robustness of their initial findings across subject pools, and to explore additional factors that might originate these initial findings. See Babcock and Loewenstein (1997) for a discussion of the features of these experimental studies.

[30] Lab studies devoted to studying role-specific biases involve the use of complex context characterized by ambiguity. Labels such as plaintiff and defendant characterize the assigned roles. As mentioned before, the use of minimal context and simple labels ensures control over subjective interpretations of labels. In this study, the use of labels to characterize the roles is aligned with the requirement of implementing a complex context.

informed that the same material was provided to an actual judge in Texas, who decided the amount of the award that the subject-plaintiff would receive at trial (a number between $0 and $100,000) in case of impasse.[31] To preserve ambiguity, the judge's exact award is not disclosed to the subjects until the end of the session. The judge's predetermined award ($30,560) is applied across all sessions and conditions.

Three experimental tasks are included in this study. Subjects are asked to state their judgments about various aspects of the legal case, to participate in pretrial bargaining negotiations, and to answer a questionnaire. The first experimental task is implemented after subjects read the case material, but before they negotiate. Each subject is required to make two judgments: (1) a settlement amount the subject would consider to be fair; and (2) a best guess regarding the amount of the award that the judge chose. Before completing this experimental task, subjects are informed that their responses will be not disclosed to the other party.[32] Subjects receive monetary incentives aligned with the precision of their judgment—a bonus of $1 at the end of the session if their prediction of the judge's award is within $5,000 (plus or minus) of the judge's actual award.

The session proceeds with the next experimental task, the participation in pretrial bargaining negotiations. The subjects have 30 minutes to negotiate an agreement. The 30-minute period is divided into six 5-minute rounds. Face-to-face communication is allowed. At the end of each round, both parties simultaneously submit settlement proposals. If the defendant's offer is greater than the plaintiff's request (i.e., a non-empty contract zone exists), an agreement is reached. The transfer is set at the midpoint. In case of disagreement, $5,000 in litigation costs is imposed, and subjects move to the next round. In case of negotiation failure in the sixth 5-minute round, the judge's decision is imposed.

Finally, a questionnaire is administered. Subjects are asked to state their perceptions of how a judge would rate the importance of 16 predetermined arguments (eight favoring the plaintiff, and eight favoring the defendant) in determining the award. The purpose of this instrument is to assess whether the subjects' roles affect their perceptions of the specific facts of the case. At the end of the session, subjects are paid for their participation in the study. The components of the subjects' payment are as follows. In addition to the potential bonus related to the judgment task, the payment involves a fixed participation fee and game earnings. The game earnings represent the pay-for-performance component of the pretrial bargaining negotiations task. Game earnings are aligned with the negotiation outcomes.

Two experimental conditions are implemented. In the first condition, subjects are informed about their randomly-assigned role before reading the case material. In the

---

[31]   The researchers could provide information about the actual judgment. Instead, they used the award provided by another judge. This procedure was adopted and described to the subjects to preclude subjects from believing that the case was chosen because the judgment award fell within a desired range (for instance, because the amount at trial was relatively high or was relatively low). Using these sorts of techniques, the design controls for factors that might affect the subjects' formation of beliefs, and, hence, their pretrial bargaining decisions. See Babcock et al. (1995a).

[32]   This feature of the experimental design allows the researchers to control for strategic factors that might affect litigants' judgments. For instance, when the plaintiff's judgment about a fair settlement amount is disclosed to the defendant, the plaintiff might behave strategically and inflate the amount to induce the defendant to propose a higher out-of-court settlement offer. In the absence of disclosure, the plaintiff's judgment is not affected by strategic considerations.

second condition, subjects first read the case material and state their judgments about a fair settlement and about the judge's award, and then are informed about their roles. These two conditions create variation in the magnitude of the self-serving bias. Following the findings from social psychology, the authors hypothesize that self-serving interpretations of fairness would be stronger in the condition in which the roles are assigned before the subjects read the case material and assess fairness. As a result, they expect a lower likelihood of out-of-court settlement under that condition.

Their findings indicate that role assignment elicited self-serving bias. Three within-condition measures of self-serving bias are constructed. The first two indicators measure the difference between the plaintiff's and defendant's assessment of a fair settlement amount, and the plaintiff's and defendant's assessment of the judge's award. Both indicators were significantly different from zero in the condition in which roles were assigned before the case was read, suggesting the presence of self-serving bias. The last indicator measures the difference between the plaintiff's and defendant's assessments of the importance of arguments favoring each litigant. Comparisons of these measures across conditions indicate that the magnitude of self-serving bias was higher in the condition in which roles were assigned before the case was read. Importantly, their results suggest that the likelihood of impasse and the time needed to achieve an out-of-court settlement were higher when the role was assigned before the subjects read the case material. Hence, the findings support the claim that out-of-court settlement might be negatively affected by the self-serving biases of the litigants.

### 3.3  Experimental Evidence on Tort Reform and Cognitive Biases

Tort reform has been motivated by the common perception that excessive damage awards promote unnecessary and costly litigation (Danzon 1986) and the escalation of liability insurance premiums (Sloane 1993). Some reforms take the form of caps or limits on damage awards (Avraham and Bustos 2010), while others mandate that a portion of the award be allocated to the plaintiff with the remainder going to the state (Landeo and Nikitin 2006; Landeo et al. 2007a).[33]

Seminal theoretical work on litigation environments that assume unbiased litigants' beliefs suggests that a reduction in the expected award at trial (a cap) increases the likelihood of out-of-court settlement.[34]

More recently, as previously described, experimental work on cognitive biases in litigation environments (Loewenstein et al. 1993; Babcock et al. 1995a) provides evidence of the presence of role-induced biases. In addition, findings from social psychology in ambiguity environments suggest that the formation of beliefs can reflect anchoring mechanisms

---

[33]  See Arlen (2000) for a survey of tort reform institutions.

[34]  Under caps, the plaintiff's expected award at trial is lower, and hence, plaintiffs are willing to accept lower settlement offers. This theoretical result holds in litigation environments characterized by common and unbiased litigants' beliefs (Bebchuck 1984), and in environments with divergent but unbiased litigants' beliefs (Priest and Klein 1984). However, in a model of liability and litigation with common and unbiased beliefs, Png (1987) finds that the effects of a reduction in the award at trial on the (unconditional) likelihood of impasse is generally ambiguous due to the effects of this tort reform on the incentives for care (and hence, on the likelihood of an accident).

or adjustments toward a reference point, and that these adjustments can be affected by self-serving bias. In litigation environments, anchoring mechanisms might characterize the influence of a damage cap on litigants' beliefs. Babcock and Pogarsky (1999) and Pogarsky and Babcock (2001) hypothesize that motivated anchoring or the self-serving adjustment of the litigants' beliefs toward the cap will occur when the value of the actual claim is below the damage cap amount.[35] When the actual claim value is above the cap, on the other hand, the cap will truncate litigants' beliefs. Hence, in environments characterized by ambiguity, damage caps might affect litigation outcomes and litigants' beliefs.[36]

Babcock and Pogarsky (1999) experimentally study the effects of damage caps on the likelihood of out-of-court settlement and litigants' beliefs in a litigation environment characterized by ambiguity and a cap set below the actual claim value.[37] Their experimental environment replicates a pretrial bargaining game between a plaintiff and a defendant (roles randomly assigned), and provides rich but symmetric information about a legal case. Subjects, MBA and public policy students attending negotiation courses, are rewarded according to performance. The pay-for-performance scheme is set in terms of grades. Better negotiation outcomes earned students better grades.[38] Two experimental conditions are implemented, cap and non-cap conditions. The only difference between these two conditions is the limit on the award at trial under the cap condition.

Babcock and Pogarsky's experimental environment is motivated by a legal case involving a personal injury lawsuit filed by a pedestrian who fell through a street vent (the plaintiff) against the manufacturer of the vent (the defendant). In this legal case, the plaintiff seeks $1,000,000 in damages for pain and suffering. Subjects playing the roles of plaintiff and defendant are given the same case information and know that their partners will receive the same information. The material provided to the subjects includes witnesses' testimony, police reports, maps, and litigants' testimony. Subjects are also informed that the same material was provided to an actual judge, who decided the plaintiff-subject award in the event of settlement impasse.[39] In the cap condition, subjects are informed that the amount of damages a judge could award to the plaintiff for pain and suffering was limited by law to $250,000. Note that the cap amount is lower than the value of the amount sought by the plaintiff. The main experimental tasks used in Babcock et al. (1995a) are also implemented in this study.[40]

---

[35]   Pogarsky and Babcock (2001) refer to this situation as a "non-binding cap."

[36]   Following the theoretical literature on settlement and litigation, Babcock and Pogarsky (1999) and Pogarsky and Babcock (2001) abstract from the effects of the jury on the plaintiff's award at trial. Theoretical and experimental work on the effects of self-serving bias and tort reform in environments that allow for group decision-making represents an interesting extension.

[37]   See Landeo (2009) for an experimental study on coherence-based reasoning (bi-directionality between choices and beliefs) in litigation environments.

[38]   Although this study implemented a pay-for-performance scheme, unnecessary noise related to the subjects' subjective valuation of grades could have been avoided if dollars had been used instead.

[39]   The exact amount decided by the judge is not told to the subjects to preserve ambiguity. The judge's predetermined award, equal to $770,000, is announced at the end of the session, across all sessions in the non-cap condition. In the cap condition, the judge's award is truncated to $250,000.

[40]   Specifically, judgments and pretrial bargaining are elicited. Before negotiation starts, subjects are required to make three judgments. First, subjects are requested to state their judgment about a

Babcock and Pogarsky's (1999) findings suggest that the litigants' assessment of fairness and their predicted trial outcomes determine their pretrial bargaining choices (i.e., the litigants' beliefs influence their choices). Their results also indicate the presence of self-serving bias, and that damage caps reduce the magnitude of the bias.[41] Finally, a higher likelihood of out-of-court settlement is observed under the cap condition. This last result might be explained by the lower uncertainty and lower self-serving bias in the cap condition.

Pogarsky and Babcock (2001) extend this work by analyzing how a damage cap that is higher than the actual claim affects litigation outcomes and litigants' beliefs. This study follows the protocol applied in Babcock and Pogarsky (1999) with a few changes. In the current experiment, the severity of the plaintiff's injuries is reduced, and the cap is set at $1,000,000. Pay-for-performance is set in monetary terms.[42] Game earnings are aligned with the negotiation outcomes. The experimental currency is the experimental dollar (50,000 experimental dollars equal 1 U.S. dollar). As in the previous study, two tasks are included in this experiment. Subjects are asked to state their judgments about the judge's award at trial, and are asked to participate in a pretrial bargaining negotiation. The two conditions studied are cap and non-cap.[43]

The results indicate that litigants' beliefs about the size of the award are affected by the cap due to a motivated anchoring mechanism. The magnitude of the self-serving biases is significantly higher under the cap condition.[44] As a result, a higher likelihood of impasse and a higher settlement amount are observed in the cap condition. Remember that the results from Babcock and Pogarsky's (1999) study on binding caps indicate that a relatively low cap reduces the magnitude of the self-serving bias. Hence, the findings from these two studies suggest that the effects of damage caps on litigants' beliefs and litigation outcomes depend on the relationship between the size of the cap relative to the underlying claim value.

---

fair settlement amount. Second, subjects are asked to state their judgment about the judge's award. Before completing this task, subjects are informed that their chosen judgments will not be disclosed to the other party. Third, subjects' reservation values are elicited. Specifically, plaintiffs are asked their minimum acceptable offer, and defendants are asked their maximum acceptable offer. Subjects receive monetary incentives aligned with the precision of their prediction of the judge's award. A bonus consisting of three lottery tickets is provided at the end of the session if the prediction of the judge's award is within $25,000 (plus or minus) of the judge's actual award. Then, the pretrial bargaining negotiation begins. The subjects have 20 minutes to negotiate an agreement. The 20-minute period is divided into four 5-minute rounds. At the end of each round, both parties simultaneously and privately submit offers. If the defendant's offer is greater than the plaintiff's request, an out-of-court settlement agreement is reached. The transfer is set at the midpoint. In case of disagreement, $10,000 in litigation costs is imposed, and subjects move to the next round. In case of negotiation failure in the fourth 5-minute round, the judge's decision is imposed. The exact amount decided by the judge is not told to the subjects to preserve ambiguity. The judge's predetermined award, equal to $325,000, is applied at the end of the session, across sessions and conditions.

[41]   The magnitude of the self-serving bias is represented by the disparity in litigants' predicted trial award. The cap significantly reduces this disparity.

[42]   In Babcock and Pogarsky's (1999) study, pay-for-performance is set in terms of grades.

[43]   The judge's award is equal to $325,000.

[44]   The magnitude of the self-serving bias is represented by the disparity in the litigants' predicted trial award. This disparity significantly increases with the cap.

### 3.4   Empirical Evidence on the Robustness of Self-Serving Bias

Debiasing interventions in pretrial bargaining environments refer to techniques intended to reduce the magnitude of self-serving bias as a way to promote out-of-court settlement. Previous literature indicates that self-serving bias is generally robust in terms of debiasing interventions and experience.

Babcock and Loewenstein (1997) report the findings of two debiasing interventions. The first intervention, implemented in Babcock et al.'s (1995a) experimental paradigm is as follows. After the roles are assigned and subjects read the case material but before they state their judgments about fairness and predictions of the judge's award, subjects receive information (a paragraph) describing self-serving bias and its consequences. A short test is then administered to check the subjects' understanding of the paragraph describing the bias. They find that informing the subjects about the bias did not affect the differences in litigants' expectations or the likelihood of out-of-court settlement. The second intervention, also implemented in Babcock et al.'s (1995a) paradigm, involves the following features. Before negotiations take place, subjects are asked to write an essay stating arguments in favor of their opponent's case. This procedure had a marginal effect on the litigants' expectations but in a direction opposite to the expected one. The settlement rate was not affected. Babcock et al. (1997) explore a third debiasing procedure. After the role is assigned and subjects read the case material, they receive information about self-serving bias and its consequences (similar to the first intervention discussed above). They are also told that self-serving bias could arise from the failure to think about the weaknesses of their own case, and are asked to list the weaknesses of their own case. The findings indicate that this intervention was effective at reducing the differences in the litigants' expectations about the judge's award. The settlement rate also increased.

Field data also suggest that self-serving bias is robust in the face of experience. In fact, seasoned labor negotiators, lawyers, and judges exhibit self-serving bias and other cognitive errors. Babcock et al. (1996) study Pennsylvania school teachers' salary negotiations. In this type of negotiation, the school district and the union representatives commonly use agreements from comparable communities as a reference. Their findings indicate that both parties choose their comparable school districts in a self-serving manner.[45] Eisenberg (1994) analyzes data from a survey eliciting experienced bankruptcy lawyers' and bankruptcy judges' perceptions of the bankruptcy system and lawyers' reports of their performance in bankruptcy cases. Comparisons of judges' and lawyers' responses also suggest the presence of self-serving bias.[46]

---

[45]   This study combines the use of survey data with field data on public school teacher contract negotiation in Pennsylvania. The survey involves data on union and school board negotiators from all school districts in Pennsylvania regarding the list of districts considered as comparable to their own district for the purpose of salary negotiations. Survey participants were assured that their responses would remain confidential. This feature allows the experimenters to control for the effects of strategic factors on the participants' perceptions.

[46]   In this study, experienced lawyers and judges involved in bankruptcy cases were asked questions regarding bankruptcy fees such as how long it takes judges to rule on fee applications and the compliance of lawyers with fee regulations. Comparisons of the responses of judges and lawyers suggest the presence of self-serving bias. For instance, 78 percent of judges indicated that they rule on interim fee applications at the fee hearing stage (i.e., at an early stage of the bankruptcy process)

## 4. NEW THEORETICAL WORK ON LITIGATION

Findings from experimental economics work on litigation institutions suggest the presence of self-serving bias and provide evidence of its negative effects on the likelihood of impasse. Experimental evidence on debiasing mechanisms and field data on experienced negotiators support claims of the robustness of self-serving bias. This empirical evidence has motivated the development of new theories of litigation. The new frameworks combine the two previously proposed sources of impasse: asymmetric information and divergent beliefs. Importantly, these new models allow for role-induced biases in litigants' beliefs.

### 4.1 Pretrial Bargaining under Self-Serving Bias

Farmer and Pecorino (2002) theoretically investigate the effects of self-serving bias on litigation outcomes. Their framework extends Bebchuk's (1984) work by allowing for asymmetric information and self-serving bias. In their model, two Bayesian risk-neutral players, an informed defendant and an uninformed plaintiff negotiate an out-of-court settlement. The source of information asymmetry is the plaintiff's probability of succeeding at trial. In addition, both litigants exhibit self-serving bias in their interpretation of the facts of the case.[47]

The biases are modeled using multiplicative and additive approaches. In the multiplicative approach, the biased probability that the plaintiff succeeds at trial is represented by the actual probability that the plaintiff succeeds at trial times the bias term. The plaintiff's bias term is assumed to be strictly greater than 1, and the defendant's is assumed to be strictly lower than 1. In the additive approach, the biased probability that the plaintiff succeeds at trial is represented by the actual probability that the plaintiff succeeds at trial plus the bias term (for the plaintiff) or minus the bias term (for the defendant). Both litigants' bias terms are assumed to be strictly positive. In both the multiplicative and additive settings, the sequence of events in the litigation game is as follows. The plaintiff (uninformed party) makes a take-it-or-leave-it settlement offer to the defendant (the informed party); after observing the offer, the defendant decides whether to accept or reject the offer. Where the offer is rejected, the case is resolved at a costly trial.

Their model predicts that impasse occurs in equilibrium.[48] In addition, their findings suggest that the plaintiff's bias increases the likelihood of impasse. The effect of the defendant's bias on the likelihood of impasse depends on the modeling choice for the bias. In the multiplicative setting, they find conditions under which an increase in the defendant's bias decreases the likelihood of trial. In contrast, when the bias is additive, an increase in the bias of the defendant increases the likelihood of trial.[49]

---

while only 46 percent of lawyers stated that judges rule at this stage. Similarly, 60 percent of lawyers indicated that they always comply with fee regulations but only 18 percent of judges stated that attorneys always comply with these regulations.

[47] See Deffains and Langlais (2009) for a different extension of Bebchuk's (1984) framework that allows for self-serving bias and risk aversion.

[48] The equilibrium concept used is perfect Bayesian equilibrium.

[49] An increase in the plaintiff's bias decreases her payoff due to the increase in the likelihood of costly impasse. The effect of a change in the defendant's bias on his payoff is generally ambiguous.

### 4.2   Pretrial Bargaining, Incentives for Care and Tort Reform under Self-Serving Bias

Landeo et al. (2013) theoretically study the effects of self-serving bias on litigation outcomes and the potential defendant's level of care. Their model builds on Reinganum and Wilde's (1986) theoretical framework on settlement and litigation and extends this framework in several ways. First, their setting encompasses two sources of disputes: asymmetric information about the plaintiff's economic losses and role-induced biases in litigants' beliefs (divergent and biased beliefs) about the size of the non-economic award at trial.[50] Second, their framework incorporates a stage prior to the litigation game. In this stage, the potential injurer chooses his level of care (i.e., expenditures on accident prevention). Hence, this environment is suitable for studying the effects of self-serving bias on litigation outcomes, incentives for care, and social welfare.

Their benchmark model involves two Bayesian risk-neutral parties, a potential plaintiff and a potential defendant. They assume that the plaintiff has private information about the amount of her economic losses. Given the uncertainty and unpredictability regarding the determination of non-economic damages, and following empirical regularities regarding the elicitation of cognitive biases (Babcock et al. 1995a),[51] they also assume that the players exhibit self-serving beliefs about the size of the non-monetary award at trial.[52] Two stages are considered. In the first stage, the potential injurer decides his level of care, which determines the probability of an accident. This decision depends on the cost of preventing accidents and on the expected litigation loss in case of an accident. They assume that every injured potential plaintiff has an economic incentive to file a lawsuit. Then, if an accident occurs, the second stage, called the litigation stage, starts. The litigation stage consists of a take-it-or-leave-it bargaining game, where a plaintiff and a defendant negotiate prior to a costly trial. The informed plaintiff makes a settlement offer; after observing the offer, the uninformed defendant decides whether to accept the proposal. Rejection from the

---

Specifically, when the bias is multiplicative, if the total litigation costs are greater than the expected award at trial (from the biased plaintiff's point of view), an increase in the defendant's bias decreases the likelihood of trial and the settlement demand. As a result, the defendant's payoff increases. When the bias is additive, an increase in the defendant's bias increases the likelihood of trial. The defendant's bias might increase or reduce the settlement demand. As a result, the defendant's payoff might increase or decrease. (Conditions for an unambiguous effect of the defendant's bias on his payoff are not derived.)

[50]   Compensatory damages include both economic and non-economic damages. Non-economic damages are primarily intended to compensate plaintiffs for injuries and losses that are not easily quantified by a dollar amount (e.g., pain and suffering). These awards have been widely criticized for being unpredictable.

[51]   Babcock et al. (1995a) argue that environments characterized by ambiguous information might elicit self-serving bias on litigants' beliefs.

[52]   Self-serving bias is modeled using an additive approach. Intuitively, the plaintiff's self-serving bias implies that he believes that the non-economic award at trial is higher than it actually is. The defendant's self-serving bias, on the other hand, implies that she believes that the non-economic award at trial is lower than it actually is. Following reported empirical regularities (Ross and Sicoly 1982; Loewenstein et al. 1993), Landeo et al. (2013) also assume that the litigants are unaware of their own bias and the bias of their opponent (i.e., the biased litigant believes that her opponent shares her beliefs).

defendant leads to trial. Using the court to resolve the dispute is costly, and may be subject to error.

The findings from their benchmark model are as follows.[53] First, accidents and disputes do occur in equilibrium.[54] Second, the defendant's bias negatively affects his expenditures on accident prevention, and hence, increases the likelihood of an accident. Third, litigants' self-serving biases exacerbate the likelihood of impasse generated by asymmetric information. Fourth, although self-serving bias serves litigants to commit to tough negotiation positions, it is economically self-serving only for the defendant. Fifth, litigants' self-serving biases might be welfare-reducing.[55]

Next, Landeo, Nikitin and Izmalkov (2013) extend their benchmark framework to study the effects of caps on non-economic damages on litigation outcomes and potential injurer's incentives for care. Following experimental findings (Babcock and Pogarsky 1999; Pogarsky and Babcock, 2001), they model the bias related to litigants' beliefs about the size of the award at trial as a function of the cap.[56] Their model predicts that caps decrease the likelihood of impasse only if the litigants do not exhibit self-serving bias. In fact, the presence of self-serving bias might reverse the positive effect of caps on impasse. In addition, their results indicate that caps might reduce the defendant's level of care and increase the likelihood of an accident.[57] Landeo et al.'s (2013) findings suggest that this policy intervention should be used with caution.

---

[53]   They apply a generalization of the perfect Bayesian equilibrium concept to this environment, and focus their analysis on the universally-divine, fully-separating perfect Bayesian equilibrium. See Banks and Sobel (1987) for details of the universally-divine refinement.

[54]   In equilibrium, the potential injurer spends resources on accident prevention but the likelihood of an accident remains greater than zero; each plaintiff type (differentiated by the amount of economic losses) makes a different settlement offer, and the defendant randomizes between accepting and rejecting the offer. In particular, the settlement demand made by the plaintiff is equal to the defendant's expected loss at trial (from the point of view of the biased defendant). The defendant is then indifferent between accepting and rejecting the plaintiff's demand. As a result, the defendant randomizes between accepting and rejecting the settlement proposal.

[55]   Specifically, the plaintiff's bias is always welfare reducing. This result might be explained by the higher likelihood of trial when the plaintiff's bias increases. The defendant's bias is welfare reducing only in cases of under-deterrence (i.e., when the defendant's level of care is lower than the socially optimal level).

[56]   Remember that Babcock and Pogarsky's (1999) and Pogarsky and Babcock's (2001) findings suggest that caps might influence litigation outcomes not only by directly reducing the expected award at trial but also by indirectly affecting litigants' beliefs about the award at trial. These findings also indicate that the effects of caps on litigants' beliefs depend on the relationship between the size of the cap and the value of the underlying claim. Landeo's (2009) experimental work on split-awards also suggests that this tort reform might affect litigants' beliefs.

[57]   Consider the effects of a damage cap on the defendant's level of care. The cap will increase the defendant's bias if he perceives the cap as relatively low (with respect to his biased estimation of the non-economic award at trial). The defendant's increased bias will reduce his expected litigation loss, and hence, the level of care. Analyze now the effects of a cap on the probability of trial. The cap will increase the bias of the plaintiff if he perceives the cap as relatively high (with respect to his biased estimation of the non-economic award at trial). The plaintiff's increased bias will increase his settlement demand. Caps will also increase the bias of the defendant if he perceives the cap as relatively low (with respect to his biased estimation of the non-economic award at trial). These two factors, which simultaneously occur when the economic damages are relatively low, will induce a higher probability of trial.

These studies demonstrate that theoretical frameworks involving asymmetric informa-tion and self-serving bias are useful tools for assessing the effects of litigation institutions. This work underscores the importance of combining theoretical and experimental economics methods in the study of litigation institutions.

## 5.   DISCUSSION AND CONCLUSIONS

An optimal design of civil litigation institutions and tort reform requires adequate knowledge of the factors that affect litigation outcomes and deterrence. The combina-tion of theoretical analysis and empirical investigation represents the application of the scientific method. Economic models, as Professor Shavell (1982, p. 56) states "provide a generally useful tool for thought," and hence, contribute to the understanding of litigation institutions. Experimental economics contributes to the scientific process of constructing empirically relevant theories of litigation by assessing the robustness of the theoretical predictions and identifying relevant behavioral factors not previously modeled.

This chapter assesses the interaction between theoretical and experimental law and eco-nomics in the study of tort litigation institutions. Special attention is devoted to liability, litigation and tort reform institutions, and to behavioral factors that might affect impasse.

Seminal theoretical work on settlement and litigation (Shavell 1982; Bebchuck 1984; Priest and Klein 1984; Reinganum and Wilde 1986) identifies two main sources of impasse: litigants' divergent beliefs and asymmetric information between the litigants about the outcome at trial. The importance of litigants' divergent beliefs on impasse and the nature of this divergence are empirical questions. Inspired by these empirical concerns, Babcock et al. (1995a) and Loewenstein et al. (1993) experimentally study pretrial bargain-ing and self-serving bias. Their findings suggest the presence of self-serving bias in pretrial bargaining environments, and a causal relation between self-serving bias and impasse. Babcock and Pogarsky (1999) and Pogarsky and Babcock (2001) provide additional evi-dence of the presence of self-serving bias in litigation environments that allow for damage caps. Their findings also suggest that the effects of damage caps on impasse depend on the size of the cap relative to the underlying claim. In particular, high damage caps (relative to the size of the claim) might increase the likelihood of impasse while low damage caps might decrease the likelihood of impasse. Importantly, Babcock and Loewenstein (1997) and Babcock et al. (1997) suggest that self-serving bias is generally robust in the face of debiasing interventions.

The findings from experimental work on litigation institutions have motivated the construction of new theoretical frameworks. Farmer and Pecorino (2002) study settle-ment and litigation using a framework that allows for asymmetric information about the plaintiff's likelihood of succeeding at trial and litigants' egocentrically-biased beliefs. Their results suggest that impasse occurs in equilibrium, and that self-serving bias might exacerbate the likelihood of impasse. Landeo et al. (2013) extend this work by studying incentives for care and litigation using a framework that allows for asymmetric information about the plaintiff's economic losses and self-serving beliefs about the size of the non-economic award at trial. They find that self-serving bias negatively affects the likelihood of impasse. Then, they use their framework to assess the effects of damage caps. Their results suggest that self-serving bias might reverse the positive effect of damage caps on impasse observed in environments that do not allow for litigants' egocentric biases. In fact, in the presence of self-serving bias, caps might increase the likelihood of impasse. Their findings also indicate that caps might decrease the incentives on care and increase the likelihood of an accident. This literature underscores the importance of studying the effects of public policy in environments that include empirically relevant assumptions about litigants' beliefs.

Our analysis of theoretical and experimental work on litigation and cognitive bias suggests a productive interaction between both methods of research. As a result of the application of scientific methods, the contributions of law and economics to the design of litigation institutions and tort reform might be strengthened.

# REFERENCES

Arlen, J. 2000. "Tort Damages: A Survey." In *Encyclopedia of Law and Economics*, Boudewijin B. and G. De Geest (eds). Cheltenham: Edward Elgar.

Arlen, J., and E. Talley. 2008. *Experimental Law and Economics*. Cheltenham: Edward Elgar.

Avraham, R., and A. Bustos. 2010. "The Unexpected Effects of Caps on Non-Economic Damages." *International Review of Law and Economics* 30: 291–305.

Babcock, L., and C. M. Landeo. 2004. "Settlement Escrows: An Experimental Study of a Bilateral Bargaining Game." *Journal of Economic Behavior and Organization* 53: 401–17.

Babcock, L., and C. Olson. 1992. "The Causes of Impasse in Labor Disputes." *Industrial Relations* 31: 348–60.

Babcock, L., and G. Pogarsky. 1999. "Damage Caps and Settlement: A Behavioral Approach." *Journal of Legal Studies* 28: 341–70.

Babcock, L., and G. Loewenstein. 1997. "Explaining Bargaining Impasse: The Role of Self-Serving Biases." *Journal of Economic Perspectives* 11: 109–26.

Babcock, L., G. Loewenstein, and S. Issacharoff. 1997. "Creating Convergence: Debiasing Biased Litigants." *Law and Social Inquiry* 22: 913–26.

Babcock, L., G. Loewenstein, S. Issacharoff, and C. Camerer. 1995a. "Biased Judgments of Fairness in Bargaining." *American Economic Review* 11: 109–26.

Babcock, L., H. Farber, C. Fobian, and E. Shafir. 1995b. "Forming Beliefs about Adjudicated Outcomes: Perceptions of Risk and Reservation Values." *International Review of Law and Economics* 15: 289–303.

Babcock, L., Xianghong Wang, and G. Loewenstein. 1996. "Choosing the Wrong Pond: Social Comparisons in Negotiations that Reflect a Self-Serving Bias." *Quarterly Journal of Economics* 111: 1–19.

Banks, J. S. and J. Sobel. 1987. "Equilibrium Selection in Signaling Games." *Econometrica* 55: 647–61.

Bar-Gill, O. 2007. "The Evolution and Persistence of Optimism in Litigation." *Journal of Law, Economics and Organization* 22: 490–507.

Bebchuk, L. A. 1984. "Litigation and Settlement under Imperfect Information." *Rand Journal of Economics* 15: 404–15.

Brooks, R., C. M. Landeo, and K. E. Spier. 2010. "Trigger Happy or Gun Shy: Dissolving Common-Value Partnerships with Texas Shootouts." *RAND Journal of Economics* 41: 649–73.

Camerer, C. F. and J. Hogarth. 1999. "The Effects of Financial Incentives in Experiments: A Review and Capital-Labor-Production Framework." *Journal of Risk and Uncertainty* 19: 7–42.

Camerer, C. F., and J. Hogarth. 2002. "The Strategic Use of Tying to Preserve and Create Market Power in Evolving Industries." *RAND Journal of Economics* 33: 194–220.

Cooter, R. 2011. "Maturing into Normal Science: The Effect of Empirical Legal Studies on Law and Economics." *University of Illinois Law Review* 5: 1476–84.

Cooter, R., S. Marks, and R. Mnookin. 1982. "Bargaining in the Shadow of the Law." *Journal of Legal Studies* 11: 225–51.

Coursey, D. L., and L. Stanley. 1988. "Pretrial Bargaining Behavior within the Shadow of the Law: Theory and Experimental Evidence." *International Review of Law and Economics* 8: 161–63.

Crawford, V. P. 1981. "Arbitration and Conflict Resolution in Labor-Management Bargaining." *American Economic Review* 71: 205–10.

Croson, R. 2002. "Why and How to Experiment: Methodologies from Experimental Economics." *University of Illinois Law Review* 4: 921–45.

Croson, R. 2005. "The Method of Experimental Economics." *International Negotiation* 10: 131–48.

Croson, R. 2009. "Experimental Law and Economics." *Annual Review of Law and Social Sciences* 5: 17.117.20.
Croson, R., and S. Gächter. 2010. "The Science of Experimental Economics." *Journal of Economic Behavior and Organization* 73: 122–31.
Croson, R., and J. S. Johnston. 2000. "Experimental Results on Bargaining under Alternative Property Rights Regimes." *Journal of Law, Economics, and Organization* 16: 50–73.
Danitioso, R., Z. Kunda, and G. T. Fong. 1990. "Motivated Recruitment of Autobiographical Memories." *Journal of Personality and Social Psychology* 59: 229–41.
Danzon, P. 1986. "The Frequency and Severity of Medical Malpractice Claims: New Evidence." *Law and Contemporary Problems* 57: 76–7.
Davis, D., and C. Holt. 1993. *Experimental Economics*. New Jersey: Princeton University Press.
Deffains, B., and E. Langlais. 2009. "Legal Interpretative Process and Litigants' Cognitive Biases" http://papers.ssrn.com/sol3/papers.cfm?abstract_id=1324490 (last visited October 16, 2014).
Eigen, Z., and Y. Listokin. 2012. "Do Lawyers Really Believe Their Own Hype and Should They? A Natural Experiment." *Journal of Legal Studies* 41: 239–69.
Eisenberg, T. 1994. "Differing Perceptions of Attorney Fees in Bankruptcy Cases." *Washington University Law Quarterly* 72: 979–95.
Falk, A., and J. J. Heckman. 2009. "Lab Experiments Are a Major Source of Knowledge in the Social Sciences." *Science* 326: 535–38.
Farber, H. 1978. "Bargaining Theory, Wage Outcomes, and the Occurrence of Strikes: An Econometric Analysis." *American Economic Review* 68: 262–84.
Farmer, A., and P. Pecorino. 2002. "Pretrial Bargaining with Self-Serving Bias and Asymmetric Information." *Journal of Economic Behavior and Organization* 48: 163–76.
Fréchette, G. R. 2015. "Laboratory Experiments: Professionals versus Students." In *Handbook of Experimental Economic Methodology*, G. Fréchette and A. Schotter (eds). Oxford: Oxford University Press.
Glöckner, A., and C. Engel. 2013. "Role Induced Bias in Court: An Experimental Analysis." *Journal of Behavioral Decision Making* 26: 272–84.
Gould, J. P. 1973. "The Economics of Legal Conflict." *Journal of Legal Studies* 2: 279–300.
Hoffman, E., and M. L. Spitzer. 1985. "Experimental Law and Economics: An Introduction." *Colorado Law Review* 85: 991–1024.
Hong, J. T., and C. R. Plott. 1982. "Rate Filing Policies for Inland Water Transportation: An Experimental Approach." *Bell Journal of Economics* 1: 1–19.
Hylton, K. 1993. "Litigation Cost Allocation Rules and Compliance with the Negligence Standard." *Journal of Legal Studies* 22: 457–76.
Hylton, K. 2002. "An Asymmetric-Information Model of Litigation." *International Review of Law and Economics* 22: 153–75.
Kennan, J., and R. Wilson. 1989. "Strategic Bargaining Models and Interpretation of Strike Data." *Journal of Applied Econometrics* 4: S87–S130.
Kennan, J., and R. Wilson. 1992. "Bargaining with Private Information." *Journal of Economic Literature* 31: 45–104.
Kuhn, T. 1996. *The Structure of Scientific Revolution*. Chicago: The University of Chicago Press.
Kunda, Z. 1987. "Motivated Inference: Self-Serving Generation and Evaluation of Causal Theories." *Journal of Personality and Social Psychology* 53: 636–47.
Kunda, Z. 1990. "The Case of Motivated Reasoning." *Psychological Bulletin* 108: 480–98.
Landeo, C. M. 2009. "Cognitive Coherence and Tort Reform." *Journal of Economic Psychology* 6: 898–912.
Landeo, C. M. 2015. "Exclusionary Vertical Restraints and Antitrust: Experimental Law and Economics Contributions." In *The Research Handbook of Behavioral Law and Economics*, K. Zeiler and J. Teitelbaum (eds). North Holland: Elsevier.
Landeo, C. M., and M. Nikitin. 2006. "Split-Award Tort Reform, Firm's Level of Care and Litigation Outcomes." *Journal of Institutional and Theoretical Economics* 162: 571–600.
Landeo, C. M., and K. E. Spier. 2013. "Shotgun Mechanisms for Common-Value Partnerships: The Unassigned-Offeror Problem." *Economics Letters* 121: 390–94.
Landeo, C. M., and K. E. Spier. 2014a. "Shotguns and Deadlocks." *Yale Journal on Regulation* 31: 143–87.
Landeo, C. M., and K. E. Spier. 2014b. "Irreconcilable Differences: Judicial Resolution of Business Deadlock." *University of Chicago Law Review* 81(1): 203–29.
Landeo, C. M., M. Nikitin, and L. Babcock. 2007a. "Split-Awards and Disputes: An Experimental Study of a Strategic Model of Litigation." *Journal of Economic Behavior and Organization* 63: 553–72.
Landeo, C. M., M. Nikitin, and S. Baker. 2007b. "Deterrence, Lawsuits and Litigation Outcomes under Court Errors." *Journal of Law, Economics, and Organization* 23: 57–97.
Landeo, C. M., M. Nikitin, and S. Izmalkov. 2013. "Incentives for Care, Litigation, and Tort Reform under Self-Serving Bias." In *The Research Handbook on Economic Models of Law*, T. Miceli and M. Baker (eds). Cheltenham: Edward Elgar Publishing.

Landes, W. 1971. "An Economic Analysis of the Courts." *Journal of Law and Economics* 14: 61–107.

Loewenstein, G., S. Issacharoff, C. Camerer, and L. Babcock. 1993. "Self-Serving Assessments of Fairness and Pretrial Bargaining." *Journal of Legal Studies* 22: 135–59.

McAdams, R. H. 2000. "Experimental Law and Economics." In *Encyclopedia of Law and Economics*, B. Bouckaert and G. DeGeest (eds). Cheltenham: Edward Elgar.

Messick, D., and K. Sentis. 1979. "Fairness and Preference." *Journal of Experimental Social Psychology* 15: 418–34.

Plott, C. R. 1982. "Industrial Organization Theory and Experimental Economics." *Journal of Economic Literature* 20: 1485–527.

Plott, C. R. 1994. "Market Architectures, Institutional Landscapes and Testbed Experiments." *Economic Theory* 1: 3–10.

Png, I. P. L. 1983. "Strategic Behavior in Suit, Settlement, and Trial." *Bell Journal of Economics* 14: 539–50.

Png, I. P. L. 1987. "Litigation, Liability, and the Incentives for Care." *Journal of Public Economics* 34: 61–85.

Pogarsky, G., and L. Babcock. 2001. "Damage Caps, Motivated Anchoring, and Bargaining Impasse." *Journal of Legal Studies* 30: 143–59.

Posner, R. A. 1977. *Economic Analysis of Law*. Boston, MA: Little, Brown and Company.

Priest, G. L., and B. Klein. 1984. "The Selection of Disputes for Litigation." *Journal of Legal Studies* 1: 1–55.

Reinganum, J. F., and L. L. Wilde. 1986. "Settlement, Litigation, and the Allocation of Litigation Costs." *RAND Journal of Economics* 17: 557–66.

Ross, M., and F. Sicoly. 1982. "Egocentric Biases in Availability and Attribution." In *Judgment under Uncertainty: Heuristics and Biases*, D. Kahneman, P. Slovic, and A. Tversky (eds). New York: Cambridge University Press.

Roth, A. E. 1986. "Laboratory Experimentation in Economics." *Economics and Philosophy* 2: 245–73.

Roth, A. E. 1995. "Bargaining Experiments." In *The Handbook of Experimental Economics*, J.H. Kagel and A. E. Roth (eds). Chicago: The University of Chicago Press.

Roth, A. E. 2008. "What Have We Learned from Market Design?" *Economic Journal* 118: 285–310.

Schweizer, U. 1989. "Litigation and Settlement under Two-Sided Incomplete Information." *Review of Economic Studies* 56: 163–78.

Shavell, S. 1982. "Suit, Settlement, and Trial." *Journal of Legal Studies* 11: 55–81.

Sloane, L. 1993. "The Split-Award Statute: A Move Toward Effectuating the True Purpose of Punitive Damages." *Valparaiso University Law Review* 28: 473–512.

Smith, V. L. 1976. "Experimental Economics: Induced Value Theory." *American Economic Review* 66: 274–79.

Spier, K. E. 1992. "The Dynamics of Pretrial Negotiation." *Review of Economic Studies* 59: 93–108.

Spier, K. E. 1994. "Pretrial Bargaining and the Design of Fee-Shifting Rules." *RAND Journal of Economics* 25: 197–214.

Talley, E., and C. Camerer. 2007. "Experimental Law and Economics." In *The Handbook of Law and Economics*, M. Polinsky, and S. Shavell (eds). Amsterdam: Elsevier.

Taylor, S., and J. D. Brown. 1988. "Illusion and Well-Being: A Social Psychological Perspective on Mental Health." *Psychological Bulletin* 103: 193–210.

Thaler, R. H. 1987. "Anomalies. The January Effect." *Journal of Economic Perspectives* 1: 197–201.

Thompson, L., and G. Loewenstein. 1992. "Egocentric Interpretations of Fairness in Interpersonal Conflict." *Organizational Behavior and Human Decision Processes* 51: 176–97.

Towers Perrin Tillinghast. 2005. *U.S. Tort Costs and Cross-Border Perspectives: 2005 Update*. Valhalla, NY: Towers Perrin.

Towers Perrin Tillinghast. 2007. *Update on U.S. Tort Cost Trends*. Valhalla, NY: Towers Perrin.

Waldfogel, J. 1998. "Reconciling Asymmetric Information and Divergent Expectations Theories of Litigation." *Journal of Legal Studies* 51: 451–76.

Wilkinson-Ryan, T., and D. Small. 2008. "Negotiating Divorce: Gender and the Behavioral Economics of Divorce." *Law and Inequality* 26: 109–32.

Watanabe, Y. 2010. "Learning and Bargaining in Dispute Resolution: Theory and Evidence from Medical Malpractice Litigation." Working Paper. Northwestern University, Evanston, IL.

Yildiz, M. 2003. "Bargaining without a Common Prior: An Immediate Agreement Theorem." *Econometrica* 71: 793–811.

# PART V

# HAPPINESS AND TRUST

# 10. Happiness 101 for legal scholars: applying happiness research to legal policy, ethics, mindfulness, negotiations, legal education, and legal practice

*Peter H. Huang*

## 1. HAPPINESS AND LEGAL POLICY

A growing yet already vast amount of recent empirical research examines the many correlates of self-reported happiness (Sin, Jacobs, and Lyubomirsky 2011, pp. 83–90). Huang (2010) summarizes many of these modern empirical findings about happiness. Variables that are positively correlated with self-reported happiness include: age, charitable giving, employment, experiences, feelings of being in control, friendships, good self-reported health, gratitude, meaningfulness, meditation, purpose, quality sleep, regular physical exercise, social ties and support, spirituality, and trust. It is worth remembering that just because two counterintuitive variables are positively correlated does not mean that either variable is the cause of the other variable. One possibility is that some other variables cause both of two positively correlated variables. For example, many of the same activities and behaviors lead to improved health and more happiness (Friedman and Martin 2011, pp. 46–48). Many empirical happiness research findings are intuitive, having a long historical tradition with ancient philosophical and spiritual roots (Haidt 2006, 2013), such as the idea that happiness is more of a journey than a destination (Edelman 2012). Other empirical happiness research findings are counterintuitive (Bernanke 2010; Wheelan 2012; Hilsenrath 2010; Bernanke 2010).

Huang (2010, 2018a) also surveys applications of happiness research to legal and public policy. For example, researchers have applied happiness research or critiqued its application to a number of areas including antitrust (Stucke 2010), business law (Huang 2011), government policy (Booth 2012; Thin 2012), legal education (Davis et al. 2011/2012; Martin and Rand 2010; Rand, Martin, and Shea 2011; Rosen 2011; Schultz 2013), legal practice (Delgado 2012), regulation and deregulation (Harrison 2011), and tax (Lawsky 2011, pp. 923–27).

Empirical happiness research assumes that numerical self-reports of happiness in response to survey questions are meaningful objects for econometric, psychometric, and statistical analysis. Empirical happiness studies analyze interpersonal, international, and intertemporal comparisons of individual happiness self-reports. Yet contested quantitative issues remain about whether individual happiness self-reports are additive, cardinal, and interpersonally comparable (Kristoffersen 2010). Differences exist in self-reported happiness levels across countries and cultures (Diener, Helliwell, and Kahneman 2010). Foundational qualitative and philosophical concerns also persist about whether quantitative self-reported measures of happiness are able to capture such aspects of happiness as authenticity, capabilities, experiential variety, goodness, meaningfulness, moral decency, purpose, sense making, values, and wisdom (Martin 2012). Recent empirical research found some key differences between happiness and meaningfulness (Baumeister et al. 2013).

Happiness research continues to refine its empirical and theoretical understanding about how fast, how much, and why people adapt hedonically to most but not all of life's events (Baucells and Sarin 2012, pp. 66–70, 113–115; Headey, Muffels, and Wagner 2010). This refinement in our knowledge about hedonic adaptation has potential legal policy implications to civil procedure (Huang 2008c), public policy (Graham 2010, 2011), and torts (Swedloff and Huang 2010).

Even whether the sign of several famous and much-publicized empirical correlations is negative or positive has recently become the subject of renewed active debate, including the relationships between these variables: income and happiness (Sachs, Stevenson, and Wolfers 2012; Stevenson and Wolfers 2008); having children and happiness (Angeles 2010; Herbst and Ifcher 2012; Margolis and Myrskylä 2011; Myrskylä and Margolis 2012); and the relative happiness over time of men as opposed to women (Herbst 2011; Stevenson and Wolfers 2009). Just what people mean by the word happiness systematically varies over their lifetime, with younger people being more likely to associate happiness with an excited and yippy skippy feeling, while older people are more likely to associate happiness with a contented and peaceful easy feeling (Mogilner, Kamvar, and Aaker 2011).

Some people argue that government policy should optimize a social function that aggregates individual self-reports of happiness. Positive psychology founder Martin Seligman (2011, pp. 239–41) advocates that policy makers evaluate policies using his proposed well-being metric in terms of its five components PERMA, which stands for Positive emotion, Engagement, positive Relationships, Meaning, and Accomplishment. In an oft-quoted speech, Robert F. Kennedy challenges the prevailing orthodoxy of how governments measure social well-being and societal progress by national income accounting in terms of a country's Gross Domestic Product (GDP) (YouTube 2008). As Kennedy memorably states GDP "measures everything, in short, except that which makes life worthwhile and it can tell us everything about America, except why we are proud that we are American."

Economists have long known that GDP is a crude, imperfect, and incomplete proxy for societal welfare. Economists have proposed alternatives to GDP, such as net economic welfare, which values the costs of congestion, crime, pollution, and other negative dimensions, to economic growth and progress. The New Economics Foundation is "an independent think-and-do tank that inspires and demonstrates real economic well-being" (New Economics Foundation 2014). A simple summary statistic for a country's flow of well-being can combine data about consumption, inequality, leisure, and mortality (Jones and Klenow 2010). Law and policy in general can and should incorporate, measure, quantify, and take into account emotional impacts that include but are not limited to just self-reported happiness (Huang 2008a, 2008b).

Bhutan is a poor, small, and undeveloped kingdom nestled in the Himalayas, with an estimated population (as of November 2017) of 810,928. In 2016, its GDP per capita was estimated to be approximately 2800 U.S. dollars. Bhutan's first paved road was built in 1961. Internet and television access there only started in 1999. In 1972, its fourth dragon king, Jigme Singye Wangchuck, coined the phrase "Gross National Happiness"

(GNH) to capture the quality of life in a more holistic and psychological manner than GDP does. GNH also provides an overarching theme for Bhutan's five-year plan to guide Bhutan's economic development. Policies have to pass a GNH review based on GNH impact statements that are similar to American environmental impact statements. The Bhutanese government promulgated four pillars of GNH that are grounded in Buddhist spiritual values and designed to manage globalization and modernization. First, promote sustainable and equitable socioeconomic development. Second, preserve and promote the integrity of Bhutan's cultural values. Third, conserve Bhutan's natural ecosystem and pristine environment. Fourth, establish good governance.

Canadian health epidemiologist Michael Pennock played a major role in the designing of what he terms a "de-Bhutanized" version of GNH for Canada and has also co-developed policy screening tools which examine the potential impacts of projects or programs on GNH. In the US, the state of Maryland calculates a Genuine Progress Indicator (Maryland 1), based on 26 separate well-being measures (Maryland 2), in three general categories: economic (e.g., cost of underemployment in contrast to unemployment) (Maryland 3), environmental (e.g., cost of climate change) (Maryland 4), and social (e.g., value of higher education) (Maryland 5). Somerville, a suburb of Boston, is the first American city to ask its residents to voluntarily complete a well-being and community survey as part of its census, which includes these questions: (1) "How happy do you feel right now? (check a box on the scale below) from 1 to 10," (2) "How satisfied are you with your life in general? (check a box on the scale below) from 1 to 10," and (3) "Taking everything into account, how satisfied are you with Somerville as a place to live?" (Tierney 2011).

China Central Television's financial channel, the National Statistics Bureau, and the China Postal Group Corporation conduct an annual survey of people's economic situation and their sense of happiness that covers 100,000 families in 31 autonomous regions, municipalities, and provinces in China. Guangdong, which is one of the richest provinces in China, is the first to have a happiness index system to measure objective and subjective indicia of well-being among 6,900 people aged 16 to 65 who have resided there for at least one year.

England's Office of National Statistics collects national well-being data that measure anxiousness, happiness, life satisfaction, and meaning (Cohen 2011). French President Nicolas Sarkozy created a commission in 2008 to measure economic performance and social progress, with 2001 Nobel Laureate in economics, Joseph E. Stiglitz as chair and 1998 Nobel Laureate in economics, Amartya Sen serving as chair advisor (Commission on the Measurement of Economic Performance and Social Progress). A report by this commission includes "Recommendation 10: Measures of both objective and subjective well-being provide key information about people's quality of life. Statistical offices should incorporate questions to capture people's life evaluations, hedonic experiences and priorities in their own survey" (Stiglitz, Sen, and Fitoussi 2009).

The OECD (Organisation for Economic Co-operation and Development) publishes a report assessing 40 OECD countries in terms of 11 aspects of people's lives: civic engagement and governance, education and skills, environmental quality, health status, housing conditions, income and wealth, jobs and earnings, personal security, social connections, subjective well-being, and work-life balance (OECD iLibrary 2011). This publication is part of a Better Life Initiative the OECD launched to promote better policies for better lives. An interactive composite well-being index designed to involve people in a debate about social progress is another part of that same initiative (OEDC Better Life Index).

Much of the variation in many well-being measures is already well captured by such traditional economic indicators as gross domestic product and the unemployment rate, but because the correlation of alternative indicators with economic measures is far from perfect, there is room to augment traditional statistical reporting by non-standard indicators (Kassenboehmer and Schmidt 2011). Countries can and should measure their emotional prosperity and focus on mental well-being (Oswald 2010, pp. 654–60). A team of psychologists and labor economist Alan Krueger, led by Daniel Kahneman, propose that policy makers adopt national time accounting to survey how much time people spend experiencing positive and negative affect (Krueger et al. 2009).

Instead of maximizing a measure of aggregate happiness, it is more politically feasible for policy makers to minimize a measure of aggregate misery, stress, or unhappiness (Huang and Blumenthal 2009, p. 592). Kahneman and Kruger (2006, pp. 18–22) propose such a specific measure that they call the U-index, where U stands for undesirable or unpleasant. They define an unpleasant emotional state to be one where the most intense feeling reported is negative. They define the U-index to be the fraction of time that an individual spends in an unpleasant emotional state. Policy makers can compute the U-index for individuals and also compute the average of those individual U-indices. The average U-index provides empirical information about negative affective experiences that a society may wish to minimize. Societies can reduce such misery in two ways. The first is to target those people who spend a lot of time being in unpleasant states, for example through particular mental health interventions, including antidepressant medication and interventions from positive psychology (Sheldon, Kashdan, and Steger 2011). The second is to enact laws and policies that reduce how much time people spend in unpleasant states. Such policies include providing or subsidizing public transportation or taxing road congestion (Diener et al. 2009, pp. 150–54).

Frey and Stutzer (2010, pp. 564–68) use Arrow's impossibility theorem and public choice economics to conclude that the maximization of aggregate happiness is problematic, neglects incentive problems from reducing people to being happiness metric stations, and ignores procedural sources of well-being from political institutions. Frey and Stutzer (2010, p. 569) observe that, "happiness is not necessarily people's ultimate goal. It may even be that people see some virtue in unhappiness if they reckon that discontent is the only way to overcome social ills." Frey and Stutzer (2010, pp. 568–70) propose a different way to apply happiness research to policy. They call their approach constitutional happiness politics, and it consists of two practical suggestions about how to use happiness research. First, identify which, how, and why institutions assist people in best achieving their personal goals and in so doing contributing maximally to individual subjective happiness. Second, introduce findings from happiness research as informational inputs into the political decision-making process.

Schubert (2012, pp. 247–54) extends this constitutional happiness approach by generalizing procedural utility to incorporate two dynamic aspects of happiness. First, people derive and enjoy pleasurable anticipation of and fond recall of happy outcomes. Second, people derive and enjoy pleasure from learning to discover and explore new sources of happiness. Schubert (2012, pp. 254–56) develops novel practical and policy implications for viewing the pursuit of happiness as the space over which to evaluate institutional design. Schubert (2012, pp. 256–58) also uses his broader welfare notion to argue for a normative basis that differs from the one that Thaler and Sunstein (2008) propose to support libertarian paternalism and policy nudges. Schubert's normative basis is that of autonomy to learn about new preferences.

Another way to incorporate happiness data into legal and policy analysis is to introduce maximum levels of a measure of unhappiness or minimum levels of a measure of happiness as constraints that government policies must satisfy while optimizing some objective function or goal besides that of maximizing happiness or minimizing unhappiness. This approach is analogous to incorporating rights as constraints that are not to be violated as opposed to rights as part of a policy goal to be optimized (Nozick 1977, p. 29).

Law, economics, and public policy discussions typically focus on improving such objective and quantitative outcomes as economic development, growth, and progress. This emphasis is at least partly due to such outcome variables being at least in theory observable to and verifiable by third parties. There is a long-standing historical and traditional suspicion regarding self-reported survey data about subjective variables among some economists, lawyers, and judges that is attributable to such variables being unobservable to and unverifiable by third parties. There are at least two responses to the arguments for evaluating law and policy based only on observable and quantitative variables instead of also survey evidence from self-reports of subjective variables, such as happiness. First, many of our most well-known economic variables are based on self-reported survey data, including national income and unemployment statistics. Second, people and society only care indirectly about economic outcomes as proxies for what really matters in life.

Economist and pioneering happiness researcher Oswald (1997, p. 1815) cogently notes that:

> Economic performance is not intrinsically interesting. No-one is concerned in a genuine sense about the level of gross national product last year or about next year's exchange rate. People have no innate interest in the money supply, inflation, growth, inequality, unemployment, and the rest. The stolid greyness of the business pages of our newspapers seems to mirror the fact that economic numbers matter only indirectly. The relevance of economic performance is that it may be a means to an end. That end is not the consumption of beefburgers, nor the accumulation of television sets, nor the vanquishing of some high level of interest rates, but rather the enrichment of mankind's feeling of well-being. Economic things matter only in so far as they make people happier.

Chip Conley, the founder of Joie de Vivre, eloquently argues that we should choose to measure what we value and not just value whatever we happen to measure (Conley 2010).

A middle-of-the-road position in response to situations and times when indicia of objective outcomes and subjective happiness measures diverge is to privilege neither category of variables. Instead law and policy can and should take into account both objective outcomes and self-reports about subjective experiences. If objective outcomes and self-reports about subjective experiences converge, then law and policy can proceed more confidently than if based upon just one category of variables. If objective outcomes and self-reports about subjective experiences disagree, then law and policy can and should understand why they diverge. Levav (2007, pp. 324–26) suggests this divergence can be due to differences in processing times from a dual-level processing of events and circumstances:

first, a cognitive and conscious level that judgments of subjective well-being capture, and second, a biological and subconscious level that medical objective outcomes capture.

Levav (2007, pp. 334–35) explains how divergences in biological and cognitive processing times of events help categorize biases in predictions of subjective well-being, which in turn has public policy implications. For example, Levav (2007, p. 335) suggests that paternalism might be justified in situations with environmental pathogens, because he believes in rejecting any public policy that neglects objective health outcomes just because those outcomes have little or no long-term impact on measures of subjective well-being.

Levav (2007, p. 335) observes that even though a doctor usually starts a medical visit by asking patients how they feel (subjective experiences), a doctor then performs a thorough physical health examination that includes taking measures of blood pressure and heart rate (objective outcomes). Levav (2007, p. 335) concludes that:

> an attempt to ascertain the effect of an event or circumstance through measures of affective judgment (that is, through SWB [Subjective Well-Being]) fails to capture sufficiently its consequences. This becomes especially important when extracting public-policy recommendations from responses to SWB questionnaires. Failure to realize the multiple effects of an event and their timing can lead to policies that are detrimental to the goal of increasing a population's well-being.

An alternative to choosing among or combining all or some of the above objective versus subjective outcome measures is to focus instead on how law affects decision-making processes (Harrison 2009). Society can design law to achieve an idealized notion of decision-making known as decisional equity that addresses problems that are caused by informational imbalances, psychic biases, and hedonic adaptation to social conditions (Harrison 2009, pp. 967–94). An open question remains as to if law can and should respond to differences in judgment and decision-making (JDM) due to differences in people's native intellect (Harrison 2009, pp. 994–95).

Finally, some experimental happiness research finds that being in a positive mood is not always desirable. For example, people induced to feel positive moods tend to use stereotypes more (Clore and Huntsinger 2007). Some people may also engage in magical thinking or hold on to irrational beliefs to stay happy (Hutson 2012).

## 2.   FROM BEHAVIORAL ECONOMICS TO MODERN HAPPINESS RESEARCH

Behavioral economics is the subfield of economics that analyzes the impacts of cognitive, social, and emotional influences on economic decisions and judgments by individuals and organizations. Behavioral economics builds on empirical and experimental research from cognitive and social psychology and experimental economics. Many subfields of economics have corresponding behavioral versions of those subfields, including behavioral finance, behavioral macroeconomics, behavioral microeconomics, behavioral industrial organization, behavioral public finance, behavioral development economics, and behavioral welfare economics.

Daniel Kahneman (2011, pp. 109–95) offers a fascinating, personal, and first-hand account of behavioral economics by one of its two co-founders, the other being

Kahneman's frequent co-author, the late Amos Tversky. Research by Kahneman and Tversky provided experimental evidence that people's answers to hypothetical questions about making choices under conditions of risk systematically violated the axioms of the dominant neoclassical economic model of decision-making under risk, namely expected utility theory. Kahneman and Tversky introduced the related ideas of cognitive biases and heuristics. An incomplete and yet lengthy list of cognitive biases and heuristics includes: affirmation bias, ambiguity effect, anchoring, availability heuristic, avoidance of cognitive dissonance, base rate neglect, belief in a just world, certainty effect, choice bracketing, choice overload, cognitive overload, commitment effect, confirmation bias, conformity, congruence bias, conjunction fallacy, consistency bias, context effect, contrast effect, curse of knowledge, diagnosis momentum, distinction bias, egocentrism, endowment effect, essentialism, exposure effect, extremeness aversion, false consensus effect, familiarity effect, framing effect, frequency illusion, fixed-pie illusion; fundamental attribution error, gambler's fallacy, groupthink, habit, halo effect, herding, hindsight bias, hyperbolic discounting, illusion of control, illusion of transparency, implicit bias, informational cascades, in-group bias, irrational escalation of commitment, Lake Wobegon effect, loss aversion, mental accounting, money illusion, motivated cognition, myopia, naïve cynicism, negativity bias, obedience to authority, omission bias, overconfidence, over-optimism, partisan perception, planning fallacy, polarization, positive illusions, priming effect, probability neglect, pseudocertainty effect, reactive devaluation, reciprocity, regret aversion, representativeness heuristic, self-serving bias, similarity-attraction effect, socialization, social proof, status quo bias, social stereotyping, sunk cost fallacy, and weakness of will.

Three reasons explain why this psychological research gradually led to behavioral economics becoming accepted as a subfield of mainstream economics. First, the notion that humans have cognitive biases and use heuristics is descriptively accurate, intuitive, and verifiable by introspection and the observation of others. Second, Kahneman and Tversky published in the mainstream empirical and theoretical economics journal, *Econometrica*, a seminal article that introduced their prospect theory, which offered a concrete alternative mathematical model to expected utility theory. Third, economist Richard Thaler popularized the research of Kahneman and Tversky by publishing a number of trade books, such as *Quasi-Rational Economics* and *The Winner's Curse*, which contains a number of Thaler's "Anomalies" columns from the *Journal of Economic Literature*, which he revised for a more popular lay audience.

Some economists and legal scholars use behavioral economics to advocate related notions of paternalism, including asymmetric paternalism (Camerer et al. 2003), emotional paternalism (Blumenthal 2007), expert paternalism (Blumenthal 2012), libertarian paternalism (Thaler and Sunstein 2008), light paternalism (Loewenstein and Haisley 2008), and soft paternalism (Holt 2006). These various conceptions of paternalism argue that sometimes people fall prey to cognitive or affective biases and use heuristics in making decisions that result in outcomes that those same people view as being suboptimal from the perspective of their own personal subjective preferences. These versions of paternalism advocate that governments can and should help such people by nudging them into better decisions without hurting others who do not require such nudging. Other economists and legal scholars raise a number of criticisms of libertarian paternalism, including concerns about assertive centrism (Schlag 2010, pp. 914, 919–24), autonomy (Mitchell 2005), behavioral biases of regulators (Cooper and Kovacic 2012), hyperopia (Fcnncl 2006), individual liberty (Saint-Paul 2011; Veetil 2010), indeterminacy of individual preferences (Hill 2007), and slippery slope arguments (Glaeser 2006).

A well-known experimental economist and game-theorist Alvin Roth "noted in conversations with psychologists that the United States has a Council of Economic Advisors, but no Council of Psychological Advisors" (Bazerman and Malhotra 2006, p. 264). Of the social sciences, economics is the one that tends to dominate the fields of business, finance, government policy making, management, media coverage, and much of the legal academy. Economics does this by institutionalizing its language and norms (Ferraro, Pfeffer, and Sutton 2005). Even ostensibly merely descriptive financial economic models can lead financial market participants to behave and interact in ways that make the predictions of these models become self-fulfilling (McKenzie 2008; McKenzie and Millo 2003). Ironically, even though some economists and journalists argue that the recent Great Recession was partly caused by the failures of certain parts of economics orthodoxy and policy makers trained in orthodox economics, the government and regulatory responses to the crisis relied heavily upon mainstream theoretical economics models and economists.

Finance or financial economics is economics over time and under risk. Modern finance is now an integral part of the social and political landscape. The role of economics and finance is now more accepted and prevalent in both modern society and its regulatory apparatus. Economists understandably participate in the regulation of business and finance. Economists have also become active in the regulation of health, environment, and safety. A central technique of economics, namely cost-benefit analysis, is often used as merely an excuse to justify the delay or repeal of regulations. Economists and lawyers have become the gatekeepers to policy, meaning that psychologists can influence policy primarily if not only by influencing economists and lawyers. Behavioral economics is the subfield of economics influenced by (cognitive and social) psychology. Behavioral law and economics is the subfield of law and economics influenced by (cognitive and social) psychology.

From behavioral economics or more precisely the study of cognitive biases and heuristics, the move to modern happiness research is a small and natural step because much of the recent empirical study of happiness focuses on how people have affective biases and use affective heuristics. Affective biases and heuristics include: the affect heuristic, affect infusion, duration neglect, emotional contagion, empathy or hot-cold gap, focusing illusion, impact bias, incidental affect, mood-congruency effect, projection bias, and vividness effect. Modern happiness research considers alternative definitions and measures of happiness, including affective versus cognitive, hedonic versus eudaimonic, and experienced versus predicted versus remembered. Much of modern happiness research does not focus exclusively on happiness and also analyzes other emotions and mental states. Modern happiness research is not a subfield of economics because modern research about happiness draws on and occurs in a number of disciplines in addition to economics, including anthropology, biology, education, epidemiology, marketing, medicine, neuroscience, philosophy, politics, public health, and sociology. What unifies modern happiness research is the study, primarily empirical and experimental, of positive affect and positive mental states. Kahneman (2011, pp. 377–407) provides a first-hand personal account of the recent psychological research about happiness by one of its pioneers.

Some recent authors of behavioral economics textbooks include a chapter or sections about what they call happiness economics, which can be defined as that part of modern happiness research that uses empirical, experimental, or theoretical economics methods, models, or techniques (Cartwright 2011; Dowling and Chin-Fang 2007; Wilkinson 2008). The subfields of behavioral economics and happiness economics share three character-istics in common. First, both subfields build and improve upon neoclassical economics by incorporating into economics insights from empirical and experimental research by economists, (cognitive and social) psychologists, and neuroscientists. Second, both subfields do not assume that individuals' preferences are fixed exogenously. Behavioral economics demonstrates that individual preferences can vary endogenously with contexts, frames, and situations. Happiness economics demonstrates that individual preferences may adapt in light of experience. Third, some people use both subfields to argue for more activist or interventionist government, legal, and regulatory policy conclusions than neoclassical economics. In other words, even in the absence of the standard neoclassical economics rationales for government intervention, namely market failures due to asym-metric information, externalities, and public goods, behavioral economics and happiness economics provide novel rationales for why people's decisions and interactions within markets can be not only socially suboptimal, but also individually suboptimal. Behavioral economics focuses on empirical findings which show that some people sometimes systematically exhibit cognitive biases and use heuristics. Happiness economics focuses on empirical findings which show that some people sometimes systematically mis-predict and mis-remember aspects of their experienced happiness.

The fact that some people sometimes systematically make decisions that those same people find suboptimal according to their own individual, private, and subjective prefer-ences does not necessarily imply that governments or for that matter private organizations have the requisite ability or information to make things better. Even if benevolent govern-ment regulators can in theory improve matters, some people will be wary about such intervention. For example, a law firm partner who practices corporate and securities law and mergers and acquisitions for a variety of corporate clients and institutional investors asks: "to what extent can I get comfortable with the concept of a paternalistic govern-ment, "nudging" me toward what will give me life-satisfaction?" (Taylor 2012, p. 710).

Blumenthal and Huang (2009) propose a regulatory philosophy, which they call positive parentalism, that differs from libertarian paternalism in two ways. First, positive parentalism emphasizes a positive framing that focuses on people's signature character strengths instead of libertarian paternalism's negative framing which emphasizes people's cognitive biases and JDM errors. Second, positive parentalism emphasizes that positive affect and emotions are keys to motivating people to change their JDM and behavior, in contrast with libertarian paternalism's emphasis on nudging people's JDM and behavior.

## 3. HAPPINESS EXPERIENCED IS NOT HAPPINESS REMEMBERED

Kahneman (2011, pp. 14, 379–410) describes happiness research which shows that peo-ple's remembered happiness differs systematically from those same people's experienced happiness. Kahneman aptly characterizes people's tendency to remember and evaluate their happiness differently from how they experience and live through their happiness as being a difference between on the one hand being happy about or with your life and on the other hand being happy in actually living your life (Kahneman 2010). Kahneman (2011, pp. 398–407) attributes this difference to people directing their attention to different aspects of their lives when thinking about life in comparison to actually living it. Kahneman (2011, pp. 388–90) illustrates his central thesis that anticipated memories of experiences as opposed to anticipated experiences themselves motivate people's behavior by stating that very frequently and to a large degree people take vacations in service of their remembering selves. Vacations typically provide fond memories, even if many of the details of the actual experiences of those vacations were annoying (for example, long lines, higher than expected prices, and less than perfect weather).

Kahneman (2011, pp. 381–85, 408–10) also raises questions about how individuals and social policy should balance remembered versus experienced happiness. Emotional memories are usually rosier than emotional experiences and people base their behavior and JDM on their anticipated or predicted emotions that tend to coincide with their memories. Kahneman (2011, pp. 378–81) expresses concern over evaluations of past experiences because they are incorrect due to fallible memories and can result in choices that do not maximize people's experienced affect (Kahneman 2011, pp. 392–97). Kahneman (2011, p. 381) views the confusion of our experiences with our memories to be a cognitive illusion, resulting in a "tyranny of the remembering self."

Huang (2014) advocates that law and policy should care more about people's experiences than memories if and when those experiences result in chronic health or stress consequences that either: (1) societies care about more than individuals do, because of negative or positive externalities, public bads, or public goods; or (2) individuals also care about, but were unaware of, do not remember, or are unable to act upon due to self-control problems. Huang (2014) analyzes examples of chronic health or stress effects from such experiences as dense and long commutes, discrimination, unhealthy eating, lack of regular physical exercise, sedentary behavior, and poor or no financial/retirement planning.

Experiences can produce negative experienced affect and negative biological, health, or stress consequences, yet nonetheless be generally forgotten or produce only mildly negative or even neutral remembered affect. Examples of such experiences are long and dense urban commutes. Experiences can also produce negative experienced affect and negative biological, health, or stress consequences, but produce dampened remembered negative affect. Examples of such experiences possibly include being a victim of crime, discrimination, or a tort. Experiences can even produce positive experienced affect yet negative biological or health consequences and positive remembered affect. Examples of such experiences possibly include unhealthy eating and certain types of addictive or obsessive behavior.

People choose which activities to experience based upon their predicted affect that typically coincide with remembered affect rather than experienced affect. The fact that the valence of remembered affect can differ from that of not only experienced affect, but also biological, health, or stress consequences implies that people may engage in activities that have adverse effects on their health, such as undergoing long and dense commutes, not sufficiently avoiding being harmed by crimes, discrimination, or torts, and eating too much or unhealthily. Individuals may indeed care about suffering from the adverse biological or negative health consequences of certain activities, but are unaware of those consequences as they happen, underestimate cumulative and/or probabilistic effects, or simply do not care about negative externalities or public bad aspects of their experiences.

In contrast, societies may care about individual health consequences or social effects more than individuals do.

Possible legal and policy interventions include focusing public attention on the adverse biological or negative health consequences of such experiences as being sedentary and repeatedly undergoing dense and long commutes. Conversely, law and policy can focus public attention on positive biological or health consequences from such experiences as healthy eating and regular physical exercise. Such a refocusing of attention is akin to directing an anxious flier's awareness to a still cup of water to see lack of turbulence on a plane. In other words, redirecting the public's attention to good and bad aspects of their experiences may influence the public's choices about what activities to experience. Mere information provision often will not suffice to motivate people to change their behavior and JDM. A more powerful legal and policy intervention is to alter the affect of experiences or memories of certain behaviors. For example, making healthy eating and regular physical exercise more fun and enjoyable is likely to change people's habits and routines by reframing those activities. Similarly, building more green spaces and public parks or making public transportation more pleasant and engaging is likely to reduce the likelihood of people being sedentary and repeatedly undergoing dense and long commutes.

## 4.   MINDFULNESS, HAPPINESS, AND ETHICAL BEHAVIOR

Riskin (2002) introduces mindfulness to legal professionals and suggests that mindfulness can help lawyers derive more career satisfaction and provide more appropriate service through better listening and negotiation. Riskin (2002) explains how mindfulness meditation in legal practice can improve attorney happiness and performance and mitigate the dominance of adversarial mindsets. Mindfulness has applications to legal education (Huang, 2015, 2016, 2017, 2018b; Huang and Felder 2015; James 2011; Reuben 2012; Zlotnick 2012) and legal practice (Harris, Lin, and Selbin 2007). Magee (2011) advocates that a core part of legal education should focus on mindfulness. Mindfulness offers foundational tools to improve dispute resolution (Riskin 2004), mediation (Rock 2005), and negotiation (Riskin 2006). Riskin (2010) considers how mindful awareness can facilitate paying attention to these five core concerns: affiliation, appreciation, autonomy, role, and status (Fisher and Shapiro 2005; Shapiro 2010) and in so doing help to identify emotional dimensions of negotiations, avoid negative emotions, and generate positive emotions that foster interest-based negotiations. Riskin (2012) provides broader historical and social context about promoting mindfulness in legal education and legal practice.

Mindfulness can foster ethical behavior and JDM (Riskin 2009). Mindfulness provides its practitioner with the pause or space to decide whether to exercise real options to engage in ethical or professional behavior (Huang 2015, 2017). Mindfulness can improve legal education and social justice (Harris 2012; Magee 2011). Over time, mindfulness can result in deeper commitments to ethical behavior and even transform people who practice mindfulness to avoid using adversarial negotiation strategies (Peppet 2002). Mindfulness can lead to more truthfulness in negotiations (Pounds 2003). Cantrell (2010) collects qualitative data based on interviews of lawyers with Buddhist legal practices involving compassion, equanimity, and an expansive conception of honesty. Cantrell (2010) challenges the dominant mainstream narrative that a good attorney must be a zealous, singularly focused, hyper-rational advocate who owes loyalty to and takes direction from a client. Further empirical and experimental research can and should examine the long-term effects of mindfulness practice upon people's behavior and JDM in bargaining and other strategic interactions. One plausible hypothesis is that mindful awareness about others being like us increases our compassion and empathy for others, and increases the likelihood of cooperation to achieve joint gains and win-win scenarios by transforming individual people's non-monetary payoffs to include emotional concerns over and connections with others. Being mindful about making errors or mistakes due to cognitive or affective biases or use of heuristics in our JDM processes is also likely to help us avoid unintentional and unethical behavior and JDM (Prentice 2004).

The relationships between mindfulness, happiness, and ethical behavior or JDM are myriad. Killingsworth and Gilbert (2010) report empirical data showing that people's minds frequently wander, leading to lower self-reported happiness and that people's thoughts predicted their self-reported happiness better than people's actions. Goudie et al. (2011) provide the first empirical support for a powerful connection between happiness and risk-avoidance. Based upon data about 300,000 Americans, they find that happier people wear seat belts more often. A rational choice explanation consistent with this finding is that happier people value life more and so act to preserve it. A general hypothesis is that being happy is correlated with taking fewer risks, especially those associated with unethical behavior or JDM. This hypothesis suggests that being happy should lead to behaving ethically. There is international evidence finding higher levels of self-reported happiness in countries that have a greater proportion of trustworthy people (Zak 2011a, p. 63; Zak 2011b, pp. 228–29; Zak and Fakhar 2006, pp. 421–423). Zak (2012, pp. 206–207) reports finding that the most generous and virtuous players in an experimental trust game were also by a significant amount the happiest people among the participants.

Most of us learn as children from our parents and many philosophical, religious, or spiritual traditions that ethical behavior is its own reward and leads to happiness. Most societies have norms that view ethical and pro-social behavior as commendable and laudable, while other norms frown upon or stigmatize anti-social and unethical behavior. Avoidance of guilt and shame can motivate compliance and obedience to social norms and in so doing foster socially virtuous behavior. Thus, for most people, being ethical and being happy end up forming a positive feedback loop. Hamilton and Monson (2011) review literatures based upon empirical social sciences and the professions to demonstrate that increased capacities for ethical behavior and professionalism, such as personal conscience defined as perceptual clarity and empathy, moral judgment, moral identity, and moral implementation skills, are related to lawyer effectiveness outcomes including these: more satisfaction with lawyers' services, decreased likelihood lawyers will experience malpractice claims or complaints, and increased likelihood lawyers will detect or report wrongdoing.

Although promoting mindfulness based on better immune function (Davidson et al. 2003) and reduced stress (Kilpatrick et al. 2011) is laudable, appeals that are based solely on health benefits do not appear to sufficiently motivate the majority of people to change their behavior. A complementary approach would emphasize the private and public benefits of mindfulness on improving people's happiness and their JDM in personal and professional domains. Better personal JDM implies happier children, colleagues, families, friends, parents, and spouses. Better professional JDM means increased global competitiveness, innovation, labor retention, living standards, productivity, and profits. Neuroscience studies analyze the relationships among different happiness measures, improved JDM, and various types of mindfulness (Huang 2010, pp. 420–21). Instead of an exclusive focus on the private and public health benefits stemming from the practice of mindfulness, policy makers can frame mindfulness in terms of increasing happiness and improving JDM. For example, Congressman Tim Ryan (2012) explains how the practice of mindfulness is not just a way to reduce stress, but it can also help children be kinder and learn better in school, improve people's health and the health-care system, develop resiliency in first responders and military personnel, and lead to more effective leadership by CEOs.

Policy makers can employ a portfolio of complementary legal policies to foster mindfulness, including tax breaks, school programs, and information provision. Legal policies to foster mindfulness vary in their degree of paternalism. Tax deductions and tax exemptions provide financial and symbolic incentives. School programs can be optional or mandatory and geared to different ages. Information provision is relatively cheap, easy, and often futile because people have to have motivation to act on knowledge. Because emotions motivate people to change their behavior (Cooney 2011; Heath and Heath 2010), policy makers may think about developing legal policies to help individuals appreciate how mindfulness can be physically enjoyable, generate positive affect, and relieve stress.

The transformative nature of mindfulness on people means that people who practice mindfulness will over time change their preferences to reflect an expanded and more inclusive notion of themselves. The fact that mindfulness practitioners have preferences that endogenously and systematically change raises a normative question of whether pre-mindfulness preferences or post-mindfulness preferences are more appropriate measures of those people's welfare. A similar question arises about how to conduct welfare analysis in economic models about individuals who have endogenous preferences that vary over context, frame, or time (McDonnell 2012).

## 5. HAPPINESS, NEGOTIATIONS, AND CONFLICT RESOLUTION

Negotiations are recurring and ubiquitous aspects of being human. We constantly negotiate with colleagues, competitors, family, friends, and ourselves. A large literature about negotiations uses multiple disciplinary approaches, including perspectives based upon behavioral and neoclassical economics, cognitive and social psychology, communications theory and cultural studies, decision and game theory, neuroeconomics and neuropsychology, and organizational behavior and management studies. Almost all negotiations involve financial, objective, observable, substantive, and verifiable issues in addition to emotional, hidden, non-verifiable, procedural, and subjective issues (Shapiro 2010). Negotiators often face and have to make tradeoffs between objective and subjective considerations in evaluating alternative outcomes. Curhan, Elfenbein, and Kilduff (2009) provide empirical evidence that higher subjective valuations achieved in job offer negotiations predicted greater employee compensation and job satisfaction and lower turnover intention, measured one year later. Discrete, particular emotions can have positive and/

or negative consequences for negotiations, with such effects systematically varying across contexts, cultures, and situations.

Based on empirical and experimental findings that in a variety of situations people tend systematically to mis-predict what makes them happy, Guthrie and Sally (2004) consider the legal ethics and professionalism implications for attorneys and their clients of negotiations where disputants are unable to ascertain what they really want. Similar issues arise for others besides attorneys who negotiate for their clients, such as agents, investment bankers, and realtors. Movius and Wilson (2011) develop some of the implications for negotiations advice, practice, research, and theory in general of the happiness research finding that people tend systematically to incorrectly predict the duration and intensity of their feelings, and related happiness research about how people inaccurately remember and misunderstand the causes and sources of their feelings.

Pearlstein (2012) details how and why conflict resolution practitioners, scholars, and students already share much in common regarding, and can also still learn much from, happiness research. In particular, the difference between happiness and meaningfulness is akin to that between positions and interests. Inaccuracies in affective forecasting are not only obstacles to achieving happiness; they are also psychological impediments to resolving conflicts. Pearlstein (2012) analyzes two hypotheses about how conflict and happiness are related. First, unhappy individuals are more likely than happy individuals to be in unproductive or even destructive conflicts. Second, individuals engaged in unproductive or even destructive conflicts are more likely than other individuals to be unhappy. Pearlstein (2012) develops a novel corollary of the above two hypotheses: there is a feedback loop between happiness and cooperation, in addition to another feedback loop between unhappiness and lack of cooperation. In other words, happiness leads to reduced conflict or even cooperation, which leads to happiness. Similarly, unhappiness leads to conflict, which leads to unhappiness.

Empirical evidence already exists that is consistent with both of the above hypotheses. Individuals in positive moods behave pro-socially, cooperate, engage in less conflict, and help others more, perhaps due to emotional contagion (Barsky, Kaplan, and Beal 2011, pp. 257, 262). The happiness of negotiators increases their confidence, cooperative behavior, and expectations of success (Cohn et al. 2009, pp. 361–62). Positive affect in negotiators also tends to increase integrative capacities, lead to more integrative solutions, and reduce contentious tactics (Carnevale and Isen 1986, p. 11). Positive mood is a resource that helps in negative interpersonal situations with intertemporal or motivational conflicts and primes more positive associations, thoughts, ideas, and expectations, which lead to more cooperative and integrative bargaining strategies (Forgas 2002, pp. 15, 20). People who self-report being happy are less likely to have workplace disputes (Frank 2008, p. 1789). Happy individuals marry earlier, have less marital conflict, and stay married longer (Haidt 2006, pp. 88, 94). Lyubomirsky, King, and Diener (2005, pp. 824, 828) find that happy people are less likely to divorce and engage in destructive conflict, in addition to being more likely to experience greater cooperation, have marital well-being, and resolve conflicts better. Positive affect in negotiators is associated with their engaging in creative problem solving, making larger concessions, and using cooperative strategies more (van Kleef, De Dreu, and Manstead 2004, p. 510). Happier people also produce higher quality and more effective interpersonal persuasive messages (Forgas 2006).

Pearlstein (2012) provides ten examples of the convergence between how to resolve conflicts and how to facilitate happiness that illustrate the connections and similarities between conflict interventions from conflict resolution theory and happiness interventions from positive psychology. First, having a feeling of a sense of being in control is crucial to happiness, being satisfied with a conflict resolution mechanism or process, and higher perceptions of fairness. Second, interpersonal trust causes and is caused by happiness and the resolution of conflict. Third, being forgiving correlates with happiness and is key to achieving closure and emotional resolution of conflict. Fourth, expressing and feeling gratitude correlates with happiness and facilitates mindsets conducive to resolving conflicts (Kinni 2003). Fifth, creativity is correlated with happiness and discovering integrative win-win solutions to resolve conflicts. Sixth, developing effective coping strategies in the face of adversity, conflict, pain, and stress correlates with happiness and resolving conflicts. Seventh, developing resilience correlates with happiness and resolving conflicts. Eighth, performing acts of kindness and generosity are correlated with happiness and more cooperative behavior in conflicts. Ninth, experiencing personal growth and finding meaning are correlated with happiness and mindfulness that in turn are related to more effective conflict resolution. Tenth, perceiving that we make a difference or matter to others improves our happiness and creates a virtuous cycle of active listening, appreciative inquiry, and similar intentional behaviors that demonstrate attention, empathy, and importance. Pearlstein (2012) provides an example of how creativity, coping, and resilience each reinforce the other two as an illustration of how subsets of these ten factors can interact with others in powerful self-reinforcing feedback loops.

Pearlstein (2012) discusses how to apply insights from happiness research to help value the settlement of disputes. He highlights the advantages of reframing conflicts to emphasize the strategies parties can use to enhance and restore their happiness, meaning, and personal strengths. Pearlstein proposes that lawyers can help their clients accumulate, develop, and leverage what he calls their "happiness capital" to be a crucial asset for better engagement with and resolution of conflicts. Pearlstein connects the happiness perception of conflict with the promotion of psychological well-being central to the therapeutic jurisprudence and preventive law movement. He develops two principles that are based on happiness research for the design of dispute systems and organizational conflict resolution. First, organizational members should participate in the design of dispute and conflict resolution systems. Second, organizations should demonstrate that its members matter to it and strive to strengthen network ties among its members. Pearlstein reminds us that unhappiness and conflict sometimes can help us avoid being complacent when facing injustice. He notes that the idea of happiness being the ultimate currency in which to evaluate life's outcomes (Ben-Shahar 2007, p. 52) has transformative implications for the processes, techniques, and training of conflict resolution professionals. Pearlstein (2012) concludes that an easy and consensus-generating agenda about how to apply happiness research to conflict resolution is found in the field of education. Individuals tend to have a default mode of zero-sum thinking. Envy and jealousy might even be neurologically hard-wired into us. Happiness studies help to justify educating people of all ages about how efficacious and important non-zero-sum thinking can be in resolving conflicts.

## 6.   IMPROVING LEGAL EDUCATION

Some journalists, lawyers, law students, and legal academics have become increasingly critical and much more vocally so recently of legal education (Floyd 2010; Morgan 2010, pp. 177–216; Olson 2011; Rapoport 2012; Zimmerman 2010). One law professor argues that law schools fail to adequately prepare their students for legal practice (Tamanaha 2012). Law professors disagree about the particular mindsets and skills that successful attorneys can and should learn in law schools. Although all law professors are legal educators, some law professors also strive to be legal scholars (Buell 2012).

The oft-parodied and repeated phrase that law professors teach their students to "think like lawyers" has no consensus meaning. The first year of American law school education involves large sections of traditional doctrinal courses in which students read highly edited appellate opinions to learn to engage in legal reasoning by analogy and precedent. In their second and third years of American law school education, students can enroll in other traditional doctrinal courses in which students also learn to engage in legal reasoning by statutory interpretation. Law students have the option after their first year in law school to enroll in clinical courses that offer experiential opportunities to interact with and help actual clients.

Traditional American legal doctrinal education has an excessively narrow and impoverished vision of what it means to "think like a lawyer" that privileges analogical, analytical, linear, and logical reasoning over the development of creativity (Menkel-Meadow 2001), emotional intelligence (James 2011), a growth mindset (Rosen 2011), and such human and social dimension skills as effective communication, active listening, and understanding context (Huang 2012). An unbalanced legal education does our students a huge disservice (Shultz and Zedeck 2008).

Recent economic challenges to and changes in the market for lawyers only highlight how important it is to prepare our students to develop successful and sustainable legal careers. The financial rate of return for a law degree can be analyzed by calculating two ratios, namely the ratio of monthly debt service divided by monthly gross income and the ratio of educational debt to annual salary (Chen 2012). In addition to law student debt, there are non-financial emotional and psychological costs of legal education.

A large body of empirical research finds that traditional doctrinal legal educational pedagogy correlates with a widespread, systemic, and significantly increased amount of law student alcohol and psychedelic drug use, alienation, allergic reactions, anger, anxiety, chemical dependency, concentration difficulties, depression, dissatisfaction, exhaustion, familial and relationship difficulties, headaches, hostility, inability to sleep, isolation, learned helplessness, lethargy, loss of self-esteem, obsessive-compulsive behavior, paranoia, psychological distress, sedentary behavior, stress, and weight fluctuations (Hess 2002, pp. 77–79; Peterson and Peterson 2009). These negative mental and physical health, emotional, and psychological effects are independent of age, gender, and law school grades (Hess 2002, pp. 77, footnote 5). These negative consequences also seem to be more pronounced for minorities and women (Hess 2002, pp. 77–79, footnote 6).

Although the fear of embarrassment, failure, and public humiliation in class can be powerful motivators to incentivize law students to prepare for being called on randomly in class, they likely also cause anxiety, depression, or stress and interfere with genuine learning. There is a movement among some law professors to humanize legal education (Fines 2008; Winick 2010). Happiness research provides empirical support for the importance of cultivating enthusiasm in law students (Zimmerman 2009), encouraging law students to adopt optimistic attribution styles (Rosen 2011), engaging law students (Law School Survey of Student Engagement 2009), engendering hope in law students (Martin and Rand 2010; Rand, Martin, and Shea 2011), helping law students to find meaning in practice (Tannebaum 2012), teaching law students to recognize, develop, and utilize their strengths (Schultz 2013), and using collaborative exercises in experiential learning (Davis et al. 2011/2012).

## 7.   IMPROVING LEGAL PRACTICE

Some lawyers are quite unhappy (Schlitz 1999; Seligman, Verkuil, and Kang 2001), while other lawyers are quite satisfied (Organ 2011). Employers in general (Amabile and Kramer 2011) and legal employers in particular (Huang and Swedloff 2008, pp. 349–50; Levit and Linder 2010, pp. 160–207) already use happiness research to help in the design of human resources policies and practices, institutional norms, organizational cultures, and workplace environments that increase employee flourishing, retention, productivity, satisfaction and thriving. An organization can achieve a sustainable competitive advantage through its members by developing and investing in psychological capital (a notion that is analogous to human capital and social capital) that consists of confidence, hope, optimism, and resiliency (Luthans, Youssef, and Avolio 2007). The Center for Positive Organizational Scholarship at the University of Michigan Ross School of Business is "devoted to energizing and transforming organizations through research on the theory and practice of positive organizing and leadership" (Ross School of Business 2014). A series of articles in a recent *Harvard Business Review* issue spotlights how modern happiness research suggests that a thriving and flourishing workforce is related to improved business performance (Harvard Business Review 2012). A reporter coined the phrase "the happiness-industrial complex" to describe the cottage industry of coaches and consultants who apply happiness research to help corporate and institutional clients hire, retain, and train people to achieve more job satisfaction and increase their organizational and team productivity (Zaslow 2006).

Improving legal education to help law students become happier, healthier, more creative, more engaged, more hopeful, and more resilient will improve the practice of law as those students enter and move through their legal careers. The same behaviors, concepts, ideas, insights, knowledge, and skills from happiness research that can be taught in law schools can also be taught to lawyers as part of on-the-job training, continuing legal education, and professional skills development programs (David 2011). Many practitioners decry the increasing lack of civility and courtesy if not outright hostility in the practice of law today (Boulder County Bar Association). Teaching mindfulness to attorneys can help them adopt less adversarial mindsets (Berkeley Law University of California).

A book review about happiness for lawyers (Levit and Linder 2010) questions whether lawyers deserve to be happy (Delgado 2012, pp. 926–28) and concludes that excessive legal formalism and the violence that law can do must change before law practice generally can become a source of happiness (Delgado 2012, pp. 928–30). An open question for lawyers individually and collectively as members of a profession and organizations is whether they can and wish to make those changes.

The prospects are promising for insights, strategies, and techniques from the happiness literature to improve legal practice. Already, the happiness in legal education literature is actually changing practices on the ground in law school orientation programs and first-year courses. The positive psychology literature suggests a number of ways to improve the subjective well-being of law students and lawyers, including practicing mindfulness, shifting their attribution style (how they think about their experiences), utilizing core strengths, and developing meaning in life and work (Huang and Felder 2015; Huang et al. 2018).

# REFERENCES

Amabile, Teresa, and Steven Kramer. 2011. *The Progress Principle: Using Small Wins to Ignite Joy, Engagement, and Creativity at Work*. Boston, MA: Harvard Business Review Press.
Angeles, Luis. 2010. Children and Life Satisfaction. *Journal of Happiness Studies* 11: 523–38.
Barsky, Adam, Seth A. Kaplan, and Daniel J. Beal. 2011. Just Feelings? The Role of Affect in the Formation of Organizational Fairness Judgments. *Journal of Management* 37: 248–79.
Baucells, Manel, and Rakesh Sarin. 2012. *Engineering Happiness: A New Approach for Building a Joyful Life*. Berkeley, CA: University of California Press.
Baumeister, Roy F., Kathleen D. Vohs, Jennifer L. Aaker, and Emily N. Garbinsky. 2013. Some Key Differences between a Happy Life and a Meaningful Life. *Journal of Positive Psychology* 8: 505–16.
Bazerman, Max, and Deepak Malhotra. 2006. Economics Wins, Psychology Loses, and Society Pays. Pp. 263–80 in *Social Psychology and Economics*, edited by David De Cremer, Marcel Zeelenberg, and J. Keith Murnighan. Mahwah, NJ: Lawrence Erlbaum Associates.
Ben-Shahar, Tal. 2007. *Happier: Learn the Secrets to Daily Joy and Lasting Fulfillment*. New York: McGraw-Hill.
Berkeley Law University of California. Mindfulness at Berkeley Law. https://www.law.berkeley.edu/students/mindfulness-at-berkeley-law/
Bernanke, Ben S. 2010. The Economics of Happiness. Commencement Speech, University of South Carolina, May 8, http://www.federalreserve.gov/newsevents/speech/bernanke20100508a.htm (last updated May 8, 2010).
Blumenthal, Jeremy A. 2007. Emotional Paternalism. *Florida State University Law Review* 35: 1–72.
Blumenthal, Jeremy A. 2012. Expert Paternalism. *Florida Law Review* 64: 721–57.
Blumenthal, Jeremy A., and Peter H. Huang. 2009. Positive Parentalism. *National Law Journal*, January 26.
Booth, Philip, ed. 2012. *. . .and the Pursuit of Happiness: Wellbeing and the Role of Government*. London: The Institute of Economic Affairs.
Boulder County Bar Association. Principles of Professionalism. http://www.boulder-bar.org/professionalism.htm#1 (last visited July 1, 2014).
Buell, Samuel W. 2012. Becoming a Legal Scholar. *Michigan Law Review* 110: 1175–90.
Camerer, Colin, Samuel Issacharoff, George Loewenstein, Ted O'Donoghue, and Matthew Rabin. 2003. Regulation for Conservatives: Behavioral Economics and the Case for "Asymmetric Paternalism." *University of Pennsylvania Law Review* 151: 1211–54.
Cantrell, Deborah J. 2010. Can Compassionate Practice also be Good Legal Practice? Answers from the Lives of Buddhist Lawyers. *Rutgers Journal of Law & Religion* 12: 3–75.
Carnevale, Peter J. D., and Alice M. Isen. 1986. The Influence of Positive Affect and Visual Access on the Discovery of Integrative Solutions in Bilateral Negotiation. *Organizational Behavior and Human Decision Processes* 37: 1–13.
Cartwright, Edward. 2011. *Behavioral Economics*. New York: Routledge.
Chen, Jim. 2012. A Degree of Practical Wisdom: The Ratio of Educational Debt to Income as a Basic Measurement of Law School Graduates' Economic Viability. *William Mitchell Law Review* 38: 1185–208.
Clore, Gerald L., and Jeffrey R. Huntsinger, 2007. How Emotions Inform Judgment and Regulate Thought. *Trends in Cognitive Science* 11: 393–99.
Cohen, Roger. 2011. The Happynomics of Life. *New York Times*, March 13.
Cohn, Michael A., Barbara L. Fredrickson, Stephanie L. Brown, Joseph A. Mikels, and Anne M. Conway. 2009. Happiness Unpacked: Positive Emotions Increase Life Satisfaction by Building Resilience. *Emotion* 9: 361–68.

Conley, Chip. 2010. Measuring What Makes Life Worthwhile. http://www.ted.com/talks/chip_conley_measuring_what_makes_life_worthwhile?language=en (last visited July 1, 2014).

Cooney Nick. 2011. *Change of Heart: What Psychology Can Teach Us About Spreading Social Change*. New York: Lantern Books.

Cooper, James C., and William E. Kovacic. 2012. Behavioral Economics: Implications for Regulatory Behavior. *Journal of Regulatory Studies* 41: 41–58.

Curhan, Jared B., Hillary Anger Elfenbein, and Gavin J. Kilduff. 2009. Getting Off on the Right Foot: Subjective Value Versus Economic Value in Predicting Longitudinal Job Outcomes from Job Offer Negotiations. *Journal of Applied Psychology* 94: 524–34.

David, Ted. 2011. Can Lawyers Learn to be Happy? *Practical Lawyer*, August, 29–36.

Davidson, Richard J., and Sharon Begley. 2012. *The Emotional Life of the Brain: How Its Unique Patterns Affect the Way You Think, Feel, and Live—and How You Can Change Them*. New York: Hudson Street Press.

Davidson Richard J., Jon Kabat-Zinn, Jessica Schumacher, Melissa Rosenkranz, Daniel Muller, Saki F. Santorelli, Ferris Urbanowski, Anne Harrington, Katherine Bonus, and John F. Sheridan. 2003. Alterations in Brain and Immune Function Produced by Mindfulness Meditation. *Psychosomatic Medicine* 65: 564–70.

Davis, Peggy Cooper, Ebony Coletu, Bonita London, and Wentao Yuan. 2011/2012. Making Law Students Healthy, Skillful, and Wise. *New York Law School Law Review* 56: 487–515.

Delgado, Richard. 2012. Recent Writing on Law and Happiness. *Iowa Law Review* 97: 913–30.

Diener, Ed, John F. Helliwell, and Daniel Kahneman. 2010. *International Differences in Well-Being*. New York: Oxford University Press.

Diener, Ed, Richard E. Lucas, Ulrich Schimmack, and John Helliwell. 2009. *Well-Being for Public Policy*. New York: Oxford University Press.

Dowling, John Malcolm, and Yap Chin-Fang, 2007. *Modern Developments in Behavioral Economics*. Hackensack, NJ: World Scientific.

Edelman, Shimon. 2012. *The Happiness of Pursuit: What Neuroscience Can Teach Us About the Good Life*. New York: Basic Books.

Fennell, Lee Anne. 2006. Hyperopia in Public Finance. Pp. 141–71 in *Behavioral Public Finance* edited by Edward J. McCaffery and Joel Slemrod. New York: Russell Sage Foundation.

Ferraro, Fabrizio, Jeffrey Pfeffer, and Richard I. Sutton. 2005. Economics Language and Assumptions: How Theories Can Become Self-Fulfilling. *Academy of Management Review* 42: 25–40.

Fines, Barbara Glesner. 2008. Fundamental Principles and Challenges of Humanizing Legal Education. *Washburn Law Journal* 47: 313–26.

Fisher, Roger, and Daniel Shapiro. 2005. *Beyond Reason: Using Emotions as You Negotiate*. New York: Viking.

Floyd, Daisy Hurst. 2010. We Can Do Better. *Journal of Legal Education* 60: 129–34.

Forgas, Joseph P. 2002. Feeling and Doing: Affective Influences on Interpersonal Behavior *Psychological Inquiry* 13: 1–28.

Forgas, Joseph P. 2006. When Sad is Better Than Happy: Negative Affect Can Improve the Quality and Effectiveness of Persuasive Messages and Social Influence Strategies. *Journal of Experimental Social Psychology* 43: 513–28.

Frank, Robert H. 2008. Should Public Policy Respond to Positional Externalities? *Journal of Public Economics* 92: 1777–86.

Frey, Bruno S., and Alois Stutzer. 2010. Happiness and Public Choice. *Public Choice* 144: 557–73.

Friedman, Howard S., and Leslie R. Martin. 2011. *The Longevity Project*. New York: Hudson Street Press.

Glaeser, Edward L. 2006. Paternalism and Psychology. *University of Chicago Law Review* 73: 133–56.

Goudie, Robert J. B., Sach N. Mukherje, Jan-Emmanuel De Neve, Andrew J. Oswald, and Stephen Wu. 2011. Happiness as a Driver of Risk-Avoiding Behavior. Working Paper No. 3451. CESifo, Munich.

Graham, Carol. 2010. *Happiness Around the World: The Paradox of Happy Peasants and Miserable Millionaires*. New York: Oxford University Press.

Graham, Carol. 2011. *The Pursuit of Happiness: An Economy of Well-Being*. Washington, DC: Brookings Institution Press.

Guthrie, Chris, and David Sally. 2004. Impact Bias: The Impact of the Impact Bias on Negotiation, *Marquette Law Review* 87: 817–28.

Haidt, Jonathan. 2006. *The Happiness Hypothesis: Finding Truth in Ancient Wisdom*. New York: Basic Books.

Haidt, Jonathan. 2013. The Happiness Hypothesis: Finding Modern Truth in Ancient Wisdom, http://www.happinesshypothesis.com/ (last updated September 2, 2013).

Hamilton, Neil, and Verna Monson. 2011. The Positive Empirical Relationship of Professionalism to Effectiveness in the Practice of Law. *Georgetown Journal of Legal Ethics* 24: 137–86.

Harris, Angela P. 2012. Toward Lawyering as Peacemaking: A Seminar on Mindfulness, Morality, and Professional Identity. *Journal of Legal Education* 61: 647–53.

Harris Angela P., Margaretta Lin, and Jeff Selbin. 2007. From "The Art of War" to "Being Peace": Mindfulness and Community Lawyering in a Neoliberal Age. *California Law Review* 95: 2073–132.

Harrison, Jeffrey L. 2009. Happiness, Efficiency, and the Promise of Decisional Equity: From Outcome to Process. *Pepperdine Law Review* 36: 935–95.

Harrison, Jeffrey L. 2011. Regulation, Deregulation, and Happiness. *Cardozo Law Review* 32: 2369–89.

Harvard Business Review. 2012. Spotlight: The Happiness Factor. http://hbr.org/2012/01/spotlight-the-happiness-factor/ar/1 (last visited July 1, 2014).

Headey, Bruce, Ruud Muffels, and Gert G. Wagner. 2010. Long-Running German Panel Survey Shows that Personal and Economic Choices, Not Just Genes, Matter for Happiness. *Proceedings of the National Academy of Sciences* 107: 17922–26.

Heath, Chip, and Dan Heath. 2010. *Switch: How to Change Things When Change Is Hard*. New York: Crown.

Herbst, Chris M. 2011. "Paradoxical" Decline? Another Look at the Relative Reduction in Female Happiness. *Journal of Economic Psychology* 32: 733–88.

Herbst, Chris M., and John Ifcher. 2012. A Bundle of Joy: Does Parenting Really Make Us Miserable? https://ssrn.com/abstract=1883839 or http://dx.doi.org/10.2139/ssrn.1883839

Hess, Gerald F. 2002. Heads and Hearts: The Teaching and Learning Environment in Law School. *Journal of Legal Education* 52: 75–111.

Hill, Claire, A. 2007. Anti-Anti-Anti-Paternalism. *New York University Journal of Law and Liberty* 2: 444–54.

Hilsenrath, Jon. 2010. Bernanke Offers a Lesson on Happiness. *Wall Street Journal*, May 8.

Holt, Jim. 2006. The New, Soft Paternalism. *New York Times*, December 3.

Huang, Peter H. 2008a. How Do Securities Laws Influence Affect, Happiness, and Trust? *Journal of Business & Technology Law* 3: 257–308.

Huang, Peter H. 2008b. Authentic Happiness, Self-Knowledge, and Legal Policy. *Minnesota Journal of Law, Science, & Technology* 9: 755–84.

Huang, Peter H. 2008c. Emotional Adaptation and Lawsuit Settlements. *Columbia Law Review Sidebar* 108: 50–57.

Huang, Peter H. 2010. Happiness Studies and Legal Policy. *Annual Review of Law and Social Science* 6: 405–32.

Huang, Peter H. 2011. Happiness in Business or Law. *Transactions: Tennessee Journal of Business Law* 12: 153–72.

Huang, Peter H. 2012. Tiger Cub Strikes Back: Memoirs of an Ex-Child Prodigy About Legal Education and Parenting. *British Journal of American Legal Studies* 1: 297–347.

Huang, Peter H. 2014. Torn Between Two Selves: Should Law Care More About Experiencing Selves or Remembering Selves? *Southern Methodist University Science & Technology Law Review* 17: 263–323.

Huang, Peter H. 2015. How Improving Decision-Making and Mindfulness Can Improve Legal Ethics and Professionalism. *Journal of Law, Business and Ethics* 21: 35–76.

Huang, Peter H. 2016. Meta-Mindfulness: A New Hope. *Richmond Journal of Law and the Public Interest* 19: 303–24.

Huang, Peter H. 2017. Can Practicing Mindfulness Improve Lawyer Decision-Making, Ethics, and Leadership? *Houston Law Review* 55: 63–154.

Huang, Peter H. 2018a, forthcoming. Subjective Well-being and the Law. In e-Handbook of Well-being, edited by Ed Diener, Shige Oishi, and Louis Tay.

Huang, Peter H. 2018b, forthcoming. Adventures in Higher Education, Happiness, and Mindfulness. *British Journal of American Legal Studies* 7.

Huang, Peter H., and Jeremy A. Blumenthal. 2009. Positive Institutions, Law, and Policy. Pp. 589–97 in *The Oxford Handbook of Positive Psychology*, edited by Shane J. Lopez and C. R. Snyder. New York: Oxford University Press.

Huang, Peter H., and Corie Rosen Felder. 2015. The Zombie Lawyer Apocalypse. *Pepperdine Law Review* 42: 727–72.

Huang, Peter H., and Rick Swedloff. 2008. Authentic Happiness and Meaning at Law Firms. *Syracuse Law Review* 58: 335–50.

Huang, Peter H., Anne M. Brafford, Debra S. Austin, and Martha Knudson. 2018, forthcoming. Positive Institutions: Organizations, Laws, and Policies. In *Handbook of Positive Psychology*, edited by Shane J. Lopez, Lisa M. Edwards, and Susana C. Marques, 3rd edition.

Hutson, Matthew. 2012. *The 7 Laws of Magical Thinking: How Irrational Beliefs Keep Us Happy, Healthy, and Sane*. New York: Hudson Street Press.

James, Colin. 2011. Law Student Wellbeing: Benefits of Promoting Psychological Literacy and Self-Awareness Using Mindfulness, Strengths Theory and Emotional Intelligence. *Legal Education Review* 21: 217–33.

Jones, Charles I., and Peter J. Klenow. 2010. Beyond GDP: Welfare across Countries and Time. Working Paper No. 16352. National Bureau of Economic Research, Cambridge, MA.

Kahneman, Daniel. 2010. The Riddle of Experience vs. Memory, http://www.ted.com/talks/daniel_kahneman_the_riddle_of_experience_vs_memory (last visited July 1, 2014).

Kahneman, Daniel. 2011. *Thinking, Fast and Slow*. New York: Farrar, Straus and Giroux.

Kahneman, Daniel, and Alan B. Kruger. 2006. Developments in the Measurement of Subjective Well-Being. *Journal of Economic Perspectives* 20: 3–24.

Kassenboehmer, Sonja C., and Christoph M. Schmidt. 2011. Beyond GDP and Back: What is the Value-Added by Additional Components of Welfare Measurement? Discussion Paper No. 5453. Institute for the Study of Labor.

Killingsworth, Matthew A., and Daniel T. Gilbert. 2010. A Wandering Mind is an Unhappy Mind. *Science* 330: 932.

Kinni, Theodore. 2003. The Art of Appreciative Inquiry, http://hbswk.hbs.edu/archive/3684.html (last visited July 1, 2014).

Kilpatrick, Lisa A., Brandall Y. Suyenobu, Suzanne R. Smith, Joshua A. Bueller, Trudy Goodman, J. David Creswell, Kristen Tillisch, Emeran A. Mayer, and Bruce D. Naliboff. 2011. Impact of Mindfulness-Based Stress Reduction Training on Intrinsic Basic Brain Connectivity. *Neuroimage* 56: 290–8.

Kristoffersen, Ingebjorg. 2010. The Metrics of Subjective Wellbeing: Cardinality, Neutrality and Additivity. *Economic Record* 86: 98–123.

Krueger, Alan B., Daniel Kahneman, David Schkade, Norbert Schwarz, and Arthur A. Stone. 2009. National Time Accounting: The Currency of Life. Pp. 9–86 in *Measuring the Subjective Well-Being of Nations: National Accounts of Time Use and Well-Being* edited by Alan B. Krueger. Chicago: University of Chicago Press.

Law School Survey of Student Engagement. 2009. What Areas of our Program Warrant Improvement, and Where Are We Doing Well? http://lssse.indiana.edu/wp-content/uploads/2016/01/2010_LSSSE_Annual_Survey_Results.pdf

Lawsky, Sarah B. 2011. On the Edge: Declining Marginal Utility and Tax Policy. *Minnesota Law Review* 95: 904–52.

Levav, Jonathan. 2007. The Mind and the Body: Subjective Well-Being in an Objective World. Pp. 315–44 in *Do Emotions Help or Hurt Decision-Making?* edited by Kathleen D. Vohs, Roy Baumeister, and George F. Loewenstein. New York: Russell Sage Foundation.

Levit, Nancy, and Douglas O. Linder. 2010. *The Happy Lawyer: Making a Good Life in the Law.* New York: Oxford University Press.

Loewenstein, George, and Emily Haisley. 2008. The Economist as Therapist: Methodological Ramifications of "Light" Paternalism. Pp. 210–45 in *The Foundations of Positive and Normative Economics*, edited by Andrew Caplin and Andrew Schotter. New York: Oxford University Press.

Luthans, Fred, Carolyn M. Youssef, and Bruce J. Avolio. 2007. *Psychological Capital: Developing the Human Competitive Edge.* New York: Oxford University Press.

Lyubomirsky, Sonja, Laura King, and Ed Diener. 2005. The Benefits of Frequent Positive Affect: Does Happiness Lead to Success? *Psychological Bulletin* 131: 803–55.

Magee, Rhonda. 2011. Educating Lawyers to Meditate. *University of Missouri Kansas City Law Review* 79: 535–93.

Margolis, Rachel, and Mikko Myrskylä. 2011. A Global Perspective on Happiness and Fertility. *Population and Development Review* 37: 29–56.

Martin, Allison D., and Kevin L. Rand, 2010. The Future's So Bright, I Gotta Wear Shades: Law School Through the Lens of Hope. *Duquesne Law Review* 48: 203–31.

Martin, Mike W. 2012. *Happiness and the Good Life.* New York: Oxford University Press.

Maryland 1. What is the Genuine Progress Indicator? http://dnr.maryland.gov/mdgpi/Pages/default.aspx.

Maryland 2. Indicators. http://dnr.maryland.gov/mdgpi/Pages/overview.aspx

Maryland 3. Cost of Underemployment. http://dnr.maryland.gov/mdgpi/Pages/scea.aspx

Maryland 4. Cost of Climate Change. http://dnr.maryland.gov/mdgpi/Pages/cop.aspx

Maryland 5. Value of Higher Education. http://dnr.maryland.gov/mdgpi/Pages/shc.aspx

McDonnell, Brett H. 2012. Endogenous Preferences and Welfare Evaluations. In *Norms and Values in Law and Economics*, edited by Aristides Hatzis. London: Routledge.

McKenzie, Donald. 2008. *An Engine, Not a Camera: How Financial Models Shape Markets.* Cambridge, MA: MIT Press.

McKenzie, Donald, and Yuval Millo. 2003. Negotiating a Market, Performing Theory: The Historical Sociology of a Financial Derivatives Exchange. *American Journal of Sociology* 109: 107–45.

Menkel-Meadow, Carrie. 2001. Aha? Is Creativity Possible in Legal Problem Solving and Teachable in Legal Education? *Harvard Negotiation Law Review* 6: 97–144.

Mitchell, Gregory. 2005. Libertarian Paternalism is an Oxymoron. *Northwestern University Law Review* 99: 1245–77.

Mogilner, Cassie, Sepandar D. Kamvar, and Jennifer Aaker. 2011. The Shifting Meaning of Happiness. *Social Psychological and Personality Science* 2: 395–402.

Morgan, Thomas D. 2010. *The Vanishing American Lawyer.* New York: Oxford University Press.

Movius, Hallam and Timothy D. Wilson. 2011. How We Feel about the Deal. *Negotiation Journal* 27: 241–50.

Myrskylä, Mikko, and Rachel Margolis. 2012. Happiness: Before and After the Kids. Working Paper No. 2012-13. Max Planck Institute for Demographic Research.

New Economics Foundation. 2014, http://www.neweconomics.org/ (last visited July 1, 2014).

Nozick, Robert. 1977. *Anarchy, State, and Utopia*. New York: Basic Books.

OECD Better Life Index. 2014, http://www.oecdbetterlifeindex.org/ (last visited July 1, 2014).

OECD iLibrary. 2011. How's Life? Measuring Well-being. http://www.oecd-ilibrary.org/economics/how-s-life_9789264121164-en (last updated October 12, 2011).

Olson, Walter. 2011. *Schools for Misrule: Legal Academia and an Overlawyered America*. New York: Encounter Books.

Organ, Jerome M. 2011. What Do We Know About the Satisfaction/Dissatisfaction of Lawyers? A Meta-Analysis of Research on Lawyer Satisfaction and Well-Being. *University of Saint Thomas Law Journal* 8: 225–74.

Oswald, Andrew J. 1997. Happiness and Economic Performance. *Economic Journal* 107: 1815–31.

Oswald, Andrew J. 2010. Emotional Prosperity and the Stiglitz Commission. *British Journal of Industrial Relations* 48: 651–69.

Pearlstein, Arthur. 2012. Pursuit of Happiness and Resolution of Conflict: An Agenda for the Future of ADR. *Pepperdine Journal of Dispute Resolution* 12: 215–266.

Peppet, Scott R. 2002. Can Saints Negotiate? A Brief Introduction to the Problems of Perfect Ethics in Bargaining. *Harvard Negotiation Law Review* 7: 83–96.

Peterson, Todd David, and Elizabeth Waters Peterson. 2009. Stemming the Tide of Law Student Depression: What Law Schools Need to Learn from the Science of Positive Psychology. *Yale Journal of Health, Policy, Law, & Ethics* 9: 357–434.

Pounds, Van M. 2003. Promoting Truthfulness in Negotiation: A Mindful Approach. *Willamette Law Review* 40: 181–224.

Prentice, Robert. 2004. Teaching Ethics, Heuristics, and Biases. *Journal of Business Ethics Education* 1: 55–72.

Rand, Kevin L., Allison D. Martin, and Amanda M. Shea. 2011. Hope, But Not Optimism, Predicts Academic Performance of Law Students Beyond Previous Academic Achievement. *Journal of Research in Personality* 45: 683–86.

Rapoport, Nancy. 2012. Changing the Modal Law School: Rethinking U.S. Legal Education in (Most) Law Schools. *Penn State Law Review* 116: 1119–54.

Reuben, Richard C. 2012. Bringing Mindfulness into the Classroom: A Personal Journey. *Journal of Legal Education* 61: 674–82.

Riskin, Leonard L. 2002. The Contemplative Lawyer: On the Potential Contributions of Mindfulness Meditation to Students, Lawyers, and Their Clients. *Harvard Negotiation Law Review* 7: 1–66.

Riskin, Leonard L. 2004. Mindfulness: Foundational Training for Dispute Resolution. *Journal of Legal Education* 54: 79–90.

Riskin, Leonard L. 2006. Knowing Yourself: Mindfulness. Pp. 239–50 in *The Negotiator's Fieldbook: The Desktop Reference for the Experienced Negotiator*, edited by Christopher Honeyman and Andrea K. Schneider. Washington, DC: ABA Section for Dispute Resolution.

Riskin, Leonard L. 2009. Awareness and Ethics in Dispute Resolution and Law: Why Mindfulness Tends to Foster Ethical Behavior. *South Texas Law Review* 50: 493–503.

Riskin, Leonard L. 2010. Further Beyond Reason: Emotions, the Core Concerns, and Mindfulness in Negotiations. *Nevada Law Journal* 10: 290–337.

Riskin, Leonard L. 2012. Awareness and the Legal Profession: An Introduction to the Mindful Lawyer Symposium. *Journal of Legal Education* 61: 634–40.

Rock, Evan M. 2005. Mindfulness Meditation, the Cultivation of Awareness, Mediator Neutrality, and the Possibility of Justice. *Cardozo Law Review* 6: 347–65.

Rosen, Corie. 2011. Creating the Optimistic Classroom: What Law Schools Can Learn from Explanatory Style Effects. *McGeorge Law Review* 42: 319–42.

Ross School of Business, University of Michigan. 2014 Center for Positive Organizations. http://www.center-forpos.org/ (last visited July 1, 2014).

Ryan, Tim. 2012. *A Mindful Nation: How a Simple Practice Can Help Us Reduce Stress, Improve Performance, and Recapture the American Spirit*. Carlsbad, CA: Hay House.

Sachs, Daniel W., Betsy Stevenson, and Justin Wolfers. 2012. Subjective Wellbeing, Income, Economic Development and Growth. Pp. 59–97 in *… and the Pursuit of Happiness: Wellbeing and the Role of Government*, edited by Philip Booth. London: Institute of Economic Affairs.

Saint-Paul, Gilles. 2011. *The Tyranny of Utility: Behavioral Social Science and the Rise of Paternalism*. Princeton, NJ: Princeton University Press.

Schlag, Pierre. 2010. Nudge, Choice Architecture, and Libertarian Paternalism. *Michigan Law Review* 108: 913–24.

Schlitz, Patrick J. 1999. On Being a Happy, Healthy, and Ethical Member of an Unhappy, Unhealthy, and Unethical Profession. *Vanderbilt Law Review* 52: 871–951.

Schubert, Christian. 2012. Pursuing Happiness. *Kyklos* 65: 245–61.

Schultz, Nancy L. 2013. Lessons from Positive Psychology for Developing Advocacy Skills. *John Marshall Law Journal* 6: 103–44.

Seligman, Martin E. P. 2011. *Flourishing: A Visionary New Understanding of Happiness and Well-being*. New York: Free Press.

Seligman, Martin E. P., Paul Verkuil, and Terry H. Kang. 2001. Why Lawyers Are Unhappy. *Cardozo Law Review* 23: 33–53.

Shapiro, Daniel. 2010. From Signal to Semantic: Uncovering the Emotional Dimension of Negotiation. *Nevada Law Journal* 10: 461–71.

Sheldon, Kennon M., Todd B. Kashdan, and Michael F. Steger. eds. 2011. *Designing Positive Psychology: Taking Stock and Moving Forward*. New York: Oxford University Press.

Shultz, Marjorie M. and Sheldon Zedeck. 2008. Final Report: Identification, Development, and Validation of Predictors for Successful Lawyering. http://www.law.berkeley.edu/files/LSACREPORTfinal-12.pdf (last visited July 1, 2014).

Sin, Nancy L., Katherine M. Jacobs, and Sonja Lyubomirsky. 2011. House and Happiness: A Differential Diagnosis. Pp. 77–94 in *House and Psychology* edited by Ted Cascio and Leonard Martin. New York: John Wiley & Sons.

Stevenson, Betsey, and Justin Wolfers. 2008. Economic Growth and Subjective Well-Being: Reassessing the Easterlin Paradox. *Brookings Papers on Economic Activity* 1–87.

Stevenson, Betsey, and Justin Wolfers. 2009. The Paradox of Declining Female Happiness. *American Economic Journal: Economic Policy* 1: 190–225.

Stiglitz, Joseph E., Amartya Sen, and Jean-Paul Fitoussi. 2009. *Report by the Commission on the Measurement of Economic Performance and Social Progress*. http://ec.europa.eu/eurostat/documents/118025/118123/Fitoussi+Commission+report

Stucke, Maurice E. 2010. Money, Is That What I Want? Competition Policy and the Role of Behavioral Economics *Santa Clara Law Review* 50: 893–979.

Swedloff, Rick, and Peter H. Huang. 2010. Tort Damages and the New Science of Happiness. *Indiana Law Journal* 5: 553–95.

Tamanaha, Brian Z. 2012. *Failing Law Schools*. Chicago: University of Chicago Press.

Tannebaum, Brian. 2012. The Practice: Finding Meaning. *Above the Law*, April 30.

Taylor, Laura Hodges. 2012. Book Review of *Law and Happiness*. *Journal of Legal Education* 61: 699–710.

Thaler, Richard H., and Cass R. Sunstein. 2008. *Nudge: Improving Decisions about Health, Wealth, and Happiness*. New Haven, CT: Yale University Press.

Thin, Neil. 2012. *Social Happiness: Theory into Policy and Practice*. Chicago: Policy Press.

Tierney, John. 2011. How Happy Are You? A Census Wants to Know. *New York Times*, April 30, 2011.

van Kleef, Gerben A., Carsten K. W. De Dreu, and Antony S. R. Manstead. 2004. The Interpersonal Effects of Emotions in Negotiations: A Motivated Information Processing Approach. *Journal of Personality and Social Psychology* 87: 510–28.

Veetil, Vipin P. 2010. Libertarian Paternalism is an Oxymoron: An Essay in Defense of Liberty. *European Journal of Law and Economics* 31: 1–14.

Wheelan, Charles. 2012. *10½ Things No Commencement Speaker Has Ever Said*. New York: Norton.

Wilkinson, Nick. 2008. *An Introduction to Behavioral Economics*. New York: Palgrave Macmillan.

Winick, Bruce J. 2010. Symposium Foreword: What Does Balance in Legal Education Mean? http://jle.aals.org/cgi/viewcontent.cgi?article=1244&context=home

YouTube. 2008. Robert F. Kennedy challenges Gross Domestic Product. https://www.youtube.com/watch?v=77IdKFqXbUY (last updated September 11, 2008).

Zak, Paul J. 2011a. The Physiology of Moral Sentiments. *Journal of Economic Behavior and Organization* 77: 53–65.

Zak, Paul J. 2011b. Moral Markets. *Journal of Economic Behavior and Organization* 77: 212–33.

Zak, Paul J. 2012. *The Moral Molecule: The Source of Love and Prosperity*. New York: Dutton.

Zak, Paul and Ahlam Fakhar. 2006. Neuroactive Hormones and Interpersonal Trust: International Evidence. *Economics and Human Biology* 4: 412–19.

Zaslow, Jeffrey. 2006. Happiness, Inc. *Wall Street Journal*, March 18.

Zimmerman, Emily. 2009. An Interdisciplinary Framework for Understanding and Cultivating Law Student Enthusiasm. *DePaul Law Review* 58: 851–917.

Zimmerman, Emily. 2010. What Do Law Students Want? The Missing Piece of the Assessment Puzzle. *Rutgers Law Journal* 42: 1–78.

Zlotnick, David M. 2012. Integrating Mindfulness Theory and Practice into Trial Advocacy. *Journal of Legal Education* 61: 654–64.

# 11. Trust and the law
*Benjamin Ho and David Huffman*

## 1. INTRODUCTION

Amartya Sen (1977) famously accused economists of studying rational fools: narrowly self-interested economic actors, disconnected from the webs of trust, reciprocity, and social interaction that constitute the reality of economic exchange. Economics has responded to this critique through three largely disjointed literatures. The growth literature has studied the relationship between survey measures of trust and economic growth in cross-country regressions. Organizational economics has focused on game theory and how self-interested rational actors can foster mutual trust through repeated interactions. Behavioral economics has drawn on experimental evidence to uncover the psychological and social mechanisms that motivate trusting and trustworthy behavior.

This understanding of the nature of trust has substantial implications for thinking about the economics of law. Laws represent the underlying institutions of the economy, allow enforcement of contracts, protect property rights, and facilitate the possibility of stable long-term trading relationships. Here, we consider the interaction between laws and trust. Specifically, this chapter seeks to address whether strong legal institutions and trust act as substitutes, such that strong law crowds out trust, or whether law and trust are complements, such that high trust and strong law are especially beneficial when the occur together. We pursue this inquiry by looking at the growth, behavioral economics, and organizational economics literatures.

In the macro growth literature there is evidence that high trust levels, and high quality of legal institutions, both contribute to positive economic outcomes (e.g., Knack and Keefer 1997; La Porta et al. 1999), but what remains to be explained is why high trust levels and good quality institutions tend to be observed together. One possibility is that these are complements for some reason: the combination of high trust and strong law is beneficial, and more so than the sum of their parts.

As causality and underlying mechanisms are difficult to unravel using macro data, we turn to experimental evidence, and to game theory. These literatures show how, depending on the circumstances, trust and the law may be either substitutes or complements. One key factor seems to be the process through which laws were implemented. Laws imposed externally, by the experimenter or by a subject with unilateral decision rights, tend to reduce motivations to trust, i.e., law is a substitute for trust. Laws adopted through referendum, by contrast, tend to increase cooperation and act as a complement to trust. We discuss psychological mechanisms that may underlie these findings. Another strand of the experimental and game theory literatures shows that strong legal institutions can be a complement to trust if these facilitate repeated interactions, for example by protecting property rights and allowing economic actors to sustain stable long-term trading relationships. Repeated interactions allow "gift exchange" to emerge, a virtuous cycle of trust and reciprocal trustworthy behavior (Akerlof 1982). Without initial trust, however, gift exchange does not work even with strong legal institutions, so trust and the law are complements.

To frame our discussion of these effects, we employ a simple model that captures various types of interactions between trust and law. The model shows how trust can promote efficient transactions in an economy with moral hazard and adverse selection from asymmetric information. The model demonstrates that there may be a variety of different mechanisms underlying trusting behavior, including trust preferences, beliefs about the preferences of others, and other preferences related to social norms and risk. The model also illustrates how different types of psychological mechanisms can generate trustworthy behavior. Finally, the model will show how different types of laws and institutions may lead to different outcomes.

The chapter proceeds as follows. In the following section we present key definitions and describe the model. Then we review results on the relationship between trust and growth from the development and macroeconomics empirical literatures. These results suggest broad patterns of how trust matters in the economy and the cross-national patterns of association between trust, legal institutions and economic growth. We then turn to evidence from experiments that shed light on mechanisms that may link trust and the law and help us understand why in some circumstances they may be complements and in others substitutes.[1] We draw some preliminary conclusions about the factors that might contribute to explaining complementarity of trust and the law at the macro level. We end the chapter with a discussion of some specific laws, and how these interact with trust.

## 1.1 Defining Trust

While economists are generally precise in their models, they have been surprisingly loose in their definition of the idea of trust. Although common usage and dictionary definitions often suffice,[2] perhaps the best way to describe how economists understand trust is in terms of how it is normally measured. The basic ways that trust is measured are either using behavior in experiments (Berg, Dickhaut and McCabe 1995), beliefs elicited in experiments (e.g., Fehr et al. 2003), or through survey measures such as those asked in the General Social Survey (e.g., Putnam 1995a, 1995b).

The canonical trust experiment (Berg, Dickhaut and McCabe 1995) has two players, a trustor and trustee. The trustor is first given some money, say $10. The trustor can keep some amount of this money, or entrust any amount to the trustee. Whatever he entrusts triples in value. For example, if the trustor entrusts all $10, then the trustee receives 3 x $10, or $30. The trustee can now choose to divide that $30 however she wants between herself and the trustor. Given that the trustee is under no obligation to return anything, the amount sent by the trustor has been used as a measure of trusting behavior; the greater is the amount sent, the more trusting is the behavior of the trustor. Similarly, the amount sent back by the trustee is a measure of trustworthiness.

---

[1] For an excellent survey on the relationships between financial incentives and pro-social motives, see Bowles and Polanía-Reyes (2012).

[2] Trust can be defined as "assured reliance on the character, ability, strength, or truth of someone or something" or "dependence on something future or contingent" (Merriam-Webster 2012).

Trusting behavior in the trust game has been widely used as a measure of trust (and trustworthiness), as the game seems to capture an essential feature of why economists care about trust in the first place. Specifically, because there is no contract forcing the second-mover to return something, the trust game captures a basic moral hazard problem, which is present in many different settings, such as investing in a company, or hiring a worker, or buying from a seller a good of uncertain quality. In these settings, contracts are typically incomplete, and thus moral hazard arises. With complete contracts trust is not relevant, because a principal does not have to worry about moral hazard.

Another approach to measuring trust isolates the belief component of trust in the context of a trust game. A player in the role of a trustor may be asked what amount he expects to be returned for different possible amounts sent by a trustor. Subjects can be given financial incentives to state beliefs as accurately as possible. For example, subjects might be rewarded for reporting beliefs that match the actual behavior of trustors (e.g., Costa-Gomes, Huck and Weizsäcker 2010). Trusting behavior is generally strongly correlated with beliefs, consistent with claims that trustworthiness is an important determinant of trust. Some designs create exogenous variation in beliefs and suggest a causal impact of beliefs about trustworthiness on trusting behavior (Costa-Gomes et al. 2001; Bartling, Fehr and Schmidt 2012). Importantly, however, the correlation between beliefs and behavior is far from perfect, indicating that other factors also play a role in determining trust. Candidate factors include various types of preferences, for example risk preferences and social preferences; evidence on determinants of trust is discussed in more detail later in the chapter.

The third approach to measuring trust (typically used in macroeconomic growth papers) is survey questions, such as those asked in the General Social Survey (GSS), the World Values Survey (WVS), or the German Socioeconomic Panel (see Putnam 1995b; Baran, Sapienza and Zingales. 2010; Fehr et al. 2003). The trust question in the GSS, which has been most widely used, asks:

> "Generally speaking, would you say that most people can be trusted or that you can't be too careful in dealing with people?"

One interpretation of responses to this question relates to beliefs; people may be trusting, or not, based on their beliefs about the likelihood of trustworthiness by others.[3] Indeed, responses to trust survey questions have been shown to be correlated with stated beliefs in the trust game (Sapienza et al. 2013). Individual differences could also potentially reflect, however, differences in willingness to trust independent of beliefs about trustworthiness; just as with trusting behavior in the trust game, survey responses might reflect preferences in addition to beliefs.[4]

---

[3]  Respondents can indicate their responses on a scale, with 1 indicating "most people can be trusted," 2 indicating "can't be too careful," and 3 indicating "depends." Typically, researchers use a response of 1 as a binary indicator for level of trust.

[4]  Notably, the evidence on whether survey responses are correlated with trusting behavior in the trust game is mixed: some studies find little correlation (Glaeser et al. 2000; Lazzarini et al. 2005), while others find that trust as measured by the survey is a significant predictor of trusting behavior in the trust game (Fehr et al. 2003; Bellemare and Kröger 2007). Thöni, Tyran and Wengström (2012) find that answers to the trust question predict cooperative behavior

Other survey measures have been deliberately designed to capture trusting behavior, as opposed to capturing beliefs. For example, Glaeser et al. (2000), use questions such as:

"How often do you lend money to your friends?"
"How often do you lend personal possessions to your friends (e.g., CDs, clothes, bicycle, etc.)?"
"How often do you intentionally leave your rooming group's hallway door unlocked (when nobody is home)?"

Glaeser et al. (2000) find that responses to these types of questions are better predictors of the behavior in trust games than the standard GSS questions.[5]

## 2. THEORETICAL FRAMEWORK

To better define the ideas about trust embodied in trust game experiments, as well as how they relate to the survey questions, we present a simple model, adapted from Ho (2012).

Consider a game with two players, a principal (the trustor) and an agent (the trustee). The game has two stages: first, the principal offers to transfer an amount $w$ to the agent, and second the agent chooses an action $x$ that produces some return $y(x)$ for the principal. The cost c the agent faces to perform the task for the principal depends on the agent's trustworthiness $\theta$ where $\theta$ is exogenous to the agent. $\theta$ can depend on any number of behavioral mechanisms described below, including, but not limited to, the fairness of the game perceived by the agent, the altruism of the agent (pure altruism or reciprocal altruism) or simply the cost of effort. Note that each behavioral mechanism is affected by many specific factors. For example, the reciprocity of the agent may depend on the amount the principal transferred, the agent's beliefs about the principal's trust or kindness, and the agent's aversion to guilt. The utilities of principal and agent are given by:

$$U_P = y(x) - w$$

$$U_A = w - c(x,\theta)$$

We define $x$ and $\theta$ such that $y(x)$ is increasing in $x$, and so that $c(x,\theta)$ has increasing differences (i.e., complements) in $x$ and $\theta$. Note that this specification abstracts away from risk aversion (but see Bohnet and Zeckhauser (2004) for evidence that behavior in the trust game is not primarily driven by risk aversion). Note also that we do not assume that cost is minimized when $x$ is zero; in fact factors like guilt or altruism could make zero effort quite

---

in a public goods game, but through the channel of preferences rather than beliefs about the cooperativeness of others. Interpreting the different results is hampered, however, by differences in experimental design and subject pools. For example, studies finding null results have used relatively homogenous samples, and have at least partially dropped the veil of anonymity, while studies finding positive correlations have used representative samples and interactions between strangers.

[5] But see footnote 3 for a discussion of mixed evidence.

costly. Solving each player's first order condition (FOC), the agent chooses her optimal $x^*$ such that she satisfies her FOC (assuming no corner solution)[6]:

$$\frac{dc(x,\theta)}{dx} = 0.$$

And then using the Implicit Function Theorem (or Topkis theorem for discrete choices), complementarity gives us:

$$\frac{dx^*}{d\theta} \geq 0$$

In which case, by backward induction the principal chooses $w$, which satisfies the principal's FOC:

$$\frac{\partial y}{\partial w} = 1$$

$$\frac{\partial y}{\partial x} \frac{\partial x}{\partial \theta} \frac{\partial \theta}{\partial w} = 1$$

Note that if the agent's trustworthiness, $\theta$, is independent of the principal's choice, as in the case of narrowly self-interested agents, or if $\theta$ represents the pure dispositional altruism of the agent, then $\frac{d\theta}{dw} = 0$ and we get a corner solution. Only if $\theta$ depends on $w$, with $\theta'(w) > 0$ (for example due to the agent having a preference for reciprocity), then $\frac{\partial x}{\partial w} > 0$ and the principal is incentivized to increase the amount transferred to the agent.

In general, the choices that the principal and agent make on their own will differ from the choices a social planner would assign. A social planner maximizes joint utility $U_P + U_A = y(x) - c(x,\theta)$ and would choose $x$ such that the FOC of the social welfare function is maximized:

$$\frac{dy}{dx} = \frac{dc}{dx}$$

This conflicts with the agent's first order condition that insists on setting $\frac{dc}{dx} = 0$. Since $\frac{dy}{dx} > 0$ and $c(x,\theta)$ is convex, the agent's optimal $x$ will produce a socially suboptimal return for the principle. By complementarity, $x$ is increasing in $\theta$, so higher $\theta$ will move the agent closer to the socially optimum choice.

## 2.1    Defining Trust in the Model

So far, we have noted that $\theta$ is a measure of trustworthiness, but we have yet to specify how we measure trust. In the context of our model, we will think about trust either as the principal's beliefs about the trustworthiness of the agent, or since these beliefs are often unobservable, as the principal's action $w$, which is reflective of his level of trust. Suppose there are two types of agents $\theta \in \{\theta_L, \theta_H\}$, with $\theta_H > \theta_L$, so that the principal is more

---

[6]    To simplify exposition, we are interested in characterizing behavior where players do not choose the highest or lowest possible values (solutions at the corners). While classical economics often predicts such extreme behavior, choice at the extremes is rarely observed in experiments.

willing to trust higher type agents (seen from the principal's first order condition). Then we can define $b$ as the principal's belief that the agent is a high type: $b = \Pr(\theta = \theta_H | h)$, where $b$ might be derived from Bayes' rule and | is the observable history of play. In this simple one-shot game, there is no history, so the principal's belief is only his prior belief before entering the game, but the history could include the agent's past interactions or information about the agent's identity. Also, it is worth noting that in this model, trust and trustworthiness are connected. As trustworthiness increases in the system, then under rational expectations, people's belief that their partner is trustworthy increases and will therefore increase trusting actions like investment that depend on having a trustworthy partner.

## 2.2 Applying the Model to the Trust Game

We can apply the model to the specific setting of the Berg, Dickhaut and McCabe (1995) trust game experiment, as follows:

w = amount entrusted $0 \le w \le 10$
x = amount returned $0 \le x \le 3w$
y = three times the amount returned, 3x

If we assume narrowly self-interested agents, then $c(x, \theta) = x.$[7] Then, the agent's FOC is $\frac{dc}{dx} = -1$, so the non-negativity constraint binds, and the agent chooses to return $x = 0$. This implies that the principal's FOC is $\frac{dU_P}{dw} = -1$, so the principal also chooses to entrust zero.

As we will discuss in detail, the data almost never support this stark prediction (starting with Berg et al. (1995)). Instead, principals often trust, and agents often reciprocate. Thus, it is likely that the agent's disposition, captured by $\theta$, does matter. At least some agents have a trustworthy disposition that causes them to reciprocate trusting behavior, even without financial incentives to do so, and with rational beliefs, a principal may therefore find it worthwhile to trust.

## 2.3 Trust and Law

Our main interest in this chapter is how this trust interacts with the legal system. To that end, let us define L as the strength of the legal institutions, where stronger laws (better monitoring, better contract enforcement, etc.) increase effort, all else being equal: $\frac{d^2c}{dxd\mathcal{L}} < 0$ so that $\frac{dx^*}{d\mathcal{L}} > 0$. Then we might ask whether law enhances the value of trustworthiness— i.e., law and trustworthiness are complements $\frac{d^2x^*}{d\mathcal{L}d\theta} > 0$—or whether law interferes with trustworthiness—i.e., law and trustworthiness are substitutes $\frac{d^2x^*}{d\mathcal{L}d\theta} < 0$.

The relationship between the legal system and trust (both in terms of beliefs and action) is more complicated because the effect that laws have on the principal's action can work through two channels. If laws increase the value of trustworthiness, $\frac{dx^*}{d\theta d\mathcal{L}} > 0$, then prin-

---

[7]    The actual payoffs for the agents might be more intuitively represented by $U_a = 3 * (w - c(x))$ but since the scalar multiple, 3, has no effect on the agent's choice.

cipals with rational expectations would entrust more. However, even if laws decrease the value of trustworthiness such that $\frac{dx^*}{d\theta d\mathcal{L}} < 0$, the direct effect of legal institutions increasing effort through stronger enforcement ($\frac{dx^*}{d\mathcal{L}} > 0$) may lead principals to entrust more as well even if the efficacy of the agent's trustworthiness declines. The tension between these two mechanisms—(1) laws increase trust because they make the population more trustworthy; (2) laws increase trust because they make entrusting safer—will be important as we consider the macro and experimental evidence.

## 3.   TRUST, LAW AND GROWTH: MACRO EVIDENCE

In this section we briefly summarize the evidence on how trust and legal systems affect economic outcomes. We also provide some evidence of a correlation that has not been as widely discussed: the tendency for trust and strong contract enforcement to be observed together.

A main stylized fact from the literature on trust and growth is that growth in income per capita is positively correlated with the level of trust in a country, where trust is measured by answers to standard trust survey questions (Knack and Keefer 1997; La Porta et al. 1997; Zak and Knack 2001; Algan and Cahuc 2009). Higher trust levels are also positively correlated with many other positive outcomes, ranging from lower levels of infant mortality to greater financial development (La Porta et al. 1997; Guiso et al. 2004).

The main approach in the growth literature to estimate the causal impacts of trust has been to use instrumental variables for trust, such as the prevalence of "hierarchical religions" in a country (La Porta et al. 1997) or the degree of "ethnic fractionalization" (Knack and Keefer 1997). Instrumental variables are intended to address the problem of reverse causality, that growth might cause trust; the key assumption is that the instrumental variables are related to growth only through an impact on trust, i.e., there is no direct link between the instrument and growth.[8] A more recent approach involves using the trust levels of different waves of immigrants to the U.S. as time-varying instruments for trust in the home countries of the immigrants (Algan and Cahuc 2010). Using time-varying instruments helps to avoid problems caused when the instruments correlate with fixed characteristics of countries that determine both the instrument and growth. Completely ruling out concerns about the validity of instrumental variables is always difficult, but we discuss converging evidence from laboratory experiments, below, which also suggests a causal impact of trust on outcomes.

In this literature, trust has been argued to foster economic growth through several channels. Due to the prevalence of incomplete contracts, high levels of trust (and trustworthiness) can free up a substantial amount of resources that would otherwise need to be spent on monitoring. These can in turn be used for investment in physical capital (Knack and Keefer 1997; Zak and Knack 2001). Also, higher levels of trustworthiness and trust mean that investment in physical capital is less risky (Knack and Keefer 1997). Another

---

[8]   Because the instrument is not related to growth directly, there is no concern of reverse causality from growth to the instrument. It can be debated whether religiosity and ethnic fractionalization are plausibly independent of growth.

potential benefit of trust is allowing a country to depart from an economy characterized by inefficient, closed group interactions, widening the scope of exchange to include largely anonymous others (La Porta et al. 1997; Algan and Cahuc 2010). In the context of the model, when society is more trustworthy, θ is higher, and thus effort, wages and output are all increased.

A different strand of the growth literature has studied the impact of legal systems on economic performance. For example, one prominent line of research has related economic performance to the extent of countries' legal protections for investors (for a survey see La Porta and Shleifer 2008). In order to get at causality, researchers have used the fact that common law countries (a system of law originating in England) tend to have stronger protections than countries with civil law (originating in Roman law); the argument is that the adoption of common law versus civil law was in many cases the result of invasion and colonization, generating variation in legal systems that is plausibly exogenous to more recent economic conditions. This literature finds that common law, and associated stronger contract enforcement, are associated with positive economic outcomes, and this is true even controlling for trust in multivariate regression analysis. This suggests that the strength of the legal system has an independent and positive impact on growth.

Interestingly, however, high levels of trust and strong legal systems tend to be observed in combination; to show the correlation between trust and legal system, we use the Rule of Law indicator constructed by the World Bank, and combine this with data from the World Values Survey on trust levels (measured by the GSS trust question).[9] As shown in the left-hand panel of Figure 11.1, countries that are at higher percentiles of the distribution for rule of law have higher average trust levels, and the correlation is statistically significant (Spearman; 0.48; $p < 0.01$). To shed some light on causality, we next look at average trust levels by legal origins, using the classification of common law and civil law origins developed by La Porta et al. (1998). We find that countries with common law origins have significantly higher average trust levels (Figure 11.1, right-hand panel). This suggests that at least some of the causality may flow from strong legal institutions to higher levels of (survey) trust. This does not rule out, however, that trust might also feed back into the development of stronger institutions. Thus, the question remains: *why* should trust and strong contract enforcement tend to be positively correlated?

One explanation for why high trust might be associated with strong contract enforcement is that contract enforcement causes trust. The survey trust question does not ask specifically about trustworthiness in one-shot situations without legal protections, or about trustworthiness in general, under the vigilant eye of the law. Thus, agreement that people can be trusted might be a reflection of the strength of the legal system, rather than beliefs about innate trustworthiness. One argument against this explanation comes from evidence that trust levels in incentivized trust games differ across countries, for example across Gulf and Western countries (Bohnet, Herrmann and Zeckhauser 2010). Because

---

[9]    For the data on trust we use *WORLD VALUES SURVEY 2005 OFFICIAL DATA FILE v.20090901, 2009*. World Values Survey Association (http://www.worldvaluessurvey.org/wvs.jsp). The rule of law indicator comes from the World Bank Governance Indicators Project, which can be found at http://info.worldbank.org/governance/wgi/index.aspx#home

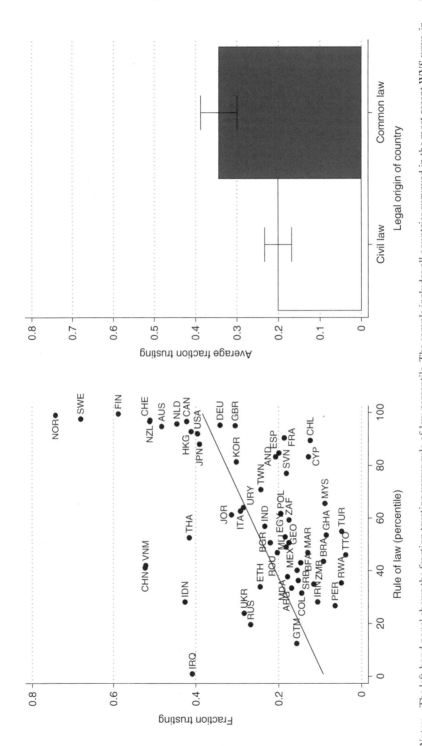

*Notes:* The left-hand panel shows the fraction trusting versus rule of law percentile. The sample includes all countries surveyed in the most recent WVS wave, in which any given country was surveyed in one of the four years 2005–2008. Rule of law percentile comes from the World Bank Governance Indicators database, and reflects rule of law in the same year as the trust measure for each country. The right-hand panel is restricted to countries with common law or civil law origins, according to the classification of La Porta and Shleifer (2008), and fraction trusting is averaged across countries.

*Figure 11.1   Trust and the rule of law*

the trust game is by construction a setting without contract enforcement, differences in trusting behavior across countries in the trust game are less likely to be the direct result of differences in contract enforcement strength. However, there is not sufficient systematic evidence to establish whether behavior in trust games is correlated with the strength of a country's contract enforcement.

An alternative explanation for why high trust and strong contract enforcement go together is that high trust levels lead to stronger contract enforcement. Following the line of argumentation in the literature on trust and growth, discussed above, trust allows individuals to not spend as many resources on monitoring, which frees up resources for investment in physical capital, but also potentially for investment in better legal institutions. With more efficient and effective institutions, the need for monitoring could be reduced even more, creating a feedback loop that increases trust.[10]

A third explanation for the positive correlation between trust and quality of legal institutions is that the two are complementary for some reason: it could be that high trust and good institutions are particularly effective when combined, i.e., when they are complements, and thus countries with one have tried and in some cases managed to develop the other. In our simple model, trust can make legal systems more effective, and vice versa, if we have $\frac{dx^*}{d\theta d\mathcal{L}} > 0$ (a dynamic model would be required to fully describe a process of coevolution of high trust and strong contract enforcement laws).

At this point, there is limited evidence in the growth literature on how trust shapes legal systems. At the same time the mechanisms that could potentially generate complementarities are still unclear. Thus, different possible explanations for the broad patterns remain to be disentangled. In the next section, we turn to an alternative source of evidence on how trust affects economic outcomes: lab experiments on trust and market institutions. This approach has some advantages over field studies in terms of being able to cleanly identify causality and the separate and interacted effects of trust and law (see Falk and Huffman 2006). Our survey is far from exhaustive, but rather focuses on experiments that speak most directly to the question of when trust and the law may be substitutes, and circumstances under which they may instead be complements.

## 4.   LAB EXPERIMENTS ON TRUST

As described above, the classic framework for studying trust in the lab at the micro level is the Berg, Dickhaut and McCabe (1995) trust game. Recall that the classic setup involves the principal entrusting part of her endowment to the agent. The amount entrusted gets tripled, and then the agent chooses how much to transfer back. From the point of view of the players of the game, social welfare is always increasing in the amount of trust the principal demonstrates, or more specifically, the amount the principal entrusts. Thus, trust

---

[10]   Interestingly, the impact of trust on growth appears to be stronger for developing countries than for higher income countries. One explanation is that low-income countries have weaker property rights and contract enforcement, and thus trust is especially important for growth. With better legal systems, trust is less necessary (Knack and Keefer 1997). In other words, the impact of trust is greatest when legal systems are weak, $\frac{dx^*}{d\theta d\mathcal{L}} > 0$ implying that trust and the law are substitutes for this sub-group of countries.

is beneficial from a societal perspective within this experimental setting, while it may or may not be beneficial from the perspective of an individual principal.

The standard result from the trust game literature is that many principals do send a positive amount to the agent, and some agents return enough to the principal to at least allow the principal to on average break even (Berg, Dickhaut and McCabe 1995) or do substantially better than if they had not trusted (e.g., Falk and Zehnder 2013). Because trust is present, social welfare is higher than predicted under the standard economic assumption that there is no such thing as a trustworthy disposition, i.e., $\frac{dx^*}{d\theta} = 0$. Given that the classic trust game is a setting with zero possibility for contract enforcement, and trust is efficiency enhancing, trust acts as a beneficial substitute for contract enforceability and the law.

It should be acknowledged that in this section we focus on the average effects across the population, but in all experiments, there is considerable heterogeneity in behavior. Our interest in this chapter is in how average tendencies toward trust and trustworthiness affect a population, but it is clear that, especially in a dynamic story of preference changes over time, heterogeneity would likely play an important role.

### 4.1   Experimental Results on Law and Trust as Substitutes

Various experimental studies have used the ability to exogenously vary institutions to shed more light on the interaction of trust and the law, and some have found that stronger external enforcement of contracts crowds out intrinsic pro-social behaviors.[11] Imposing such constraints tends to reduce intrinsic trustworthiness, which leads in turn to less trust and worse welfare outcomes. This provides a case of stronger legal protections and societal trust being negatively correlated, because of a negative interaction effect.

The role of enforcement and legal institutions can be introduced in various ways, but one approach has been to do so through allowing the possibility for a principal to restrict the choice set of the agent. The prototypical study that takes this approach is Falk and Kosfeld (2006), which studies in one experimental condition a trust game with a 0th stage, where the principal has the option to exert control on the agent's action space by choosing a minimum level that has to be returned. They find that if a principal uses the minimum option and controls the agent's actions this reduces the trustworthiness of the agent's response, and that this reduction outweighs the benefits of using control.[12]

Rietz et al. (2013) provide related evidence on negative impacts of control. They consider the impact of minimum effort restrictions in a trust game, where the restrictions are imposed by the experimenter rather than by the principal. They find that imposing a minimum effort restriction reduces the willingness of principals to trust, even though the minimum puts a lower bound on agent effort. The reduced trust by principals is associated

---

[11]   There is a substantial literature on crowd-out by financial incentives on intrinsic cooperative behavior. We survey only a limited number of papers here, but see Bowles and Polanía-Reyes (2012) for a more extensive review of the experimental literature.

[12]   The possibility exists that the crowding-out effect is context-dependent and perhaps not completely robust. For example, Ziegelmeyer, Schmelz and Ploner (2012) try but fail to replicate the Falk and Kosfeld results. However, other studies do replicate the result, and similar findings have been found in a variety of other settings (e.g. Schnedler and Vadovic 2011).

with reduced back-transfers by agents, and efficiency is reduced relative to a situation without such a restriction.[13]

Other studies also find examples of stronger contract enforcement crowding out trust, where enforcement takes the form of monitoring. Bohnet, Frey and Huck (2001) study the impact of experiencing higher or lower rates of monitoring on subsequent trustworthiness in a low monitoring environment; monitoring is an exogenously imposed (by the experimenter) probability that untrustworthy behavior is punished. They find that high monitoring increases trust when it is in effect, but after monitoring probabilities are lowered, trustworthiness is worse for those who experienced high monitoring than those who had low monitoring always. The authors argue that experiencing high monitoring crowds out trust.

Dickinson and Villeval (2008) study a real-effort principal agent game with a similar structure to the trust game, where the principal chooses the level of monitoring intensity. They find that trustworthiness is reduced when principals choose monitoring above a certain threshold. This effect occurs, however, only when the agent's actions have implications for the principal's payoffs.

### 4.2 Experimental Results on Law and Trust as Complements

Another group of studies finds examples where institutional rules are complementary to trust. Specifically, a set of papers finds that if rules are voted on by subjects, then rules can increase pro-social behavior. For example, Tyran and Feld (2006) and Putterman, Tyran and Kamei (2011) find that non-deterrent (i.e. small) legal sanctions have little effect on cooperation when exogenously imposed, but do effectively induce cooperation if those rules were accepted in a vote by the participants.

Another factor that can determine whether laws crowd out or complement trust is how the law is framed. For instance, Schnedler and Vadovic (2011) replicate the findings of Falk and Kosfeld (2006), but also include a treatment where the initial endowments are shifted to reframe the imposition of control as one of maintenance of property rights. In the later case, the harmful effects of control are reduced, presumably because protecting property rights is viewed as a more legitimate motivation for imposing legal restrictions, than is increasing one's likelihood of receiving a "hand-out."

Institutions and trust may also be complements to the extent that they work together to facilitate "gift exchange," i.e., a pattern of high $w$ from the principal being reciprocated by high $x$ from the agent. Bartling, Fehr and Huffman (2014) present principals with examples of past play, and these are found to prime high or low trust beliefs. They then study how the impact of this exogenous variation in trust depends on the institutional environment. High levels of predicted trustworthiness cause high $w$, and agents reciprocate with high $x$, in a setting where principals and agents can endogenously choose to engage

---

[13]   A control condition in Falk and Kosfeld (2006) considered the impact of an experimenter-imposed minimum transfer in a dictator game, and found no impact on dictator transfers. This contrasts with the negative impact they observe in a condition where the recipient chose to impose the minimum in the dictator game. The Rietz et al. (2013) study, where an experimenter-imposed minimum did have a negative impact, is different because it considers exogenous minimums in the context of a trust game.

in repeated interactions. When the institutional environment is worsened, in the sense that stable trading relationships are ruled out and interactions are one-shot, agents become less trustworthy, and principals reduce trust from initially high levels. High trust levels thus have a weaker impact where institutions are worse at sustaining stability. Bartling et al. also study a third environment, in which there is both instability and additional problems with contract enforcement, in the sense that principals can cheat on wage offers. In this case, even high initial trust does not prevent rapid convergence to minimum possible total payoffs, and outcomes are much worse than with either of the other institutional settings. While these results suggest that high trust levels are more effective with more favorable institutional environments, another aspect of the data suggests that the impact of institutions also depends on trust. Bartling et al. find that, regardless of the institutional environment, low initial trust leads to bad economic outcomes. Even in the strongest legal environment, with stable trading relationships and only one-sided moral hazard, low trust is self-fulfilling and the outcome is similarly bad to what is achieved in worse institutional environments.

We now turn to a discussion of the psychological and game theoretic mechanisms on which trust is based, in order to shed light on why law can sometimes be a complement to and sometimes a substitute for trust.

## 5. MECHANISMS UNDERLYING TRUST

In the context of our model, trust is a choice. The trustor is the principal, and the trustee is the agent. Trust on the part of the principal depends partly on beliefs about an agent's disposition, and partly on the perceived/experienced stakes involved in trust being violated. In this section we first survey theory and evidence on the psychological mechanisms underlying trust. We then discuss economic mechanisms featured in the game theory literature.

### 5.1 Psychological Mechanisms

Various psychological mechanisms may cause an agent to have a trustworthy disposition and affect the level of the principal's trustworthiness, even in the absence of material incentives to be trustworthy. This, in turn, makes trust by the principal more likely if the principal has rational beliefs. We focus on mechanisms that seem most relevant for explaining the experimental evidence on trust and the law.

One source of a trustworthy disposition among agents is unconditional kindness or altruism: an agent might not exploit the principal because his preferences put a positive weight on the principal's payoff. Models of "warm glow" altruism, for example, allow for such a utility function (Andreoni 1990). In the context of our model, an agent who cares about warm glow has a higher level of trustworthiness $\theta$, which provides intrinsic utility for higher levels of output $x$.

Substantial evidence indicates, however, that trustworthiness is at least partly motivated by conditional kindness, i.e., *reciprocity*. A key piece of evidence supporting this interpretation is the strong relationship between the amount of trust and the amount of money transferred back in the trust game (e.g., Berg, Dickhaut and McCabe 1995).

Another study by Ashraf, Bohnet and Piankov (2006) explicitly tests for the role of unconditional altruism and conditional altruism. Unconditional altruism is measured by a Dictator Game, where a subject simply decides how much of an endowment to share with an anonymous other. This altruism measure does help predict trustworthy behavior, but trustworthiness still depends on the amount sent by the trustor, indicating an important role for positive reciprocity. Various models incorporate a "kindness" term into agent utility functions, which captures the perceived kindness, or unkindness, of the principal and affects the utility value of helping the principal (see, e.g., Falk and Fischbacher 2006).

In our baseline model, agent's choice of output $x$, should not be affected by the principal's choice over the transferred amount $w$. However, if we assume that the agent's desire to reciprocate is given by $\theta(w)$ which is increasing in the principal's choice $\theta'(w) > 0$, then the agent's effort is increasing in the initial payment, which gives the principal incentive to increase the transferred amount. Other models assume that people care about equality in payoffs, or fairness, with the result that a generous act by the principal requires a compensating act by the agent (Fehr and Schmidt 1999). There are interesting implications if trustworthiness is based on reciprocity, in that low trust levels can be self-fulfilling, generating low trustworthiness, while high trust levels can lead to trustworthiness and enhanced efficiency.

Importantly, reciprocity can be negative as well as positive; individuals are willing to take actions that are personally costly in order to punish individuals for unkind actions. In experiments, people are willing to engage in costly punishment of individuals who violate norms of trust or fairness (Fehr and Gächter 2000; Fehr and Fischbacher 2003). Measures of self-reported emotion and evidence from brain imaging studies suggest that people are angered by unfair behavior and enjoy, or feel relief from, punishing wrong doers (Fehr and Gächter 2000; De Quervain et al. 2004). Negative reciprocity implies that agents do not just reward high trust with being trustworthy, they might take advantage of opportunities to punish low trust. For example, if a principal imposes a minimum effort level as in Falk and Kosfeld (2006), this would have no psychological effect through positive reciprocity. If agents are negatively reciprocal, however, and lack of trust is viewed as unkind, this could explain the reduction in effort caused by control. Clearly, legal institutions play a role in a society's approach to punishing wrongdoing, and they may reflect an underlying psychological motivation to punish.

Instead of assuming that the agent gains utility from the payoff of the principal, another way to explain altruistic or reciprocal behavior is to assume that the agent cares about the beliefs of the principal: if there are two types of agents, $\theta \in \{\theta_L, \theta_H\}$ and as before we let $b = \Pr[\theta = \theta_H | \hbar]$, then we can introduce a term for the psychic utility an agent receives for being perceived to be a high type:

$$U_A = w - c(x, \theta) + v(b)$$

where $v$ is increasing in $b$. Then the agent's FOC is moderated by the effect of her choice on the principal's beliefs:

$$\frac{dc(x, \theta)}{dx} = \frac{dv(b)}{db} \frac{db}{dx}$$

Therefore, an agent chooses a level of $x$ where the marginal cost of effort is equal to her marginal psychic utility. In particular, the agent may behave altruistically and reciprocally because she wants the principal to *perceive* her as altruistic or reciprocal (see Benabou and Tirole 2006). Empirically, there is growing support for image maintenance as an important mechanism underlying altruistic or reciprocal dispositions. For example, effort on a task that generates payoffs for a charity is reduced when a personal financial incentive is added and the presence of this incentive is public knowledge (Ariely, Bracha and Meier 2009). This is consistent with people caring about their social image and finding less value in being pro-social when incentives make this a noisier signal of a good disposition.[14] This social-image aspect of trustworthiness is potentially important in the context of the law, if legal rules affect the signaling value of being trustworthy as well as the perceived kindness of trusting.

Agents might also be upset with the principal for having negative beliefs. Distrust could be viewed as an "insult" and agents might resent the need to exert effort to change the principal's beliefs. In this case negative reciprocity motives might lead agents to be less trustworthy if they think the principal does not trust them, in order to punish the principal for having this belief. Thus, even laws that impose some minimum standards of performance, but do not prevent signaling trustworthiness by putting in more than minimum effort, may have a negative impact; imposing the minimum may signal distrust, and cause the individual to do the minimum only in retaliation (Falk and Kosfeld 2006).

So far we have focused on determinants of beliefs about trustworthiness, but psychological factors also play a role in determining the willingness of a principal to trust independent of the principal's beliefs about the agent's disposition. In particular, one determinant of trust is risk preference. Trusting is like playing a lottery, where the payoff is uncertain given some uncertainty about the degree of trustworthiness of the agent. Standard risk aversion can cause someone to be less willing to trust for a given belief about the probability that the agent is trustworthy. Indeed, risk aversion as measured by choices in lottery experiments predicts willingness to trust in a trust game (e.g., Schechter 2007).

There is also evidence, however, that people have a special aversion to having their trust betrayed, above and beyond that which can be explained by risk aversion over financial payoffs. Bohnet et al. (2008) demonstrate "betrayal aversion," where the willingness to pay to avoid playing a lottery increases if the outcome of the lottery depends on the actions of another human being. In other words, there is something worse about getting a low payoff as the result of violated trust, as opposed to getting the same payoff as the result of a lottery, even if subjective beliefs equate the probabilities of a bad outcome in the lottery situation and in the human interaction environment. A potential explanation for betrayal aversion is an anticipated negative emotional experience, which a person expects to feel if they are exploited. Betrayal aversion is also an example of how affective states can influence the choices of the principal. If the principal is more betrayal-averse, he or she may be more concerned about the risk of any interaction since possible negative outcomes

---

[14]    Related evidence shows that subjects are willing to pay to exit a dictator game if they can keep most of the endowment but avoid having an anonymous other know that sharing would have been possible (Dana, Cain and Dawes 2006).

are compounded by negative emotional experience. To the extent that institutions, or contracts, are structured in such a way as to reduce variance in behavior, or risk of betrayal, they may foster willingness to trust. On the other hand, if the presence of legal protections signals that people are not trustworthy, this could actually undermine willingness to trust, if principals are betrayal averse and the law does not allow perfect contract enforcement.

Taken together, the existing evidence indicates a potentially complex interaction between trust and law due to human psychology. Some psychological mechanisms may cause trust to be a substitute for legal contract enforcement, but such mechanisms can also lead to complementarities between trust and the law. For example, to the extent that reciprocity and altruism cause agents to be trustworthy, legal enforcement of contracts is less important. If contractual enforcement reduces the ability of agents to signal their trustworthiness, stronger laws might reduce trustworthiness and trust. On the other hand, if principals are betrayal averse, and law brings greater certainty, this might facilitate trust, thereby triggering reciprocity and trustworthiness. If the presence of strong law sends a negative signal about trustworthiness, by contrast, this could reduce willingness to trust. We discuss various laws and institutions in detail later in the chapter in light of the evidence on psychological mechanisms.

## 5.2  Game Theory Mechanisms

Having surveyed the behavioral and experimental economics literature on trust, we turn to what has traditionally been a distinct literature that asks the same question: the organizational economics literature, which uses neo-classical game theory and assumes narrowly self-interested players in order to understand how cooperation can be sustained in principal-agent transactions. It should be noted that most of the game theory models are based on infinitely repeated play and thus are not directly applicable to the experimental evidence or the baseline model we presented above, which is largely a one-shot or finitely repeated design. However, it is typically argued that insights from theories of repeated games are useful for explaining these results either because players in one-shot games follow heuristics of behavior that they developed while playing repeated games (Frank 1988) or because the existence of irrational opponents allows repeated game equilibria to be sustained in finite-move games (Kreps et al. 1982).

The literature on relational contracts originated primarily with Baker, Gibbons and Murphy (1994) and MacLeod and Malcomson (1989) in studies designed to explore how principal-agent problems involving non-contractible subjective performance can be circumvented through infinitely repeated interaction. Returning to our model, and considering narrowly self-interested agents, recall that in a one-shot game, agents will put in minimal effort, and principals will anticipate that and offer minimal investment. However, the well-known folk-theorem argues that in a repeated setting where actions can be conditioned on past behavior, how much a player values her reputation or her "reputational capital" can be a sufficient incentive for maintaining a social welfare maximizing equilibrium. A more complete survey of the theoretical literature can be found in MacLeod (2007), and a survey of this literature as it pertains to law can be found in Spier (2007). We focus here on the elements that pertain to the behavioral phenomenon of trust and how it interacts with legal regimes.

One theme of the literature is that it may be optimal to not take full advantage of the possibility of specifying the obligations of trading partners in a contract, even when legal institutions allow such contractual enforcement. The basic idea is that the efficiency of the equilibrium outcome of repeated games depends critically on what happens to each party in the event that cooperation breaks down. Laws and institutions that protect afflicted parties in the case of contract breach can actually make cooperation more difficult because they improve the value of outside options and thus increase the temptation to renege.

For example, Bernheim and Whinston (1998) analyze why contracts often have the feature of "strategic ambiguity," where parties choose incomplete contracts when complete contracts are available. They find that incomplete contracts work better in repeated games because they increase the degree of punishment available when either party shirks. Similar results are shown in Shaprio and Stiglitz (1984) and Levin (2003) who show that the power of a performance incentive which a relational contract is able to provide decreases as the attractiveness of the outside option increases.

This literature also considers the impact laws have on signaling, but again in the context of contractual breach. For example, Allen and Gale (1992) and Spier (1992) note that parties may prefer incomplete contracts because complete contracts serve as a signal of the intent for bad behavior. A trustworthy person would not need to spell everything out in a complete contract, therefore game theory suggests that one might infer that someone who relies on complete contracts has something to hide.

A different theme in the literature is that certain types of legal institutions, which foster the possibility of interacting repeatedly over long time frames, will be complements to trust. Legal institutions that facilitate repeated interactions are broadly speaking those that promote stability, for example limiting the possibility of seizure of assets by the state, or reducing the possibility of violence, and thereby increasing the chance that the trading partner of the current period will still be a viable partner in the next period. The potential for repeated interactions means that trading partners operate under "the shadow of the future," allowing the possibility for cooperation to be sustained by appropriately chosen punishment strategies in an infinitely repeated game. In fact, the experimental literature shows that this idea goes through even in finite horizon games. Brown, Falk and Fehr (2004) show in the lab that market efficiency is higher when market participants can endogenously engage in repeated interactions with trading partners who have performed well in the past. The mechanism is "gift exchange," in the sense that principals offer generous up-front wages to agents who have performed well in the past, and agents respond by being trustworthy. Efficiency is lower when institutions create instability and allow only one-shot interactions, because agents become less reciprocal in the absence of the "shadow of the future." Notably, while institutions fostering repeated interaction make gift exchange possible, the virtuous cycle still requires principals to trust enough to pay generous wages. Thus, from a game theoretic perspective, trust and the law can also be complements.

A related theme in the literature stresses the importance of dissemination of information about past behavior. If future players "forget" the performance of trading partners in the past, then the possibility for repeated interactions loses its bite in terms of fostering cooperation. Milgrom, North and Weingast (1990) demonstrate the importance of institutions that disseminate reputation information for the development of medieval international trade. The theme of the importance of information systems to maintain reputation has also been developed in Greif (1989, 1993) and Kranton (1996).

In summary, the game theory literature describes mechanisms through which the use of contracts to specify agent obligations can be a substitute for trust. Similar to the empirical findings on trust as a substitute, it can be suboptimal for a principal to take advantage of the opportunity to constrain the choices of agents. The theory also outlines mechanisms through which strong legal institutions may be complements to trust, namely by fostering the possibility for repeated interactions.

## 6. TRUST AND THE LAW: SUBSTITUTES OR COMPLEMENTS?

In this section we return to the contrasting experimental evidence, about the law being a substitute or complement for trust, in light of psychological and game theoretic mechanisms.

One interpretation of the experimental evidence is that the process through which laws are implemented matters for whether they crowd out or foster trust. In the studies we surveyed where trust and the law were substitutes, the law took the form of externally imposed contractual constraint on agent choices, imposed either by a principal or by the experimenter. By contrast, studies where contractual enforcement was imposed through referendum found that law was a complement to trust. The process through which contractual constraints are imposed thus seems to matter.

The process for implementing laws may matter because it determines what "signal" is sent about the intrinsic trustworthiness of agents. Specifically, laws that are imposed externally and that serve to limit the choices of agents may send a signal that agents are untrustworthy. In the case that the rules are put in place by the experimenter, principals may infer that agents are untrustworthy, and reduce trust, strategically or due to betrayal aversion motives. This can in turn be self-fulfilling if agents are reciprocal and respond to low trust by being untrustworthy. In the case that a principal is given the option to constrain the agent, and makes use of the option, this may signal to the agent that the principal believes he is untrustworthy. This might trigger a negatively reciprocal action from the agent, in the form of reduced trustworthiness. As suggested by the game theory literature, principals might find it optimal to not utilize the possibility of adopting stronger contract enforcement, even if the legal framework makes it possible.

Laws that are implemented through referendum may send a different signal, that agents view trustworthiness as important and fair. In such a process, individuals who vote for sanctions for untrustworthy behavior will be affected by the sanctions themselves. Thus, voting for sanctions tends to signal that agents may be intrinsically trustworthy. This might increase principals' willingness to trust, as well as directly affect the trustworthiness of agents because they want to conform to the social norm. Indeed, Tyran and Feld (2006) measured beliefs about cooperation, and show that subjects expected greater cooperation if mild sanctions were implemented by a vote, compared to a setting where sanctions were not an option.

In line with this interpretation, Jolls, Sunstein and Thaler (1998) argue that the content of law should be viewed as a codification of what society sees as right or wrong. For example, laws that ban mutually beneficial transactions like usury or price gouging fail on the usual economic metrics of efficiency but exist because they reflect prevailing norms of fairness. Societies that have prevailing norms of trust and trustworthiness might also collectively choose stronger laws of enforcement.[15]

Whether the law is a complement to trust also seems to depend on the content of the legal institution: strong laws do not simply imply perfect contract enforcement between trading partners, they may also have an important function in terms of protecting trading relationships from external threats and promoting stability. The results of Bartling et al. (2014) highlight the complementarity between trust and legal institutions that allow stable long-term relationships; the combination of such institutions with high trust is very beneficial, whereas having either bad institutions, or low trust, leads to much worse outcomes. Their results also show the importance of some minimal ability to enforce contractual terms; if there is double moral hazard in the sense that both wage offers and worker effort levels are not contractually enforceable, then market outcomes are even worse, and high initial trust beliefs do not help. Both game theory and psychological mechanisms provide explanations for how "gift exchange," a virtuous cycle of trust and reciprocal trustworthiness, can arise in a setting with repeated interactions and partial contractual enforceability. The ability to credibly promise high wages is necessary for principals to be able to send a gift and start the gift exchange process. The ability to engage in repeated interactions is also important, because in this case agents have a stronger motive to reciprocate high trust and high wages with high effort: being trustworthy in the current period increases the likelihood that the principal chooses to interact with the agent again in the future, and continue to pay high wages. The trustworthiness of agents in turn reinforces the willingness of principals to continue trusting.

In summary, one way to reconcile the apparent complementarity of trust and law at the macro level, with experimental evidence, is to think about the process underlying the implementation of law, and the precise content of strong "rule of law." To the extent that legal systems of contract enforcement are seen as signals of a social value placed on trust, as opposed to a negative signal that people are untrustworthy, this could explain complementarity at the macro level. In addition, if rule of law is capturing features of institutions that promote stability and the ability to have long-term trading relationships, this is another channel through which trust and the law may be complementary.

---

[15]    While Jolls, Sunstein and Thaler do not specify the direction of causality, others have suggested that law may serve as a mechanism to shift the norms in society. For example, Kahan (2000) notes counter-intuitively that the effectiveness of a new law that contravenes an established norm in society may be decreasing in the severity of the punishment associated with that law. The purported reason is that severe punishments would be seen by law enforcers as unjust and thus the law would go unenforced, while mild punishments would be accepted and help shift the norm to match the change in the legal framework. More broadly, Stout (2011) argues that laws should be constructed to "cultivate the conscience" of society through the channels of obedience, conformity and empathy, and the overemphasis of law and economics on material incentives has caused a neglect in a key channel of how law and trust norms might interact.

## 7.   CASE STUDIES AND DISCUSSION

Having discussed the relationship between trust and law at a relatively general and abstract level, we now turn to a discussion of the interaction of trust with several specific types of laws. We focus on laws that affect employment contracts and laws that are seemingly designed to help restore violated trust, so-called apology laws.

### 7.1   Employment Contracts—Minimum Wage, etc.

Turning to specific aspects of employment law that interact with trust, one important case in point is minimum wage laws. Increasing legally required minimum wages has been found to produce unexpected effects: a tendency for firms to increase wages to a level *above* the new minimum wage, the so-called "spillover effect," and for firms to not take advantage of exceptions in the law to pay less than the minimum wage to certain groups, for example teenagers.

One explanation for these effects is that minimum wage laws might affect the perception of agents about what is a "fair wage," with consequences that the lowest wage workers are willing to accept. Specifically, Falk, Fehr and Zehnder (2006) conduct experiments where the labor market starts out with no minimum wage law and then one is introduced. Exploiting the fact that a lab experiment makes it possible to directly measure worker reservation wages (in an incentive compatible way), they show that introducing a higher minimum wage causes workers to increase their reservation wages to be above the new minimum wage. As a consequence of this change, firms with rational beliefs about worker dispositions know that they need to pay wages higher than the new minimum wage, even if they were paying lower wages than the new minimum wage level before the law was introduced. Workers in this experiment demand higher wages even though their outside option if they refused the contract was a payment of zero.

One interpretation of these results is that workers perceive the minimum wage as a signal about the bare minimum a firm should pay if it is "decent." This might explain why the fair wage is somewhat higher than this minimum, as is indeed the case with worker reservation wages. Falk, Fehr and Zehnder (2006) also conduct experiments where a minimum wage is first introduced and then removed. Strikingly they find that reservation wages stay high even after the minimum is eliminated. Thus, even temporary laws can have a lasting impact through the channel of changing agent fairness perceptions.

Trust is also relevant when principals design employment contracts. Different forms of compensation involve different degrees of trust, ranging from a binding up-front wage, which is paid regardless of the agent's performance and thus involves maximum trust, to compensation being fully contingent on performance, which reduces the need for trust by the principal (Fehr, Klein and Schmidt 2007). In some cases, there is also an issue of trust by the agent: for the labor relation to be successful, the agent may need to trust that a principal will actually pay a promised but unenforceable performance bonus, or reward good performance with a future wage increase (e.g., Lazear and Rosen 1981). Lab experiments show that labor contracts that rely on the trustworthiness of the employer to pay fair bonuses can be quite successful. For example, Fehr, Klein and Schmidt (2007) conduct an experiment where a principal and agent have a one-shot interaction. They give principals the choice between different contract forms and find that a contract combining a fixed up-front payment with the unenforceable promise of a bonus payment is the most successful. This is because subjects that are acting as the firms in the experiment did in fact pay their promised bonuses when the worker performed well, despite the one-shot nature of the game. Showing that they expect this trustworthiness on the part of employers, workers choose high effort levels. By contrast, principals do worse with a "trust free" contract, which automatically imposes a modest fine for poor performance by the agent. The value of flexible contracts is also demonstrated by Charness et al. (2012), who find in a trust game experiment that principals can do even better if they allow agents to set their own wages. This is because agents choose higher effort for a given wage payment, when they chose the wage level themselves.

Employment protection legislation (EPL) is another important labor market institution that complicates the relationship between principal and agent by making firing costly if an agent is retained beyond an initial probation period. Falk, Huffman and MacLeod (2015) use a labor market experiment where firms and workers can endogenously engage in repeated interactions, and they exogenously vary whether the market has EPL, and whether or not bonus payments are possible. Without the option to pay bonuses, EPL is shown to sharply reduce market efficiency, possibly because it forces firms to rely on rising wage profiles as an incentive device. This elicits only modest effort levels from workers, presumably because of the limited credibility of large wage increases that go into effect only at the end of the (finite) game. When bonus pay is possible, by contrast, EPL has little impact on market efficiency. This is because, as in Fehr, Klein and Schmidt (2007), firms use bonus pay and credibly reward workers for good performance from the start. The degree of required trust is lower because the principal must make good on her promise immediately.

## 7.2   Liability for Accidents: Apologies and the Restoration of Trust

One key application of how trust and specifically violations of trust interact with the law is in the realm of tort law, particularly as applied to legal liability for product defects. The relationship between a buyer and a seller when the quality of the good is uncertain depends on trust. Liability provisions where the buyer can seek recourse against the seller increases the outside options for buyers and reduces the relational incentives for the seller. We have seen then that increasing the strength of product liability laws could decrease trust. One particular case study worth considering of how laws interact with trust relationships is in the area of Apology Laws. The function of apologies has long been seen as a social custom that mends frayed relationships. Ho (2012) shows that apologies act as signals by agents for future trustworthy behavior. In the area of medical malpractice, states have become concerned that one cause of rising malpractice costs is that doctors are reluctant to apologize because they fear inviting litigation, but patients often sue only because they never received an apology. In an effort to encourage apologies and more trust, 36 states have drafted apology laws that forbid plaintiffs from using apologies by doctors as evidence in court. However, like the minimal effort laws, apology laws also interfere with the agent's ability to signal. This is a case where the laws could serve as a complement to trust, encouraging more trust-generating apologies, or as a substitute, subverting apologies by diminishing their meaning. Ho and Liu (2011) find in a difference-in-differences study that the former effect dominates: apology laws reduce the average size of malpractice payments while increasing the speed of settlement. Ho (2012) and Ho and Liu (2011) point out that the welfare implications of more apologies and less malpractice is ambiguous. As doctor effort is unobserved and standards of care are enforced by malpractice, more apologies could increase moral hazard on the part of doctors.

## 8. CONCLUSIONS

In this chapter, we offer a survey of the literature on trust and the law, exploring the behavioral and game theoretic mechanisms that help maintain cooperation when contracts are incomplete. Our particular focus is on understanding the extent to which trust and the law are substitutes or complements. We begin with evidence at the aggregate, country level that high trust levels and strong legal institutions are observed together, consistent with complementarity. We then consider evidence from laboratory experiments, some of which is consistent with trust being a substitute for law, and some of which shows a complementary relationship. A survey of the evidence on behavioral and game theoretic mechanisms that underlie trust helps shed some light on the reasons for the different results in the experimental literature and suggests directions for future research on disentangling the reasons for the observed macroeconomic behavior. Understanding the relationship between trust and the law has important consequences for policy makers and institutional design related to how trust can support or undermine the law, and for practitioners in understanding how laws can support or undermine trust. We understand relatively little about how social trust and institutional rules co-evolve over time in a dynamic political economy context. That suggests a next step in research for understanding the macro patterns we observe today.

## REFERENCES

Akerlof, George A. 1982. Labor Contracts as Partial Gift Exchange. *Quarterly Journal of Economics* 97: 543–569.

Akerlof, George A. and Janet L. Yellen. 1990. The Fair Wage-Effort Hypothesis and Unemployment. *The Quarterly Journal of Economics* 105: 255–283.

Algan, Y. and P. Cahuc. 2009. Civic Virtue and Labor Market Institutions. *American Economic Journal: Macroeconomics* 1: 111–145.

Algan, Yann, and Pierre Cahuc. 2010. Inherited Trust and Growth. *American Economic Review* 100(5): 2060–2092. DOI: 10.1257/aer.100.5.2060

Allen, Franklin and Douglas Gale. 1992. Measurement Distortion and Missing Contingencies in Optimal Contracts. *Economic Theory* 2: 1–26.

Al-Ubaydli, Omar, Uri Gneezy, Min Sok Lee and John A. List. 2010. Towards an Understanding of the Relative Strengths of Positive and Negative Reciprocity. *Judgment and Decision Making* 5: 524–539.

Andreoni, James. 1990. Impure Altruism and Donations to Public Goods: A Theory of Warm-Glow Giving. *The Economic Journal* 100: 464–477.

Ariely, Dan, Anat Bracha and Stephan Meier. 2009. Doing Good or Doing Well? Image Motivation and Monetary Incentives in Behaving Prosocially. *The American Economic Review* 99: 544–555.

Ashraf, Nava, Iris Bohnet and Nikita Piankov. 2006. Decomposing Trust and Trustworthiness. *Experimental Economics* 9: 193–208.

Baker, George, Robert Gibbons and Kevin J. Murphy. 1994. Subjective Performance Measures in Optimal Incentive Contracts. *The Quarterly Journal of Economics* 109: 1125–1156.

Baran, Nicole, Paula Sapienza and Luigi Zingales 2010. Working Paper 15654. National Bureau of Economic Research: Cambridge, Mass.

Bartling, B., E. Fehr and D. Huffman. 2014. Institutions and Trust: Does Trust Generate Lasting Improvements in Economic Outcomes. Working Paper.

Bartling, B., E. Fehr and K. M. Schmidt. 2012. Screening, Competition, and Job Design: Economic Origins of Good Jobs. *The American Economic Review* 102: 834–864.

Becker, G. S. and G. J. Stigler. 1977. De Gustibus Non Est Disputandum. *The American Economic Review* 67: 76–90.

Bellemare, Charles and Sabine Kröger. 2007. On Representative Social Capital. *European Economic Review* 51: 183–202.

Bellemare, Charles, Sabine Kröger and Arthur Van Soest. 2008. Measuring Inequity Aversion in a Heterogeneous Population Using Experimental Decisions and Subjective Probabilities. *Econometrica* 76: 815–839.

Benabou, Roland and Jean Tirole. 2003. Intrinsic and Extrinsic Motivation. *Review of Economic Studies* 70: 489–520.

Benabou, Roland and Jean Tirole. 2006. Incentives and Prosocial Behavior. *The American Economic Review* 96: 1652–1678.

Berg, Joyce, John Dickhaut and Kevin McCabe. 1995. Trust, Reciprocity, and Social History. *Games and Economic Behavior* 10: 122–142.

Bernheim, B. Douglas and Michael D. Whinston. 1998. Incomplete Contracts and Strategic Ambiguity. *The American Economic Review* 88: 902–932.

Bohnet, Iris, Bruno Frey and Steffen Huck. 2001. More Order with Less Law: On Contract Enforcement, Trust, and Crowding. *The American Political Science Review* 95: 131–144.

Bohnet, Iris, Fiona Greig, Benedikt Herrmann and Richard Zeckhauser. 2008. Betrayal Aversion: Evidence from Brazil, China, Oman, Switzerland, and the United States. *The American Economic Review* 98: 294–310.

Bohnet, Iris, Benedikt Herrmann and Richard Zeckhauser. 2010. Trust and the Reference Points for Trustworthiness in Gulf and Western Countries. *Quarterly Journal of Economics* 125: 811–828.

Bohnet, Iris and Richard Zeckhauser. 2004. Trust, Risk, and Betrayal. *Journal of Economic Behavior and Organization* 55: 467–484.

Bowles, S. and S. Polanía-Reyes. 2012. Economic Incentives and Social Preferences: Substitutes or Complements? *Journal of Economic Literature* 50: 368–425.

Brown, Martin, Armin Falk and Ernst Fehr. 2004. Relational Contracts and the Nature of Market Interactions. *Econometrics* 72: 747–780.

Charness, Gary, Ramón Cobo-Reyes, Natalia Jiménez, Juan A. Lacomba and Francisco Lagos. 2012. The Hidden Advantage of Delegation: Pareto Improvements in a Gift Exchange Game. *American Economic Review*, 102(5): 2358–2379, doi: 10.1257/aer.102.5.2358.

Costa-Gomes, M., Crawford, V. P. and Broseta, B. 2001. Cognition and Behavior in Normal-form Games: An Experimental Study. *Econometrica*, 69: 1193–1235, doi:10.1111/1468-0262.00239.

Costa-Gomes, M. A., S. Huck and G. Weizsäcker. 2010. Beliefs and Actions in the Trust Game: Creating Instrumental Variables to Estimate the Causal Effect. Working Paper No. 368. ESRC Center for Economic Learning and Social Evolution: London, UK.

Dana, Jason, Daylian M. Cain and Robyn M. Dawes. 2006. What You Don't Know Won't Hurt Me: Costly (but quiet) Exit in Dictator Games. *Organizational Behavior and Human Decision Processes* 100: 193–201.

De Quervain, D. J., U. Fischbacher, V. Treyer, M. Schellhammer, U. Schnyder, A. Buck and E. Fehr. 2004. The Neural Basis of Altruistic Punishment. *Science* 305: 1254–1258.

Dickinson, D. and M. Villeval. 2008. Does Monitoring Decrease Work Effort? The Complementarity Between Agency and Crowding-out Theories. *Games and Economic Behavior* 63: 56–76.

Falk, Armin, Ernst Fehr and Christian Zehnder. 2006. Fairness Perceptions and Reservation Wages: The Behavioral Effects of Minimum Wage Laws. *The Quarterly Journal of Economics* 121: 1347–1381.

Falk, Armin and Urs Fischbacher. 2006. A Theory of Reciprocity. *Games and Economic Behavior* 54: 293–315.

Falk, Armin and David Huffman. 2006. Studying Labor Market Institutions in the Lab: Minimum Wages, Employment Protection, and Workfare. *Journal of Institutional and Theoretical Economics* 163: 30–45.

Falk, Armin, David Huffman and W. Bentley MacLeod. 2015. Institutions and Contract Enforcement. *Journal of Labor Economics* 33: 571–590.

Falk, Armin and Michael Kosfeld. 2006. The Hidden Costs of Control. *The American Economic Review* 96: 1611–1630.

Falk, Armin and Christian Zehnder. 2013. A City-Wide Experiment on Trust Discrimination. *Journal of Public Economics* 100: 15–27.

Fehr, Ernst and Urs Fischbacher. 2003. The Nature of Human Altruism. *Nature* 425: 785–791.

Fehr, Ernst, Urs Fischbacher and Simon Gächter. 2002. Strong Reciprocity, Human Cooperation, and the Enforcement of Social Norms. *Human Nature* 13: 1–25.

Fehr, Ernst, Urs Fischbacher, Bernhard Von Rosenblatt, Jürgen Schupp and Gert G. Wagner. 2003. A Nation-Wide Laboratory: Examining Trust and Trustworthiness by Integrating Behavioral Experiments into Representative Survey, http://papers.ssrn.com/sol3/papers.cfm?abstract_id=413204

Fehr, Ernst and Simon Gächter. 2000. Cooperation and Punishment in Public Goods Experiments. *The American Economic Review* 90: 980–994.

Fehr, Ernst, Alexander Klein and Klaus M. Schmidt. 2007. Fairness and Contract Design. *Econometrica* 75: 121–154.

Fehr, Ernst and John A. List. 2004. The Hidden Costs and Returns of Incentives: Trust and Trustworthiness among CEOs. *Journal of the European Economic Association* 2: 743–771.

Fehr, Ernst and Bettina Rockenbach. 2004. Human Altruism: Economic, Neural, and Evolutionary Perspectives. *Current Opinion in Neurobiology* 14: 784–790.

Fehr, Ernst and Klaus M. Schmidt. 1999. A Theory of Fairness, Competition, and Cooperation. *The Quarterly Journal of Economics* 114: 817–868.

Fischer, Paul and Steven Huddart. 2008. Optimal Contracting with Endogenous Social Norms. *The American Economic Review* 98: 1459–1475.

Frank, R. H. 1988. *Passions Within Reason: The Strategic Role of Emotions*. New York: Norton.

Frey, B. S. 1994. How Intrinsic Motivation is Crowded Out and In. *Rationality and Society* 6: 334–352.

Galbiati, Roberto, Karl Schlag and Jole van der Weele. 2011. Sanctions that Signal. Working Paper No. 1107. Department of Economics, University of Vienna: Vienna, Austria.

Glaeser, Edward L., David I. Laibson, José A. Scheinkman and Christine L. Soutter. 2000. Measuring Trust. *The Quarterly Journal of Economics* 115: 811–846.

Gneezy, Uri and Aldo Rustichini. 2000. A Fine is a Price. *The Journal of Legal Studies* 29: 1–17.

Gneezy, U. and A. Rustichini. 2004. Incentives, Punishment, and Behavior. Pp. 572–589 in *Advances in Behavioral Economics*, edited by C. F. Camerer, G. F Loewenstein, and M. Rabin. New York: Russell Sage Foundation.

Goeree, Jacob and Charles Holt. 2001. Ten Little Treasures of Game Theory and Ten Intuitive Contradictions. *The American Economic Review* 91: 1402–1422.

Goeree, Jacob and Charles Holt. 2005. An Experimental Study of Costly Coordination. *Games and Economic Behavior* 51: 349–364.

Goette, Lorenz, David Huffman and Stephan Meier. 2012. The Impact of Social Ties on Group Interactions: Evidence from Minimal Groups and Randomly Assigned Real Groups. *American Economic Journal: Microeconomics* 4: 101–115.

Greif, Avner. 1989. Reputation and Coalitions in Medieval Trade: Evidence on the Maghribi. *The Journal of Economic History* 49: 857–882.

Greif, Avner. 1993. Contract Enforceability and Economic Institutions in the Early Trade: The Maghribi Traders' Coalition. *The American Economic Review* 83: 525–548.

Guiso, L., P. Sapienza and L. Zingales. 2004. The Role of Social Capital in Financial Development. *The American Economic Review* 94: 526–566.

Henrich, Joseph. 2004. Cultural Group Selection, Coevolutionary Processes and Large-scale Cooperation. *Journal of Economic Behavior and Organization* 54: 3–35.

Ho, Benjamin. 2012. Apologies as Signals: With Evidence from a Trust Game. *Management Science* 58: 141–158.

Ho, Benjamin and Elaine Liu. 2011. Does Sorry Work? The Impact of Apology Laws on Medical Malpractice. *Journal of Risk and Uncertainty* 43: 141–167.

Ichino, Andrea and Gerd Muehlheusser. 2008. How Often Should You Open the Door? Optimal Monitoring to Screen Heterogeneous Agents. *Journal of Economic Behavior & Organization* 67: 820–831.

Jolls, Christing, Cass R. Sunstein and Richard Thaler. 1998. A Behavioral Approach to Law and Economics. *Stanford Law Review* 50: 1471–1550.

Kahan, Dan M. 2000. Gentle Nudges vs. Hard Shoves: Solving the Sticky Norms Problem. *The University of Chicago Law Review* 67: 607–645.

Kahneman, Daniel and Amos Tversky. 1979. Prospect Theory: An Analysis of Decision under Risk. *Econometrica* 47: 263–291.

Kessler, J. and S. Leider. 2012. Norms and Contracting. *Management Science* 58: 62–77.

Knack, Stephen and Philip Keefer. 1997. Does Social Capital Have an Economic Payoff? A Cross-Country Investigation. *Quarterly Journal of Economics* 112: 1252–1288.

Kosfeld, Michael, Markus Heinrichs, Paul J. Zak, Urs Fischbacher and Ernst Fehr. 2005. Oxytocin Increases Trust in Humans. *Nature* 435: 673–676.

Kranton, Rachel E. 1996. The Formation of Cooperative Relationships. *Journal of Law, Economics, & Organization* 12: 214–233.

Kreps, D. M., P. Milgrom, J. Roberts and R. Wilson. 1982. Rational Cooperation in the Finitely Repeated Prisoner's Dilemma. *Journal of Economic Theory* 27: 245–252.

La Porta, Rafael. 1998. Agency Problems and Divided Policies Around the World. Working Paper 6594. National Bureau of Economic Research: Cambridge, Mass.

La Porta, Rafael, Florencio Lobez-de-Silanes, Andrei Shleifer and Robert W. Vishny. 1997. Trust in Large Organizations. *The American Economic Review* 87: 333–338.

La Porta, Rafael, Florencio Lopez de-Silanes, Andrei Shleifer and Robert W. Vishny. 1998. Law and Finance. *Journal of Political Economy* 106(6): 1113–1155, https://doi.org/10.1086/250042

La Porta, R., F. Lopez-de-Silanes, A. Shleifer and R. Vishny. 1999. The Quality of Government. *The Journal of Law, Economics, and Organization* 15(1): 222–279, https://doi.org/10.1093/jleo/15.1.222

La Porta, Rafael and Andrei Shleifer. 2008. The Unofficial Economy and Economic Development. *Brookings Papers on Economic Activity* Fall: 275–352.

Lazear, E. P. and S. Rosen. 1981. Rank-Order Tournaments as Optimum Labor Contracts. *The Journal of Political Economy* 89: 841–864.

Lazzarini, S. G., R. Madalozzo, R. Artes and J. de Olivia Siqiera. 2005. Measuring Trust: An Experiment in Brazil. *Economia Aplicada* 9: 153–179.

Levin, Jonathon. 2003. Relational Incentive Contracts. *The American Economic Review* 93: 835–857.

MacLeod, W. Bentley. 2007. Reputations, Relationships, and Contract Enforcement. *Journal of Economic Literature* 45: 595–628.

MacLeod, W. Bentley and James M. Malcomson. 1989. Implicit Contracts, Incentive Compatibility, and Involuntary Unemployment. *Econometrica* 57: 447–480.

Merriam-Webster. 2012. https://www.merriam-webster.com/dictionary/trust

Milgrom, Paul R., Douglas C. North and Barry R. Weingast. 1990. The Role of Institutions in the Revival of Trade: The Law Merchant, Private Judges, and the Champagne Fairs. *Economics and Politics* 2: 1–23.

Ploner, M., K. Schmelz and A. Ziegelmeyer. 2010. Hidden Costs of Control: Three Repetitions and an Extension. Working Paper No. 2010,007. JENA Economic Research Papers. Jena, Germany.

Putnam, R. D. 1995a. Bowling Alone: America's Declining Social Capital. *Journal of Democracy* 6: 65–78.

Putnam, Robert D. 1995b. Tuning In, Tuning Out: The Strange Disappearance of Social Capital in America. *PS: Political Science and Politics* 28: 664–683.

Putnam, R. D. 1996. The Strange Disappearance of Civic America. *The American Prospect* 24: 34–48.

Putnam, R. D. 2001. *Making Democracy Work: Civic Traditions in Modern Italy*. Princeton, NJ: Princeton University Press.

Putterman, Louis, Jean-Robert Tyran and Kenju Kamei. 2011. Public Goods and Voting on Formal Sanction Schemes. *Journal of Public Economics* 95: 1213–1222.

Rabin, Matthew and Joel L. Schrag. 1999. First Impressions Matter: A Model of Confirmatory Bias. *Quarterly Journal of Economics* 114: 37–82.

Rietz, Thomas A., Eric Schniter, Roman M. Sheremeta and Timothy W. Shields. 2013. Trust, Reciprocity, and Rules, http://papers.ssrn.com/sol3/papers.cfm?abstract_id=1923831; https://www.biz.uiowa.edu/faculty/trietz/papers/Trust,%20Reciprocity%20and%20Rules.pdf

Sapienza, Paola, Anna Toldra-Simats and Luigi Zingales. 2013. Understanding Trust the Economic Journal, doi: 10.1111/ecoj.12036.

Schechter, L. 2007. Traditional Trust Measurement and the Risk Confound: An Experiment in Rural Paraguay. *Journal of Economic Behavior & Organization* 62: 272–292.

Schnedler, Wendelin and Radovan Vadovic. 2011. Legitimacy of Control. *Journal of Economics & Management Strategy* 20: 985–1009.

Sen, Amartya. 1977. Rational Fools: A Critique of the Behavioral Foundations of Economic Theory. *Philosophy & Public Affairs* 6: 317–344.

Shapiro, Carl and Joseph E. Stiglitz. 1984. Equilibrium Unemployment as a Worker Discipline Device. *The American Economic Review* 74: 433–444.

Sliwka, Dirk. 2003. Organizational Structure and Innovative Activity. *Economics of Governance* 4: 187–214.

Sliwka, Dirk. 2007. Trust as a Signal of a Social Norm and the Hidden Costs of Incentive Schemes. *The American Economic Review* 97: 999–1012.

Spier, Kathryn E. 1992. Incomplete Contracts and Signaling. *The RAND Journal of Economics* 23: 432–443.

Spier, K. E. 2007. Litigation. Pp. 432–443 in vol.1 of *Handbook of Law and Economics* edited by A. M. Polinsky and S. Shavell. Amsterdam: Elsevier.

Stout, L. A. 2011. *Cultivating Conscience: How Good Laws Make Good People*. Princeton, NJ: Princeton University Press.

Thöni, Christian, Jean-Robert Tyran and Erik Wengström. 2012. Microfoundations of Social Capital. *The Journal of Public Economics* 96: 635–643.

Tyran, Jean-Robert and Lars Feld. 2006. Achieving Compliance When Legal Sanctions are Non-deterrent. *Scandinavian Journal of Economics* 108: 135–156.

Zak, P. J. and S. Knack. 2001. Trust and Growth. *The Economic Journal* 111: 295–321.

Ziegelmeyer, Anthony, Katrin Schmelz and Matteo Ploner. 2012. Hidden Costs of Control: Four Repetitions and an Extension. *Experimental Economics* 15: 323–340.

# PART VI

# EXPERIMENTS AND NEUROECONOMICS

# 12. Law and economics in the laboratory
## Gary Charness and Gregory DeAngelo

Experimental methods have become increasingly prominent in the social sciences. Of course this methodology has been common for decades in psychology, but economists and political scientists have also found it to be a fruitful resource for examining behavior and testing theory. Yet, why should researchers in the area of law and economics care about laboratory experiments? After all, there are plenty of field data available for empirical tests. While field data are indeed rich and abundant, they reflect a variety of environmental factors; disentangling these factors is difficult, if not impossible. The intertwining of potential causal factors in the field is particularly acute in law and economics.

Laboratory experiments have some important advantages over other approaches. One key advantage is the feasibility of controlling conditions more tightly than in any other context. It is possible to assign subjects randomly to treatments and to replicate results. Random assignment helps control for alternative explanations. Replicability is valuable both in providing a solid baseline from which to test the effects of varying factors in the environment and in allowing for robustness checks. One of the great strengths of laboratory experiments is that one can keep constant all elements of the environment save one. The researcher can then readily test the impact of a particular manipulation, cleanly identifying a potential treatment effect.

Particular applications and issues potentially make laboratory experiments especially valuable to the field of law and economics. One can implement changes in punishment and monitoring technology—in the law, the size of sanctions, probability of apprehension and so on—without having to worry about simultaneity issues.[1] One can readily extract information such as the role of risk preferences or uncertainty, and can potentially crack open the black box of decision-making by judges and juries during trials. Furthermore, one can learn about the role of morality (or lack thereof) in decisions by juries, judges, etc.

Lab experiments are particularly useful for testing theory. For example, one may wish to learn whether a theoretical prediction that, holding the expected cost of malfeasance constant, a higher penalty combined with a lower probability of detection will more effectively deter undesirable behavior. It is straightforward to test this (within some bounds in terms of the size of the penalty) by comparing the predictions of the model to actual behavior in the lab. In addition, in some environments theoretical predictions might be embryonic or absent; in this case, gathering behavioral data in the lab may lead to new (or more precise and accurate) theories. One way to think about a lab experiment is as a first link in a longer chain running from theory to actual field behavior.

Of course, external validity, the extent to which behavior observed in the laboratory can

---

[1] In the field, changes in levels of punishment and monitoring can impact crime levels, but changes in crime levels can also impact levels of punishment and monitoring. For this reason, using field data to identify the impact of punishment and monitoring on crime rates is difficult.

be generalized to behavior in field environments, is a serious issue.[2] Indeed, our view is that one must take with several grains of salt any extrapolation of the choices observed in the lab to field contexts. Nevertheless, the ability to clearly identify experimental treatment effects provides a major advantage over the field. While we may not completely trust, for example, that a particular rate of contractual adherence observed in the lab will be the same in a field context, knowing the magnitude or the direction of a change that results in simple contexts is still quite useful.

In any case, laboratory experiments are just one of a variety of complementary methodological approaches that are useful for research in law and economics; one should use the tool that is best suited for the task at hand.[3] At a minimum, this approach should be viewed as one arrow in the researcher's quiver.

Laboratory experiments have become an important research tool in economics. The number of experimental papers published in high-ranking economics journals has grown exponentially in recent years. These experiments have been used to study everything from social preferences and reciprocity to behavior in large-scale markets. Literally thousands of laboratory experiments have been conducted in economics in the past 20 years. We do not perform a recital of these but refer the reader to recent surveys such as Kagel and Roth (1995), Camerer, Lowenstein and Rabin (2003), and Kagel and Roth (2015).

More recently, researchers in the fields of political science and anthropology have embraced laboratory experiments. For example, Thomas Palfrey and Rebecca Morton have examined voter participation, the curse of the swing voter, strategic voting, and information aggregation in committees.[4] Some of these areas have immediate application to jury decision-making.[5] Cultural anthropologists and development economists have been conducting simple laboratory-style experiments in primitive areas for perhaps a decade. Henrich et al. (2005) report such experiments conducted in 15 small-scale societies to study behavioral features such as social preferences, risk-aversion, and informal risk sharing.

The purpose of this chapter is to familiarize the reader with a handful of the vast array of techniques experimentalists use to explore theories related to law and decision-making in (mock) legal environments. Section 1 describes a set of experiments conducted to study decisions of judges, juries and attorneys. Section 2 reviews experiments designed to study the effects of law enforcement. Section 3 describes a set of experiments that study the bargaining behavior of principals and their agents and the role that communication plays in negotiations. Our objective is to demonstrate the usefulness of employing economics experiments to study law and legal institutions. It is important to note that the summaries of studies we provide are not meant to reflect the bigger picture of the literatures on

---

[2]   Critics of laboratory experiments assert that little can be learned from inexperienced undergraduate students, who typically act as subjects in economics experiments, making choices in unfamiliar settings. Levitt and List (2007) provide a critique, and Falk and Heckman (2009) strongly dissent, pointing out the advantages of the laboratory for careful control and tests of theory. Plott (1982) argues that the simple environments used to study behavior in the lab are well suited for theory testing.

[3]   For a detailed discussion of the advantages and disadvantages of laboratory experiments, the interested reader may wish to consult Charness and Kuhn (2011).

[4]   See e.g., Battaglini, Morton and Palfrey (2010) and Battaglini, Morton and Palfrey (2008).

[5]   For a survey of the literature in this area, see Morton and Williams (2008, 2011).

the studied topics. The literatures in these areas are vast, and we do not draw general conclusions about what we can learn from the broad literatures here. Our goal simply is to provide a window into how experiments can be used to study economics principles relevant to law.

## 1.   EXPERIMENTS STUDYING DECISION-MAKING BY ACTORS IN LEGAL ENVIRONMENTS

Researchers are starting to employ the tools of experimental economics in many areas of law and economics. From topics pertaining to judge and jury decision-making to the appropriate punishment regimes, the laboratory has proved to be a fruitful environment for understanding the role of economic agents in legal environments. In what follows, we briefly discuss several areas in which experiments that study law and economics issues have been particularly prevalent in the past ten years, including the behavior of judges, juries, attorneys and litigants.

### 1.1   Judges

The study of judges in their natural environment—the courtroom—is difficult because researchers cannot observe directly what drives judicial decision-making. In particular, understanding what sorts of factors influence decisions is limited by the fact that judges hear each case only once. This makes it impossible to observe a judge making the same decision repeatedly under slightly different conditions. Additionally, our ability to observe judicial decisions in similar environments is constrained by the number of cases that settle out of court—approximately 97% of cases (Rosenberg 2003). Decisions also are likely biased by previous decisions and precedents. Thus, the scope for conducting empirical research on the judicial decision-making process using field data is severely limited.

Given the problems with examining judges in their natural habitat, researchers have begun examining judges in controlled environments where multiple treatments can be implemented. This research has proven to be useful in understanding heuristics and biases that might influence judges' decisions and might be difficult for judges to overcome when handling a trial and determining a verdict.

Chris Guthrie, Jeffrey Rachlinski and Andrew Wistrich have played an integral role in examining judges in the past ten years. They have a knack for gathering large numbers of judges from many different courts and examining their decisions under various conditions. Observing decisions across multiple treatments has allowed the authors to examine how anchoring, framing, hindsight and racial biases might impact judicial decision-making.[6]

Rachlinksi, Guthrie and Wistrich (2007) and Guthrie, Rachlinski and Wistrich (2007) examine the impact of anchoring, framing, egocentricity and hindsight bias on decisions

---

[6]   Anchoring and framing are components of decision-making that result in individuals attaching too much importance to one aspect of a decision, potentially yielding an error in judgment (see Tversky and Kahneman 1974). Hindsight bias (see Roese and Vohs 2012) can impact decision-making when individuals believe that an outcome was likely ex ante despite any objective evidence to support the claim that the outcome actually was predictable.

by bankruptcy and federal magistrate judges. The decisions by the judges are compared to laypersons' decisions to determine if judges appear to be better able to resist the influence of biases. In general, results from experiments suggest that judges are impacted by these biases in approximately the same ways that laypersons are. Additionally, the judges who were examined do not appear to be any more or less affected by the representativeness heuristic and cognitive illusions than laypersons when making rulings.[7]

In follow-up research, Rachlinski et al. (2009) and Rachlinski, Guthrie and Wistrich (2011) examine hindsight and racial biases in judges. Rachlinski et al. (2009) examine whether judges carry and potentially implement racial biases that laypersons tend to suffer from—notably that white Americans harbor implicit biases in regard to black Americans.[8] To examine this bias, the authors recruited 133 trial judges in a study of "the psychology of judging." The main finding was that judges suffer from the same invidious biases that most adults suffer from when assessing the outcome of a hypothetical trial. However, in treatments in which the judges were told the race of a hypothetical defendant (e.g. "Caucasian" or "Black"), the judges appeared to overcome their implicit biases. The judges produced nearly identical decisions in cases in which they were faced with a Black defendant and with a Caucasian defendant. In effect, judges tend to make judgments that do not appear to be correlated with their implicit associations.

Rachlinski, Guthrie and Wistrich (2011) examine whether judicial decision-making is subject to hindsight bias. This question is important because judges can issue warrants to permit the gathering of data (foresight) and can also permit a piece of information to be presented at trial as evidence (hindsight). Because the judge knows whether a search without a warrant produced incriminating evidence, hindsight bias might encourage him to permit evidence obtained using unconstitutional methods. The authors use a data set they gathered by surveying over 900 state and federal judges who make judgments of probable cause in circumstances involving both foresight and hindsight. Surprisingly, judges appear to make approximately the same ruling in both foresight and hindsight conditions. This suggests that they somehow override biases that might cloud their judgment.

## 1.2   Juries

Although judges oversee the vast majority of court cases, a trial by a jury of one's peers is a legal right in many legal systems. Juries are interesting subjects to study because jurors typically do not have formal legal training. This lack of expertise gives rise to questions related to the components of the legal process that might impact jury decisions. Jury trials also produce greater uncertainty relative to bench trials about the outcome of the trial (see Harel and Segal 1999), which makes research on jury trials all the more interesting.

One of the most widely publicized determinations juries make is how much to award

---

[7]   Tversky and Kahneman (1972, p. 430) define the representativeness heuristic as "the degree to which [a single event] (i) is similar in essential characteristics to its parent population, and (ii) reflects the salient features of the process by which it is generated." For example, if I am told a coin is fair and ten flips of the coin result in seven heads, then I believe that the probability that the next flip will result in a head is higher than the objective probability (50%).

[8]   The authors define "implicit bias" as "stereotypical associations so subtle that people who hold them might not even be aware of them" (p. 1196).

plaintiffs in compensatory and punitive damages. Hastie, Schkade and Payne (1999) designed a mock jury experiment that questioned whether variation in anchors (i.e., variations in the plaintiff's request for a punitive damage award of a specific amount) and whether the plaintiff was local or remote affected the jury's decision.[9] They found that both high anchors and the plaintiff being local (regardless of whether the defendant was local or remote) were positively correlated with the size of punitive damage awards. Similarly, Greene, Coon and Bornstein (2001) used a mock trial experiment to test whether caps on the amount of awardable punitive damages would affect compensatory damages. They found that compensatory damages were inflated only when punitive damages were completely prohibited. Kahneman, Schkade and Sunstein (1998) examined personal injury cases and how the severity of the plaintiff's injuries affected the punitive damage award. This study found that the participants agreed on outrage and punishment scales, but hypothetical award amounts were random. Greene, Johns and Smith (2001) used a hypothetical automobile negligence case to look into whether injury severity might affect damage awards and found that the magnitude of hypothetical awards was positively associated with hypothetical injury severity rather than the degree of negligence of the hypothetical defendant.[10] The results suggest that irrelevant aspects of cases can influence juries' decisions in problematic ways.[11]

The factors that impact how juries decide have also been examined fairly extensively. For example, Inbar, Pizzarro and Cushman (2012) examined the role of moral blameworthiness on a jury's propensity to convict. Interestingly, experiments conducted using jury-eligible subjects suggest that juries are prone to moral judgments even when the individuals they convict have not caused or intended to inflict harm on other individuals. For instance, a jury might convict an individual that it deems to have been morally at fault when betting, for example that a company's stock will decline or that a natural disaster will occur, if the betting individual might benefit from another individual's misfortune.[12]

Others have studied how adversarial competition among expert witnesses at trial impacts the accuracy of jury decision-making. In a laboratory experiment where subjects solve problems as groups, Boudreau and McCubbins (2008) chose two subjects to be fully informed experts. By giving their expert opinion, the experts can influence the payouts, which depend on the choice of the other group members. They find that even in the absence of monitoring and possible punishment for misrepresentation, competition

---

[9]  The experiment tested the conjecture that "some juries are motivated by their power to redistribute wealth from remote (usually corporate) coffers into local (usually individual citizens') pockets" (Hastie, Schkade and Payne 1999, p. 449).

[10]  Half the subjects participated in a mild injury treatment and the other half in a severe injury treatment. Similarly, half the subjects were told that negligence was certain (e.g., the defendant was traveling faster than the speed limit) and the other half were told that the defendant was not negligent (e.g., the defendant was traveling at the speed limit).

[11]  These and other similar experimental designs assume that subjects' decisions in hypothetical settings are correlated with the decisions of actual jurors in real cases. They might not be for a variety of reasons. The assignment of subjects to value-laden roles and the elicitation of hypothetical decisions are considered shortcomings that limit our confidence in placing weight on the results. For a general discussion of best practices in experiment design, see Davis and Holt (1993).

[12]  See also Monin, Pizarro and Beer (2007).

fostered by the adversarial nature of trials, by itself, can increase truth-telling and the accuracy of jury decisions.

While experiments that examine how individuals process the quality and value of the information they receive from others yield insights about individual jurors, the collective intelligence of the group is also an object of study since collective decision-making is an essential part of the decision-making process for juries. Bornstein and Greene (2011) find that both individual and collective cognitive reasoning influence juries. Results reported by Minson and Mueller (2011) provide insight into how individuals display *dissent neglect* by systematically placing greater weight on judgments that are similar to their own. *Dissent neglect* is hypothesized to stem from the fact that individuals believe that their own judgments are fundamentally more objective than those of others.[13] Additionally, Minson and Mueller (2011) show that individuals will systematically underweight their peers' judgments when making group decisions. Finally, Yaniv (2004) finds that individuals tend to discount the information they receive from others. Specifically, the more knowledgeable the information receiver, the greater the discount attached to the information received from others.

Particular insights from experiments designed to test theories from political science are also relevant for understanding juror behavior. For example, under certain conditions, theory predicts that rational voters sometimes do not vote sincerely (in line with their private information) because one's vote matters only if it is the tie-breaking or deciding vote. Recent experimental studies on juries, committees and legislatures have attempted to test this prediction by applying it to particular types of decisions (see for example, Fréchette, Kagel and Lehrer 2003; Fréchette, Kagel and Morelli 2005; Levine and Palfrey 2007; Feddersen, Gailmard and Sandroni 2009; Battaglini, Morton and Palfrey 2010; Goeree and Yariv 2011). These studies suggest that the voting institution can substantially impact the outcome.

Many experimental studies find compelling evidence that voters may vote strategically in some settings. This is problematic if we assume that the most reliable jury decisions occur when all jurors vote non-strategically. A non-strategic juror votes according to his true beliefs given the information he received at trial and through discussions with his co-jurors during the deliberation process. Experimental studies have found that the voting institution can impact on whether jurors vote strategically. For example, Guarnaschelli, McKelvey and Palfrey (2000) find that jurors are more likely to vote strategically under a unanimity rule. Battaglini, Morton and Palfrey (2010) also identify strategic voting behavior in the form of the so-called swing-voter's curse—the prediction that "[a] poorly informed voter may be better off . . . to leave the decision to informed voters because his uninformed vote may go against their choice and could decide the outcome in the wrong direction" (p. 62).

The voting-aggregation rules clearly seem key in predicting jurors' behavior. The issue of strategic voting, however, is most applicable to environments in which voters cannot communicate amongst themselves and thereby aggregate individually received signals. This theory is applicable only in settings where jurors are unable to aggregate these signals through the deliberation process. The typical deliberation process, however, involves com-

---

[13]   See also Carlson and Russo (2001).

munication. Jurors are at least somewhat informed of the potential distribution of votes by other jurors. This knowledge potentially impacts the voting decision of each individual juror. In other words, the pivotal juror will have learned, through the deliberation process, about the distribution of votes from other jurors, which is likely to impact her own vote.

In the past decade, several papers have analyzed the potential impact of communication on collective choice outcomes. Coughlan (2000) and Austen-Smith and Feddersen (2006) were among the first to report evidence suggesting that the availability of particular communication protocols can dramatically alter collective decisions. A recent paper by Goeree and Yariv (2011) represents the state of the art. They find that people vote in a sophisticated, strategic manner when free-form communication is not feasible. However, free-form communication greatly improves efficiency, virtually eliminates strategic voting, and substantially diminishes the distorting effects of different voting institutions. The findings from these experiments support predictions that communication in deliberation on collective decisions consistently reveals private information, does a good job of predicting eventual verdicts, and improves efficiency. The results suggest that collective decision-making by juries is likely to be preferable to individual decisions from a welfare point of view.

## 1.3   Attorneys

As noted above, some 97% of civil court cases are decided outside the courtroom through settlement, making the role of attorneys all the more important. Unlike courtroom decisions, the impact that attorneys have on settlements is not so easily observable. In fact, little is known about the decisions that settling parties make because most settlements in civil cases are kept private. Some describe settlements as resulting from "bargaining in the shadow of the trial" or occurring inside a black box of decision-making.[14] Bushway and Redlich (2012) offer one of the first empirical tests of bargaining in the shadow of the trial, which is somewhat surprising given the large body of work on what drives trial outcomes (Devine et al. 2001). Unlike trial outcomes, however, data on settlements are hard to come by. For example, case data on the plea process in criminal cases are hard to find, and the relevant counterfactuals for individuals who enter pleas (i.e., what would have happened if they went to trial) are hard to identify.

In an attempt to make progress in this area, Bushway, Redlich and Norris (2014) used a web-based protocol to survey judges, prosecutors and defense attorneys who were randomly assigned to 16 different evidence conditions. The survey, completed by over 1,600 respondents, was employed to test predictions generated by applying the expected utility model framework to decision-making during plea bargain sessions.[15] The survey

---

[14]   Researchers have studied the general question whether individuals account for future uncertainties when making choices in the current period. For example, Dal Bó (2005) used infinitely repeated prisoner's dilemma games with a random continuation rule (so that subjects were uncertain about whether each current round was the final round) to study whether the shadow of the future impacts on current choices. He found that subjects were increasingly more cooperative as the likelihood of future interaction increased.

[15]   Basic expected utility models predict that defendants will accept a plea bargain if the punishment offered is less than the expected punishment at trial discounted by the likelihood of a guilty

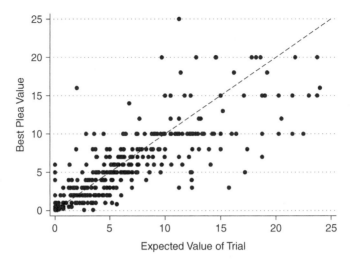

*Source:*   Bushway, Redlich and Norris (2014).

*Figure 12.1   Scatter plot of best plea value and expected value of trial for prosecutors*

questions relate to the expected outcome of the trial, including the probability of conviction and the expected punishment. Responders were also asked to state the plea deal they would advocate for (all within their own jurisdiction).[16] Contrary to the predictions of Bibas (2004), Bushway et al. found that, on average, the simple expected utility theory appears to fit the data quite well. They also found little difference in responses by role. Prosecutors, defense attorneys, and judges responded similarly to the survey questions.

Bushway et al. did, however, find a surprisingly large amount of unexplained deviation from the expected utility theory prediction at the individual level. This is documented in Figure 12.1, taken from their study, which presents a scatter plot of the relationship between the expected value of the trial and the best plea deal offered by prosecutors. As the authors explain:

> The diagonal line [see Figure 12.1] represents the slope expected by the shadow of the trial model. Although the relationship is clearly positive and strong, considerable variation is found around the line. Some prosecutors offer deals that are below the expected value of the trial (below the diagonal line), whereas other prosecutors offer deals that are above the expected value of the trial (above the diagonal line) . . . This variation could be random noise or measurement error induced by the clumping of the responses in the probability of conviction,[17] but it could also

---

verdict. If the defendant is risk averse, he might be willing to accept an amount of punishment that exceeds his expectation over the trial outcome.

[16]   Miller, McDonald and Cramer (1978) provide details about how plea-bargaining works. The institutional details inform economics models of decision-making during bargaining sessions over pleas.

[17]   "Although we used a method designed to minimize clumping, the probability of conviction has substantial bunching at 25 percent, 50 percent, and 75 percent" (Bushway, Redlich and Norris 2014, p. 742).

reflect other causal mechanisms. In addition, [the figure][18] shows that the relationship is likely to be nonlinear, with a slope that seems to flatten as the expected value of the trial increases. (2014, pp. 742–743)

Anecdotally at least, this large amount of variation in the plea discount is consistent with other observations researchers have reported that suggest that very similar cases result in very different plea discounts (Smith 1986; Ulmer and Bradley 2006; Spohn and Fornango 2009).

Two broad classes of explanations attempt to account for the types of variation found in the Bushway, Redlich and Norris (2014) experiment: different types of people and different types of bargaining environments. The attorney-respondents could have varied over at least three key decision-making dimensions: attitudes towards risk; attitudes towards uncertainty; and attitudes towards loss. In each case, experimental economists have shown that these attitudes can explain sizeable variations in the degree to which individual decisions deviate from the simple expected utility model tested by Bushway, Redlich and Norris (2014). It is at least possible that the observed variation could be explained by differences in individual preferences.[19] Another possibility is that this variation is the natural result of key characteristics of the bargaining game, such as uncertainty over the outcome at trial (Stuntz 2004). We believe the key question is the extent to which the nature of the bargaining game itself, over and above the individual differences in preferences, can help explain the wide variation in plea discounts observed in both case data (Bushway and Redlich 2012; Smith 1986)[20] and experimental data (Bushway, Redlich and Norris 2014).

Others have studied the impact of information on attorneys' estimates of jury verdicts. One notable example is a study by Jacobson, Dobbs-Marsh, Liberman and Minson (2011), in which law students were paired with other law students and experienced trial attorneys were paired with other experienced trial attorneys. The subjects were asked to guess the amounts of jury awards in actual cases. After guessing, each subject was then told his partner's guess and asked if he wished to revise his own guess. Jacobson et al. found that the accuracy of the second, informed guess was better than the first for both students and experienced attorneys. While both students and attorneys placed less weight on the information received from their partners relative to the weight assigned to their own guesses, the attorneys discounted the information more heavily than the students. The attorneys' guesses would have been more accurate if they had placed equal weight on their guesses and their partner's guesses. This suggests that attorneys "should seek out a second opinion and give that opinion more weight than they might be initially inclined to do" (Jacobson et al. 2011, p. 115).

---

[18]   The authors refer to their Figure 2 at this point, but they obviously intend to refer to Figure 1.

[19]   The authors collected no systematic information about differences in preferences about risk, attitudes towards uncertainty or attitudes towards loss in the surveyed case (armed robbery).

[20]   Bargaining in case data entails bargaining over plea deals in the shadow of a trial as well as bargaining over the charges that will be brought to a trial.

## 1.4   Experiments on Litigation and Settlement

Judges might do more harm than good when they intervene in settlement negotiations. Research suggests that a decision-maker's subjective perceptions of probabilities over potential outcomes differ from objective reality (see e.g., Tversky and Kahneman 1974). If judges' beliefs are consistent with this common finding, the divergence could have an unfortunate impact when judges interject themselves into settlement talks. In addition, experimental evidence suggests that judges are likely to (correctly or incorrectly) perceive settlement to be more attractive to plaintiffs than to defendants in ordinary litigation (Guthrie 2003). This, in turn, suggests that judges are likely to advocate settlement more strenuously to plaintiffs than to defendants, even though the experimental evidence suggests that plaintiffs are more likely than defendants to be attracted to settlement in the first place (Rachlinski 1996–1997; Guthrie 2003). By urging plaintiffs to accept a relatively small amount or by failing to urge defendants to offer some larger amount, judges could promote unfair settlements that under-compensate plaintiffs and under-deter defendants.

Attorneys can also wreak havoc on settlement negotiations under some conditions for a different set of reasons. Rachlinski (1996) reported experimental evidence demonstrating that a substantial number of subjects assuming the role of lawyer chose to behave (arguably) unethically when faced with an ethical dilemma. Rachlinski (1996) presented a litigation problem to law student subjects assigned to the role of counsel for a defendant pharmaceutical company in a hypothetical products liability suit. The subjects learned that the parents of a child allegedly injured by a drug manufactured by the defendant had sued the defendant for damages. The subjects further learned that the defendant had offered the parents $3 million to settle the case. Unknown to the parents, however, the defendant had discovered and withheld several relevant, incriminating documents during the discovery process. The subjects learned that they could be sanctioned if they agreed to settle the case without disclosing the documents to the plaintiffs.

To study the impact of framing on subjects' choices, Rachlinski (1996) randomly assigned half of the subjects to a "gains" condition. Subjects in this group learned that their client, who had originally expected to have to pay plaintiffs $5 million to settle the case, believed the case was "going well." Subjects assigned to the "losses" condition learned that their client, who had originally expected to pay plaintiffs only $1 million, believed that the case was "going poorly." Rachlinski asked subjects in both groups to indicate whether they would agree to accept the plaintiffs' offer and settle the case. Although the subjects faced the same decision—whether to settle the case for $3 million prior to disclosing relevant and incriminating documents—the framing of the decision problem affected subjects' willingness to engage in risky, and arguably unethical, behavior. Only 12.5% of the subjects assigned to the gains condition (case is going well) indicated that they would engage in the ethically risky behavior of settling prior to disclosing. By contrast, 45% of those assigned to the losses condition (case is going poorly) indicated that they would settle before disclosing.

Consistent with the predictions of Kahneman and Tversky's (1979) Prospect Theory,[21]

---

[21]   Prospect Theory is an alternative to Expected Utility Theory. It assumes that individuals assign value to gains and losses relative to some reference point (as opposed to assigning value to

Rachlinski found that subjects prompted about hypothetical clients facing hypothetical losses were nearly four times as likely to adopt a risk-seeking, and ethically dicey, litigation strategy. Although the subjects might not have known whether settling before disclosing violated the governing ethical rules, "settling before a party can find out unpleasant facts about one's case smacks of impropriety and unfairness" (p. 142). Many of the subjects appeared willing to sacrifice ethical principles in an attempt to avoid incurring losses. It is worth emphasizing, though, that attorneys do not directly incur losses when their clients pay. Moreover, Prospect Theory assumes that the decision-maker will incur actual losses (as opposed to hypothetical losses). This calls into question the suitability of the experiment as a test of the theory. This research does, however, report an interesting finding about reference effects and their possible impact on decision-making during settlement that highlights a need for further investigation.

Others have studied factors that might explain why settlement negotiations sometimes fail. For example, Gilliland, Dunn and Navarro (2008) and Miettinen, Ropponen and Sääskilahti (2011) conducted experiments involving computer-based questionnaires to explore reasons why settlement fails. Specifically, the experimenters place subjects in roles (plaintiff, defendant or one party in a negotiation game), give them a settlement offer and then ask them to decide whether to accept the offer or continue to negotiate. Gilliland, Dunn and Navarro (2008) found that subjects were more likely to hypothetically settle out of court when the outcome was framed in a positive way,[22] when they perceived the probability of winning the case as low and when the outcome of the trial was uncertain. In a separate study, Miettinen, Ropponen and Sääskilahti (2011) studied the impact of inequity aversion on settlement behavior. They found that, contrary to conventional wisdom, greater variance in possible court outcomes leads to higher settlement rates, and high variance reduces the likelihood of settlement. The authors rule out asymmetric information and self-serving biases as explanations and attribute the result to subjects' distaste for inequality in outcomes.

## 1.5 A Note on Methods

Before moving on to Section 2, it is important for us to highlight possible methodological issues with the experiments summarized in Section 1. First, experimentalists generally avoid asking the subjects to engage in "role play," where they attempt to place themselves in the shoes of some actor with particular skills or characteristics or interests. Many are critical of this technique given the difficulties subjects likely have in making authentic

---

outcomes) and that they are risk averse in the face of potential gains but risk seeking in the face of potential losses (as opposed to being consistently risk averse in the face of any type of uncertainty).

[22] All subjects were told that a settlement offer of $10,000 had been made and that their attorney estimated a 50% chance of a $20,000 award and a 50% chance of getting nothing. Subjects playing the plaintiff role in the positive-frame treatment were told "If you accept this offer, you will receive $10,000 in compensation." Subjects in the negative-frame treatment were told "If you accept this offer, you will lose $10,000 in income." Despite the obvious problems with the language (i.e., one cannot actually "lose" $10,000 by accepting $10,000 in lieu of playing the lottery—one merely loses the *chance* to gain $20,000), the results might teach us something about framing.

decisions during role play.[23] Second, many of the experiments described in this section are hypothetical in nature. This violates a basic principle of experiment design. Specifically, experimental environments are valid tests of theory only if they include all necessary assumptions that drive the theory's predictions. The experiments described in this section all purport to test theories that assume non-hypothetical outcomes (e.g., an actual verdict with actual consequences). Thus, whether these experiments stand as valid tests of the theories is questionable.[24] While these concerns should not compel us to ignore the results, they might substantially reduce the amount of weight we place on the evidence as support for the tested theories' predictions. More practically, it would be prudent for us to wait to apply the tested theories until other sorts of evidence give us better confidence in the theories' predictions as they relate to legal system actors.

## 2.   EXPERIMENTS ON LEGAL REMEDIES AND ENFORCEMENT

Many behavioral experiments produce results that are potentially relevant to choices over institutional settings and laws and to predicting the impacts of perceptions of fairness and punishment. We focus specifically on papers published after 2000, emphasizing the relevance to the field of Law and Economics.

Laboratory experiments help researchers isolate the effects of institutional settings, the characteristics of information and the structure of legal rules on subjects' behavior and outcomes. Croson and Johnston (2000), for example, study the impact of vagueness in the legal definition of property rights. They find that vagueness strongly influences the tendency of subjects to take property from others without consent and reduces the likelihood of a consensual exchange. The results suggest that alternative legal approaches to the definition and protection of entitlements can lead to dramatic differences in behavior and in allocations.

In addition to studying the impact of law vagueness, researchers have also studied the impact of information vagueness. Standard litigation theory assumes that information—

---

[23]   Croson (2002, pp. 929–930) explains: "Experimental economists, generally, prefer very little context when they are testing theories for three reasons. First, the theory being tested often does not rely on context, so the experiments should not either. Second, context often adds variance to the data. For example, if some subjects think that going to court is a bad thing, then describing the experimental decision as "going to court" as opposed to "choosing option A" could change an individual's decision. These changes might not affect the average or aggregate decision, but it can impact the variance of those decisions, reducing the likelihood of detecting statistically significant differences between treatments of the experiment. Finally, and most importantly, context can add systematic bias or demand effects. For example, if subjects want to be seen as kind, gentle types by their professor, then describing the decision in terms of going to court might reduce everyone's likelihood of choosing that option. Such systematic changes in the data will significantly change the conclusions reached, thus context should be avoided in these types of experiments. In theory testing experiments, there are only low costs associated with avoiding context."

[24]   Davis and Holt (1993, p. 24) note: "In designing an experiment, it is critical that participants receive salient rewards that correspond to the incentives assumed in the relevant theory or application."

produced during the discovery phase, for example—leads to a convergence of the parties' expectations over trial outcomes, which results in a higher likelihood of settlement. Loewenstein and Moore (2004) conducted experiments to determine whether all such information discovery is likely to produce these results. They use a conventional bargaining experiment (unrelated to litigation) to test the predictions of the standard model and to differentiate between information that can give rise to multiple interpretations and information that leads to an undisputed interpretation. They find that, contrary to the standard theory, vague information leads to a divergence of expectations. This result provides support for models that assume that individuals are subject to self-serving biases—e.g., plaintiffs interpret vague information in the best light for their case, and defendants interpret the same information in the best light for theirs. Even though subjects were paid only if they could agree to trade, negotiations failed more often, and took longer, when information was vague as opposed to precise. They also found that a working communication institution that helped to reduce uncertainty increased the efficiency of the bargaining process and outcomes.

Others have found that allowing communication in settings in which law typically disallows it can actually increase efficiency. For example, Santore, McKee and Bjornstad (2010) designed an experiment to study whether allowing communication about pricing strategies, typically a violation of antitrust law, can help to achieve socially optimal trades between multiple holders of complementary patents[25] and producers who wish to purchase licenses to use the legally protected intellectual property. The results support theoretical models that predict increased efficiency when communication is allowed. These findings suggest that loosening up on enforcement of collusion prohibitions might be optimal under some conditions. Deck and Farmer (2006) design experiments that produce results supporting a similar theory around information structures of final offer arbitration.[26] They find that allowing subjects to decide publicly how much to invest in building their cases to convince the arbitrator to side with them results in more efficient outcomes than those produced under private investment choices.

Researchers have also employed experiments to study the justifications for strong enforcement of particular legal rules. Bilz (2012) designed an experiment to determine whether the exclusionary rule[27] is justified by concerns over protecting the integrity of the judicial system and not just deterrence of illegal searches and seizures. Employing hospital cafeteria diners, law students and lawyers as subjects, she elicited responses to questions about hypothetical vignettes to measure motives. She also drew inferences from whether subjects chose a small bottle of hand-sanitizer or a highlighter pen as a thank-you gift

---

[25] Complementary patents refer to a set of patents held by different parties, all of which are required to incorporate the collective technology into useable products. When a product manufacturer wishes to license all the technology protected by the set of patents, inefficiencies such as coordination and hold-out problems can arise.

[26] Final offer arbitration (Stevens 1966) "requires that agents submit a final offer and the arbitrator must choose one of the two: there is no splitting of the difference" (Deck and Farmer 2007, p. 416).

[27] The exclusionary rule is a rule of evidence that courts apply to forbid the government from using, during criminal proceedings, evidence collected or analyzed in a manner that violates a defendant's constitutional rights.

as evidence of the dirty-evidence motive. She found that subjects preferred exclusion even when law enforcement officials did not realize they were violating the suspect's constitutional rights, a type of situation in which the motive for exclusion cannot be deterrence. In addition, participants who were obliged to use unconstitutionally obtained evidence at trial disproportionately chose the sanitizer over the pen. From these choices, Bilz concluded that subjects were motivated by a desire to maintain the system's integrity.

Others have studied similar issues in civil settings. Darley et al. (2010), for example, explore whether and how we should punish wrongdoers when wrongful acts result only in the possibility of future harm. Just as Bilz did, the authors use subject responses to a variety of vignettes that vary the details related to the responsibility of the wrongdoer, the wrongdoer's state of mind, causation, risk levels and actual harm versus an increased risk of harm. The authors conclude that individuals prefer to award damages even in cases in which the injurer's conduct was not negligent or intentional, taking a stronger strict liability stance than current tort doctrine seems to take. The subjects also more stringently punished actions that actually resulted in harm relative to actions that did not result in harm, which seems to be in line with modern tort doctrine.

A long line of experimental economics research examines free riding and the punishment of such behavior in public goods games. Some have used public goods games in the lab to study sanctions as an element of justice when information about choices, and therefore who deserves punishment, is incomplete. Grechenig, Nicklisch and Thöni (2010) use a standard repeated voluntary contribution mechanism[28] game to examine how punishment is doled out when subjects can punish participants who under-contribute but "reasonable doubt" exists about the amount each subject contributed. Interestingly, the authors find that subjects are willing to punish in the face of highly inaccurate information about contribution amounts. Their results suggest that sufficiently accurate information about others' behavior is crucial for achieving socially efficient outcomes using sanctions.[29]

Experimentalists have also studied methods of enforcement in the lab. Guttentag, Porath and Fraidin (2008) study methods for preventing corporate fraud. They separated subjects into small groups and put them into a situation that made it possible to engage in behavior that was not necessarily disallowed but might be perceived as fraudulent. Each group was given time to complete a difficult task and then given the right answers and asked whether they wanted to change their answers. They earned more for right answers but, if an answer change was detected, they would earn less than they would have for answering incorrectly. Subjects were required to disclose explanations for why they answered the way they answered, analogous to financial statement reporting. The authors found that requiring disclosure of explanations reduced "fraud" (the answer-change rate). Levels of intra-group trust and the strength of group cohesion were associated with an

---

[28]    The repeated voluntary contribution mechanism allocates to each subject a fixed number of tokens that the subject can either keep or contribute to a public good, entirely or partially. Choices are made simultaneously. The contributed tokens are then multiplied by some known number and divided evenly amongst all of the participants in the experiment (see Fehr and Gachter 2000). The socially efficient outcome requires all subjects to contribute all tokens to the public good, but individual rationality compels subjects to keep all their tokens and free ride on others' contributions.

[29]    See also Andreoni and Gee (2012, 2015) and DeAngelo and Gee (2015).

increase in the number of changed answers. The results help us understand both the causes of fraud and the methods for deterring it.[30]

Law enforcement regimes have also been examined to determine the impact of different enforcement tools on proscribed behavior. The laboratory is a particularly good environment for studying enforcement regimes given that it is difficult, if not impossible, to untangle causal mechanisms in the field (e.g., enforcement efforts are typically higher in high crime areas) and observing outcomes such as recidivism rates is impossible. Friesen (2012) and DeAngelo and Charness (2012) study different components of law enforcement mechanisms on the level of deterrence in experimental environments.[31] Friesen (2012) examines whether an increase in the probability of getting caught is better at deterring crime than an increase in fines. Her results suggest that increases in punishment severity are more effective.

DeAngelo and Charness (2012) examine the role of uncertainty over the enforcement regime (fine and probability of apprehension) in individuals' choices to commit a proscribed criminal activity—hypothetical speeding in this case. Each subject was paid $0.60 if he refrained from speeding and $1 if he chose to speed and didn't get caught. Detection of the "law violation" was possible with some probability, and the subject suffered a fine upon detection. Multiple experiments were run, and treatments varied by the fine imposed on offenders and the probability of getting caught. As theory predicts, subjects were less likely to speed when the expected cost of speeding increased. In addition, the researchers studied the impact of uncertainty about the likelihood of detection and the fine. The results suggest that greater uncertainty over the enforcement regime yields increased deterrence at no additional cost to the enforcer.

Finally, Anderson et al. (2017) examine the role of uncertainty over the deterrence mechanism (probability of apprehension and/or fine) in the willingness to recidivate. Variations between treatments mimicked the DeAngelo and Charness (2012) design, with subjects making choices over repeated rounds. Rather than focusing on the likelihood of offending given uncertainty over the enforcement regime, the researchers examine how such uncertainty impacts the likelihood that one will offend again after getting caught and fined. Consistent with DeAngelo and Charness (2012), higher expected costs of speeding reduce speeding. With respect to recidivism, subjects who are caught and fined in one period are less likely to ever speed again relative to those who skirt detection. Interestingly, uncertainty over the legal regime increases the willingness to recidivate. Subjects re-offended sooner after being caught if they were uncertain about which enforcement regime would be applied relative to facing a known risk of detection.

---

[30]   Others have studied similar phenomena. Mullen and Nadler (2008), for example, design an experiment to study whether people are more likely to act immorally if they witness another's immoral behavior. They find evidence of moral spillovers; witnessing immoral behavior can trigger others' deviant behavior.

[31]   See also Schildberg-Horisch and Strassmair (2012).

## 3. EXPERIMENTS STUDYING BARGAINING OF PRINCIPALS AND AGENTS

Behavioral contract theory predicts how people will respond in contract negotiations; for example, holding to one's reservation price may very well not lead to good social outcomes, as individuals are prone to reject very low offers (as in the ultimatum game). One particular research area that has been developing in recent years is how communication influences decisions and outcomes in principal-agent environments. A series of experimental studies finds that non-binding and costless messages (cheap talk) can effectively induce optimal social outcomes. These studies also shed light on how the nature of the message can play an important role.

Charness and Dufwenberg (2006) examine the effect of cheap talk messages on behavior in environments with either hidden action (moral hazard) or hidden information (adverse selection). This study considers a situation in which a principal (or potential employer) can hire an agent (potential employee) to complete a project, but cannot observe with certainty whether the agent, if hired, exerts costly effort. The payoff structure in one calibration of the game is the following (see Figure 12.2). If the principal chooses not to offer the position (Out), then the principal and the agent each receive $5. If the principal hires the agent (In) and the agent exerts no effort (Don't), the project is not successful; in this case, the principal receives $0 and the agent receives $14. If the agent does exert effort (Roll), there is a 5/6 chance that the project will be successful; if it is unsuccessful (if a die rolled individually for the agent comes up 1), the principal receives $0 and the agent receives $10, while if it is successful (the die comes up 2–6), the principal receives $12 and the agent receives $0. Since the principal who hires an agent can receive the payoff of $0

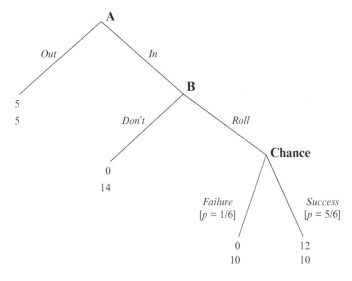

*Source:*   Gary Charness and Martin Dufwenberg, "Promises and Partnership," *Econometrica* 74, no. 6 (2006), p. 1581. Printed with permission of The Econometric Society.

*Figure 12.2   Game form from Charness and Dufwenberg (2006)*

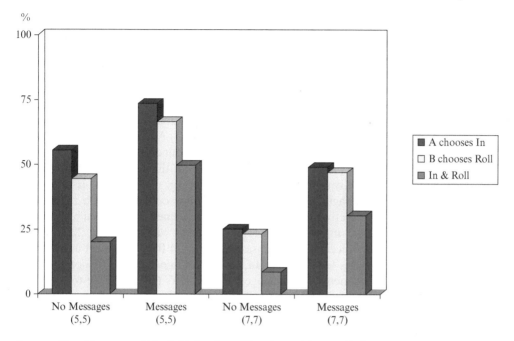

*Source:* Gary Charness and Martin Dufwenberg, "Promises and Partnership," *Econometrica* 74, no. 6 (2006): 1587. Printed with permission of The Econometric Society.

*Figure 12.3 Results from Charness and Dufwenberg (2006): percentage of outcomes by tree branch*

even if the agent exerts effort, the principal cannot verify whether the agent failed to exert effort. A second payoff calibration involves the principal and agent each receiving $7 if the agent is not hired (all else is the same).

Play is one-shot and anonymous, so that an agent who cares only about his or her payoff has no reason to exert effort. Knowing this, according to standard game theory assumptions, an own-payoff-maximizing principal should choose to avoid paying a wage for no work. This leads to each person receiving $5, instead of each receiving (in expectation) $10. Since this is a suboptimal social outcome, there is scope for an intervention to improve matters. The intervention studied is a free-form message that the agent is allowed to send to the paired principal, who sees the message before making a choice. Figure 12.3 summarizes the results. "A" refers to the principal and "B" refers to the agent.

Standard game theory, as noted, would predict that A always chooses Out in all treatments. Completely selfish behavior is not observed in any treatment, however. This is unsurprising given a large body of other work finding that people do have social preferences (see, e.g., Bolton and Ockenfels 2000; Fehr and Schmidt 1999; Charness and Rabin 2002). Nevertheless, the authors observe a strong effect from communication. When the outside option for the principal leads to $5 for each (the (5,5) treatment) and no messages are permitted, 25 of 45 (56%) A's choose to hire the agent ("In") and 20 of

45 (44%) B's choose to exert costly effort ("Roll").[32] When B is able to send a message to A, considerably more outcomes are socially optimal: 31 of 42 (74%) A's choose In and 28 of 42 (67%) B's choose Roll. The (In, Roll) socially optimal profile occurs 20% of the time (9 of 45 pairs) without communication, compared to 50% (21 of 42 pairs) with possible communication. Similar effects are observed in the (7,7) treatment. Without communication, 12 of 48 (25%) B's choose Roll and 11 of 48 (23%) A's choose In. When B is able to send a message to A, once again the authors observe considerably more socially optimal outcomes: 24 of 49 (49%) B's choose Roll and 23 of 49 (47%) A's choose In. The (In, Roll) optimal profile occurred 8% of the time (4 of 48 pairs) without communication, compared to 31% (15 of 49 pairs) with possible communication. All of the differences mentioned in this paragraph are statistically significant at the 5% level.

The content of the messages helps us understand how communication might have changed the results. The effectiveness of communication seemed to be driven by promises (non-binding statements of intent). In the (5,5) treatment with messages, 22 of 24 A's (92%) choose to hire after receiving a promise, and 18 of 24 B's (75%) exert costly effort after making a promise; this leads to the (In, Roll) profile occurring 67% of the time. Similarly, in the (7,7) treatment with messages, 16 of 24 A's (67%) choose to hire after receiving a promise, and 20 of 24 B's (83%) exert costly effort after making a promise; this leads to the (In, Roll) profile occurring 58% of the time. Note that these numbers are much higher than in the corresponding treatments where no messages are permitted. The results also provide strong support for the notion of guilt aversion, whereby one wishes to avoid anticipated guilt triggered by disappointing another party. These results suggest that, contrary to conventional theory, judicial enforcement of contracts is not required in all cases to achieve the efficient outcome.

Charness and Dufwenberg (2010) performed another set of experiments to more closely examine the impact of communication. The results reported provide a cautionary note regarding the effectiveness of messages per se. In the same (5,5) framework as above, free-form messages were not employed; instead, each B was given two sheets of paper. One stated: "I promise to choose Roll;" the other was blank.[33] B placed one of the two sheets in an envelope that was conveyed to the paired A. These experimenter-generated and impersonal messages were largely ineffective. Twenty-three of 41 A's (56%) chose In after receiving a bare promise from B, and 25 of 41 B's (61%) chose Roll after making a bare promise. These rates did not differ from those observed in Charness and Dufwenberg (2006) in the (5,5) treatment without messages; neither difference is statistically significant at the 5% level. These results suggest that individuals do not have preferences over promise-keeping per se. It seems that something beyond a preference for truth-telling is driving behavior in experiments that allow for free-form communication.

Finally, Charness and Dufwenberg (2011) test the effect of communication in an environment of hidden information (i.e., the principal is unable to observe the ability of

---

[32]   In this experiment, the strategy method was used. Each agent made a choice contingent on the principal's choosing to hire the agent. In this manner, a choice for every agent is elicited, which increases the amount of data produced by a relatively small number of recruited subjects.

[33]   The instructions mentioned that a promise was not binding as otherwise some B's might have felt compelled to choose Roll if they promised they would, believing that this was their only choice.

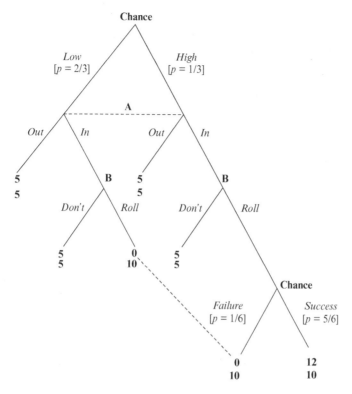

*Note:*   A represents the principal and B represents the agent. The (5,7) game is identical except that each player receives $7 if either agent type chooses Don't. In the (7,7) game, Out choices by A and Don't choices by both agents result in a payout of $7 to each player.

*Figure 12.4   The (5,5) game from Charness and Dufwenberg (2011)*

the agent) as opposed to hidden action (i.e., the principal is unable to observe the choice of the agent). There is a 2/3 chance that an agent has low talent and a 1/3 chance that the agent has high talent, and both players know this probability distribution, but only the agent knows his type. The design varies the payoffs and the ability of the agent to send a message to the principal.

In the (5,5) treatment (see Figure 12.4), the principal can choose not to hire (Out), in which case the principal and the agent each receive $5. If the principal hires the agent (In), the outcome depends on the agent's type and choice. If the agent has high talent and chooses Roll (to exert effort), the agent receives $10 and there is a 5/6 chance that the principal receives $12 and a 1/6 chance that he receives $0. If the high-talent agent chooses Don't (to not exert effort), each person receives $5. If the hired agent has low ability and chooses Roll, the agent receives $10 and the principal receives $0; if the hired low-ability agent chooses Don't, each person receives $5.

The game-theoretic prediction, which assumes that players care only about their material payoffs, can be determined using backward induction. Theory predicts B will choose Roll regardless of his ability because he will receive 10 in any event, which is larger than

7, the amount he would receive if he chose Don't. Knowing this, A's expected payoff from choosing In is $3.33 ($12 times 1/3 times 5/6), which is less than $5, what he gets if he chooses Out. So, A will choose Out even though this choice fails to achieve the socially optimal outcome. This prediction is one inspiration for our system of legal enforcement of contracts.

The (5,7) treatment is nearly identical, but there is one difference, which in fact turns out to be crucial: if an agent is hired, both the agent and the principal receive $7 if the agent chooses Don't. The theoretical predictions (when we assume that one cares only about one's own material payoffs) is the same as in the (5,5) treatment, but here even the low-ability agent can participate in an outcome that is a Pareto improvement over the principal's outside option.[34] The authors also conducted a (7,7) treatment, where the outside option for the principal leads to $7 each, while each of the principal and the agent receives $7 if the agent is hired and chooses Don't. The game theoretic prediction is the same as in the other two environments.[35]

Note that in all treatments, if the principal (A) chooses In and the agent (B) chooses Don't, both players are better off than if the principal and agent decide in the game-theoretic predicted way (A chooses Out). So, again, we have room to intervene in some way to help the players achieve what's in their joint best interest. The source of the problem is the hidden information related to the agent's ability, so an opportunity to communicate is a potential solution. Since any promise communicated by the agent to the principal is not binding (in the sense that the principal is not punished if he promises and then breaches his promise), theories that assume that individuals care only about material outcomes would produce the same predictions as those that arise from similar environments in the absence of information. As mentioned, however, existing evidence suggests people have social preferences. Communication might promote trust and cooperation. This might depend, though, on whether the agent has the ability to increase his payout by making a promise and then keeping the promise, as in the (5,7) treatment.

The results are summarized in Table 12.1. Note that the results turn on whether the low-ability agent can participate in a Pareto-improving outcome. Summarizing the results, the only case in which communication led to a significant increase was for low-talent B's in the (5,7) game, where the Don't rate nearly doubles, to 78%. Note that this rate is more than quadruple the Don't rates with communication in the two non-participation games, with statistical significance at $p < 0.001$ for each comparison. The proportions of Don't are very close in the (5,5) and (7,7) games, regardless of whether communication is possible. In general, it seems that low-talent B's refuse to step aside when there is no available Pareto

---

[34]  A Pareto improvement is an outcome that makes at least one person better off without making anyone worse off, relative to some other outcome.

[35]  A parallel to the (5,7) environment is the Spence (1973) signaling game, except without a materially costly signal. In Spence's (1973) design, the agent can assume a managerial position or a clerical position. While both types of agents can perform the clerical job, only the high-ability agent can succeed at the managerial position. The principal would like to assign the agent to the appropriate position, but the agent receives more money if she chooses the managerial position (by choosing Roll). In contrast, in the (5,5) treatment and the (7,7) treatment, only a managerial position is available, so that the principal can profitably hire only the high-ability agent. A low-ability agent who is offered a position can give the principal a break only by declining the position (choosing Don't).

Table 12.1 *Results from Charness and Dufwenberg (2011)*

Rates by Treatment and Tests for the Effect of Communication

| Treatment | Low B's Don't | | | A's In | | |
|---|---|---|---|---|---|---|
| | M | NM | Z-stat | M | NM | Z-stat |
| (5,7) | 18/23 (78%) | 8/20 (40%) | 2.56 | 33/41 (80%) | 28/40 (70%) | 1.09 |
| (5,7) | 3/16 (19%) | 2/13 (15%) | 0.24 | 24/47 (51%) | 20/45 (44%) | 0.64 |
| (5,7) | 2/11 (18%) | 3/13 (23%) | −0.29 | 21/42 (50%) | 18/40 (45%) | 0.45 |

improvement over A's outside option, but are often willing to accept lower payoffs than high-talent B's when participation is feasible.

The patterns in the messages sent reveal that the effect of communication is driven by promises by low-ability agents in the (5,7) treatment. While high-ability agents typically state that they have high-ability (as do about 20% of the low-ability agents in each of the three treatments), many low-ability agents in the (5,7) treatment state that they have low ability but that they will choose Don't, leading to $7 for each of A and B. It turns out that A's who receive such messages choose In 93% of the time. What is perhaps more surprising is that each and every low-ability agent who sent this message chooses Don't when this promise has been made.

These results provide some "useful lessons" that, on extrapolation, may offer guidance for those who wish to detect whether someone else is being honest. A claim that the agent has high talent should be viewed with some suspicion, as it may well be "the big lie." However, when participation is possible regardless of the agent's talent, the claim that someone has low talent but will do his best turns out to be completely reliable, and is in fact almost always believed by the principal; it seems that one can trust people who confess imperfections. Perhaps people are substantially more prone to be cooperative when they can participate by having a voice and choosing an action that yields improvements in material payoffs for all parties involved than when the only way to gain is at the expense of others. This may help to explain many market situations, which differ over the availability of Pareto-improvements. For example, e-commerce furnishes settings in which the quality of the good traded is not readily observable, and it may or may not be the case that all sellers have the ability to provide a good that buyers value.

Brandts, Charness and Ellman (2012) consider the effect of communication in a buyer-seller framework, in which a cost shock occurs after the parties agree to an initial price. Two individuals are randomly paired, and the buyer proposes a price to the seller. The seller can choose to accept or reject this price. If rejected, each party receives the disagreement payoff of 5. If the seller accepts the offer, she then chooses a quality level, which determines the buyer's gross trade value (10, 30 or 45). However, before this quality choice is made, the seller observes a cost of either 0 or 20 (with equal likelihood).

Two forms of contract can be offered. The first is a rigid contract, in which the price is set in the beginning and cannot be changed. The second is a flexible contract, in which an initial price is set, but the price can be augmented by an additional payment after the cost shock is realized (and observed by the buyer). In either case, the seller observes the final price and decides on quality level -1, 0, or 1. A quality level of 0 is costless, while choosing -1 or 1 costs the seller one unit. With a quality level of -1, the buyer receives the original endowment of 5 plus an additional 10 payoff units; with a quality level of 0, the buyer receives the original endowment of 5 plus an additional 10 payoff units plus 20 more units for the higher quality and with a quality level of 1, the buyer receives the original endowment of 5 plus an additional 10 payoff units plus 35 more units for the highest quality.

In principle the flexible contract seems clearly superior, as the buyer and seller can in effect share the cost shock. However, the seller has no particular reason to believe that a buyer who offers a flexible contract will in fact pay an additional amount after the cost shock is revealed. This uncertainty can lead to a rigid contract being more profitable for the buyer, as found in Fehr, Hart and Zehnder (2015). Brandts, Charness and Ellman (2012) test for the effect of communication (free-form chat) on the type of contract offered, the quality chosen, and buyer and seller profits. Two treatments (chat and no chat) were conducted, each with four sessions.

The rigid contract is in fact more prevalent (chosen 55% of the time) and leads to slightly higher earnings for the buyer when no communication is permitted. The buyer receives an average payoff of 10.80 and the seller receives an average payoff of 7.81 when a rigid contract is offered. By comparison, the buyer receives an average payoff of 9.73 and the seller receives an average payoff of 7.96 when a flexible contract is offered. The distribution of (-1,0,1) quality choices, given an accepted contract, was (31%, 65%, 4%) with rigid contracts and (40%, 56%, 4%) with flexible contracts.

However, matters change dramatically when communication is allowed. In treatment 2, the proportion of rigid contracts offered was only 25%. The buyer receives an average payoff of 12.66 and the seller receives an average payoff of 16.68 when a rigid contract is offered. Earnings are substantially higher with a flexible contract—the buyer receives an average payoff of 17.02 and the seller receives an average payoff of 20.95 when a flexible contract is offered. The distribution of (-1,0,1) quality choices, given an accepted contract, was (14%, 36%, 50%) with rigid contracts and (6%, 20%, 74%) with flexible contracts. The differences in the proportion of rigid contracts offered, the payoffs for the buyer and the seller, and the distribution of quality choices are all significantly different across treatments. These results are further evidence that communication, even when non-binding, can foster trust and trustworthiness.

In an additional treatment with restricted chat (the buyer is allowed to state only how much he would pay with and without a cost shock), the authors find no effect on quality or profits compared to the baseline with no chat. This holds for both rigid and flexible contracts. This result adds to the growing evidence that a richer and endogenous form of communication is needed to move behavior away from a unique, but socially inferior, equilibrium when own-payoff maximization is assumed. These sorts of studies refine our understanding of the need for judicial enforcement of agreements.

## 4. CONCLUSION

The role and importance of laboratory experiments in research related to law and economics has been and will continue growing. As expectations for reliable estimates from field data move further in the direction of natural experiments, the laboratory will continue to be an environment where manipulation of context and parameters can be profitably undertaken. We once again point out the value of incentivized experiments rather than hypothetical ones, whenever this is feasible.

In our distillation of previous research, we discussed several law and economics contexts that have been applied in the laboratory. The last decade of research has produced a considerable amount of work from legal scholars, psychologists, political scientists and economists in the area of law and economics. This research has examined the role and magnitude of cognitive and social biases in decision-making by many legal actors (attorney, judges and juries). Additionally, the heuristics that legal actors/agencies utilize in reaching their decisions/conclusions and enforcing the legal code are examined in order to determine the role that information, risk, uncertainty and bargaining play in these processes.

## REFERENCES

Anderson, L. R., G. DeAngelo, W. Emons, B. Freeborn and H. Lang. 2017. Penalty Structures and Deterrence in a Two-stage Model: Experimental Evidence. *Economic Inquiry* 55: 1833–1867. doi:10.1111/ecin.12464.

Andreoni, J. and L. Gee. 2012. Gun for Hire: Delegated Enforcement and Peer Punishment in Public Goods Provision. *Journal of Public Economics* 96: 1036–1046.

Andreoni, J. and L. Gee. 2015. Gunning for Efficiency with Third Part Enforcement in Threshold Public Goods. *Experimental Economics* 18: 154–171.

Austen-Smith, D. and T. Feddersen. 2006. Deliberation, Preference Uncertainty, and Voting Rules. *American Political Science Review* 100: 209–217.

Battaglini, M., R. Morton and T. Palfrey. 2008. Information Aggregation and Strategic Abstention in Large Laboratory Elections. *American Economic Review* 98: 194–200.

Battaglini, M., R. Morton and T. Palfrey. 2010. The Swing Voter's Curse in the Laboratory. *Review of Economic Studies* 77: 66–89.

Bibas, S. 2004. Plea Bargaining Outside the Shadow of Trial. *Harvard Law Review* 117: 2463–2547.

Bilz, K. 2012. Dirty Hands or Deterrence? An Experimental Examination of the Exclusionary Rule. *Journal of Empirical Legal Studies* 9: 149–171.

Bolton, G.E. and A. Ockenfels. 2000. ERC: A Theory of Equity, Reciprocity, and Competition. *American Economic Review* 90: 166–193.

Bornstein, B. and E. Greene. 2011. Jury Decision Making: Implications For and From Psychology. *Current Directions in Psychological Science* 20: 63–67.

Boudreau, C. and M. McCubbins. 2008. Nothing But the Truth? Experiments on Adversarial Competition, Expert Testimony, and Decision Making. *Journal of Empirical Legal Studies* 5: 751–789.

Brandts, J., G. Charness and M. Ellman. 2012. Let's Talk: How Communication Affects Contract Design. Working Paper No. 3883. CESifo Group, Munich.

Bushway, S. and A. Redlich. 2012. Is Plea Bargaining in the "Shadow of the Trial" a Mirage? *Journal of Quantitative Criminology* 28: 437–454.

Bushway, S., A. Redlich and R. J. Norris. 2014. An Explicit Test of Plea Bargaining in the "Shadow of the Trial." *Criminology* 52: 723–754.

Camerer, C., G. Lowenstein and M. Rabin, eds. 2003. *Advances in Behavioral Economics*. Princeton, NJ: Princeton University Press.

Carlson, K. and E. Russo. 2001. Biased Interpretation of Evidence by Mock Jurors. *Journal of Experimental Psychology: Applied* 7: 91–103.

Charness, G. and M. Dufwenberg. 2006. Promises and Partnership. *Econometrica* 74: 1579–1601.

Charness, G. and M. Dufwenberg. 2010. Bare Promises: An experiment. *Economics Letters* 107: 281–283.
Charness, G. and M. Dufwenberg. 2011. Participation. *American Economic Review* 101: 1211–1237.
Charness, G. and P. Kuhn. 2011. Lab Labor: What Can Labor Economists Learn from the Lab? Pp. 229–330 in vol. 4A of *Handbook of Labor Economics*, edited by Orley Ashenfelter and David Card. Amsterdam: North Holland.
Charness, G. and M. Rabin. 2002. Understanding Social Preferences with Simple Tests. *Quarterly Journal of Economics* 117: 817–869.
Coughlan, P. 2000. In Defense of Unanimous Jury Verdicts: Mistrials, Communication, and Strategic Voting. *American Political Science Review* 94: 375–393.
Croson, R. 2002. Why and How to Experiment: Methodologies from Experimental Economics. *University of Illinois Law Review* 2002: 921–945.
Croson, R. and J. Johnston. 2000. Experimental Results on Bargaining under Alternative Property Rights Regimes. *Journal of Law, Economics, and Organization* 16: 50–73.
Dal Bó, P. 2005. Cooperation under the Shadow of the Future: Experimental Evidence From Infinitely Repeated Games. *The American Economic Review* 95: 1591–1604.
Darley, J., L. Solan, M. Kugler and J. Sanders. 2010. Doing Wrong Without Creating Harm. *Journal of Empirical Legal Studies* 7: 30–63.
Davis, D. and C. Holt. 1993. *Experimental Economics*. Princeton, NJ: Princeton University Press.
DeAngelo, G. and G. Charness. 2012. Deterrence, Expected Cost, Uncertainty and Voting: Experimental Evidence. *Journal of Risk and Uncertainty* 44: 73–100.
DeAngelo, G., G. Charness and B. Freeborn. 2011. Mechanisms for Reducing Criminal Recidivism: Experimental Evidence. Working Paper, http://papers.ssrn.com/sol3/papers.cfm?abstract_id=1894086 (last visited May 20, 2015).
DeAngelo, G. and L. Gee. 2015. Peer vs. Centralized Detections and Sanctions. Working Paper.
Deck, C. and A. Farmer. 2007. Bargaining and Arbitration with Asymmetric Uncertainty. *Research in Labor Economics* 26: 415–445.
Devine, D., L. Clayton, B. Dunford, R. Seying and J. Pryce. 2001. Jury Decision Making: 45 Years of Empirical Research on Deliberating Groups. *Psychology, Public Policy, and Law* 7: 622–727.
Engel, C. and M. Kurschilgen. 2011. Fairness Ex Ante and Ex Post: Experimentally Testing Ex Post Judicial Intervention into Blockbuster Deals. *Journal of Empirical Legal Studies* 8: 682–708.
Falk, A. and J. Heckman. 2009. Lab Experiments Are a Major Source of Knowledge in the Social Sciences. *Science* 326: 535–538.
Feddersen, T., S. Gailmard and A. Sandroni. 2009. Moral Bias in Large Elections: Theory and Experimental Evidence. *American Political Science Review* 103: 175–192.
Fehr, E. and S. Gachter. 2000. Fairness and Retaliation: The Economics of Reciprocity. *Journal of Economic Perspectives* 14: 159–181.
Fehr, E., O. Hart and C. Zehnder. 2015. How Do Informal Agreements and Revision Shape Contractual Reference Points? *Journal of the European Economic Association* 13: 1–28.
Fehr, E. and K. M. Schmidt. 1999. A Theory of Fairness, Competition, and Cooperation. *Quarterly Journal of Economics* 114: 817–868.
Fréchette, G., J. Kagel and S. Lehrer. 2003. Bargaining in Legislatures: An Experimental Investigation of Open versus Closed Amendment Rules. *American Political Science Review* 97: 221–232.
Fréchette, G., J. Kagel and M. Morelli. 2005. Nominal Bargaining Power, Selection Protocol, and Discounting in Legislative Bargaining. *Journal of Public Economics* 89: 1497–1517.
Friesen, L. 2012. Certainty of Punishment versus Severity of Punishment: An Experimental Investigation. *Southern Economic Journal* 79: 399–421.
Gilliland, V., J. Dunn and D. Navarro. 2008. Who Framed Roger Rabbit: The Effect of Legal Role and Frame on the Outcome of Civil Disputes. *Proceedings of the 30th Annual Meeting of the Cognitive Science Society* 23–26 July: 1005–1010.
Goeree, J. and L. Yariv. 2011. An Experimental Study of Collective Deliberation. *Econometrica* 79: 893–921.
Grechenig, K., A. Nicklisch and C. Thöni. 2010. Punishment Despite Reasonable Doubt—A Public Goods Experiment with Sanctions Under Uncertainty. *Journal of Empirical Legal Studies* 7: 847–867.
Greene, E., D. Coon and B. Bornstein. 2001. The Effects of Limiting Punitive Damage Awards. *The Journal of Law and Human Behavior* 25: 217–234.
Greene, E., M. Johns and M. Smith. 2001. The Effects of Defendant Conduct on Jury Damage Awards. *The Journal of Applied Psychology* 86: 228–237.
Guarnaschelli, S., R. McKelvey and T. Palfrey. 2000. An Experimental Study of Jury Decision Rules. *American Political Science Review* 94: 407–423.
Guthrie, C. 2003. Prospect Theory, Risk Preference, and the Law. *Northwestern University Law Review* 97: 1115–1164.
Guthrie, C., J. Rachlinski and A. Wistrich. 2007. Blinking on the Bench: How Judges Decide Cases. *Cornell Law Review* 93: 1–43.

Guttentag, M., C. Porath and S. Fraidin. 2008. Brandeis' Policeman: Results from a Laboratory Experiment on How to Prevent Corporate Fraud. *Journal of Empirical Legal Studies* 5: 239–273.

Harel, A. and U. Segal. 1999. Criminal Law and Behavioral Law and Economics: Observations on the Neglected Role of Uncertainty in Deterring Crime. *American Law and Economics Review* 1: 276–312.

Hastie, R., D. Schkade and J. Payne. 1999. Juror Judgments in Civil Cases: Effects of Plaintiff's Requests and Plaintiff's Identity on Punitive Damage Awards. *The Journal of Law and Human Behavior* 23: 445–470.

Henrich, J., R. Boyd, S. Bowles, C. Camerer, E. Fehr, H. Gintis, R. McElreath, M. Alvard, A. Barr, J. Ensminger, K. Hill, F. Gil-White, M. Gurven, F. Marlowe, J. Patton, N. Smith and D. Tracer. 2005. "Economic Man" in Cross-cultural Perspective: Economic Experiments in 15 Small-scale Societies. *Behavioral and Brain Sciences* 28: 795–855.

Inbar, Y., D. A. Pizzarro and F. Cushman. 2012. Benefiting from Misfortune: When Harmless Actions are Judged to be Morally Blameworthy. *Personality and Social Psychology Bulletin* 38: 52–62.

Jacobson, J., J. Dobbs-Marsh, V. Liberman and J. Minson. 2011. Predicting Civil Jury Verdicts: How Attorneys Use (and Misuse) a Second Opinion. *Journal of Empirical Legal Studies* 8: 99–119.

Kagel, J. and A. Roth. 1995. *Handbook of Experimental Economics*. Princeton, NJ: Princeton University Press.

Kagel, J. and A. Roth. 2015. *Handbook of Experimental Economics*, vol. 2. Princeton, NJ: Princeton University Press.

Kahneman, D., D. Schkade and C. Sunstein. 1998. Shared Outrage and Erratic Awards: The Psychology of Punitive Damages. *The Journal of Risk and Uncertainty* 16: 49–86.

Kahenman, D. and Amos Tversky. 1979. Prospect Theory: An Analysis of Decision Under Risk. *Econometrica* 47: 263–292.

Levine, D. and T. Palfrey. 2007. The Paradox of Voter Participation? A Laboratory Study. *American Political Science Review* 101: 143–158.

Levitt, S. and J. List. 2007. What Do Laboratory Experiments Measuring Social Preferences Reveal About the Real World?. *Journal of Economic Perspectives* 21: 153–174.

Loewenstein, G. and D. Moore. 2004. When Ignorance is Bliss: Information Exchange and Inefficiency in Bargaining. *Journal of Legal Studies* 33: 37–58.

Menkhaus, D. and O. Phillips. 2009. Maintaining Tacit Collusion in Repeated Ascending Auctions. *Journal of Law and Economics* 52: 91–109.

Miettinen, T., O. Ropponen and P. Sääskilahti. 2011. Gambling for the Upper Hand—Settlement Negotiations in the Lab. Research Paper No. 022. Jena Economic Research Papers, Jena, Germany.

Miller, H., W. McDonald and J. Cramer. 1978. *Plea Bargaining in the United States*. Washington, DC: Government Printing Office.

Minson, J. and J. Mueller. 2011. The Cost of Collaboration: Why Joint Decision Making Exacerbates Rejection of Outside Information. *Psychological Science* 23: 219–224.

Monin, B., D. Pizarro and J. Beer. 2007. Deciding versus Reacting: Conceptions of Moral Judgement and the Reason-effect Debate. *Review of General Psychology* 11: 99–111.

Morton, R. and K. Williams. 2008. Experimentation in Political Science. Pp. 339–356 in *The Oxford Handbook of Political Methodology*, edited by Janet M. Box-Steffensmeier, Henry E. Brady and David Collier. New York: Oxford University Press.

Morton, R. and K. Williams. 2011. Electoral Systems and Strategic Voting: Laboratory Election Experiments 2011. Pp. 369–383 in *Cambridge Handbook of Experimental Political Science*, edited by James N. Druckman, Donald P. Green, James H. Kuklinski and Arthur Lupia. New York: Cambridge University Press.

Mullen, E. and J. Nadler. 2008. Moral Spillovers: The Effect of Moral Violations on Deviant Behavior. *Journal of Experimental Social Psychology* 44: 1239–1245.

Plott, C. R. 1982. Industrial Organization Theory and Experimental Economics. *Journal of Economic Literature* 20: 1485–1527.

Rachlinski, J. J. 1996. Gains, Losses, and the Psychology of Litigation. *Cornell Law Faculty Publications* 795.

Rachlinski, J. 1996–1997. Gains, Losses, and the Psychology of Litigation. *Southern California Law Review* 70: 113–149.

Rachlinski, J., C. Guthrie and A. Wistrich. 2007. Heuristics and Biases in Bankruptcy Judges. *Journal of Institutional and Theoretical Economics* 163: 167–186.

Rachlinski, J., C. Guthrie and A. Wistrich. 2011. Probable Cause, Probability, and Hindsight. *Journal of Empirical Legal Studies* 8: 72–98.

Rachlinski, J., S. Johnson, A. Wistrich and C. Guthrie. 2009. Does Unconscious Racial Bias Affect Trial Judges? *Notre Dame Law Review* 84: 1195–1246.

Roese, N. and K. Vohs. 2012. Hindsight Bias. *Perspectives on Psychological Science* 7: 411–426.

Rosenberg, D. 2003. Adding a Second Opt-out to Rule 23(b)(3) Class Actions: Cost without Benefit. *University of Chicago Legal Forum* 19: 19–70.

Santore, R., M. McKee and D. Bjornstad. 2010. Patent Pools as a Solution to Efficient Licensing of Complementary Patents? Some Experimental Evidence. *Journal of Law and Economics* 53: 167–183.

Schildberg-Horisch, H. and C. Strassmair. 2012. An Experimental Test of the Deterrence Hypothesis. *Journal of Law, Economics & Organization* 28: 447–459.

Smith, D. 1986. The Plea Bargaining Controversy. *The Journal of Criminal Law and Criminology* 77: 949–968.

Spence, M. 1973. Job Market Signaling. *Quarterly Journal of Economics* 87: 355–374.

Spohn, C. and R. Fornango. 2009. U.S. Attorneys and Substantial Assistance Departures: Testing for Interprosecutor Disparity. *Criminology* 47: 813–846.

Stevens, C. M. 1966. Is Compulsory Arbitration Compatible with Bargaining? *Industrial Relations* 5: 38–52.

Stuntz, W. 2004. Plea Bargaining and Criminal Law's Disappearing Shadow. *Harvard Law Review* 117: 2548–2569.

Tversky, A. and K. Daniel 1972. Subjective Probability: A Judgement of Representativeness. *Cognitive Psychology* 3: 430–454.

Tversky, A. and D. Kahneman. 1974. Judgment under Uncertainty: Heuristics and Biases. *Science* 185: 1124–1131.

Ulmer, J. and M. Bradley. 2006. Variation in Trial Penalties Among Serious Violent Offenses. *Criminology* 44: 631–670.

Yaniv, I. 2004. The Benefit of Additional Opinions. *Current Directions in Psychological Science* 13: 75–78.

# 13. What explains observed reluctance to trade? A comprehensive literature review
*Kathryn Zeiler\**

## 1. INTRODUCTION

Valuation gaps and exchange asymmetries are among the most widely studied phenomena in the field of behavioral economics. They are also among the most widely applied in the law literature (Klass and Zeiler 2013). A valuation gap exists when the most a person is willing to pay for an item (WTP) is less than the least amount that same person is willing to accept to give up the same item if endowed with it (WTA). Asymmetric exchange behavior is observed when a person is reluctant to give up an endowed item in exchange for another item of comparable value.[1] Early observations of such reluctance to trade were noted as evidence against standard utility theory, which assumes that one's valuation of an item is independent of whether one is endowed with the item (Thaler 1980; Kelman 1979). Since then, researchers have attempted to develop and test numerous theories designed to explain observed reluctance to trade. In the meantime, legal scholars have been busy spinning out hundreds of applications of this finding in every conceivable area of law—from adverse possession in property law to default rules in contract law to beneficiary's rights in trust law to right to discoveries in intellectual property law, and on and on and on (Klass and Zeiler 2013; Korobkin 2014).

The purpose of this chapter is to present the current state of the social science literature related to observed reluctance to trade. Georgantzís and Navarro-Martínez (2010, p. 2) summarize the state of the literature best: "[D]espite the overwhelming volume of evidence on the WTA–WTP gap accumulated to date, researchers are still far from agreement on the nature of the disparity and even on its very existence."[2] Numerous theories have been proposed and few can be ruled out based on the evidence to date. While reluctance to trade has been observed in many laboratory settings, such behavior does not seem to be robust. From a scientific perspective, we are compelled to place the most weight on theories that

---

\* Thanks are due to Keith Hylton, Owen Jones, Michael Meurer, Charles Plott, Theodore Sims, and Joshua Teitelbaum for valuable comments and suggestions.
[1] Valuation gaps and exchange asymmetries are often referred to as "endowment effects." The name is confusing when it comes to the cause of gaps and asymmetries because it implies that endowment is the cause. For this reason, some have adopted less theory-suggestive names for the observed phenomena (e.g., Plott and Zeiler 2005, 2007). I use "valuation gap" and "exchange asymmetry" throughout depending on the context in which the phenomenon is observed. I use "reluctance to trade" to refer to the general phenomenon.

[2] See also, Biel et al. (2011) ("At present, there is no sign of an approaching consensus . . .") and Lunn and Lunn (2014) ("There remains no agreed explanation for the finding that experimental subjects and survey respondents generally set a minimum selling price for an item that is two or more times higher than the maximum those without the same item will pay to acquire it").

are able to organize the largest swaths of reported data. When a theory's predictions fail to garner robust support, the theory is either discarded or updated. As existing theories are revised and tested, new theories arise and are often supported by initial data, bolstered by replications and checks on robustness, and sometimes fail to stand up to on-going robustness checks. The social science literature on the topic, mostly in the fields of economics and psychology, is an on-going conversation between theory and empirical verification, and, at present, several theories stand as possible winners..

Despite the uncertainty that exists about the drivers of observed reluctance to trade and the continual evolution of the social science knowledge base on the phenomenon,[3] legal scholarship has not kept pace.[4] The social science literature on reluctance to trade has thoroughly saturated legal scholarship. Legal scholars regularly make claims that are not supported by the existing literature. Oftentimes legal scholars rely on decades-old sources or other legal scholars' descriptions of the literature, which are often outdated, incorrect or incomplete. Given the rapid pace of discovery, a firm understanding of the drivers of observed reluctance to trade cannot be gained by plucking one study or even a large handful of studies from the now vast literature. Understanding what we know and what remains unknown requires a survey and a synthesis of the entire literature. And, because the literature is continually developing, snapshots at particular points in time quickly become outdated. Useful importation of knowledge from the social sciences requires a full understanding of the state of the literature at the moment of importation, including what we know and what we're uncertain about.[5]

Understanding social science literatures is not a matter of simply understanding the contributions of individual studies. Each study is connected to the larger literature in some way, and understanding a study's import requires an analysis of how it advances what we already know and what new questions it gives rise to. When new findings are published, our understanding of best explanations shifts. We get answers to some questions, and, often, new questions arise. Experimenters work on separating theories by designing clever environments that produce divergent predictions from competing theories. Those efforts teach us not only about the relative predictive value of the theories but also about the influences of experiment design choices meant to control for alternative explanations or measure variables of interest (e.g., valuations of goods as owner and non-owner).

The purpose of this chapter is three-fold. First, it presents one viewpoint on the state of the literature. The bottom line is that reported data lend support to several theories, and more work is required to better understand the causes of reluctance to trade. A number of open questions remain. Second, the chapter provides an example of how we might analyze individual experimental studies to determine how they fit into a literature. This sort of analysis is necessary to properly update our beliefs about the causes of observed

---

[3]    Just in the last decade, at least 73 studies have been published in journals or posted as working papers: 8 in 2006, 9 in 2007, 3 in 2008, 4 in 2009, 6 in 2010, 11 in 2011, 9 in 2012, 5 in 2013, 13 in 2014 and 5 in 2015.

[4]    See Klass and Zeiler (2013) for a discussion of the problems with importation of the reluctance to trade literature into legal scholarship and ideas for mitigating them. Zeiler (2010) makes the more general case.

[5]    To assist in this endeavor, I regularly update this review. Readers can find the most recent version at http://sites.bu.edu/kzeiler/research-2/. A link to a glossary of terms also appears there.

phenomena. Third, the chapter offers examples of methods employed to critique individual studies. To this end, studies are not merely summarized but are evaluated along many dimensions, including the soundness of the experiment design, the connection between tested theories and the design, and the strength of inferences drawn from results. Best practices, for example, require the design to incorporate all necessary features of the tested theory and to control for alternative explanations.

This is not the first review of the reluctance to trade literature. Others have both summarized it and attempted to draw conclusions from it about what drives observed reluctance to trade. A few meta-analyses examine how various features of experimental environments impact subject choices (Horowitz and McConnell 2002; Sayman and Öncüler 2005; Tuncel and Hammit 2014). These studies reveal wide variation in experiment design and help in the endeavor to develop a set of controls for alternative explanations—many of which relate to the difficulties that arise when we ask individuals to do something they usually resist: reveal the most they would be willing to pay for something and the least they would be willing to accept to give something up. Ericson and Fuster (2014) walk us through what they classify as three waves of research in the field: early experiments and theory, challenges to the existence and interpretation of valuation gaps, and expectations-based reference points.[6] This chapter differs from their review in two main ways. First, I include (for better or worse) a larger number of studies. Second, and more importantly, we reach different conclusions. While Ericson and Fuster claim that "[l]oss aversion . . . is . . . still the leading paradigm for understanding the endowment effect" (p. 555), this chapter concludes that the data support other theories just as well and possibly better. Morewedge and Giblin (2015) step through several posited theories from the literature and provide a quick snapshot of evidence for and against each. They conclude that an extension of one theory, which they refer to as "attribute sampling bias," can account for a wide set of the reported evidence. While they do not explain their conclusions (they cover 125 studies in eight journal pages), the review organizes the literature through a helpful lens. This review, which is substantially longer, provides a thicker analysis and offers methodological critiques. Finally, some literature reviews, unfortunately, are misleading and possibly at least partly responsible for the confused legal scholarship.[7]

---

[6]  They also describe a number of alternative theories and point to evidence in support of and against each. This chapter discusses expectations-based reference points and all other terms used but not defined in this section.

[7]  See e.g., Kahneman et al. (2008). They claim that "[t]here is . . . little or no empirical support for the empirical assertion of people's symmetrical valuations of gains and losses and the presumed economic choices and behavior that results [sic] from them. Instead, tests consistently indicate that people value the loss of an entitlement more, and usually far more, than a fully commensurate gain and make choices accordingly" (p. 939). This chapter's summary of the literature makes it clear that by the mid-2000s several published studies called into question the assumption that losses are more painful than gains of the same size. While their review was published in 2008, the most recent study it cites was published in 1998. Between 1998 and 2008, tens of published studies had reshaped the landscape.

Korobkin (2014) draws conclusions from a relatively small subset of published studies. His review covers roughly 40 studies by my count. As a point of reference, this chapter catalogs over 150 published studies, roughly 130 of which were published before his chapter was printed. Caution

The chapter begins by describing the standard model of preferences, which generally assumes that valuation is independent of ownership status, and then catalogs early findings published in the 1980s that seem to suggest that ownership status influences valuation. This decade of research was characterized by a number of studies designed to test various potential explanations for observed reluctance to trade, and the results did not point to any one theory. Despite this, the literature gravitated towards a single theory—endowment theory, which assumes that preferences are reference-dependent and that individuals are averse to losses. With endowment theory on the rise, some went to work to investigate the conditions that might trigger loss aversion and those that might reduce its effects. Evidence suggested that we might be especially reluctant to trade goods that trigger moral commitments (e.g., objects with intrinsic value like pine trees), goods that signal something about our characteristics (e.g., earned goods), goods that we consider when we're in particular emotional states, and goods that we intend to consume rather than ones that we're in the business of trading in markets or that don't belong to us but to firms that employ us. While some pointed to these sorts of findings as evidence of the context-dependent nature of loss aversion, others leveraged them to develop competing theories in an attempt to better unify the data. Since the early 1990s, a number of theories have been developed and tested by both economists and psychologists including substitution theory, expectation theory, preference uncertainty, mere-ownership theory, enhancement theory, subject misconceptions, and regret avoidance. The chapter walks through each proposed theory, cataloging the evidence for and against. While some theories have garnered more support from the data than others, no single theory yet deserves the title of leading theory. In addition, the phenomenon itself has proved too unstable to warrant general claims that valuations depend on ownership (or expectations over ownership) or that individuals are generally reluctant to trade. Given the current state of the literature, to make such claims is to misrepresent the full set of results. As this chapter makes clear, much more work is required to develop a theory or set of theories worthy of designating the leading theory.

## 2.   NEOCLASSICAL THEORY ASSUMES WTA EQUALS WTP

Neoclassical microeconomic theory assumes that, ignoring wealth effects,[8] one's valuation for a good (with many available substitutes)[9] is independent of whether one is endowed

---

should be used when considering conclusions drawn from roughly a third of all relevant studies. One omitted study (e.g., Plott and Zeiler 2011) was published in the same issue of a journal that contained an included and highly influential study (e.g., Isoni et al. 2011) that posed a serious challenge to previous work. Korobkin's readers, unfortunately, are getting not only an incomplete view but also a biased view of the literature. In addition to the lack of comprehension and the apparent cherry picking of included studies, Korobkin confuses alternative theories for explanations of loss aversion. For example, he argues that attachment to endowed goods drives loss aversion, but the authors of attachment theory offer it as an alternative to loss aversion. See discussion of mere-ownership theory *infra*.

[8]   A wealth effect (or income effect) can occur when purchasing power changes as a result of a change in wealth (or income). In laboratory experiments, we might worry about wealth effects caused by endowing owners with a good and giving nothing to non-owners. The non-owners are

with the good. That is, standard utility theory assumes that the most one is willing to pay to obtain a good is the same as the minimum amount one is willing to accept to give up that same good if endowed with it (Willig 1976; Randall and Stoll 1980). This implies that indifference curves are reversible. An indifference curve, as illustrated in Figure 13.1, indicates the rate of substitution between two commodities. The individual characterized by the indifference curve in the figure is equally happy with one mug and $10 as he is with two mugs and $5. If endowed with one mug and $10, he is indifferent between his endowment and giving up $5 to obtain another mug. In the reverse, if endowed with two mugs and $5, he is indifferent between his endowment and giving up a mug in exchange for $5. Regardless of the starting point, his valuation for the mug (the amount that makes him indifferent between the money and a mug) is the same—$5.

That assumption was called into question by various researchers who observed disparities in WTP and WTA in the 1970s. Hammack and Brown (1974) reported one of the first observations of reluctance to trade. A hypothetical survey of duck hunters revealed a gap

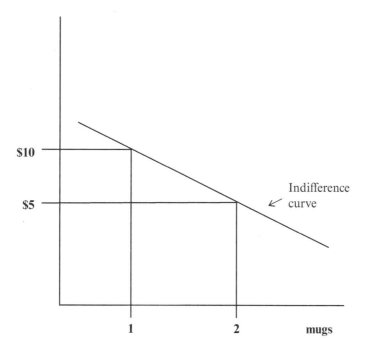

*Figure 13.1   A reversible indifference curve*

---

less wealthy, on average, than owners and so might be willing to pay less to obtain the good relative to the amount owners are willing to forgo to keep the good. One way to avoid wealth effects is to ensure that potential buyers and potential sellers begin on the same indifference curve by endowing potential buyers with an amount of cash that is equivalent to the average value of the good given to potential sellers. For example, some experimenters endow potential buyers with cash in an amount equal to the average reported WTA (e.g., Morrison 1997b).

9   See more on the impact of substitutes, *infra*.

in valuations of the right to duck hunt on wetlands. On average, those with a hypothetical right to hunt were willing to accept on average $1,044 to give it up while those without the right were willing hypothetically to pay an average of only $247 to get it. This, and similar observations,[10] motivated a long line of laboratory investigations to measure valuations in controlled conditions in an effort to determine the cause of observed gaps.

## 3.    GAPS IN THE LAB: AN EARLY EXPLORATION OF VALUATION ELICITATION PROCEDURES

One of the first tested hypotheses was that observed valuation gaps were caused by the hypothetical nature of the valuation elicitation device used in earlier studies reporting gaps.[11] Knetsch and Sinden (1984) hypothesized that the gap was the result of the hypothetical nature of such contingent valuation studies. They were among the first to estimate reluctance to trade in the laboratory under non-hypothetical conditions. They endowed half their subjects with lottery tickets, which gave the ticket holders a chance to win a choice between a $70 bookstore gift certificate and $50 in cash. The second group was given an opportunity to purchase a lottery ticket for $2 and had access to credit if short on cash. Those endowed with lottery tickets were given a chance to sell their tickets for $2. Exchanges were performed individually and privately to control for "information influences and information flows" (p. 510). To control transaction costs, all subjects were required to stop at a cash desk to discuss options. If the hypothetical nature of previous experiments caused the observed gap, then removing this feature would remove the gap.

---

[10]    For example, Bishop and Heberlein (1979) elicited valuations for non-hypothetical WTP, hypothetical WTA and hypothetical WTP for a goose-hunting permit. Hypothetical WTA exceeded non-hypothetical WTP, which exceeded hypothetical WTP. Despite the implicit assumption of all theories that choices have actual consequences, many others have elicited valuations under hypothetical conditions. For example, Gerking et al. (1988) reported a WTP–WTA gap in hypothetical valuations for job safety. Johnson et al. (1993) reported hypothetical gaps in insurance deductibles, Hartman et al. (1991) for residential electrical services, Korobkin (1998) for contract terms, Hoorens et al. (1999) for time (i.e., purchase and sale of hypothetical labor), Cook and Wu (2001) for lottery tickets and Nash and Rosenthal (2014) for position in a line to choose a dorm room. Chilton et al. (2012), after training subjects to report their true valuations, reported mixed results for valuations of hypothetical health conditions. Some have studied why average hypothetical WTA tends to be higher than average non-hypothetical WTA. Li et al. (2002) for example suggest that individuals are uncertain about their preferences and they "do not search for their true preferences in a hypothetical situation as intensively as in real transactions." In addition, they posited that risk aversion and preference uncertainty pushes individuals who are uncertain about the welfare effects of proposed changes to report higher WTA values relative to WTA values reported by individuals who are more certain about their preferences. It should be noted that Horowitz and McConnell's (2002) meta-analysis of gap studies reported no difference in results from studies using "incentive-compatible" elicitation devices and those that do not, although they (oddly) count some hypothetical studies as incentive-compatible. In more recent meta-analyses, Sayman and Öncüler (2005) and Tuncel and Hammitt (2014) reported significantly smaller disparities in studies that use truly incentive-compatible mechanisms.

[11]    For example, see Jones-Lee et al. (1985) and Viscusi et al. (1987). For a dated and yet still relevant intellectual exchange on the pros and cons of employing the contingent valuation method to elicit valuations for non-market goods, see Cummings et al. (1986).

It did not. A smaller proportion of owners chose to sell their lottery tickets relative to the proportion of non-owners who chose to buy a ticket, suggesting that owners' valuations for the tickets were, on average, higher than non-owners'. The authors conducted additional tests to check the impact of lowering the value of the prizes available and the cash trade amount to test the influence of familiarity with the task, and to test robustness across different subject pools (e.g., employed people v. students). The results were robust to these variations. Only one treatment produced no exchange asymmetry. In this treatment, non-endowed subjects were given cash and very little time passed between the moment of endowment and choices. The authors proposed two possible explanations for the lack of reluctance to trade: the expressed desire by subjects to participate in the group activity and a possible lack of belief that the cash and tickets were in fact owned given the short period of time between endowment and trade decisions.[12] Generally, though, while valuation gaps decreased relative to those estimated using hypothetical elicitation devices, statistically significant gaps remained.[13] Knetsch and Sinden attributed these gaps to asymmetric evaluation of realized income and opportunity income.[14] They pointed to several potential sources of this asymmetric valuation, including cognitive biases, regret avoidance, and reference-dependent loss aversion, a feature of preferences posited by Kahneman and Tversky (1979) that assumes individuals experience a greater subjective effect of a loss from some reference point relative to an equivalent gain from that same point. Loss aversion is one feature of a theory some refer to as "endowment theory" (Klass and Zeiler 2013), an application of prospect theory (Kahneman and Tversky 1979) to contexts of riskless choice (see Tversky and Kahneman 1991).[15]

Coursey et al. (1987) explored the possibility that flaws in the methods Knetsch and Sinden (1984) used to elicit choices might explain their results. They noted that the use of lottery tickets, and the uncertainty they introduce, might have confounded the results. In addition, they point to the lack of a demand-revealing, market-like elicitation mechanism[16] and of opportunities for subjects to understand that reporting their true

---

[12]  A large literature has developed to investigate the relevance of the strength of reference states and what exactly sets reference points. See *infra* for details.

[13]  Bishop et al. (1983) also explored the hypothetical nature of contingent valuation studies and hypothesized that "contingent markets are too artificial to provide a sufficient context for developing accurate values" (p. 620). While the authors did not estimate gaps, substantial differences in valuations were observed depending on whether outcomes were hypothetical or non-hypothetical and whether subjects were asked to report WTP or WTA. Hypothetical elicitation devices were found to result in higher WTA and lower WTP relative to non-hypothetical elicitation devices.

[14]  It is possible that income (or wealth) effects explain observed reluctance to trade. Specifically, non-owners might offer to pay less than the amount owners are willing to accept because non-owners, on average, have less wealth than owners, who were endowed with some item at the start of the experiment. Given the size of observed gaps and the low value of goods used in experiments, however, this explanation generally has been ruled out, at least as the dominant explanation (see e.g. Bishop et al. 1983). Other experimenters attempt to control wealth effects by endowing non-owners with cash (e.g., Plott and Zeiler 2005) or by asking subjects, all of whom were endowed with goods, whether they want to trade the endowment for a different good with similar market value (e.g. Kahneman et al. 1990).

[15]  This theory is explained in more detail *infra*.

[16]  Demand-revealing mechanisms are designed to encourage the reporting of true valuations (i.e., the most one would be willing to pay to obtain an item or the least one would accept to give

valuations would serve their best interests. When they elicited valuations in the context of hypothetically buying and selling the right to avoid holding a bitter tasting liquid in their mouths for a few seconds,[17] they observed a valuation gap. In contrast, when the authors employed a demand-revealing Vickery (1961) auction mechanism to elicit valuations, ran four non-binding trials to encourage learning,[18] and endowed potential buyers with $10, the gap disappeared due to a substantial decrease in reported owner valuations. The authors concluded that reluctance to trade should be expected only when decisions are made outside markets or when individuals lack experience with the elicitation device.[19]

Follow-up studies designed to test the effects of elicitation methods report mixed results.

---

up an item). These amounts are sometimes referred to as "non-strategic valuations." If subjects report valuations that deviate from their true valuations because they think they will be better off doing so, these reported valuations cannot be used to test theories that predict a disparity in the true valuations of owners and non-owners.

[17]    The researchers chose to use an unfamiliar good to avoid preconceived notions of value.

[18]    The clearing price was announced to all subjects after each round. Note that controversy exists around the influence of repeated trials; see e.g., Morrison (2000). While they might be necessary for learning one's preferences and how best to engage with an unfamiliar elicitation device, they might be unnecessary (and not worth the added cost) if reported valuations do not change across rounds. In addition, even if reported valuations do change across rounds, the changes might not necessarily reflect learning. Finally, they might bias reported valuations, especially if preferences are imprecise, clearing prices are announced between rounds, and announced prices influence reported valuations. Morrison (2000) reported results from experiments that employed multiple rounds. Subjects were told how much they would have to pay to purchase the goods at a nearby store. The randomly chosen clearing prices were announced between each round. Morrison observed no change over five rounds when subjects reported valuations for a chocolate bar, for which no gap was observed in any round, and an increase in the gap over the first couple of rounds when subjects reported valuations for mugs over five rounds. A slight decrease in the mug valuation gap occurred over the final three rounds, but the gap in the final round was larger than the gap in the first round. Morrison found some evidence that subjects learn their true valuations when they participate in multiple rounds and that owners need more rounds than non-owners to "locate" their true valuations. She found no statistically significant evidence that reported valuations depend on the clearing price announced in the previous round, but this might be due to her small sample size (n = 10).

[19]    Gregory and Furby (1987) questioned whether subjects understood the elicitation device used by Coursey et al., whether the rounds meant to help subjects learn their valuations for the good actually performed as intended, whether the fact that not all rounds were binding with certainty moved reported valuations away from actual valuations, whether the presence of extreme outliers skewed the results, whether the instructions might have signaled to non-owners an upper bound on their valuations, whether endowing potential buyers but not potential sellers with cash impacted reported valuations, and whether announcing the clearing price between rounds triggered a lack of independence of one subject's reported valuations from others', especially given subjects' unfamiliarity with the good. A reanalysis of the data demonstrates a lack of robustness in terms of the elimination of outliers. While Coursey (1987) convincingly responded, the multi-faceted critique highlights difficulties that experimenters face when they attempt to elicit true valuations in the lab.

In a second critique, Knetsch and Sinden (1987) suggested a number of reasons why the elicitation mechanism used by Coursey et al. might not be demand revealing. They also argued that giving cash to potential buyers, a design feature that attempts to control for wealth effects, might lead to a house-money effect—the possibility that subjects are more willing to spend cash received as a windfall during an experiment relative to money from their own pockets. The authors also worry about other confounding impacts caused by the cash endowment.

Knez et al. (1985) estimated valuation gaps using bids and asks for lotteries in a repeated market setting. They found that subjects were willing to deviate from reported valuations once engaged in the market. While some had suggested that valuation gaps could lead to market inefficiencies, the authors pointed to their results as evidence that gaps observed in single-shot, non-market settings do not imply "that . . . individuals are incompetent or markets are inefficient" (p. 401). Similarly, Brookshire and Coursey (1987) estimated gaps using three methods: the contingent valuation method,[20] a single-shot hypothetical (but otherwise) demand-revealing auction, and repeated and binding demand-revealing auctions. In the non-hypothetical treatment, potential buyers were endowed with cash and potential sellers were endowed with the right to have a particular number of trees planted in their neighborhood (all subjects lived in the same neighborhood). The demand-revealing auction was explained to the subjects. In contrast with Knez et al. (1985), Brookshire and Coursey (1987) observed statistically significant gaps in each treatment. The gap, however, decreased across each of the three treatments (again, as a result of reduced owner valuations). The authors concluded that, while reference-dependent loss aversion seems to be present under all conditions, market settings have disciplinary effects that move reported valuations closer to true valuations.[21]

Harless (1989) contributed to the gap literature in two ways. First, he refined the valuation elicitation device by explaining to subjects through examples the optimal strategy of the demand-revealing auction. He hypothesized that subjects likely were unfamiliar with the auctions used to elicit valuations and that explaining the optimal strategy to the subjects would help eliminate any noise caused by strategic considerations. Second, rather than using a between-subject design, in which each subject acts only as a potential seller or a potential buyer, he employed a within-subject design, measuring the gap by averaging individual differences between valuations as owner and as non-owner.[22] He observed no gap in valuations for lotteries, which implies that previously observed gaps were due to subject misconceptions of the elicitation device and the way in which gaps were estimated, and not loss aversion.

To summarize, by the end of the 1980s evidence reported in the literature supported a

---

[20] The contingent valuation method entails simply asking subjects to state their valuations either as hypothetical owners or hypothetical non-owners. Subjects' reports do not result in consequences of any sort.

[21] Ortona and Scacciati (1992) observed no disparity in valuations when subjects faced real payoffs after announcing valuations for necessary goods of substantial value (i.e., half day's net wages). They concluded that, although endowments can impact valuations in some cases, if the payoffs are real and the goods are necessary and expensive, rational behaviors might swamp reference-dependent loss aversion (or any other drivers of valuation gaps).

[22] Relative to between-subject designs, within-subject designs often increase the power of statistical tests, increasing the likelihood of detecting treatment effects if they exist. They also controlled for any unobservable differences between control and treatment groups that remain after randomized assignment. The downside to within-subject designs is potential carryover effects— participation in the control group might impact subjects' subsequent choices once the treatment is applied. For example, subjects might feel a need to be consistent across rounds. In this context, a subject might wonder whether it would seem odd to report different valuations as a potential buyer and a potential seller. This change in the experiment design might explain, as least in part, Harless's null result. Schmidt and Traub (2009) reported evidence supporting the claim that between-subject and within-subject measures might produce different results.

number of theories including reference-dependent loss aversion, uncertain or imprecise preferences, the lack of market discipline (which acts to drive inflated WTA down to values more reflective of actual values), and a lack of familiarity with the valuation elicitation device. Despite the mixed evidence, the next steps in the literature veer towards the adoption of endowment theory as the dominant explanation.

## 4.   THE DEVELOPMENT OF ENDOWMENT THEORY

Knetsch (1989) was the first to report observed exchange asymmetries in the context of trading one good for another good (as opposed to some amount of money). He motivated the design change by framing it as a more direct test of the assumption of reversible indifference curves. Subjects were endowed with coffee mugs, which they kept in their possession while answering a short questionnaire.[23] Subjects were then told they could either keep the mug they owned or exchange the mug for a candy bar. The subjects were told to signal their desire to trade by holding up a piece of paper with the word "trade" written on it. To reduce the possibility of transaction costs related to trading, the experimenter immediately made all desired trades by walking the candy bar to the subject and exchanging it for the mug. Another group participated in the same experiment except that they were endowed with candy bars and offered mugs in exchange. A third group was simply offered a choice between the two goods with neither being endowed. The simple design eliminated income effects and any opportunity for strategic bidding. The design also nicely separates the theories Knetsch tests. If indifference curves were reversible, we would expect no difference in the proportions of subjects in each group favoring one good over the other. If individuals are averse to losses, however, we would expect willingness to trade to depend on endowment status. The results were consistent with the behavior predicted by loss aversion. While 56% of those given a choice chose the mug, 89% of mug owners kept their mugs and only 10% of candy bar owners traded for a mug.[24] Two additional

---

[23]   In most experiments, subjects possess the endowed good for a short time before making choices about whether to keep it or give it up. This reduces the likelihood that the value of the good changes due to experience with it or some sort of psychological attachment that often comes with owning a good for some longer period of time. When reluctance to trade results after a short possession period, some refer to observed reluctance to trade as an "instant endowment effect" (Tversky and Kahneman 1991). Korobkin (2003) argued that theories based on attachment cannot explain instant valuation gaps. Others, however, suggest that such instant effects result from "generalized response tendencies in relation to possessions, even when such consumption capital may not have been built up yet" (Ariely et al. 2005). Reb and Connolly (2007) reported evidence suggesting that possession alone might drive reluctance to trade. They also review the then-existing literature on subjective ownership—feelings of ownership that are induced by control over a good even when it is not owned. Bischoff and Meckl (2008) reported evidence of valuation gaps in rights to publically provided goods even when no one individual has exclusive property rights over the good. Coren (2007, Chapter 4) developed a theory of "cognitive investment" to explain instant valuation gaps but fails to find evidence supporting the theory in data collected using a survey instrument.

[24]   Harbaugh et al. (2001) replicated this result for cohorts of different ages, ranging from 5-year-olds to college undergraduates. The authors interpreted these results as evidence of loss aversion. If market experience was at work to correct mistakes in valuation, the argument goes, we would not see gaps in valuations reported by undergraduate students who have higher levels of

treatments using different designs produced similar results.[25] Knetsch interprets his results as additional evidence of endowment theory, but he does not attempt to square the theory with published evidence that works against it.

Kahneman et al. (1990) similarly reported the results of several experiments designed to test alternative theories of gaps but failed to explain why gaps are not observed in other contexts. They provided a "summary [table] of past tests of evaluation disparities." Surprisingly, the table did not report confidence intervals for the estimates, and it excluded null results.[26] They did, however, acknowledge potential explanations beyond endowment theory, including perceived illegitimacy of the transaction,[27] standard bargaining habits (i.e., sellers' instinct to ask high and buyers' instinct to bid low), subject misunderstandings, presumably of the valuation elicitation device, and transaction costs. They also began to refine endowment theory. The theory assumes that endowments set individuals' reference points, which frame perceptions of the giving up of endowments as losses and the getting of endowments as gains. Loss aversion assumes that individuals are hurt by losses more than they are helped by gains of the same size, thus endowment theory predicts a reluctance to trade away endowments. The authors refined the theory to exclude some types of endowments. They asserted that reluctance to trade should not be expected for goods that are purchased for resale rather than consumption. In addition, it should not be expected "if a perfect substitute is readily available at a lower price" (p. 1344).

Kahneman et al. designed an environment to test theories related to transaction costs, misunderstandings and strategic bargaining behavior. They posited that if gaps are not observed when subjects trade induced-value tokens,[28] we can rule out these theories as explanations for gaps observed when subjects trade goods (using the same methods as those used in the induced-value token rounds) for which endowment theory would predict

---

market experience relative to younger subjects. The authors concluded that "[t]he endowment effect appears to be a "real" part of preferences, rather than a mistake that diminishes with experience and learning" (p. 181).

[25] Chapman (1998) reported data suggesting that not all trades are perceived as losses. Her results support the conjecture that the relation between the endowed good and the alternative good matters. For example, subjects seem not to be reluctant to give up an endowed good for an *identical* alternative good, suggesting that the mere giving up of an item does not trigger a perceived loss. She drew a line between "trade-loss aversion," the notion that loss aversion is a characteristic of the exchange, and "attribute-loss aversion," that loss aversion is a characteristic of a single item or attribute of that item. This distinction can be thought of as a modification to assumptions about what exactly constitutes a loss.

[26] Table 1 (p. 1327) does not report whether observed gaps were statistically significantly different from zero: e.g., Coursey et al. (1987) concludes that the gap observed in Part III—the only treatment with non-hypothetical choices and design features intended to train subjects on the valuation elicitation procedure—was not statistically significant; Test 4 of Knetsch and Sinden (1984) produced no statistically significant gap). The table also failed to include some studies reporting null results (e.g., Harless 1989). Unfortunately, readers have likely misinterpreted this table as a signal of robustness of gaps, when, in fact, the evidence was mixed at the time. Kahneman et al. did, however, mention some previously reported null results later in the text.

[27] This theory might explain results in experiments, for example, where the endowed good is a public good such as neighborhood tree density. See, e.g., Brookshire and Coursey (1987).

[28] Induced-value tokens are items that subjects who end up owning them at the end of the experiment can trade for cash in an amount equal to the value assigned to them by the experimenter before the start of the experiment.

gaps. Kahncman et al. ran several treatments,[29] one of the most controlled[30] of which elicited valuations for mugs using the Becker, DeGroot, Marschak (BDM) mechanism (Becker et al. 1964). Each potential seller is asked to report the least amount she is willing to accept to give up her endowment, and that reported value is compared to a randomly generated number. If the reported valuation is higher than the random number, the owner keeps her endowment. If the reported valuation is less than the random number, she gives up her item in exchange for an amount of cash equal to the random number. This device encourages reports of true (i.e., non-strategic) valuations. If a seller decides to report a valuation that is higher than her true valuation, she risks forgoing an opportunity to trade her item for an amount higher than her true valuation. If she decides to report a valuation that is lower than her true valuation, she risks trading her item for an amount that is lower than her true valuation. The incentives are similar for buyers, who report a valuation and then buy at a price equal to the random number only if the random number is lower than the reported valuation.

Each of 59 subjects was randomly assigned to the buyer role or the seller role and remained in the same role throughout the experiment. Subjects participated in two hypothetical induced-value token rounds.[31] In all rounds subjects were told that it was in their best interest to answer the questions truthfully and that reported valuations would have no effect on the price at which the items were traded. Potential buyers did not receive cash to spend during the experiment,[32] and they did not physically possess the mugs while bidding on them, although they were shown the mugs prior to reporting valuations. Valuations were elicited using the multiple price list format: each subject was asked whether he would sell (or buy) at a specific price across a set of prices ranging from $0 to $9.50 in increments of 50 cents.[33] Reluctance to trade was estimated in an unconventional way by comparing the actual numbers of trades to the predicted number

---

[29]   In a pair of treatments, Kahneman et al. investigated whether non-owners are reluctant to buy or owners are reluctant to sell by asking a third group of subjects to simply choose between the good and different amounts of cash. They found that choosers' valuations were more in line with potential buyers' valuations than potential sellers' valuations and concluded that the gap was driven by reluctance to sell. Franciosi et al. (1996) wondered whether the terms "buying," "selling," and "choosing" suggested particular strategies to the subjects—i.e., "buyers are motivated to buy low and sellers to sell high" (p. 216)—that might have nudged subjects away from their true valuations. Franciosi et al. tested the impact of language by stripping out these terms. While the WTA–WTP gap narrowed, it remained statistically significant.

[30]   By "most controlled," I mean the treatment that attempts to eliminate the greatest number of alternative explanations.

[31]   Note that the hypothetical nature of the token rounds negates the demand-revealing nature of the elicitation device. Had gaps been observed in these rounds, this feature might have accounted for them, but gaps were not observed.

[32]   Subjects were told to bring cash to the experiment and that credit and change would be available. The authors reported that some subjects borrowed money from other subjects.

[33]   Kahneman et al. (1990) are cited as the first to use multiple price lists to elicit commodity valuations (Anderson et al. 2006). The demand-revealing properties of this method have been questioned (e.g., Anderson et al. 2006), but Kahneman et al. obtained the same results in a separate treatment that asked subjects to simply report their valuations. Anderson et al. (2007) reported evidence supporting the multiple price list method as a valid way to elicit non-strategic (i.e., true) valuations. Others have employed this mechanism (see *infra* for examples).

of trades assuming that the distribution of values in the two groups is the same barring sample variation.[34] That is, the authors concluded that sellers were reluctant to trade if the ratio of the number of observed trades to the number of expected trades is less than 1.

The results support the existence of valuation disparities driven by endowments. The ratios of observed trades to expected trades in the induced-value token rounds were both roughly 1 (no tests of significance were mentioned). From this result, Kahneman et al. (1990) concluded that subjects understood the valuation elicitation procedure and that they understood that strategic bidding was not advantageous. On the other hand, the ratio of observed to expected number of trades in the mug round was 0.41 (no tests of significance mentioned). The median selling price was over twice the median buying price. A number of alternative designs were employed to control for various alternative explanations, and reluctance to trade proved robust.[35]

Note that while Knetsch (1989) and Kahneman et al. (1990) both produced results in support of endowment theory and robust for various design changes to control for alternative explanations, the body of evidence in the literature at the time Kahneman et al. was published did not universally support this explanation, and neither Knetsch nor Kahneman et al. attempted to explain the published null results. Despite this, legal scholars tend to cite these studies as proof (and not just evidence) of endowment theory without acknowledging results that call the explanation into question (Klass and Zeiler 2013). When applying any economic theory in law and policy, disclosing the evidence both for and against the theory is necessary to determine how confident we should be when we contemplate generating legal rules and policies based on a particular theory. The bottom line is that, in 1990, the explanation for observed reluctance to trade remained elusive despite claims to the contrary (Klass and Zeiler 2013).

Despite the literature's mixed evidence, the findings from Knetsch and Sinden (1984), Knetsch (1989), and Kahneman et al. (1990), along with more general evidence of status quo bias, prompted Tversky and Kahneman (1991) to adapt prospect theory (Kahneman and Tversky 1979) to contexts of riskless choice.[36] The theory, which I will refer to as

---

[34] Franciosi et al. (1996) explored the impact of using a different auction mechanism that avoids possible incentives related to uncertainty over the clearing price inherent in the mechanism Kahneman et al. use to elicit valuations in some of their treatments. Franciosi et al. employed a demand-revealing elicitation device that informed subjects of the clearing price as the market ran. While fewer trades occurred relative to the predicted number of trades, trading volume increased. In addition, Franciosi et al. demonstrated that trading volume might decrease even when no significant difference between WTP and WTA exists. Thus, they interpreted Kahneman et al.'s results as supporting a prediction of under-trading but not a WTP-WTA disparity, per se.

[35] Borges and Knetsch (1998) ran simulations to estimate the impact of valuation gaps on number of trades. They concluded from the collected valuations data and simulations that competitive markets will not produce efficient outcomes and that final allocations depend on initial endowments, a direct challenge to the predictions of Coase (1960).

[36] Tversky and Kahneman (1991) claim that "[a]lthough isolated findings may be subject to alternative interpretations, the entire body of evidence provides strong support for the phenomenon of loss aversion" (p. 1041). Such incomplete summaries of empirical results highlight the importance of developing a first-hand knowledge of empirical literatures before importing theories designed to explain observed phenomena reported in the literatures (Zeiler 2010). Those who chose not to rely on Tversky and Kahneman's literature description would have discovered Knez et al.

"endowment theory,"[37] assumes that individual preference relations depend on one's reference state (i.e., reference dependent preferences). In riskless choice contexts, "the reference state usually corresponds to the decision maker's current position, [but] it can also be influenced by aspirations, expectations, norms, and social comparisons" (Tversky and Kahneman 1991, pp. 1046–1047). Endowment theory assumes that a potential seller's reference point is set when a good becomes part of that owner's endowment (Kahneman et al. 1990, p. 1326).[38] In this sense, reference points are assumed to be exogenous. In addition, the theory assumes that changes from one's current position affect the decision maker differently. That is, losses lead to more disutility than the utility enjoyed by gains of the same size. It also assumes diminishing marginal sensitivity, which implies that marginal value decreases with the distance from the reference point.[39] The authors

---

(1985) and Harless (1989), both of which are absent from Tversky and Kahneman's (1991) reference list and discussion, and both of which fail to provide support for endowment theory.

[37]   The revised name is meant to distinguish the explanation from the observed phenomenon (Plott and Zeiler 2005). Others noted the importance of this earlier on (Mandel 2002, p. 746) ("It is important to clearly distinguish the behavioral definition of the endowment effect from its possible explanations").

[38]   Sen and Johnson (1997, p. 111) reported data suggesting that "mere possession of only a coupon for one of the choice options leads to an instantaneous increase in subjects' preference for that option." Strahilevitz and Loewenstein (1998) investigated the impacts of past ownership, duration of ownership, possession and attractiveness of the item on the setting of reference points. Others refer to this phenomenon as an increase in the subjective value of a good caused by psychological attachment. See, e.g., Ariely and Simonson (2003), who suggested that attachment can occur even in the absence of ownership. They refer to this as a "pseudoendowment effect." Shu and Peck (2011; study 2) find that duration of ownership increases both feelings of psychological ownership and seller valuations.

[39]   A separate strand of the literature attempts to explain why preferences might be characterized by loss aversion and reference dependence. A growing body of research (a small fraction of which is cited here) suggests an evolutionary biological explanation for valuation gaps. For example, Jones (2001) theorized that valuation gaps might arise from an evolutionary adaptation that also manifests in the "widespread phenomenon in territorial systems that residents of a territory almost invariably defeat challengers" (p. 1185). Thus, those with a predisposition to hold on to what they actually possess, in the face of an uncertain trade for something potentially better, may have been more likely to thrive, and to pass along the same predisposition, than those all too willing to relinquish. In turn many species, including humans, might now bear genetically influenced but condition-dependent predispositions to place relatively high values on endowed items. See also Friedman (2004) and Gintis (2007), who offered similar theories based on selection for territorial behavior.

Consistent with this approach, Flemming et al. (2012) suggested that the preference features assumed by endowment theory might be the consequence of "earlier evolutionary pressures on human cognitive abilities." For example, we might exhibit a tendency to keep what we have because, for the vast majority of primate evolution, trades were difficult to enforce against defectors, by the party to first relinquish—especially in the absence of language and third-party enforcement mechanisms. They reported experimental findings suggesting that apes are reluctant to trade goods that are evolutionarily salient (e.g., food). This finding supports the evolutionary biological explanation for loss aversion. (Huck et al. (2005) formalized the idea in game-theoretic terms.) They found relatively strong effects for evolutionarily salient items (e.g., food).

Several studies have explored reluctance to trade in nonhuman primates and in African tribes. In an experiment using capuchin monkeys as subjects, Chen et al. (2006) and Lakshminarayanan et al. (2008) reported data they interpret as supporting innate reference dependence and loss aversion. In

predicted no aversion to losses of money (and tokens that could be exchanged for money) and losses of goods held for sale in routine commercial transactions.[40] Munro and Sugden (2003) reformulate endowment theory to fit the existing data and to deviate as little as possible from conventional consumer theory.[41] They also extend the theory to build in an assumption of endogenous reference points, which can accommodate experimental findings that suggest that reference points adjust rapidly to changes in endowments. While these theories seemed consistent with some published evidence, it is important to note that they failed to explain the null results that also appeared in the literature at the time.

Before moving on to the literature that explores factors that either enhance or disrupt the formation of valuation gaps, I address some apparent confusion around the normative implications of endowment theory as an explanation for observed gaps. Specifically, some claim that the characteristics of preferences upon which endowment theory is built are "irrational" (see e.g., Arlen et al. 2002, p. 3) or "inconsistent" (Jones 2001, p. 1148). Apicella et al. (2014) described the endowment effect as a "well-known departure from rational choice." The theory's authors, however, are explicitly agnostic about the normative

---

an experiment using chimpanzees as subjects, Brosnan et al. (2007) reported data they interpret as support for evolutionary explanations for valuation gaps. They predicted and found reluctance to trade food items but not toys. Kanngiesser et al. (2011) observed a reluctance to trade food items in great apes but no effect for tool items. Evidence for orangutans is mixed (contrast Kanngiesser et al. (2011) with Flemming et al. (2012)). And gorillas behave comparably to chimpanzees, Drayton et al. (2013). Brosnan et al. (2012) reported additional data purporting to support the assumption that gaps are context-specific. In a set of chimpanzee experiments, reluctance to trade was observed for tools that immediately could be used to acquire food, but was not observed for the same tools when they had no immediate value (i.e., when food was either out of reach or absent). Apicella et al. (2014) found that an isolated tribe of bushman in Tanzania exhibited no reluctance to trade, but a subset of the tribe living in less isolated conditions with more opportunities for regular trading exhibited a tendency to resist giving up endowed goods. Heifetz and Segev (2004) developed an alternative to endowment theory that is grounded in a different set of evolutionary assumptions. Rather than assuming selection for territorial behavior, the authors assumed that toughness in bargaining serves as an evolutionary explanation for observed valuation gaps. The authors argued that this explanation is better at organizing existing data than endowment theory grounded in loss aversion.

See Jones (2017) in this volume for an illuminating discussion of the study of explanations for observed phenomenon using an evolutionary biology approach.

[40] Some have challenged the claim that individuals are not averse to losses of goods held for sale. For example, van Dijk and van Knippenberg (1996) reported evidence suggesting that gaps might appear in exchange good markets if traders are uncertain about future exchange prices. This uncertainty, the theory goes, might "elicit a motivation to avoid regret" (p. 522). The authors posited that individuals focus on the net monetary result from trading goods meant for exchange, rather than the mere loss. Other researchers have explored similar theories (see the section below on Uncertain Preferences). In a follow-up study, van Dijk and van Knippenberg (1998) reported data supporting a related theory that suggests gaps might arise in exchange goods markets if individuals are unable to compare endowed goods with alternative goods offered for a trade, making it impossible to focus on the net monetary result from the trade, which shifts focus instead to the mere loss. Others have explored the role of exchange value curiosity in reluctance to trade (van de Ven et al. 2005).

[41] For example, Munro and Sugden's revised endowment theory does not assume that preferences are additively separable, an assumption of endowment theory that they argue is implicit but unnecessary.

status of their model's assumptions about the features of individual preferences.[42] This is important when it comes to drawing policy implications from the economics literature. If the best-supported theories suggest that we tend to act irrationally or err in the face of losses, then we might find it worthwhile to structure law in a way that helps us overcome this irrational tendency.[43] On the other hand, if loss aversion is thought to be a feature of preferences, just as risk aversion is, then we might aim to use law to structure markets in ways that help individuals reduce the disutility that losses cause.

First, though, we need to determine whether losses trigger disutility in excess of the disutility that arises from the lost consumption value. After describing the literature that explores environmental features that might enhance or diminish reluctance to trade, the chapter will describe the vast literature that explores alternatives to endowment theory.

## 5.   GAP ENHANCERS AND DISRUPTORS

As the literature started taking a turn towards endowment theory as the leading explanation for observed reluctance to trade, some attempted to map out conditions under which endowment theory might apply. While the purpose of these studies was to determine a set of conditions that trigger loss aversion, some viewed this as the beginning of the end of endowment theory as the leading explanation for observed reluctance to trade. Rather than interpreting mixed results as teaching us something about the context-dependent nature of endowment theory, some argued that the results suggested that something other than reference dependence and loss aversion might better explain observed reluctance to trade. Before stepping through the alternative theories, this section walks through the studies exploring gap enhancers and disruptors.

### 5.1   Moral Commitments

Boyce et al. (1992) set out to study gaps in valuations of public goods. While valuation gaps for these sorts of goods might be caused by loss aversion given the lack of perfect substitutes, Boyce et al. suggested an alternative explanation—the desire to "preserve a natural resource for moral or other motives" (p. 1366), even if one might never receive direct consumption benefits from it. The authors argued that intrinsic value might be relevant only for those assigned the property right because ownership of the right triggers moral responsibility for preserving the commodity, a responsibility not felt by those considering whether to contribute to preservation efforts. The authors elicited valuations for Small Norfolk Island pine trees and employed two treatments to separate consumption

---

[42]   "Is loss aversion irrational? . . . We conclude that there is no general answer to the question about the normative status of loss aversion or of other reference effects . . . [A] bias in favor of the status quo can be justified if the disadvantages of any change will be experienced more keenly than its advantages." (Tversky and Kahneman 1991, p. 1057).

[43]   For example, Kermer et al. (2006) reported evidence supporting an alternative theory that assumes that loss avoidance is the result of overestimation of the hedonic effect of losses. This explanation posits that loss aversion is a mistake rather than a feature of human preferences.

value from intrinsic or moral value.[44] To estimate consumption value, subjects were asked to report their WTP to obtain a tree to take home or WTA to give up a tree they were given at the beginning of the experiment. To estimate intrinsic value, different subjects in a separate treatment were told that any trees sold to the experimenter, or not purchased, would be destroyed.[45] The intrinsic value conjecture predicts that the gap in the "kill" treatment is greater than the gap in the "no kill" treatment.

Boyce et al. structured the experiment to control for alternative explanations. They employed the BDM mechanism to elicit non-strategic valuations. They endowed potential buyers with $40 and potential sellers with a tree (with a retail value of $6) and $30 to minimize income effects. Subjects participated in ten hypothetical practice rounds to gain familiarity with the elicitation device. To avoid decisions based on perceptions of other subjects (e.g., subjects might worry that others will harass them or think badly of them if they sell trees that get destroyed) or the possible inconvenience of getting the tree home after the experiment, subjects were instructed to pick up their trees at a later time from a different location. This ensured that subjects did not learn the choices of other subjects. Valuation gaps appeared in both the no-kill and kill treatments, with the gap in the kill treatment exceeding the gap in the no-kill treatment due to a substantial increase in WTA. The authors, however, noted variation in the kill-WTA reports, with some subjects reporting valuations similar to those reported in the no-kill treatment and others reporting valuation substantially higher. The authors concluded that for goods with intrinsic value (as opposed to consumption value), some element of moral responsibility might explain why reported WTA is higher than reported WTP. Importantly, while these results are often lumped in with other gap results to demonstrate support for endowment theory, they actually support a more nuanced theory based on notions of mortality.[46]

Walker et al. (1999) designed an experiment to study whether human versus natural causes of losses influence the magnitude of valuation gaps. In one experiment, the authors elicited valuations for neighborhood trees provided by the city. Some subjects were asked to value the saving of trees threatened by naturally occurring disease. Others were asked to value the saving of trees from damage caused by a street-widening project. All subjects

---

[44] Other researchers have explored whether the *magnitude* of the gap depends on the moral aspects of the traded goods (e.g., Irwin 1994). Caution is necessary, however, when contingent valuation methods are used to elicit hypothetical valuations for goods with highly moral aspects, such as the right to a clean beach. The theories that provide the predictions experimenters set out to test assume that choices have actual consequences. When this is not the case, features other than individual values for the goods might influence reported valuations and those influences might impact "seller" valuations differently than they impact "buyer" valuations.

[45] Subjects did not witness the destruction, but a witness verified it.

[46] In a study testing a similar theory, Biel et al. (2011) told one group of subjects (the donation owners) that they would receive SEK 50 for participating and that an additional SEK 100 would be donated to the World Wide Fund to protect the Swedish otter. They told another group (the donation non-owners) that they would receive SEK 150 for participating. During the experiment, the donation owners were given an opportunity to get an additional SEK100 in lieu of the donation, and the donation non-owners were given an opportunity to donate SEK 100 to the same Fund. Subjects made anonymous choices. Forty-five percent of donation owners opted to remain donors, and 19% of donation non-owners decided to donate. Based on subject responses to surveys meant to measure the feelings each choice would provoke, the authors attributed the difference to affective influences and moral reactions.

were told to assume they owned a house with a tree in the yard in danger of being lost. Some were asked to report how much they would need to be compensated to give up the opportunity to save the tree. Others were asked how much they would be willing to pay to save the tree. The authors report a hypothetical valuation disparity in the human destruction treatment but not in the natural cause treatment. While the elicitation device employed was not designed to measure actual valuations, and so should be interpreted with caution, the results suggest that further study is necessary to determine whether features other than the gain or loss of the consumption value of a good drive reported valuations. The authors interpret the results as support for the hypothesis that valuations are mediated by feelings of moral responsibility.

## 5.2   Frames, Attitudes, and Emotions

Loewenstein and Issacharoff (1994) suggested additional nuance by positing an increase in the valuation of items that are added to one's endowment as a result of successful performance of a task and a decrease in the valuation of those added as a result of failure (e.g., consolation prizes). This theory calls into question the standard economic assumption of source independence—the notion that the valuation of an item does not depend on how the item was obtained.[47] The authors also framed source dependence as a moderator of endowment theory, suggesting that "positive source effects enhance the impact of endowment and negative source effects weaken it"[48] (p. 158). Valuations were elicited using the BDM mechanism and a multiple price list after subjects were told that it was in their best interest to report true valuations. The results support the conjecture that people become differentially "attached" to objects as a function of how the objects are obtained (p. 165). Thus, the study offers evidence of another force beyond reference-dependent loss aversion that drives WTA higher than WTP. The authors pointed to the concept of "associationism" as the most straightforward explanation for source dependence. The idea is that the positive affect caused by good feelings that come from association with an object obtained through successful performance increases one's

---

[47]   Plott and Zeiler (2007) include the impact of the acquisition source as a component of a broader theory they refer to as enhancement theory. See *infra* for details.

[48]   Psychologists have tested related factors that might moderate valuation gaps. Saqib et al. (2010) posited that levels of consumer involvement in trading decisions can impact loss aversion levels. Specifically, they suggested that high involvement and higher stakes can increase the perceived importance of gains and losses, which can impact the magnitude of the asymmetric impact of losses relative to gains. Subjects who provided marketing assistance to the seller of a good (e.g., providing information about preferred highlighter colors) in exchange for the good, a highlighter set, reported higher valuations than owners who received a good after reading about a different good, causing a larger valuation gap (valuations by those given a choice between the good and money did not differ by level of involvement). The results held up when the authors used alternative methods of inducing perceptions of involvement. Aggarwal and Zhang (2006) reported evidence suggesting that salient relationship norms impact levels of loss aversion. Subjects who were, prior to reporting valuations, asked to put themselves into the shoes of a person with a communal outlook towards his friends reported higher WTA relative to those in a control group (no priming) and those who were asked to put themselves into the shoes of a person with an exchange outlook (i.e., quid pro quo relationship view).

valuation for the object.[49] Of course associationism cannot explain results from experiments in which subjects received endowments in the absence of successful performance, but it suggests an alternative (or supplementary) explanation in the presence of such performance. Simple versions of endowment theory do not predict varying outcomes conditional on endowment source.

In a similar vein, Liberman et al. (1999) examined how interventions that focus an individual on either promotion (making oneself better off) or prevention (avoiding making oneself worse off) impact reluctance to trade. They hypothesize that if a person is prompted to consider promotion, he is more likely to be open to change (and less reluctant to trade). Alternatively, if a person is prompted to consider prevention, concerns over safety and security give rise to reluctance to change (and therefore to trade). In one experiment, subjects were asked to describe their current hopes and goals and how they differed from their hopes and goals in the past, and then asked to decide whether they would be willing to accept a hypothetical pen given to them as a gift from a friend in exchange for a hypothetical mug given to their roommate as a gift from the same friend. Subjects displayed no reluctance to trade. Another group of subjects who were asked to describe their current sense of duty and obligation before deciding whether they would be willing to hypothetically trade were reluctant to trade. In another experiment, participants engaged in actual trades. In this experiment, the authors used subjects' answers to a series of questions to measure promotion focus and prevention focus. Those with high levels of promotion focus were less reluctant to trade relative to those with low levels. The opposite was true for those with high levels of prevention focus. This result suggests that framing can influence reluctance to trade.

Lerner et al. (2004) studied whether specific emotions affect the likelihood and magnitude of valuation gaps. They designed an experiment to test appraisal-tendency theory, which posits that emotions experienced during an irrelevant situation can carry over to subsequent economic decisions. For example, the experience of anger during an unrelated situation might compel risky economic choices in subsequent unrelated situations. On the other hand, the theory posits that we might not expect carryover effects in situations that involve actual monetary risks. During the experiment, the negative emotions of disgust and sadness were evoked using film clips. The authors hypothesized that feelings of disgust would cause owners to place lower values on endowed goods. Potential buyers would react less strongly to disgust because seller "proximity" to the good is expected to augment contamination. On the other hand, the authors predicted, in line with previous results, that sadness would trigger a desire for change, leading potential sellers to reduce their values and potential buyers to increase their values, both in an effort to trade. The multiple price list method was employed to elicit valuations, and one round was randomly chosen for payment. Non-owners received a cash payment, and owners received a set of

---

[49] Others have constructed theories that stand as alternatives to endowment theory and hinge on the psychological relationship between individuals and their possessions. Coren (2007) summarized the literature that develops and tests these sorts of theories. Evidence exists to support these theories, which are built on assumptions such as emotional attachment to possessions as alternatives to loss aversion. These theories assume that losses loom larger than gains not because we're generally averse to losses but because we perceive endowments as somehow different from identical items that we do not own.

highlighters. The findings support the theory. Owners exposed to the disgust prompt reported lower values for their highlighters relative to owners exposed to a neutral film clip. Exposure to a sad film clip was followed by relatively low owner valuations and relatively high non-owner valuations, resulting in a reverse gap (i.e., WTP > WTA).[50]

Shu and Peck (2011) test two potential moderators of loss aversion that relate to attitudes and emotions. The first, psychological ownership, assumes that legal ownership is unnecessary to trigger loss aversion. Mere psychological ownership, the simple feeling that something is "mine," might be sufficient. The authors estimated feelings of psychological ownership by eliciting responses to three statements using a seven-point scale from strongly disagree to strongly agree.[51] The second, affective reaction, predicts that emotional reactions towards an object can meditate loss aversion. To test this prediction, the authors elicited subject self-reports related to positive emotions and negative emotions.[52] Subjects were randomly assigned to two treatments, seller and chooser, and the multiple list price format was used to elicit pen valuations. After reporting valuations, the authors measured levels of psychological ownership and affective reaction to the good. The average seller valuation exceeded the average chooser valuation, and sellers reported greater psychological ownership and positive affective reactions (but not negative affective reactions) than did choosers.[53] The authors concluded that psychological ownership and affective reaction to the good act to mediate the effects of loss aversion.[54]

---

[50]   In a similar study, Lin et al. (2006) asked whether valuations gaps are mediated by happy and sad emotional states. They hypothesized that gaps will be smaller if valuations are reported when individuals are in a negative emotional state (e.g., sad) relative to a positive emotional state (e.g., happy). The authors induced emotional states in two ways: by asking subjects to recount happy or sad experiences and by exposing subjects to audiovisual clips intended to invoke particular emotional responses. Unlike Lerner et al. (2004), however, it seems that subjects did not make binding choices nor were valuations elicited using demand-revealing mechanisms. So, while the results suggest sadness reduces valuation gaps, the experiment design is not a valid test of the theory; thus, we should use caution when interpreting the results. Shu and Peck (2011; study 6) found mixed results when they measured the correlations between induced sadness and disgust and affective reaction towards the good.

Martinez et al. (2011) induced feelings of regret and disappointment that were unrelated to the good and found that both emotional states influence valuations of lotteries, but in different ways. Standard procedures were used to replicate a valuation gap. Inducing feelings of regret eliminated the gap, and inducing feelings of disappointment reversed it.

[51]   The statements included: "I have a very high degree of personal ownership of my item," "I feel like I own the item" and "I feel like this is my item."

[52]   Participants were told, "Here is a list of emotional reactions you may have experienced while evaluating the product. Please indicate how much you felt each of these emotional reactions." Subjects reported their emotional reactions on separate five-point scales ranging from "a lot" to "not at all."

[53]   Note that gap results were generated using parametric tests, which assume normal distributions, and regressions (presumably using ordinary least squares estimators), which assume that error terms are normally distributed. The authors did not provide results of checks of these assumptions, and they likely are not satisfied. The standard in the literature given the nature of the data is to use non-parametric tests, which do not rely on distributional assumptions. This reduces the weight we can place on the reported results.

[54]   In a similar set-up, the authors found that owners of an unpleasant object (a ball point pen covered in an adhesive and rolled in fine black sand) valued the good equally to choosers, had stronger feelings of ownership towards the good and strong negative affective reactions towards

While the results are potentially useful, we are unable to draw any causal connections between psychological ownership, affective reaction and valuations given potential endogeneity. In other words, the authors did not randomly assign subjects to varying levels of psychological ownership and affective reaction, so it might be that some third variable is driving both attitudes or emotions and valuations. For example, sellers might have announced relatively high valuations based on basic market instincts to sell high and then those who bid the highest reported the strongest ownership feelings in an effort to appear consistent with their reported valuations. This is mere conjecture, but we can't rule it out given the experiment design.

## 5.3  Market Experience

A separate line of research explores the possibility that while gaps and exchange asymmetries are regularly observed in the lab, we should not expect them to arise in markets comprised of traders with long-run experience. List (2003) estimated the impact of market experience by taking experimental methods to the field, where experienced traders of goods are plentiful. He predicted that experienced traders of goods (in this case sports cards and collector pins) are less likely to exhibit reluctance to trade an unfamiliar but related good. All subjects were drawn from attenders of sports cards and pin shows. The inexperienced traders were non-dealers attending the show. Experienced traders of sports cards were drawn from the population of dealers selling and buying goods at the shows. In one treatment, each subject was given one card (in exchange for completing a survey) and asked whether he would like to trade the card for a different card of equal value.[55] List presented evidence that, following the experiment, the subjects planned to consume the goods (hold them in their collections) rather than trade them. The pooled data revealed reluctance to trade the endowed card, consistent with endowment theory. A disaggregation of the data, however, revealed that experienced sports card dealers exhibited no reluctance to trade.[56] In a second treatment, List checked the robustness of the result to good type. He again found that more experienced traders were not reluctant to trade while inexperienced consumers tended to hold on to their endowments. He also presented some evidence that rejects reverse causality—experience seems to reduce reluctance to trade, as opposed to willingness to trade causing an increase in trading experience.[57] Finally, to test robustness for other goods and different levels of experience, List ran conventional lab experiments, bringing the same group of subjects into the lab once a week for four weeks. During each session, subjects were given an everyday good (e.g., a mug, a pen, a can of

---

it relative to choosers. Seller valuations were positively correlated with feelings of ownership and negatively correlated with negative affective reaction.

[55]  List estimated general preferences by giving a different group of subjects a choice between the two goods. Roughly half the group chose one good, and half chose the other.

[56]  Shu and Peck (2011; study 5) replicated List's results using a hypothetical survey instrument and found a correlation between induced experience—subjects asked to imagine that they had experience trading cards—and feelings of ownership.

[57]  List (2003) also estimated reluctance to trade using an n-th price auction to elicit valuations for sports cards. Dealers' WTA was statistically identical to their WTP. For non-dealers, the valuations of owners exceeded those of non-owners. In these rounds, however, cash was not given to non-owners so wealth effects are not controlled, which opens the door to an alternative explanation.

soda, a highlighter) and asked if they wanted to trade the endowed good for some other everyday good of roughly equal value. Different goods were used each week. Although he found reluctance to trade even after four sessions, the likelihood of trading increased over the sessions. The results, taken together, support the conjecture that trading experience reduces one's reluctance to trade.

While List (2003) provided preliminary evidence that experience attenuates reluctance to trade, questions remain. First, does attenuation extend to situations beyond those previously encountered, and, second, did List (2003) effectively separate endowment theory and neoclassical theory given that refinements of endowment theory assume that goods acquired for trade do not trigger reluctance to trade (e.g., Kahneman et al., 1990). Is it possible that List's experienced traders might have planned to resell the goods acquired during the experiment, despite their reports to the contrary? List (2004) attempted to provide answers to these questions by estimating differences in the reluctance to trade of sports cards dealers and non-dealers when endowed with everyday goods of roughly equal value (mugs and chocolate bars). In exchange for completing a survey, dealers and non-dealers were given either a mug or a candy bar or both or neither. Each mug owner was asked whether she wanted to exchange her mug for a candy bar (and vice versa for candy bar owners). Those receiving both were forced to exchange both for either a mug or a candy bar. Those receiving neither chose one. Consistent with List (2003), non-dealers exhibited a reluctance to trade while dealers did not. Those receiving both and neither chose the mug roughly half the time, confirming the assumption of roughly equal value. These results support the claim that experience trading one type of good can diminish reluctance to trade other types of goods. So, while the results do not allow us to draw inferences about what causes gaps, they do suggest that gaps might be unstable.

It is important to note that the designs of both List (2003) and List (2004) make it impossible to draw causal inferences about the impact of experience on reluctance to trade. The problem is that subjects were not randomly assigned to treatment and control groups characterized by experience and no experience. Therefore, we can't be sure if experience or some other variable correlated with experience caused this group's no-gap result. To mitigate this concern, List (2011) randomly assigned a group of subjects who reported that they made zero trades in a typical month (inexperienced traders) to two different treatments: experience and no experience. Subjects in the experience treatment gained market experience in the sports card market over a six-month period. A second group gained no experience over the same period. To induce experience, subjects in the experience treatment were given a lottery ticket for every trade they executed during the study period. To mitigate attrition, subjects were required to sign affidavits promising they would return. They were also given lottery tickets for showing up for subsequent sessions. The results suggest a causal relationship between experience and reduced reluctance to trade. Using a simple exchange design similar to Knetsch (1989), List found a similar baseline of reluctance to trade (13% and 10% of subjects assigned to the no-experience and experience treatments respectively opted to trade their endowed good for the alternative good).[58] After three months of experience trading, 35% of subjects

---

[58]   Some subjects were endowed with mugs and asked whether they wanted to trade for pens. Others were endowed with pens and had an opportunity to trade for a mug.

traded, compared to 11% of those who had not gained experience. After six months, 55% of experienced subjects traded, compared to 21% of those without experience. Both differences were statistically significant at a 95% confidence level. List (2011) acknowledged the possibility that the results might be due to experimenter-demand effects—subjects who were encouraged to trade during the six-month period might have believed that the experimenter wanted them to trade in the mug/pen rounds. In any event, the results stand as at least some evidence of a causal connection between trading experience and a lack of reluctance to trade.

Using a different method to investigate the impact of market experience on reluctance to trade, Apicella et al. (2014) ran experiments on two groups of Hudza Bushmen of Northern Tanzania, hunter-gatherers who rely on neither herding nor agriculture for food. One group lives in an isolated region, and its members interact rarely with outsiders. Food is consumed immediately and is shared equally among all members of the tribe. Possessions are few, and the tribe remedies unequal distributions by taking from those that have excess supply and giving to those with fewer resources. This group has little to no experience with trading. The second group is located near safari parks and has been exposed to tourists. Tour guides regularly compensate members of the group to take tourists on hunts. The group also produces bows and arrows for sale to the tourists. Members of this group sometimes venture to a nearby village to purchase food and other products. Using a Knetsch (1989) style simple exchange design,[59] the authors observed reluctance to trade in the second group (those with experience trading) but not the first (those with little experience trading). One obvious problem with the study's design is that the experimenters did not randomly assign Hudza members to the treatment and control groups. Thus, some variable other than trading experience might be driving observed differences. To address this concern, the authors pointed to some evidence that casts doubt on the possibility that Hudza members with particular traits or preferences selected themselves into the group with trading experience. They also claimed that varying levels of familiarity with the goods used in the experiment likely do not drive the results. In the end, however, the lack of random assignment leaves open the possibility that something other than differences in trading experience might drive the differences in reluctance to trade. Despite this limitation, the results suggest a complicated (and unclear) relationship between market experience and reluctance to trade.

## 5.4 Agency

Some have explored whether agents anticipate their principals' valuation gaps when making decisions on their behalf. Marshall et al. (1986) used a design similar to Knetsch and Sinden's (1984) simple design (i.e., would you trade a lottery ticket for $2) except that subjects were told that they could not participate in the lottery. Instead they were asked to advise someone who owned the lottery ticket or someone contemplating buying a lottery ticket. No valuation gaps were observed in the choices of agents in both hypothetical

---

[59]  The experimenter randomly chose which good to endow and, in one treatment, subjects were not allowed to touch the goods prior to making a choice. See Plott and Zeiler (2007), discussed *infra*, for a discussion of design choices in simple exchange experiments.

treatments and treatments involving actual payoffs. The authors suggested that agents' lack of appreciation for principals' valuation disparities might give rise to agency costs that go beyond moral hazard and other previously identified frictions.

Some have explored a different question about the relevance of agency for valuation gaps: do valuation gaps hold up when an individual-agent is transacting with his employer-principal. Arlen et al. (2002) explored whether managers of firms are reluctant to trade when transacting with their firms. Specifically, they tested two conjectures. The "exchange-value" hypothesis suggests that transactions between principals and agents involve entitlements held primarily for exchange purposes, and so loss aversion is not triggered by the loss of these sorts of goods (Kahneman et al., 1990). The alternative "shared-entitlement" hypothesis posits that an agent's sense of loyalty to the firm reduces her sense of entitlement in cases where the agent feels the firm is entitled to the asset. The authors first successfully replicated the gap result using a basic design in line with Kahneman et al. (1990). The law student subjects then pretended to play the role of agent to a hypothetical firm. Subjects were told that they would need to choose between keeping (or obtaining) a good, potentially a factor of production for the firm, and receiving a higher wage. Those not endowed with the asset were given an opportunity to "take" the asset.[60] Subjects were told that the firm would enjoy higher profits if it used the asset in production. Coffee mugs were used to represent the firm "asset." Each subject participated in eight rounds and was told that one round would be chosen at random for payment. Reported choices suggest no valuation gap. The authors also reported findings that suggest that the disappearance of the gap is driven by lower owner valuations. To test whether the no-gap result was driven by the perception of the asset as an exchange good or by a sense of loyalty to the firm, the authors conducted yet another experiment to separate the competing theories. The goal of the design was to remove the possibility of shared entitlement (i.e., a sense of loyalty). In this experiment, subjects were not playing the role of an employee of the firm but rather an applicant for a job at the firm. The subjects were told nothing regarding how their choice would impact the firm's profit. Given this design, an observed gap would support the shared-entitlement hypothesis, while the exchange-value hypothesis would be supported by the absence of an observed gap. No gap was observed. This result adds support to the exchange-value hypothesis, in line with the qualification suggested by Kahneman et al. (1990).

* * *

The studies described in this section suggest that levels of loss aversion might be impacted by many factors such as the moral valence of the good, emotions at the time of choice, feelings the good invokes, whether we regularly trade the good (or other goods) and who our trading partners are. The findings were important for refining endowment theory. In addition, however, they also inspired researchers to posit and explore alternative theories, theories suggesting that reluctance to trade is driven not by loss aversion but by some other force or set of forces. Each proposed theory has given rise to a sub-literature. The

---

[60]   The authors ran an additional experiment to test whether unendowed subjects were morally opposed (or at least reluctant) to take the firm's asset. They found no evidence that morality motivated choices.

purpose of the next section is to describe the alternatives, review the evidence generated to test the theories and illustrate how individual studies fit into larger literatures. While the literature has not converged on any one of the new theories, endowment theory clearly is no longer the leading explanation (if it ever was or should have been). The theory has essentially been replaced by expectation theory, which retains the assumptions of reference dependence and loss aversion but makes different assumptions about what sets reference points. While some data support this new theory, some call into question its predictive value. The same is true of the alternatives. Several theories stand as top-dog contenders. More work is required to test the theories against each other, to abandon the ones that fall short and to refine, and possibly combine, the remaining in a way that maximizes the theory's ability to predict choices.

# 6. ALTERNATIVE THEORY DEVELOPMENT

## 6.1 Hanemann's Substitution Theory

Hanemann's (1991) theory of gaps differs radically from endowment theory. The theory relies on two key assumptions from standard economic theory—that the availability of substitutes impacts price elasticity and that potential buyers face budget constraints. Specifically, one's WTA to give up a good in the absence of substitutes might be higher than one's WTP if budget constraints bind so that a potential buyer whose valuation is at least as high as the market price possesses inadequate funds to buy at the market price. When substitutes for a good do not exist (e.g., one's health or neighborhood tree density or the life of a Norfolk pine tree), the theory predicts that an individual endowed with the good requires more in compensation to give it up (in the extreme, an infinite amount) relative to the amount she would pay to acquire it (in the extreme, her entire, but limited, wealth). When substitutes exist, however, WTA will be lower given the ability of a potential seller to obtain a substitute. Figure 13.2 demonstrates the basic concept.

A reduction in substitutability (a move from Panel A to Panel B) results in an increase in valuation of the good. That is, potential sellers require more money ($13 as opposed to $5) to remain on the indifference curve if they give up one mug. Buyers are also willing to pay more to obtain the good, but they face budget constraints. Thus, Hanemann's theory attempted to explain observed gaps by positing that the lack of substitutes pushes WTA up, and budget constraints preclude WTP from increasing to the same extent.[61]

Shogren et al. (1994) designed an experiment to test whether the degree of substitution between goods (rather than endowment theory) might explain observed valuation gaps.[62]

---

[61]  Others have expanded Hanemann's substitution theory. Amiran and Hagen (2003), for example, worked out conditions under which WTA and WTP can infinitely diverge for public goods even where the elasticity of substitution between market goods and the public good is strictly positive. Hanemann (2003) agreed with Amiran and Hagen's analysis and framed their results in relation to his earlier work.

[62]  Adamowicz et al. (1993) published an experiment to test whether substitution effects explain observed gaps prior to Shogren et al. (1994). The experiment, however, did not employ a demand-revealing mechanism to elicit valuations. Subjects simply completed questionnaires that prompted

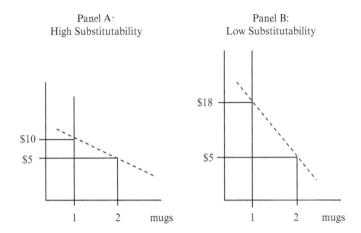

Panel A:
High Substitutability

Panel B:
Low Substitutability

*Note:* The dotted lines represent indifference curves, which indicate various combinations of mugs and money that make an individual indifferent between the combinations. For example, the indifference curve in Panel A suggests that the individual is indifferent between one mug plus $10 and two mugs plus $5. From this we can infer that the individual would require a transfer of $5 to make him indifferent between keeping both mugs and giving up a mug. In other words, his valuation of one mug is conditional on owning two mugs (i.e., his WTA) is $5.

*Figure 13.2   The impact of substitutability on WTA*

The authors used an auction mechanism designed to elicit true valuations for a brand-name candy bar (a good with substitutes) and a reduction in the risk of food-borne illness (a good without substitutes).[63] Valuations were measured after subjects participated in repeated auction rounds, each followed by an announcement of the market-clearing price, which was a function of the subjects' reported valuations. Repeated rounds were employed to help the subjects understand the auction mechanism, which leads to confidence that the reported valuations are the subjects' non-strategic valuations. Subjects acted either as sellers or buyers, and all subjects reported valuations for both the candy bar and the reduction in risk of illness. All outcomes were potentially binding. One round was selected

---

them to report hypothetical maximum amounts they would be willing to pay to buy (and minimum amounts they would be willing to accept to sell) goods with varying substitute availability. While the experiment design is not a perfect fit in relation to the tested theory's assumptions because subject choices are not followed by consequences, the study provides some evidence that availability of substitutes explains at least part of observed gaps. While the availability of substitutes reduced the magnitude of the observed (hypothetical) gap, a statistically significant (hypothetical) gap remained.

[63]   The auction mechanism employed was designed to elicit non-strategic valuations, but it is not the familiar first-price auction that allocates the good to the highest bidder. The subjects (all university students) were not told that they could optimize their payouts by reporting the most they would be willing to pay as non-owners and the least amount they would be willing to accept as owners. The authors simply described the auction mechanism and tested the subjects' understanding of it. See *infra* for details on theories related to subjects' lack of familiarity with the elicitation device.

randomly to be the binding round.[64] Potential buyers were endowed with cash that they could spend during the experiment and either a small piece of candy (or a food product with normal risk of contamination) that they could exchange for a brand-name candy bar (or a strictly screened food product with a lower risk of contamination) if their bids exceeded the clearing price determined by the auction. Sellers received the same amount of cash as buyers plus either a brand-name candy bar or a strictly screened food product,[65] and they were given an opportunity to downgrade their endowment in exchange for cash if their reported valuation did not exceed the market clearing price.

Given this design, Hanemann's substitution hypothesis would be supported if no gaps were observed in the candy bar rounds and gaps appeared in the food rounds. On the other hand, if gaps were robust across the type of good, the data would support endowment theory. The data support Hanemann's hypothesis. Candy bar WTA did not exceed WTP after multiple rounds of bidding, and WTA converged to the average candy bar market price, but food product WTA exceeded WTP even after multiple auction rounds and subjects were provided full information about the probability and severity of health risks.[66] To test whether gaps might persist in environments with available substitutes but uncertain value and cost, an additional treatment was conducted to elicit valuations for mugs with the university's emblem. Subjects were told they would be able to purchase as many mugs as they wanted right outside the door after the experiment. No valuation gap was observed. Shogren et al. noted that their results contradict the results obtained by Kahneman et al. (1990) in similar experiments that elicit valuations for goods with substitutes (e.g., pens and mugs). They pointed to numerous differences in the experiment design including the auction used to elicit valuations, but drew no conclusions about the impact of procedures on reported valuations. They rightly highlighted the need for further research to better understand the impact of elicitation methods on reported valuations in experimental markets.[67]

Morrison (1997a) challenged the conclusions drawn by Shogren et al. (1994). She started by revising endowment theory to assume that one's level of loss aversion depends on the degree of substitutability. More specifically, she posited that, if reference dependence causes a kink in the indifferent curve, loss aversion might be detectable only when the degree of substitutability is relatively low (i.e., no close substitutes). If the degree of

---

[64] To leave the experiment with take-home cash, subjects were required to eat a food product that had either the usual chance of being contaminated with a food-borne pathogen or a lower probability of contamination due to strict screening for pathogens. The chances of contamination of both food products were explained to the subjects prior to eliciting valuations.

[65] Note that owners were endowed with more than non-owners, which might cause a wealth effect. While the size of the differential is small, theoretically it might account for observed gaps. Morrison (1997b), *infra*, ruled out this potential explanation by giving non-owners the same amount of cash as owners plus cash equivalent to the average reported WTA. In other words, Morrison began by placing owners and non-owners on the same indifference curve.

[66] Sugden (1999) called this interpretation into question by arguing that Hanemann's theory predicts only small gaps in the food product market given that observed buyer valuations are low relative to subject wealth (i.e., buyers seem not to face budget constraints). Thus, Sugden argued, the large observed gap is inconsistent with Hanemann's theory. This sort of critique highlights the danger of drawing conclusions from only a subset of the data's features.

[67] This line of research has been taken up and is summarized *infra*.

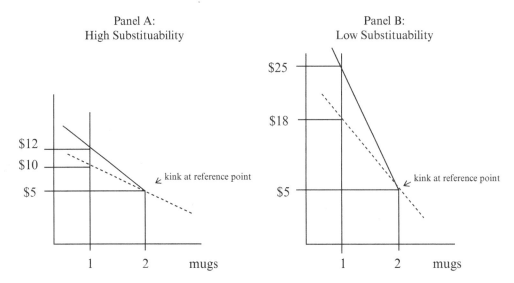

*Figure 13.3   The impact of loss aversion on WTA as a function of substitutability*

substitutability is high (i.e., close substitutes are available), then the valuation disparity, while present, might simply be more difficult to detect in the lab.

Figure 13.3 illustrates the basic idea. When substitutes exist (see Panel A) and an individual is endowed with two mugs and asked to report the minimum amount she is willing to accept to give up one mug, in the absence of loss aversion, she asks $5 (i.e., she is indifferent between $5 + two mugs and $10 + one mug, so her valuation for the mug is $5). When substitutes do not exist (Panel B), she requires $13 to give up her endowment ($18 minus $5). If potential buyers are equally income-constrained under both market conditions, a valuation gap is likely to appear only under low substitutability. As noted earlier, Hanemann argued that observed gaps have been misinterpreted as resulting from loss aversion when they are actually caused by low substitutability. Morrison's critique noted that loss aversion, if it exists, has a different impact on a seller's reported valuation depending on the degree of substitutability. If loss aversion causes a kink in the indifference curve at the reference point ($5 and two mugs), in markets with high substitutability loss aversion would push WTA up much more modestly than in markets with low substitutability (up to $7 in Panel A versus $20 in Panel B). Morrison's main point is that the lack of a valuation gap in markets with high substitutability does not necessarily demonstrate the lack of loss aversion. It could be that loss aversion is simply more difficult to detect because of its relatively small impact on seller valuations in markets with high substitutability.

Morrison (1997b) performed the tests suggested in her previous work. Specifically, she designed an experiment based on Shogren et al.'s (1994) design to test endowment theory against the substitutability hypothesis and to determine whether both theories might be at work when valuation gaps are observed. One basic design difference between Morrison and Shogren et al. is that subjects in some of Morrison's treatments were placed on the same indifference curves before valuations are elicited. In her first treatment, to replicate

Shogren et al., Morrison endowed both owners and non-owners with the same amount of cash. Potential buyers were told that they could spend their own money during the experiment, and they were encouraged to bring money to the experiment when they signed up to participate. In a second treatment, non-owners were endowed with cash equal to the cash given to owners plus cash equal to the average owner WTA response. In both treatments, subjects were told the price of the good and that it was offered for sale at a nearby shop; therefore, substitutability is assumed to be relatively high in both treatments. Under this design, Hanemann's theory predicts a gap in the first treatment due to the higher potential for budget constraints, but not the second. Endowment theory predicts gaps in both. Morrison found neither; rather, she observed no gap in the first treatment and a statistically significant gap in the second. The results from Treatment 2, which ruled out substitutability as a possible explanation, compelled her to conclude that endowment theory plays a significant role in gap creation, despite the fact that the theory cannot explain the result in the first treatment.

Shogren and Hayes (1997, p. 241), in a short comment on Morrison (1997a), raised concerns with her theory. They claimed that the theory's assumptions are arbitrary and argue that she failed to propose "a more sensitive way to detect [the] elusive effect." They noted, however, that the literature does contain evidence in support of endowment theory. They hypothesize that the mixed results might be attributable to the differing auction mechanisms used to elicit valuations (e.g., BDM as employed by Kahneman et al. (1990) and Vickery auctions used in Shogren et al. (1994)). They worried that repeated signals in the form of between-round announcements of market clearing prices in Vickery auctions might move reported valuations away from subjects' true valuations.

Bateman et al. (1997) used a different experimental design to test endowment theory against Hanemann's substitution effect conjecture. They noted that while Shogren et al. (1994) provided some evidence for substitution effects as an explanation for observed gaps, they did not directly measure the elasticities of substitution (i.e., the steepness of indifference curves), thus the interpretation of their data was merely speculative. Bateman et al. designed an experiment that purported to eliminate substitution and income effects as a possible explanation for observed gaps. They did this by asking subjects to rank order the same two bundles of goods from various endowment points. They then compared the preference orderings across different reference points.

The authors established endowments by giving subjects differing bundles of two goods: {a little of x, a little of y}, {a little of x, a lot of y}, {a lot of x, a little of y} or {a lot of x, a lot of y}.[68] Subjects were then asked indirectly to rank order two of the bundles (i.e., {a little x, a lot of y} and {a lot of x, a little y}) conditional on being endowed with one of the four bundles (the reference point).[69] The demand-revealing BDM mechanism

---

[68]   E.g., bundle a = {2 cans of Coke, £3.00}, bundle b = {6 cans of Coke, £3.00}, bundle c = {2 cans of Coke, £2.20}, and bundle d = {6 cans of Coke, £2.20}.

[69]   Rank ordering was elicited by asking subjects to state an amount of a good that would make one option just better than the other. To illustrate, assume a subject is endowed with {2 cans of Coke, £3.00}. The subject is presented with two options, one of which he must chose. For example, two options might be (1) we give you 4 cans of Coke and you give us $X, and (2) nothing (no change from initial endowment). The subject is asked to state the highest value of X such that he would still prefer option (2) to option (1). In this case, X is equivalent to the subject's WTP for

was used to determine preference orderings after subjects were trained and tested on the device. Under these conditions, the standard theory of consumer value predicts that a subject's rank ordering of the two bundles will not depend on the subject's endowment (Hicks and Allen 1934). Endowment theory, on the other hand, predicts that rank orderings will depend on one's starting point because subjects will account for potential losses differently than assumed under the standard theory. Bateman et al. found that the data supported endowment theory, both in the Coke and the luxury chocolate treatments. They also found that the effect was stronger for luxury chocolates than it was for Coke, suggesting that familiarity might diminish the effect but not completely eliminate it.[70] They concluded that their "results [were] consistent with those of a large number of other experiments and field surveys," and that "[i]n light of this evidence, it seem[ed] that the influence of loss aversion [was] a robust effect"[71] (p. 503). Interestingly, Bateman et al. (1997) reported evidence suggesting loss aversion in money. This result, along with others, such as no-gap results for induced-value tokens and the equivalence between chooser and potential buyer valuations, leads to the question: what sets reference points?

### 6.2   Expectation Theory: Endowment Theory Generalized

The theory Bateman et al. (1997) tested and the theory Kahneman et al. (1990) posited are different in important ways. Bateman et al. (1997) assumed that reference points are set by one's current endowment, no matter what that endowment is, including money. The results Kahneman et al. (1990) reported, however, suggest that valuations of choosers and potential buyers are the same, implying that buyers do not experience the giving up of money as a loss that triggers a disutility, at least under certain conditions.[72] To resolve

---

4 cans of Coke conditional on having 2 cans of Coke and £3.00. The authors used pilot studies to determine the combinations of goods so that one bundle would not always be preferred to the other bundle.

[70]   Bateman et al. (1997) used luxury chocolates to test conjectures related to the impact of good familiarity on gaps. Specifically, they noted that the potential loss of a familiar good might not trigger loss aversion because (1) one's preference for familiar goods is more certain, reducing the likelihood of stochastic variation and error in valuation determinations, (2) one might use known market prices as an anchor when thinking about one's valuation, and (3) if the product is regularly consumed, one might view gains of the good in the experiment as saved money rather than increased consumption. Again, it is important to note that hypotheses such as these substantially refine endowment theory, but appliers of the theory often overlook them (Klass and Zeiler 2013). Landesberg (2007) also reported a gap in valuations for an unfamiliar good (albeit smaller than the usual 2 to 1 ratio of WTA to WTP—between 1.27 and 1.40) and a smaller gap for a familiar good (estimated WTA/WTP ratio of 1.12–1.23). For subjects who confirmed that the familiar good was in fact familiar, no gap was observed. We might question the power of the test to identify an effect, however, given the small sample size—12 owners and 8 non-owners.

[71]   Bateman et al. (2000) measured hypothetical valuations in the field for pubic goods such as traffic calming methods to test Hanemann's substitution effect conjecture against endowment theory. Their data supported neither theory, but the hypothetical nature of the questions posed to subjects calls into question whether the study's design is a good test of either theory, both of which assume that actual consequences follow choices.

[72]   For example, if a potential buyer has extra money to spend on an unexpected purchase opportunity, then no feeling of loss might arise from the giving up of the money. On the other hand, if the potential buyer must give up some planned purchase to spend the money on an unex-

this issue, Bateman and Kahneman joined forces with a number of other authors to conduct an adversarial collaboration (Bateman et al. 2005).[73] Using a demand-revealing mechanism, the authors elicited WTP, WTA, and equivalent gain (EG), a measure of the smallest amount of money that the individual would be willing to accept in place of a gain of some amount of a good (in this case, high quality chocolates).[74] A number of hypotheses were formulated by developing predictions from the competing theories given the experiment design. For example, if individuals experience the giving up of money as a loss, then the smallest amount of a *good* an individual is willing to accept in return for a loss of some amount of endowed *money* will exceed the smallest amount of a good an individual is willing to accept in place of a gain of some amount of money. Both measures ask subjects to report the amount of money that would make them indifferent between the money and the good, but in the former condition, the subject loses the money and gains the good while in the latter condition, the subject gains the money or the good and nothing is lost. If money given up is experienced as a loss, individuals averse to losses will demand extra compensation in the form of a larger amount of the good received in exchange for the money. On the other hand, if individuals do not experience giving up money as a loss, then the two reported valuations would be equal. The data turned out not to support either theory particularly well. The authors noted that they ". . . cannot reject [Kahneman's no-loss-aversion-in-buying hypothesis] with 95 percent confidence; but there is no positive support for that hypothesis" (p. 32). Other results reported in the study support the claim that individuals are averse to money losses. According to the authors, the most striking feature of the results was the relative weakness of loss aversion in all comparisons in which both theories predict such effects.[75] Although the results were mixed, both parties agreed that the results favor loss aversion in money, although only weakly. This implies that endowment theory might be quite general—the nature of the endowment is potentially irrelevant despite earlier caveats. Overall, however, this study might be viewed more generally as a reason to question the explanatory power of endowment theory.

A few years later, Kahneman teamed up with Novemsky to continue the exploration of the same question: are individuals averse to money losses? (Novemsky and Kahneman 2005). The authors elicited valuations in three treatments: (1) **buyers** reported the highest

---

pected purchase opportunity, the loss of the money might be experienced as a loss of the planned purchase. By designing an experiment such that the potential transactions offered are sufficiently small to avoid the latter scenario, we can rule out the latter alternative explanation.

Others have examined experiment design features that might strengthen or weaken reference states. See, e.g., Knetsch and Wong (2009), discussed *infra*.

[73] Co-authors positing competing theories conduct such studies to test one theory against the other using an experiment designed to separate them. Typically, all participants agree to co-author the study regardless of which theory the data support.

[74] In initial treatments, the authors used vouchers that could be exchanged by the subjects for high quality chocolates at a local shop. Surprisingly, given previously published results (e.g., Sen and Johnson 1997), the data suggested no loss aversion for the vouchers. For this reason, actual chocolates were used in subsequent treatments.

[75] The authors did find the typical 2-to-1 ratio between WTA and WTP in the classic WTA/WTP comparison, however, which lends some support to endowment theory. But, the theory is not able to unify the results reported in the study.

amount they would pay for a good (WTP); (2) **choosers** reported the lowest amount of money that would trigger a choice to take the money over taking the good (CE); and (3) **sellers** reported the lowest amount of money that would compel them to give up an endowed good (WTA). If individuals are not loss averse in money but are loss averse in goods, then the ratio of WTA to CE should be greater than 1 and the ratio of CE to WTP should equal 1. The list method was used to elicit all valuations. One choice on the list was chosen randomly to determine the outcome. Data were collected during eight different experiments conducted over a number of years.[76] Some experiments were hypothetical and some resulted in binding outcomes. Different items were used in the eight experiments. Despite mixed results across the experiments (two of the eight experiments cannot rule out the possibility of no gap), the authors concluded that, at least in the aggregate, the data supported loss aversion in goods (WTA/CE > 1) but no loss aversion in money (CE/WTP = 1).

Novemsky and Kahneman (2005) combined their results with results from other experiments to formulate two propositions:[77]

(1) individuals are averse to losses of benefits rather than attributes of a good so we should expect no loss aversion for exchanges of goods that are close substitutes, and

(2) goods that are exchanged as intended are not evaluated as losses[78] (e.g., shoe sellers intend to exchange shoes for money, so they will not exhibit loss aversion when they give up the shoes).

These sorts of results highlighted a potential need to refine endowment theory in a more general way. Much of the reported evidence failed to support endowment theory's assumption that reference points are set by endowments. Köszegi and Rabin (2006) proposed a theory that moves away from this assumption. Their model instead assumed that one's overall utility for a riskless outcome depends on consumption utility and on gain-loss utility, the sensation of gain or loss due to a departure of the endowment from some reference point. Their model assumed that reference points are set not by one's endowment but by one's "rational expectations held in the recent past about outcomes."[79] So, for example, a merchant who regularly sells goods expects not to end the day as

---

[76]   Aggregated results were produced using averages weighted by sample sizes. Weighting by sample size ensures that results from sessions with a large number of subjects don't get weighted more heavily than results from smaller sessions.

[77]   The authors developed a third proposition related to the relationship between risk aversion and loss aversion. Ariely et al. (2005) responded to these results and their potential interpretation, which are beyond the scope of this review.

[78]   No loss aversion for money is a special case of this proposition. Svirsky (2014) reported additional evidence that supports the general claim. He observed a valuation gap for chocolate coins described to subjects as chocolate but not for money or for chocolate coins described as tokens. He did not take a position, however, on what drives the observed gap given the wide array of possibilities in the literature, some of which relate to basic design choices.

[79]   "Specifically, a person's reference point is her probabilistic beliefs about the relevant consumption outcome held between the time she first focused on the decision determining the outcome and shortly before consumption occurs" (p. 1141).

owner of the merchandise. Thus, the merchant does not experience negative gain-loss utility when he sells goods. In addition, reference point updating might lag behind belief updating. Thus, one might have expectations over ending up with a good that get resolved, but preferences continue to depend on the expectations. For example, I might expect to receive a new bike for my birthday, but I do not receive the bike. The model predicts that, even after the uncertainty is resolved, my willingness to pay for the bike is higher than it was before I expected to receive it. This model, which I will refer to as "expectation theory," seems a good replacement for Tversky and Kahneman's (1991) endowment theory because its predictions are consistent with a larger swath of the data published by the mid-2000s.[80]

In a similar vein, Brenner et al. (2007) distinguished between "possession loss aversion" (disutility that arises from the loss of any endowment, which is more severe than the utility that arises from a gain of the same good if not endowed) and "valence loss aversion" (disutility that arises from changes perceived as negative developments, which is more severe than the utility that arises from changes perceived as positive developments), and posited that both play a role in valuation gaps. In questionnaire-type, hypothetical choice experiments, the authors produced data suggesting that valence loss aversion tends to dominate possession loss aversion.[81] The authors claimed that valence loss aversion also tends to better organize the array of data published through the mid-2000s. How much weight can be placed on these results, however, is unclear given that the experiment design is not completely in line with the assumptions of the theories (i.e., that choices are followed by actual consequences).

Ericson and Fuster (2011) directly tested expectation theory by manipulating subject expectations and correlating the induced expectations with reluctance to trade. In experiment 1, subjects were endowed with a randomly selected good (either a mug or a pen, both university memorabilia) and individually randomly assigned to having either a 10% or 90% chance to decide whether to trade for the other good. Thus, subjects in one treatment expected that they likely would be in a position to decide whether to trade, and subjects in the other did not. Subjects then completed a questionnaire after which they were reminded about instructions for the (possible) exchange. This reminder was intended as a check on understanding of the task and to get them to think about the possible decision. Another questionnaire was administered, after which the subjects were asked to report choices that would be administered if they end up in a position to trade. After another questionnaire a die was rolled and decisions for those allowed to choose were effectuated. The results supported expectation theory: subjects expecting not to be able to trade their endowed good were less likely to report being willing to trade than those expecting to be able to trade.

The authors ran a second experiment designed to induce expectations over ownership. Subjects were individually randomly assigned either a 10% or 80% chance of receiving the

---

[80]  For example, Köszegi and Rabin's (2006) model was able to explain the lack of aversion to losses of money (e.g., Novemsky and Kahneman 2005) and goods obtained for the purpose of reselling them (e.g., List 2003).

[81]  Shu and Peck (2011; study 7) collected data using similar hypotheticals and found a correlation between the valence of the endowed good, affective reaction towards the good and feelings of ownership.

mug in their possession and leaving with it at the end of the experiment, each with equal likelihood. Each subject also had a 10% chance of being in a position to choose between the mug and some randomly determined amount of money. Finally, each subject had a 10% chance of getting no mug and no money. After the questionnaire and a reminder about the task, subjects were asked to make choices between the mug and different monetary amounts (from $0 to $9.57 in 33 cent increments) and told that these choices would be effectuated in the case they were in a position to choose between the mug and money. In this case, the experimenter would randomly choose an amount from the list to determine which choice would be implemented. They were then told that if they ended up getting no mug and no money they would get to choose between a pen and some random amount of money. They then made choices between the pen and different monetary amounts (the same list used to elicit mug valuations). The pen valuations were used to difference out preferences for university memorabilia. In line with the predictions of expectation theory, subjects with a high chance of receiving and leaving with the mug valued it (weakly) significantly higher in the absolute sense than those who had a low chance.[82] This finding supports expectation theory, but the magnitude of the gap was substantially lower than the oft-cited 2-to-1 ratio of WTA to WTP.[83]

Smith (2012) designed an experiment similar to Ericson and Fuster's (2011) second experiment, but his focus was on expectation theory's predictions related to lagged beliefs. Recall that expectation theory assumes that preferences might lag behind beliefs (my valuation for a good I expected to receive but didn't receive is higher relative to the valuation I had for it prior to developing the expectation even though I now expect not to get it). To test whether preferences are influenced by lagged beliefs, Smith determined whether subjects were endowed with the good before eliciting valuations. Subjects had either a 10% or 70% chance of getting a water bottle. Once the subjects individually determined the outcome by drawing a marble out of a bag, valuations were elicited using the multiple price list format. Those who won a mug valued it as a seller, and those who did not valued it as a buyer. The demand-revealing BDM mechanism was used to determine which subjects transact, and sales and purchases were made privately in an adjacent room. To reduce the impact of reference point formation related to expectations over the buying/ selling task, subjects were not told about the task until endowments were determined. The elicitation mechanism, however, was explained before subjects reported valuations, which might have contaminated their expectations. Smith tested two predictions from

---

[82]    The authors estimated the difference a second time assuming that the effect of a high probability of getting the mug is approximately proportional to the consumption utility of the mug to determine whether mug lovers will boost their valuations more than those not so passionate about mugs. The authors used regression analysis to correlate log-transformed mug valuations with the likelihood of getting the mug, controlling for log-transformed pen valuations (a proxy for preferences over university memorabilia to reduce idiosyncratic noise) and subject demographics. They found that valuations for the mug were between 20 and 30% higher on average for those with a high probability of getting one.

[83]    Ericson and Fuster (2011) ran a third experiment to separate expectation theory from motivated taste change theory (Strahilevitz and Loewenstein 1998), which assumes that preferences are impacted by self-image partly driven by the self-perceived desirability of one's own possessions. Their results provided no support for motivated taste change. See details behind the literature related to mere-ownership theory *infra*.

expectation theory: (1) WTP for those with high expectations of winning is greater than WTP of those with low expectations of winning (due to lagged beliefs); and (2) WTA for those with high expectations exceeds WTP for those with high expectations (due to loss aversion). The results support the assumption of loss aversion but not the predicted influence of lagged beliefs. Smith pointed out that subjects possibly did not hold the lotteries for a sufficient length of time to incorporate expectations into their reference points. Alternatively, it might be that in this context subjects were able to quickly update their reference points upon resolution of the lotteries. Of course it is also possible that preferences simply are not a function of lagged beliefs. In any event, the data stand as evidence against a basic tenant of expectation theory.

Heffetz and List (2014) designed another set of experiments to directly test expectation theory. Unlike in Ericson and Fuster's (2011) design, their subjects did not own either of the goods before deciding which they would choose if given the opportunity to make a choice. Like in Ericson and Fuster (2011), the experiment was designed to induce varying expectations over which item will be received to test the impact of expectations over outcomes on choices. They first asked subjects to flip a coin and choose a number between 1 and 100. Subjects were then allowed to inspect two items (a mug and a pen) and were told that they would get one of the items as a gift. Whether they got to choose the gift or were assigned one of the items according to the coin flip was determined randomly according to known probabilities (e.g., a 99% chance that the chosen good is received and a 1% chance that the coin flip determines which good is received). The randomization procedure was explained, a test of understanding was administered, and default goods were revealed (e.g., if you are not allowed to choose, you will receive the pen if your coin flip came up heads and the mug otherwise). After completing an unrelated questionnaire (to pass time), all subjects chose a good that would be given to them in the event they were allowed to choose. The uncertainty was resolved, and subjects either received the chosen good or were assigned one of the goods based on the outcome of the coin flip. The treatments varied subject expectations over whether they will end up with the default good (either a 1% chance or a 99% chance).[84] Thus, expectation theory predicts different choices. The theory predicts that those with a strong expectation that they will receive the default good will choose the default good and that those with a strong expectation of getting a choice will make choices that are independent of the default good (half are predicted to choose the mug and half the pen). The standard model predicts that choices are independent of reference points, so the standard model predicts that subjects with a strong expectation of getting the default will choose the mug or the pen independent of the default good. The data revealed that subjects' choices were independent of their expectations across the board. Unlike in Ericson and Fuster (2011), the data did not support expectation theory.

Although choices seemed not to be influenced by expectations, Heffetz and List (2014) found that they are correlated with the coin flip, even when it's virtually irrelevant.[85] This

---

[84]  The authors used a survey to verify expectations. The vast majority of subjects correctly answered questions related to expectations. Almost all of the others correctly answered after being prompted to re-read the instructions and try again.

[85]  For subjects who correctly answered on the first attempt questions meant to check understanding, choices were correlated with the coin flip (p = 0.03). The result was not statistically

result is predicted by neither standard theory nor expectation theory (when combined with the results related to expectations). In a second experiment, designed to explore both the disparity in results relative to Ericson and Fuster (2011) and the observed coin-flip dependence in the first experiment, the authors brought the design more in line with Ericson and Fuster's design.[86] In addition, they varied the strength of the language used to convey the endowment and to remind subjects of the endowment at the time of choice. When endowments were emphasized and subjects were reminded of them, the results observed in the previous experiment held up. Specifically, expectations over outcomes did not impact choices, but choices were correlated with the coin-flip. When the language used to convey endowment was de-emphasized, however, no statistically significant correlation between the coin flip and choices was observed, and choices did not depend on expectations over outcomes. This evidence suggests that the language used to convey ownership impacts choices. The divergent results call into question the ability of expectation theory, in its simple form, to predict behavior.[87]

### 6.3   Uncertain Preferences

At the same time that researchers were testing and refining both endowment theory and substitution theory, additional alternative theories were being generated. Several theorists have focused on uncertainty over preferences as an explanation for observed gaps. For example, Hoehn and Randall (1987) posited that individuals must consult their preferences to determine their true valuations for goods and that this consultation is time-consuming and might be stopped short when they face time pressure to report WTP, biasing it downward. Dubourg et al. (1994) explored whether gaps are driven by imprecise preferences through eliciting valuations for hypothetical changes in the risk of non-fatal road injuries. They concluded that gaps seem to be correlated with imprecise preferences but that imprecision explains only a portion of observed gaps. They pointed to endowment theory as a potential explanation for the remaining portion.[88] Kolstad

---

significant for all subjects ($p = 0.13$) but likely would be if the authors ran a one-sided test, which is arguably the better test given the nature of expectation theory's predictions.

[86]   For example, subjects had either a 90% or a 10% chance of being able to choose rather than 99% or 1%, subjects answered additional survey questions used to measure expectations, and the time they spent thinking about one good versus the other was adjusted to be more in line with the amount of time Ericson and Fuster allowed.

[87]   In another (working) investigation of expectation theory, Goette et al. (2014) argued that varying the probability of the ability to choose is not a sharp test of the theory. Instead, the authors varied the probability of a forced exchange. Owners were endowed with a good and non-owners were endowed with money. Valuations were elicited after subjects were told that they would be forced to trade with some probability. When that probability was set to zero, the results replicated Kahneman et al. (1990)—WTA exceeds WTP. Expectation theory predicts that the gap should disappear when the probability of a forced trade is 0.5 and should reverse itself when the probability exceeds 0.5. When Goette et al. varied this probability, however, they observed the usual valuation gap. The authors suggested that expectation theory needs to account for individuals' lack of ability to fully forecast future reactions to gains and losses when developing plans of action.

[88]   Dubourg et al. (1994) dismissed substitution effects as a plausible explanation for their experimental results. They claimed that this sort of risk had substitutes because "drivers of less safe cars can switch some journeys to public transport, or trade speed and convenience for safety

and Guzman (1999) attempted to explain valuation gaps in contexts where experimenters employ first-price auction mechanisms to elicit valuations.[89] They assumed that subjects are able to expend costly effort to reduce uncertainty about their valuations. Their theory predicted that when the payoff from trade is small relative to the cost of information, subjects will tend to understate WTP and overstate WTA. The theory, however, relates only to valuations elicited using first-price auctions, so it cannot explain divergence in second-price auctions, which are commonly used to elicit valuations in experiments.[90] Plott (1996) suggested a similar process of preference discovery. Specifically, Plott laid out what he terms the "discovered preference hypothesis," which models decision making in three stages. Stage one is characterized by a lack of experience with the environment that maps choices into outcomes. In this stage, choices are driven by self-interest but are impulsive, and thus might appear irrational. Decision makers transition into stage two as they gain experience with the environment, practicing and learning from feedback following biding choices. During this stage, choices begin to stabilize and more closely align with preference-based models. By stage three individuals anticipate that others will act rationally, and choices become best responses to the predicted rational behavior of others. This hypothesis suggests that seemingly irrational behavior might instead be a symptom of a lack of experience or understanding of the environment, and that practice and experience might be a necessary component of preference discovery.

Zhao and Kling (2001) took a related approach in an attempt to organize the then-existing data better than both endowment theory and substitution theory. Their commitment cost theory built upon an assumption of imprecise preferences and predicted that subjects would inflate WTA when they were uncertain about their valuations.[91] The theory predicts that a potential seller will report a WTA that is higher than her true WTA

---

by driving more slowly and carefully" (pp. 127–128). Of course, as the authors mentioned, whether subjects actually contemplated these sorts of substitutes before reporting hypothetical valuations for risk reductions was unclear. Despite this lack of clarity, the authors deemed endowment theory to be a "better explanation."

Morrison (1998, p. 190) pointed out, however, that knowing whether gaps are caused by endowment theory or alternative theories, such as lack of market discipline and preference imprecision, is impossible given the context in which Dubourg et al. elicited valuations. That is, she argued that Dubourg et al. (1994) did not provide strong evidence given the hypothetical nature of the valuation elicitation procedure. As evidence against alternative theories she pointed to elicited valuations reported in her earlier paper (Morrison 1997b), which imposed market discipline by using an incentive-compatible elicitation device and employing repeated trials to allow subjects to gain experience using the device. She measured preference precision by asking owners, who were endowed with mugs over which subjects were assumed to have imprecise preferences, to state (1) the minimum value that they were sure they would be willing to accept to give up their endowment and (2) the maximum value that they were sure they would not accept. Analogous responses were elicited from non-owners. She found that minimum WTA exceeded maximum WTP (Figure 2, p. 193) and argued that this evidence cuts against preference imprecision as a driver of observed gaps.

[89] In these auctions, the highest bidder buys and pays his bid, and the lowest asker sells and receives her ask.

[90] In second-price auctions, the highest bidder buys but pays an amount equal to the second-highest bid. Selling works similarly. Second-price auctions were designed to encourage the reporting of true valuations.

[91] Li et al. (2002) empirically estimated the impact of uncertainty over the welfare effects of a proposed change on distributions of valuations. They found that "individuals who [were] uncertain

if she is forced to state a valuation that will potentially result in her having to give up the good for money sooner than she would choose to give it up. By announcing a higher WTA, she buys time to discover her valuation because she is more likely to leave the experiment with the good and have opportunities to determine her true valuation and then to sell the good after the experiment. Similarly, potential buyers will offer less to avoid buying until they can obtain more information about their true valuation for the good. The theory posits that we can think of the difference between reported WTA (WTP) and actual WTA (WTP) as the amount the subject is willing to forego to postpone the decision until she is able to obtain more information about her true valuation.[92] Zhao and Kling argued that data reported in other experiments supported their theory. For example, when values are certain (e.g., values for induced-value tokens in Kahneman et al. 1990), we do not observe gaps. Kahneman et al. (1990) did observe gaps, however, for mugs even after opportunities to learn during repeated bidding rounds. The author noted, though, that subjects need opportunities to learn not only about how the valuation elicitation mechanism works but also about their true valuations.

Kling et al. (2013) designed an experiment to test commitment cost theory. They began by refining the theory. They noted that commitment cost theory is incomplete without some source of asymmetry in beliefs over the ease in buying and selling outside the experiment. If subjects anticipate the possibility that they might wish to reverse trades made during the experiment after learning more about their values and the market value of the good, then the valuations reported during the experiment will depend on subjects' beliefs about the ease of buying and selling after the experiment. If beliefs about ease are symmetric, then we would expect WTA = WTP. Under Kling et al.'s (2013) version of commitment cost theory, valuation gaps are caused by asymmetries in beliefs about ease of buying versus ease of selling, which they assume stem from cognitive dissonance and/or limited memory. Under the assumption of cognitive dissonance, subjects' beliefs about the ease of buying or selling are correlated with their role in the experiment because individuals tend to believe that their trading position in the experiment, say as a seller, is a "good" position, which triggers the belief that selling in the future will be easier relative to buying. The same is true for potential buyers. Buyers believe that the buyer role is a "good" position, which triggers the belief that buying in the future will be easier relative to selling.

---

about the welfare effects of a proposed change tend[ed] to have higher expected WTA values than under certainty."

[92] Zhao and Kling (2004) presented a formal dynamic model of an individual's decision to purchase or sell under conditions of uncertainty, irreversibility, and learning. The theory assumes that "commitment costs arise when the following conditions are met: the individual (1) is uncertain about the value of the good, (2) expects that she can learn more about the value in the future, (3) has some willingness to wait, (4) expects a cost associated with reversing the action of buying or selling, and (5) is forced to make a trading decision now even though she might prefer to delay the decision" (Zhao and Kling 2004, p. 510).

Simonson and Drolet (2004) also studied the impact of uncertainty on reported valuations and consider how their findings might inform theories intended to explain gaps. They focused on individuals' uncertainty regarding whether they wish to sell an endowed good. They examined the impacts of anchors on reported WTA. They found that uncertainty is correlated with an irrelevant anchor's influence on reported WTA. They did not, however, go as far as suggesting that uncertainty causes WTA to exceed WTP.

These divergent beliefs cause potential sellers to report high WTA because they believe that they will be able to *sell* outside relatively easily if they resolve their uncertainty after the experiment and wish to reverse the experiment outcome of no sale. Potential buyers, on the other hand, report low WTP because they believe that they will be able to *buy* easily outside if they resolve uncertainty after the experiment and wish to reverse the choice not to purchase in the experiment. Alternatively, Kling et al. suggested that the asymmetry could be caused by limited memory of past buying and selling experiences coupled with the assumption that we perceive selling as easier than buying if we more readily recall selling experiences, and buying as relatively easier if we readily recall buying experiences. Most gap experiments provide subjects with experience trading before measuring the gap; therefore, sellers get experience selling and buyers get experience buying. Thus, beliefs over ease of buying and selling diverge along role lines. This leads to the same predictions as under the assumption of cognitive dissonance. Buyers will report low WTP because they believe they will easily be able to buy after the experiment if they so wish after their uncertainties about their valuation and the market price are resolved (or reduced).

To test this theory, the researchers conducted what they describe as a "field" experiment.[93] The experiment was conducted using subjects drawn from a pool of people who were attending a sports card show. In one set of experiments, half the subjects were given a baseball card with a market value of roughly $12, and the other half were given $12 in cash to rule out income effects. After eliciting valuations using an incentive compatible mechanism,[94] the subjects were asked to report whether they intended to keep, trade, or sell the card if they ended up with one at the end of the experiment. Subjects also were asked to report how easy they thought it might be to sell or purchase the card outside the experiment. Subjects were told that their responses would be kept confidential and that they would be contacted within three days if they were among the traders based on reported valuations,[95] and cash (cards) were mailed to subjects who mailed in cards (cash). The authors observed a valuation gap.[96] More analysis was performed to determine the cause of the gap. The authors found that potential sellers who planned to keep the card stated statistically significantly higher values on average than those who planned to sell

---

[93]  See Harrison and List (2004) for a description of field experiments, in which data are collected using experimental methods that are applied in actual markets rather than in the laboratory. Despite the use of the term, Kling et al.'s (2013) experiment might better be described as a quasi-field experiment in the sense that the data were collected using subjects that were attending a sports card show. Subjects reported valuations in a (mobile) laboratory setting and not as participants in actual transactions at the sports card show.

[94]  Valuations were elicited using the Shogren et al. (2001) nth-price auction, which is designed to encourage reports of non-strategic valuations.

[95]  Subjects endowed with cards traded if their reported valuations were less than a randomly chosen number. In exchange for their cards, they received a number of dollars equal to the randomly chosen number. Those not endowed traded if their reported valuations were more than a different randomly chosen number. In exchange for cash equal to the randomly chosen number, they received a card.

[96]  The gap was statistically significant at the 5% level according to both parametric and non-parametric tests. Non-parametric tests are employed when the populations from which the samples are drawn are not normally distributed. The null hypothesis is that the samples were drawn from the same population (i.e., a group of individuals that behave similarly regardless of which treatment is applied).

outside the experiment. They also found asymmetric beliefs about the ease of transacting outside the experiment. For example, those intending to keep the card reported beliefs of higher levels of difficulty selling outside the experiment relative to those who did not intend to keep the card. Generally, the results support the predictions of Zhao and Kling's commitment cost theory.[97] WTA decreased and WTP increased as the perceived difficulty of reversing the transaction decreased.[98]

Others have proposed similar theories that assume uncertain preferences. For example, Inder and O'Brien (2003) suggested that individuals might report low WTP and high WTA if they are uncertain about how a transaction will impact their utility in an effort to avoid negative emotional states that might arise from disappointment or regret.[99] Such reactions might be triggered, for example, if an individual does not know the market value of the good and purchases the good during the experiment for an amount above an amount she could gain from selling the good after the experiment (or for an amount that exceeds the utility she eventually derives from the good).

Carmichael and MacLeod (2006) also developed a rational choice theory model based on principals similar to those employed by Zhao and Kling (2004). The authors crafted a trading model that assumes that individuals have the capacity to walk away from a seemingly unfair deal even if it requires giving up a potential gain. They assumed that individuals are endowed with goods and have the ability to "act decisively before they have fully analyzed a situation" (p. 213). Their model predicted that individuals might refuse to trade if the perceived gains from trade are small relative to the expected gains from waiting to fully analyze things. The model seems to be the first to suggest that valuation gaps are the result of bargaining strategies developed through evolution. The basic idea is that "survival" depends on strategic reluctance to give up one's endowments, and that we naturally default to these "adaptive structures known to exist in our brains" (p. 213).

Tsur (2008) modeled valuation uncertainty from a different angle. He assumed that gaps were caused by uncertain preferences, but he diverged from previously posited theories regarding how that uncertainty impacts behavior. Rather than assuming positive costs of committing to a transaction prior to discovering one's valuation, Tsur assumed that individuals, faced with opportunities to transact, predicted their uncertain utility from a trade by using selective past experiences. Selectivity results from the assumption that individuals place greater weight on past utility from transactions that were carried out

---

[97]   Ratan (2012) reported evidence from simple exchange settings that support a similar theory.
[98]   Corrigan et al. (2008, p. 285) conducted additional tests of the impact of commitment costs on WTP and found that "respondents offered the opportunity to delay their purchasing decisions until more information became available were willing to pay significantly less for improved water quality than those facing a now-or-never decision." Lusk (2003) put predictions related to WTP to the test in the lab and found that most of his results were not in line with the theory's predictions. He noted several problems with the experiment design (pp. 1321–1322), so it is unclear how much weight we can confidently place on the results.
[99]   See also Zhang and Fishbach (2005) who reported evidence which suggests that the magnitude of gaps is affected by regret-type feelings that are associated with losing possession of a potentially valuable object (for sellers) or losing money on a potentially worthless purchase (for buyers). Ratan (2014) found evidence of regret avoidance in simple exchange experiments that allow subjects to reverse trading decisions if they wish. See *infra* for details on experiments designed to test regret theory.

relative to those that were not. Valuations gaps result because buyers recall past purchases, which were more likely to occur after an overestimation of value relative to previously avoided buying opportunities, and sellers recall past sales, which were more likely to occur after an underestimation of value relative to previously avoided selling opportunities. Buyers reduce their predicted utility (and therefore their reported valuations), and sellers increase theirs, based on experienced utility. Tsur's model built in variation in levels of sophistication to predict larger gaps for those who failed to account for selectivity (naïve agents) compared to those who did (rational agents). Tsur did not run experiments to test his model, but he did attempt to square the model's predictions with previously reported data. He argued that his theory explained variation in gap size. Specifically, valuation gaps tend to be larger for non-market goods (such as air quality and nuclear water repositories) than for ordinary market goods, such as pens and mugs, and induced-value tokens, which have certain values. In addition, he argued that his theory also accommodated results suggesting that experienced traders' valuations do not depend on their reference states.

Kingsley and Brown (2013) revisited the basic theories of preference uncertainty—for example Plott's (1996) discovered preference hypothesis and List's (2003) market experience conjecture—and put these theories to the test by providing subjects with opportunities to discover their preferences for goods by engaging in a "value learning exercise." In the baseline treatment, student subjects were paid a $10 show-up fee and handed a coffee mug with the school's insignia. Valuations were elicited using the multiple price list format. Subjects received instruction on the mechanism and participated in hypothetical induced-value practice rounds as hypothetical owners and non-owners. Subjects were randomly assigned to either the owner or non-owner group, and valuations were collected. Transactions were completed anonymously. A second treatment included a value-learning exercise before valuations were elicited. The subjects were asked to make 155 hypothetical choices between pairs of items including the mug, five other locally available private goods, four public goods, and 11 different dollar amounts. The purpose of the exercise was to provide subjects with an opportunity to learn their valuation for the mug. If uncertain preferences explain observed valuation gaps, and the exercise helps subjects learn their preferences, then the valuation gap should disappear after subjects complete the value-learning exercise. Kingsley and Brown observed a valuation gap in the baseline treatment but not in the treatment that provided the mechanism for learning one's valuation. This result supports Plott's (1996) discovered preference hypothesis and suggests that explanations that assume loss aversion are not robust.

In an effort to develop a general theory that can accommodate outcomes that vary based on preference uncertainty, Loomes et al. (2009) proposed a model that assumed that individuals are loss averse and that reluctance to trade varies with the characteristics of relevant goods and an individual's knowledge about and experience with the good.[100] The model predicted that "exchange resistance" increases as utility loss aversion and uncertainty about future preferences over relevant goods increase. The assumed dependence of reluctance to trade on preference uncertainty allows the theory to explain a wider

---

[100]   In support of this assumption, Landesberg (2007) observed valuation gaps for an unfamiliar good but not for a familiar good. Familiarity was measured in part by how often the subjects purchased the good outside the lab.

range of experimental findings than Tversky and Kahneman's (1991) endowment theory. For example, the theory predicted that gaps are reduced or eliminated in contexts in which experience or experimental procedures reduce uncertainty about future preferences. Loomes et al. did not, however, put this theory up against other theories that have found support in the literature. Thus, more work is required to determine which theory best unifies the reported findings.

### 6.4    Mere-Ownership Theory

Moving away from the assumption that individuals experience disutility from losses, some have developed theories that suggest that mere ownership of a good can change the nature and value of the good. This camp of theories posits that reluctance to trade is caused by the placement of a higher valuation on an owned good relative to the same good when it lies outside one's endowment. This explanation is an alternative to endowment theory, which assumes valuation gaps are driven by sellers' demand for compensation in return for suffering the loss of a good valued the same regardless of whether she owns it. In other words, higher WTA under endowment theory is assumed to be driven not by divergent valuations of goods based on endowment status but by amounts of cash (or other goods) required by owners to compensate them for the disutility they experience when they give up an endowment. This distinction is important and is sometimes missed by legal scholars.[101]

Loewenstein and Adler (1995) characterized the impact of ownership on valuation as a "type of endogenous taste-change." They suggested that WTA exceeds WTP because individuals experience extra utility from the owning of a good as opposed to the assumption that individuals demand compensation for losses.[102] They explored whether individuals are able to predict the impact of ownership on valuation. The authors provided subjects

---

[101]    For example, see Korobkin (2014) who suggested that attachment to substantive endowments is one possible psychological explanation for loss aversion—"the endowment effect could result from an attachment to substantive entitlements that forms solely as a consequence of ownership or possession. Once a widget becomes my widget, perhaps I like the widget more" (p. 17). He incorrectly described attachment as a driver of loss aversion rather than an alternative to it. He made the same mistake with his descriptions of transactional disutility, regret theory, and query theory, all of which are offered by their authors as alternatives to loss aversion. These theories are described *infra*.

[102]    Others posit that ownership might create a psychological association between the object and the owner. Beggan (1992) found that subjects evaluate a good more favorably when they own the good even when they do not chose it. He suggested that this finding reflects a general tendency of people to make self-enhancing judgments—i.e., implicit evaluations of oneself are transferred to objects one owns. Similarly, Nesselroade et al. (1999) found that subjects tend to enhance their possessions when they compare them to possessions of the same type that others own. Kogut and Kogut (2011) found a correlation between subjects' self-reports of levels of attachment to those with whom they have close relationships, self-reported levels of attachment anxiety, and valuations of both sellers and buyers. They found a positive correlation between attachment anxiety and valuations, both as buyers and sellers, but more strongly for sellers. They concluded that some of the variation in valuations can be attributed to variation in attachment anxiety in close relationships that individuals transfer to goods. See Morewedge et al. (2009) for a summary of the broader literature in psychology.

with a monetary incentive to accurately predict their own WTA in terms of giving up a mug in the event they obtain one by correctly guessing the result of a coin flip. Once mug ownership was randomly determined, mug owners announced that they wished they had reported higher WTA. Why can't individuals predict the impact of ownership on valuation? The authors posited that "a person must be threatened with the loss of an object to appreciate his or her heightened attachment to it" (p. 935). They concluded that valuations reported for hypothetically owned goods or rights are likely biased downward.[103]

Carmon and Ariely (2000) reported data that supports the claim that potential buyers and potential sellers assess the value of the same item differently, which leads to divergent valuations. Their experimental data suggests that "buyers and sellers focus on aspects of the exchange associated with what they will forgo and differ in the attention they pay to attributes of the evaluated item and in how they evaluate what they notice" (p. 368), sometimes referred to as "focus on the foregone theory."[104] Nayakankuppam and Mishra (2005) designed an experiment to test whether the behavior reported by Carmon and Ariely (2000) was due instead to buyers and sellers focusing on different features of the good. For example, a potential seller might be more likely to notice the benefits he derives from a good and fail to notice its negative features. Buyers on the other hand might notice both positive and negative features when deciding whether and for how much to purchase a good. Their evidence suggests that potential buyers and potential sellers do, in fact, tend to focus on different aspects of goods, and this differential focus causes valuation gaps.[105] Okada (2010) found a similar result for goods with uncertain values that become

---

[103] Other researchers have explored whether individuals are able to predict and anticipate valuation gaps in themselves and in others. For example, Van Boven et al. (2000) predicted an underestimation of the magnitude of the gap due to "egocentric empathy gaps," an overestimation of the similarity between their own valuation and the valuation of the person on the other side of the transaction. In addition, they predicted that individuals make biased predictions about what their valuations would be if they found themselves on the opposite side of the transaction. They found evidence of both predictions. They also found that mis-estimation led to reduced earnings for subjects when placed in a market setting, suggesting that markets might not reduce the observed biases. Subjects who gained experience in the roles of both potential buyer and potential seller exhibited a smaller egocentric empathy gap. Later Van Boven et al. (2003) further explored whether ownership creates attachment utility. They reported experimental results suggesting that individuals do not anticipate endowment effects in their trading partners. Bischoff and Meckl (2008) offered a model to illuminate the normative implications of assuming that gaps are caused by attachment utility (which they label the "ownership-utility effect") as opposed to loss aversion. Specifically, they argued that if an ownership-utility effect as opposed to loss aversion causes gaps, then public goods will be overproduced under certain conditions.

The attachment utility hypothesis, however, has not enjoyed unanimous support. Loewenstein and Kahneman (1991), for example, pointed out findings from Kahneman et al. (1991) that suggested that pen owners were no more likely than non-pen-owners to rate pens highly on an attractiveness scale. In addition, the "instantaneous" nature of gaps seems to work against attachment theory, at least if it assumes that attachment requires some time to develop (Kahneman et al. 1990, p. 1342; but see Coren 2007, who suggested that attachment might occur instantly).

[104] Shu and Peck (2011; study 4) employed a hypothetical survey on valuation of basketball tickets to study whether a focus on the attributes of the object or money owned is correlated with feelings of ownership. Subject responses suggest a positive correlation.

[105] In the same vein, Casey (1995) proposed a "transaction encoding framework," predicting that individuals encode the transaction problem differently along a number of dimensions, only

certain after transactions occur (e.g., forward contracts).[106] She attributed valuation gaps to potentially different foci of owners and non-owners on the good's features—owners on positive features and non-owners on negative ones—that are driven by risk aversion.

Johnson et al. (2007) explored a similar theory, which they describe as a "query theory of value construction." They designed an experiment to test whether individuals determine valuations by answering a series of questions whose order differs depending on one's reference point. The idea is that the order of questions an individual asks herself when attempting to determine her value of an item differs depending on whether she owns the item, and the order systematically generates values that are higher for owned items relative to non-owned items. More specifically, the theory posits that potential sellers consider the advantages of keeping the item first and then the advantages of selling it, while potential buyers (or choosers) consider the advantages of not obtaining the item (the non-owner's status quo) and then the advantages of obtaining it. Judgments related to advantages and disadvantages are based on information retrieved from memory.[107] The asymmetry is purported to arise from the greater weight placed on answers to the question first considered.

To test their theory, Johnson et al. used the multiple price list format[108] to elicit the valuations of the subjects endowed with a mug and the subjects who were presented

---

one of which is endowment. While Casey (1995) acknowledged that some researchers observe no gap between WTP and WTA, his theory is not able to explain those findings.

[106]   Parametric tests were used although the distribution of the data likely does not satisfy the necessary assumption of normality, thus confidence in the results is limited.

[107]   Ashby et al. (2012) expanded query theory to include situations where information is, instead, provided during the valuation and preference construction phase rather than retrieved from memory. They derived a set of hypotheses that set out the assumptions of their Biased Evidence Accumulation theory. The theory assumes that potential buyers focus more on value-decreasing attributes relative to potential sellers, and this bias impacts valuation. Using eye-tracking devices, the authors found that potential buyers of lotteries attended more to the low outcome on average. They also found a negative correlation between time spent focusing on the low outcome and reported valuations, and a negative correlation between the gap and deliberation time, suggesting that as time passes, attention shifts—potential buyers begin to consider positive attributes of the good, and potential sellers shift their attention to negative attributes of the good.

In a similar study, Pachur and Scheibehenne (2012) designed an experiment to study information search behavior of owners and non-owners. To the extent that information is available to help determine valuations, they predicted that owners would stop searching after encountering signals of high value and non-owners after low-value signals. Subjects were allowed to play the lottery until they felt ready to value it. Each time they played a lottery, the computer would randomize over the possible outcomes according to the assigned probabilities and produce a result. Subjects then valued hypothetical lotteries as owners and non-owners. Observed within-subject valuation differences support the authors' search theory. Valuations as hypothetical owners exceeded valuations as hypothetical non-owners. Search termination was correlated with owner/non-owner roles and received signals—disparities in termination choices result in hypothetical owners and non-owner exposure to different samples from lottery plays. Sellers stopped searching after observing high value signals, and buyers after low value signals. Distributions of signals correlated with valuations.

[108]   The authors referred to the multiple price list method as the BDM mechanism, but, technically, the BDM mechanism requires subjects to report valuations rather than make a series of choices presented in the list. Use of the BDM mechanism avoids any influence experimenters might have on reported valuations when they choose prices that appear in the list (Anderson et al. 2006, 2007).

choices between the mug and various amounts of cash.[109] Subjects performed a "practice task," during which they reported non-binding valuations for induced-value items. Those who did not report the induced value were eliminated from the experiment. Subjects were also given tests of understanding, and those who failed were eliminated. All subjects were given a chance to inspect a mug placed in front of them.[110] They then proceeded to computers where they learned their endowment state (seller or chooser). Before using the list to make choices between the good and different amounts of cash, the subjects listed the aspects they considered in making the decision. The reported aspects were used to draw inferences about the questions subjects asked themselves and whether the order of the questions depends on the subject role. Subjects then used the multiple price list to report their preferences. A previously determined random number was announced, and transactions were completed. A valuation gap was observed—sellers and choosers reported average valuations of $5.71 and $3.42 respectively (statistically significant at the 1% level under both parametric and non-parametric tests of differences). The authors also noted differences between sellers' and choosers' descriptions of aspects. Sellers were more positive about the mug relative to the cash, and they listed positive mug aspects earlier than positive cash aspects. They concluded that this evidence supports query theory. Interestingly, they found that listed aspects explain much more variation in valuations than the endowment state, suggesting that endowment alone is insufficient to explain gaps and that individuals might be heterogeneous in how endowments impact query order.[111] One potential concern is priming. The impact of eliciting subject views on aspects immediately following endowment (or assignment to the chooser role) and before eliciting valuations is unknown. By eliciting views of aspects of items, the experimenters might have focused subjects' attention in a way that deviates from environments outside the lab. Additional research is required to explore this issue.

The studies summarized in this section all reported evidence in support of mere-ownership theory. These results are important, but they do not allow us to draw inferences about the impact of reference dependence and loss aversion, if any. It is quite possible that both explanations—mere-ownership theory and endowment theory—play a role in observed reluctance to trade. Morewedge et al. (2009) pointed out the difficulty in testing one theory against the other—both theories predict gaps in the presence of ownership.

---

[109]  Johnson et al. claimed that, by comparing valuations of potential sellers to choosers rather than potential buyers, they eliminated wealth effects. This is not true, however. Theoretically, at least, owners might feel wealthier on average relative to choosers because they received more from the experimenters than did the choosers. The endowment puts the sellers on different indifference curves relative to the choosers. The amount of the difference, however, likely is too small to trigger concerns that wealth effects drive the reported results. The eliminated concern is not income effects but budget constraints. Under this design, we don't have to worry about buyers announcing low valuations because they don't have cash available to pay an amount equal to their true valuation.

[110]  The practice task and test for understanding were motivated by results produced by Plott and Zeiler (2005) discussed *infra*. Plott and Zeiler showed that the gap disappears when controls for subject misconceptions about the valuation elicitation device are employed. Johnson et al. (2007) did not, however, employ all of Plott and Zeiler's controls, making it difficult to completely rule out subject misconceptions as a driver of the results.

[111]  Similarly, Shu and Peck (2011; study 3) replicated some of the study's findings and reported a correlation between query order and self-reported feelings of psychological ownership.

What is needed is a way to separate the theories by generating a design that leads to divergent predictions. To this end, Morewedge et al. designed an experiment to hold ownership constant and vary whether subjects experience a loss or a gain. Using the multiple price list method with a randomly generated price, they estimated the valuation of mugs by both sellers and by choosers who already owned one mug.[112] The owner-choosers were asked to choose between various amounts of money and a second mug. Endowment theory predicts that such owner-choosers would report lower values relative to sellers, while mere-ownership theory predicts they would report values equal to sellers. They assumed that owner-chooses will value a second mug the same as the owned mug. In support of mere ownership theory, they find equivalent average values of owner-choosers and sellers. One obvious alternative explanation is that some other difference between the two groups is driving the result—namely, that owner-choosers will end up owning a pair of mugs, which might increase their individual value over the value of an endowed single mug. To rule out complementarity, Morewedge et al. estimated the value of two mugs to those who own none and were asked to choose between two mugs and various amounts of cash. The per-mug value for non-owners was the same regardless of how many mugs the experimenters offered. This suggests that complementarity does not explain the main result.[113]

The authors were also interested in comparing valuations of seller-owners and seller-non-owners and the valuations of chooser-owners and chooser-non-owners. They estimated values by asking subjects to make choices as agents for others, some who have an opportunity to sell a good they own and others who do not own but are presented a choice between the good and some amount of money.[114] The authors claimed that endowment theory predicts that those acting as agents for sellers will report relatively high values regardless of whether they own the good. Alternatively, they argued, mere-ownership

---

[112]   Morewedge et al. referred to choosers as buyers for ease of exposition, but I use choosers here to maintain consistency with the descriptions of other studies.

[113]   Others have explored the impact of the number of goods owned or considered for purchase. For example, Burson et al. (2012) found variation in observed gaps for single units (gap in valuations for one chocolate) versus multiple units (no gap in valuations of 25 chocolates) versus multiple units described as one unit (gap in valuations for 20 chocolates described to subjects as a box of chocolates). They offered four possible explanations for this variation including modifications to endowment theory and alternatives to endowment theory. Schurr and Ritov (2014) studied the impact of the number of units but from a different angle. They found valuation gaps when subjects were forced to sell (buy) all or nothing, but not when they could sell (or buy) just some owned (or considered) units. They referred to this finding as the "giving-it-all-up effect." The authors interpreted this finding as evidence against endowment theory, which would predict gaps regardless of whether endowments or expectations set reference points. They did, however, suggest that loss aversion might depend on the magnitude of the change since individuals are not asymmetrically impacted by small losses. Of course this interpretation is rejected by many experiments that find valuation gaps for single low-value goods identical to those used by Schurr and Ritov. Their findings, though, might be important for identifying conditions under which we would predict valuation gaps. They suggested that gaps should not be expected when sellers decide to sell a few of many and buyers decide to buy a few more than they already own.

[114]   The experimenters did not deceive subjects. They later brought another group into the lab, randomly assigned them to the agents and gave them cash or mugs depending on the randomly determined price and the agents' choices.

theory predicts that those who own the good will report relatively high values regardless of whether they are acting as agents for sellers or choosers. Their findings support mere-ownership theory.[115] Valuations are higher for owners relative to non-owners, both for those representing choosers and for those representing sellers. Conditional on ownership, valuations do not differ depending on who is represented. These results seem to be in line with those Loewenstein and Adler (1995) reported. The findings are also consistent with previous results for non-owners Marshall et al. (1986) reported, although they suggested that individuals are loss averse but do not anticipate loss aversion in others. The results Morewedge et al. reported suggest this is not the case. If it were, we would have observed owners reporting valuations similar to those of non-owners, but we do not. We might wonder whether loss aversion is anticipated only if the agent is an owner, but Morewedge et al. found that owners report the same average valuation regardless of whether they are deciding for sellers or choosers, and those average values are higher than the values reported by both groups of non-owners. Thus, while the results cannot rule out loss aversion as a sufficient condition for valuation gaps, they do suggest it is not a necessary condition. In the end, however, the amount of weight we can place on any of the results is limited by the test Morewedge et al. used to measure gaps. They generated all results using parametric tests. Generally, non-parametric tests are employed in this literature given the likelihood that the data are non-normally distributed. Morewedge et al. did not report whether the data satisfy the normality assumption, so caution is warranted when drawing inferences from the results.[116]

### 6.5  Enhancement Theory

On a parallel track, others have investigated the influence of methods used in the laboratory to endow owners and to elicit choices. Plott and Zeiler (2007) revisited the line of research that explores the drivers of exchange asymmetries in experiments where subjects are endowed with one good and asked whether they'd like to trade their good for another good. The authors posited several potential influences acquisition and choice methods

---

[115]  Maddux et al. (2010) used the standard design based on Kahneman et al.'s (1990) BDM mechanism elicitation approach and found differences in the magnitudes of gaps for East Asians (smaller gaps) and Westerners (larger gaps). They attributed these differences to self-enhancement tendencies in Western cultures versus those in East Asia. Assuming that mere ownership causes gaps, Maddux et al. attributed the observed differences in gap magnitudes to the tendency of Westerners to engage in more self-aggrandizement than East Asians, which leads to higher valuations of owned goods that are infused with value from mere association with the highly valued self. It should be noted here, though, that the authors used parametric tests, the results of which might be invalid given that valuation data tends to be non-normally distributed.

Dommer and Swaminathan (2013) investigated why mere ownership leads an owner to increase his valuation for an endowed good. They reported evidence suggesting that owners increase valuation to enhance the self and that this effect is stronger when one's self-esteem is threatened. They also reported differences between males and females that they attributed to gender disparities in reactions to valuations as owners of out-group goods (i.e., goods associated with others). They suggested that such "motivational factors can often override the impact of loss aversion in influencing valuations for goods" (p. 1047).

[116]  See Schmidt and Traub (2009) for a useful discussion of the impacts of employing different statistical tests to measure gaps.

might have on reluctance to trade: (1) experimenters, through involvement over the choice of which good to endow, might signal something about relative value to subjects or suggest that the item is a "gift" from the experimenter;[117] (2) the language used to endow subjects and to elicit subject choices might suggest the relative value of the items;[118] (3) the location of the good at the time of choice might signal the relative value or generate positive transaction costs; and (4) choices might depend on what other subjects choose. To test these conjectures, the authors altered procedures used to endow subjects and to collect choices. Plott and Zeiler started by replicating the exchange asymmetry reported by Knetsch (1989)—this "standard procedures" treatment resulted in an asymmetry that was statistically significant at the 6% level. In a separate treatment, they implemented a set of procedures designed to control for the impact of acquisition and choice methods. The good to be endowed was randomly chosen rather than appearing to be chosen by the experimenter; the subjects were told, "These coffee mugs are yours" rather than "I'm giving you the coffee mug. It is a gift. You own it. It is yours"; subjects were asked to circle the item they wanted to take home with them (mug, pen, I don't care) rather than choosing between the options "I want to keep my mug" and "I want to trade my mug for a pen"; and subjects made choices privately and with neither the endowed good nor the alternative good in their possession. No exchange asymmetry was observed. They also ran a treatment that included the full set of controls but left both the endowed and alternative goods in the subjects' possession. Possession did not change the null result—no statistically significant exchange asymmetry was observed. These results provide support for the claim that exchange asymmetries are explained not by endowment theory but by classical preference theories such as signaling, information aggregation, and other-regarding preferences.[119] Some refer to this collection of conjectures as "enhancement theory" (Klass and Zeiler 2013).[120]

---

[117]    Others have posited similar conjectures. For example, see Nesselroade et al. (1999), who suggested that the giving of objects by the experimenter to the subjects "may have caused participants to enhance the value of the gift to thank the gift giver" (p. 23). Ericson and Fuster (2011) found support in their data for this conjecture, which they refer to as the "value inference effect."

[118]    Mandel (2002) also considered the impact of language used to elicit valuations. He designed an experiment to investigate potential confounds created by the language Thaler (1980) used to elicit valuations. Mandel hypothesized that by mentioning to each subject endowed with a hypothetical bottle of wine that "a wine merchant offers to purchase it from you," the experimenter might have signaled that the buyer might be willing to buy at a high price, triggering strategic considerations that move the reported valuation away from the subject's non-strategic valuation. While an available supplier was mentioned to buyers, the prompt did not mention any intention to sell. This insight was one of the earliest warnings about the subtle impact language can have on reported valuations.

[119]    Ericson and Fuster (2010, working paper version of Ericson and Fuster 2011, on file with author) argued that the language used by Plott and Zeiler (2007, p. 1459) ("We began these sessions by informing the subjects that mugs and pens would be used during the experiment. Subjects were then told that a coin was flipped before the start of the experiment to determine which good, the mug or the pen, would be distributed first. We then distributed mugs to the subjects and announced, 'These mugs are yours') triggered an expectation in subjects that they would also be given a pen or that they would have an opportunity to trade the mug for a pen. This is an open question.

[120]    This theory should not be confused with self-enhancement theory, which assumes that ownership triggers an increase in the value of a good because the owner associates the good with himself (Beggan 1992).

In a direct response to Plott and Zeiler (2007), Knetsch and Wong (2009) suggested that the disappearance of exchange asymmetries is due not to influences suggested by enhancement theory but rather by experimental procedures that diminish the subjects' reference state. For example, Knetsch and Wong posited that reference states are muddled when subjects possess both goods instead of just the endowed good, when the endowed good is randomly chosen as opposed to determined by the experimenter, and when the choice is neutrally framed (i.e., "Which good would you like to take home?" as opposed to "Would you like to trade your X for a Y?"). This muddling, the theory goes, diminishes the perception of the giving up of the endowed good as a loss to be avoided. Knetsch and Wong purported to test their theory by adopting all necessary controls to eliminate enhancements triggered by the experiment procedures and by generating reference states of varying strengths across treatments to test how this variable impacts exchange behavior. The theory predicts that exchange asymmetries will appear when the reference state, which might not hinge on ownership, is strong and thus more likely to trigger a perceived loss.

The authors designed three treatments to estimate the effects of reference state strength. However, despite their claim to the contrary, they could not rule out Plott and Zeiler's (2007) conjectures as drivers of the divergent outcomes across treatments. In Treatment 1 ("owned and weak reference"), all subjects were endowed with the same randomly chosen item. Subjects were told that they had "earned" the good and now owned it, and they could take it home with them if they wished to. After subjects had time to inspect the good, which was then removed from their possession, they were offered a trade and privately chose a good. Choices were presented neutrally—i.e., "which item would you like to take home?" In line with both theories' predictions, no exchange asymmetry was observed.

Treatment 2 ("owned and semi-strong reference") was identical to Treatment 1 except that the "earned" item was determined randomly using student identification card numbers. Half the subjects in the room were told that they owned one good, and the other half were told they owned the other. This design change was meant to enhance the reference state by creating a feeling of "deservedness" that comes from "winning" the good during the random assignment. As in treatment 1, subjects were given time to inspect the goods, but they did not possess them at the time of choice. Choices were made privately, but the language was changed to emphasize ownership ("keep X" or "trade X for a Y"), which was meant to enhance the reference state. Their theory predicts that these two design changes will result in a higher reluctance to trade relative to Treatment 1. The result was in line with this prediction, and the authors concluded that diminished reference states, rather than Plott and Zeiler's enhancement theory, explained Plott and Zeiler's (2007) results. The obvious problem here, though, is that enhancement theory *also* predicts a stronger reluctance to trade given the design changes. Specifically, it predicts that experimenter emphasis of ownership will signal the goods' relative values. In addition, while Plott and Zeiler did not discuss feelings of deservedness, increased reluctance to trade in response to the altered method of endowment is in line with their intuitions about how endowment methods might impact the perceived value of an endowed good. The same logic applies to telling subjects they earned the endowed good. While this feature can't account for any of the variation in choices across treatments because it is held constant across each of them, it is yet another way in which Knetsch and Wong did not control enhancements. So, despite Knetsch and Wong's claim that they ruled out enhancements, they in fact did not. For this reason, their design did not effectively separate their theory from enhancement theory.

Treatment 3 ("not-owned and strong reference") was plagued by the same problem. The authors' goal here was to test for the effects of design features predicted to produce strong reference points in the absence of ownership. In this treatment, the experimenter chose which good to (eventually) endow, which the authors predicted would strengthen the reference state. Subjects were told they don't own the good, but they would eventually if they earned it by completing a questionnaire. Subjects were allowed to inspect but not to use the good, which stayed in their possession. This design change is noted as a second feature meant to strengthen the reference state. After subjects completed the questionnaire, they were allowed to inspect the alternative good, which was then placed in front of the room, out of their possession. Subjects then made a private choice between "earn and keep the X" and "give up earning X and earn Y instead," language designed to strengthen the reference state in a third way. As their theory predicted, this treatment resulted in the largest exchange asymmetry. The problem, however, is that Plott and Zeiler's enhancement theory also predicted that this treatment would produce the largest exchange asymmetry. According to their enhancement theory, experimenter involvement in the choice over which good to endow, the placement of the goods, and the language used to elicit choices can all signal the relative value of the goods. Thus, Treatment 3, like the other treatments, was ill equipped to separate Knetsch and Wong's hypotheses from Plott and Zeiler's. While the experiment did provide evidence that ownership is not required to trigger reluctance to trade, it did not help us determine what exactly causes it in these types of settings.

Engelmann and Hollard (2010) set out to disentangle the number of potential drivers of exchange asymmetries posited by Plott and Zeiler (2007). They focused on two types of uncertainty that might impact choices: "choice uncertainty," defined as uncertainty about the relative values of the endowed and alternate goods that might arise from the public choices of others, and "trade uncertainty," defined as uncertainty about whether trading is optimal given potential transaction costs (e.g., experimenter involvement in the choice over which good to endow and decision costs in the presence of indifference). They also explored the role of trading experience on choices, following on work by List (2004). They hypothesized that List's (2004) results suggesting that trading experience seems to reduce exchange asymmetries are, in fact, driven by the possibility that those voluntarily choosing to gain trading experience are more likely to have less trade uncertainty. The basic idea is that exchange asymmetries are caused not by loss aversion of the inexperienced but by lower trade uncertainty of experienced traders, which makes it more likely for them to trade. The authors remedied this selection problem by strongly encouraging one set of subjects to trade to induce experience and reduce trade uncertainty. The authors conducted two treatments, both with two stages. In the first stage of the free-trade treatment, subjects were randomly endowed with a good and allowed to trade with other subjects if they wished to do so. In stage one of the forced-trade treatment, subjects lost their randomly endowed good if they did not trade it for an alternative good. In both treatments, an identical second stage was conducted where subjects faced the standard choice between an earned endowed good (chosen by the experimenter) and an alternative good.[121] The results suggest that forced trading in stage 1 drives higher rates of trading in stage 2. If we assume that even very limited trading experience reduces trade uncertainty for those who would otherwise not trade due to such uncertainty, this result supports the conjecture that trade uncertainty plays a role in exchange asymmetries. Engelmann and Hollard argued that experience is unlikely to change expectations that set one's reference point. Thus, endowment theory seems not to explain observed exchange asymmetries.

Ratan (2014) employed a different experiment design to test whether trade uncertainty affects reluctance to trade in simple exchange experiments. Ratan wondered whether anticipated regret theory might explain observed exchange asymmetries. If subjects were uncertain about whether to trade, then they might lean towards not trading to avoid the regret that might arise from a bad decision. He designed an experiment that reduced the likelihood that subjects would consider future regret when deciding whether to trade the endowed goods for the alternate goods. Specifically, subjects in the treatment group were allowed to reverse their decisions within 24 hours. Ratan observed an exchange asymmetry in the control group, which did not have an opportunity to reverse choices, but not in the treatment group. He concluded that removing any anticipation of regret is sufficient to eliminate reluctance to trade in simple exchange settings. He also noted that his result bolsters the more general claim that asymmetries are sensitive to small changes in the experiment design and calls into question the necessity of trading experience for elimination of exchange asymmetries.

Brown et al. (2015) were also interested in exploring which design features do the most work to trigger a reluctance to exchange one good for another. They began by reviewing the existing literature to generate a list of potential explanations that find support in the data.[122] They then reported the results from 11 experiments designed to test a series of hypotheses related to the potential drivers of exchange asymmetries. The experiments differed in the goods used, the number of endowed goods (all the subjects endowed with the same good or half of the subjects endowed with one and the other half with other), the location of the goods at the time of choice, the passage of time after endowment, and the method of choice (raised hands or private forms). The extreme trading observed by Knetsch (1989) was not observed in any of the 11 experiments. The lowest percentage of trading over all experiments was 21%. Exchange asymmetries were observed in all but two experiments. In one of the two, half the subjects received one good and half the other (to control for the signaling of relative value through endowment), subjects possessed

---

[121]  While stage 2 would have been cleaner if the experiments had endowed subjects with randomly chosen goods, the experimenters chose which good to endow and subjects earned them in both treatments, so any differences cannot be attributed to this design feature. It is impossible, however, to determine exactly what drives exchange asymmetries in stage 2 of the free-trade treatment.

[122]  The contenders are many: experimenter emphasis of the endowment (characterization as a gift, personal selection of the good by the experimenter, and language used to emphasize ownership), characterization of the decision as trading or choosing, the amount of possession time, whether the decision could later be reversed, location of the goods at the time of choice, utility or disutility from the act of trading (e.g., disutility experienced from the giving up of the good), and utility gained from impressions created by trading (e.g., trading out of solidarity because others are trading or to be part of the in-group ("herding") or not trading to avoid offending the experimenter). The authors added to the list the possible inability of subjects to rank the goods due to indifference or preference imprecision.

the endowed good but not the alternative at the time of choice, subjects completed an unrelated questionnaire after endowment and before choosing (to increase the "sense of attachment"), and they made public choices by raising hands. This result, however, was not robust to a change in the goods used. In the other no-asymmetry treatment, half the subjects received one good and the other half received the other, subjects possessed both goods at the time of choice, no time passed between endowment and the choice, and subjects chose privately. Given the large number of experiments and the variation in exchange asymmetries, it is difficult to pinpoint what's driving them, as the authors conceded. They tossed out some conjectures (e.g., possession of both goods might dull the sense of endowment,[123] asking the subjects to choose between the goods rather than to decide whether to trade or keep might focus subjects away from the fact that they own one of the goods, telling subjects that there are enough goods for everyone to get what they want might give them the impression that they are just choosing rather than keeping or trading). The data cannot resolve these questions, but, as the authors conceded, "[w]hat seemed at first like the simplest of experiments turns out to be surprisingly complex" (p. 115).

### 6.6   Valuation Elicitation Methods, Subject Misconceptions, and Market Instincts

As noted in the description of the literature's seminal studies, several early researchers pointed to valuation elicitation methods as potential drivers of observed reluctance to trade. While evidence that supported alternatives to endowment theory was often given short shrift in the early days, some attempted to reconcile the mixed results, a crucial step in theory development. In contrast to Knetsch (1989), Kahneman et al. (1990) and Tversky and Kahneman (1991), Singh (1991), for example, attempted to reconcile the entire body of existing literature. Singh's purpose was to check the robustness of reluctance to trade in a different subject pool—Malaysian civil servants as opposed to American university students—and, perhaps most importantly, to reconcile the results of previous studies. Singh begins by noting three insights from the existing literature: (1) demand-revealing mechanisms reduce the magnitude of valuation gaps but do not always eliminate them; (2) within-subject designs might provide a better measure of gaps and the method of measuring gaps matters (e.g., the ratio of median WTA to median WTP is less influenced by outliers than the ratio of mean WTA to mean WTP); and (3) the method of endowment might matter (e.g., reluctance to trade might disappear when an endowment is the result of a windfall).

Singh endowed all the subjects with $3 and no lottery tickets, two lottery tickets with an expected value of $1.50 each, or $1.50 plus one lottery ticket. He elicited (non-binding) valuations at the beginning of the experiment by asking each subject to report his WTA and WTP for a lottery ticket. He then allowed the subjects to trade lottery tickets in a double-bid auction in an hour-long market, which enabled subjects to learn their values

---

[123]   Kogler et al. (2013) found a disparity between choices made by owners and inspectors when asked to choose between two goods sitting next to each other on a table. Owners owned one of the two goods and inspectors were given time to inspect one of them. Ratan (2012) reported a similar result. This is some evidence that possession of both goods is insufficient to eliminate reluctance to trade.

for the lottery ticket.[124] At the end of the market, subjects again reported (non-binding) WTA and WTP for the lottery. The lottery outcome was determined, and subjects were paid according to their endowments at the end of the market. Before subjects participated in the market, a valuation gap was observed for the civil servants, but it disappeared after they gained experience valuing the lottery during market trading.[125] Singh also measured the gap using a sample of undergraduate and graduate students and observed no gap both before and after the market. He also asked another group to advise hypothetical clients on the highest WTP and lowest WTA, and no gap was observed, although he cautions against putting much weight on this result due to the hypothetical nature of the task. Thus, he finds that the gap disappears after subjects are given opportunities to discover their true valuations for the lottery ticket.

This evidence is in line with Harless's (1989) results, but what about the studies that report significant gaps and exchange asymmetries? Singh attributed the variation in results to the type of asset endowed—when risky but not uncertain assets are used, no gap is observed, but when assets with uncertain values (e.g., mugs) are employed, gaps appear. With respect to endowment theory, this sort of observation suggests yet another theory refinement. When we combine this refinement with those from Kahneman et al. (1990), endowment theory predicts reluctance to trade only if the asset has an uncertain value, if it will be consumed rather than sold or exchanged, and if it has no available perfect substitutes. This nuance seemed to be lost in the applications of endowment theory in law at the time.

Shogren et al. (2001) continued to explore how auction mechanisms impacted valuation gaps. They constructed an experiment that holds constant all features across treatments except for the auction mechanism.[126] In rounds using the BDM mechanism, the multiple price list format was used to elicit choices at various prices, and, between rounds, subjects were told the randomly drawn clearing price and how many buyers and sellers were willing to buy and sell at that price. In Vickery auction rounds, subjects were asked to write down a numerical value on a sheet (either the most they were willing to pay or the least amount they were willing to accept), and between rounds subjects were told the market-clearing price, which was determined by the subjects' bids. Endowment theory predicts gaps will persist regardless of the mechanism used to elicit valuations, assuming the mechanism is effective at encouraging reports of true valuations. The results revealed different outcomes across auction mechanisms, both of which are designed to elicit true valuations. In the BDM treatment, for both candy bars and mugs, gaps were observed in the first round and persisted throughout. In the Vickery auction treatment, however, while gaps appeared

---

[124]   In a double auction, owners and non-owners bid simultaneously, and owners willing to sell at prices lower than some non-owners' bids are matched with those non-owners, and trades are effectuated (Fudenberg and Tirole 1991).

[125]   Because the data were not distributed normally, Singh employed a non-parametric sign test to determine whether the median individual WTA-to-WTP ratio was greater than 1.1, which allows for a small income effect.

[126]   All subjects received $15 up front, ten rounds were conducted for each auction, candy bars and coffee mugs were auctioned, subjects were not informed of the retail price of the goods, participation was voluntary (as opposed to being a course requirement), and subjects were told that one round would be selected as the binding round at the end of the experiment.

initially, they disappeared by round 2 with candy bars and by round 4 with mugs (reappearing only in the eighth mug round). WTP increased and WTA decreased over the Vickery auction rounds. To test the conjecture that Vickery auctions do not induce the reporting of true valuations of bidders whose values are such that they will never trade,[127] the authors devised a clever auction mechanism—the random nth-price auction. In this auction, subjects do not know which value in the list of reported values will set the price from round to round. Under this auction mechanism, the valuation gap disappeared by the fourth candy bar round and by the fifth mug round, and it did not return. Shogren et al. (2001) did not directly test the conjecture that announced market-clearing prices between rounds might move reported valuations away from true valuations, but they pointed to contrary evidence published elsewhere (List and Shogren 1999). The authors concluded that their data do not support endowment theory and that the elicitation device at least partly explains observed gaps.

Sugden (1999) suggested that eliciting valuations might require more than the use of an incentive compatible mechanism. He argues:

> [T]he Becker-DeGroot-Marschak mechanism and the second-price sealed-bid auction are quite complicated, and their incentive-compatibility is not immediately obvious. . . . For example, a respondent who is presented with a purportedly take-it-or-leave-it offer may wonder whether the offer really is non-negotiable. . . . Thus, respondents might misrepresent their preferences in the mistaken belief that it was to their advantage to do so. . . . [I]n most bargaining situations, it is good tactics to try to give the impression that you are less eager to trade than you really are. . . . The point . . . is to try to influence the other party's belief about your reservation price; you want the other party to underestimate your maximum WTP, or to overestimate your minimum WTA. . . . [R]espondents' understanding of . . . incentive-compatibility may depend on the clarity of the instructions they are given and on the opportunities they are allowed for gaining experience of how the elicitation mechanism works. (pp. 162–163)

Plott and Zeiler (2005) designed an experiment to test a conjecture similar to Sugden's (1999). Specifically, they tested endowment theory against an alternative explanation related to subject misconceptions. Misconceptions, they posited, can arise both from lack of familiarity with the elicitation mechanism (Sugden 1999) and during the process of discovering one's value for a good (Plott 1996). The basic idea is that misconceptions might trigger subjects to revert to their basic market instincts to buy low and sell high.[128]

---

[127]    The authors conjectured that these subjects have no incentive to report true valuations as long as their reported valuations exceed the clearing price, information about which subjects gather from round to round.

[128]    Coren (2007, Chapter 3) attempted to flesh out this basic concept by developing a theory around the notion of bargaining scripts, which assumes that individuals' self-interested motivations when placed in bargaining environments are to maximize the amount obtained in exchange for the endowed good or to minimize the amount paid in exchange for the good. Her experimental data (gathered using hypothetical surveys) support the bargaining scripts hypothesis. Binmore (1994), in a much earlier critique of the field's response to anomalous behavior observed in the lab, argued that unless behavior is robust to environments that include strong incentives and ensure subject understanding of the nature of the tasks, "the experimenter has probably done no more than inadvertently to trigger a response in the subjects that is adapted to some real-life situation, but which bears only a superficial resemblance to the problem the subjects are really facing in the laboratory" (pp. 184–185).

After replicating valuation gaps using the Kahneman et al. (1990) design,[129] they altered the design in a number of ways: (1) subjects were provided training on the BDM using numerical examples that illustrated why it was in subjects' best interest to report their true values; (2) subjects were walked through examples on how to determine their true values;[130] (3) subjects participated in unpaid practice rounds, which provided time for questions and an opportunity for the experimenter to check for understanding;[131] (4) subjects participated in a number of paid practice rounds using lotteries, switching between buyer and seller roles throughout, to gain experience with the BDM mechanism;[132] and (5) subjects received payouts anonymously to eliminate the potential for signaling of personal characteristics through revealed valuations (Fremling and Posner 2001). These design changes were driven by a "revealed theory methodology," the adoption of the union of controls found in the literature to control for subject misconceptions about the elicitation device. The authors observed no gap in mug valuations in two experiments using different subject pools (USC Law students and Pasadena City College students).[133]

To test whether experience using the mechanism drove the results, a second group of USC Law students reported mug valuations using the same experiment design, except valuations were recorded before the paid practice rounds. No gap was observed, suggesting that experience with the mechanism is not required to control misconceptions.[134]

---

[129] Half the subjects, university students, were randomly assigned to be sellers and the other half buyers. Sellers were given mugs with the school logo. Buyers were allowed to inspect a mug. Subjects participated in two unpaid practice rounds using induced-value tokens and one binding round using mugs. Valuations were elicited using the multiple price list method. Payouts were made publically. Buyers used their own money and were told that credit and change were available at the beginning of the experiment.

[130] Potential buyers were instructed to start low and increase until they reach an amount that makes them indifferent between the money and the good. Potential sellers were instructed to start high and decrease to find their indifference point. The experimenter directly elicited individual valuations; the multiple price list format was not used. Non-owners who ended up purchasing a mug used money earned during the lottery rounds to pay for it. This is in contrast to the Kahneman et al. (1990) replication, in which buyers exchanged their own money for the mug.

[131] Corrigan et al. (2014) subsequently studied the impact of hypothetical practice rounds (in the absence of training on the mechanism) and found evidence that practice rounds seem to impact behavior in non-practice rounds and that multiple non-practice rounds seem to mitigate anchoring and subject misconceptions.

[132] Vondolia et al. (2014) reported evidence suggesting that subjects who had experience using trading mechanisms outside the lab reported different valuations for hypothetical goods in the lab. They found that "being familiar with monetary and labour payment vehicles attenuates time/money response asymmetry" (p. 13).

[133] In a separate study, Kovalchik et al. (2005) used similar procedures and observed no gap in valuations of healthy elderly individuals (average age 82). Roth (2005) also used similar procedures and observed no gap for consumer goods but gaps remained for risky assets. As discussed *supra*, Plott and Zeiler (2010, 2011) also observed gaps in lotteries. Kniesner et al. (2014) found no valuation gap in wage data from the field and suggested that the no-gap result might be due to the fact that labor providers likely have no misconceptions about the trading environment.

[134] Note that once subjects had written down their valuations, they were prompted to consider whether the offer was in fact their actual non-strategic value, and they were allowed to change the offer before committing to it. This procedure was intended to increase subjects' understanding of and attention to their non-strategic valuations, a measure that is required to test endowment theory. Kingsley and Brown (2012) noted that this revision prompt had not been previously used,

The results support the claim that gaps observed in the laboratory are caused not by loss aversion and reference dependence, but by the methods experimenters use to elicit valuations.[135] Candidates include the unfamiliar elicitation procedures and lack of anonymity. Recent evidence reported by Brown and Cohen (2015) supports unfamiliar elicitation procedures over anonymity.[136] These results in combination with Plott and Zeiler's suggest

---

and they wondered whether it might be driving the no-gap result. Using procedures similar to, but not the same as, Plott and Zeiler (2005), Kingsley and Brown (2012, p. 2582) replicated the no-gap result, but they also had subjects submit pre-prompt valuations. Rather than simply giving subjects an opportunity to change their offers, as Plott and Zeiler did, they told the subjects "before you commit to your . . . offer and we reveal the fixed offer, consider whether your offer reflects your actual, non-strategic, value of the mug. [Your offer] will be discarded." They required all subjects to submit another offer, although they informed the subjects that they were not required to alter their initial offer. The authors observed a gap in pre-prompt offers but not in post-prompt offers. They concluded that the prompt might have suggested to subjects that they did not go far enough in their iterations to find their non-strategic valuations (see *supra* footnote 130). The authors did note that it is impossible to determine whether pre- or post-prompt valuations more accurately reflect non-strategic valuations. It is possible, however, that the prompt might have led to overcorrections of strategic valuations. In a separate replication of Plott and Zeiler's no-gap result, Isoni et al. (2011), discussed *infra*, did not indicate that they allowed subjects an opportunity to revise their reported mug valuations. More research is required to fully understand the impact of this procedure and its role in the no-gap results reported in the literature. Note that Korobkin (2014) incorrectly pointed to Kingsley and Brown's (2012) findings as evidence of experimenter demand effects (post-prompt reconsideration "caus[e] buyers to believe they should move higher and sellers to believe they should move lower" (p. 12)); the data do not allow us to determine whether subjects are moving towards their true valuations or in the directions the experimenters "demand."

[135]   Köszegi and Rabin (2006, p. 1142) argued that Plott and Zeiler's (2005) results can be explained by reference-dependent preferences. They claimed that "Plott and Zeiler . . . successfully decoupled subjects' expectations from their initial ownership status." They did not explain what they mean by this or how Plott and Zeiler's design might have caused a "decoupling." It is possible that they are implying that the Plott and Zeiler procedures (e.g., putting each subject in the position of potential buyer and potential seller throughout the binding practice rounds) created an expectation that endowments would be sold. This is only a guess, but it seems at least a plausible interpretation. This interpretation might explain the results from treatments that elicit mug valuations after subjects participate in a number of practice rounds. It does not, however, explain the no-gap result in the treatment where mug valuations are elicited prior to the binding practice rounds.

Ericson and Fuster (2010, p. 26) argued that "the procedures and training used by [Plott and Zeiler] may not have induced a difference between buyers and sellers in their expectations of keeping the mug, as subjects may anticipate the possibility of trade." They did not provide detailed conjectures about which procedures might be setting expectations. We can rule out the binding practice rounds given the results of the second experiment that finds no gaps in the absence of practice rounds. It is possible, however, that training on the BDM mechanism might impact expectations over and above more basic messages used by others about optimal behavior—for example, Kahneman et al. (1990) explained the BDM mechanism and told subjects it was in their best interest to report their true values. It is an open question.

[136]   Brown and Cohen (2015) designed a 2 x 2 experiment to test the impact of anonymity on valuation gaps. Valuations were elicited from half the subjects using the procedures employed by Kahneman et al. (1990), half under conditions of anonymity and half whose valuations and payouts could be tied back to them. The other half reported valuations under the Plott and Zeiler (2005) procedures, half assigned to an anonymous condition and the other half to a non-anonymous condition. They observed valuation gaps in the Kahneman et al. treatments regardless of anonymity, and no gap in the Plott and Zeiler treatments regardless of anonymity. The results

that lack of familiarity with the elicitation device causes subjects to misconceive how their reported valuations will impact outcomes and encourages them to rely on their basic market instincts to sell high and buy low. If this conjecture is correct, it implies that the valuations subjects report in experiments that do not control misconceptions are strategic and not useful for testing theoretical assumptions about the deep structure of preferences including reference dependence and loss aversion.

A third potential explanation for Plott and Zeiler's null result is the house money effect. Potential mug buyers had cash to spend from lottery rounds in the controlled experiment but not in the Kahneman et al. replication, and they might have been more willing to spend cash "won" during the experiment relative to cash from their own pockets. Plott and Zeiler (2005) reported findings demonstrating that lottery round income and WTP are not positively correlated in experiments where subjects reported valuations after the lottery rounds, which stands as evidence against the house money effect. Despite this, WTP in the Kahneman et al. replication, in which subjects did not receive a show-up fee but were offered credit, is lower than WTP under the Plott and Zeiler procedures in treatments where potential buyers reported mug valuations after the lottery rounds.[137] In the Plott and Zeiler treatment where potential buyers reported mug valuations before the lottery rounds, subjects did not have the lottery winnings in hand when reporting mug valuations but they did receive a $5 show-up fee at the beginning of the experiment. If the house money effect were driving willingness to pay, we might expect mug valuations to fall somewhere between WTP from the replication and WTP from the controlled experiments since average lottery winnings fell well above $5. They are roughly in the same ballpark, however, as WTP valuations following the lottery rounds.[138] This is additional evidence that WTP is not correlated with the amount of cash received during the experiment prior to reporting WTP. In addition, gaps have been observed in the absence of show-up fees, and gaps remain when show-up fees are added.[139] More work is required to determine the impact of cash gained during the experiment and how it influences our ability to measure true WTP.

Landesberg (2007), in a study primarily designed to investigate the impact of familiarity with the good on valuation gaps, employed versions of the controls similar to those that Plott and Zeiler (2005) adopted to control subject misconceptions. Subjects participated in two practice rounds using induced-value tokens, one as owner and one as non-owner,

---

suggest that anonymity is not the driving factor in Plott and Zeiler's experiment and that subject misconceptions likely drove their no-gap result.

[137]   Mean and median WTP in the Kahneman et al. replication were $1.74 and $1.50, respectively. In Plott and Zeiler's treatments with mug valuations following the lottery rounds, mean WTP was $5.20 and 7.29 and median WTP was $5.00 and $8.00.

[138]   Mean WTP is $7.88 and median is $6.50. When one outlier is dropped, mean WTP is $6.50 and median is $5.00.

[139]   For example, Kovalchik et al. (2005) employed the Plott and Zeiler (2005) procedures but did not provide a show-up fee. They did not observe a valuation gap. Smith (2012) used Kahneman et al.'s (1990) procedures but added a show-up fee. He observed a valuation gap. Perhaps the strongest evidence against the house money effect conjecture is from Bartling et al. (2015), described *infra*. They not only gave subjects a large show-up fee, but they reminded subjects about the show-up fee when presenting all choices. The house money effect conjecture surely predicts no valuation gap, but they observe one.

and four binding rounds, during which half the subjects were owners and the other half were non-owners. They were allowed to ask questions during the practice sessions and the binding rounds, and many questions were fielded. Subjects were told that their choices and outcomes would be anonymous. During the binding rounds, the multiple price list method was used to elicit valuations for a voucher that could be exchanged for a sandwich. Subjects were told that one of the four rounds would be chosen at random and that the chosen round would determine payoffs.[140] The elicitation mechanism was explained using numerical examples, and subjects were told that it was in their best interests to report their true valuations as they made choices between the good (a voucher for a sandwich at a nearby shop)[141] and the various monetary amounts in the list. Subjects were told that credit would be available. The random market price was announced between each round. At the end of the experiment, subjects received $5 for participating in the experiment and transactions were anonymously executed. As a test of misconceptions, the author tallied the number of subjects who reported correct valuations for the practice round induced-value tokens. Ninety-eight out of 127 (77%) reported a $3 valuation for both practice round tokens, which could be exchanged at the end of the experiment for $3. Those who did not pass were dropped from the dataset.[142] The author observed valuation gaps in all four rounds using the voucher for the unfamiliar sandwich shop (WTA/WTP ratios between 1.27 and 1.40, all significant at the 99% confidence level) and smaller gaps in all four rounds using the voucher for the familiar sandwich shop (ratios between 1.12 and 1.23, two significant at the 90% level and two at the 95% level). What might explain the difference in results between this study and Plott and Zeiler (2005)? While the procedures used were similar, they were not the same.[143] For example, Landesberg did not walk subjects through the procedure Plott and Zeiler employed to help subjects understand the meaning of "true valuation" (buyers start low and increase until they reach an amount of money that makes them indifferent between the good and the money and sellers start high). In addition, Landesberg used the multiple price list method while Plott and Zeiler asked subjects to write down a valuation. The two studies also employed different goods. Given that the design is different from Plott and Zeiler's in more than one way, it is impossible to tie down what might be driving the divergent results. It is important to note,

---

[140]   It is important to note here that the binding trial was not randomly determined. The experimenter chose a trial with a random price below $5 because subjects were given $5 for participating in the experiment and transactions would be easier (no credit was required for buyers). This sort of deception is strongly frowned upon in experimental economics. It is not clear whether subjects detected the fraud during the experiment, but the paper clearly states that the author deceived the subjects.

[141]   In one treatment, the voucher was for a familiar sandwich from a shop with an average sandwich price of $4.50. In another treatment, the voucher was for a less familiar sandwich from a shop with an average sandwich price of $6.50. Subjects were not told the average prices of sandwiches from the two shops.

[142]   Seventy-nine percent of the dropped subjects were "endowment prone." They reported WTA higher than WTP, WTA above $3 or WTP below $3. Their valuations for the vouchers, however, did not differ much from those of subjects who passed the test, perhaps suggesting that both groups' understanding was roughly the same by the time they started the non-hypothetical sandwich voucher rounds.

[143]   Landesberg, in fact, claimed to have implemented a "more complete set of controls than did Plott and Zeiler (2005)" (p. 39), but this does not seem to be the case.

however, that Landesberg's instruction on the elicitation device might be responsible for reducing the gap from the usual ratio of 2 to 1 down to 1.4 to 1 at the highest.

Georgantzís and Navarro-Martínez (2010, p. 1) designed an experiment to shed light on the psychological basis for valuation gaps. They argued that their results cast "serious doubts on the claim that the gap might be just a consequence of inappropriate experimental practice." They correlated subject attitudes and feelings about the good, measured using survey instruments, with reported valuations to test theories based on mere-ownership and loss aversion triggered by preference uncertainty. They designed the experiment to "replicate" the valuation gap "using a standard design, while avoiding misconceptions as much as possible" (p. 897). Subjects were divided into two groups, choosers and owners (as opposed to buyers and sellers), and they reported their valuations for a bottle of wine in those roles using the multiple price list format.[144] Two surveys were administered before owners were endowed with the wine bottle. The first was designed to measure attitudes related to "general liking, attitude towards having the good, attractiveness, [and] design and quality" (p. 897), and the second attempted to measure the level of familiarity with the good using the prompt: "under normal conditions, would you buy a bottle of wine like this one?" (p. 898). Owners were then endowed with a bottle of wine, and choosers were allowed to inspect one. Next, subjects completed a second attitude instrument to measure attitudes related to "appearance, attractiveness, quality, taste, refinement, and general liking" (p. 897), and another instrument designed to measure levels of positive and negative feelings (e.g., happy, pleased, good, excited, upset, uncomfortable, awkward, bad).[145] Attitudes towards risk were collected for a portion of the subjects one week prior to the experiment during sessions conducted to run an unrelated experiment.

The authors reported several findings: (1) owner valuations are higher than chooser valuations; (2) choosers and owners report similar attitudes about the good after owners are endowed, even when divided into groups with non-positive and positive attitudes prior to endowment; (3) sellers reported having higher levels of positive feelings post-endowment relative to choosers, positive feelings were correlated with reported valuations, and reports of negative feelings were the same across treatments; (4) neither familiarity nor attitudes towards risk were correlated with chooser valuations, but owners who reported that they would buy a bottle of wine like the endowed one under normal conditions reported lower valuations relative to owners who reported that they wouldn't buy such a bottle; and (5) owners reporting higher levels of risk aversion valued the good more highly than those with lower levels of risk aversion. From these findings, Georgantzís and Navarro-Martínez concluded that: (1) subject misconceptions cannot explain the observed gap because they were controlled; (2) changes in attitudes related to the good do not cause gaps; (3) enhanced positive feelings caused by receiving and owning

---

[144] The working paper version of the study indicates that choosers chose between "I prefer the bottle" and "I prefer the money" for each possible price, and owners chose between "I keep the bottle" and "I exchange the bottle."

[145] The authors did not estimate within-subject differences in attitudes before and after endowment, arguing that such comparisons are not meaningful because they are different instruments measuring different attitudes, and might be plagued by contamination problems. They also measured personality traits, but they are not discussed here.

the endowed good (mere ownership) contribute to observed gaps; and (4) loss aversion contributes to observed gaps in the presence of unfamiliarity and uncertainty (i.e., those who would not normally purchase the good are less familiar with it, and thus feel more uncertain about their preferences related to it, increasing the level of loss aversion one would experience if the good were exchanged for money). They argued that Plott and Zeiler's (2005) procedures, such as repeated practice rounds, undermine the "necessary psychological underpinnings" (p. 906) of the valuation gaps that they uncover.

Whether these findings help us separate experiment design issues from mere ownership theory and uncertainty-driven loss aversion is unclear. First, although Georgantzís and Navarro-Martínez argued that the design "avoids misconceptions as much as possible" (2010, p. 897), it is possible that the observed gaps resulted from features of the design that Plott and Zeiler (2005) identified as potential drivers of gaps. For example, subjects were not told that their choices would be anonymous,[146] and, perhaps more importantly, subjects were not trained on the elicitation device. As Plott and Zeiler (2005) emphasized, although the multiple price list format seems quite simple, subjects might not fully grasp the idea that they are best off when they report their true preferences. In addition, even though subjects are not labeled as buyers and sellers, for owners who misconceive how their price-by-price choices will map into outcomes as a function of some randomly generated price, the choices of "keep" or "exchange" might be sufficient to trigger basic seller-type instincts to choose to exchange only at the higher prices in the list. Thus, we cannot rule out misconceptions, at least as Plott and Zeiler (2005) conceptualize them, as drivers of the observed gap.

While Georgantzís and Navarro-Martínez argued that their results cast serious doubt on Plott and Zeiler's misconceptions conjecture, it might be consistent with them. Features Plott and Zeiler included in the design to eliminate misconceptions and other influences are not present here; thus, misconceptions about how choices map onto outcomes might have triggered the basic instincts of the owners, now in a position to exchange their good for money, to exchange at a high price. What do we make, then, about differences in emotions between owners and choosers and the correlations between risk aversion and owner valuations, and between familiarity and owner valuations? It is entirely possible that owners report more positive feelings than choosers simply because they just received a good. Those positive feelings, however, might be unrelated to valuation gaps if subjects turn their attention to uncertainty about the elicitation device once the experimenter asks them to choose between the good and various amounts of money. Also, lack of familiarity with the good and higher levels of risk aversion might feed into subject reactions to the unfamiliar elicitation device. Both might impel owners towards basic instincts when they face the unfamiliar device. Choosers don't have basic instincts to fall back on. Alternatively, owners might worry that when the experimenters observe their non-anonymous choices, they might perceive low-value owners in some negative way—as soft bargainers or as individuals who lack gratitude for "gifts," etc. The lack of anonymity makes it impossible to rule out these sorts of owner reactions.

---

[146]   Subject instructions are not included in the published version of the paper, but they do appear in a working paper version (on file with author). Note, however, that Brown and Cohen (2015) reported evidence suggesting that anonymity does not impact the results.

Second, Georgantzís and Navarro-Martínez's explanation of Plott and Zeiler's results is problematic. They argued that "[t]he fact that the gap can be eliminated shows just that the necessary psychological underpinnings for it to appear can be undermined through experimental procedures (like, for example, repeated practice rounds that may lead subjects to perceive the good as something they trade)" (2010, p.17). Although an interesting research question, the claim is mere conjecture given their results do not provide evidence to support it. Something they did not note is that Plott and Zeiler's subjects did not trade mugs until the final round used to measure gaps. Lotteries were used in the repeated practice rounds. It is less likely that trading lotteries in the practice rounds led subjects to perceive mugs as something they trade. If this were true, however, then we might predict no gaps in the field where people transact regularly, although perhaps they don't sell sufficiently regularly to consider goods as objects of trade. It's an open question. In any event, Plott and Zeiler observed no gap even when subjects did not participate in the repeated binding practice rounds, so practice rounds can be ruled out as a potential underminer. What's left then? It is possible that other procedures might do the undermining. Referring to subjects as buyers and sellers or training on the elicitation device might somehow do the work. We can't be sure without evidence. To test this, the authors might have incorporated these features into their design in a second experiment to examine whether reported emotions and other psychological underpinnings are different in the presence and absence of the relevant features.

Koh and Wong (2013) suggested an alternative interpretation of Plott and Zeiler's (2005) results. They proposed that certain procedures might have caused the gap to disappear due to the reduced salience of gains and losses. They listed specific procedures that led to this concern: buyers and sellers both possessed the good at the time of valuation, the experiment did not frame transacting in terms of gains and losses, and owners and non-owners received both buying and selling instructions. More specifically, the authors wondered whether these procedures might have weakened the reference state so that subjects treated their endowment status as irrelevant. In addition, they hypothesized that training procedures presenting yes/no questions related to plausible mug values employed to train subjects on how to find their true valuations might have caused subjects to anchor on those values. Plott and Zeiler's verbal training procedure ended with an example of $6.50 as a valuation for an owner and $5.25 as a valuation for a non-owner. Koh and Wong wondered whether subjects might have anchored on one of these values depending on their roles as potential seller or potential buyer. In a treatment intended to replicate Plott and Zeiler's (2005) Treatment 2 (anonymity, training, two hypothetical practice rounds but no binding experience), the authors found mixed results.[147] In a second

---

[147] The result from a Wilcoxon-Mann-Whitney rank sum test on a sample pooled across four different sessions supports the claim that a valuation gaps exists (at the 95% confidence level), but the result from a median test cannot reject the null hypothesis of no difference between WTA and WTP. One unemphasized difference between Plott and Zeiler and Koh and Wong's attempted replication is the payment of the show-up fee. Plott and Zeiler paid $5 to subjects upon arrival. Koh and Wong "eventually paid [a] $5" show-up fee. It's possible they paid the fee at the end of the experiment rather than the beginning. If so, this might be evidence of a house money effect in Plott and Zeiler's Treatment 2 no-gap result. See the text accompanying footnote 137 for a more detailed discussion of this conjecture.

treatment, only sellers possessed the mugs. Buyers were allowed to inspect but did not possess at the time of valuation. Sellers were told "the mug you are inspecting is yours to take home with you at the end of the experiment, if you decide to keep it later." The instructions were edited to change "the item" and "the mug" to "my mug" and "your mug" for owners. Owners received only the owner instructions and non-owners only the non-owner instructions. Finally, the training procedure was altered so that the example ended with $650 as a valuation for an owner and $525 as a valuation for a non-owner, and subjects were told that these were hypothetical examples. The authors observed a valuation gap in this treatment. They ran a third treatment to determine whether the results from their second treatment would change if the Plott and Zeiler examples were used rather than the examples using implausible mug valuations. The result did not change—a valuation gap was observed. The authors interpreted these findings as evidence that Plott and Zeiler's procedures weaken the subjects' reference states and that the weakened reference states caused the gap to disappear. An alternative interpretation based on Plott and Zeiler's 2007 study is that the change in procedures generated enhancement effects. For example, subjects in the owner-only sessions who were repeatedly told that the mug was theirs might have perceived the mug as a gift from the experimenter and perceived the repeated emphasis on "yours" and "mine" as signals of value. Koh and Wong's results, however, stand as some evidence against Plott and Zeiler's misconceptions conjecture.

Evident from the descriptions included in this chapter, experimenters commonly employ the theoretically demand-revealing BDM mechanism to elicit valuations.[148] Although Plott and Zeiler's (2005) results suggest that training on the mechanism might be required to control subject misconceptions over how their reported valuations map into outcomes, training has not caught on. Some have argued that training somehow changes subjects' reference points (e.g., Köszegi and Rabin 2006) or that elaborate training procedures train subjects to do what the experimenters want them to do (assess true values) when they would not do so in the field (e.g., Kahneman 2011). To further investigate potential misconceptions related to the BDM mechanism, Cason and Plott (2014) designed an experiment to elicit valuations for cards worth $2 if owned at the end of the experiment. Given that all theories predict that subjects will value the cards at $2, the authors used reported valuations that deviated from $2 to test theories related to subject misconceptions about how their choices map onto outcomes. They found that with basic instructions and no training or feedback, only 17% of subjects reported values of $2. After outcomes were determined using the BDM mechanism, subjects participated in an identical second round. Following one round of feedback, 31% of subjects reported values of $2. Those who initially chose $2 tended to stay with $2 in the second round, but those who made a sub-optimal choice in the first round tended to choose a different value in the second round. Subjects who made costly mistakes in the first round were more likely to value the card at $2 relative to those who made

---

[148]   But see Loomes et al. (2010) ("A guiding principle for the design, widely accepted among stated preference researchers, is that individuals cope more easily with conditional questions requiring yes/no responses ('If the price was x, would you buy?') than with unconditional open-ended questions using maximum or minimum concepts ('What is the highest price you would pay?'))" (p. 380). They did not provide support for the claim of wide acceptance.

inconsequential mistakes.[149] They demonstrated that simple interpretations might lead to conclusions that the data support theories grounded in framing (such as endowment theory with reference points set by either endowments or expectations), but more sophisticated analyses suggest that theories that assume "game form misconceptions" fit the data better. Specifically, the data suggested that a substantial portion of subjects "believe that the payment mechanism is similar to a first-price procurement auction in which the lowest offer wins and is paid the offer price" (Cason and Plott 2014, p. 1257). The basic conclusion is that unless misconceptions are controlled, it is difficult to determine whether game form misconceptions or framing theories (or other sorts of theories) explain observed phenomena. In addition, if testing a theory or set of theories requires the elicitation of non-strategic (or true) valuations, the presence of game form misconceptions will make testing those theories impossible.

In line with the insights of Cason and Plott (2014), Loomes et al. (2010) tested whether market discipline shrinks observed valuation gaps. They designed an experiment to investigate how feedback generated by the market impacts reported valuations. If market discipline works to encourage the reporting of true valuations and individuals are not loss averse, gaps should decrease in magnitude and eventually disappear as the market institution administers discipline. Specifically, the market discipline hypothesis predicts that negative experiences triggered by non-optimal choices that are punished by the market will encourage optimal choices—in this context the reporting of true valuations—in subsequent rounds. The authors employed a median-price auction, which is demand revealing but does not systematically bias bids and asks.[150] After explaining the auction procedures, subjects participated in two hypothetical practice rounds for induced-value vouchers (i.e., tickets with a certain value that can be exchanged for cash at the end of the experiment). Next subjects took part in two binding practice rounds, one as owner and one as non-owner. Subjects were then trained on the special features of the auctions for lottery tickets, and two hypothetical practice rounds were conducted using lottery tickets (e.g., a 19% chance of winning X and an 81% chance of winning Y). Following the practice rounds, eight lottery rounds were conducted, two of which collected measures of WTP and WTA used to estimate the valuation gap. Subjects reported their valuations by answering a series of yes/no questions (e.g., would you pay X to get a lottery ticket?) ordered to narrow down to true valuations. After each round the market price was announced for that round, and subjects were informed about their outcomes. Each auction was repeated six times. One round of one auction was chosen at random at the end of the experiment, and payments were made based on the outcome of the chosen auction round. Valuation gap magnitudes

---

[149]  For example, if a subject reported a valuation of $3 and the random offer was $4, the subject would receive $4, the same amount he would have received had he reported $2 as his valuation. He loses only if the random offer falls between $2 and his higher reported valuation. In that case, he would keep the card and receive $2 rather than the higher random offer.

[150]  Second-price auctions, the authors pointed out, might encourage owners to increase (and non-owners to decrease) reported valuations across rounds. This is due to the fact that the announced market clearing price in owner (non-owner) auctions likely will be higher (lower) than the average valuation, and the announced prices might give rise to "shaping effects"—a tendency for subjects with uncertain valuations to shift their reported valuations towards the announced market clearing price.

decreased over the rounds but did not completely disappear. The authors interpreted this result as support for the market discipline hypothesis.

Lunn and Lunn (2014) proposed a "computational theory of exchange" in line with, but more precise than, Plott and Zeiler's (2005) notion of reliance on basic instincts: sell high and buy low. Specifically, Lunn and Lunn assumed that individuals, when responding to elicitations of valuations in unfamiliar settings, "behave as if they are at the start of a potential sequence of trading opportunities, when in fact they are in a one-shot market that will clear at a single price" (p. 5). The basic idea is that "agents will simply extend a logic that they use successfully outside the laboratory to a one-shot experiment where, effectively, it backfires" (p. 5). The model predicts that WTA will exceed WTP because owners, aiming to maximize their surplus, will ask for an amount that exceeds the true value and that depends on their beliefs about what others are willing to pay, and non-owners, also aiming to maximize their surplus, will offer an amount that is lower than the true value and depends on their beliefs about what the current owners are willing to accept. Owners and non-owners both assume that they will get a chance to make another offer if the first is rejected and another if the second is rejected, and so on, even if the rules of the auction do not allow for this. The model also predicts that, if an individual is choosing between the good and cash, he will report his true valuation or certainty equivalent (CE). The prediction that separates this theory from others is the relationship between the CE and the reported valuations of owners and non-owners. The model predicts that as one's CE increases, the ratio between WTA and CE should approach 1 from above, and the ratio between WTP and CE should approach 1 from below. Lunn and Lunn derived predictions about the relationships between CE, WTA, and WTP for five alternative theories, all of which differ from the predictions from their theory. They used data from previously published studies to test their theory against the others. Data gathered by multiple experimenters supported the model and did not support predictions of the alternative theories. The authors argued that the theory is consistent with self-reports of how subjects set WTA and WTP, the observed correlation between willingness to exchange and perceptions of what others will pay or accept, subject perceptions of market prices, subject responses to feedback on what others pay or accept, and associations between the likelihood of future exchange and reluctance to trade. They claimed that the model might also provide insights into the findings of both Plott and Zeiler (2005) and List (2003), but they did not elaborate.

Finally, Bartling et al. (2015), building on Cason and Plott (2014), studied whether misconceptions about the elicitation device are necessary to produce valuation gaps. Bartling et al.'s aim was to implement procedures to control misconceptions in experiments that asked subjects to value induced-value cards and to determine whether such controls eliminate valuation gaps. In each session, subjects were randomly assigned to be either all buyers or all sellers and were told they would get a show-up fee of 25 CHF. The multiple price list method was used to elicit valuations for an induced-value card that could be exchanged at the end of the experiment for 8.50 CHF. Both buyers and sellers received a card. Buyers were told that they could purchase it; sellers were told that the card was theirs and that they owned it but that they could sell it to the experimenter. The multiple price list was different from the usual list. In each row, the list informed subjects of the outcome of each choice. For example, the buyers' list contained two rows not included in the usual list: one labeled "Final payoff (25 CHF – price + value of card)" and the other labeled "Final Payoff (25 CHF)." The cells in these two columns revealed the total payout that would result for each option in that row. For example, in the row asking whether the subject would be willing to purchase the card for 1 CHF, the subject was informed that he would gain 32.50 CHF if he bought at that price and 25 CHF if he did not. Subjects were constrained to a single switching point. After subjects made choices in each row, they were required to report the final payoff for each choice. The list, including columns with final payoffs for each choice, was in front of them during this exercise. Each subject was allowed to alter choices in this phase. If the subject entered all payoffs correctly, he earned 2 CHF. If mistakes were made, the subject was asked to try again. The subject could continue only when all answers were correct. Subjects then conducted the same exercise with one alteration—the induced-value card was replaced with a box of chocolates.[151] As in the first part, the outcome of each choice was presented to the subjects. For example, in the row asking whether the subject would be willing to purchase the box for 1 CHF, the subject was informed that he would gain "24 CHF + chocolate" if he bought at that price and 25 CHF if he did not. As in the first part, subjects were required to report how much money they would receive for each option and whether they would get the chocolate. Changes were possible during this phase, subjects were paid for correct answers on the first attempt, and they could move on only if all answers were correct.[152] Given that the outcomes from each choice were presented to the subjects, Bartling et al. unsurprisingly observed a higher rate of optimal choices in the induced-value card exercise than did Cason and Plott (71% v. 17%). Eighty-one percent of subjects correctly reported the outcome for each choice at the first attempt. Bartling et al. then split the subjects into two groups based on their performance in the first part. A subject was categorized as "sophisticated" if she both valued the card correctly and correctly identified outcomes across all potential prices at the first attempt in both parts. The main result was that a statistically significant valuation gap for the box of chocolates was observed when including only subjects classified as sophisticated. The authors interpreted the results as evidence that gaps can persist even in the presence of evidence of a lack of misconceptions. Unfortunately, they did not go one step further to give the reader a sense of which theories might best explain the observed gap.

### 6.7 Gaps in Lottery Valuations: Loss Aversion, Question-Influenced Beliefs, Focus Bias, or Gambling Wealth?

Several researchers have studied reluctance to trade lottery tickets. While endowment theory, which assumes a riskless environment and a market for a certain good (e.g., mugs, pens, and chocolates), makes no predictions about disparities in lottery valuations, Kahneman and Tversky's (1979) prospect theory does. The nature of lotteries gives rise to a number of alternative theories as well. This section begins with a debate involving valuations of lotteries by subjects in Plott and Zeiler's (2005) practice rounds. Following

---

[151] The boxes were purchased from a local, well-known shop at a retail price of 17 CHF. Subjects were not informed of the price.

[152] The authors used audio recordings to instruct the subjects and posted the recordings on-line for easy access. This potentially allows for better replicability relative to having the conductor of the experiment read the instructions aloud.

that, a quick overview of more general studies of lotteries and the theories developed to explain reluctance to trade lotteries is provided.

Isoni et al. (2011) questioned the generalizability of Plott and Zeiler's (2005) misconceptions conjecture by pointing to the fact that valuation gaps remain in Plott and Zeiler's 14 practice rounds using lottery tickets. The authors posed the question: if procedures are in place to mitigate misconceptions, what explains observed gaps in the lottery rounds? Plott and Zeiler's design was replicated in some aspects, but not all, although the differences arguably are irrelevant given that the results were similar in all relevant aspects to Plott and Zeiler's results. Isoni et al. observed gaps for four out of five lotteries. Using Plott and Zeiler's data, they also reported gaps in all their lottery rounds. They concluded that it is "not credible to propose that misconceptions about a common set of elicitation procedures persist . . . and then suddenly disappear when the mug task is faced" (2011, p. 1005). The authors offered some conjectures to explain the mug results—that design features might have "reduced the salience of the distinction between buying and selling tasks," that placement of mugs in front of both buyers and sellers might have affected subjects' reference points (presumably the implication is that buyers' reference points were impacted by possession in the absence of ownership), that training and practice somehow weaken an individual's perception of "not trading" as a reference point (although this is less likely in Plott and Zeiler's Treatment 2, where subjects report mug valuations before the 14 paid lottery rounds), that the no-gap mug result was driven by house money effects triggered by the payment of a show-up fee,[153] and that the differing nature of the goods (mugs v. lotteries) explains the disparity in results.

Plott and Zeiler (2011) provided a more nuanced analysis of the lottery data both from Plott and Zeiler (2005) and Isoni et al. (2011), which demonstrates that the data do not support endowment theory, despite the presence of a gap and Isoni et al.'s claim that they controlled for "all sources of contamination." The problems seem to stem from issues listed in Plott and Zeiler (2005; footnote 15), including subjects' perceptions of the nature of randomization and the concept of probability. First, in the four lottery rounds using degenerate lotteries with certain outcomes (e.g., 50% chance of 20 cents and 50% chance of 20 cents), an average of 23% of Isoni et al.'s subjects reported strictly dominated valuations. Interestingly only 3% of Plott and Zeiler's subjects on average did the same. The difference in procedures used during the training rounds might explain the disparate results. In addition, 13% of Isoni et al.'s subjects and 8% of Plott and Zeiler's subjects reported valuations at or outside the range of possible outcomes in the large stakes lottery rounds with non-negative outcomes.

Perhaps more telling, subjects were more likely to ask at or above the upper bound as sellers, and bid at or below the lower bound as buyers. When these subjects are removed from the dataset, gaps disappear for two of the ten examined lotteries (using 90% confidence as the cut-off), and the magnitude of the gap diminishes substantially for the others. These results suggest potential asymmetric beliefs about the outcomes of the lotteries that are tied to buyer/seller roles. Plott and Zeiler (2011) also reported evidence rejecting prospect theory's assumption of stable risk preferences in the domains of gains and losses. Specifically, prospect theory assumes risk aversion when uncertain gains are

---

[153]   See text accompanying footnote 137.

valued and risk seeking behavior when uncertain losses are valued. The lottery valuation data reported by both Plott and Zeiler (2005) and Isoni et al. (2011) fail to support this basic assumption of prospect theory.

Plott and Zeiler (2011) referred to the potential impact of ownership on beliefs as a "question-influenced beliefs conjecture," and it stands as an alternative explanation for lottery gaps.[154] In fact, given the evidence that subjects might perceive the same lottery as two different items (with two different likely outcomes), lotteries might be ill-suited for testing endowment theory, which assumes that buyers and sellers value the *same good* differently given loss aversion. Even if we start with the assumption that the goods are the same in the eyes of buyers and sellers, the question-influenced beliefs conjecture stands as an alternative to endowment theory, and the employed designs cannot separate them. Plott and Zeiler (2010) laid out a potential roadmap for applying revealed theory methodology to control for lottery misconceptions using controls adopted in the literature involving lottery valuation elicitation.

Finally, Plott and Zeiler (2011) called into question Isoni et al.'s alternative explanations for the no-gap results in Plott and Zeiler's (2005) and Isoni et al.'s (2011) mug rounds. In the end this conversation raises more questions than it resolves: What exactly causes gaps in lottery rounds? How can we control for misconceptions related to the nature of randomness? How might show-up fees impact on buyer valuations? How might possession impact buyer valuations? How might training and practice related to the elicitation device impact on one's reference point? While some research exists on many of these questions (and is discussed throughout this chapter), more work is required to better understand these various influences.

Rather than implementing Plott and Zeiler's revealed theory methodology to control for lottery misconceptions, Fehr et al. (2015) took a different approach to test Plott and Zeiler's misconceptions conjecture. They used procedures similar to Plott and Zeiler's (2005) treatments with binding experience (i.e., the lottery rounds) to elicit valuations for lotteries and commodities (mugs and USB sticks). Subjects were trained in both the BDM procedure and how to locate their true valuations, and they participated in two practice rounds, during which they were allowed to ask questions in private (as opposed to publicly in Plott and Zeiler). Also, unlike in Plott and Zeiler, choices and payouts were not anonymous.[155] Akin to Bartling et al. (2015), Fehr et al. then used reported lottery valuations to categorize subjects as either "rational" or "irrational." For example, they categorized a subject as "rational" if he reported valuations that were either on or inside the lottery bounds for all lotteries. Of the 95 subjects who reported valuations for a mug in the final round, 42 (44%) fit the bill. Using only the mug valuations of these subjects, a valuation gap was observed. The authors interpreted this as evidence against the misconceptions theory. Using other definitions of "rational," they found similar results. The second major finding was that, unlike Plott and Zeiler (2005) and Isoni et al. (2011),

---

[154] Given the experiment design, it is impossible, of course, to separate the impact of question-influenced beliefs on valuations within the bounds from the impact of loss aversion or other forces. It is reasonable, though, to believe that question-influenced beliefs play at least some role in gaps for subjects who did not bid at or outside the lottery bounds.

[155] Recall, however, that Brown and Cohen (2015) reported findings suggesting that results are similar under anonymous and non-anonymous conditions.

they observed gaps in valuations of both mugs and USB sticks. Thus, the main result of the two previous studies was not replicated. These results potentially called into question the stability of the no-gap result under the Plott and Zeiler (2005) procedures, but were inconsistent with numerous replications of the no-gap result (see, e.g., Kovalchik et al. 2005; Roth 2005; Isoni et al. 2011; Kingsley and Brown 2012; Brown and Cohen 2015).

Others have studied gaps in lottery valuations, and the results support a number of theories. Some have gone back to basics to study the impacts of income effects. Schmidt and Traub (2009) designed an experiment to study within-subject gaps in lotteries and whether income effects cause observed gaps in lottery valuations. They controlled income effects by endowing buyers with an amount of money equal to the highest possible outcome of the lottery endowed to sellers. In addition, in most rounds all buyers and sellers started from and ended in a risky position, which controlled any influences of movements from risky to non-risky positions and vice versa. They concluded that income effects cannot account for gaps in lottery valuations, but that the experiment design might. In particular, their data suggest that lottery valuation gaps might be driven by disparities in starting and ending risk positions across buyers and sellers and by between-subject gap measurement. Interestingly, just as reported by Plott and Zeiler (2011), some of Schmidt and Traub's subjects reported valuations above the largest possible outcome and below the smallest possible outcome. These data suggest a possible misunderstanding of the nature of lotteries, an issue in need of further study.

Others have explored whether gaps are robust in terms of the size of the stakes. Blavatskyy and Pogrebna (2010) cleverly employed data compiled from the television show *Deal or No Deal*, where contestants are given sealed boxes containing some unknown amount of money picked from a known distribution of possible monetary prizes ranging from one cent to half a million euros and asked whether they wish to exchange it for another sealed box containing a different unknown amount of money picked from the same known distribution. Their results suggest that when individuals choose in high stakes environments, exchange asymmetries are substantially reduced.

Others have tested psychological theories related to risk perception. Peters et al. (2003) tested a theory related to affect, which assumes that, when valuing lottery tickets, owners focus on the best possible outcome and have negative affect towards giving up the chance to win that amount. Non-owners, on the other hand, focus on the amount of money they must give up to obtain the ticket and on the likelihood of ending up with the worst possible outcome.[156] Peters et al. elicited valuations for lotteries with two possible non-negative monetary outcomes (e.g., a 5% chance of winning $100 and a 95% of winning nothing). Subjects reported their feelings towards the lottery—sellers were asked to report

---

[156]   This research builds on an earlier study by Einhorn and Hogarth (1985). They posited that owners and non-owners of insurance would pay different amounts of attention to possible losses when considering whether to sell or buy insurance, which drives owner valuations higher than non-owner valuations. The authors found a predicted gap between valuations of buyers and sellers of (hypothetical) insurance. Others have posited different models of lottery value construction. For example, Johnson and Busemeyer (2005) developed the Sequential Value Matching model, which assumes that sellers start with a high price and then insufficiently adjust downwards to reach their indifference point, whereas buyers start with a low price and insufficiently adjust upwards on the way towards their indifference point.

how they would feel about not having the ticket, and buyers were asked how they would feel about having the ticket—and then each subject reported valuations as both buyer and seller, half as seller first and half as buyer first. The BDM mechanism was used to encourage subjects to report non-strategic valuations, and subjects were trained on how the mechanism works. The theory predicts higher valuations for potential sellers. The authors observed a valuation gap and reported other evidence supporting their posited role of affect. The authors acknowledged the possibility that the form of the questions about affect might have caused the gap, but they downplayed it given the gap's robustness in the literature to date. What we have learned about procedures since then, however, suggests that getting subjects to focus on affect before reporting valuations likely impacts on their valuations. Whether gaps exist outside the lab when individuals are not prompted to focus on affect is unclear.

Finally, in a new addition to the ever-growing stack of theoretical explanations, Lewandowski (2014) challenged the predictive value of the basic tenet of consequentialism that assumes that individuals make choices conditional on their total wealth. In most experiments, subjects are asked to report valuations for lotteries with small values relative to total wealth. Under expected utility theory and certain assumptions about relative risk aversion, individuals are assumed to be risk neutral when it comes to small-value lotteries. Thus, standard expected utility predicts no gap in small-value lottery valuations. Lewandowski strayed from the standard model only by assuming that individuals do not consider their total wealth but rather the amount of wealth with which they are willing to gamble (aka "gambling wealth"). Similarly, Fudenberg and Levine (2006) developed a dynamic model in which the long-term self controls various short-term selves. The long-term self allows the current short-term self to take only a small amount of money (aka "pocket cash") to places that entice with discretionary spending opportunities (e.g., the casino or the nightclub). This sort of model assumes that short-term selves make choices that are optimal given a small amount of wealth. Lewandowski's expected utility theory with gambling wealth predicted gaps in lotteries, but he did not attempt to determine whether his theory explains the variation in reported results. This would seem to require a set of hypotheses about how experimental procedures impact perceptions about wealth or a method for estimating beliefs over wealth.

## 6.8 Transaction Disutility, Bad Deal Aversion, and Regret Avoidance

As another alternative to endowment theory, some have posited that owners ask for amounts in excess of their consumption values not to compensate for disutility from experienced losses but to avoid regret. Bar-Hillel and Neter (1996) found that subjects were reluctant to trade an endowed lottery ticket for an alternative identical ticket plus a small monetary incentive. Conversely, over 90% of subjects were willing to trade an endowed pen for an identical pen plus a small cash bonus. They interpreted the evidence as support for the claim that

> two lottery tickets, even if they are identical as gambles, have the potential to have different worth once the gambles are played and the uncertainty resolved. . . . [T]he mere fact that two lottery tickets have the potential to result in different outcomes, and in particular, one can result in a desired outcome while the other results in a less desired outcome, suffices to induce an anticipation of regret (which is assumed to be larger for an exchange than for its refusal). (p. 26)

Van de Ven and Zeelenberg (2011) also found that subjects were reluctant to exchange a lottery ticket for an identical lottery ticket even when they could receive a free pen if they exchanged. When they removed anticipation of regret by making it impossible for subjects to know whether they would have won the lottery had they kept the initial endowment, reluctance to trade was reduced, suggesting that anticipated regret accounts for observed reluctance to trade lotteries, at least in part. In another treatment, subjects were given information that would allow them to know whether they would have won the lottery had they traded. In addition, those who traded would know whether they would have won had they not traded. In this symmetric information treatment, 77% of subjects traded, and that percentage exceeded the percentage who traded in a baseline treatment where only traders would know whether they would have won had they not traded.

Note that these sorts of designs make it difficult to rule out loss aversion as an explanation for gaps given that subjects were paid to trade. It could be that the payment to trade is sufficient to compensate for the disutility from the loss. Kogler et al. (2013) addressed this by designing an experiment to keep the costs of trading and not trading the same. In one experiment, half the subjects were given a lottery ticket and the other half were allowed to inspect one. They were then given the choice of keeping the owned or inspected ticket or getting another identical ticket with the same chance of winning. Both tickets were in possession at the time of choice. Subjects did not receive a bonus for trading, and transactions costs, possession and information were identical across treatments. Half of the non-owners kept the inspected ticket, but the vast majority of owners held on to the endowed ticket. After choices were made, valuations for the chosen ticket relative to the other ticket were elicited. Subjects were asked to state the least amount they would accept to give up the ticket they now owned in exchange for the other ticket. Endowment theory predicts similar valuations for the two groups, but the average valuation of initial owners was higher than the average valuation of initial inspectors. This result is not predicted by endowment theory, but it might be in line with regret theory. Bar-Hillel and Neter (1996) found evidence of higher levels of regret for previously owned tickets that were given away and turned out to be winners relative to a ticket that was not chosen from a choice set. Thus, feelings of regret depend on both the outcome and on the action taken. When subjects were asked to report anticipated feelings of regret based on hypothetical situations, the highest levels of regret were recorded for switching possessors relative to non-switching possessors and inspectors who either switched or did not. When the experimenters ran the same design with mugs instead of lottery tickets, subjects who were endowed with a mug were reluctant to switch for an identical mug, whereas statistically half of inspectors chose the inspected mug. Reported valuations of owned mugs did not differ between initial owners and initial inspectors. The authors concluded that both endowment theory and regret theory have roles to play depending on whether subjects are evaluating riskless or risky goods.

Isoni (2011) proposed a model that assumes reference-independent valuations for consumption goods. Her model generated valuation gaps instead by assuming price sensitivity and bad-deal aversion. Individuals were characterized by price sensitivity if they got utility from making good deals and suffered disutility from being "ripped off." Bad-deal aversion is the notion that the pain associated with bad deals outweighs the pleasure derived from same-sized good deals. Isoni defined good and bad deals relative to the expected price, potentially justified by the fact that individuals normally consider a posted price when deciding whether to trade. In environments in which the price is unknown, individuals form expectations about the price, and they experience utility or disutility depending on how the expected price compares with the actual price. Thus, owners will report valuations in excess of their true valuations to avoid selling at a price below the expected price, and non-owners will report valuations below their true valuations to avoid buying at a price above the expected price. The model predicts not only gaps in WTA and WTP but also decaying gaps in repeated markets, shaping effects (i.e., the tendency for reported valuations to move in the direction of announced market clearing prices in repeated markets), and variations in reported valuations elicited using different versions of demand-revealing elicitation devices. Isoni's analysis of the data and the leading theories concludes that bad-deal aversion might be best at organizing the data existing at the time. As she noted, however, it cannot account for exchange asymmetries in simple exchange experiments such as those undertaken by Knetsch (1989). In those experiments, the price (i.e., the alternative good) was known at the time of the choice.

Weaver and Frederick (2012) reported evidence of bad-deal aversion, which they referred to as "transaction disutility." Half of the endowed owners of boxes of candy were told that the market price of the candy at a local movie theatre was $4, and the other half were told that a retail store sold the candy for $1.49 per box (both true statements). Non-owners were split into two groups, and they reported valuations under the same two conditions as owners. The BDM mechanism was used to elicit valuations (price lists were not provided to avoid introduction of alternative reference prices). Under endowment theory, revealed market prices should not impact reported valuations. Bad deal avoidance, on the other hand, predicts that moderate market reference prices will decrease reported owner valuations, reducing or eliminating valuation gaps. The results supported bad deal avoidance. A gap was observed in the high reference price treatment, but not in the moderate reference price treatment. Owner valuations were significantly lower in the moderate revealed market price treatment relative to the high revealed market price treatment, but non-owner valuations were not significantly different across treatments. The authors ran a second experiment using mechanical pencils with different prices on affixed tags with similar results (i.e., WTA exceeded WTP in the high market price condition but not in the moderate market price condition, and the increased market price pushed owner valuations higher but not non-owner valuations). A separate experiment confirmed that non-owner valuations respond to a change in the market price from moderate to low but not moderate to high. Weaver and Frederick acknowledged that their theory could not account for all results reported in the literature, and thus they argued that their theory should supplement rather than supplant other theories that have found support in the literature.

Evidence for regret theory has been found in simple exchange experiments as well. Ratan (2014) conducted simple exchange experiments and gave subjects 24 hours to reverse the decision made in the lab. Subjects performed a simple task to earn a good (a drink bottle or bookmark—randomly assigned across subjects). Endowment through earning was meant to ensure feelings of endowment without using language to emphasize ownership to avoid signaling relative value (see Plott and Zeiler 2007). Subjects completed a questionnaire and then were supplied with the alternative good for inspection. They were informed of the store prices, the same for both goods, to remove any question about relative values. Choices were made privately and while subjects were in possession of both goods. Two treatments were conducted. In the first, decisions made in the lab were final. In the second, subjects were told that they could reverse their decision during the next 24 hours. Subjects who could not reverse their decision exhibited reluctance to trade while those who could did not. Neither endowment theory nor expectation theory can explain this result. Anticipated regret theory, however, is consistent with the result. The ability to reverse the decision protects subjects against choosers' remorse.

Arlen and Tontrup (2015) designed a set of experiments to test the assumption that anticipated regret impacts choices only when the individual feels solely responsible for the choice.[157] If responsibility is shared, for example with an agent or a set of fellow voters, then anticipated regret should influence choices less strongly, and we should observe less reluctance to trade. In a base treatment, subjects were endowed with a lottery ticket and asked whether they wanted to trade the ticket for an identical ticket plus a small monetary bonus. In line with previous results, a statistically significant positive percentage of subjects rejected the trade. The result did not change when subjects were told that another subject's agent recommended trading. A statistically significantly higher percentage of subjects (relative to the base treatment) traded when told that an actual agent was paid to recommend trading, and, in fact, recommended trading (69% v. 30% in the lab; 78% v. 56% in treatments conducted online). This supports anticipated regret theory's prediction related to sole versus shared decision responsibility. In addition, relative to the base treatment, a statistically significantly higher percentage of subjects (79%) voted to trade when told that the outcome of a majority vote of at least 80 subjects would determine each subject's outcome. A similar result was observed when subjects were told the same, but also that they could veto the vote outcome and decide on their outcomes individually. In the veto-vote treatment, 85% of subjects voted to trade and only 11% of subjects vetoed the group decision and kept their endowed ticket. In other treatments, the authors found evidence suggesting that individuals are willing to pay to shed sole responsibility for the decision. The authors argued that their results posed a serious challenge to the common assumption that legal intervention is required to alleviate inefficiencies that arise from reluctance to trade. They argued that individuals often use responsibility-shifting institutions to avoid anticipated regret and that efficient outcomes are more likely to result from allowing private orderings relative to interventions that are ill-equipped to sort people by preferences that we cannot observe.

---

[157]    Arlen and Tontrup seemed to assume throughout most of the article that anticipated regret explains gaps generally, although, as is obvious from this review, the theory is inconsistent with a number of reported results. For example, the theory cannot explain no-gap results in experiments that use commodities such as mugs and pens and that do not take steps to eliminate subject uncertainty over value. They did acknowledge near the end of the paper that in some cases reluctance to trade might be caused by "loss aversion caused by attachment to entitlements" (p. 176). This seems problematic for a couple of reasons. First, attachment is posited in the literature generally as an alternative to endowment theory (reference dependent preferences plus loss aversion) and not as a cause of loss aversion (one of the assumptions of endowment theory). In fact, Tversky and Kahneman (1991), who the authors cite, did not mention the notion of attachment in their development of endowment theory. Second, the authors' results did not support endowment theory, and the literature has moved away from it in the face of mounting evidence against it.

*\*\*\**

In summary, this section highlights the substantial number of theoretical explanations for gaps that have been developed and tested, including endowment theory, substitution theory, expectation theory, preference uncertainty, mere-ownership theory, query theory, enhancement theory, choice uncertainty, trade uncertainty, subject (game form) misconceptions and reversion to basic market instincts, the computational theory of exchange, the question-influenced beliefs conjecture, the gambling wealth conjecture, transaction disutility, bad deal aversion and regret avoidance. The literature is also filled with evidence related to experiment design features that might impact reluctance to trade such as endowing sellers with the good but not buyers with cash (income effects), endowing buyers with cash (house money effects), announcements of market clearing prices, non-anonymous choices that offer signaling opportunities, length of ownership, possession, and many more.

### 6.9 Synthesis and the Frontier

What general conclusions can we draw from the body of published evidence? Most importantly for legal scholarship, it is safe to conclude that, even though endowment theory continues to be cited as the leading explanation of observed reluctance to trade (Klass and Zeiler 2013), the theory has not held up well to the growing body of published data. The social sciences literature essentially moved beyond it. This is not to say that loss aversion and reference dependence have no possible role to play. While much evidence rejects the claim that endowments set reference points, theorists have shifted the theory's assumptions to suggest, for example, that expectations set reference points (Köszegi and Rabin 2006). While some evidence supports expectation theory (depending on its assumptions about how we form expectations), it is inconsistent with a number of observations in the lab, including some from experiments designed specifically to test it. The same is true for a number of other theories. Preference uncertainty, mere-ownership theory, enhancement theory, subject misconceptions, expectation theory and regret avoidance, among others, have all garnered some support, but no one theory clearly rises to the top as the leading explanation. More work is required to determine which best organizes the body of existing evidence and stands up to tests of robustness.

Although several theories remain in contention, some fare worse than others. Explanations centered on wealth effects seem not to organize the data well. Gaps appear in experiments with goods of relatively low value where we would not expect wealth effects to impact valuations much, and at least some experiments that control for them produce gaps when the theory predicts no gaps. Isoni (2011) convincingly argued that Hanemann's (1991) substitution theory was not a good candidate given the implausibly large WTP response to income changes the theory would need to assume to fit the data. In addition, substitution theory's predictions are out of sync with reported valuations of private goods with plentiful substitutes (e.g., mugs with a university logo available at the campus bookstore) in environments where potential buyers are given cash to remedy budget constraints.

That more than one explanation is at work is also possible. For example, Brown (2005) reported evidence from subject self-reported explanations for gaps that might be interpreted as support for commitment cost theory (e.g., "My thoughts are, what do I think I can get for the notebook" (p. 374)). Other self-reports suggested a reversion to basic sell high/buy low instincts ("I grew up with 'buy low, sell high'" (p. 374)). A handful of subjects complained about being broke, although none seemed worried that they would be unable to obtain the good outside the lab if sold during the experiment, which might constitute mixed evidence of an explanation grounded in substitution effects. Some researchers directly tested multifaceted theories, which suggest that more than one driver might be at work more generally. For example, Chatterjee et al. (2013) reported evidence suggesting that both mere ownership, which they argued triggers an association of the self with the object, and loss aversion played necessary roles in gap formation.[158]

Some have been working on developing new ways to test theories that attempt to explain observed reluctance to trade.[159] By running experiments on subjects while taking images of their brains using functional MRI technology, researchers are able to identify which parts of the brain are active during decision-making tasks involving valuation in different roles.[160] Research in brain science has taught us much about which parts of the brains are active when we're thinking strategically or motivated by fear or reacting to potential rewards and losses. Even though we have roughly five decades of research on this question under our belts, in many ways we are in the very early stages. Much more work is required before we can confidently employ data from brain scans to home in on the causes of reluctance to trade.

## 7.  CONCLUSION: IMPLICATIONS FOR APPLICATIONS IN LAW

Despite the numerous potential explanations for observed reluctance to trade, law and policy scholars generally point to one, endowment theory, and proceed to work out both descriptive theories and normative arguments in a wide variety of legal contexts based on this single theory (Klass and Zeiler 2013). Indeed, even some economists emphasize endowment theory despite numerous alternatives supported by equally strong evidence.[161] While we might well have justified this approach during the 1990s, when endowment theory was new and seemed to be gaining ground, following the turn of the century the continued application of endowment theory in legal scholarship fell out of sync with the economics literature; the latter has long since moved beyond endowment theory, while legal scholarship has lagged behind.[162]

---

[158]    After reporting results that support their theory, the authors offer explanations for results in the literature that seem to work against the theory. They also point out results their theory does not predict, which opens the door for further exploration.

[159]    Morewedge and Giblin (2015) review some of the literature.

[160]    See Votinov et al. (2010) for a recent example. They provide a summary of the neuroeconomics literature on reluctance to trade, and highlight variation in results from these studies.

[161]    See, e.g., Johnson et al. (2006).

[162]    See Klass and Zeiler (2013). See also a recent review by law professor Korobkin (2014), which mistakenly points to theories that were proposed as alternatives to endowment theory (e.g., attachment, transaction disutility, regret avoidance, and query theory) as drivers of loss aversion. A recent review of some of the relevant literature by economists Ericson and Fuster (2014) more accurately characterizes the alternative theories as alternatives to endowment theory and argues,

Keeping up on developments in the economics literature is not the only issue with which legal scholars have struggled in their attempts to import findings related to reluctance to trade from economics into law. First, at least some legal scholars mistakenly assume that observed deviations from predictions of standard economic models trigger a need for intervention. To determine whether and how to intervene, we need to understand what drives the observed reluctance. As this review has attempted to highlight, economics experiments are performed not only to identify whether gaps exist but also to identify what explains them. And observed gaps do not necessarily support theories that assume a lack of rationality.[163] Different causes can lead to different policy responses and some causes suggest no policy response is required. For example, if we believe that gaps are an artifact of experiment designs that do not have analogs in settings outside the lab, then we would not expect gaps outside the lab, and we would need no policy intervention. The first step is to understand what causes observed reluctance to trade, and more work is required. This, of course, does not mean we should not act until we fully understand the cause(s). Intervention might be warranted before we achieve a full understanding, but we must account for the risks of intervening in the face of incomplete information before deciding whether and how to move forward. We must also accurately represent the state of scientific knowledge when offering proposals.

Second, law and policy scholars tend to focus on the trees (or, more likely, a single tree) and often fail to appreciate the large and continually changing forest (Klass and Zeiler 2013). The vastness of the reluctance to trade literature makes it impossible to draw conclusions from any one study or even a handful of studies.[164] As this review makes clear, those who wish to draw lessons from the literature must evaluate the body of evidence as a whole to understand which inferences are valid. The reluctance to trade literature reveals that no one theory finds universal (or close to universal) support. Many open questions remain. We are still in search of a theory that is able to organize a substantial portion of the reported results. As is also clear, relying on second-hand descriptions of studies and claims about what we can learn from any one study or the literature more generally is dangerous. Both lawyers and economists sometimes get it wrong, even when describing single studies.[165] Best practice requires careful reading of primary sources.

Third, law and policy scholars often fail to appreciate how little weight we can confidently place on any one experimental finding when we aim to import theory into descriptive and normative claims related to law and policy. Findings reported in one study that support some tested theory are but a first step on the road towards a theory with support sufficient to warrant substantial weight. In well-developed literatures, such as the

---

as mentioned, that loss aversion remains a potential explanation, but as part of a substantially modified version of endowment theory and only with the caveat that still more research is required.

[163] See Zeiler (forthcoming). As mentioned, Tversky and Kahneman (1991) were agnostic as to whether loss aversion is irrational. More generally, depending on the context in which they appear, observed gaps sometimes constitute support for a wide array of rational choice theories.

[164] See, e.g., Open Science Collaboration (2015) ("As much as we might wish it to be otherwise, a single study almost never provides definitive resolution for or against an effect and its explanation").

[165] Some have gone as far as drawing inferences from "handfuls" of studies that do not exist. See, e.g., Klass and Zeiler (2013) who point out Arlen and Talley's (2008) unsupported claims.

one on reluctance to trade, researchers have reported a substantial number of findings and have posited and tested a wide array of theories. Law and policy scholars should strive to identify the theory that best organizes the entire body of evidence in the literature. In high quality studies, authors summarize the findings from the existing literature and attempt to assess how well the tested theory organizes the entire body of evidence. If the study does not provide such an analysis, the reader should either assess the theory along these lines or, at a minimum, warn the reader of the literature's existence.[166] In addition, extreme caution should be exercised until results are replicated (Open Science Collaboration 2015). The first step in testing alternative theories is often to replicate reported results. Often, even when the same or very similar procedures are used to elicit responses from subjects, results vary, suggesting that the finding is fragile to changes in the subject pool or small variations in procedures. In law and policy scholarship, we should take care not to place much weight, if any, on new results and those that have yet to be replicated. While waiting to import a newly posited theory until it is supported by convincing evidence is unnecessary, the importer should accurately report on the contours of the economics literature to give readers an accurate sense of how much weight should be placed on the theory.

One approach a legal scholar might (mistakenly) take in the face of so many theory contenders is that it doesn't matter much what explains reluctance to trade. We know individuals are reluctant—we observe it all the time in the lab. So, no matter what's driving it, the argument might go, we can expect reluctance. For example, if a legal rule places a right or good into the hands of some party, that party will be reluctant to trade the right or good away. Thus, counter to Coase's (1960) famous prediction, law matters. The reluctance to trade might prevent the right or good from getting into the hands of the person who values it the most. A closer analysis of the literature, however, demonstrates the flaw in this reasoning. Certainty the law matters if we experience a disutility from the giving up of something we own or expect to end up with. If endowment theory or expectation theory explains observed reluctance to trade in the lab, we might expect individuals to be tight-fisted when it comes to legal entitlements, at least under certain conditions. If, on the other hand, uncertain preferences explain reluctance to trade in the lab, our take changes. First, we might expect less uncertainty outside the lab. Second, we might be able to find ways to assist individuals with preference discovery. The same sort of analysis applies if subject misconceptions are responsible for reluctance to trade in the lab. We would start by asking whether we expect such misconceptions outside the lab. In contexts in which individuals face unfamiliar elicitation devices, we might require information disclosures that help ensure accurate reporting. Of course, this sort of requirement would be unnecessary if observed gaps are caused by loss aversion as opposed to misconceptions. If loss aversion explains observed gaps, then we would not perceive valuation gaps as errors, and we would be best served by allowing free expression of preferences. Although we might worry that goods might not make it into the hands of the individual with the highest

---

[166]    The most unhelpful approach is to point readers to a subset of studies that support the author's pet theory while failing to include others that do not, even when they are published in the same journal issue as the cited studies. (See, e.g., Korobkin (2014), which cites Isoni et al. (2011) but not Plott and Zeiler (2011), which is printed immediately following the former and provides evidence against many of its claims.) Law review editing procedures are not set up to catch this sort of cherry picking. Misleading reviews serve to exacerbate the confusion in legal scholarship.

value conditional on ownership. As these examples illustrate, it matters greatly for legal applications which theory rises to the top as the leading theory.

The experimental literature on reluctance to trade is not unlike other literatures on a variety of issues studied by economists and psychologists that potentially impact law and policy. Most experimental literatures have features similar to the literature described here. They report findings that support a substantial number of different theories. They are comprised of studies that take incremental steps towards understanding some particular observed phenomenon. They include studies that vary widely in the theories they test, the methods they use to elicit subject responses, and the controls employed to rule out alternative explanations. In our efforts to import interesting findings into law and policy, we often lose sight of this variation and the limitations it places on our ability to draw useful insights from a single study or a small number of studies. The detailed literature review provided here will hopefully foster an appreciation for the nature of experimental findings and a deeper understanding of how best to import them into legal scholarship.

# REFERENCES

Adamowicz, Wiktor L., Vinay Bhardwaj, and Bruce Macnab. 1993. "Experiments on the Difference between Willingness to Pay and Willingness to Accept." *Land Economics* 69: 416–427.

Aggarwal, Pankaj and Meng Zhang. 2006. "The Moderating Effect of Relationship Norm Salience on Consumers' Loss Aversion." *Journal of Consumer Research* 33: 413–419.

Amiran, Edoh Y. and Daniel A. Hagen. 2003. "Willingness to Pay and Willingness to Accept: How Much Can They Differ? Comment." *American Economic Review* 93: 458–463.

Anderson, Steffan, Glenn W. Harrison, Morten I. Lau, and E. Elisabet Rustrőm. 2006. "Elicitation Using Multiple Price List Formats." *Experimental Economics* 9: 383–405.

Anderson, Steffan, Glenn W. Harrison, Morten I. Lau, and E. Elisabet Rustrőm. 2007. "Valuation Using Multiple Price List Formats." *Applied Economics* 39: 675–682.

Apicella, Coren L., Eduardo M. Azevedo, Nicholas A. Christakis, and James H. Fowler. 2014. "Evolutionary Origins of the Endowment Effect: Evidence from Hunter-Gatherers." *American Economic Review* 104: 1793–1805.

Ariely, Dan and Itamar Simonson. 2003. "Buying, Bidding, Playing, or Competing? Value Assessment and Decision Dynamics in Online Auctions." *Journal of Consumer Psychology* 13: 113–123.

Ariely, Dan, Joel Huber, and Klaus Wertenbroch. 2005. "When Do Losses Loom Larger than Gains?" *Journal of Marketing Research* 42: 134–138.

Arlen, Jennifer H. and Eric L. Talley. 2008. "Introduction". In *Experimental Law and Economics*, edited by Jennifer H. Arlen and Eric L. Talley. Cheltenham, UK and Northampton, MA, USA: Edward Elgar.

Arlen, Jennifer and Stephan Tontrup. 2015. "Does the Endowment Effect Justify Legal Intervention? The Debiasing Effect of Institutions." *The Journal of Legal Studies* 44: 143–182.

Arlen, Jennifer, Matthew L. Spitzer, and Eric L. Talley. 2002. "Endowment Effects within Corporate Agency Relationships." *Journal of Legal Studies* 31: 1–37.

Ashby, Nathaniel J. S., Stephan Dickert, and Andreas Glöckner. 2012. "Focusing on What You Own: Biased Information Uptake Due to Ownership." *Judgment and Decision Making* 7: 254–267.

Bar-Hillel, Maya and Efrat Neter. 1996. "Why Are People Reluctant to Exchange Lottery Tickets?" *Journal of Personality and Social Psychology* 70: 17–27.

Bartling, Björn, Florian Engl, and Roberto A. Weber. 2015. "Game Form Misconceptions are not Necessary for a Willingness-to-Pay vs. Willingness-to-Accept Gap." *Journal of the Economic Science Association* 1: 72–85.

Bateman, Ian, Daniel Kahneman, Alistair Munro, Chris Starmer, and Robert Sugden. 2005. "Testing Competing Models of Loss Aversion: An Adversarial Collaboration." *Journal of Public Economics* 89: 1561–1580.

Bateman, Ian, Ian H. Langford, Alistair Munro, Chris Starmer, and Robert Sugden. 2000. "Estimating Four Hicksian Welfare Measures for a Public Good: A Contingent Valuation Investigation." *Land Economics* 76: 355–373.

Bateman, Ian, Alistair Munro, Bruce Rhodes, Chris Starmer, and Robert Sugden. 1997. "A Test of the Theory of Reference-Dependent Preferences." *Quarterly Journal of Economics* 112: 479–505.

Becker, Gordon M., Morris H. DeGroot, and Jacob Marschak. 1964. "Measuring Utility by a Single-Response Sequential Method." *Behavioral Science* 9: 226–232.

Beggan, James K. 1992. "On the Social Nature of Nonsocial Perception: The Mere Ownership Effect." *Journal of Personality and Social Psychology* 62: 229–237.

Biel, Anders, Olaf Johansson-Stenman, and Andreas Nilsson. 2011. "The Willingness to Pay-Willingness to Accept Gap Revisited: The Role of Emotions and Moral Satisfaction." *Journal of Economic Psychology* 32: 908–917.

Binmore, Kenneth. 1994. *Playing Fair*. Cambridge, MA: MIT Press.

Bischoff, Ivo and Jürgen Meckl. 2008. "Endowment Effect Theory, Public Goods and Welfare." *The Journal of Socio-Economics* 37: 1768–1774.

Bishop, Richard C. and Thomas A. Heberlein. 1979. "Measuring Values of Extramarket Goods: Are Indirect Measures Biased?" *American Journal of Agricultural Economics* 61: 926–930.

Bishop, Richard C., Thomas A. Heberlein, and Mary Jo Kealy. 1983. "Contingent Valuation of Environmental Assets: Comparisons with a Simulated Market." *Natural Resources Journal* 23: 619–633.

Blavatskyy, Pavlo and Ganna Pogrebna. 2010. "Endowment Effects? 'Even' with Half a Million on the Table!" *Theory and Decision* 68: 173–192.

Borges, Bernhard F. J. and Jack L. Knetsch. 1998. "Tests of Market Outcomes with Asymmetric Valuations of Gains and Losses: Smaller Gains, Fewer Trades, and Less Value." *Journal of Economic Behavior & Organization* 33: 185–193.

Boyce, R. R., T. C. Brown, G. H. McClelland, G. L. Peterson, and W. D. Schulze. 1992. "An Experimental Examination of Intrinsic Values as a Source of the WTA-WTP Disparity." *The American Economic Review* 82: 1366–1373.

Brenner, Lyle, Yuval Rottenstreich, Sanjay Sood, and Baler Bilgin. 2007. "On the Psychology of Loss Aversion: Possession, Valence, and Reversals of the Endowment Effect." *Journal of Consumer Research* 34: 369–376.

Brookshire, David S. and Don L. Coursey. 1987 "Measuring the Value of a Public Good: An Empirical Comparison of Elicitation Procedures." *American Economic Review* 77: 554–566.

Brosnan, Sarah F., Owen D. Jones, Molly Gardner, Susan P. Lambeth, and Steven J. Schapiro. 2012. "Evolution and the Expression of Biases: Situational Value Changes the Endowment Effect in Chimpanzees." *Evolution and Human Behavior* 33: 378–386.

Brosnan, Sarah F., Owen D. Jones, Susan P. Lambeth, Mary Catherine Mareno, Amanda S. Richardson, and Steven J. Schapiro. 2007. "Endowment Effects in Chimpanzees." *Current Biology* 17: 1704–1707.

Brown, Alexander L. and Gregory Cohen. 2015. "Does Anonymity Affect the Willingness to Accept and Willingness to Pay Gap? A Generalization of Plott and Zeiler." *Experimental Economics* 18: 173–184.

Brown, Thomas C. 2005. "Loss Aversion Without the Endowment Effect, and Other Explanations for the WPA-WTP Disparity." *Journal of Economic Behavior & Organization* 57: 367–379.

Brown, Thomas C., Mark D. Morrison, Jacob A. Benfield, Gretchen Nurse Rainbolt, and Paul A. Bell. 2015. "Exchange Asymmetry in Experimental Settings." *Journal of Economic Behavior & Organization* 120: 104–116.

Burson, Katherine, David Faro, and Yuval Rottenstreich. 2012. "Multiple-Unit Holdings Yield Attenuated Endowment Effects." *Management Science* 59: 545–555.

Carmichael, Lorne H. and W. Bentley MacLeod. 2006. "Welfare Economics with Intransitive Revealed Preferences: A Theory of the Endowment Effect." *Journal of Public Economic Theory* 8: 193–218.

Carmon, Ziv and Dan Ariely. 2000. "Focusing on the Forgone: How Value Can Appear So Different to Buyers and Sellers." *Journal of Consumer Research* 27: 360–370.

Casey, Jeff T. 1995. "Predicting Buyer-Seller Pricing Disparities." *Management Science* 41: 979–999.

Cason, Timothy N. and Charles R. Plott. 2014. "Misconceptions and Game Form Recognition: Challenges to Theories of Revealed Preference and Framing." *Journal of Political Equality* 122(6): 1235–1270.

Chapman, Gretchen B. 1998. "Similarity and Reluctance to Trade." *Journal of Behavioral Decision Making* 11: 47–58.

Chatterjee, Promothesh, Caglar Irmak, and Randall L. Rose. 2013. "The Endowment Effect as Self-Enhancement in Response to Threat." *Journal of Consumer Research* 40: 460–476.

Chen, M. Keith, Venkat Lakshminarayanan, and Laurie R. Santos. 2006. "How Basic are Behavioral Biases? Evidence from Capuchin Monkey Trading Behavior." *Journal of Political Economy* 114: 517–537.

Chilton, Susan, Michael Jones-Lee, Rebecca McDonald, and Hugh Metcalf. 2012. "Does the WTA/WTP Ratio Diminish as the Severity of a Health Complaint is Reduced? Testing for Smoothness of the Underlying Utility of Wealth Function." *Journal of Risk and Uncertainty* 45: 1–24.

Coase, Ronald. 1960. "The Problem of Social Cost." *Journal of Law & Economics* 1: 1–44.

Cook, H. E. and A. Wu. 2001. "On the Valuation of Goods and Selection of the Best Design Alternative." *Research in Engineering Design* 13: 42–54.

Coren, Amy E. 2007. "Bridging the WTA-WTP Gap: Ownership, Bargaining, and the Endowment Effect." PhD dissertation, The University of Texas at Austin.

Corrigan, Jay R., Catherine L. Kling, and Jinhua Zhao. 2008. "Willingness to Pay and the Cost of Commitment: An Empirical Specification and Test." *Environmental Resource Economics* 40: 285–298.

Corrigan, Jay R., Matthew C. Rousu, and Dinah Pura T. Depositario. 2014. "Do Practice Rounds Affect Experimental Auction Results?" *Economics Letters* 123: 42–44.

Coursey, Don L. 1987. "Markets and the Measurement of Value." *Public Choice* 55: 291–297.

Coursey, Don L., John L. Hovis, and William D. Schulze. 1987. "The Disparity Between Willingness to Accept and Willingness to Pay Measures of Value." *Quarterly Journal of Economics* 102: 679–690.

Cummings, R. G., D. S. Brookshire, and W. D. Shulze. 1986. *Valuing Environmental Goods: An Assessment of the Contingent Valuation Method.* New Jersey: Rowman & Allanheld.

Dommer, Sara Loughran and Vanitha Swaminathan. 2013. "Explaining the Endowment Effect through Ownership: The Role of Identity, Gender, and Self-Threat." *Journal of Consumer Research* 39(5): 1034–1050.

Drayton, Lindsey A., Sarah F. Brosnan, Jodi Carrigan and Tara S. Stoinski. 2013. "Endowment Effects in Gorillas (*Gorilla gorilla*)." *Journal of Comparative Psychology* 127(4): 365–369.

Dubourg, W. R., M. W. Jones-Lee, and Graham Loomes. 1994. "Imprecise Preferences and the WTP-WTA Disparity." *Journal of Risk and Uncertainty* 9: 115–133.

Einhorn, Hillel J. and Robin M. Hogarth. 1985. "Ambiguity and Uncertainty in Probabilistic Inference." *Psychological Review* 92: 433–461.

Engelmann, Dirk and Guillaume Hollard. 2010. "Reconsidering the Effect of Market Experience on the 'Endowment Effect'." *Econometrica* 78: 2005–2019.

Ericson, Keith M. M. and Andreas Fuster. 2010. "Expectations as Endowments: Evidence on Reference-Dependent Preferences from Exchange and Valuation Experiments." November 9, Working Paper, on file with author.

Ericson, Keith M. M. and Andreas Fuster. 2011. "Expectations as Endowments: Evidence on Reference-Dependent Preferences from Exchange and Valuation Experiments." *Quarterly Journal of Economics* 126: 1879–1907.

Ericson, Keith M. M. and Andreas Fuster. 2014. "The Endowment Effect." *Annual Review of Economics* 6: 555–579.

Fehr, Dietmar, Rustamdjan Hakimov, and Dorothea Kübler. 2015. "The Willingness to Pay–Willingness to Accept Gap: A Failed Replication of Plott and Zeiler." *European Economic Review* 78: 120–128.

Flemming, Timothy M., Owen D. Jones, Laura Mayo, Tara Stoinski, and Sarah F. Brosnan. 2012. "The Endowment Effect in Orangutans." *International Journal of Comparative Psychology* 25: 285–298.

Franciosi, Robert, Praveen Kujal, Roland Michelitsch, Vernon Smith, and Gang Deng. 1996. "Experimental Tests of the Endowment Effect." *Journal of Economic Behavior & Organization* 30: 213–226.

Fremling, Gertrud and Richard A. Posner. 2001. "Market Signaling of Personal Characteristics." *John M. Olin Law & Economics Working Paper* No. 87 (2D Series), http://chicagounbound.uchicago.edu/cgi/viewcontent.cgi?article=1313&context=law_and_economics

Friedman, David. 2004. "Economics and Evolutionary Psychology." In *Evolutionary Psychology and Economic Theory (Advances in Austrian Economics, Volume 7)*, edited by Roger Koppl, 17–33. Emerald Group Publishing Limited.

Fudenberg, Drew and David K. Levine. 2006. "A Dual-Self Model of Impulse Control." *The American Economic Review* 96(5): 1449–1476.

Fudenberg, Drew and Jean Tirole. 1991. *Game Theory.* Cambridge: MIT Press.

Georgantzís, Nikolaos and Daniel Navarro-Martínez. 2010. "Understanding the WTA–WTP Gap: Attitudes, Feelings, Uncertainty and Personality." *Journal of Economic Psychology* 31: 895–907.

Gerking, Shelby, Menno de Haan, and William Schulze. 1988. The Marginal Value of Job Safety: A Contingent Valuation Study." *Journal of Risk and Uncertainty* 1: 185–199.

Gintis, Herbert. 2007. "The Evolution of Private Property." *Journal of Economic Behavior & Organization* 64: 1–16.

Goette, Lorenz, Annette Harms, and Charles Sprenger. 2014. "Randomizing Endowments: An Experimental Study of Rational Expectations and Reference-Dependent Preferences." *Institute for the Study of Labor (IZA) (Discussion Paper No. 8639).*

Gregory, Robin and Lita Furby. 1987. "Auctions, Experiments and Contingent Valuations." *Public Choice* 55: 273–289.

Hammack, Judd and Gardner Mallard Brown, Jr. 1974. *Waterfowl and Wetlands: Toward Bioeconomic Analysis.* Baltimore: Johns Hopkins University Press.

Hanemann, W. Michael. 1991. "Willingness to Pay and Willing to Accept: How Much Can They Differ?" *American Economic Review* 81: 635–647.

Hanemann, W. Michael. 2003. "Willingness to Pay and Willingness to Accept: How Much Can They Differ? Reply." *American Economic Review* 93: 464.

Harbaugh, William T., Kate Krause, and Lise Vesterlund. 2001. "Are Adults Better Behaved Than Children? Age, Experience, and the Endowment Effect." *Economics Letters* 70: 175–181.

Harless, David W. 1989. "More Laboratory Evidence on the Disparity Between Willingness to Pay and Compensation Demanded." *Journal of Economic Behavior and Organization* 11: 359–379.

Harrison, Glenn W. and John A. List. 2004. "Field Experiments." *Journal of Economic Literature* 42: 1009–1055.

Hartman, Raymond S., Michael J. Doane, and Chi-Keung Woo. 1991. "Consumer Rationality and the Status Quo." *Quarterly Journal of Economics* 106: 141–162.

Heffetz, Ori and John A. List. 2014. "Is the Endowment Effect an Expectations Effect?" *Journal of the European Economic Association* 12: 1396–1422.

Heifetz, Aviad and Ella Segev. 2004. "The Evolutionary Role of Toughness in Bargaining." *Games and Economic Behavior* 49: 117–134.

Hicks, J. R. and R. G. D. Allen. 1934. "A Reconsideration of the Theory of Value. Part I." *Economica* 1: 52–76.

Hoehn, J. P. and A. Randall. 1987. "A Satisfactory Benefit Cost Indicator from Contingent Valuation." *Journal of Environmental Economics and Management* 14: 226–247.

Hoorens, Vera, Nicole Remmers, and Kamieke van de Riet. 1999. "Time is an Amazingly Variable Amount of Money: Endowment and Ownership Effects in the Subjective Value of Working Time." *Journal of Economic Psychology* 20: 383–405.

Horowitz, John K. and Kenneth E. McConnell. 2002. "A Review of WTA/WTP Studies." *Journal of Environmental Economics and Management* 44: 426–47.

Huck, Steffan, Georg Kirchsteiger, and Jorg Oechssler. 2005. "Learning to Like What You Have: Explaining the Endowment Effect." *The Economic Journal* 115: 689–702.

Inder, Brett and Terry O'Brien. 2003. "The Endowment Effect and the Role of Uncertainty." *Bulletin of Economic Research* 55: 289–301.

Irwin, Julie R. 1994. "Buying/Selling Price Preference Reversals: Preference for Environmental Changes in Buying Versus Selling Modes." *Organizational Behavior and Human Decision Processes* 60: 431–457.

Isoni, Andrea. 2011. "The Willingness-to-Accept/Willingness-to-Pay Disparity in Repeated Markets: Loss Aversion or 'Bad-deal' Aversion?" *Theory and Decision* 71: 409–430.

Isoni, Andrea, Graham Loomes, and Robert Sugden. 2011. "The Willingness to Pay—Willingness to Accept Gap, the 'Endowment Effect,' Subject Misconceptions, and Experimental Procedures for Eliciting Valuations: Comment." *American Economic Review* 101: 991–1011.

Johnson, Eric J., Simon Gächter, and Andreas Herrmann. 2006. "Exploring the Nature of Loss Aversion." IZA Discussion Paper No. 2015.

Johnson, Eric J., Gerald Häubl, and Anat Keinan. 2007. "Aspects of Endowment: A Query Theory of Value Construction." *Journal of Experimental Psychology: Learning, Memory, and Cognition* 33: 461–74.

Johnson, Eric J., John Hershey, Jacqueline Meszaros, and Howard Kunreuther. 1993. "Framing, Probability Distortions, and Insurance Decisions." *Journal of Risk and Uncertainty* 7: 35–51.

Johnson, Joseph G. and Jerome R. Busemeyer. 2005. "A Dynamic, Stochastic, Computational Model of Preference Reversal Phenomenon." *Psychological Review* 112: 841–861.

Jones, Owen. 2001. "Time-shifted Rationality and the Law of Law's Leverage: Behavioral Economics Meets Behavioral Biology." *Northwestern University Law Review* 95: 1141–1205.

Jones, Owen. 2017. "Why Behavioral Economics Isn't Better, and How It Could Be." In *Research Handbook on Behavioral Law and Economics*, edited by Joshua C. Teitelbaum and Kathryn Zeiler. Cheltenham, UK and Northampton, MA, USA: Edward Elgar.

Jones-Lee, M. W., M. Hammerton, and P. R. Phillips. 1985. "The Value of Safety: Results of a National Sample Survey." *The Economic Journal* 95: 49–72.

Kahneman, Daniel. 2011. *Thinking Fast and Slow*. New York: Farrar, Straus & Giroux.

Kahneman, Daniel and Amos Tversky. 1979. "Prospect Theory: An Analysis of Decision Under Risk." *Econometrica* 47: 263–292.

Kahneman, Daniel, Jack L. Knetsch, and Richard H. Thaler. 1990. "Experimental Tests of the Endowment Effect and the Coase Theorem." *Journal of Political Economy* 98: 1325–1348.

Kahneman, Daniel, Jack L. Knetsch, and Richard H. Thaler. 1991. "The Endowment Effect, Loss Aversion and Status Quo Bias." *Journal of Economic Perspectives* 5: 193–206.

Kahneman, Daniel, Jack L. Knetsch, and Richard H. Thaler. 2008. "The Endowment Effect: Evidence of Losses Valued More than Gains." In *Handbook of Experimental Economics Results: Volume 1*, 939–948. Amsterdam: Elsevier B.V.

Kanngiesser, Patricia, Laurie R. Santos, Bruce M. Hood, and Josep Call. 2011. "The Limits of Endowment Effects in Great Apes (Pan Paniscus, Pan Troglodytes, Gorilla Gorilla, Pongo Pygmaeus)." *Journal of Comparative Psychology* 125(4): 436–445.

Kelman, Mark. 1979. "Consumption Theory, Production Theory, and Ideology in the Coase Theorem." *Southern California Law Review* 52: 669–698.

Kermer, Deborah A., Erin Driver-Linn, Timothy D. Wilson, and Daniel T. Gilbert. 2006. "Loss Aversion is an Affective Forecasting Error." *Psychological Science* 17: 649–653.

Kingsley, David and Thomas Brown. 2012. "Does Prompting for Revision Influence Subjects' Offers in Willingness to Accept – Willingness to Pay Lab Experiments?" *Economics Bulletin* 32: 2580–2585.

Kingsley, David and Thomas Brown. 2013. "Value Learning and the Willingness to Accept–Willingness to Pay Disparity." *Economics Letters* 120: 473–476.

Klass, Gregory and Kathryn Zeiler. 2013. "Against Endowment Theory: Experimental Economics and Legal Scholarship." *UCLA Law Review* 61: 2–64.

Kling, Catherine L., John A. List, and Jinhua Zhao. 2013. "A Dynamic Explanation of the Willingness to Pay and Willingness to Accept Disparity." *Economic Inquiry* 51: 909–921.

Knetsch, Jack L. 1989. "The Endowment Effect and Evidence of Nonreversible Indifference Curves." *American Economic Review* 79: 1277–1284.

Knetsch, Jack L. and J. A. Sinden. 1984. "Willingness to Pay and Compensation Demanded: Experimental Evidence of an Unexpected Disparity in Measures of Value." *Quarterly Journal of Economics* 99: 507–521.

Knetsch, Jack L. and J. A. Sinden. 1987. "The Persistence of Evaluation Disparities." *Quarterly Journal of Economics* 102: 691–696.

Knetsch, Jack L. and Wei-Kang Wong. 2009. "The Endowment Effect and the Reference State: Evidence and Manipulations." *Journal of Economic Behavior & Organization* 71: 407–413.

Knez, Peter, Vernon L. Smith, and Arlington W. Williams. 1985. "Individual Rationality, Market Rationality, and Value Estimation." *American Economic Review* 75: 397–402.

Kniesner, Thomas J., W. Kip Viscusi, and James P. Ziliak. 2014. "Willingness to Accept Equals Willingness to Pay for Labor Market Estimates of the Value of a Statistical Life." *Journal of Risk and Uncertainty* 48: 187–205.

Kogler, Cristoph, Anton Kühberger, and Rainer Gilhofer. 2013. "Real and Hypothetical Endowment Effects When Exchanging Lottery Tickets: Is Regret a Better Explanation Than Loss Aversion?" *Journal of Economic Psychology* 37: 42–53.

Kogut, Tehila and Ehud Kogut. 2011. "Possession Attachment: Individual Differences in the Endowment Effect." *Journal of Behavioral Decision Making* 24: 377–393.

Koh, Weining and Wei-Kang Wong. 2013. "The Willingness to Accept–Willingness to Pay Gap: Do Possession and Framing Still Matter Despite Important Controls for Subject Misconceptions?" *National University of Singapore Working Paper*.

Kolstad, Charles D. and Rolando M. Guzman. 1999. "Information and the Divergence between Willingness to Accept and Willingness to Pay." *Journal of Environmental Economics and Management* 38: 66–80.

Korobkin, Russell. 1998. "The Status Quo Bias and Contract Default Rules." *Cornell Law Review* 83: 608–687.

Korobkin, Russell. 2003. "The Endowment Effect and Legal Analysis." *Northwestern University Law Review* 97: 1227–1291.

Korobkin, Russell. 2014. "Wrestling with the Endowment Effect, or How to Do Law and Economics Without the Coase Theorem." In *The Oxford Handbook of Behavioral Economics and the Law*, edited by Eyal Zamir and Doron Teichman, 330–334. Oxford: Oxford University Press.

Köszegi, Botond and Matthew Rabin. 2006. "A Model of Reference-Dependent Preferences." *Quarterly Journal of Economics* 121: 1133–1165.

Kovalchik, Stephanie, Colin F. Camerer, David M. Grether, Charles R. Plott, and John M. Allman. 2005. "Aging and Decision Making: A Comparison Between Neurologically Healthy Elderly and Young Individuals." *Journal of Economic Behavior & Organization* 58: 79–94.

Lakshminarayanan, Venkat, M. Keith Chen, and Laurie R. Santos. 2008. "Endowment Effect in Capuchin Monkeys." *Philosophical Transactions: Biological Sciences* 363: 3837–3844.

Landesberg, Stuart A. 2007. "Why We Will (Sometimes) Not Sell What We Would Not Buy: Empirical Evidence of a Conditional Endowment Effect." B.A. dissertation. Amherst College, Amherst, MA.

Lerner, Jennifer S., Deborah A. Small, and George Loewenstein. 2004. "Heart Strings and Purse Strings: Carryover Effects of Emotions on Economic Decisions." *Psychological Science* 15: 337–341.

Lewandowski, Michal. 2014. "Buying and Selling Price for Risky Lotteries and Expected Utility Theory with Gambling Wealth." *Journal of Risk and Uncertainty* 48: 253–283.

Li, Chuan-Zhong, Karl-Gustaf Lofgren, and W. Michael Hanemann. 2002. "Real Versus Hypothetical Willingness to Accept: The Bishop and Heberlein Model Revisited." In *Economic Theory for the Environment: Essays in Honour of Karl-Goran Maler*, edited by Bengt Kristrom, Partha Dasgupta, and Karl-Gustaf Lofgren, 205–218. Cheltenham UK and Northampton, MA, USA: Edward Elgar.

Liberman, Nira, Lorraine Chen Idson, Christopher J. Camacho, and E. Tory Higgins. 1999. "Promotion and Prevention Choices Between Stability and Change." *Journal of Personality and Social Psychology* 77(6): 1135–1145.

Lin, Chien-Huang, Shih-Chieh Chuang, Danny T. Kao, and Chaang-Yung Kung. 2006. "The Role of Emotions in the Endowment Effect." *Journal of Economic Psychology* 27: 589–597.

List, John A. 2003. "Does Market Experience Eliminate Market Anomalies?" *Quarterly Journal of Economics* 118: 41–71.

List, John A. 2004. "Neoclassical Theory Versus Prospect Theory: Evidence from the Marketplace." *Econometrica* 72: 615–625.

List, John A. 2011. "Does Market Experience Eliminate Market Anomalies? The Case of Exogenous Market Experience." *American Economic Review* 101: 313–317.

List, John A. and Jason F. Shogren. 1999. "Price Information and Bidding Behavior in Repeating Second-Price Auctions." *American Journal of Agricultural Economics* 81: 942–949.

List, John A. and Jason F. Shogren. 2002. "Calibration of Willingness-to-Accept." *Journal of Environmental Economics and Management* 43: 219–233.

Loewenstein, George and Daniel Adler. 1995. "A Bias in the Prediction of Tastes." *The Economic Journal* 105: 929–937.

Loewenstein, George and Samuel Issacharoff. 1994. "Source Dependence in the Valuation of Objects." *Journal of Behavioral Decision Making* 7: 157–168.

Loewenstein, George and Daniel Kahneman. 1991. "Explaining the Endowment Effect." *Carnegie Mellon University Working Paper*.

Loomes, Graham, Shepley Orr, and Robert Sugden. 2009. "Taste Uncertainty and Status Quo Effects in Consumer Choice." *Journal of Risk and Uncertainty* 39: 113–135.

Loomes, Graham, Chris Starmer, and Robert Sugden. 2010. "Preference Reversals and Disparities Between Willingness to Pay and Willingness to Accept in Repeated Markets." *Journal of Economic Psychology* 31: 374–387.

Lunn, Pete and Mary Lunn. 2014. "What Can I Get for It? The Relationship Between the Choice Equivalent, Willingness to Accept and Willingness to Pay." *ESRI Working Paper 479*.

Lusk, Jayson. 2003. "An Experimental Test of the Commitment Cost Theory." *American Journal of Agricultural Economics* 85: 1316–1322.

Maddux, William W., Haiyang Yang, Carl Falk, Hajo Adam, Wendi Adair, Yumi Endo, Ziv Carmon, and Steven J. Heine. 2010. "For Whom is Parting with Possessions More Painful? Cultural Differences in the Endowment Effect." *Psychological Science* 21: 1910–1917.

Mandel, David R. 2002. "Beyond Mere Ownership: Transaction Demand as a Moderator of the Endowment Effect." *Organizational Behavior and Human Decision Processes* 88: 737–747.

Marshall, James D., Jack L. Knetsch, and J. A. Sinden. 1986. "Agent's Evaluations and the Disparity of Measures of Economic Loss." *Journal of Economic Behavior and Organization* 65: 115–127.

Martinez, Luis F., Marcel Zeelenberg, and John B. Rijsman. 2011. "Regret, Disappointment and the Endowment Effect." *Journal of Economic Psychology* 32: 962–968.

Morewedge, Carey K. and Colleen E. Giblin. 2015. "Explanations of the Endowment Effect: An Integrative Review." *Trends in Cognitive Sciences* 19: 339–348.

Morewedge, Carey K., Lisa L. Shu, Daniel T. Gilbert, and Timothy D. Wilson. 2009. "Bad Riddance or Good Rubbish? Ownership and Not Loss Aversion Causes the Endowment Effect." *Journal of Experimental Social Psychology* 45: 947–951.

Morrison, Gwendolyn C. 1997a. "Resolving Differences in Willingness to Pay and Willingness to Accept: Comment." *American Economic Review* 87: 236–240.

Morrison, Gwendolyn C. 1997b. "Willingness to Pay and Willingness to Accept: Some Evidence of an Endowment Effect." *Applied Economics* 29: 411–417.

Morrison, Gwendolyn C. 1998. "Understanding the Disparity Between WTP and WTA: Endowment Effect, Substitutability, or Imprecise Preferences?" *Economic Letters* 59: 189–194.

Morrison, Gwendolyn C. 2000. "WTP and WTA in Repeated Trial Experiments: Learning or Leading?" *Journal of Economic Psychology* 21: 57–72.

Munro, Alistair and Robert Sugden. 2003. "On the Theory of Reference-dependent Preferences." *Journal of Economic Behavior & Organization* 50: 407–428.

Nash, Jane G. and Robert A. Rosenthal. 2014. "An Investigation of the Endowment Effect in the Context of a College Housing Lottery." *Journal of Economic Psychology* 42: 74–82.

Nayakankuppam, Dhananjay and Himanshu Mishra. 2005. "The Endowment Effect: Rose-Tinted and Dark-Tinted Glasses." *Journal of Consumer Research* 32(3): 390–395.

Nesselroade, Jr., K. Paul, James K. Beggan, and Scott T. Allison. 1999. "Possession Enhancement in an Interpersonal Context: An Extension of the Mere Ownership Effect." *Psychology & Marketing* 16: 21–34.

Novemsky, Nathan and Daniel Kahneman. 2005. "The Boundaries of Loss Aversion." *Journal of Marketing Research* 42: 119–128.

Okada, Erica M. 2010. "Uncertainty, Risk Aversion, and WTA vs. WTP." *Marketing Science* 29: 75–84.

Open Science Collaboration. 2015. "Estimating the Reproducibility of Psychological Science." *Science* 349: 943.

Ortona, Guido and Francesco Scacciati. 1992. "New Experiments on the Endowment Effect." *Journal of Economic Psychology* 13: 277–296.

Pachur, Thorsten and Benjamin Scheibehenne. 2012. "Constructing Preference from Experience: The Endowment Effect Reflected in External Information Search." *Journal of Experimental Psychology: Learning Memory and Cognition* 38: 1108–1116.

Peters, Ellen, Paul Slovic, and Robin Gregory. 2003. "The Role of Affect in the WTA/WTP Disparity." *Journal of Behavioral Decision Making* 16: 309–330.

Plott, Charles R. 1996. "Rational Individual Behavior in Markets and Social Choice Processes: The Discovered Preference Hypothesis." In *The Rational Foundations of Economic Behaviour*, 225–250. London: Macmillan Publishing.

Plott, Charles R. and Kathryn Zeiler. 2005. "The Willingness to Pay–Willingness to Accept Gap, the 'Endowment Effect,' Subject Misconceptions, and Experimental Procedures for Eliciting Valuations." *American Economic Review* 95: 530–545.

Plott, Charles R. and Kathryn Zeiler. 2007. "Asymmetries in Exchange Behavior Incorrectly Interpreted as Evidence of Endowment Effect Theory and Prospect Theory?" *American Economic Review* 97: 1449–1466.

Plott, Charles R. and Kathryn Zeiler. 2010. "Web Appendix to Endowment Effect Theory, Subject Misconceptions and Enhancement Effect Theory: A Reply to Isoni, Loomes and Sugden" https://www.aeaweb.org/aer/data/april2011/20100063_app.pdf

Plott, Charles R. and Kathryn Zeiler. 2011. "The Willingness to Pay–Willingness to Accept Gap, the 'Endowment Effect,' Subject Misconceptions, and Experimental Procedures for Eliciting Valuations: Reply." *American Economic Review* 101(2): 1012–1028.

Randall, Alan and John R. Stoll. 1980. "Consumer's Surplus in Commodity Space." *American Economic Review* 71: 449–457.

Ratan, Anmol. 2012. "Mistakes, Closure and Endowment Effect in Laboratory Experiments." *Monash University, Department of Economics (Discussion Paper 22/12)*.

Ratan, Anmol. 2014. "Anticipated Regret or Endowment Effect? A Reconsideration of Exchange Asymmetry in Laboratory Experiments." *Journal of Economic Analysis & Policy* 14: 277–298.

Reb, Jochen and Terry Connolly. 2007. "Possession, Feelings of Ownership and the Endowment Effect." *Judgment and Decision Making* 2: 107–114.

Roth, Gerrit. 2005. "Predicting the Gap between Willingness to Accept and Willingness to Pay." PhD dissertation, Munich Graduate School of Economics.

Saqib, Najam U., Norman Frohlich, and Edward Bruning. 2010. "The Influence of Involvement on the Endowment Effect: The Moveable Value Function." *Journal of Consumer Psychology* 20: 355–368.

Sayman, Serdar and Ayşe Öncüler. 2005. "Effects of Study Design Characteristics on the WTA–WTP Disparity: A Meta Analytical Framework." *Journal of Economic Psychology* 26: 289–312.

Schmidt, Ulrich and Stefan Traub. 2009. "An Experimental Investigation of the Disparity Between WTA and WTP for Lotteries." *Theory and Decision* 66: 229–262.

Schurr, Amos and Ilana Ritov. 2014. "The Effect of Giving It All Up on Valuation: A New Look at the Endowment Effect." *Management Science* 60: 628–637.

Sen, Sankar and Eric J. Johnson. 1997. "Mere-Possession Effects without Possession in Consumer Goods." *Journal of Consumer Research* 24: 105–117.

Shogren, Jason F. and Dermot J. Hayes. 1997. "Resolving Differences in Willingness to Pay and Willingness to Accept: Reply." *American Economic Review* 87: 241–244.

Shogren, Jason F., Sungwon Cho, Cannon Koo, John List, Changwon Park, Pablo Polo, and Robert Wilhelmi. 2001. "Auction Mechanisms and the Measurement of WTP and WTA." *Resource and Energy Economics* 23: 97–109.

Shogren, Jason F., Seung T. Shin, Dermot J. Hayes, and James B. Kliebenstein. 1994. "Resolving Differences in Willingness to Pay and Willingness to Accept." *American Economic Review* 84: 255–270.

Shu, Suzanne B. and Joann Peck. 2011. "Psychological Ownership and Affective Reaction: Emotional Attachment Process Variables and the Endowment Effect." *Journal of Consumer Psychology* 21: 439–452.

Simonson, Itamar and Aimee Drolet. 2004. "Anchoring Effects on Consumers' Willingness-to-Pay and Willingness-to-Accept." *Journal of Consumer Research* 31: 681–690.

Singh, Harinder. 1991. "The Disparity Between Willingness to Pay and Compensation Demanded." *Economic Letters* 35: 263–266.

Smith, Alec. 2012. "Lagged Beliefs and Reference-Dependent Preferences." *University of Arizona Working Paper 08-03*.

Strahilevitz, Michal A. and George Loewenstein. 1998. "The Effect of Ownership History on the Valuation of Objects." *Journal of Consumer Research* 25: 276–289.

Sugden, Robert. 1999. "Alternatives to the Neo-Classical Theory of Choice." In *Valuing Environmental Preferences: Theory and Practice of the Contingent Valuation Method in the US, EU, and Developing Countries*, edited by Ian J. Bateman and Kenneth G. Willis, 152–180. Oxford: Oxford University Press.

Svirsky, Daniel. 2014. "Money is No Object: Testing the Endowment Effect in Exchange Goods." *Journal of Economic Behavior & Organization* 106: 227–234.

Thaler, Richard. 1980. "Toward a Positive Theory of Consumer Choice." *Journal of Economic Behavior & Organization* 1: 39–60.

Tsur, Matan. 2008. "The Selectivity Effect of Past Experience on Purchasing Decisions: Implications for the WTA-WTP Disparity." *Journal of Economic Psychology* 29: 739–746.

Tuncel, Tuba and James K. Hammitt. 2014. "A New Meta-Analysis on the WTP/WTA Disparity." *Journal of Environmental Economics and Management* 68: 175–187.

Tversky, Amos and Daniel Kahneman. 1991. "Loss Aversion in Riskless Choice: A Reference-Dependent Model." *Quarterly Journal of Economics* 106: 1039–1061.

Van Boven, Leaf, David Dunning, and George Loewenstein. 2000. "Egocentric Empathy Gaps Between Owners and Buyers: Misperceptions of the Endowment Effect." *Journal of Personality and Social Psychology* 79: 66–76.

Van Boven, Leaf, George Loewenstein, and David Dunning. 2003. "Mispredicting the Endowment Effect: Underestimation of Owners' Selling Prices by Buyer's Agents." *Journal of Economic Behavior & Organization* 51: 351–365.

van de Ven, Niels and Marcel Zeelenberg. 2011. "Regret Aversion and the Reluctance to Exchange Lottery Tickets." *Journal of Economic Psychology* 32: 194–200.

van de Ven, Niels, Marcel Zeelenberg, and Eric van Dijk. 2005. "Buying and Selling Exchange Goods: Outcome Information, Curiosity and the Endowment Effect." *Journal of Economic Psychology* 26: 459–468.

van Dijk, Eric and Dann van Knippenberg. 1996. "Buying and Selling Exchange Goods: Loss Aversion and the Endowment Effect." *Journal of Economic Psychology* 17: 517–524.

van Dijk, Eric and Dann van Knippenberg. 1998. "Trading Wine: On the Endowment Effect, Loss Aversion, and the Comparability of Consumer Goods." *Journal of Economic Psychology* 19: 485–495.

Vickery, William. 1961. "Counterspeculation, Auctions, and Competitive Sealed Tenders." *The Journal of Finance* 16: 8–37.

Viscusi, W. K., W. A. Magat, and J. Huber. 1987. "An Investigation of the Rationality of Consumer Valuations of Multiple Health Risks." *The RAND Journal of Economics* 18: 465–479.

Vondolia, Godwin K., Håkan Eggert, Ståle Navrud, and Jesper Stage. 2014. "What Do Respondents Bring to Contingent Valuation? A Comparison of Monetary and Labor Payment Vehicles." *Journal of Environmental Economics and Policy* 3: 253–267.

Votinov, Mikhail, Tatsuya Mima, Toshihiko Aso, Mitsunari Abe, Nobukatsu Sawamoto, Jun Shinozaki, and Hidenao Fukuyama. 2010. "The Neural Correlates of Endowment Effect Without Economic Transaction." *Neuroscience Research* 68: 59–65.

Walker, Michael E., Osvoldo F. Morera, Joanne Vining, and Brian Orland. 1999. "Disparate WTA-WTP Disparities: The Influence of Human versus Natural Causes." *Journal of Behavioral Decision Making* 12: 219–232.

Weaver, Ray, and Shane Frederick. 2012. "A Reference Price Theory of the Endowment Effect." *Journal of Marketing Research* XLIX: 696–707.

Willig, Robert. 1976. "Consumer's Surplus Without Apology." *American Economic Review* 66: 589–597.

Zeiler, Kathryn. 2010. "Cautions on the Use of Economics Experiments in Law." *Journal of Institutional and Theoretical Economics* 166: 178–193.

Zeiler, Kathryn. Forthcoming. "Mistaken about Mistakes." *European Journal of Law and Economics*.

Zhang, Ying and Ayelet Fishbach. 2005. "The Role of Anticipated Emotions in the Endowment Effect." *Journal of Consumer Psychology* 15: 316–324.

Zhao, Jinhua and Catherine L. Kling. 2001. "A New Explanation for the WTP/WTA Disparity." *Economic Letters* 73: 293–300.

Zhao, Jinhua and Catherine L. Kling. 2004. "Willingness-to-Pay, Compensating Variation, and the Cost of Commitment." *Economic Inquiry* 42: 503–517.

# 14. Incentives, choices, and strategic behavior: a neuroeconomic perspective for the law
*Terrence Chorvat and Kevin McCabe*

## 1. INTRODUCTION

In this chapter, we discuss some ways in which neuroscientific research applied to economics, commonly referred to as neuroeconomics, can inform legal scholarship. Given the limitations on space of this chapter, we cannot discuss anything like all of the neuroeconomic research that has been done in the last few years, even all of that which is of relevance to legal scholarship.[1] Therefore, this chapter is a highly selective review of the research that we believe is useful to legal scholars. The focus of the chapter is on neuroeconomic research related to financial decisions and its relevance to legal scholarship.

A mainstay of many earlier survey articles in neuroeconomics was to have some discussion which can be referred to as the "methodological" debate (e.g., Bernheim 2009; Gul and Pesendorfer 2008; Glimcher 2010). That is, neuroeconomic survey articles often contain or consist entirely of an existential argument for neuroeconomics as an area of study (e.g., Camerer, Lowenstein, and Prelec 2005; Camerer 2008). However, at this point methodological debates are beside the point. A fairly large number of individuals and institutions are committed to pursuing neuroeconomic research for as far into the future as one can foresee. The question then becomes how best to focus this research.

Rather than entirely side-stepping these debates, it will profit us to consider two points that came into greater focus as a result of these methodological debates. The first is a more specific demarcation of what we might consider "neuroeconomics" as opposed to other types of research. Perhaps the most prominent critics of neuroeconomics, Gul and Pesendorfer (2008) stated that economic models make no assumptions about brain function. Of course, this is not strictly true in that economic models assume that the humans are capable of performing optimization computations or something equivalent to them.

To understand the importance of the optimization assumption, imagine we discovered that the reason why humans exhibit downward sloping demand functions is the result of some process along the lines of Becker's argument (Becker 1962) that even a population of irrational consumers should have downward sloping demand curves. Such knowledge would certainly impact our economic models. Becker's argument was based on the idea that budget constraints in essence force a population of consumers who choose between goods at random to exhibit downward sloping demand curves. Becker claimed that this

---

[1] The book by Glimcher et al. (2009) comes close to summarizing all of the neuroeconomics literature available at the time. A large portion of it arguably is relevant to legal scholarship. Given that the amount of research in this area has significantly increased since then and this chapter is more than an order of magnitude shorter than that volume, it would simply be impossible to discuss all that is relevant to legal scholarship.

showed that many of the predictions of economics do not require rationality assumptions. However, many predictions of richer models of behavior such as expected utility models would not be confirmed if individuals behaved at random. We can see that economic models therefore generally make a number of implicit assumptions about decision processes. For example, economic models generally assume that preferences are stable in some way. If we learn that preferences are not perfectly stable, perhaps we should include the labile nature of preferences in our models.

We can use Gul and Pesendorfer's argument that economics makes no assumptions about neurological processes to help us differentiate "neuroeconomic" models from other types of models. Their argument suggests that we can consider neuroeconomic models as those that explicitly include considerations of the decision-making process other than a straightforward optimization of some objective function. This would include bounded rationality models or any model that addresses cognitive, affective or other limits placed on the decision-making process. (Rubinstein 1998; Gigerenzer 2000). Under this view, the scope of neuroeconomics is greater than models that include neuronal activity directly. Any model that postulates some of neurological limits to decision-making should be considered a neuroeconomic model, even though the neurological element of such models will vary.[2]

Attempting to include cognitive, affective or other limitations to optimization of utility goes back at least as far as Simon (1955). Simon argued that it is reasonable to model human decision processes as based on the use of heuristics rather than on the basis of formal optimization of some simple utility function. One goal of economics would then be to model these heuristics. One might note that including computational processes other than optimization of a standard utility function will likely result in models that do not have the elegant analytic solutions that have been an important part of economics. These models will likely need to make use of computational methods other than standard optimization methods. Fortunately, these computational methods have become common in economic modeling in recent years (Stachurski 2009).

The second point that became clearer due to the methodological debates relates to the kinds of neuroscientific research that will impact economics and the kind of economic work that should be incorporated by neuroscientists. For good or ill, modern economics mostly consists of the mathematical modeling of economic activity. Of course, a thorough mathematical analysis includes statistical or econometric analysis to test the strength of particular relationships posited in models. Indeed, because mathematical relationships better lend themselves to empirical testing, econometrics may be a key driver in the increasingly mathematical nature of economics. In any case, economics is a discipline based on mathematical models that have been tested empirically (Weintraub 2002).

As a result, if neuroscience is to affect economics, as well as be affected by it, the conversation between the two disciplines will have to be essentially mathematical. While neuroscience itself is very commonly quite mathematical (Gabbiani and Cox 2010),

---

[2]   Of course, if we are creating a neologism, we can define the word as we wish, much like Humpty Dumpty in *Through the Looking Glass* (Carroll 1871, Chapter 6, p. 205). "'When I use a word,' Humpty Dumpty said in a rather scornful tone, 'it means just what I choose it to mean— neither more nor less.'" Of course, in the future the term "neuroeconomics" will come to mean whatever it will be generally applied to over time.

not all of the research, particularly that which is often considered neuroeconomic is mathematical in the way required by economics. In particular, the "outputs" of research need to be such that they can directly affect mathematical models used in economics. To put this more pointedly, in the words of Ernest Rutherford, "all science is either physics or stamp collecting" (quoted in Birks 1962, p. 108). That is, one is either attempting to describe the dynamics of the subject or is merely collecting interesting facts and naming items of interest. Merely observing which brain regions are involved in a decision process would be "stamp collecting" in this metaphor. Using information from neuroscience to inform our models of the decision-making process would be physics. Any particular work in neuroeconomics is likely to fall somewhere in between the extremes of "physics" and "stamp collecting."

To make this idea more concrete, one can argue that neuroeconomic studies showing that a particular neural region is involved when subjects make certain choices yield what may be thought of as essentially qualitative results.[3] While interesting, these qualitative results often tell us little directly about the decision process.[4] This can be contrasted with studies that test models that directly relate levels of neural activity in specific brain regions to particular decision mechanisms. For example, one might test a model that posits that the degree of activation in the region(s) of interest has some monotonic relationship with the decision. This allows us to either predict the decision from the activation or the activation from the decision. That is, the latter type of research not only informs us about the location of the processing, but also tells us something about the nature of the processing that is occurring.

Of course, the experiments that yield mostly qualitative results can still be useful. The nature of persuasion in economics, or in any discipline other than mathematics, is not always, if ever, based on apodictic demonstrations (McCloskey 1994). The qualitative results may help us to conceive of why a particular process might be more likely without presenting additional statistical evidence of its accuracy. However, if neuroeconomics is to have a major influence on economics, it will have to be through models that relate to quantitative predictions of behavior resulting from neural activity.

To illustrate the distinction, albeit imperfectly, we can first consider one of the first prominent neuroeconomic studies that examined the quasi-hyperbolic discounting model (sometimes referred to as the $\beta-\delta$ model)[5] (McClure et al. 2004). This study showed that

---

[3]   Even though the data from neuroeconomic experiments are clearly quantitative, the finding that appropriate data (e.g., blood oxygen level response) from a particular brain region is correlated with a particular decision is itself in truth a qualitative result. That is, if the result of the experiment is to say that we find that a particular set of regions seem to be implicated in particular decisions, this does not tell us what these regions are doing, merely that they seem to be involved. Such a result can best be thought of as a qualitative result.

[4]   Obviously, the statistical analysis of the data in fMRI or PET experiments utilize a lot of interesting mathematics such as Fast Fourier Transforms, etc. However, the results themselves do not directly feed into a mathematical model of behavior in the way that behavioral data from economic experiments seem to.

[5]   Under this model the method of discounting is such that the current utility value of a stream of consumption in the future will be:

$$u_t = c_t + \beta[\delta c_{t+1} + \delta^2 c_{t+2} + \delta^3 c_{t+3} + \ldots]$$

different brain regions had higher levels of activation when different time discounting choices were made. That is, when immediacy predominated, areas associated with the so-called prelimbic system were more active, and when the standard exponential discounting best described the choices made, the prefrontal areas associated with executive control as well as the parietal cortex were more active. McClure et al. argue this evidence bolsters the case that a model something like quasi-hyperbolic discounting best describes the time discounting process people use. The explanation is that the brain has different regions that are used for discounting and anything that one can obtain immediately has greater salience than something that can be obtained only in the future.

One should note that the nature of time discounting is the subject of a vigorous debate. Other researchers (Kable and Glimcher 2010) argue that their experiments provide evidence of a different form of the discount function that is closer to standard hyperbolic discounting.[6] They also present evidence that the activation in the three regions[7] that had been thought to encode immediacy of reward actually encode something closer to subjective value. Kable and Glimcher found that their subjects did not behave in accordance with the quasi-hyperbolic model in terms of preference reversals. Rather they were more consistent with the hyperbolic model and even more consistent with a hyperbolic model that is not anchored in the present but at a time determined by the nearest point in time a payoff is possible. Still other researchers such as Sripada, Gonzalez, Phan, and Liberzon (2011) found evidence that the three regions encode subjective value (consistent with the findings of Kable and Glimcher) but also found that the medial prefrontal cortex and posterior cingulate cortex seem to be more active when subjects consider immediate rewards. Taken together these experiments support the assumption that the same regions (possibly even the same neural circuits) are involved in different types of processing at the same time. Interestingly, the choices made by the subjects in the experiment of Sripada et al. were well described by the exponential discounting model. This may indicate that the intertemporal decision-making process is much more complex than contemplated by any of these models. The purpose of discussing these additional models is not to mediate the various claims. Rather it is to note that the nature of the neural processes involved in time discounting is a very active area of research.

For the purposes of discussing the contrasting different types of research let us set aside these complexities and consider the McClure et al. study on its own. While their results seem to be helpful in arguing for a model such as quasi-hyperbolic discounting, we note

---

as compared to the standard model of exponential discounting which can be written as:

$$u_t = c_t + \delta c_{t+1} + \delta^2 c_{t+2} + \delta^3 c_{t+3} + \ldots$$

That is, in the quasi-hyperbolic discounting model, the difference between current consumption and consumption in the next period is more highly discounted than the differences between other consecutive periods (between the second period and the third period).

[6]   Kable and Glimcher (2010) propose a model which takes the form , where $SV = \frac{A}{1 + k(T - T^{ASAP})}$, is the subjective value of any given choice and is the difference in time between the given choice and the choice which gives the payoff at a time closest to the present ("as soon as possible").

[7]   The three regions include the ventral striatum, the ventromedial prefrontal cortex and the posterior cingulate cortex.

that even if we believe this model, the mechanisms they discuss are not the only way that quasi-hyperbolic discounting could have been instantiated. That is, the brain circuitry for this type of behavior could have been and indeed might be different. Quasi-hyperbolic discounting might have been instantiated in a single brain region, or exponential discounting might have been instantiated in two different regions. Indeed, this same argument could be applied to any type of discounting model that one might come up with.[8] So while these neural activation results seem useful, they are in no way conclusive as to the proper structure of the model. Nor do they help us to formulate the discounting model in any way beyond what the behavioral data alone would have allowed. That is, observing that the processing occurred in particular regions is not necessarily dispositive as to the type of processing that is occurring, given the current level of knowledge of neural circuitry. That is, because the same neural regions can be associated with different mental processes, merely identifying an active region does not uniquely identify the mental process being utilized.

To illustrate how neuroeconomics can provide more direct evidence of a model and assist in parameterizing functional forms already postulated or potentially suggest new and better functional forms for modeling decision-making, we might contrast McClure et al. with a recent study that examined neural activation of subjects during an investment game. As reviewed more fully below in Section 2, this study looked at the activity level in the ventromedial prefrontal cortex and the ventral striatum for realized gains as compared to unrealized or "paper" gains and found that this difference related to choices which imply that realized gains are preferred to "paper" gains (Frydman et al. 2014). Looking only at activations in these regions, one could predict that outcomes during the periods of lower activation were less highly valued than outcomes during the periods of higher activations. These predictions would have accurately forecast the actions of the subjects.

In particular, this experiment helps us to differentiate between models that assume that the disposition effect[9] is due to a misapplication of mean-reversion as opposed to differences in valuation of realized versus unrealized gains.[10] The Frydman et al. study reports what appears to be a higher valuation for realized gains relative to unrealized gains. As discussed more fully below, the evidence from this experiment appears to support a realized utility model (Shefrin and Statman 1985).[11] Of course, as we saw with the prior discussion of models of time discounting, there likely is a great deal more to the story that

---

[8]   One can see this by considering the parallel versus single processing of equations by computers. Some mathematical process may be more efficiently dealt with through parallel processing, however in general almost any type of process can in principle be done by a single processing unit. This follows from the Church-Turing Thesis (Church 1936). While this thesis cannot be proven, mathematicians almost universally accept it (Davis 1965).

[9]   The disposition effect is the name of the phenomenon in which investors are more likely to sell an investment that has experienced an increase in value and retain one that has experienced a decrease in value (Odean 1998).

[10]   If one believes that returns are uncorrelated over time, then investments that have made gains should be sold with equal frequency to those that have lost value. However, if you believe that investments which have made high returns are likely to make low returns, and vice versa (i.e., that returns exhibit mean-reversion), then it would make sense to sell investments which have experienced gains and continue to hold those which have experienced losses.

[11]   Under the realized utility model, increases in the value of investments that have been

we can derive from this one experiment. Indeed, other brain regions certainly affect these calculations. In addition, the study's results do not tell us exactly what calculations are made in the process of valuation, although it does give some indications. As with nearly every subject discussed in this chapter, a lot more research will likely have to done before we can claim to understand this behavior.

The contrast of the two types of experimental research—fact discovery and theory testing—while illustrative, is not perfect. Both types of studies help us to understand the decision-making process. Indeed, there is much overlap in the type of analysis in these two types of experiments. However, we would argue that the work along the lines of the study of realized gains is of more direct value because it presents stronger evidence for the hypothesis it is used to test than does the evidence from the experiment concerning quasi-hyperbolic discounting. One should note that in large measure, the reason for the difference in results is the difference in the nature of the hypotheses the two papers were testing. The McClure et al. study examined a theory that predicted only that two different processes were occurring, while the Frydman et al. study examined a model that makes predictions about the difference in the level of activations within the same system.

Currently, neuroeconomic research is at its most rigorous and immediately useful when its focus is on what we will refer to as short-term decision-making. By the term "short-term decisions" we mean those decisions where all of the information necessary for the decision is revealed to the subject during the experiment and the decision is made during the course of the experiment. Long-term decisions would then be those decisions where at least some element of the decision and the processing of the decision is made outside of the structure of the experiment. Short-term decisions, such as a choice of what to consume immediately, are likely more susceptible to analysis by laboratory methods than longer-term decisions. That is, neuroeconomics is currently more able to give insight into choices made by subjects during an experiment than about the retirement planning of these same individuals.

The short-term versus long-term decision problem is a standard one for experimental economics. If some part of the decision is not observed during the experiment, we have likely lost some degree of understanding over what determined that decision. This is a variant of the problem of external validity of the results obtained in the lab. That is, even if we can describe the decisions individuals make in the lab perfectly, it is not clear what this tells us about decisions made outside the lab. This issue of external validity has been an important one for experimental economics since its inception.[12] This problem is even more acute for neuroeconomics because it is attempting to model neural processes explicitly, and not simply decisions, and so the issue becomes more obvious. As a result, the time scales under study in neuroeconomics often are even shorter than those utilized in traditional experimental economics. Our ability to extend the results from the activity that occurs at a time scale of about a second (which is typical in fMRI studies) to decisions taking hours to perhaps weeks becomes less obvious. While the hope and belief of all researchers in both experimental economics and neuroeconomics is that we are

---

"realized," i.e., where the gains have been converted into cash, are valued more highly than increases in investments that are "unrealized" or still contained in the investment.

[12]   Based on these types of considerations, the use of field experiments has grown (List 2011). A large literature discusses the notion of externality validity with respect to experiments and the extent to which it is and is not a valid criticism. See Plott (1982, 2001).

discovering relevant information, whether what we find is relevant must be demonstrated outside of the lab.

Of course, it is not the case that neuroeconomics has nothing to say about long-term decisions. Neuroeconomic research has given us some important information about the neurological bases of long-range planning. For example, studies of individuals with various types of brain injuries and the deficits they seem to suffer are an important source of information about this (Bechara, Damasio, and Damasio 2000). Unfortunately, this does not necessarily directly help us model behavior. In order to use this information to model behavior, knowledge that particular neural regions are involved is insufficient, as the same region can be involved in a number of different processes. We need to understand more fully what type of processing occurs in these brain regions as the particular decisions we are studying are being made. Similarly, as discussed in the next section, knowing that success as a trader of financial assets appears to be correlated with a certain genetic profile does not tell us what is different about the decision process of the individuals who possess that profile. In Section 2 we discuss how such research can be used to suggest what may be occurring in long-term decision-making. Because, as mentioned above, the evidence from research on longer-term decisions is less strong than it is for short-term decisions, our conclusions about the neural processes involved in long-term decisions must, by their nature, be more tentative.

Importantly, to some degree, the current study of neuroeconomics is limited by our degree of both temporal and spatial resolution of neural activity.[13] If we could somehow keep track of every cell in the human brain and be able to process the information we obtain at the cellular level then we could truly understand how decisions are made.[14] As we discuss below, the temporal differences in decisions can matter. There is a fair amount of evidence that the same neural structure can be used for different decisions at the same time, with different latencies in the process (Schultz 2009).[15] This might significantly complicate our models of decision-making.

Unfortunately, neuroeconomics faces a problem much like that in the old joke about the drunk who has lost his keys.[16] That is, the questions we wish to answer are not the questions we can answer easily. However, science progresses by focusing on small answerable questions (Weisskopf 1972). We then hope that these answers allow us to progress towards larger questions. Neuroeconomics, like any new area of research needs to focus on the questions it can answer with the hope that the answers will build up to allow us to answer the questions in which we are truly interested.

One thing that is clear from the study of the neural mechanisms of decisions is that the brain uses a variety of modules, each of which have separate tasks. The hodology of these interactions will clearly be a focus of future research. To illustrate this, some of the earliest

---

[13]  For example, processes that occur at faster time scales than we can measure escape our notice.

[14]  This is not merely a detection problem, but also a storage and computing problem given the size of the human brain.

[15]  One can analogize this to Fourier modes in the brain activations. For an accessible discussion of Fourier modes, see Chapter 3 of Haberman (1998).

[16]  The old joke goes: A drunk loses his house keys. A policeman comes upon the drunk looking for his keys under a lamppost. He starts to help him look for his keys. After a few minutes of unsuccessful searching, the policeman says to the drunk, "are you sure you dropped your keys here?" The drunk responds "I lost them over there, but the light is better here."

work in neuroeconomics indicated that some neural ensemble in the orbitofrontal cortex appears to create some warning about potential adverse consequences. Based on many years of studying individuals with brain lesions, decisions appear to require processing in multiple areas to achieve optimality (or at least what we might term better decisions) (Bechara, Damasio, and Damasio 2000). While a significant body of evidence suggests that decisions involve the integration of conflicting areas (Bossaerts, Preuschoff, and Hsu 2009), the precise nature of these interactions is unclear.

As mentioned previously, this chapter will be highly selective and even opinionated in its discussion. This chapter will focus on research concerning financial decisions. This is in part because so much research has been done in this area, and because the work on financial decisions has a natural and direct relevance to law. We hope that this chapter illustrates how neuroeconomic work is not only relevant but also essential to understanding human decisions.

Decisions are at the center of legal scholarship, particularly so in law and economic scholarship. Research in law and economics seeks to understand the impact of laws and other systems of rules by utilizing the methods of economics. To the extent neuroeconomic research affects economics, at a minimum it will likely affect legal scholarship in the area of law and economics. Furthermore, the manner in which individuals make decisions is of clear relevance to legal scholarship in general. Some applications of neuroeconomics to legal scholarship, particularly in terms of taxation and the regulation of financial markets, are discussed at the end of the chapter.

## 2.   THE NEURAL BASIS OF FINANCIAL DECISIONS

Researchers have done a fair amount of intriguing work on the neurological basis of financial decisions. Financial decisions involve choices between different investments. Investments are not commonly thought to be valuable in and of themselves, but their value derives from an increase in the ability of the investment owners to consume in some future period (Berns and Montague 2002). Different investments are distinguished by differences in their return and their risk, however that risk is defined.

Standard financial models are based on the idea that individuals make investments so as to maximize returns relative to the risks undertaken. We can then see that under standard economic models, financial decisions are in most ways not any different than decisions made in other domains. Individuals simply make choices that maximize a utility function. The complications that arise in financial models involve the form that the constraints on risk-taking assume as well as the process of the formation of expectations based on the prior behavior of assets.

A large number of models in the academic literature on finance are not strictly based on assumptions about the utility functions of individuals. These models, such as the Fama-French model[17] (Fama and French 1993), are based on statistical observations that

---

[17]   In the Fama-French model, returns on any particular equity investments are related to the return on the equity market as a whole, as well as two additional portfolios. The first is a portfolio that gives the return of small companies minus the return to large companies. The second gives

have been found to correlate with the behavior of markets better than models that are built up from utility assumptions (Cochrane 2005). These statistical models essentially eschew the choices of individual actors and use the structure of the markets themselves to determine the dynamics of prices. Neuroeconomics is unlikely to be able to address these models to any significant degree in the near future as they are not explicitly based on individual perceptions and behavior. Therefore, neuroeconomic work should focus on models derived from individual utility.

## 2.1  Stochastic Discount Factors

Before entering a discussion of the neuroeconomic research as applied to finance, it is useful to discuss the financial model that we will use as the framework for analyzing neuroeconomic work. Standard financial economics textbooks (Cochrane 2005) often start with a two-period model,[18] which can be expressed as:

$$U_t(c_t, c_{t+1}) = u_t(c_t) + \delta E[u_{t+1}(c_{t+1})] \tag{1}$$

Here, $U_t$ is the utility of the individual at time $t$, $u_t$ is the utility of current consumption, $u_{t+1}$ is the utility of future consumption and $c_t$ and $c_{t+1}$ are the time indexed consumption amounts. $\delta$ is the discount factor assuming that period $t+1$ consumption is discounted relative to current consumption. Note that in this setup, there is no assumption that the consumption utility function is the same in the two periods. This setup of the model is more general than in standard textbooks which generally restrict $u_t(\cdot) = u_{t+1}(\cdot)$. This generality in equation (1) is designed to allow us to include features such as habit formation or other changes to the utility function that might occur in the two periods. As is standard in economics, we assume that the decision to consume in the first period as opposed to the second will have to be such that the marginal utility to current consumption must be equal to the discounted marginal utility from consumption in the second period. This means that if the price of a unit of the investment in the current period is $p_t$ and the payoff of the investment in the next period is $x_{t+1}$ then we have a first order condition:

$$-p_t u_t'(c_t) + \delta E[u'_{t+1}(c_{t+1})x_{t+1}] = 0.$$

Rearranging gives us:

$$p_t = E\left[\delta \frac{u'_{t+1}(c_{t+1})}{u_t'(c_t)} x_{t+1}\right] \tag{2}$$

This is sometimes written:

$$p_t = E[mx_{t+1}]$$

where $m = \delta \frac{u'_{t+1}(c_{t+1})}{u'_t(c_t)}$.

---

the return of companies with a high book-to-market ratio minus those with a low book-to-market ratio.

[18]  Merton (1973) was the first to put forth this model.

The expression $m$ is often referred to as the pricing kernel or the stochastic discount factor. This pricing kernel translates "true" probabilities into those that can be used to price assets in the market.[19] We can see that this factor includes the discount for time, $\delta$, as well as other features of utility functions like risk-aversion (because the shape of the utility curve will determine marginal utility), which enter into the formula through the ratio of marginal utilities, that is $\frac{u_{t+1}'(c_{t+1})}{u_t'(c_t)}$.

We should note that we have not assumed that $c_t$ is a particular variable. Indeed, it could even be a vector of inputs (e.g., different consumption goods, or even lagged consumption from earlier periods), as long as the range of the utility function is the set of real numbers, or some subset of the real numbers. In addition, the utility function could assume almost any form, including wealth maximization as well as cumulative prospect theory.

Equation (2) is one of the fundamental equations of finance for determining the price of an asset. It is quite easy to extend this analysis to a multi-period model of the form:

$$p_t = E_t \left[ \sum_{j=1}^{\infty} \delta^j \frac{u_{t+j}'(c_{t+j})}{u_t'(c_t)} D_{t+j} \right] \tag{3}$$

Here the payoff in each period is $D_{t+j}$ (which one can conceive of as the dividend paid in that period). We can note that each period has its own discount factor and its own comparison to current period consumption.[20] Therefore, this model can accommodate standard methods of time discounting such as exponential or hyperbolic discounting. Indeed, in this framework almost any sequence of time discount factors is allowed.[21] For stochastic discount factors to exist we need only assume the existence of a differentiable utility function and that it is sensible to talk about a single price for an asset at any given time, sometimes called the law of one price (Cochrane 2005).

In this setup, we can see how neuroeconomics may be of use to academic finance scholars. A great deal of neuroeconomic work attempts to analyze the sequence of time discount factors $(\delta^1, \delta^2, \ldots)$ (McClure et al. 2004; Kable and Glimcher 2010). As discussed earlier, some of this work has lent strength to a quasi-hyperbolic series of discount factors, while other works seems to indicate different models might be more accurate. In addition, the nature of the sequence of utility functions $(u_t, u_{t+1}, \ldots)$ has also been the subject of research (see e.g., Frydman et al., 2014).

One interesting consequence of writing the pricing model using the stochastic discount factor is that we can see that both the time discounting sequence and the utility growth sequence are under the expectation operator. Most neuroeconomic research has considered these two sequences (time discount and utility growth) as having independent

---

[19]   Of course, the notion of "true" probabilities is problematic. A probability distribution is based on a level of information. Objective probabilities would mean a probability on which all observers could agree, but since each observer will have different information, such a probability does not exist. See De Finetti (1937).

[20]   There is not a comparison to consumption with other periods because it is assumed that the future self will make the future comparison correctly. In order to avoid bubbles in this model, we have to make a transversality assumption. That is, we have to assume that $E[m_{t,t+j} \, p_{t+j}] \to 0$ as $j \to \infty$ (Cochrane 2005). Of course, if any type of discounting other than exponential discounting is used, there will be some form of dynamic inconsistency.

[21]   It would be reasonable to restrict the value so that $\delta^1 < \delta^2 < \ldots$.

evolutions. However, if the evolution of the utility growth sequence is somehow related to the evolution of the discount factor, this could add a dimension to our modeling of financial decisions but likely at the sake of losing a significant degree of analytic tractability resulting in the necessity of utilizing computational methods to solve such models.

Another important feature of the stochastic discount factor is best understood by considering the representation $p_t = E[mx_{t+1}]$. Here, $m$ can be thought of as the Radon-Nikodym derivative,[22] which converts the "true" expected value to that which gives us the price observed in the market. Standard financial economics models assume that investors are utilizing the "correct" probabilities in calculating the expected value. But if individuals calculate the probabilities incorrectly, then we should include these probabilistic errors into the expected value we use to price assets. Doing this results in what is sometimes referred to as the behavioral stochastic discount factor (Shefrin 2008). This type of model would add a term in the stochastic discount factor. If the probability density function for the "true" probability of the payoff $x_{t+1}$ can be written as:

$$\Pi(x_{t+1}),$$

and if the probability density function as used by the market to price the asset is:

$$P(x_{t+1}),$$

then if we add the term:

$$\frac{P(x_{t+1})}{\Pi(x_{t+1})}$$

we now can write a stochastic discount factor to price assets based on the probability measure actually used by the market.[23] The new equation would become:

$$p_t = E\left[\frac{P(x_{t+1})}{\Pi(x_{t+1})}\delta\frac{u_{t+1}'(c_{t+1})}{u_t'(c_t)}x_{t+1}\right]$$

The new stochastic discount factor is then:

$$m = \frac{P(x_{t+1})}{\Pi(x_{t+1})}\delta\frac{u_{t+1}'(c_{t+1})}{u_t'(c_t)}$$

Much of the financial economics literature has been devoted to attempting to understand the nature of the stochastic discount factor and its dynamics (Cochrane 2005). Many scholars believe that understanding the stochastic discount factor is viewed as the key to understanding the dynamics of asset prices. Under this model, some element of the stochastic discount factor must change in order for the price of the asset to change. One can then think about neuroeconomic research on financial decisions as attempting to say

---

[22]  The Radon-Nikodym derivative is also referred to as the likelihood ratio when comparing two different probability distributions.
[23]  We are assuming here that $\Pi(x_{t+1})$ is absolutely continuous in relation to $P(x_{t+1})$. That is, the value of $\Pi(x_{t+1})$ is never zero unless the value of $P(x_{t+1})$ is also zero.

something about the stochastic discount factor or pricing kernel and the degree to which it is shaped by the neural mechanisms. To the extent that neuroeconomic work on financial assets is relevant to academic financial models, it is almost certainly directly related to the stochastic discount factor or some equivalent construct.

In attempting to relate the price observed in the market to other phenomena, the discussion so far has implicitly assumed that all individuals essentially share the same stochastic discount factor. However, this is absurd. Individuals most certainly differ in their estimates of probabilities, in their risk aversion and in their time discounting. So while the notion of a single stochastic discount factor for the entire market may be a coherent concept, it is not necessarily clear how one could derive this from individual stochastic discount factors (Shefrin 2008, Chapter 14; Constantinidies and Duffie 1996). This is similar to the standard problem in economics that unless preferences take on a certain form, known as the Gorman form, aggregating them into a demand function is essentially an intractable problem (Mas-Colell, Green and Whinston 1995, Chapter 4). Nonetheless, if certain phenomena correlate with changes in the stochastic discount factor of a large segment of market participants, it would seem reasonable to attempt to explain pricing moves by these factors even though we may not have a rigorous proof of what the precise effect should be on market prices.

The foregoing has essentially been an argument that, to the extent neuroeconomic work wishes to impact financial models in a direct way, it should be structured to say something about the form of the stochastic discount factor (or some equivalent model in financial economics). As a consequence, researchers investigating particular phenomena from the perspective of neuroscience should be mindful of how their research informs our understanding of the stochastic discount factor. That is, they should consider how the phenomenon under study affects the perception of probabilities, time discounting, risk aversion, or some combination of these.

## 2.2   Heterogeneous Behavior of Experienced versus Inexperienced Actors in the Market

Some of the earliest work that can be termed neuroeconomics dealt with the reaction of traders of financial assets to market price fluctuations. For example, Andrew Lo and Dmitry Repin (2002) looked at the physiological responses of traders to real-time trading events. They discuss how the trading decisions they studied were likely based on what the authors refer to as intuition, as opposed to reflective decisions due to the amount of time in which these decisions had to be made. For a large percentage of active market traders, such as those trading bonds, currencies, futures, options, and stocks, trading decisions have to be made within a matter of seconds to minutes. This is likely not enough time for deliberative decisions based on all currently available information. Therefore, decisions to buy or sell financial assets at the current market price are based to some significant degree on unconscious processes where neuroeconomics might be able to provide some significant explanatory power.

Lo and Repin's main focus was to compare the physiological responses (blood pressure, skin conductance, etc.) of younger traders to those of more experienced traders. They found that, except for very high volatility events and periods when the bid-ask spread changed, the more experienced traders had lower physiological responses than less experienced traders. The authors argue that this indicates that at some level experienced traders processed the information they observed in the market differently than did the less experienced traders.

The lower physiological responses of experienced traders have many possible explanations. Lo and Repin discuss how it might be that more experienced traders simply have to exert less cognitive effort in tasks that they have performed for years. Because the more experienced traders have experienced similar situations in the past, they know how to react. Therefore, experienced traders' decisions do not take as much cognitive effort as they would have earlier in the traders' careers. The fact that not all situations resulted in lower responses by the experienced traders indicates that the automated responses explanation is not the full story. Recall that two types of events were correlated with elevated physiological responses in experienced traders: changes in the bid-ask spread and the highest volatility events. The bid-ask spread for any asset is set by market insiders, who are the most aware of market movements. A change in the spread then indicates that these insiders believe that there has been a change in market dynamics. Similarly, very high volatility events may indicate a change in market dynamics as well. Therefore, both of these events can be taken to indicate that market behavior may be changing and attention must be paid to it.

Unfortunately, Lo and Repin do not report the relative performance of the experienced versus inexperienced traders during the period under study. They argue that this is too difficult because it is not possible to compare the amount of risk undertaken. Furthermore, the intraday volatility that they would have been able to observe is not necessarily indicative of the risk the traders were taking on. Volatility itself has a volatility (Tsay 2010). As a result, it may be that on any given day low volatility assets might experience higher price volatility than assets that normally have higher price volatility. It is difficult to draw conclusions from what is effectively a sample size of one (that is, only one day's worth of results were studied). This is unfortunate because if the more experienced traders were taking on less risk, this might also explain the brain activity. For example, if more experienced traders took on much less risk than inexperienced traders, this might explain why it took a very high level of volatility for them to experience elevated responses. Lower risk positions might not present significant risks unless the market is highly volatile. For example, if the experienced traders were more secure in their jobs, they may not have felt the need to take on as much risk, and the fact that they didn't take on as much risk might explain their lower brain activation.

Keeping these caveats in mind, this study can be viewed as evidence of the effect of experience on the use of information. That is, both experienced and inexperienced traders were exposed to the same information set (commonly denoted $\Omega_t$ or sometimes $_t$ in the academic literature). Yet, the investment professionals with different levels of experience reacted differently to this information. Therefore, the flow of information is not necessarily the key to determine how investors will view the market. A natural question is whether experienced investors are simply those who have better models to begin with and who survive in a Darwinian process or whether these professionals develop better models over time. Some research that might bear on this question is discussed below.

Interesting related work involves differences in investment strategies between experienced and inexperienced fund managers. Inexperienced fund managers were found to be more likely to invest in the stocks whose values crashed in the Internet bubble of the late 1990s (Greenwood and Nagel 2009). This provides some evidence that those who are experienced with financial markets behave differently than those who are not. One does need to be mindful of the differences between the decisions being made in the two studies. While the decisions of a mutual fund manager and a trader both concern which investments one should make, as well as how long one should continue to hold these investments, the position of mutual fund manager is different in many ways than that of a trader. The most important difference is the time frame in which these decisions are made. The trader has to make decisions essentially second-by-second, while mutual fund managers generally have days to weeks to make decisions. This may be a crucial difference in attempting to understand decisions made by the two groups.

We can connect this research to the stochastic discount factor by considering the difference between experienced and inexperienced investors. That is, do we believe that the different behavior observed affects the perceived probabilities, $P(x_{t+1})$, the discount factors, $\delta$, or risk aversion, $\frac{u'(x_t)}{u'(x_{t+1})}$? Greenwood and Nagel argue that learning theories are consistent with their evidence, which would imply that experience alters perceived probabilities. Perhaps inexperienced traders require more cognitive effort to trade because they are still learning probability distributions that accompany particular types of market dynamics. As discussed in the next section, research on the formation of asset pricing bubbles bears on this question, and so before discussing this further, we will first consider the research related to bubbles.

## 2.3   Asset Pricing Bubbles

In financial transactions, individuals and institutions attempt to outsmart the market, or at least to not be outsmarted by the market. That is, to some degree decisions concerning investments in financial markets are dependent on beliefs about how other actors in the markets will behave. Under classical finance theory, if markets are efficient and all actors believe markets are efficient, then asset price bubbles should not form. However, while asset price bubbles can generally not be proven to exist, casual empiricism would suggest that they do.

The discussion of the different processing styles of experienced versus inexperienced traders relates directly to a large body of work done on the causes and dynamics of asset pricing bubbles. A great deal of work in experimental economics explores the generation of bubbles as well their sustainability (Smith, Suchanek, and Williams 1988). One common theme in this work is that experience with the particular market being observed seems to reduce the likelihood of bubble formation as well as reduce the longevity of the bubbles that do arise (Hassam, Porter, and Smith 2008). We see that generally subjects learn not to enter into bubbles after having seen asset pricing bubble formation three times in the market in question.[24] Other work in which the participants in the experimental market are a mix of experienced and inexperienced investors has shown that if as few

---

[24]   It appears that the experience is very domain specific. In the experiments conducted in Hassam, Porter, and Smith (2008), the subjects were corporate executives participating in an on-campus program (Arizona Executive Program). The subjects were from a variety of different industries. The experiment still resulted in asset price bubbles in much the same way as has been observed with college students as subjects. We should note that most of the executives were not from the financial industry and would likely have seen bubbles in asset markets only indirectly

as one third of the investors are experienced (that is, they understand the problem of asset price bubble formation), then asset pricing bubbles do not form in these markets (Dufwenberg, Linquist, and Moore 2005).

Some work has attempted to investigate how neural mechanisms affect asset price bubble formation. Knutson et al. (2008) showed erotic pictures to a group of males who then participated in an experimental asset market. They found that asset-pricing bubbles were more likely to arise following exposure to these erotic images. A recent similar experiment was conducted where subjects were shown one of three types of videos: exciting, neutral or fearful. They found that exposing subjects to exciting videos resulted in larger asset pricing bubbles. (Lin, Odean and Andrade 2012). These experiments indicate that activation of certain neural systems, likely the dopaminergic system, which is involved in sexual attraction (Fisher, Aron, and Brown 2006), may make bubble formation more likely. It is not clear how these effects should be included in a financial market equilibrium with other traders who have not been exposed to this type of material. That is, given the experimental results on experience, the market dynamics are clearly complex, and applying these findings to the operation of financial markets outside the lab is difficult at best. One obvious difference is that erotic pictures are not flashed to all market participants in the field immediately before an asset pricing bubble begins. Indeed, these bubbles tend to form over a period of weeks, months, or even years. Clearly not all market participants are subject to the same stimuli over the entire period. Extending the research to markets in the field is therefore a very useful area of research.

We should note that the environments in these experiments generally differ from those in financial markets outside the lab in many additional ways that are likely to be important. In financial markets, there is a constant inflow of information outside of the movement of the prices themselves, such as political and other world events. Much of this information will have uncertain effects on prices. Indeed, sorting out the relevant from the irrelevant information is one of the biggest issues for financial decision-making. Because market actors are not able to process simultaneously all available information that is potentially relevant to prices, investors will focus on particular sets of information. Different investors will focus on different sets of information. Even those investors utilizing the same information will have different models for processing the information they have. Therefore, the level of complexity in financial markets is a great deal larger than it is in experimental markets.

With regard to the last point, some interesting work has been done on information transmission in the market. Bruguier, Quartz, and Bossaerts (2010) found that the ability to read signals from market insiders is correlated with performance on a test of the ability to formulate a theory of mind. This experiment tested the ability of uninformed traders to discern information from transaction prices and order flows. They found that informed traders conveyed information to uninformed traders through their trading actions. The authors argue that this may make the efficient market hypothesis more reasonable, because this would clearly be one mechanism that might result in efficient markets. Evidence such as this might help us to understand the common finding that financial

---

rather than directly. Therefore, experience in business in general does not prevent the formation of asset bubbles.

markets can be highly micro-efficient (that is, they incorporate current information into stock prices well) but macro-inefficient (they do not forecast macro events very well) (Jung and Shiller 2006). The findings of Bruguier et al. indicate that information can be effectively transmitted to the market without the information itself being transmitted. Of course, the type of information conveyed by such moves is likely to be of only short-term relevance because, in the long run, essentially all information is revealed to market actors.

How might we relate the research on asset price bubbles to stochastic discount factors? One possibility is to conclude that the stochastic discount factor has been formulated incorrectly. If individuals generally do not make infinite calculations, but rather do so only for finite time periods (and perhaps for only a few periods) then the possibility of bubbles exists. As discussed before, under standard finance theory, asset-pricing bubbles essentially should not form (Cochrane 2005). In order for bubbles to form, individuals would have to assume that the dividend-to-price ratio will have to grow without limit as time goes on. Consequently, asset price bubbles would form only if market actors believe prices will grow faster than the required return forever. Since this would be essentially impossible, bubbles should never form (Cochrane 2005). We can note that this argument assumes that the stochastic discount factor is of the form specified in equation (3).

One can see that the classic stochastic discount factor model assumes that individuals include an infinite number of terms in their stochastic discount factor. Under this assumption, the argument against rational bubbles works only if individuals believe that the price will continue to increase forever, and if not, then rational bubbles are not possible. However if individuals make calculations for a finite number of time periods, this conclusion does not necessarily hold. That is, if the prices are not based entirely on beliefs about future values, but also second-order beliefs about other investors' beliefs, the price might rise quickly within the time horizon of the investor. In that case, investors might believe the market price will increase rapidly for some period, and if each believes that he can sell the asset before the bubble collapses, then bubbles might form. Investors would then each act to form the bubble by buying the asset believing that individually they can profit from the price increase and sell the asset before the value collapses.

To the extent this is an accurate model, asset-pricing bubbles can be analogized to what are referred to as p-beauty games. In the most common form of p-beauty games, each contestant chooses an integer in the interval [0,100]. The contestant who wins is the one who chooses the integer closest to the p-multiplied average of all chosen integers. A common choice for p in these studies is 2/3. Therefore, a contestant should not attempt to choose the average of the chosen numbers, but rather something smaller. The game theoretic Nash equilibrium strategy derived using infinite backward induction is zero. However, in experiments, this is not what occurs (Camerer 2009). Often the modal choice is p times 50.[25] So here we see an example where individuals do not employ infinite backward induction of the type assumed in standard financial models, and the optimal response in this situation is not to backwardly induct infinitely.[26]

---

[25]   Fifty is the average of all integers in the choice set.

[26]   Models of this type are referred to as quantal response models. For a discussion, see Houser and McCabe (2009). In the case of p-beauty games, the optimal response appears to be $p^2$ times the average of the possible choices (e.g., 22 if p = 2/3).

Much like a p-beauty game, in asset pricing bubbles the optimal strategy is not to perform infinite calculations, but to backwardly induct only one step more than the average person. In the case of asset bubbles, this means "riding" the bubble, as long as the position is liquidated before the bubble collapses. Unfortunately, almost by definition the average market actor will not be able to do this. We could model this behavior by making an alteration to the stochastic discount factor. If there are not infinite periods, but only n-periods, then the investor has to believe only that the price of the asset will increase for n periods, instead of increasing for an infinite number of periods. Formally, the stochastic discount factor would become:

$$p_t = E_t\left[\sum_{j=1}^{n-1}\delta^j\frac{u'_{t+j}(c_{t+j})}{u'_t(c_t)}D_{t+j} + \delta^n\frac{u'_{t+n}(c_{t+n})}{u'_t(c_t)}x_{t+n}\right]$$

We note that the last term on the right hand side is the price of the asset at some finite time in the future, not an infinite sequence of dividends. This formula assumes expectations over the asset's market value at the time one wishes to sell the asset that may or may not reflect a reasonable discounted expected value of future cash flows of the asset. That is, because individuals are not making the calculations assumed in the argument against rational bubbles, the argument is inapplicable. Under our model of a modified stochastic discount factor, investors would behave as if they believe that markets are not rational in the sense of classic finance models and they are attempting to exploit this irrationality. Unfortunately, since by the nature of asset bubbles the average investor is caught in the collapse of the bubble, most investors are not able to carry out their investment strategy.

What happens both in repeat p-beauty games (Nagel 1995) as well as in asset pricing experiments is that individuals learn from their mistakes and that within a few periods, they are able to essentially utilize the rational strategy (choose a low integer or zero in the p-beauty game and not form asset bubbles). These experiments indicate that while market actors do not initially understand the implications of infinite backward induction, they can learn the implications over time.

One issue in bubble formation appears to be that individuals often learn not only from what happens to their investments, but also by what would have happened had they made different decisions (Lohrentz *et al.* 2007). Therefore, seeing that the investor could have made better returns by investing in something else may be related to regret theory. Indeed, regret seems to play a significant role in human decision-making (Coricelli, Dolan, and Sirigu 2007), although fictive learning is in many ways a broader concept than regret.[27] Interestingly, Coricelli, Dolan, and Sirigu argue that the attempt by individuals to minimize regret can actually result in the choices by players in games that converge to the rational solution of the game. One promising area of research may then be why certain individuals become involved in asset price bubbles while others do not and the extent to which fictive learning or regret may be involved.

---

[27]  Fictive learning here means altering future decisions based on counterfactual outcomes of what might have occurred if prior decisions had been different.

## 2.4   Genetic and Hormonal Studies

Another interesting line of research in the neural basis of financial decision-making is that of conducting genetic studies on individuals who have been successful in financial markets. A key recent paper is by Sapra, Beavin, and Zak (2012). This study compared the genetic profiles of 60 Wall Street professionals to those of students in a business school. Sapra et al. found a much higher prevalence of particular variants of dopamine receptors (DRD4P and COMT) among successful traders than among the business students.[28] While this work is highly suggestive of genetic differences between successful Wall Street traders and business school students, what to make of these differences is unclear. We do not yet know how these receptors are helpful in allowing these traders to have longer careers as traders of financial assets. It would be interesting to study how these genes are related to different behaviors. For example, among business students with these genes do we observe different tastes for risk? Do they attend to information differently?[29] Answers to questions such as these would help us to directly relate this work to financial models.

There are a number of further questions in connection to this type of work, at least as currently conducted. We need to consider the difference between what makes someone want to be a trader and what makes someone successful at being a trader. With regard to this, we first note that the study did not compare successful professionals with students in business schools at the time the professionals went to business school, nor from the same business schools the professional attended.[30] Therefore, to view the differences found in the study as indicative of differences in the populations we have to assume that the students who attend business school now have essentially the same genetic makeup as those who attended business school years ago when these professionals went to school. In addition, we cannot assume that all of these business students were planning on becoming traders, which is actually a fairly specialized role even within the financial industry. There are many other areas that individuals focus on in business school. Furthermore even within finance there are large differences between various positions in financial firms. Therefore, we may not be able to separate out desire to be a trader from ability to perform as a trader at this stage.

Another recent study (Kuhnen and Chiao 2009) found that risk-taking appears to be correlated with certain genes. The authors found that genes that had previously been linked to emotional behavior, anxiety, and addiction (5-HTTLPR as well DRD4) are correlated with risk-taking in investment decisions. They found that individuals who have the 5-HTTLPR s/s variant on average take on 28% less risk than those with s/l or l/l alleles. They also found that individuals with the DRD4 7-repeat allele took on 25%

---

[28]   DRD4P stand for dopamine receptor 4 promoter and COMT stands for catecholamine-D-methlytransferase. Both of these types of receptors affect synaptic dopamine, and the authors state that these are associated with moderate levels of synaptic dopamine.

[29]   There is some evidence that DRD4 is correlated with cognitive development (Posner et al. 2012).

[30]   Of course, just as Heraclitus noted that one cannot step into the same river twice, one cannot sample from the same school in different years. However, one might imagine that the students attending the same business school in different years may well share characteristics in ways that one might not expect across schools.

more risk than individuals without the 7-repeat version.[31] Again, it is unclear how these different receptors affect the decision-making process and why it may be that they affect risk-taking. Do they alter perceptions of probabilities, attitudes towards risk directly, some combination of the two, or something else altogether?

A few other studies have examined the potential impact of genes on financial decisions. One particularly interesting study was done on identical twins in Sweden. This study found that 25% of the risk preferences in the portfolios as a result of a mandated change in retirement accounts in Sweden could be explained by differences in genetic makeup (Cesarini et al. 2009). In addition, one study found that ambiguity aversion seems to have some genetic correlation as well (Chew, Ebstein, and Zhong 2012).

The genetic research discussed above indicates that the dopaminergic system may have a significant impact on financial decisions. The role played by the dopaminergic system in decision-making is highly complex (Schultz 2009). For example, the dopaminergic system seems at certain frequencies of neural firing to encode reward prediction error and at other frequencies to encode expected value as well. The same cells appear to be involved in multiple levels of processing. This creates significant complexity in attempting to determine the effect of these receptors in the financial decision-making process. The problem of attempting to model systems that have processes that operate at very different time scales is sometimes referred to as the stiffness of the system (Gockenbach 2011). This creates well-known problems for modeling and understanding the precise dynamics of decision-making. In particular, stiffness can cause models to be very sensitive to initial parameters, the time scales of the dynamics, and a number of neural inputs in the model. If these are not carefully chosen, models can easily incorrectly predict dynamics.

Other research has indicated that other neurotransmitters may also play a role in investment decisions. Knutson, Samanez-Larkin, and Kuhnen (2011) found that individuals who possess the short version of the serotonin transporter gene have portfolios that are less heavily weighted in equities and have fewer credit lines. They suggest that these individuals may be trying to avoid situations in which they have to make complicated financial decisions. Of course, there are many other possible reasons for this relationship (e.g., differences in risk aversion, or level of interest in wealth creation).

The genetic studies relate to the question of whether it is learning by professionals that makes the difference or if those with good investment strategies *ab initio* are successful and therefore long-lived investment professionals. It is possible that successful traders are different to begin with because of their different genetic structure. Of course, the finding that there is indeed something different in the genetic make-up of successful Wall Street traders or those who take on more risk is in no way contradictory to standard economics. Economic models generally do not take a position on how preferences or abilities arise. Preferences and ability almost certainly have some genetic component. Observing different dopamine processing may tell us something about traders' decisions. However, at this point it is unclear how we can incorporate this knowledge into our models. This work does

---

[31]   Other studies have found that the DRD4 7-repeat variant is correlated with higher novelty-seeking scores more than other DRD4 variants and is more likely to be found in pathological gamblers. One needs to be careful in drawing inferences about the effects of variants of the DRD4 gene on behavior. A meta-analysis of the studies concerning this gene found inconclusive evidence that the gene was correlated with novelty seeking (Munafo et al. 2008).

suggest that researchers should attempt to understand the mechanisms by which those genes act to create the preferences or abilities, or both, that translate into success in the financial market.

Another very interesting line of research deals with hormonal levels and trading decisions. It has been well established that hormonal levels can significantly alter decisions. Churchland and Winkielmann (2012) discuss the regulatory effects of neuropeptides such as oxytocin and vasopressin. These neuropeptides and hormones seem to have a significant effect on the regulation of behavior.

Specifically as applied to financial markets, Coates and Herbert (2007) found that higher levels of testosterone in the morning correlated with trading success later that day. If hormones have a significant effect on trading activity, then given the relationship between hormones and weather, this may be a partial explanation of results that seem to correlate the weather in the city of the market and the performance of the market (Hirschliefer and Shumway 2003).

Follow-up work by Coates and Page (2009) indicates that the higher returns observed due to higher levels of testosterone in the earlier study may be the result of a greater willingness to take on risk. They found that traders who have higher levels of testosterone did not in general make better choices, just riskier ones (as measured by the Sharpe Ratio).[32] In most financial models, greater risk is associated with a higher expected value of returns, and so, because the results in Coates and Herbert (2007) were averaged over a large number of traders, it should not surprise us that, on average, traders who take on more risk have higher returns.

One potential upshot of the effect of hormones and other similar influences on decisions is that perhaps something along the lines of the random utility model provides the most accurate description of trader decisions (Glimcher 2010). That is, on any given day, variables other than economic news may affect the flow of market prices. Observed variables, such as prices and macroeconomic variables, are insufficient to predict behavior, and so we would have to include some unknown variables, which are essentially the same, from our perspective, as random variables.[33] Therefore, factors that are not generally thought to affect market prices might actually do so. Of course, to the extent that this is true, it is unclear why other market participants have not attempted to discover these variables and utilize this information to earn a profit, thus bringing markets back to efficiency, where market prices reflect the "true" value of the assets. While hormonal fluctuations can explain some elements of market price dynamics, such fluctuations are not likely to explain significant asset bubbles. Pricing bubbles in the stock market often last for years. It seems implausible that a significant portion of market actors sustains hormonal fluctuations for such a period of time.

If, as the genetic studies indicate, successful Wall Street professionals are neurologically different from the rest of the population, we might wish to focus experimental work on those who have these genetic features. The question of what information and market

---

[32] They did find that greater experience with the market did result in investors being able to obtain higher returns at lower risk (that is, their experience resulted in higher Sharpe ratios).

[33] Interestingly, perhaps these additional variables might be indirectly included in models such as the Fama-French model (Fama and French 1993) if they affect the factors in the model.

mechanisms make it more or less likely for asset pricing bubbles to form in populations similar to those of market actors is clearly an important area of ongoing research. It appears that hormonal or dopaminergic stimulation alters risk aversion, and it might alter the perception of probabilities as well. Either of these changes can be seen to affect the stochastic discount factor.[34] On a cautionary note, McCullough, Churchland, and Mendez (2013) discuss some of the problems with measurement of hormonal levels, which are of course crucial to determining the effect of hormones and other neuroactive chemicals. They argue for caution in interpreting these studies given the difficulty in measuring some types of hormones and other bioactive chemicals.

## 2.5 Realized Utility

Another interesting line of work addresses the question of how individuals decide when to sell assets. A lot of behavioral research indicates that individuals hold assets that have experienced losses longer than they should, based on a simple calculation of wealth maximization (Odean 1998). It has been long observed that so-called "paper" gains and losses are not treated in the same way as realized gains and losses (realized gains or losses are those from positions that have been sold or closed and so are no longer subject to market fluctuations), although standard economic models treat them the same. Researchers often refer to this phenomenon as realized utility. Frydman et al. (2014) examined neural activity while the subjects chose whether to realize or defer gains and losses. They found that individuals had higher levels of activation in the ventromedial prefrontal cortex and the ventral striatum for realized gains than for so-called "paper" gains. The authors hypothesize that the reason individuals hold on to losing portfolios is that, even though this does not make sense in the context of the experiment,[35] individuals do not fully experience a gain or loss until recognized. A finding consistent with realized utility models is the commonly observed behavior that individual investors often trade too often. That is, individuals have a desire to trade assets that are currently returning a net gain because such a trade will increase their utility, even though there is little reason to believe that entering into a trade is advantageous in the long run. This increase in utility arises because the sale ensures that the transaction will end with a gain, which appears to have additional value to the investor above and beyond the actual gain itself. Thus, these investors will incur high trading costs and enter into more trades than is optimal given standard preferences.

An important question is whether the neural mechanisms observed are used not only for decisions in these experiments, which can be closely analogized to day trading, or

---

[34]   Recall the key term in the stochastic discount factor is $\frac{u'_{i+1}(c_{i+1})}{u'_i(c_i)}$, which is likely to be affected by altering risk aversion, which is often measured by the ratio $\frac{u''(c)}{u'(c)}$. Furthermore, since the stochastic discount factor is an expected value, the alteration of the probabilities assigned to potential outcomes will likely affect this expected value.

[35]   In this experiment, returns on stocks exhibited positive autocorrelation. That is, if a stock had returned a gain in one period, it was more likely to return a gain in the next period, and, symmetrically, stocks that returned a loss in one period were likely to return a loss in the next period. Therefore, to maximize returns, investors should retain stock that have just experienced a gain and sell stocks that have just experienced a loss. This is the opposite of what subjects did.

whether they also apply to longer-term decisions such as whether to sell a house. While similar behavior has been observed in those circumstances as well (Genesove and Mayer 2001), at this point we cannot be sure that this is the result of the same decision process.

Realized utility models relate to the stochastic discount factor in a complicated fashion. Here, the element of the model that is being changed is the utility function itself: $u(x_{t+1})$. In this case, the expected utility of continuing to invest once the security increases in value must overcome the utility of currently realizing the gain. One speculative idea is that the optimism bias often observed in psychology studies (Griffin and Tversky 1992) might be balanced by realized utility in many situations, so that together these two mental phenomena result in behavior that may be closer to that of the "rational" investor of standard finance theory.

## 2.6   Applications

Neuroeconomic research on financial decisions has numerous implications for legal scholarship. For example, whether individuals use standard expected utility or something closer to realized utility can have implications for the taxation of investment income. Under the standard economic theory of income taxation (Simons 1938) unrealized gains should be taxed in the same way that realized gains are. If individuals treat realized gains differently from "paper" gains, one might argue that these two types of gains should be taxed differently (Chorvat 2003). If the tax system taxed both types of gains in the same way, individuals would undervalue assets that create paper gains because their tax cost would be the same as assets they value more highly, i.e. those that give realized gains. The tax system would then differentially discourage investment in assets that are more likely to create "paper" gains in the near term as compared to assets that give immediate realized payoffs.

In addition, understanding how financial investment decisions are made can have obvious impacts in the regulation of securities markets. Of course, the most attention-grabbing applications would involve rules to inhibit asset price bubble formation. Interestingly, the research in this area indicates that experienced investors behave differently given the same information. Such findings indicate that information disclosure may be insufficient to foster efficient markets. Indeed, the bubble experiments indicate that experience itself may be necessary to prevent asset bubbles. Unfortunately, experience is not something that can be legislated. Furthermore, it does not seem that learning about bubbles in some abstract way prepares individuals to deal with them in the market (Greenwood and Nagel 2009). If the disclosure of information is not sufficient to help investors, regulators need to consider what type of interventions will foster better actions by investors. Unfortunately, detecting bubbles in financial markets is often difficult (Gurkaynak 2005).

Further research in this area might examine whether participation in asset price bubble experiments might alter the way that investors perceive real investment choices. That is, is it possible to give market participants simulated experience that might allow them to make better investment choices in the future? The research done on fictive learning indicates that individuals do not necessarily have to experience losses but merely the possibility of losses in order to learn about markets. If this is possible, it suggests that regulators should require this type of training of at least some market participants.

The genetic studies on investment behavior indicate that further research should perhaps take into account the types of individuals being studied as compared to the types of individuals the legal system hopes it might influence. Perhaps research on bubbles should focus on those who are most like market actors in order to understand what information and institutions will reduce the likelihood of asset pricing bubbles. Furthermore, by better understanding what information successful Wall Street professionals attend to, legal rules can help make this information more salient to other market participants.

Of course, concern with financial markets is not focused only on mitigating the effects of asset price bubbles. One of the goals of the legal system is to ensure the quick dissemination of information to aid efficient pricing in markets. The work of Bruguier et al. indicates that the effect of information can be disseminated without the information itself being disseminated. This might reduce concern over information disclosure. However, information must still be disseminated to a reasonable segment of the market in order for this effect to operate.

The studies showing that priming of the dopaminergic system indicate that the disclosures and required paperwork necessary before investing may have value, even if individuals do not retain or understand the information they are given. By subjecting individuals to a non-excitatory stimuli, researchers may be reducing the over-stimulated dopaminergic state, a state that might trigger an individual to be overly willing to take on risk. This suggests that investor protections may be effective for reasons different from those that motivated their adoption.

## 3.   CONCLUSION

This chapter argues that neuroeconomic research should attempt to focus on standard models that relate to the behavior being studied. Focusing on such models will help to focus the research as well as suggest profitable extensions of the research. The improved models will help us to better understand and craft legal rules and institutions.

## BIBLIOGRAPHY

Asparouhova, Elena, Peter Bossaerts, and Ahn Tran. 2012. Market Bubbles and Crashes as an Expression of Tension Between Social and Individual Rationality: Experiments. Working Paper. Caltech, Pasadena, CA.
Bechara, Antoine, Hanna Damasio, and Antonio Damasio. 2000. Emotion, Decision Making and the Orbitofrontal Cortex. *Cerebral Cortex* 10(3): 295–307.
Becker, Gary. 1962. Irrational Behavior. *Journal of Political Economy* 70(1): 1–13.
Bernheim, B. Douglas. 2009. The Psychology and Neurobiology of Judgment and Decision-Making: What's in it for Economists. Pp. 115–125 in *Neuroeconomics: Decision Making and the Brain*, edited by Paul Glimcher, Colin F. Camerer, Ernst Fehr, and Russell A. Poldack. London: Academic Press.
Berns, Gregory and Read Montague. 2002. Neural Economics and the Biological Substrates of Valuation. *Neuron* 36(2): 265–284.
Birks, John B. 1962. *Rutherford at Manchester*. London: Heywood & Co.
Bossaerts, Peter, Kersten Preuschoff, and Ming Hsu. 2009. The Neurobiological Foundations of Valuation in Human Decision Making under Uncertainty. Pp. 353–366 in *Neuroeconomics: Decision Making and the Brain*, edited by Paul Glimcher, Colin F. Camerer, Ernst Fehr, and Russell A. Poldack. London: Academic Press.
Bruguier, Antoine, Steven R. Quartz, and Peter Bossaerts. 2010. Exploring the Nature of "Trader Intuition." *Journal of Finance* 65: 1703–1723.
Camerer, Colin. 2008. The Case for Mindful Economics. Pp. 43–69 in *The Foundations of Positive and Normative Economics: A Handbook*, edited by Andrew Caplin and Andrew Schotter. New York: Oxford University Press.

Camerer, Colin. 2009. Behavioral Game Theory and the Neural Basis of Strategic Choice. Pp. 193–206 in *Neuroeconomics: Decision Making and the Brain*, edited by Paul Glimcher, Colin F. Camerer, Ernst Fehr, and Russell A. Poldack. London: Academic Press.

Camerer, Colin, George Lowenstein, and Drazen Prelec. 2005. Neuroeconomics: How Neuroscience Can Inform Economics. *Journal of Economic Literature* 43: 9–64.

Campbell, John and John Cochrane. 1999. By Force of Habit: A Consumption Based Explanation of Aggregate Stock Behavior. *Journal of Political Economy* 107: 205–251.

Carroll, Lewis. 1871. *Through the Looking Glass and What Alice Found There*. London: Macmillan.

Cesarini, David, Christopher Dawes, Magnus Johannesson, Paul Lichtenstein, Björn Wallace. 2009. Genetic Variation in Preferences for Giving and Risk-Taking. *Quarterly Journal of Economics* 124: 809–842.

Chew, Soo Hong, Richard P. Ebstein, and Song Fa Zhong. 2012. Ambiguity Aversion and Familiarity Bias: Evidence from Behavioral and Gene Association Studies. *Journal of Risk and Uncertainty* 44(1): 1–18.

Chorvat, Terrence. 2003. Perception and Income: The Behavioral Economics of the Realization Doctrine. *Connecticut Law Review* 36: 75–124.

Church, A. 1936. An Unsolvable Problem of Elementary Number Theory. *American Journal of Mathematics* 58: 345–363.

Churchland, Patricia and Piotr Winkielmann 2012. Modulating Social Behavior with Oxytocin: How Does it Work? What Does It Mean. *Hormones and Behavior* 61: 392–399.

Coates, J. M. and J. Herbert. 2007. Endogenous Steroids and Financial Risk on a London Trading Floor. *Proceedings of the National Academy of Sciences* 105: 6167–6172.

Coates, John and Lionel Page. 2009. A Note on Trader Sharpe Ratios. *PLoS One* 4(11): e8036.

Cochrane, John. 2005. *Asset Pricing*. Princeton, NJ: Princeton University Press.

Constantinidies, George and Darrell Duffie. 1996. Asset Pricing with Heterogeneous Consumers. *Journal of Political Economy* 104: 219–240.

Coricelli, Giorgio, Raymond Dolan, and Angela Sirigu. 2007. Brain, Emotion and Decision Making: The Paradigmatic Example of Regret. *Trends in Cognitive Sciences* 11(6): 258–265.

Davis, Martin, ed. 1965. *The Undecidable, Basic Papers on Undecidable Propositions, Unsolvable Problems and Computable Functions*. New York: Raven Press.

De Finetti, Bruno. 1937. La Prevision: ses Lois Logiques, ses Source Sujectives. *Annales de l'Institut Henri Poincaré* 7: 1–68.

Dufwenberg, Martin, Tobias Lindquist, and Evan Moore. 2005. Bubbles and Experience: An Experiment. *American Economic Review* 95: 1731–1737.

Fama, Eugene and Kenneth French. 1993. Common Risk Factors in the Returns for Stocks and Bonds. *Journal of Financial Economics* 3(1): 3–56.

Fisher, Helen E., Arthur Aron, and Lucy L. Brown. 2006. Romantic Love: A Mammalian Brain System for Mate Choice. *Philosophical Transactions of the Royal Society of London. Series B: Biological Sciences* 361(1476): 2173–2186.

Frydman, Cary, Nicholas Barberis, Colin Camerer, Peter Bossaerts, and Antonio Rangel. 2014. Using Neural Data to Test a Theory of Investor Behavior: An Application to Realization Utility. *Journal of Finance* 69: 907–946.

Gabianni, Fabrizio and Steven Cox. 2010. *Mathematics for Neuroscience*. London: Academic Press.

Genesove, David and Christopher Mayer. 2001. Loss Aversion and Seller Behavior: Evidence from the Housing Market. *Quarterly Journal of Economics* 116: 1233–1260.

Gigerenzer, Gerd. 2000. *Adaptive Thinking: Rationality in the Real World*. New York: Oxford University Press.

Glimcher, Paul. 2010. *Foundations of Neuroeconomic Analysis*. New York: Oxford University Press.

Glimcher, Paul, Colin F. Camerer, Ernst Fehr, and Russell A. Poldrack, eds. 2009. *Neuroeconomics: Decision Making and the Brain*. London: Academic Press.

Gockenbach, Mark. 2011. *Partial Differential Equations: Analytical and Numerical Methods*. Philadelphia, PA: Society for Industrial and Applied Mathematics.

Greenwood, Robin and Stefan Nagel. 2009. Inexperienced Investors and Bubbles. *Journal of Finance Economics* 93(2): 239–258.

Griffin, Dale and Amos Tversky. 1992. The Weighting of Evidence and the Determinants of Confidence *Cognitive Psychology* 24: 411–435.

Gul, Faruk and Wolfgang Pesendorfer. 2008. The Case for Mindless Economics. Pp. 3–42 in *The Foundations of Positive and Normative Economics: A Handbook*, edited by Andrew Caplin and Andrew Schotter. New York: Oxford University Press.

Gurkaynak, Refet. 2005. Econometric Tests of Asset Pricing Bubbles: Taking Stock. *Federal Reserve Finance and Economics Discussion Series 2004–2005*.

Haberman, Richard. 1998. *Applied Partial Differential Equations*, 4th edn. New York: Pearson.

Hassam, Deshmann, David Porter, and Vernon Smith. 2008. Thar She Blows: Can Bubbles be Rekindled with Experienced Subjects. *American Economic Review* 98(3): 924–937.

Hirschliefer, David and Tyler Shumway. 2003. Good Day Sunshine: Stock Returns and the Weather. *Journal of Finance* 58(3): 1009–1032.

Houser, Daniel and Kevin McCabe. 2009. Experimental Neuroeconomics and Non-Cooperative Games. Pp. 47–63 in *Neuroeconomics: Decision Making and the Brain*, edited by Paul Glimcher, Colin F. Camerer, Ernst Fehr, and Russell A. Poldack. London: Academic Press.

Jung, Jeeman and Robert Shiller. 2006. Samuelson's Dictum and the Stock Market. *Economic Inquiry* 43: 221–228.

Kable, Joseph and Paul Glimcher. 2010. An "As soon as Possible" Effect in Human Intertemporal Decision-Making: Behavioral Evidence and Neural Mechanisms. *Journal of Neurophysiology* 103: 2513–2531.

King, Ronald, Vernon Smith, Arlington Williams, and Mark Van Boening. 1993. The Robustness of Bubbles and Crashes in Experimental Stock Markets. Pp. 183–200 in *Non-Linear Dynamics and Evolutionary Economics*, edited by Richard Day and Ping Chen. New York: Oxford University Press.

Knutson, Brian, Gregory Samanez-Larkin, and Camelia Kuhnen. 2011. Gain and Loss Learning Differentially Contribute to Life Financial Outcomes. *PLOS One* 6(9): e24390.

Knutson, Brian, G. Elliott Wimmer, Camelia M. Kuhnen, and Piotr Winkielman. 2008. Nucleus Accumbens Activation Mediates the Influence of Reward Cues on Financial Risk Taking *Neuroreport* 19: 509–513.

Kuhnen, Camelia and Joan Y. Chiao. 2009. Genetic Determinants of Financial Risk-Taking. *PLOS One* 4(2): e4362.

Kuhnen, Camelia and Brian Knutson. 2005. Neural Basis of Financial Risk-Taking. *Neuron* 47: 763–770.

Lin, Shengle, Terrance Odean, and Eduardo Andrade. 2012. Bubbling with Excitement: An Experiment. Working Paper. University of California: Berkeley, Berkeley, CA.

List, John. 2011. Why Economists Should Conduct Field Experiments and 14 Tips for Pulling One Off. *Journal of Economic Perspectives* 25(3): 3–16.

Lo, Andrew and Dmitry Repin. 2002. The Psychophysiology of Real Time Financial Risk Processing. *Journal of Cognitive Neuroscience* 14(3): 323–339.

Lohrentz, Terry, Kevin McCabe, Colin Camerer, and P. Read Montague. 2007. Neural Signature of Fictive Learning Signals in a Sequential Investment Task. *Proceedings of the National Academy of Sciences* 104(22): 9493–9498.

Mas-Colell, Andreu, Jerry Green, and Michael Whinston. 1995. *Microeconomic Theory*. New York: Oxford University Press.

McCloskey, Deidre. 1994. *Knowledge and Persuasion in Economics*. New York, NY: Cambridge University Press.

McClure, Samuel, David Laibson, George Lowenstein, and Jonathan Cohen. 2004. Separate Neural Systems Value Immediate and Delayed Monetary Rewards. *Science* 306: 503–507.

McCullough, Michael E., Patricia S. Churchland, and Armando Mendez. 2013. Problems with Measuring Peripheral Oxytocin: Can the Data on Oxytocin and Human Behavior Be Trusted? *Neuroscience and Biobehavioral Reviews* 37: 1485–1492.

Merton, Robert. 1973. An Intertemporal Capital Asset Pricing Model. *Econometrica* 41: 867–887.

Morris, S., A. Postlewaite, and H. Shin. 1995. Depth of Knowledge and the Effect of Higher Order Uncertainty. *Economic Theory* 6: 453–467.

Munafo, M. R., B. Yalcin, S. A. Willis-Owen, and J. Flint. 2008. Association of the Dopamine D4 Receptor (DRD4) Gene and Approach-related Personality Traits: Meta-analysis and New Data. *Biological Psychiatry* 63(2): 197–206.

Nagel, Rosemarie. 1995. Unraveling in Guessing Games: An Experimental Study. *American Economic Review* 85: 1313–1326.

Odean, Terrance. 1998. Are Investors Reluctant to Realize their Losses. *Journal of Finance* 53(5): 1775–1798.

Payton-LeNestoru, Elise and Peter Bossaerts. 2011. Risk, Unexpected Uncertainty and Estimation Uncertainty: Bayesian Learning in Unstable Setting. *PLos Computational Biology* 7(1): e1001048.

Plott, Charles R. 1982. Industrial Organization Theory and Experimental Economics. *Journal of Economic Literature* 20: 1485–1527.

Plott, Charles R. 2001. Introduction. Pp. ix–xxvii in *Public Economics, Political Processes, and Policy Applications*, Cheltenham, UK and Northampton, MA, USA: Edward Elgar Publishing.

Posner, Michael, Mary K. Rothbart, Brad E. Sheese, and Pascale Voelker. 2012. Control Networks and Neuromodulators of Early Development. *Developmental Psychology* 48(3): 827–835.

Rubinstein, Ariel. 1998. *Modelling Bounded Rationality*. Cambridge, MA: MIT Press.

Sapra, Steve, Laura Beavin, and Paul Zak. 2012. A Combination of Dopamine Genes Predicts Success by Professional Wall Street Traders. *PLOS One* 7: e30844.

Schultz, Wolfram. 2009. Midbrain Dopamine Neurons: A Retina of the Reward System? Pp. 321–330 in *Neuroeconomics: Decision Making and the Brain*, edited by Paul Glimcher, Ernst Fehr, Colin Camerer, and Russell Alan Poldrack. London: Academic Press.

Shefrin, Hersh. 2008. *A Behavioral Approach to Asset Pricing*. Waltham, MA: Academic Press.

Shefrin, Hersh and Meir Statman. 1985. The Disposition to Sell Winners Too Early and Ride Losers Too Long: Theory & Evidence. *Journal of Finance* 40(3): 777–790.
Simon, Herbert. 1955. A Behavioral Model of Rational Choice. *Quarterly Journal of Economics* 69: 99–118.
Simons, Henry. 1938. *Personal Income Taxation*. Chicago: University of Chicago Press.
Smith, Vernon, Gerry Suchanek, and Arlington Williams. 1988. Bubbles, Crashes and Endogenous Expectations in Experimental Spot Asset Markets. *Econometrica* 56: 1119–1151.
Sripada, Chandra, Richard Gonzalez, Luan Phan, and Israel Liberzon. 2011. The Neural Correlates of Intertemporal Decision-Making: Contributions of Subjective Value, Stimulus Type, and Trait Impulsivity. *Human Brain Mapping* 32(10): 1637–1648.
Stachurski, John. 2009. *Economic Dynamics: Theory and Computation*. Cambridge, MA: MIT Press.
Thurstone, L. 1927. A Law of Comparative Judgment. *Psychological Review* 34: 273–286.
Tsay, Ruey. 2010. *Analysis of Financial Time Series*, 3rd edn. Hoboken, NJ: Wiley.
Weintraub, E. Roy. 2002. *How Economics Became a Mathematical Science*. Durham, NC: Duke University Press.
Weisskopf, Victor. 1972. The Significance of Science. *Science* 176: 138–146.

# PART VII

# CAUTIONS AND WAYS FORWARD

# 15. The price of abstraction
*Gregory Mitchell*

Traditional law and economics scholars and behavioral law and economics scholars disagree about many things, but they agree on the value of abstraction in the study of law and behavior. Posner (2010), in the most recent edition of his seminal *Economic Analysis of Law*, acknowledges that economic assumptions are "one-dimensional and pallid," but he defends their use on grounds that "abstraction is of the essence of scientific inquiry" (p. 17). Jolls, Sunstein, and Thaler (1998), in their foundational article for the behavioral law and economics movement, likewise embrace abstract models of behavior, but the models they favor are to be built on more realistic assumptions: "The unifying idea in our analysis is that behavioral economics allows us to model and predict behavior relevant to law with the tools of traditional economic analysis, but with more accurate assumptions about human behavior, and more accurate predictions and prescriptions about law" (Jolls, Sunstein, and Thaler 1998, p. 1474). Behavioral law and economics ("BLE") thus promises tractable models that will outperform the too-elegant models of law and economics ("L & E").[1]

The effort to replace standard microeconomic assumptions with more realistic, yet still simple assumptions—without jettisoning a basic economic orientation toward behavior that emphasizes prices and utility maximization—has come at the cost of tremendous oversimplification of complex psychological phenomena and data. Throughout BLE scholarship one finds the results of empirical studies of judgment and decision-making ("JDM") distilled to simple summary accounts of how people behave, with the representative person typically portrayed as at the mercy of cognitive shortcuts and weak willpower. For example, Puchniak and Nakahigashi (2012, p. 59) recently wrote that "behavioral law and economics predicts that when actors face a complex decision, they will commonly rely on a mental heuristic that results in irrational behavior."[2] Here, decision complexity is said to have a main effect on behavior by inducing reliance on a mental rule of thumb that simplifies decision-making but leads to irrational decisions, such as basing a wager on beliefs about whether the roulette wheel has hit red too many times in a row instead of

---

[1]   Models in BLE usually involve only lexical statements of assumptions about behavior rather than statements of mathematical or logical relationships between variables, although some BLE papers published in L & E journals promulgate formal models (e.g., Bar-Gill 2006).

[2]   Puchniak and Nakahigashi (2012) could fall outside BLE if one excludes articles that seem to be primarily attempts to extend propositions and models found in core BLE works. If treated as outside BLE, then we could substitute as the example statements by Korobkin and Ulen (2000) relied on by Puchniak and Nakahigashi for the quotation in the text. Korobkin and Ulen (2000, p. 1078) wrote that "[a]s the problem becomes more complex, either because there are more options from which to select or because each option has more attributes associated with it, actors might attempt to minimize effort by adopting simplified strategies, thus violating the procedural predictions of rational choice theory."

on a rational calculation of odds (for detailed discussions of the JDM studies giving rise to BLE, see Mitchell 2002a, 2014).[3]

This way of presenting JDM research to the world has consequences. It implies, in this case, that decision complexity is a sufficient condition to trigger irrational outcomes (and thus also implies that individuals do not differ in any meaningful way in their propensity to rely on mental heuristics or to engage in irrational behavior in the face of complexity). It implies that simple decisions (whatever those might be) do not implicate mental shortcuts or that these mental shortcuts do not lead to irrational outcomes in simple cases. It implies that researchers have actually studied the mechanisms giving rise to the behavior and found the same mechanisms at work across persons, and it implies that the researchers understood the goals of the subjects and determined that the subjects failed to meet those goals or were unsatisfied with their outcomes. It implies that findings about decision complexity and irrational behavior are generalizable or transportable to new settings: surely multiple ways of defining complexity and a wide range of decision tasks and behaviors have been tested to support the claim made by Puchniak and Nakahigashi. It implies that the social welfare costs associated with an assumption of rationality will exceed the costs associated with an assumption of irrationality. None of these implications may be true, and some are certainly false.

As Jolls, Sunstein, and Thaler (1998) contemplated, misleading implications are unavoidable if BLE is to be a complement to law and economics, in which L & E's broad assumptions about rationality are replaced by broad assumptions about irrationality, and complications in the empirical data are treated as noise rather than signals.[4] In short, the price of abstraction paid by BLE has been the acceptance of an oversimplified view of human judgment and decision-making—the same price paid by L & E for its abstractions. This purchase has resulted in the neglect of heterogeneity in results and of interactions among variables, an emphasis on the existence of effects over the size of effects and their practical significance, avoidance of open questions about external validity, and reification of labels rather than delving into the multiple psychological processes and other non-psychological factors that may cause or account for behavior.[5]

---

[3]   Within experimental studies, a "main effect" refers to the effect of one independent variable on a dependent variable when averaging across other independent variables. A main effect can be contrasted with an interaction effect, in which the effect of one independent variable on a dependent variable depends on the value of one or more other independent variables. In other words, with an interaction, the effect of one independent variable is conditional on the value of at least one other independent variable. Many effects within behavioral law and economics are treated as if they are main effects when in actuality they are interaction effects without the conditions made explicit.

[4]   For an overlapping critique of models within behavioral economics, see Berg and Gigerenzer (2010), though Berg and Gigerenzer also take issue with the basic orientation of behavioral economics: "Described as a new empirical enterprise to learn the true preferences of real people, the dominant method in behavioral economics can be better described as filtering observed action through otherwise neoclassical constrained optimization problems with new arguments and parameters in the utility function" (Berg and Gigerenzer 2010, p. 162).

[5]   I have been complaining for some time that BLE is not sufficiently connected to the research that supplies its behavioral assumptions (e.g., Mitchell 2002a, 2002b). My complaint does not apply to every BLE work, because some acknowledge, more or less directly, that simple assumptions about irrationality cannot do justice to the empirical data (e.g., Jolls 2007; see also Prentice 2004; Rachlinski 2003 for arguments that I fail to do justice to the empirical richness of BLE work).

Nevertheless, it is hard to argue that BLE has paid too high a price for its abstractions if success is judged in terms of intellectual influence. BLE quickly gained adherents (Korobkin 2011) and won a seat in public policy debates (e.g., Osborne and Thaler 2010). But it would be wrong to believe that these gains came from success in empirical competitions with L & E, for whether BLE's abstract models lead to better predictions and explanations, and thus better prescriptions, remains to be determined. The odds of BLE winning these empirical competitions would be increased if BLE scholars accepted a good bit more realism and a bit less abstraction.

## 1. HETEROGENEITY AND OOMPH

Perhaps the single most serious problem afflicting BLE, from both descriptive and prescriptive perspectives, is the lack of attention to observed heterogeneity in preferences and behavior in the research studies drawn on to formulate the assumptions for BLE's models. A close contender is the lack of attention paid to the practical significance of irrational behavior in these underlying studies, or inattention to what Ziliak and McCloskey (2008) call the "oomph" factor: how much impact does one variable have on another variable where impact is measured on some scale of practical significance? We need not select either shortcoming as the most serious offense, for they reinforce one another. If we do not know who shows which irrational behaviors with what frequency, then we cannot determine the costs associated with the observed irrational behavior individually or in the aggregate, for some costs may be more serious for some subsets of persons than others (most obviously the poor versus the wealthy) and some anomalies may be relatively rare or common. Conversely, if we do not concern ourselves with practical significance, then we are likely to be content with demonstrations of irrationality among some subgroup of our subjects and unconcerned that some high percentage of subjects may have acted as predicted by rational choice theory.

BLE cannot content itself merely with existence proofs, however, because BLE purports to describe and predict behavior better than L & E and to offer more effective prescriptions. When social science research is to be applied, researchers must concern themselves with heterogeneity and effect size if they are to avoid inefficient and ineffective prescriptions with perverse effects. "Social science research can . . . reveal complexities that mean no single solution will work everywhere or warn us that solving one problem will raise problems in other areas" (Lempert 2008, p. 909). Stated positively, understanding the sources of variance in data opens up a wider range of interventions than might otherwise be considered. One may be able to design price- or information-based interventions that encourage the rational to sort themselves from the irrational, or one may be able to target interventions at only a subset of individuals who exhibit a particular irrational behavior, as proposals advanced under the banners of "asymmetric paternalism" (e.g., Loewenstein, Brennan, and Volpp 2007) and "libertarian paternalism" (e.g., Sunstein

---

But I am willing to wager that attempts to replace overly simple models of rational behavior with overly simple models of irrational behavior remain common within BLE—indeed, examples of oversimplification will likely be found in other chapters of this very handbook.

and Thaler 2003) seek to do. Implicit in the development of these limited paternalism concepts is the recognition of heterogeneity: not everyone needs protection against their own foibles, and acting as if they do would be inefficient and unnecessarily paternalistic. Understanding heterogeneity and the practical significance of irrational behaviors allows policymakers to spend limited material and political resources wisely to prevent the most serious errors.

Because many JDM studies are designed simply to test for deviations from rationality, these studies often rely on tests of statistical significance to separate chance deviations from "real" deviations. A minority of subjects—sometimes only a handful depending on sample size and the degree of variance in the data—who exhibit the behavior defined by the researcher to be irrational is often sufficient to reject the null hypothesis of perfect rational behavior across subjects.[6] The effect need not reach a preset size of theoretical or practical significance, and with the right experimental design extremely small effects will be statistically significant (Meehl 1967, 1978). Indeed, in between-subjects designs, where no participants are exposed to both the control and experimental conditions, the effect technically exists only in the aggregate and may not apply to even a single individual within the sample (Hutchinson, Kamakura, and Lynch, 2000). One should accordingly not mistake statistical significance for evidence of prevalence and practical importance, yet such conflation is found in BLE from its earliest days. Hanson and Kysar (1999a, 1999b), Jolls, Sunstein, and Thaler (1998) and Korobkin and Ulen (2000), some of the most important papers in the founding of the BLE movement,[7] often describe "people" as showing this or that irrational behavior when confronted with some JDM task or situation, and statistical significance is the source of these conclusions (these articles offer a variety of "stylized facts" to use Tirole's (2007) terminology, with only occasional acknowledgment of heterogeneity in the data and little or no discussion of effect sizes). The message conveyed is that irrational behavior is common and consequential for the decision-makers.

Of course, if there was little variance in behavior in JDM studies and if all effects were large and costly, then this message would be descriptively, accurately and prescriptively significant. But that is not the case. Considerable variance in behavior is observed with respect to all of the anomalies cataloged by BLE scholars, and some of the most-studied anomalies produce small effects that are not robust to design changes. Consider, for instance, the finding from psychology and behavioral economics that many people playing dictator and ultimatum games offer more and accept less than a simple model of utility maximization would predict, a finding that provides grounds for incorporating other-regarding preferences into the utility function. While one does often find in ultimatum and dictator games a majority or a sizeable minority who exhibit other-regarding

---

[6]   The pervasive use of null hypothesis statistical significance testing (NHST) in so many JDM studies has another important implication for BLE and L & E: be wary of invocations of statistically significant rejections of the perfect rationality null hypothesis in claims that BLE outperforms L & E descriptively or predictively. Fisherian NHST, as practiced by most JDM researchers, is not a measure of the relative descriptive or predictive success of two competing theories or hypotheses.

[7]   BLE has several important precursors (see Mitchell 2002a), and the short list in the text omits a number of important articles in the development of BLE. My focus here is on the development of BLE since the publication of Jolls et al. (1998).

preferences that complicate L & E's simple self-interest assumption, one also often finds sizeable minorities who act selfishly, and among the nominally altruistic one finds a range of altruism (Cooper and Dutcher 2011; Engel 2011).[8] Furthermore, different samples often exhibit different patterns of behavior (e.g., Anderson et al. 2010), raising concerns about over-reliance on undergraduate samples as the basis for broad BLE models (and for L & E models as well based on such samples). Heterogeneity occurs as well across situations that were not theorized to alter the frequency of rational behavior. The percentage exhibiting selfish or altruistic behavior in ultimatum and dictator games may depend greatly on fairly minor changes in the game setting (Levitt and List 2007), for instance, and using hypothetical versus real monetary values in experiments may affect the range of behaviors and preferences elicited (e.g., List and Gallet 2001). Finally, heterogeneity sometimes appears across outcome measures within the same domain of concern. For example, a meta-analysis (or quantitative synthesis of existing research) by Gallagher and Updegraff (2012) found no difference in the impact of loss-framed and gain-framed messages on poor-health *detection* behaviors, but gain-framed messages were more effective than loss-framed messages at promoting poor-health *prevention* behaviors.

With respect to effect size, the oomph associated with even the most prominent "cognitive illusions" can be surprisingly small. Table 15.1 summarizes the results of several meta-analyses of behavioral phenomena that are often invoked by BLE scholars.

With the exception of the large impact of initial offers on negotiation outcomes observed by Orr and Guthrie (2006) and the large self-serving bias observed by Mezulis et al. (2004), the effects observed are small to moderate under Cohen's (1988) guidelines for effect sizes. This fact should not come as a surprise because the field supplying much of the JDM research that undergirds BLE, social psychology, studies mostly small effects, some moderate effects, and few large effects (Mitchell 2012; Richard, Bond, and Stokes-Zoota 2003).[9] Small effects are not always costless (e.g., an error may be rare but extremely consequential for those who make the error, or the marginal impact of an error may be particularly important where the choice set is small or dichotomous), but small effects are easily overwhelmed by other effects (e.g., one bias may cancel out another bias; Baron 2010), and many people fail to exhibit such effects in many situations. Furthermore, all of these phenomena, whether small, medium or large in mean effect size, exhibit large variance across persons and conditions.

## 2.   INTERACTIONS AND EXTERNAL VALIDITY

Why do we observe so much heterogeneity in JDM data? This heterogeneity may reflect subsets of subjects who exhibit different behaviors due to persistent individual differences, it may be due to systematic changes in the research setting that lead to predictable

---

[8]   Korobkin (2011) notes that in the classic demonstrations of deviations from rationality by Kahneman and Tversky, large numbers of subjects did not show the deviations (see also Mitchell, 2002a).

[9]   And the reported small effects may actually be overestimates of strength for a number of JDM phenomena, as it appears that a bias against publishing non-significant results exists within JDM studies (Renkewitz, Fuchs, and Fiedler 2011), as in many other areas of research.

*Table 15.1 Results of meta-analyses of behavioral phenomena*

| Phenomenon | Overall effect size information[†] | Moderator examples | Citation |
|---|---|---|---|
| Actor-observer differences in attributions | $d = .06$ (internal attributions); $d = .02$ (external attributions); $d = .10$ (internal − external attribution difference score) | Actors less likely than observers to explain negative outcomes as internally caused and greater actor-observer asymmetries for hypothetical than real events | Malle (2006) |
| Anchoring (first offer/demand) effect on negotiated outcomes | $r = .50$ | Effects smaller with more information or greater experience | Orr and Guthrie (2006) |
| Biased information search (bias for congenial over uncongenial information) | $d = .36$ (.34, .39) | Larger effects with greater commitment to position, greater personal relevance, or greater confidence | Hart et al. (2009) |
| Covariation detection (in 2 X 2 information matrices) | Generally participants used information in normatively correct manner and did well at judging strength of correlations | Larger effects of cells emphasized by experimenter | Lipe (1990) |
| Illusion of control | $D = .62$ (.49, .75) | Larger effects associated with greater emphasis on achieving success | Stefan and David (2013) |
| Outcome severity effect on attributions of responsibility | $r = .08$ | Smaller effects for liability judgments and with student samples | Robbennolt (2000) |
| Gain-loss framing effect in health messages | $r = .08$ (.03, .13) | Small effect observed for prevention behaviors; no effect on attitudes, intentions or detection behaviors | Gallagher and Updegraff (2012) |
| Certainty-uncertainty (risky) framing effect | $r = .44$ (.39, .48) | Larger effects in samples with women and with single option presented | Piñon and Gambara (2005) |
| Positive-negative (attribute) framing effects | $r = .26$ (.18, .34) | Larger effects with multiple options presented | Piñon and Gambara (2005) |
| Gain-loss framing effects | $r = .44$ (.36, .53) | Larger effects with multiple options presented | Piñon and Gambara (2005) |
| Hindsight bias (knew-it-all-along effect) | $d = .39$ (.36, .42) | Smaller effects in studies using real events or subjective probability estimates | Guilbault et al. (2004) |
| Intensity bias in affective forecasts | $g = .55$ (.42, .68) | Smaller effects for questions focused on affect from specific event asked immediately after event | Levine et al. (2012); see also Mathieu and Gosling (2012) |

| | | | |
|---|---|---|---|
| Self-serving bias in causal attributions for success versus failure | $d = .47$ (.42, .52) | Larger effects under high self-threat or low task-choice conditions | Campbell and Sedikides (1999) |
| Self-serving bias in causal attributions for positive outcomes | $d = .88$ (.86, .89) | Smaller effects with participants between ages of 12 and 54, from Eastern cultures or suffering from psychopathology | Mezulis et al. (2004) |
| Social loafing | $d = .44$ (.39, .48) | Smaller effects with unique or identifiable individual inputs or with participants from Eastern cultures | Karau and Williams (1993) |
| Time preference and health behavior | $r = .12$ (.08, .16) | Larger effects for addictive behaviors than healthful behaviors | Chapman (2005) |
| Too-much-choice (choice overload) effect | $D = .02$ (-.09, .12) | Evidence of choice overload more likely where consumers had weaker preferences or less expertise | Scheibehenne et al. (2010) |
| Dictator game behavior | Mean offer = 28.35% of pie | Older dictators and identified dictators offered more and deserving recipients received higher offers | Engel (2011) |
| Ultimatum game behavior | Mean offer = 40% of pie; mean rejection rate = 16% | Regional differences in responses but not offers (with Asians having higher rejection rates) | Oosterbeek et al. (2004) |

*Note:* [†]Where available, mean effect sizes and confidence intervals (in parentheses) are reported; where this information was not available, a description of the meta-analytic findings is provided. The original source should be consulted for full information, including information on the number of studies included and heterogeneity in effects.

465

differences, or it may be due to random, unpredictable error (e.g., where some small effect is not captured by an unreliable dependent measure). The first two possibilities pose challenges to BLE's simple models in which one situational variable is said to give rise to irrational behavior across persons regardless of other situational variables, such as the model put forward by Puchniak and Nakahigashi (2012) in which increasing complexity is said to produce irrational decisions.[10] If the likelihood of irrational behavior is predictably conditional on the type of individual or type of situation, then failure to include parameters for these interactions in BLE's supposedly more realistic models must be justified on the grounds that the predictive and explanatory payoffs of adding these parameters do not justify the increase in complexity. The models found within BLE rarely include explicit parameters that specify which effects hold for which identifiable types of persons or situations (or even informal statements of interactions), and this failure to include known interactions is rarely justified.

When BLE began, such failures were more justifiable than they are now, at least with respect to person parameters, because research into individual differences in rationality only recently proliferated (e.g., Schunk and Betsch 2006; Stanovich 1999; Frederick 2005; see generally Appelt et al. 2011). However, well before Jolls et al. (1998), psychologists and economists were aware that many of the classic demonstrations of irrationality from JDM studies were subject to situational constraints (e.g., Kerr et al. 1996; Smith and Walker 1993; Tetlock 1992). With the move toward dual-process models of judgment and choice (e.g., Kahneman 2011), in which analytical thought and the likelihood of procedural rationality varies with identifiable individual and situational characteristics, the view that everyone uses the same cognitive heuristics for all JDM tasks and falls prey to the same cognitive biases cannot be maintained. This shift in views about cognitive processes should impact BLE's assumptions about procedural rationality, and greater understanding of the factors that lead people to be altruistic, impatient and risk seeking or risk averse should complicate the motivational assumptions of BLE. Behavior in dictator and ultimatum games depends on the personality of those playing the game (e.g., Ben-Ner and Kramer 2011), among other variables; intertemporal choices vary by personality (e.g., Hirsh, Morisano, and Peterson 2008), among other variables; and risk preferences appear to vary by sex (Byrnes et al. 1999; Croson and Gneezy 2009), among other variables. It is not true that all people value fairness over selfishness or are willing to make equal sacrifices in the name of fairness. Every published anomaly is shown, sooner or later, to be subject to conditions. We live in a world of interactions, not main effects, and ignoring interactions will lead to many prediction errors.

Ignoring known interactions leads to obvious predictions errors for the known cases,

---

[10] And to claims such as that by Hanson and Kysar (199b) that "we are naively and stubbornly optimistic at heart, regardless of how well informed we are" (p. 655) (Hanson and Kysar made clear that they were serious about that "we" in this claim by adding that over-optimism "is not limited to any particular age, sex, education level, or occupational group" (p. 655)), and by Jolls and colleagues (1998) that "individuals tend to judge the likelihood of uncertain events (such as getting caught for a crime) by how available such instances are to the human mind, and this may depend on factors unrelated to the actual probability of the event" (p. 1538). Certainly these and other BLE articles contain some acknowledgment of interactions among variables, but one commonly finds statements implying main effects when the underlying data show interaction effects.

but ignoring the likelihood of unknown interactions leads to errors through overconfidence in the external validity of existing research. The simple models and broad theories found in BLE are based almost exclusively on extrapolations from laboratory experiments and paper-and-pencil surveys demonstrating deviations from rationality. The assumption is that other individuals in other situations will exhibit the same deviations, yet that assumption is false for many people and many situations.[11]

Given that we now know that many popular effects from JDM studies are conditional on individual and situational parameters, is it reasonable to assume that an effect will generalize across persons and situations before the generalizations have been tested? Just because experience with one good or in one domain increases rationality (e.g., List 2003, 2011), we should not assume that experience with other goods in other domains will increase rationality because the settings in which a model holds have to be determined empirically (Mitchell 2012), but is it safer to make the positive or negative generalization assumption when no research has yet tested the generalization? To make that determination, BLE researchers need to examine the pattern of results found across existing studies for a particular effect, and to consider the source as well as the size of the effect. If the effect has been found only in one or a small number of studies, skepticism is in order, particularly for counter-intuitive results (Lempert 2008). Policy applications should be developed from theory informed by a collection of studies and should not be extrapolations directly from one or a few experiments (Zeiler 2010). If the effect has been demonstrated only in social psychology laboratory studies, then theory built on this effect is likely to falter when applied to new settings or problems, because effects from social psychology laboratory studies often do not replicate in the field and in fact change direction in the field (e.g., a positive correlation between two variables in the lab is often a negative correlation in the field) with surprising frequency (Mitchell 2012). If the effect is a small effect, then further caution is in order because small effects are less likely to hold up in the field and more likely to change direction in the field (Mitchell 2012). When considering whether to extrapolate from one research setting, one sample of stimuli, or one sample of participants to another for modeling or prescription purposes, BLE's dictum that context matters greatly to judgment and choice (e.g., Sunstein and Thaler 2003) should be internalized: "People react differently to structurally identical problems that are presented in different ways . . ." (Hogarth 2005, p. 260).

---

[11]   As discussed elsewhere (Mitchell 2012), highly controlled and even artificial experiments can serve a very important role in theory development and testing. Yet we must recognize that the variables controlled in the laboratory will often systematically alter the expression of behavior outside the laboratory, and thus these variables should be taken into account in the development of theory and refinement of the conditions under which behaviors are expected to occur. Moreover, outside the laboratory people are not randomly assigned to treatment conditions but often systematically sort themselves in ways that should be taken into account when seeking to apply basic research findings. Thus, my critique here is focused on simplistic extrapolations from simple experiments rather being a general critique of experiments for a lack of external validity.

## 3.   REIFICATION AND DEFEATISM

The attempt to apply findings from single studies, rather than from a theory derived from an integrated group of findings, points to another problem within BLE: impoverished understandings of causal mechanisms animate many BLE discussions. The prevailing understanding of the causes of deviations from rational choice predictions has been, first, that individuals rely on cognitive heuristics that systematically bias thought and lead to errors; second, that individuals have great difficulty exchanging future interests for present interests; and, third, that individuals care about fairness and are willing to incur material costs to vindicate fairness concerns (see Jolls et al. 1998, for this influential framing of the bounds on judgment and choice). Discussion of causation rarely goes much deeper than these broad concepts—of bounded rationality due to cognitive heuristics, bounded willpower, and bounded self-interest—despite considerable debate within JDM research over the causes of observed deviations from rationality.

The notion that bounded rationality arises from the automatic operation of cognitive heuristics has exerted a particularly stifling impact on BLE's causal discussions, as cognitive heuristics have become reified, or treated as if they are mental processes themselves that cause many irrational behaviors. The heuristic constructs originally developed by Kahneman and Tversky (availability, representativeness, and anchoring) were shorthand labels used to describe what were assumed to be a collection of basic perceptual and inferential processes in which people supposedly answer a difficult question with an answer to an easier question, with the more fundamental causal mechanisms still unknown when the heuristic constructs were developed (Kahneman and Frederick 2002). Likewise, dual-process approaches, such as the two-system approach favored by Kahneman (2011), are useful organizing fictions that should not be taken to mean there are clear dividing lines between causal mechanisms associated with "System 1" or "System 2" thought. Indeed, we are at risk of intuition and affect (key concepts within System 1) becoming the latest reified constructs, with all manner of mysterious judgment and choice being reduced to intuition or feeling, with the reach of these reifications extending from choices of simple gambles to moral judgments.

Numerous different brain processes and structures may be activated within each of these "systems" (Glöckner and Witteman 2010; Mitchell 2009; Reyna 2012; Weber and Johnson 2009). To understand how to combat heuristic or System 1 modes of thought so commonly associated with biases and errors, we need to understand the deeper mechanisms causing irrational outputs. For instance, Chapman and Johnson (2002) discuss competing causal accounts for anchoring effects (i.e., bias associated with the anchoring heuristic) and how different causes have different implications for debiasing interventions. Causal mechanisms may be irrelevant to interventions that take options deemed too risky off the table, but for many interventions an accurate understanding of the cause(s) of the unwanted behavior is needed to formulate effective and efficient policies (Lempert 2008; Klass and Zeiler 2013; Zeiler 2010).

Another negative consequence of widespread acceptance of the heuristics and biases account of JDM has been a defeatist view about the prospects for debiasing because heuristic modes of thought were seen as automatic and beyond conscious control. This defeatism may help to explain, along with the reification of high-level constructs, why so little attention has been paid to underlying causal processes. With the move toward dual-process approaches to JDM and the acceptance of a role for analytical thought to counter biases, the bogeyman of insuperability might appear to be in retreat. But with the rise of implicit theories of JDM that emphasize unconscious processing and discount conscious reasoning (e.g., Greenwald and Banaji 1995), BLE is at even greater risk of defeatism if it fails to appreciate that such associationist accounts of JDM do not remove the prospect of internal and external debiasing (Mitchell 2009). One key is recognizing that effective debiasing may require altering the decision environment, depending on the cause of a bias, to either take advantage of a countervailing intuitive mode of thought or activate a more mindful state (Weber and Johnson 2009). Another key is recognizing that many experiments seek to isolate implicit processes without examining their interplay with other, potentially overriding, cognitive and motivational processes, and these studies may thus suggest that implicit processes are more impactful than is really the case (Blanton et al. 2009; Mitchell 2009).

One focus of BLE has been the beliefs, feelings, and inferential processes that produce judgments about factual matters and assessments of choice options. Another focus of BLE has been preferences, with the prevailing view being that preferences are constructed on the spot, rather than existing somewhere in the mind and consulted when a choice is presented (e.g., Sunstein and Thaler 2003). This view persists despite there being, as noted above, consistent differences in revealed preferences across persons and situations and despite BLE taking the view that there is a stable taste for fairness. Perhaps because the constructed preferences view is so dominant, the possibility of stable preferences, meta-preferences or bedrock values has received little attention within BLE. However, if default-option paternalism continues to influence public policy and retirement planning, then gaining a better understanding of the limits of preference construction (and manipulation) must become a priority. Beshears and colleagues (2010) found that the status quo bias in favor of a default option in retirement contributions was subject to extremity effects (i.e., the default option was set so high that many opted out), suggesting that some people do have a range of acceptable values that must be satisfied if a default option is to be accepted, but this extremity effect may itself be conditional on cognitive resources and willpower. As Beshears et al. (2010) note, "if it is socially desirable to have high contribution rates in defined contribution retirement savings plans, aggressive defaults may not be an effective policy" (p. 11). Without understanding the range of acceptable values for a particular good and why the range may or may not affect acceptance of a default, it will be difficult to formulate efficient "nudges." The growing influence of evolutionary accounts of moral judgment, with their emphasis on consistent gut reactions to moral scenarios (e.g., Haidt 2007), may also pose problems for BLE's constructionist view of preferences and its agnosticism on the origins of preferences. At a minimum, BLE is going to have to come up with a theory that distinguishes persistent views on fairness and morality, which supposedly influence judgment and choice more often than L & E's self-interest assumption allows, from "ordinary" preferences that can more easily be manipulated.

## 4.   ADDING REALISM AND THEORY TO BLE

The simple models offered by BLE, which often read like lists of biases that afflict all people to cause serious real-world errors, cannot be defended on realism grounds. These models ignore heterogeneity, effect sizes, variable interactions, and external validity constraints, and they provide little purchase on the causes underlying observed deviations from rationality. These models can only be defended as abstractions offered to compete with L & E on its own abstract terms. Psychological tests disconfirming rational choice theory do not provide evidence of predictive or explanatory superiority relative to that of rational choice theory, for these tests ignore heterogeneity and effect size and do not test competing causal theories. Psychological demonstrations of irrationality are, by and large, only that: demonstrations that some people do, under some circumstances, act irrationally.[12] Sometimes the number of deviators is large, and sometimes the deviations are practically significant. Therefore, the message here is not that L & E models should always be accepted; the message is that BLE should not be assumed to be descriptively and prescriptively superior merely because it builds its models from psychological studies of judgment and decision-making.

The first step towards a BLE that has greater predictive value than L & E would be to incorporate into BLE's models parameters that represent the interactions found in JDM research. Some of these parameters may turn out to provide minimal improvement in fit, but they should not be dismissed out of hand. And the process of researching and testing parameters will lead scholars to give greater consideration to the relative frequency of rational and irrational behavior in particular domains. The second step would be to pay much greater attention to effect size associated with the psychological phenomena that lead people astray and consider whether other common influences on legal judgment and choice exert more powerful or countervailing effects in complex settings outside the laboratory. This step should include placing the effect size onto a practically meaningful scale of some sort, such as the amount of monetary loss associated with an irrational behavior for the average individual and in the aggregate. The third step would be to pay greater attention to the causal mechanisms that produce anomalous behavior, recognizing that heterogeneity in behavior indicates that multiple causal processes may be at work.

These three steps are unlikely to be as significant or burdensome as they may first appear, for most BLE articles deal with a specific problem or legal topic that can be dealt with in greater complexity than the level of detail found in foundational BLE articles, which launched broad attacks on L & E's assumptions. Unfortunately, many BLE scholars have relied on these broad, foundational articles as their primary sources and have not delved deeply into the underlying, primary research literature to gain an understanding of the complexities that surround the various anomalies.[13]

---

[12]    Harrison (2010) similarly assails behavioral economics for claiming to have overthrown basic economic theories when what it has really shown is that economic theories in general, whether denoted behavioral or not, need parameterization: "the recognition that a certain parameterization is restrictive hardly constitutes a fundamental revolution in thinking. It is as if somebody claimed that the whole of production theory was wrong because the observed behavior of factor shares did not follow the predictions of a Cobb–Douglas production function. The fact that the economics profession has allowed the behaviorists to market their contributions as fundamental is not the fault of the behaviorists, but of those that allowed such tripe to pass unchallenged" (Harrison 2010, p. 50).

[13]    For those seeking to apply JDM research on a particular phenomenon, Chapman and Johnson (2002), in their discussion of the anchoring heuristic, provide an excellent template for the presentation of a body of work, except that they do not address effect size: they

A fourth step, which would be more costly, would be to conduct research that pits L & E and BLE predictions directly at odds instead of settling for attempts to reject the null hypothesis of perfect rationality. Such competition requires predictions both about what rational behavior would look like in a particular setting and about the irrational behavior that is predicted to occur, and about the causal processes that give rise to the respective behaviors. And that would require that BLE come forward with a theory of context or the situation that permits us to predict which bias will hold sway under which conditions (cf. Shafir 2007).

One particularly promising theory that may unify a number of findings on constructed preferences and provide a framework for analyzing contexts for competitive testing and prescriptive purposes is Sher and McKenzie's information leakage theory (2006, 2011). Sher and McKenzie discuss how standard research on framing effects cannot provide sound answers to the question whether people irrationally change preferences in response to seemingly normatively insignificant features of the decision setting. They emphasize the role of information "leakage" to the listener/reader from the speaker's choice of labels relative to an explicit or implicit reference point, and they show how many findings can be reconciled under this perspective (though the jury is still out on the full extent of the theory's explanatory scope). Just as importantly, Sher and McKenzie (2011) discuss how researchers must perform an information analysis of the "frames" presented to people and a psychological analysis of the processes that may be operative at different levels of the informational analysis. This framework provides a means for analyzing a wide range of situations and revealing their informational and psychological complexity, which should lead to greater care and modesty on the part of BLE and L & E prescribers.

An alternative approach for analyzing contexts would be to build on the work of Vernon Smith and others who posit that rationality axioms will hold only for those who have adequate incentives and opportunities to know and reveal their true preferences— what Plott (1996) called the "discovered preferences" thesis. From this perspective, BLE (and behavioral economics) and L & E (and traditional microeconomics) are focused on different domains: BLE as usually practiced is the domain of errors that arise while people seek to discover their true preferences; L & E is the domain of discovered preferences and rational behavior. Discovered preferences should be found under conditions that motivate people to gather accurate, relevant data, give them opportunities to obtain this data, and provide feedback for learning purposes once choices are made (Bruni and Sugden, 2007). To put the contrast too simply: BLE's models may apply to situations where people have one chance to get it right ("life as a between-subjects design"), and L & E's model may apply to situations where people get second chances ("life as a repeated-measures design"). The discovered preference thesis cannot be dismissed out of hand given empirical evidence in support, although the implications of this evidence are debated, and it

---

survey the research literature to provide (a) clear definitions of the phenomena as found in the literature to make clear that some studies may address different but related constructs, (b) necessary conditions for anchoring (including statements of relative impact across conditions), (c) an assessment of the causes of anchoring, and (d) a discussion of the possible applications of anchoring heuristic research in light of the prior discussion on necessary conditions and causes.

potentially offers a unifying theory of the contexts where rational behavior will be more and less likely.[14]

## 5.   CONCLUSION

No model, by its nature, can be true to all of the facts found in a body of research. As Posner (2010) notes, scientific theory requires some abstraction to avoid being nothing more than description, and choices among levels of abstraction and competing model assumptions should be made on the basis of relative explanatory and predictive power. There are, however, surprisingly few examinations of the relative power of L & E and BLE models to explain past behavior and predict future behavior. When those examinations accumulate, we are sure to find that both models have their successes and failures, and that both BLE and L & E must jettison some of their abstractions and simplicities for some areas of the law in order to provide apt descriptions and prescriptions. When that happens, then BLE will become a true complement to L & E.

Until that happens, when encountering a simple model from BLE that posits a deviation from rationality, ask who these people are who exhibit these irrational behaviors, with what consistency (both individually and across the sample), in what situations, on what outcome measures, with what practical effects, and why? Without this information, it is impossible to adjudicate the empirical competition between BLE and L & E and, more importantly, to formulate effective and efficient prescriptions.

## REFERENCES

Anderson, S., Harrison, G. W., Lau, M. I., and Rutström, E. E. 2010. Preference Heterogeneity in Experiments: Comparing the Field and Laboratory. *Journal of Economic Behavior and Organization* 73: 209–224.

Appelt, K. C., Milch, K. F., Handgraaf, M. J. J., and Weber, E. U. 2011. The Decision Making Individual Differences Inventory and Guidelines for the Study of Individual Differences in Judgment and Decision Making. *Judgment and Decision Making* 6: 252–262.

Bar-Gill, O. 2006. The Evolution and Persistence of Optimism in Litigation. *Journal of Law, Economics & Organization* 22: 490–507.

Baron, J. 2010. Looking at Individual Subjects in Research on Judgment and Decision Making (or Anything). *Acta Psychologica Sinica* 42: 1–11.

Ben-Ner, A., and Kramer, A. 2011. Personality and Altruism in the Dictator Game: Relationship to Kin, Collaborators, Competitors, and Neutrals. *Personality and Individual Differences* 51: 216–221.

Berg, N., and Gigerenzer, G. 2010. As-if Behavioral Economics: Neoclassical Economics in Disguise? *History of Economic Ideas* 18: 134–165.

Beshears, J., Choi, J. J., Laibson, D., and Madrian, B. C. 2010. The Limitations of Defaults. Working Paper. NBER, Cambridge, MA.

Blanton, H., Jaccard, J., Klick, J., Mellers, B. A., Mitchell, G., and Tetlock, P. E. 2009. Strong Claims and Weak Evidence: Reassessing the Predictive Validity of the IAT, *Journal of Applied Psychology* 94: 567–582.

Bruni, L., and Sugden, R. 2007. The Road Not Taken: How Psychology Was Removed From Economics, and How it Might be Brought Back. *The Economic Journal* 117: 146–173.

---

[14]   Although Sunstein and Thaler (2003) endorse BLE's constructed preferences view, they concede some limited domain for discovered preferences when they write that consumers may have "well-formed" or "true" preferences in some choice domains.

Byrnes, J. P., Miller, D. C., and Schafer, W. D. 1999. Gender Differences in Risk Taking: A Meta-analysis. *Psychological Bulletin* 125: 367–383.

Campbell, W. K., and Sedikides, C. 1999. Self-Threat Magnifies the Self-Serving Bias: A Meta-analytic Integration. *Review of General Psychology* 3: 23–43.

Chapman, G. B. 2005. Short-Term Cost for Long-Term Benefit: Time Preference and Cancer Control. *Health Psychology* 24: S41–S48.

Chapman, G. B., and Johnson, E. J. 2002. Incorporating the Irrelevant: Anchors in Judgments of Belief and Value. Pp. 120–138 in *Heuristics and Biases: The Psychology of Intuitive Judgment*, edited by T. Gilovich, D. W. Griffin, and D. Kahneman. New York: Cambridge University Press.

Cohen, J. 1988. *Statistical Power Analysis for the Behavioral Sciences*, 2nd edn. Hillsdale, NJ: Lawrence Erlbaum Associates.

Cooper, D. J., and Dutcher, E. G. 2011. The Dynamics of Responder Behavior in Ultimatum Games: A Meta-study. *Experimental Economics* 14: 519–546.

Croson, R., and Gneezy. U. 2009. Gender Differences in Preferences. *Journal of Economic Literature* 47: 448–474.

Engel, C. 2011. Dictator Games: A Meta Study. *Experimental Economics* 14: 583–610.

Frederick, S. 2005. Cognitive Reflection and Decision Making. *Journal of Economic Perspectives* 19: 25–42.

Gallagher, K. M., and Updegraff, J. A. 2012. Health Message Framing Effects on Attitudes, Intentions, and Behavior: A Meta-analytic Review. *Annals of Behavioral Medicine* 43: 101–116.

Glöckner, A., and Witteman, C. 2010. Beyond Dual-Process Models: A Categorisation of Processes Underlying Intuitive Judgment and Decision Making. *Thinking & Reasoning* 16: 1–25.

Greenwald, A. G., and Banaji, M. R. 1995. Implicit Social Cognition: Attitudes, Self-Esteem, and Stereotypes. *Psychological Review* 102: 4–27.

Guilbault, R. L., Bryant, F. B., Brockway, J. H., and Posavac, E. J. 2004. A Meta-analysis of Research on Hindsight Bias. *Basic and Applied Social Psychology* 26: 103–117.

Haidt, J. 2007. The New Synthesis in Moral Psychology. *Science* 316: 998–1002.

Hanson, J. D., and Kysar, D. A. 1999a. Taking Behavioralism Seriously: Some Evidence of Market Manipulation. *Harvard Law Review* 112: 1420–1571.

Hanson, J. D., and Kysar, D. A. 1999b. Taking Behavioralism Seriously: The Problem of Market Manipulation. *New York University Law Review* 74: 101–217.

Harrison, G. W. 2010. The Behavioral Counter-revolution. *Journal of Economic Behavior & Organization* 73: 49–57.

Hart, W., Albarracín, D., Eagly, A. H., Brechan, I., Lindberg, M. J., and Merrill, L. 2009. Feeling Validated Versus Being Correct: A Meta-Analysis of Selective Exposure to Information. *Psychological Bulletin* 135: 555–588.

Hirsh, J. B., Morisano, D., and Peterson, J. B. 2008. Delay Discounting: Interactions Between Personality and Cognitive Ability. *Journal of Research in Personality* 42: 1646–1650.

Hogarth, R. B. 2005. The Challenge of Representative Design in Psychology and Economics. *Journal of Economic Methodology* 12: 253–263.

Hutchinson, W. J., Kamakura, W. A., and Lynch, J. G., Jr. 2000. Unobserved Heterogeneity as an Alternative Explanation for "Reversal" Effects in Behavioural Research. *Journal of Consumer Research* 27: 324–344.

Jolls, C. 2007. Behavioral Law and Economics. Pp. 115–145 in *Behavioral Economics and its Applications*, edited by P. Diamond and H. Vartiainen. Princeton, NJ: Princeton University Press.

Jolls, C., Sunstein, C. R., and Thaler, R. 1998. A Behavioral Approach to Law and Economics. *Stanford Law Review* 50: 1471–1550.

Kahneman, D. 2011. *Thinking Fast and Slow*. New York: Farrar Straus and Giroux.

Kahneman, D., and Frederick, S. 2002. Representativeness Revisited: Attribute Substitution in Intuitive Judgment. Pp. 49–81 in *Heuristics and Biases: The Psychology of Intuitive Judgment*, edited by T. Gilovich, D. W. Griffin, and D. Kahneman. New York: Cambridge University Press.

Karau, S. J., and Williams, K. D. 1993. Social Loafing: A Meta-analytic Review and Theoretical Integration. *Journal of Personality and Social Psychology* 65: 681–706.

Kerr, N. L., MacCoun, R., and Kramer, G. P. 1996. Bias in Judgment: Comparing Individuals and Groups. *Psychological Review* 103: 687–719.

Klass, G., and Zeiler, K. 2013. Against Endowment Theory: Experimental Economics and Legal Scholarship. *UCLA Law Journal* 61: 2–64.

Korobkin, R. 2011. What Comes After Victory for Behavioral Law and Economics? *University of Illinois Law Review* 2011: 1653–1674.

Korobkin, R. B., and Ulen, T. S. 2000. Law and Behavioral Science: Removing the Rationality Assumption from Law and Economics. *California Law Review* 88: 1051–1144.

Kühberger, A. 1998. The Influence of Framing on Risky Decisions: A Meta-Analysis. *Organizational Behavior and Human Decision Processes* 75: 23–55.

Lempert, R. 2008. Empirical Research for Public Policy: With Examples from Family Law. *Journal of Empirical Legal Studies* 5: 907–926.

Levine, L. J., Lench, H. C., Kaplan, R. L., and Safer, M. A. 2012. Accuracy and Artifact: Reexamining the Intensity Bias in Affective Forecasting. *Journal of Personality and Social Psychology* 103: 584–605.

Levitt, S. D., and List, J. A. 2007. What Do Laboratory Experiments Measuring Social Preferences Reveal About the Real World? *Journal of Economic Perspectives* 21: 153–174.

Lipe, M. G. 1990. A Lens Model Analysis of Covariation Research. *Journal of Behavioral Decision Making* 3: 47–59.

List, J. A. 2003. Does Market Experience Eliminate Market Anomalies? *Quarterly Journal of Economics* 118: 41–71.

List, J. A. 2011. Does Market Experience Eliminate Market Anomalies? The Case of Exogenous Market Experience. *American Economic Review* 101: 313–317.

List, J. A., and Gallet, C. A. 2001. What Experimental Protocol Influence Disparities Between Actual and Hypothetical Stated Values? *Environmental and Resource Economics* 20: 241–254.

Loewenstein, G., Brennan, T. A., and Volpp, K. 2007. Asymmetric Paternalism to Improve Health Behaviors. *JAMA* 298: 2415–2417.

Malle, B. 2006. The Actor-observer Asymmetry in Causal Attribution: A (Surprising) Meta-analysis. *Psychological Bulletin* 132: 895–919.

Mathieu, M. T., and Gosling, S. D. 2012. The Accuracy or Inaccuracy of Affective Forecasts Depends on How Accuracy is Indexed: A Meta-Analysis of Past Studies. *Psychological Science* 23: 161–162.

Meehl, P. 1967. Theory-testing in Psychology and Physics: A Methodological Paradox. *Philosophy of Science* 34: 103–115.

Meehl, P. 1978. Theoretical Risks and Tabular Asterisks: Sir Karl, Sir Ronald, and the Slow Progress of Soft Psychology. *Journal of Consulting and Clinical Psychology* 46: 806–834.

Mezulis, A. H., Abramson, L. Y., Hyde, J. S., and Hankin, B. L. 2004. Is There a Universal Positivity Bias in Attributions? A Meta-Analytic Review of Individual, Developmental, and Cultural Differences in the Self-Serving Attributional Bias. *Psychological Bulletin* 130: 711–747.

Mitchell, G. 2002a. Taking Behavioralism Too Seriously? The Unwarranted Pessimism of the New Behavioral Analysis of Law. *William and Mary Law Review* 43: 1907–2021.

Mitchell, G. 2002b. Why Law and Economics' Perfect Rationality Should Not Be Traded for Behavioral Law and Economics' Equal Incompetence. *Georgetown Law Journal* 91: 67–167.

Mitchell, G. 2009. Second Thoughts. *McGeorge Law Review* 40: 687–722.

Mitchell, G. 2012. Revisiting Truth or Triviality: The External Validity of Research in the Psychological Laboratory. *Perspectives on Psychological Science* 7: 109–117.

Mitchell, G. 2014. Alternative Behavioral Law and Economics. Pp. 167–192 in *Oxford Handbook of Behavioral Economics and the Law*, edited by E. Zamir and D. Teichman. Oxford: Oxford University Press.

Oosterbeek, H., Sloof, R., and van de Kuilen, G. 2004. Cultural Differences in Ultimatum Game Experiments: Evidence from a Meta-analysis. *Experimental Economics* 7: 171–188.

Orr, D., and Guthrie, C. 2006. Anchoring, Information, Expertise, and Negotiation: New Insights from Meta-Analysis. *Ohio State Journal on Dispute Resolution* 21: 597–628.

Osborne, G., and Thaler, R. Jan. 28, 2010. We Can Make You Behave. *The Guardian* (available at http://www.theguardian.com/commentisfree/2010/jan/28/we-can-make-you-behave).

Piñon, A., and Gambara, H. 2005. A Meta-Analytic Review of Framing Effect: Risky, Attribute and Goal Framing. *Psicothema* 17: 325–331.

Plott, C. R. 1996. Rational Individual Behavior in Markets and Social Choice Processes: The Discovered Preference Hypothesis. Pp. 225–250 in vol. 114 of *The Rational Foundations of Economic Behavior, IEA Conference*, edited by K. J. Arrow et al. London: Macmillan.

Posner, R. A. 2010. *Economic Analysis of Law*, 8th edn. New York: Aspen Publishers.

Prentice, R. A. 2004. Chicago Man, K-T Man, and the Future of Behavioral Law and Economics. *Vanderbilt Law Review* 56: 1663–1777.

Puchniak, D. W., and Nakahigashi, M. 2012. Japan's Love for Derivative Actions: Irrational Behavior and Non-Economic Motives as Rational Explanations for Shareholder Litigation. *Vanderbilt Journal of Transnational Law* 45: 1–82.

Rachlinski, J. J. 2003. The Uncertain Psychological Case for Paternalism. *Northwestern University Law Review* 97: 1165–1225.

Renkewitz, F., Fuchs H. M., and Fiedler, S. 2011. Is There Evidence of Publication Biases in JDM Research? *Judgment and Decision Making* 6: 870–881.

Reyna, V. F. 2012. A New Intuitionism: Meaning, Memory, and Development of Fuzzy-Trace Theory. *Judgment and Decision Making* 7: 332–359.

Richard, F. D., Bond, C. F., and Stokes-Zoota, J. J. 2003. One Hundred Years of Social Psychology Quantitatively Described. *Review of General Psychology* 7: 331–363.

Robbennolt, J. K. 2000. Outcome Severity and Judgments of "Responsibility": A Meta-analytic Review. *Journal of Applied Social Psychology* 30: 2575–2609.

Scheibehenne, B., Greifeneder, R., and Todd, P. M. 2010. Can There Ever Be Too Many Options? A Meta-Analytic Review of Choice Overload. *Journal of Consumer Research* 37: 409–425.

Schunk, D., and Betsch, C. 2006. Explaining Heterogeneity in Utility Functions by Individual Differences in Decision Modes. *Journal of Economic Psychology* 27: 386–401.

Shafir, E. 2007. The Problematic Content and Context of Decisions. Pp. 291–294 in *Behavioral Economics and its Applications*, edited by P. Diamond and H. Vartiainen. Princeton, NJ: Princeton University Press.

Sher, S., and McKenzie, C. R. M. 2006. Information Leakage from Logically Equivalent Frames. *Cognition* 101: 467–494.

Sher, S., and McKenzie, C. R. M. 2011. Levels of Information: A Framing Hierarchy. Pp. 35–63 in *Perspectives on Framing*, edited by G. Keren. New York: Psychology Press.

Smith, V. L., and Walker, J. 1993. Monetary Rewards and Decision Cost in Experimental Economics. *Economic Inquiry* 31: 245–261.

Stanovich, K. E. 1999. *Who Is Rational? Studies of Individual Differences in Reasoning*. Mahwah, NJ: Lawrence Erlbaum Associates, Inc.

Stefan, S., and David, D. 2013. Recent Developments in the Experimental Investigation of the Illusion of Control: A Meta-analytic Review. *Journal of Applied Social Psychology* 43: 377–386.

Sunstein, C. R., and Thaler, R. H. 2003. Libertarian Paternalism Is Not an Oxymoron. *University of Chicago Law Review* 70: 1159–1202.

Tetlock, P. E. 1992. The Impact of Accountability on Judgment and Choice: Toward a Social Contingency Model. Pp. 331–376 in vol. 25 of *Advances in Experimental Social Psychology*, edited by M. Zanna. New York: Academic Press.

Tirole, J. 2007. Comment by Jean Tirole. Pp. 294–299 in *Behavioral Economics and Its Applications* edited by P. Diamond and H. Vartiainen. Princeton, NJ: Princeton University Press.

Weber, E. U. and Johnson, E. J. 2009. Mindful Judgment and Decision Making. *Annual Review of Psychology* 60: 53–86.

Zeiler, K. 2010. Cautions on the Use of Economics Experiments in Law. *Journal of Institutional and Theoretical Economics* 166: 178–193.

Ziliak, S. T., and McCloskey, D. N. 2008. *The Cult of Statistical Significance*. Ann Arbor, MI: University of Michigan Press.

# 16. Why Behavioral Economics isn't better, and how it could be
## Owen D. Jones*

## 1. INTRODUCTION

Had things not changed, we might all be toasting the successes of Behavioral Law and Economics. After all, scholars who have developed Behavioral Economics tools, as well as those who have applied Behavioral Economics in the legal arena, have made some really key contributions worth careful, respectful, admiring attention.

But times, disciplines, and the state of knowledge have changed—a lot—in the decades since Tversky and Kahneman first highlighted how real people (in both regular and expert flavors) sometimes systematically depart from predictions of the standard expected utility model in neoclassical economics. And those changes now render it uncomfortably obvious that Behavioral Economics, and those who rely on it, are by and large failing to keep up with developments in other disciplines that also bear directly on the same key mysteries of human decision-making.

What's holding Behavioral Economics—and hence Behavioral Law and Economics—back? This chapter identifies four key impediments. It explores their causes. It suggests ways around them, including one possible pathway for integrating relevant and necessary multi-disciplinary insights.

To illustrate, the chapter provides an example using one favorite phenomenon of Behavioral Economics and Behavioral Law and Economics alike: the so-called "endowment effect."[1] That term describes the seemingly irrational propensity for people often to refuse to accept in payment for a just-acquired good or right a larger sum of money (often much larger) than the maximum sum they would have paid to acquire that good or right (Thaler 1980; Tversky & Kahneman 1991; Kahneman, Knetsch, & Thaler 1990, 1991). That propensity is troubling because, as a consequence, goods and rights are (arguably)

* Work on this chapter was supported, in part, by a grant from the John D. and Catherine T. MacArthur Foundation. Its contents reflect the views of the author and do not necessarily represent the official views either of the MacArthur Foundation or of The MacArthur Foundation Research Network on Law and Neuroscience (http://www.lawneuro.org/). Kathy Zeiler and Michael Guttentag gave important and useful feedback. John Alcock, Paige Skiba, Mona Sobhani, and Andrew Kabbes provided a number of helpful references.

[1] I fully agree with Plott, Zeiler, and Klass (Plott & Zeiler 2005, 2007; Klass & Zeiler 2013) that the term "endowment effect" is unfortunate and misleading. It inappropriately imports, into the label for an effect, one hypothesis among many for what causes the effect. That is, the term presumes that certain exchange asymmetries are caused by ownership (i.e., endowments) instead of something else. Though far from perfect, the term "endowment effect" nonetheless remains the label by which most readers have come to know the phenomenon. And many more precise alternatives (such as "the gap between willingness-to-pay and willingness-to-accept") are unwieldy. So I will continue to use the term here, trusting readers to note its manifest failings.

often stickier than would be efficient (Korobkin 2003). That is, instead of winding up in the hands of those who value them most, goods and rights will tend to stay in the hands of those into whose hands they first get. (Cue market chaos.)

Along the way, we will consider how Behavioral Economics will continue to develop its nascent relationship with the burgeoning field of Neuroscience—in which new technologies (such as functional magnetic resonance imaging) enable the non-invasive study of the brain activities underlying human decision-making (Knutson et al. 2008; Camerer 2008; Camerer, Loewenstein, & Drazen 2005). New discoveries about the brain regions, circuitries, and neural activities associated with such things as outcome uncertainty, risky decision-making, time-discounting rates, the framing effect, reference dependence, loss aversion, and the endowment effect are providing interdisciplinary and potentially useful perspectives on these phenomena.

The goal of this chapter is to provide those of us deploying, or engaged with, Behavioral Economics or Behavioral Law and Economics some new bases for meaningful self-critique, as well as some concrete recommendations for constructive steps we could take to help move these important schools of thought forward, in light of new developments in other fields.

## 2.  FOUR PROBLEMS

### 2.1  Four Problems with Behavioral Economics

To be clear, I'm a big fan of (and occasional contributor to) both Behavioral Economics (hereafter BE) and Behavioral Law and Economics (hereafter BLE) (Jones 2001; Jones & Brosnan 2008; Brosnan et al. 2007, 2012). I care deeply about human decision-making. I want to see our understandings of it improved. And I want to see Law deploying the best models of human behavior it can, while pursuing its goals to the very best of its abilities (Jones & Goldsmith 2005; Jones, O'Connor, & Stake 2011).

Good, novel, and useful empirical work, as well as deep thinking on the possible implications of that work—as is frequently evident in BE and BLE literatures alike–is to be celebrated. And robust, credible challenges to conventional wisdom deserve close attention. But past performance is (as so often said) no guarantee of future results. And at least four things are currently keeping BE from realizing its full potential.

The first problem is that BE is misleadingly named (Rachlinski 2011), with unfortunate downstream consequences. Calling the approach "Behavioral Economics" inevitably defines the field *in relation to* Economics and, impliedly, *only* in relation to Economics. This helped, at first, because the label provided immediate traction with those scholars already in, or paying attention to, Economics. But now it hurts more than it helps, because those gains are offset by larger losses that flow, in the form of opportunity costs, from so sharply and needlessly narrowing the scope of what BE could actually apply to.

Economics uses one set of tools – a powerful set that has repeatedly proved its usefulness. But it is essential to keep in mind that Economics applies its tools within a very broad and disciplinarily boundary-less landscape: human decision-making. And in this domain Economics is far from having either the only or the complete set of tools. Consequently, to brand the important insights of BE explicitly and exclusively in relation to Economics is to semantically and conceptually hitch BE insights to a single boxcar, instead of to an entire train of them, each loaded with its own collection of differing and relevant tools. The taxonomically limited label arguably and perhaps inevitably shrinks the ambitions of those who use BE away from what could be even greater, more sweeping, and more useful ends—while simultaneously alienating large audiences who, though interested in human decision-making, aren't interested in providing Economics with uniquely privileged status, even if that is a status against which BE somewhat reacts.

The second problem, partly related to the first, is that the many different people invoking BE haven't yet agreed about what it is, and what BE tools are designed to do. Depending on what you read, either in BE or about BE, it variously looks like: (1) a distinct field of its own (blazing its own path on human decision-making); (2) a special-ized subfield of Economics or Experimental Economics (attending to a particular set of failed predictions in the otherwise majestic sweep of Economic successes); (3) a critique of Economics (similar to how Critical Legal Studies is a critique of prevailing legal thought); (4) a specialized set of tools within Economics; (5) an effort to import into Economics the insights of a single additional field; or (6) an effort to create a brand new field from the dyadic synthesis of Economics and Psychology (much as Biophysics is the hybrid offspring of Biology and Physics). This is not a major indictment; after all, intellectual movements often ferment this way. Yet BE as a whole would likely benefit from those who apply it being more explicit about which of these things (or which other things) they are trying to do. They will then either come to coalesce around a common understanding of their collective purposes or they will fracture into distinct groups with different visions. Either outcome would probably be preferable, for a movement this far along, to the ill-defined status quo.

The third problem is that, in trying to improve upon the approaches of Economics to human decision-making, BE has (so far at least) turned almost entirely to only one other set of tools—in this case from the field of Psychology. Aside from some distinct pockets of work (e.g., Knutson et al. 2008; Camerer 2008; Stake 2004) there is little evidence, across BE scholarship, of trying to transcend disciplinary divisions more broadly. Why aim so low? It makes BE just as susceptible to the critique of over-narrowed focus as scholars in BE and BLE themselves often level (and, let's face it, sometimes smugly) against neoclas-sical Economics. There are a wealth of additional fields whose practitioners—just like those in Economics, Behavioral Economics, and Psychology—lay equally self-confident claim to having important and well-developed insights into the phenomenon of human decision-making. And drawing on these fields, in addition to Psychology, would further strengthen BE, and increase the probability that the mysteries of human decision-making are revealed as thoroughly and deeply as possible.

The fourth problem is that the insights from Psychology on which BE draws are—though quite valuable—an increasingly small proportion of all relevant insights from Psychology. Sorry to rain on the parade. But someone has to say this. Because it's true. And because even without venturing beyond the borders of Psychology (as now seems essential), there is a lot more to Psychology today than is actually used in most BE and BLE scholarship. The growth in knowledge is not merely the function of Psychology having moved further along some long-time trajectory. It is also and primarily a function of the fact that Psychology has been radically and forever changed by a series of new technologies that have arrived in the last couple of decades. They enable us to study the brain activity that *underlies* the very human decision-making phenomena that BE and BLE scholars care about. And as big a fan as I am of Tversky and Kahneman, for example, it bears pointing out that the ability to investigate internal processes of decision-making—using functional brain imaging, for example—simply didn't exist back in the day, when Tversky and Kahneman (1974) were observing only the external, downstream *results* of brain activity. Put another way, new techniques in neuroscience enable us to more directly study the mechanisms that underlie and cause behavior, rather than continuing—as we long have—to infer the existence of such mechanisms, and to try to describe them, based only on resultant behaviors. Practicing BE uninformed by brain-imaging is therefore akin to practicing Astronomy without a telescope, or to practicing Medicine without a microscope. Possible, but needlessly limited.

## 2.2 The Origins of Those Four Problems

What caused these problems? We could hypothesize multiple and specific causal pathways. But they can all very likely be traced, one way or another, to the same origin: a toxic combination of three individually regrettable circumstances.

First is the profoundly mistaken assumption—under which universities generally, and consequently most of humanity, continue to labor—that reality can actually be divided into pieces. We tend to assume that reality can be neatly and meaningfully disaggregated into tidy little packages, which can then be separately posted to the attention of relatively small groups of scholars—who are (in the main) segregated into independently operating departments within universities. Each group has its own assumptions, its own literatures, its own methods and—most often—its own beatific confidence that it, and only it, sheds the most worthy light on those things on which its light is focused.

The second toxic thing is the widely shared assumption that the specific way in which universities long ago divided reality was the only (or at least the best) way to do so. Although we take this for granted as received truth, it in fact has never been demonstrated. Sure, if you're going to divide reality up, this is undeniably *a* way to do so. But are we really better off for having long ago divided the Natural Sciences from the Social Sciences, as if this distinction were meaningful? Having divided Anthropology from Psychology and both of them from Sociology and Philosophy? Having divided Psychology from Biology and both of those from Economics? Separations were made—sometimes intentionally, sometimes by happenstance. But it is by no means obvious that—even if we assume separations are a good idea—our ancestors just happened to settle on the exactly optimal way of delineating intellectual territories.

Third is path-dependence. After it was assumed that reality was best studied in meaningfully (not just conveniently) different pieces, and that those pieces had been carved at their optimal joints, we for hundreds of years have, in the main, kept the disciplinary tribes divided. Sure, there are interdisciplinary, multidisciplinary, and even "transdiciplinary" efforts underway. True, there has been a rise in joint faculty appointments and explicitly "interdisciplinary studies" majors. That's all laudable. But it's also undeniable that the main intellectual super-structures of universities remain pretty much the same as they long have looked. And, at least for now, most of us tenured scholars plying our crafts were trained within, and dutifully replicate, the rigidly divided mental and *depart*-mental traditions.

The consequence of this three-part combination is evident in our current mess—both generally and for BE and BLE specifically. The initial division of reality into severable parts, the misplaced confidence that our division (among the many thousands of alternatives) was optimal, and our history of treating that division as permanent has together led us into a cascade of further and deeper fractures, within the already fractured disciplines. We daily witness the outward entropy of scholars into smaller and more isolated sub-disciplines, fewer and fewer of whom are even aware of, or could if pressed even communicate with, the scholars in many of the other fields that are simultaneously working on what are arguably closely related—or even identical—problems.

This leaves BE precisely where it is. Not alone, certainly, in being too narrow and too isolated for the greater good of what its practitioners are ultimately laboring to accomplish. But BE is misleadingly named, insufficiently defined in both identity and purpose, over-relying on one field to the near-total exclusion of other highly relevant fields, and—even *within* that one field—already long out of date. Much of that seems inevitable, frankly, when viewed against the backdrop of deep-seated disciplinary divisions that sacrifice foregone discoveries on the altar of taxonomic clarity.

This is, admittedly, a dark view of a dim circumstance. And we can take no comfort from the fact that those who deploy BE are not alone in thinking its dyadic (rather than more ambitiously trans-disciplinary) approach such cause for celebration. But—as I will attempt to demonstrate in the next sections—there remain many reasons for optimism, and multiple paths toward a brighter future for both BE and BLE

## 3.   A PATH FORWARD: INITIAL STEPS

To help BE move forward faster, we need to first step back to first principles. As I read the collective literatures, the over-arching and shared goal of all BE work appears to be something like this: to continue progress toward a more robust, accurate, predictive, and useful model of the kinds of human decision-making that underlie behaviors of social consequence.

In pursuing this goal, scholars deploying BE tools are by no means alone. Scholars in multiple disciplines—from Sociology to Evolutionary Biology to Economics to Neuroscience to Political Science to Artificial Intelligence, among many others—have this very same goal. Those in scientific fields generally pursue this goal for its own sake: the self-justifying quest to increase our aggregate understanding of everything, including the brain-behavior connection. But scholars in the fields that mainly *apply* the behavioral models offered up by other disciplines operate most effectively and efficiently when their behavioral models are as robust as current knowledge can afford. And that's where Law—and ultimately BLE—come in.

Law, of course, is a field mainly concerned with applications—which is why so many legal scholars pay so much attention to both Economics and to Behavioral Economics (Posner 2011; Jolls, Sunstein, & Thaler 1998; Korobkin 2011; Sunstein 2000, 2013, 2014; Shafir 2013). Put another way, the reason the legal system is always looking for predictively accurate models of human behavior is because Law is—put bluntly—in the business of inspiring people to behave differently, and more prosocially, than they would behave in the absence of law (Jones & Goldsmith 2005).

Whether it is trying to get people to stop killing each other, or trying to get people to all drive on the same side of the road, or trying to get people to save enough for their own retirements, the more robust Law's behavioral models are the better chance Law has of successfully achieving the many social goals that society tells it to pursue. And without robust models of where behavior comes from, and why behaviors take the forms and patterns they do, Law can't do its job as effectively and efficiently as it otherwise might.

As a consequence, the legal system inevitably relies not only on its own internal logic and experience but also on the insights offered up by other disciplines. Put another way: *Law is fundamentally a consumer of behavioral models*. It shops in the academy, discipline by discipline, aisle by aisle, and shelf by shelf, seeing what looks good on sale. But four problems for Law immediately present.

The first problem for Law (which is a by-product of the more direct problem for BE discussed above) is that the many disciplines on which Law draws—and the constituent knowledge bases, training, and world views of the scholars in them—still tend to reflect the musty and somewhat arbitrary divisions of a complex, naturalistic reality into either tidy little parts (we study rocks over here; you study trees over there) or tidy little methods (here we use Sociology to examine human behavior; over there they use Anthropology). True, stuff can get discovered this way, sometimes. And it has been. But these divisions are often counter-productive because—as in the parable of the blind men who each thought the whole elephant was accurately represented by the small part of it they first touched—reality doesn't actually come packaged in tidy little parts that can be fully known with tidily distinct little methods. This is bad enough when it only limits the depth of our understandings of human behavior. But it is independently pernicious when it also—as it does for Law as a downstream consumer of behavioral models—limits our very abilities, as a society, to pursue social goals as effectively as we might. Whenever the legal system makes and pursues policies in reliance on misleadingly partial impressions of reality it translates academic limitations at conceptual levels into practical limitations at real-world levels. Real problems for real people ensue.

The second problem for Law is that these divisions not only yield foregone opportunities, where dovetailing the insights from multiple disciplines could provide new advantages. These divisions also sometimes enable the blithely simultaneous existence of two or more disciplinary perspectives and behavioral models that are patently incompatible with one another. As one paper put it: it's as if a team of chemists and a team of physicists were each separately designing optimal combustion engines—while each using assumptions that were flatly incompatible with basic tenets of the other's field (Cosmides, Tooby, & Barkow 1992; Tooby & Cosmides 1992). That makes the consequences for Law, when it relies on the insights of one discipline or another at a time, far more fraught with potential for error than Law tends to notice.

The third problem is that Law—in under-noticing the extent to which reality has become so fractured and scattered across disciplines that incompatible models can survive—has been far, far too passive a consumer. Law is passive in two interconnected ways. (1) Legal scholars and legal policy-makers don't feel empowered to *expect* that the behavioral models they must use will be cross-compatible and integrated. That's like going to buy a car, mutely resigned to the idea that the working electronics system and the working drive train might not work with one another. (2) Legal scholars and policy-makers don't do enough to *identify* and *call out* incompatibilities between multiple disciplinary perspectives on human behavior—encouraging, cajoling, or demanding that behavioral models be reconciled, one way or another, before they rely on (or bet the farm on) any of them. In this, I think the legal system is paradoxically shy. And also shirking an important and implied duty it owes to all of the governed.

The fourth problem is largely a function of the prior two. People trained in Law typically don't acquire the range of skill sets needed to be able to evaluate the claims of other decision-making disciplines more systematically and to be able to be active participants in furthering their reconciliation. We academics are trained in fields, not in solutions. That is, we are trained in methods of achieving analyses that are internally consistent, not in methods for achieving knowledge that is externally and pan-disciplinarily consistent.

To be sure, Law didn't create these problems all by itself. It inherited them and accepts them as received inevitabilities. And legal scholars have lived out scholarly lives within this comfortable but self-limiting pattern for so long—and in the company of so many very good and very smart people who are similarly situated—that it doesn't strike them as shockingly odd, and deeply flawed.

Nevertheless, and against that backdrop, here's where we are. BE, like many other fields and schools of thought, is in the business of developing more accurate models of human behavior. But it often does so using only or primarily a particular subset—the so-called *cognitive heuristics and biases* subset—of the information now available within the single field (Psychology) to which it has chosen to attend. Meanwhile, Law needs better models of human behavior. But it isn't very good at recognizing or dealing with partial or conflicting models.

What's to be done about it? Here are five recommendations:

1. *Stop defining the field of inquiry in relation to Economics.* The insights of BE are too important to suggest they belong within—or in sole relationship to—Economics. Bringing cognitive heuristics and biases (Kahneman, Slovic, & Tversky 1982; Kahneman & Tversky 1996) into discussions often dominated by neoclassical Economic perspectives has been a big and important step, to supplement useful thinking in those domains where the tools of Economics have been less useful. But it's a step that's been taken. There are many more steps to take. And those steps have importance beyond the field of Economics alone.

2. *More clearly articulate the shared purpose.* For example, a more overtly ambitious goal of BE might be something like: developing the best achievable model of human decision-making. But however its goal is more explicitly defined, BE has reached a state of sufficient maturity and diversity that rich reflection and discussion could yield a vision of mission that is not only shared, but more productive as a consequence of being more explicitly purposeful. Clarifying the mission would usefully broaden the vision of what might aid in fulfilling it.

3. *Stop thinking it's really the method that matters.* Let's stop thinking as if disciplines are in a contest for methodological hegemony. It doesn't count as success if, in the long run, BE scholars manage to just replace one set of useful but imperfect and disciplinarily-limited tools within Economics with another set of useful but imperfect and disciplinarily-limited tools within Psychology. The methods we use should be dictated by our goals, not our disciplines.

4. *Assume that multiple disciplines are relevant to future progress.* Because they are.

Scholars trained in many different fields are all working, simultaneously and too-often in isolated parallel, on different but inevitably interrelated aspects of human decision-making. Trying only to supplement or challenge Economics with Psychology (technically only a subset of Psychology) is akin to adding only a wrench to a toolbox that contains only a hammer.

5. *Assume that deploying the insights and method of multiple disciplines will require, in part, integrating disciplines too-long divided.* There is so much going on, in so many different fields, that bears directly on human decision-making. It is a mistake to focus just on any one or two fields. Within-field gains are evident, but relatively linear— whereas the rate of gain from cross-disciplinary integration has a greater potential to be geometric.

Terrific, you say. All we have to do, in the end, is to integrate disciplines. But how?

## 4. INTEGRATING DISCIPLINES: A CONVERGING QUESTIONS APPROACH

I don't have all the answers. But the remaining sections of this chapter propose one possible path to integration, in the hope of sparking discussions that might supply them.

This particular path—let's call it a *Converging Questions approach*, as a shorthand— begins straightforwardly enough with explicitly identifying evident but under-noticed differences between *the kinds of questions* that different fields investigate. The chapter then illustrates how that approach can lead to improved thinking about heuristics and biases, and about the legal implications of them, using the endowment effect[2] as an example.

What drives this approach is the observation that disciplines focusing on very similar phenomena are often assumed to be in direct competition with each other—when in fact sometimes they are and sometimes they aren't. Sometimes they approach a phenomenon at such a perpendicular to another field's approach that they can't even butt heads in the same plane of analysis. What renders their perspectives incommensurable in such cases is that the very different kinds of questions they ask enable under-noticed complementarity and convergence. So one path toward integrating them looks like this.

First, we identify a manageable subset of behavioral phenomena in which we are particularly interested, situating it explicitly (for orienting context) within a broader, more general phenomenon. Second, we take the seemingly pedestrian but in fact crucial step of identifying the different categories of questions we might ask about the phenomenon. By "kinds of questions" I mean the classical biggies: Who, What, Where, When, Why, and How. Third, we identify which existing fields, according to their existing nomenclatures and taxonomies, are in whole or in part, by design or accomplishments, appropriate for answering those kinds of questions about that kind of phenomenon. Fourth, we work to integrate the perspectives of those disciplines that most directly address the same question (e.g., the What? or the Why?). This involves not only cumulating perspectives that are compatible but also working to identify and resolve any incompatible assumptions or

---

[2]   Objections reiterated. See footnote 1 above.

*Table 16.1   Examples of categories of questions*

| | |
|---|---|
| What? | What is this so-called endowment effect? In what ways shall we identify it, categorize it, define it, and know it when we see it? |
| Who? | Who are the people who exhibit endowment effects? Everyone? Or do some categories of people—such as judges, agents, professionals, juveniles, trained subjects—either not exhibit the phenomenon, or exhibit it differently? |
| Where? | Where is the endowment effect most evident? Does it vary by environmental circumstance? Is it equally evident inside and outside of laboratory settings, in both simple and complex contexts? In non-laboratory conditions, is it as equally evident in private transactions as it is with publicly traded stocks? |
| When? | Does the propensity toward the endowment effect change over time? Does it change with experience? With age? With training? |
| Why? | Why does the endowment effect exist? Why does it arise, or not arise, in the specific patterns, distributions, and magnitudes that it does? |
| How? | How does the endowment effect come about? How do perception and decision mechanisms of the brain combine to cause this behavior to come to pass? |

findings. Fifth, we then integrate *across* questions the perspectives that have been integrated *within* them, dovetailing the edges of insights into multiple joints of a converged and coherent whole.

That's too abstract. So the remainder of this chapter provides a very rough-cut but more concrete illustration of how this *Converging Questions* approach might play out in the context of the endowment effect (which in some quarters is also known as the "status quo bias").

### 4.1   Stage 1: Identify a Manageable Subset of Broader Phenomena

Example: Let's focus our efforts on understanding endowment effects, which can be located within the broader phenomenon of cognitive heuristics and biases and related phenomena, which are in turn located within the broader-still phenomenon of human decision-making.

### 4.2   Stage 2: Identify Categories of Questions

Table 16.1 contains examples.

### 4.3   Stage 3: Identify Relevant Fields

Examples: For the "What?" inquiry, relevant fields include, Behavioral Economics, Cognitive Psychology, Anthropology, Sociology, Economics, and the like, all of which specialize in observing and categorizing various forms of human behavior. For the "Why?" inquiry, relevant fields include Evolutionary Biology, Evolutionary Psychology, and (perhaps, but more on this below) Behavioral Economics, all of which specialize in trying to understand the underlying causes of various forms of behavior. For the "How?" inquiry, relevant fields include Neuroscience, Developmental Biology, and Anatomy, all of which specialize in discovering the mechanisms by which behaviors arise from the neural activity of organisms. And so on.

## 4.4   Stage 4: Integrating Within Categories of Question

This stage is the hardest, because there are many fields relevant to each category of question. So this stage warrants the lengthiest illustration. Below, I'll sketch and illustrate the approach focusing (still within the context of the endowment effect) only on the "Why?" question. And, within that question, we'll focus our attention on just two of the many relevant fields: Behavioral Economics and Evolutionary Biology.

### 4.4.1   The Behavioral Economics approach to the Why question

Under some conditions, people seem to value goods and rights inconsistent with the assumptions of the standard expected utility theory in Economics. Under those assumptions, there should ordinarily be no meaningful variance between the maximum price someone is Willing-To-Pay to acquire a good or right (often referred to as WTP) and the minimum price he or she would be Willing-To-Accept to sell it (the so-called WTA) (Knetsch & Sinden 1984; Hoffman & Spitzer 1993; Franciosi et al. 1996).

The existence of a WTP/WTA gap (also called "exchange asymmetry"; Plott & Zeiler 2007, 2011) has been amply demonstrated (Horowitz & McConnell 2002). And it is this gap to which people typically refer (or at least should be referring) when they use the unfortunately misleading[3] label "endowment effect" (Thaler 1980; Kahneman, Knetsch, & Thaler 1990, 1991; Plott & Zeiler 2005, 2007; Klass & Zeiler 2013).

The question at this moment in the analysis is: Why? *Why* do people so often exhibit an endowment effect? There are a variety of explanations (Korobkin 2003, 2014, and Zeiler, Chapter 13 this volume, provide overviews). But the most common explanation inside the field of BE comes from a suite of interconnected ideas termed "Reference Dependence," "Loss Aversion," and "Prospect Theory" (Kahneman & Tversky 1979; Tversky & Kahneman 1991, 2000; Kahneman, Knetsch, & Thaler 1990, 1991; but see Arlen & Tontrup 2013).

*Reference Dependence* is the idea that the value a person ascribes to something is not absolute, but instead shifts as a function of its relative relationship to some set-point of reference. *Loss Aversion* is a label for the hypothesized mindset by which people appear to weigh a loss of a certain amount more heavily than a gain of the same amount. *Prospect Theory* links Reference Dependence and Loss Aversion, such that a person's behavior can often be understood as resulting from some circumstance that sets a reference point, from which losses and gains are then measured. On this view, the endowment effect is explained by the fact that ownership (an endowment) sets a reference point—as to which losses then loom larger than equivalently-sized gains.[4]

---

[3]   See footnote 1. For a history of the term, see Klass & Zeiler 2013, Part I.

[4]   As Klass and Zeiler usefully summarize: "Endowment theory says that [WTP-WTA gaps] are at least partially explained by the general phenomenon of loss aversion. Prospect theory holds that when deciding what to do, people give possible losses more weight than potential gains of the same magnitude. Endowment theory is an application of prospect theory, adding the hypothesis that ownership determines whether one experiences a change as a gain or as a loss. Endowment

### 4.4.2  How well does Behavioral Economics answer the Why question?

Viewed from within the landscape of BE, Prospect Theory provides a nice causal explanation for the endowment effect. The moment of ownership sets a reference point in psychological stone; losing the owned thing through a sale for $x$ dollars weighs more heavily, from that reference point, than does gaining the thing for a purchase price of $x$ dollars; asymmetric pricing and exchange behavior ensue.

But it bears emphasis that that explanation, however tactically useful (and it is), only provides a satisfactory explanation for why the endowment effect exists from within the boundaried conceptual and methodological frameworks of BE. If, alternatively, we look sideways at that explanation, from the perspective of brain sciences (including Evolutionary Biology) for example, we see an entirely different picture. From that perspective, it seems patently clear that Prospect Theory can't possibly explain why the endowment effect exists.

Here's why: saying that the endowment effect is caused by Loss Aversion, as a function of Prospect Theory, is like saying that human sexual behavior is caused by Abstinence Aversion, as a function of Lust Theory. The latter provides no intellectual or analytic purchase, none, on *why* sexual behavior exists. Similarly, Prospect Theory and Loss Aversion—as valuable as they may be in describing the endowment effect phenomena and their interrelationship to one another—provide no intellectual or analytic purchase, none at all, on *why* the endowment effect exists. Here are three reasons (further explored in Jones & Brosnan 2008) why those explanations don't work.

First, you can't provide a satisfying causal explanation for a behavior by merely positing that it is caused by some psychological force that operates to cause it. That's like saying that the orbits of planets around the sun are caused by the "orbit-causing force." While true as an observational and logical matter, it doesn't really add anything. The futility of layering one observation on top of another while in pursuit of a causal explanation was vividly described this way: explaining the endowment effect with loss aversion is like saying that rain is caused by a rainstorm (McCaffery 1994, pp. 1865–66). (Arlen 1998, Jones 2001, and Klass & Zeiler 2013 describe similar frustrations.) The problem is that claiming that the endowment effect is caused by loss aversion really only provides a place-holding name for a cause, and therefore inevitably raises the question at one remove: what causes loss aversion? Behavioral Economics has no answer.

Second, loss aversion rests on no theoretical foundation. Nothing in it explains why, when people behave irrationally with respect to exchanges, they would deviate in a pattern, rather than randomly.[5] Nor does it explain why, if any pattern emerges, it should have been loss aversion rather than gain aversion. Were those two outcomes equally likely? If not, why not?

---

theory posits that ownership sets one's reference point, the movement from which triggers either a perceived gain or loss, and that people perceive the transfer or sale of endowments as losses" (Klass & Zeiler 2013, p. 4).

[5]  There is no consensus among the disciplines on what renders a behavior "irrational." Economists, for instance, have a high threshold, preferring often to say that a candidate's behavior simply deviates from the predictions of standard expected utility theory. Others believe that either internal inconsistency, illogic, personal disadvantage, or impulsiveness is necessary or sufficient for the label. I don't think it matters much whether we conclude that the endowment effect is or isn't irrational, so long as we agree that it is a puzzle warranting a satisfying explanation.

Third, nothing in the loss aversion explanation provides any reasonable basis for predicting or explaining one of the most puzzling aspects of endowment effects: the well-documented fact that the presence and magnitude of the endowment effect varies considerably among different goods, rights, and conditions. A robust explanation should encompass the variations as well as the regularities.

### 4.4.3   The Evolutionary Biology approach to the Why question

By using the perspective of one *Why?*-related field (Evolutionary Biology) to consider the perspective of another (Behavioral Economics), we can—in this case at least—see that the latter is insufficient, on its own, and needs help. But that's a far cry from actually providing that help. So here's a more concrete (though still necessarily quite over-brief) illustration, in four subsections. We'll look first at the general perspective. Then we'll subsequently consider the theoretical foundation, some empirical investigations, and the overarching point of it all. Keep in mind throughout that the details here are less important than the method being illustrated.

#### 4.4.3.1   *The general perspective*

Behavioral biologists distinguish between two fundamentally different kinds of causes. One concerns why a behavior came to be fairly typical within a species. The other concerns how the perception of particular environmental circumstances tends to result in that behavior. In this section we'll look at the former. (The latter will become relevant in Stage 5, below.)

Here's the perspective from which a behavioral biologist approaches the endowment effect. If you encounter a species with members that tend to behave in patterned ways, in similar contexts, it is often worth hypothesizing (without, of course, assuming) that natural selection has left them predisposed to behave this way.

Although the term *natural selection* is familiar to many, it is often only vaguely understood. So it is worth pausing to be precise: natural selection is not so much a process as it is a label for the result of a process. It is a label given to what happens when any system incorporates these three features: (1) inheritance of traits; (2) variation in inherited traits; and (3) differential reproductive success, as a consequence of differing inherited traits (Bergstrom & Dugatkin 2011; Futuyma 2013; Williams 1966). What happens, in a world of differing heritable traits, and all else being equal, is that those traits that increase the reproductive success of the organisms that bear them more than do contemporaneously existing alternative traits in other members of the same species tend to appear (i.e., to be "naturally selected") in increasing proportions in subsequent generations of individuals. Traits that just happen to "work," will also happen to become increasingly common within a species over evolutionary time.

Natural selection is not the *only* evolutionary process. (Others are: mutation, migration, and genetic drift.) But it is the only evolutionary process that tends to leave both the physical and (importantly) behavioral features of organisms tightly fitted to the environmental circumstances that each respective species has long encountered. This is because those features have tended—on average and across time—to contribute to the life and reproduction of the organisms that bear them more than do contemporaneously existing alternative traits (Zimmer & Emlen 2012; Herron & Freeman 2013).

To briefly illustrate, suppose that most members of certain species of birds tend to gather together and fly to lower latitudes as winter approaches. An evolutionary biologist hypothesizes that the predisposition toward doing so has historically provided some advantage to the individuals who did so (e.g., moving to a location with higher energetic benefits in food, per hour of foraging investment, and lower costs, in calories expended, in merely surviving harsh conditions) compared to individuals who did the opposite (e.g., flying to higher—and therefore colder and less resource-rich—latitudes in the winter). Biologists don't assume that the birds consciously evaluate options, consider reasons, and then fly in the direction that cool-headed analysis provides. But nor do they assume that the birds fly in random directions, or that the directions they fly in can be adequately explained by kinks in their preference curves (such as by "cold temperature aversion" or the like). It has long been established that natural selection can embed members of species with entire suites of behavioral predispositions (of differing strengths and probabilities) without having to build self-consciously analytic machinery to do so.

Analogously, if members of the human species tend to exhibit behavioral predispositions of the "cognitive heuristics and biases" sort, such as the endowment effect, perhaps some of those predispositions historically provided some advantage to the individuals who did so, compared to predispositions to do the opposite.

So far so good. But how might this perspective appeal to those steeped in Behavioral Economics? Not so much. At least, not initially. In fact, there's a good reason that this line of thinking doesn't come more naturally. And that's because the behaviors in humans with which we are here interested can often lead to outcomes that can be personally disadvantageous. If the outcome makes no logical sense, and hurts self-interest instead of aiding it, for what earthly reason (one might ask) should we consider the possibility that these behaviors reflect evolved psychological adaptations, rather than mere quirks or cultural artifacts?

Here, we need to reflect on two things about evolutionary processes. One is that nothing in evolution ever guarantees that any individual will, in the moment, behave in the most successful of all ways it possibly could. Natural selection plays to the historical averages. If a given predisposition outperforms another *on average*, across the *average* environmental circumstances historically encountered by members of that species, that is sufficient for the predisposition to appear in increasingly large percentages of subsequent populations, compared to contemporaneously existing predispositions toward alternative behaviors.

The second thing is that natural selection cannot see into the future. It can't design behavioral predispositions for the coming changes in environmental circumstances. When environments are long stable, evolved behavioral predispositions tend to stabilize within them. But rapid changes in environmental circumstances can lead to mismatches between evolved behavioral predispositions that vestigially persist and any challenges newly presented by the changed environment. Put another way, a mismatch between a behavior and an outcome does not, by itself, disprove the hypothesis that the behavior reflects an evolved adaptation to a prior environmental condition.

Which is all to say: there is more than one type of irrationality. For example, one type of irrationality is random—where behavior is irrationally unaffected by circumstance. Another type of irrationality is self-destructive—where behavior is consistently and exactly the direct opposite of what would ever have been in one's self-interest under similar circumstances. And one important but easily overlooked type of irrationality—relevant here—is what I have in this economics context called "Time-Shifted Rationality" (Jones

2001). That general concept goes by a variety of different labels in different fields—such as "mismatch" (Nesse & Williams 1996; Lieberman 2013) or "ecological rationality" (Gigerenzer & Todd 1999; Gigerenzer 2000, 2008). But the core notion is simply this: behavior that is time-shiftedly rational is one that is irrational in the *current* environmental circumstances, but which yielded, on average, substantively rational outcomes when it appeared in *historical* environmental circumstances.

Two examples will illustrate. First, consider that some birds not only provide a vigorous display against a predator bird flying near overhead, but also provide the same display against a distant airplane of the same apparent aspect as the predator. The latter is clearly irrational. It wastes energy that is hard to come by in a way that neither affects the plane nor decreases (from zero) the probability that the plane will swoop down to enter the defending bird's territory. But the predisposition to so display is not randomly irrational. It is time-shiftedly rational. In a world without planes, an evolved predisposition toward such vigorous display tended, on average, to better defend territory and offspring than did contemporaneous predispositions toward, for instance, passivity in the face of threat or incursion (Flasskamp 1994; Curio 1978).

Second, consider your own preferences for foods that are sweet or fatty. Sweet and fatty foods are rich in energy. It's generally agreed among biologists that that's *why* members of our species tend to like them. A lot. A predisposition to finding their tastes pleasurable (which leads to further consumption of them) outperforms a predisposition to disliking them in a world in which energy-rich foods are relatively scarce. Of course, that is precisely the world that we and our primate ancestors lived in for millions of years. Only in the recent eye-blink of time, from an evolutionary perspective, have we been able to so harness sweets and fats, and the means of delivering them, that it is possible to over-consume these to our detriments. It takes a long time to become unhealthily obese eating oranges. But not so long eating similar quantities of crème brûlée. Although predispositions toward sweets and fats often lead us to irrationally self-destructive outcomes under these just-arrived environmental circumstances, they led us to outcomes that were quite substantively rational across the thousands of millennia just prior. Consequently, the predispositions toward sweets and fats aren't at all *randomly* irrational. It is not as if they might just as easily have been irrational predispositions toward bitters, sours, or rotting meats. They are *time-shiftedly* rational. That is, predispositions toward sweets and fats used to lead to rational outcomes in the environmental circumstances we long encountered. It is only the arrival of very different, very novel environmental circumstances (in the forms of refined sugars, cheap grocery stores, and fast-food restaurants) that makes the often irresistible strength of those predispositions irrational *today*.[6]

What's the point? The point is that understanding more about where a behavior comes from, what function natural selection has historically favored it to perform, and why it came to exist in the patterns it does can provide some much-needed context and richer

---

[6] Note that trying to explain a preference for sweets by merely detailing the mechanistic relationship between sweet-sensing taste-buds and pleasurable experiences in the brain only raises the question why humans have such specialized taste-buds, and why stimulating them is perceived as pleasurable rather than aversive. That is, such facts are important to answering the "How" question, but not the "Why" question. Much mischief follows whenever the two kinds of explanations are confused.

information, which can then underlie more informed, more nuanced, and potentially improved predictions about: (a) the circumstances that will evoke the behavior; (b) the patterns in which the predispositions will tend to operate; (c) the connection of the behavior to other behaviors; and (d) the difficulty humans will encounter in trying to change them (all further discussed in Jones 2001). And those predictions can lead to deeper understandings about, for example, the Where? and When? inquiries, and thus to a more coherent understanding of the entire behavioral phenomenon.

### 4.4.3.2   *The theoretical foundation*

OK. So it's easy to see time-shifted rationalities in other contexts of human behavior. But how, precisely, might that perspective improve the predictions just mentioned, as well as any advantage to BE and to BLE? We'll return in a moment to the endowment effect specifically. But to get there, let's first see how Time-Shifted Rationality illustrates a broader point relevant to BE.

Equipped with the principles above, we can observe an animal species (in this case *Homo sapiens*) that displays a variety of deviations (pointed out by BE scholars) from predictions of the rational choice model (developed by Economics scholars). These various deviations are often grouped together under the label "heuristics and biases" (Tversky & Kahneman 1974; Kahneman, Slovic, & Tversky 1982; Gilovich, Griffin, & Kahneman 2002). And they are so grouped not because they are thought to be tightly linked to one another, but simply because they are all within the super-set of things that are thought to be "deviations." That is, they form a category defined more by what they are not than by what they are.

Although not every member of the species under consideration deviates in all conditions, two things are clear. First, when a great many members of this human species do deviate, they deviate in response to *quite similar conditions*. There is a tight link between the deviation and the conditions.

Second, when they do deviate, most people tend to deviate *in the same way*, among all the possible ways they could have deviated. For example, they are vastly more likely to exhibit an endowment effect (valuing what they have just received more than the maximum they would have paid to acquire it), than they are to exhibit an "anti-endowment effect" (valuing what they have just received far less than the maximum they would have paid to acquire it) or some randomly irrational effect (such as, when just gifted a mug, responding by hopping up and down on one leg).

In a 2001 article, I argued that if Time-Shifted Rationality provides a viable explanation for the endowment effect then that may more broadly suggest that some of what we've been lumping together as deviations from rational choice predictions may in fact be connected, sub-surface, by something far more substantive than the mere fact that they are all deviations (Jones 2001). It would suggest they may all be effects of the very same process: adaptation through natural selection. (A converging set of scholars in different disciplines have been raising similar hypotheses about possible evolutionary origins of various cognitive biases (see, e.g., Haselton & Nettle 2006; Gigerenzer 2006; McDermott, Fowler, & Smirnov 2008; Wilkinson 2008), including the endowment effect, Prospect Theory, and the like (see, e.g., Jones 2001; Huck, Kirchsteiger, & Oechssler 2005; Jones & Brosnan 2008; McDermott, Fowler, & Smirnov 2008)).

That at first seems easy to theorize, but hard to test. But the next section describes one set of empirical tests informed by this perspective, and the generally corroborating results.

### 4.4.3.3   *The empirical tests*

To test the idea that a variety of departures from rational choice predictions might reflect evolved adaptations,[7] I had the good fortune to team up with primatologist Sarah Brosnan. Together, we made a series of increasingly specific, theory-driven predictions and tested them.

Although our main interests are the ways in which evolutionary perspectives can increase our understandings of the set of cognitive heuristics and biases generally, we chose to focus initial energies on the endowment effect because it is a widely-studied and well-recognized phenomenon that is regularly invoked not only in BE literature, but also in BLE.

The perspective from behavioral biology on the endowment effect is simple: in environments that lacked today's novel features (such as reliable property rights, third-party enforcement mechanisms, and the like) it is inherently risky to give up what you have for something that might be slightly better. Nothing guarantees that your trading partner will perform. So in giving up one thing for another you might wind up with neither.

So the hypothesis is that natural selection would historically have favored a tendency to discount what you might acquire or trade for, compared to what you already have in hand, even if that tendency leads to irrational outcomes in the current (demonstrably different) environment. The basis of the hypothesis is a variation of the maxim that a bird in the hand has been, historically, worth two in the bush.

First, we predicted that if the endowment effect were in fact an example of Time-Shifted Rationality then the endowment effect would likely be observable in at least some other species. Here's why, in a nutshell. (These predictions are all explained more fully in Jones & Brosnan 2008.) If the endowment effect tends to lead on average to behaviors that were adaptive when there are asymmetric risks of keeping versus exchanging, then this isn't likely to be true only for humans. It should at a minimum be observable in some or all of our closest primate relatives, i.e. the other four of the five great apes: chimpanzees, orangutans, gorillas, and bonobos.

Second, we predicted that if the endowment effect were in fact an example of Time-Shifted Rationality, the prevalence of the endowment effect in other species is likely to vary across categories of items. This follows because selection pressures can, and very often do, narrowly tailor behavioral predispositions that vary as a function of the evolutionary salience (i.e., significance) of the circumstance. Put another way, evolved behavioral adaptations can be "facultative," consisting of a hierarchical set of "if-then" predispositions, which lead to alternate behaviors in alternate circumstances. Because no animal evolved to treat all objects the same, there's no reason to expect that they, or humans, would exhibit the endowment effect equally for all objects, or equally in all circumstances. Some classes of items are obviously more evolutionarily significant than others—simply because value is not distributed evenly across all the items a primate encounters.

Third (and as a logical consequence of prediction (2)), we predicted that the prevalence

---

[7]   Note that this is not simply an argument that there are evolutionary roots. That can be demonstrated by showing consistent patterns among various non-human relatives. The hypothesis that a behavior reflects an evolved adaptation is a narrower, more specific hypothesis, about the causal processes that lead to the trait becoming relatively common among members of a species.

of the endowment effect will correlate—increasing or decreasing, respectively—with the increasing or decreasing evolutionary salience of the item in question. *Evolutionary salience* refers to the extent to which the item, under historical conditions, would contribute positively to the survival, thriving, and reproducing of the organism acquiring it.

To test these predictions, we conducted a series of experiments with chimpanzee subjects. No other extant theory generated this set of three predictions. And the results of our experiments corroborated all three.

Although the details of the experiment are not the point here (where I'm trying to illustrate the *Converging Questions* approach), a few words are in order to address naturally arising questions such as: how can you test for the endowment effect in a species without currency? In brief, our paradigm involved testing subjects under a series of counterbalanced preference and exchange conditions (modified from Knetsch 1989).

In the "preference" condition, a chimpanzee subject would be offered two different items within a class of items, and then be given the one item the subject indicated (by pointing) it wanted to receive. In the two "exchange" conditions, subjects were given one of the items and then given the opportunity to trade that item for the other item. (Chimpanzees are very good at expressing preferences, and also at exchanging an object in hand for another one that is offered.)

Specifically, in one of the exchange conditions the subject would get item A and the opportunity to trade it for item B. And in the other exchange condition the subject would receive item B and the option to exchange it for item A. We counted as evidence of the endowment effect the refusal to exchange a less-preferred item (as established in the preference condition, which preferences tended to be stable within individuals over time and repeated testing) for a more-preferred item when given the opportunity to do so. In effect, the "value" of the less-preferred item would in that case have jumped to be greater than the value of the item the chimpanzee prefers, when given the option.

Our results provided the first evidence of an endowment effect in another species. Specifically, and as predicted, chimpanzees exhibit an endowment effect consonant with many of the human studies that find the effect. As predicted, the prevalence of the effect varies considerably according to the class of item. And, as predicted most specifically, the prevalence was far greater (14 times greater, in fact) within a class of trading evolutionarily salient items—here, food items—for each other than it was when trading within a class of non-evolutionarily salient items—here toys (Brosnan et al. 2007; Jones & Brosnan 2008).[8] Put another way, our subjects were 14 times more likely to hang on to their less-preferred evolutionarily salient item when they could trade it for their more-preferred evolutionarily salient item than they were to hang on to their less-preferred item with corresponding, but not evolutionarily salient, items (Brosnan et al. 2007; Jones & Brosnan 2008).

So far so good. But we then extended this approach (Brosnan et al. 2012) with a new prediction—which, like the prior three, was not predicted by any other extant theory of the endowment effect. We predicted that we would be able to turn the endowment effect

---

[8]   Endowment effects have subsequently also been observed in orangutans, gorillas, bonobos, and capuchins (Lakshminaryanan, Chen, & Santos 2008; Flemming et al. 2012; Kanngiesser et al. 2011; Drayton et al. 2013).

on and off in chimpanzees, *for the very same objects*, by manipulating their contextual, evolutionarily-salient values. Specifically, we used two tools familiar to our subjects that had no intrinsic value but which could be used to extract one of two kinds of food from containers when those containers were within reach. We predicted that the endowment effect would manifest in chimpanzees mainly when the tools could actually be used to extract the food. That is, we predicted that the endowment effect would turn on and off, depending on whether the tools were or were not evolutionarily salient in the moment.

We tested chimpanzees across the same three conditions above, with the added manipulation that the food containers were either: (a) absent from view; (b) in view but out of reach; or (c) in view and within reach. The results were again consistent with the prediction (Brosnan et al. 2012). In fact, *no* subject exhibited the endowment effect when the food was either out of view or out of reach. But the endowment effect came on line again, at levels similar to those often observed in humans, when the food was within reach, at which point the tools had immediate, contextual, evolutionarily salient value. Using this novel, theory-driven approach, we could turn the endowment effect on and off for the very same object.

### 4.4.3.4   The point

What is the point of all this? The point is that by fertilizing the study of how humans deviate from rational actor predictions of economics with not only c. 1980s' Psychology but also with perspectives of Evolutionary Biology (i.e., why species come to exhibit decision-making patterns in the first place), several new things can obtain.

First, for example, new things can be discovered about the endowment effect. It exists in other species. It exists in similar ways. New patterns of behavior can be predicted that cannot be predicted by other theories.

Second, predicting and demonstrating variations in endowment effect magnitudes, on the basis of differing characteristics intrinsic to different tradable things, and on the basis of differing contexts in which those things can be traded, provides some potential basis for beginning to untangle the single biggest knot in endowment effect literature: why—across many hundreds of studies (Sayman and Ön üler 2005)—does the magnitude of the endowment effect differ as it does, sometimes coming on strong, sometimes weakly, and sometimes not at all? Future work, informed by evolutionary perspectives on brain and behavior, may help to explain at least some of this variance.

Third, it promisingly points the way to a potential and deeper unification of all or many cognitive heuristics and biases and related phenomena. Specifically, it suggests that all or many of these discovered and widely-shared cognitive quirks may be interconnected, and all linked, as results of evolutionary processes that have mindlessly but relentlessly designed these human information processing and behavior-biasing predispositions to be just the ways they are. This view provides the basis for a significant change in how we think about them. Not only may they be products of the same underlying phenomenon, they may also have been far more likely to take the forms they do than to have taken other forms.

**4.5   Stage 5: Integrating Across Questions**

So far, we've set ourselves on a path of providing new value, to the goals of BE and BLE, by trying to figure out how to overcome traditional disciplinary boundaries, in order to blend the many virtues of BE with the virtues of other disciplines.

We've identified the psychological phenomenon in which we are interested (here, the endowment effect, within the suite of cognitive heuristics and biases and related phenomena). We identified a variety of distinct kinds of questions we might ask about the phenomenon. We considered which existing fields are most appropriate for trying to answer those questions (here, the *What?*, *Why?* and *How?* questions). And we've tried to combine the insights from some of the fields that purport to address one of those questions (here, the *Why?* question).

The question at this point is: how do we go about trying to integrate perspectives across the questions, rather than simply within them? Let's turn next to consider how we might integrate perspectives on the *Why?* question with perspectives on the *How?* question (i.e., how the endowment effect comes to be manifested). The key move here will be to expect, in light of the evolutionary biology perspectives just sketched, that how the endowment effect tends to be manifested in humans will be through a set of brain regions, circuits, and activations that are held relatively in common among members of our species.

**4.5.1   The *How?* perspective**

When it comes to animal—and hence human—behavior, there are several disciplines that each focus on differing aspects of the *How?* question. The *How?* question asks: by what physical and chemical pathways does an organism come to perceive environmental contexts, process that information, and use it to bias the probability of differing behavioral outputs?

Because the human body-plan centralizes this input-output processing in a brain, relevant inquiries include such things as: How does brain tissue come to be built in the ways it is? How is the brain constructed? How are surroundings and contexts perceived? How is information stored and processed? And how does that processing translate into particular actions? These are questions that Genetics and Neuroscience (among other life sciences) can help to answer.

Genetics is a science that, among other things, studies: inheritance within a species of physical and behavioral traits; variations in those inherited traits; and the pathways by which the interaction of genetic potentiality with actually encountered environmental circumstances yields traits that actually manifest (Brooker 2011; Plomin et al. 2012).

Neuroscience is a science that, among other things, studies how brains are physically constructed; how regions of the brain are anatomically and functionally specialized; how the constituent neurons and basal ganglia operate; and how neurons interact in ways that enable decision-making and behavior (Purves et al. 2011; Bear, Connors, & Paradiso 2006). The last of that list is the domain of the subspecialty "Cognitive Neuroscience."

Cognitive Neuroscience, which studies the brain circuitry and circuit activity underlying psychological processes, is thriving as a field (Banich & Compton 2010; Gazzaniga, Ivry, & Mangun 2013) because, among other reasons, technological advances such as *Positron*

*Emission Tomography* (PET) and *Functional Magnetic Resonance Imaging* (fMRI)[9] enable researchers to study brain function non-invasively, in awake and mentally active subjects[10] (Posner & Raichle 1994; Huettel, Song, & McCarthy 2008).

It is important to stress that the techniques are by no means perfect. One must understand their limitations, and guard against improper or unduly extrapolated inferences, which can sometimes be tempting (Aguirre 2014; Jones et al. 2009; Jones, Schall, & Shen 2014, Chapter 9). At the same time, experiments that are carefully designed, narrowly tailored, and cautiously interpreted are providing new and potentially useful insights about the pathways through which people's perceptions of environmental contexts are translated into behaviors.

### 4.5.2   How cognitive heuristics and biases arise

The techniques just mentioned have enabled the growth of the entire new field of Neuroeconomics, which among other things studies the in-brain underpinnings of economic decision-making and behavior (Montague & Berns 2002; Camerer, Loewenstein, & Drazan 2005; Camerer 2008; Glimcher et al. 2009; Phelps 2009; Knutson et al. 2005; Fehr & Rangel 2011; Clithero, Tankersley, & Huettel 2008; Glimcher 2004; Rustichini 2009; Bechara & Damasio 2005; Coaster et al. 2011; Kuhnen & Knutson 2005) .

Here is a sampling, for the general flavor of research directions and findings. The locations of the brain regions mentioned here are less important, to the immediate purpose, than the fact that they have been identified:

i.   Risk and Choice:
  a.   The neural correlates of outcome uncertainty, and risky decision-making, are increasingly known (Platt & Huettel 2008; Peterson 2005; Volz, Schubotz, & von Cramon 2003; Mohr, Biele, & Hauke 2010)
  b.   Prefrontal, parietal, and temporal cortex networks underlie decision-making in the presence of uncertainty (Paulus et al. 2001)
  c.   Activation of a brain region known as the nucleus accumbens precedes risky choices and risk-seeking mistakes (Kuhnen & Knutson 2005)
  d.   Activation of the anterior insula precedes riskless choices and risk-aversion mistakes (Kuhnen & Knutson 2005)
  e.   Interconnected activity patterns are evident in certain prefrontal regions of the brain during risky decision-making (Minati et al. 2012)
  f.   Voluntary risk-taking, but not involuntary risk-taking, is associated with increased activity in a number of mesolimbic-frontal regions, including mid-brain, striatum, insula, prefrontal cortex, and anterior cingulate (Rao et al. 2008)
  g.   The degree of brain activity in the medial prefrontal cortex is negatively correlated with the risk preference of subjects (Xue et al. 2009)
  h.   The degree of activity in the ventro-medial prefrontal cortex is positively correlated with an individual's risk preference (Xue et al. 2009)

---

[9]   The "f" is typically lowercase by convention.
[10]   For user-friendly introductions to these techniques, see Greely & Wagner 2011; Jones et al. 2009; and Jones et al. 2014. More in-depth coverage appears in Bremner 2005.

The new techniques have also enabled researchers to make strong and interconnected inferences about the brain activity that underlies various cognitive heuristics and biases (Lee 2006), such as those involved in intertemporal choice and framing effects. For example:

ii.  Intertemporal Choice
   a.  Low cortisol levels correlate with large time-discounting rates (Takahashi 2004)
   b.  Limbic region activation is greater for choices between an immediate reward and a delayed reward than for choices between two delayed rewards (McClure et al. 2004, 2007)
   c.  Relative activation of the lateral prefrontal cortex and posterior parietal cortex predicts choice behavior between an immediate and a delayed reward (McClure et al. 2004, 2007)

iii.  The Framing Effect
   a.  Cognitive functions involved in framing effects are localized in the prefrontal and parietal cortices of the brain (Gonzalez et al. 2005)
   b.  Cognitive effort required to select a sure gain is considerably lower than the cognitive effort required to choose a risky gain (Gonzalez et al. 2005)
   c.  Cognitive effort expended in choosing a sure loss is equal to the cognitive effort expended in choosing a risky loss (Gonzalez et al. 2005)
   d.  Activity in the anterior cingulate reflects susceptibility to framing (Deppe et al. 2007)
   e.  Amygdala activity is associated with the framing affect (De Martino et al. 2006)
   f.  Individuals with increased orbital and medial prefrontal cortex activity have reduced susceptibility to the framing effect (De Martino et al. 2006)

Closer to the discussions here, the brain scanning techniques have also enabled researchers to learn a great deal about the brain activity underlying loss aversion, reference dependence, and the endowment effect. For example:

iv.  Loss Aversion:
   a.  The neural bases of loss aversion have been identified (Tom et al. 2006, 2007; Dreher 2007)
   b.  Loss aversion has been the subject of many studies (Tom et al. 2006, 2007; Sokol-Hessner, Camerer, & Phleps 2013; Dreher 2007; De Martino, Camerer, & Adolphs 2010; Chib et al. 2012)
   c.  The amygdala is involved in evaluating the prospective outcomes of choices (Kahn et al. 2002; De Martino, Camerer, & Adolphs 2010)
   d.  The amygdala is involved in anticipating and experiencing monetary loss (Kahn et al. 2002; De Martino, Camerer, & Adolphs 2010)
   e.  Amygdala damage eliminates loss aversion in monetary contexts (De Martino, Camerer, & Adolphs 2010)

v.  Reference Dependence
   a.  Neural responses to reward anticipation under risk is nonlinear in probabilities (Hsu et al. 2009; Fox & Poldrack 2009)

    b.   Nonlinear decision weight functions of uncertain prospects are modulated by anterior cingulate activity (Paulus and Frank 2006)

    c.   Ventral striatal activity reflects reward probability and magnitude during anticipation (Yacubian et al. 2006)

    d.   Loss-related expected value and the associated prediction error are reflected in amygdala activation (Yacubian et al. 2006)

vi.  Endowment Effect

    a.   The neural correlates of the endowment effect are increasingly known (Knutson et al. 2008; Votinov et al. 2010, 2013)

    b.   Electrical stimulation to the right inferior frontal gyrus increases the magnitude of the endowment effect (Votinov et al. 2013)

    c.   Subjects display greater activation in the nucleus accumbens for the products they prefer, across both buying and selling conditions (Knutson et al. 2008)

    d.   However, subjects also show greater mesial prefrontal cortex activation in response to low prices when buying, compared to when selling (Knutson et al. 2008)

    e.   During selling, right insular activation for the preferred products predicts individual differences in propensity to exhibit the endowment effect (Knutson et al. 2008)

Let's look at just one of these studies more closely. To investigate brain activity correlated with the endowment effect, a team composed of George Loewenstein, Brian Knutson, Drazen Prelec, Elliott Wimmer, Scott Rick, and Nick G. Hollon used fMRI to brain-scan 24 subjects as they considered six products in differing choosing, buying, or selling conditions (Knutson et al. 2008). The results not only helped to identify brain circuitries and activations correlated with the effect, they also enabled a test to partially distinguish between two reference-dependent accounts of it: an "enhanced attraction" hypothesis; and a "loss aversion" hypothesis. The distinction between these hypotheses is that "[p]eople might find it difficult to part with their possessions either because of enhanced attraction to the item [or] simply because of an aversion to potentially losing the item" (p. 814).

The paradigm involved scanning subjects who had been given ownership of objects before the scan session (such as iPod Shuffles, flash drives, digital cameras, and the like) as they made their buy, sell, and choose choices. Some of those choices involved selling objects they now owned. And subjects were (truthfully) instructed that a fraction of their choices would be implemented, post-scan, "for real."

Prior studies had shown that activation in an area known as the *nucleus accumbens* (NAcc) was associated with prediction of monetary gain while activation in the *insula* was associated with prediction of monetary loss (p. 814). This gave the researchers some rough benchmarks by which to measure which was most involved, and how, when the endowment effect manifested. The researchers therefore hypothesized that "if people have enhanced *attraction* to products when selling versus buying, they should show increased NAcc activation when viewing those products" (p. 814). On the other hand, "if people have increased *aversion* to losing products when selling versus buying, they might show increased insula activation when viewing those products" (p. 814).

Behaviorally, the team's subjects showed a robust endowment effect, making analysis of brain data relevant. With respect to NAcc activation, the results seemed clear. Although NAcc activity correlated with a subject's expressed preference for an item, the interaction of NAcc activity with Sell versus Buy conditions did not vary, as it arguably would have if the endowment effect were a function of enhanced attraction to objects one owns. The story with insula activation is a bit more complicated. On the one hand, insular activation did not correlate with the interaction of product preference by either Buy or Sell conditions. On the other hand, differences between individual subjects in insular activation did predict the likelihood that subject behavior would manifest the endowment effect (Knutson et al. 2008, pp. 815–19).

The team concluded not only that product preference activated different regions than anticipated product loss. It also concluded that these brain activities "provide evidence consistent with reference-dependent theories (e.g., prospect theory), rather than reference-independent theories (e.g., rational choice) and specifically support a loss aversion rather than an enhanced attraction account of the endowment effect" (p. 820). Not only does this finding (if replicated and robust) illuminate how the endowment effect may arise in the brain, it also, in the authors' words, illustrates how "neuroscience methods can advance economic theory not only by breaking down apparently unitary phenomena (e.g. choice) into constituent components (e.g., anticipation of gain and loss) but also by specifying which of these components matters when" (p. 820).

The studies in this section illustrate relatively new technologies and methods for exploring human decision-making. They have their limits.[11] And there are inevitable logical boundaries to the inferences that can be drawn from them. Yet the thing to keep in mind is that the mind is increasingly being studied within the corporeal brain itself. The linkages between brain activity and behavior are newly but constantly developing, in ways that may ultimately aid BE and BLE.

### 4.5.3   Bringing it all together

The whole point of all of this discussion is to help BE and BLE surge forward again. Doing so requires redoubled efforts to gain a more accurate, robust, and useful model of human behavior than whatever we already have. That, in turn, and as described earlier, requires a more committedly transdisciplinary approach, because there are no good reasons to believe that any one discipline, or any dyad of them, can supply enough insights to capture the complexities of human decision-making realities.

In other words, in the same way that three-dimensional realities are only weakly approximated by two-dimensional representations, complex behavioral phenomena are sufficiently multi-dimensional that we need the joined forces of multiple disciplines to more accurately, and ultimately more usefully, model those behaviors.

To this point, I have suggested that a *Converging Questions* approach may be one pathway for getting there. And I have used the endowment effect to sketch how portions of that pathway might look. But it is essential to recognize that I am not saying, in this illustration, that evolutionary biology or neuroscience provides a better understanding of the endowment effect than Behavioral Economics does. That would miss the point

---

[11]   For overviews, see Aguirre 2014; Jones et al. 2009; Jones, Schall, & Shen 2014, Chapter 9.

entirely. What I'm trying to illustrate is that each of those fields, and many more besides, can have comparative advantages within their own domains, largely because they have specialized in answering very different kinds of questions. And the end result is that the endowment effect can—in all likelihood—be more productively explored from multiple disciplinary dimensions than it can be explored from one discipline alone.

For example, exploring the endowment effect from an evolutionary biology perspective suggests that the behavioral predisposition is shared with at least some other key species, and—because it provides insight on why the effect may exist in the first place—it enables both the prediction of, and the discovery of, new truths about the phenomenon that are not predicted by any of the other existing theories. Similarly, exploring the endowment effect from a neuroscientific perspective enables identification of the mechanistic pathways by which the effect is manifested in the brain, which enables a process of comparing the likelihood that one hypothesis for how the behavior comes to be is more accurate than another.

The idea is that as the different strengths of the different relevant disciplines get integrated together, it will enable deeper and better explorations of topics such as: *In what patterns will the endowment effect emerge in the future?; Which people, under what conditions, with respect to what goods and rights, will manifest what kind of effect, in what magnitudes?;* and *What sorts of things might inspire them to behave differently, if we want them to?* The aspiration is that when scholars in one discipline attempt to fully explore the questions within its domain they will be better able to answer those questions, because of the richer and more complete set of contexts and insights supplied by scholars in other domains. The process of iterated cross-fertilization and integration can lead to better, more accurate, and more useful behavioral models.

If I'm right about that, for all or many of the cognitive heuristics and biases, then a similar approach may also work for the endgame of exploring deeper connections between the set of them, which might only be discovered when multiple disciplines work together.

## 5.   CONCLUSION

Here are the take-aways. Behavioral Economics and Behavioral Law and Economics have each made terrific and important progress. But that's no reason not to aspire to even greater achievements.

In this chapter, I've identified a number of problems holding the fields back, traced several origins of those problems, and suggested a variety of ways forward. In the end, achieving more requires at least three things.

First, it requires drawing on a far greater and more current swath of insights from within the field of Psychology than just the literatures on heuristics, biases, and related phenomena. For instance, it requires incorporating new and rapidly accumulating information, within the technology-accelerated domain of Cognitive Neuroscience, about how brains make decisions.

Second, achieving more requires drawing on a broader set of fields, within the domain of human decision-making, than Psychology alone. For instance, it requires incorporating new information and perspectives from fields, such as Evolutionary Biology, that provide demonstrated promise for enriching our understandings of human behavioral phenomena we care about. The extended (though inevitably still partial) example I supplied, regarding multi-disciplinary angles on the endowment effect, illustrates only a very small tract of a much larger landscape to be usefully explored.

Third, achieving more requires working to integrate knowledge about human decision-making from multiple fields into a more coherent whole. For instance, it requires self-conscious and goal-directed development of better methods for grinding away the incompatibilities between disciplines that bear on the same realities, and then dove-tailing remaining compatibilities to build better, more robust, more accurate, more predictive, and more effective models of human decision-making and behavior. The *Converging Questions* approach, proposed and illustrated here, may usefully aid this. But the key thing is that we not just aspire to multi-disciplinary approaches, but also work together to develop and deploy them.

## REFERENCES

Aguirre, G. K. 2014. Functional neuroimaging: Technical, logical, and social perspectives. *Hastings Center Report* 45(2): S8–S18.

Arlen, J. 1998. Comment: The future of behavioral economic analysis of law. *Vanderbilt Law Review* 51(6): 1765–88.

Arlen, J., & S. W. Tontrup. 2013. A process account of the endowment effect: Voluntary debiasing through agents and markets. Working Paper. NYU School of Law, Public Law Research Paper, NYU Law and Economics Research Paper.

Banich, M. T., & R. J. Compton. 2010. *Cognitive Neuroscience*, 3rd edn. Stamford, CT: Cengage Learning.

Bear, M. F., B. W. Connors, & M. A. Paradiso. 2006. *Neuroscience: Exploring the Brain*, 3rd edn. Philadelphia, PA: Lippincott Williams and Wilkins.

Bechara, A., & A. R. Damasio. 2005. The somatic marker hypothesis: A neural theory of economic decision. *Games and Economic Behavior* 52(2): 336–72.

Bergstrom, C. T., & L. A. Dugatkin. 2011. *Evolution*. New York, NY: W. W. Norton & Company.

Bremner, J. D. 2005. *Brain Imaging Handbook*. New York, NY: W. W. Norton & Company.

Brooker, R. 2011. *Genetics: Analysis and Principles*, 4th edn. New York, NY: McGraw-Hill.

Brosnan, S. F., O. D. Jones, M. Gardner, S. P. Lambeth, M. C. Mareno, A. S. Richardson, & S. J. Schapiro. 2007. Endowment effects in chimpanzees. *Current Biology* 17: 1704–707.

Brosnan, S. F., O. D. Jones, M. Gardner, S. P. Lambeth, & S. J. Schapiro. 2012. Evolution and the Expression of Biases: Situational Value Changes the Endowment Effect in Chimpanzees. *Evolution and Human Behavior* 33: 378–86.

Camerer, C. F. 2008. Neuroeconomics: Opening the gray box. *Neuron* 60(3): 416–19.

Camerer, C. F., G. Loewenstein, & P. Drazen. 2005. Neuroeconomics: How neuroscience can inform economics. *Journal of Economic Literature* 43: 9–64.

Chib, V. S., B. De Martino, S. Shimojo, & J. P. O'Doherty. 2012. Neural mechanisms underlying paradoxical performance for monetary incentives are driven by loss aversion. *Neuron* 74(3): 582–94.

Clithero J. A., D. Tankersley, & S. A. Huettel. 2008. Foundations of neuroeconomics: From philosophy to practice. *PLOS Biology* 6(11): e298.

Coaster, M., B. P. Rogers, O. D. Jones, W. K. Viscusi, K. L. Merkle, D. H. Zald, J. C. Gore. 2011. Variables influencing the neural correlates of perceived risk of physical harm. *Cognitive, Affective, & Behavioral Neuroscience* 11(4): 494–507.

Cosmides, L., J. Tooby, & J. H. Barkow. 1992. Introduction: Evolutionary psychology and conceptual integration. Pp. 3–15 in *The Adapted Mind: Evolutionary Psychology and the Generation of Culture*, edited by J. H. Barkow, L. Cosmides, & J. Tooby. Oxford: Oxford University Press.

Curio, E. 1978. The adaptive significance of avian mobbing. I. Teleonomic hypotheses and predictions. *Zeitschrift für Tierpsychologie* 48: 175–83.

De Martino, B., C. F. Camerer, & R. Adolphs. 2010. Amygdala damage eliminates monetary loss aversion. *Proceedings of the National Academy of Sciences* 107(8): 3788–92.

De Martino, B., D. Kumaran, B. Seymour, & R. J. Dolan. 2006. Frames, biases, and rational decision-making in the human brain. *Science* 313(5787): 684–87.

Deppe M., W. Schwindt, A. Pieper, H. Kugel, H. Plassmann, P. Kenning, K. Deppe, & B. E. Ringlestein. 2007. Anterior cingulate reflects susceptibility to framing during attractiveness evaluation. *NeuroReport* 18(11): 1119–23.

Drayton, L. A., S. F. Brosnan, J. Carrigan, & T. S. Stoinski. 2013. Endowment effects in gorillas (Gorilla gorilla). *Journal of Comparative Psychology* 127(4): 365–69.

Dreher, J. C. 2007. Sensitivity of the brain to loss aversion during risky gambles. *Trends in Cognitive Sciences* 11(7): 270–72.

Fehr, E., & Rangel, A. 2011. Neuroeconomic Foundations of Economic Choice—Recent Advances. *Journal of Economic Perspectives* 24(4): 3–30.

Flasskamp, A. 1994. The adaptive significance of avian mobbing v. an experimental test of the "Move on" hypothesis. *Ethology* 96: 322–33.

Flemming, T. M., O. D. Jones, L. Mayo, T. Stoinski, & S. F. Brosnan. 2012. The endowment effect in orangutans. *International Journal of Comparative Psychology* 25: 285–98.

Fox, C. R., & Poldrack, R. A. 2009. Prospect theory and the brain. Pp. 145–76 in *Neuroeconomics: Decision Making and the Brain*, edited by P. W. Glimcher, C. F. Camerer, R. A. Poldrack, & E. Fehr. Boston: Elsevier.

Franciosi, R., P. Kujal, R. Michelitsch, V. Smith, & G. Deng. 1996. Experimental tests of the endowment effect. *Journal of Economic Behavior and Organization* 30(2): 213–26.

Futuyma, D. J. 2013. *Evolution*, 3rd edn. Sunderland, MA: Sinauer Associates, Inc.

Gazzaniga, M., R. B. Ivry, & G. R. Mangun. 2013. *Cognitive Neuroscience: The Biology of the Mind*, 4th edn. New York, NY: W. W. Norton & Company.

Gigerenzer, G. 2000. *Adaptive Thinking: Rationality in the Real World*. Oxford and New York: Oxford University Press.

Gigerenzer, G. 2006. "Bounded and rational". Pp. 115–33 in *Contemporary Debates in Cognitive Science*, edited by R. J. Stainton. Malden, MA: Blackwell.

Gigerenzer, G. 2008. Why heuristics work. *Perspectives on Psychological Science* 3(1): 20–29.

Gigerenzer, G. & P. M. Todd. 1999. Ecological rationality: The normative study of heuristics. Pp. 487–97 in *Ecological Rationality: Intelligence in the World*, by G. Gigerenzer, P. M. Todd & The ABC Research Group. New York: Oxford University Press.

Gilovich, T., D. Griffin, & D. Kahneman. 2002. *Heuristics and Biases: The Psychology of Intuitive Judgment*. Cambridge and New York: Cambridge University Press.

Glimcher, P. W. 2004. *Decisions, Uncertainty, and the Brain: The Science of Neuroeconomics*. Cambridge and London: MIT Press.

Glimcher, P. W., C. F. Camerer, R. A. Poldrack, & E. Fehr, eds. 2009. *Neuroeconomics: Decision Making and the Brain*. Boston: Elsevier.

Gonzalez, C., J. Dana, H. Koshino, & M. Just. 2005. The framing effect and risky decisions: Examining cognitive functions with fMRI. *Journal of Economic Psychology* 26(1): 1–20.

Greely, H. & A. Wagner. 2011. Reference guide on neuroscience. Pp. 747–812 in 3rd edition of *Reference Manual on Scientific Evidence* by Federal Judicial Center. Washington, DC: National Academies Press.

Haselton, M. G. & D. Nettle. 2006. The paranoid optimist: An integrative evolutionary model of cognitive biases. *Personality & Social Psychology Review* 10(1): 47–66.

Herron, J. C. & S. Freeman. 2013. *Evolutionary Analysis*, 5th edn. San Francisco, CA: Benjamin Cummings.

Hoffman, E. & M. L. Spitzer. 1993. Willingness to pay vs. willingness to accept: Legal and economic implications. *Washington University Law Review* 71(1): 59–114.

Horowitz, J. & K. E. McConnell. 2002. A review of WTA/WTP studies. *Journal of Environmental Economics & Management* 44: 426–47.

Hsu, M., I. Krajbich, C. Zhao, & C. F. Camerer. 2009. Neural response to reward anticipation under risk is nonlinear in probabilities. *The Journal of Neuroscience* 29(7): 2231–37.

Huck, S., G. Kirchsteiger, & J. Oechssler. 2005. Learning to like what you have—explaining the endowment effect. *The Economic Journal* 115(505): 689–702.

Huettel, S. A., A. W. Song, & G. McCarthy. 2008. *Functional Magnetic Resonance Imaging*, 2nd edn. Sunderland, MA: Sinauer Associates, Inc.

Jolls, C., C. R. Sunstein, & R. Thaler. 1998. A behavioral approach to law and economics. *Stanford Law Review* 50: 1471–532.

Jones, O. D. 2001. Time-shifted rationality and the law of law's leverage: Behavioral economics meets behavioral biology. *Northwestern University Law Review* 95: 1141–206.

Jones, O. D., & S. F. Brosnan. 2008. Law, biology, and property: A new theory of the endowment effect. *William and Mary Law Review* 49(6): 1935–90.

Jones, O. D., & T. H. Goldsmith. 2005. Law and behavioral biology. *Columbia Law Review* 105: 405–502.

Jones, O., J. Buckholtz, J. Schall, & R. Marois. 2009. Brain imaging for legal thinkers: A guide for the perplexed. *Stanford Technology Law Review* 5: 1–48.

Jones, O. D., E. O'Hara O'Connor, & J. Stake. 2011. Economics, behavioral biology, and law. *Supreme Court Economic Review* 19(1):103–41.

Jones, O. D., J. D. Schall, & F. X. Shen. 2014. *Law and Neuroscience.* New York: Aspen Publishers.

Kahn, I., Y. Yeshurun, P. Rotshtein, I. Fried, D. Ben-Bashat, & T. Hendler. 2002. The role of the amygdala in signaling prospective outcome of choice. *Neuron* 33(6): 983–94.

Kahneman, D. 2011. *Thinking Fast and Slow.* New York, NY: Farrar, Straus and Giroux.

Kahneman, D., & A. Tversky. 1979. Prospect theory: An analysis of decision under risk. *Econometrica* 47(2): 263–92.

Kahneman, D., & A. Tversky. 1996. On the reality of cognitive illusions. *Psychological Review* 103(3): 582–91.

Kahneman, D., J. L. Knetsch, & R. H. Thaler. 1990. Experimental tests of the endowment effect and the Coase Theorem. *The Journal of Political Economy* 98(6): 1325–48.

Kahneman, D., J. L. Knetsch, & R. H. Thaler. 1991. Anomalies: The endowment effect, loss aversion, and status quo bias. *Journal of Economic Perspectives* 5(1): 193–206.

Kahneman, D., P. Slovic, & A. Tversky. 1982. *Judgment Under Uncertainty: Heuristics and Biases.* Cambridge and New York: Cambridge University Press.

Kanngiesser, P., Santos, L., Hood, B., & Call, J. 2011. The limits of endowment effects in great apes (*Pan paniscus, Pan troglodytes, Gorilla gorilla, Pongo pygmaeus*). *Journal of Comparative Psychology* 125(4): 436–45.

Klass, G., & K. Zeiler. 2013. Against endowment theory: Experimental economics and legal scholarship. *UCLA Law Review* 61: 2–64.

Knetsch, J. L. 1989. The endowment effect and evidence of nonreversible indifference curves. *American Economic Review* 79(5): 1277–84.

Knetsch, J. L., & J. A. Sinden. 1984. Willingness to pay and compensation demanded: Experimental evidence of an unexpected disparity in measures of value. *The Quarterly Journal of Economics* 99(3): 507–21.

Knutson B., J. Taylor, M. Kaufman, R. Peterson, & G. Glover. 2005. Distributed neural representation of expected value. *Journal of Neuroscience* 25(19): 4806–12.

Knutson, B., G. E. Wimmer, S. Rick, N. G. Hollon, D. Prelec, & G. Loewenstein. 2008. Neural antecedents of the endowment effect. *Neuron* 58(5): 814–22.

Korobkin, R. 2003. The endowment and legal analysis. *Northwestern University Law Review* 97(3): 1227–91.

Korobkin, R. 2011. What comes after victory for behavioral law and economics? *University of Illinois Law Review* 2011: 1653–74.

Korobkin, R. 2014. Wrestling with the endowment effect, or how to do law and economics without the Coase Theorem. Pp. 300–34 in *Oxford Handbook of Behavioral Economics and the Law,* edited by Eyal Zamir and Doron Teichman. New York, NY: Oxford University Press, Inc.

Kuhnen, C. M., & B. Knutson. 2005. The neural basis of financial risk taking. *Neuron* 47(5): 763–70.

Lakshminaryanan, V., K. Chen, & L. Santos. 2008. Endowment effect in capuchin monkeys. *Philosophical Transactions of the Royal Society B* 363: 3837–44.

Lee, D. 2006. Neural basis of quasi-rational decision making. *Current Opinion in Neurobiology* 16(2): 191–98.

Lieberman, D. 2013. *The Story of the Human Body: Evolution, Health, and Disease.* New York, NY: Pantheon Books.

MacArthur Foundation Research Network on Law and Neuroscience. http://www.lawneuro.org/ (last visited October 14, 2014).

McCaffery, E. J. 1994. Cognitive theory and tax. *UCLA Law Review* 41(7): 1861–947.

McClure S. M., K. M. Ericson, D. I. Laibson, G. Loewenstein, & J. D. Cohen. 2007. Time discounting for primary rewards. *Journal of Neuroscience* 27(21): 5796–804.

McClure S. M., D. I. Laibson, G. Loewenstein, & J. D. Cohen. 2004. Separate neural systems value immediate and delayed monetary rewards. *Science* 306(5695): 503–507.

McDermott, R., J. H. Fowler, & O. Smirnov. 2008. On the evolutionary origin of prospect theory preferences. *The Journal of Politics* 70(2):335–50.

Minati, L., M. Grisoli, A. K. Seth, & H. D. Critchley. 2012. Decision-making under risk: A graph-based network analysis using functional MRI. *NeuroImage* 60(4): 2191–205.

Mohr M., G. Biele, & R. Hauke. 2010. Neural processing of risk. *eJournal of Neuroscience* 30(19): 6613–19.

Montague P. R. & G. S. Berns. 2002. Neural economics and the biological substrates of valuation. *Neuron* 36(2): 265–84.

Nesse, R. M., & G. C. Williams. 1996. *Why We Get Sick: The New Science of Darwinian Medicine.* New York, NY: Vintage Books.

Paulus, M. P., & L. R. Frank. 2006. Anterior cingulate activity modulates nonlinear decision weight function of uncertain prospects. *Neuroimage* 30(2): 668–77.

Paulus M. P., N. Hozack, B. Zauscher, J. E. McDowell, L. Frank, G. G. Brown, & D. L. Braff. 2001. Prefrontal, parietal, and temporal cortex networks underlie decision-making in the presence of uncertainty. *NeuroImage* 13(1): 91–100.

Peterson, R. L. 2005. The neuroscience of investing: fMRI of the reward system. *Brain Research Bulletin* 67(5): 391–97.

Phelps, E. A. 2009. The Study of Emotion in Neuroeconomics. Pp. 233–50 in *Neuroeconomics: Decision Making and the Brain*, edited by P. W. Glimcher, E. Fehr, C. Camerer, & R. A. Poldrack. Boston: Elsevier.

Platt, M. L., & S. A. Huettel. 2008. Risky business: The neuroeconomics of decision making under uncertainty. *Nature Neuroscience* 11(4): 398–403.

Plomin, R., J. C. DeFries, V. S. Knopik, & J. M. Neiderhiser. 2012. *Behavioral Genetics*, 6th edn. New York, NY: Worth Publishers.

Plott, C. R., & K. Zeiler. 2005. The willingness to pay–willingness to accept gap, the "endowment effect," subject misconceptions, and experimental procedures for eliciting valuations. *American Economic Review* 95(3): 530–45.

Plott, C. R., & K. Zeiler. 2007. Exchange asymmetries incorrectly interpreted as evidence of endowment effect and prospect theory? *The American Economic Review* 97(4): 1449–66.

Plott, C. R., & K. Zeiler. 2011. The willingness to pay–willingness to accept gap, the "endowment effect," subject misconceptions, and experimental procedures for eliciting valuations: reply. *American Economic Review* 101: 1012–28.

Posner, M. I., & M. E. Raichle. 1994. *Images of Mind*. New York, NY: W. H. Freeman & Company.

Posner, R. A. 2011. *Economic Analysis of Law*, 8th edn. New York, NY: Aspen Publishers.

Purves, D., G. J. Augustine, D. Fitzpatrick, W. C. Hall, A. LaMantia, & L. E. White. 2011. *Neuroscience*, 5th edn. Sunderland, MA: Sinauer Associates, Inc.

Rachlinski, J. L. 2011. The psychological foundations of behavioral law and economics. *University of Illinois Law Review* 2011: 1675–96.

Rao, H., M. Korczykowski, J. Pluta, A. Hoang, & J. A. Detre. 2008. Neural correlates of voluntary and involuntary risk taking in the human brain: An fMRI study of the Balloon Analog Risk Task (BART). *Neuroimage* 42(2): 902–10.

Rustichini A. 2009. Neuroeconomics: What have we found, and what should we search for? *Current Opinion in Neurobiology* 19: 672–77.

Sayman, S., & A. Öncüler. 2005. Effects of study design characteristics on the WTA–WTP disparity: A meta analytical framework. *Journal of Economic Psychology* 26(2): 289–312.

Shafir, E. (ed.). 2013. *The Behavioral Foundations of Public Policy*. Princeton, NJ: Princeton University Press.

Sokol-Hessner, P., C. F. Camerer, & E. A. Phelps. 2013. Emotion regulation reduces loss aversion and decreases amygdala responses to losses. *Social Cognitive and Affective Neuroscience* 8(3): 341–50.

Stake, J. E. 2004. The property "instinct". *Philosophical Transactions B* 359: 1763–74.

Sunstein, C. (ed.) 2000. *Behavioral Law and Economics*. Cambridge: Cambridge University Press.

Sunstein, C. 2013. Deciding by default. *University of Pennsylvania Law Review* 162(1): 1–57.

Sunstein, C. 2014. *Why Nudge? The Politics of Libertarian Paternalism*. New Haven, CT: Yale University Press.

Takahashi, T. 2004. Cortisol levels and time-discounting of monetary gain in humans. *NeuroReport* 15: 2145–47.

Thaler, R. 1980. Toward a positive theory of consumer choice. *Journal of Economic Behavior & Organization* 1: 39–60.

Tom, S. M., C. R. Fox, C. Trepel, & R. A. Poldrack. 2006. Losses loom larger than gains in the brain: Neural loss aversion predicts behavioral loss aversion. Working Paper. Uncertainty Laboratory Research Group, University of California, Los Angeles.

Tom, S. M., C. R. Fox, C. Trepel, & R. A. Poldrack. 2007. The neural basis of loss aversion in decision-making under risk. *Science* 315(5811): 515–18.

Tooby, J., & L. Cosmides. 1992. The psychological foundations of culture. Pp. 19–136 in *The Adapted Mind: Evolutionary Psychology and the Generation of Culture*, edited by J. H. Barkow, L. Cosmides, & J. Tooby. New York, NY: Oxford University Press.

Tversky, A., & D. Kahneman. 1974. Judgment under uncertainty: Heuristics and biases. *Science* 185(4157): 1124–31.

Tversky, A., & D. Kahneman. 1991. Loss aversion in riskless choice: A reference-dependent model. *Quarterly Journal of Economics* 106: 1039–61.

Tversky, A. & D. Kahneman. 2000. Advances in prospect theory: Cumulative representation of uncertainty. Pp. 44–65 in *Choices, Values, and Frames*, edited by Amos Tversky & Daniel Kahneman. Cambridge and New York: Cambridge University Press.

Volz, K. G., R. I. Schubotz, & D. Y. von Cramon. 2003. Predicting events of varying probability: Uncertainty investigated by fMRI. *NeuroImage* 19(2 Pt 1): 271–80.

Votinov, M., T. Aso, S. Koganemaru, H. Fukuyama, & T. Mima. 2013. Transcranial direct current stimulation changes human endowment effect. *Neuroscience Research* 76(4): 251–56.

Votinov, M., T. Mima, T. Aso, M. Abe, N. Sawamoto, J. Shinozaki, & H. Fukuyama. 2010. The neural correlates of endowment effect without economic transaction. *Neuroscience Research* 68(1): 59–65.

Wilkinson, N. 2008. *An Introduction to Behavioral Economics*. Basingstoke: Palgrave Macmillan.

Williams, G. C. 1966. *Adaptation and Natural Selection: A Critique of Some Current Evolutionary Thought.* Princeton, NJ: Princeton University Press.

Xue, G., Z. Lu, I. P. Levin, J. A. Weller, X. Li, & A. Bechara. 2009. Functional dissociations of risk and reward processing in the medial prefrontal cortex. *Cerebral Cortex* 19(5): 1019–27.

Yacubian, J., J. Gläscher, K. Schroeder, T. Sommer, D. F. Braus, & C. Büchel. 2006. Dissociable systems for gain- and loss-related value predictions and errors of prediction in the human brain. *The Journal of Neuroscience* 26(37): 9530–37.

Zeiler, K. 2018. What explains observed reluctance to trade? A comprehensive literature review. In *Research Handbook on Behavioral Law and Economics* edited by Joshua C. Teitelbaum and Kathryn Zeiler. Cheltenham, UK and Northampton, MA, USA: Edward Elgar Publishing.

Zimmer, C., & D. Emlen. 2012. *Evolution: Making Sense of Life.* Englewood, CO: Roberts and Company Publishers.

# Index